ACCA
STUDY TEXT

Paper 1.1

Preparing Financial Statements

IN THIS JUNE 2003 EDITION

- Targeted to the syllabus and study guide
- Quizzes and questions to check your understanding
- Clear layout and style designed to save you time
- Plenty of exam-style questions
- Chapter Roundups and summaries to help revision
- Mind Maps to integrate the key points

BPP's **MCQ Cards** and **i-Learn** and **i-Pass** products also support this paper.

FOR EXAMS IN DECEMBER 2003 AND JUNE 2004

BPP Professional Education
June 2003

First edition 2001
Third edition June 2003

ISBN 0 7517 1150 0 (Previous ISBN 0 7517 0230 7)

British Library Cataloguing-in-Publication Data
A catalogue record for this book
is available from the British Library

Published by

BPP Professional Education
Aldine House, Aldine Place
London W12 8AW

www.bpp.com

Printed in Great Britain by Ashford Colour Press

All our rights reserved. No part of this publication may be reproduced, stored in a retrieval system or transmitted, in any form or by any means, electronic, mechanical, photocopying, recording or otherwise, without the prior written permission of BPP Professional Education.

We are grateful to the Association of Chartered Certified Accountants for permission to reproduce past examination questions and questions from the pilot paper. The answers have been prepared by BPP Professional Education.

©
BPP Professional Education
2003

Contents

	Page
THE BPP STUDY TEXT	(v)
HELP YOURSELF STUDY FOR YOUR ACCA EXAMS	(vii)
The right approach – developing your personal study plan – suggested study sequence	
SYLLABUS	(xii)
STUDY GUIDE	(xvi)
THE EXAM PAPER	(xxiv)
OXFORD BROOKES BSC (Hons) IN APPLIED ACCOUNTING	(xxvii)
OXFORD INSTITUTE OF INTERNATIONAL FINANCE MBA	(xxvii)
SYLLABUS MINDMAP	(xxviii)

PART A: GENERAL FRAMEWORK
1	Introduction to accounting	3

PART B: ACCOUNTING CONCEPTS AND PRINCIPLES
2	The accounting and business equations	23
3	An introduction to financial statements	37

PART C: DOUBLE ENTRY BOOKKEEPING AND ACCOUNTING TREATMENTS
4	Sources, records and the books of prime entry	55
5	Ledger accounting and double entry	67
6	From trial balance to financial statements	92
7	The cost of goods sold, accruals and prepayments	106
8	Discounts, bad debts and provisions	122
9	Accounting for stocks	140
10	Fixed assets - depreciation, disposal and revaluation	160
11	Bank reconciliations	200
12	Control accounts	210
13	Correction of errors	222

PART D: ACCOUNTING CONVENTIONS AND STANDARDS
14	Accounting conventions	235
15	Intangible fixed assets	259
16	Provisions, contingencies and post balance sheet events	271

PART E: FINANCIAL STATEMENTS
17	Incomplete records	287
18	Partnership accounts	314
19	Limited companies	325
20	Cash flow statements	350
21	Group accounts	368

Contents

PART F: INTERPRETATION OF ACCOUNTS
22   Ratio analysis   395

OTHER TOPICS

PART G: MISCELLANEOUS TOPICS
23   Computer applications in accounting   427
24   The regulatory framework   443
25   Usefulness of financial accounting   463

EXAM QUESTION BANK   475

EXAM ANSWER BANK   513

INDEX   569

ORDER FORM

REVIEW FORM & FREE PRIZE DRAW

THE BPP STUDY TEXT

Aims of this Study Text

To provide you with the knowledge and understanding, skills and application techniques that you need if you are to be successful in your exams

This Study Text has been written around the **Preparing Financial Statements** syllabus.

- It is **comprehensive**. It covers the syllabus content. No more, no less.
- It is written at the **right level**. Each chapter is written with the ACCA's **study guide** in mind.
- It is targeted to the **exam**. We have taken account of the **pilot paper and all sittings so far**, questions put to the examiners at ACCA conferences and the assessment methodology.

To allow you to study in the way that best suits your learning style and the time you have available, by following your personal Study Plan (see page (viii))

You may be studying at home on your own until the date of the exam, or you may be attending a full-time course. You may like to (and have time to) read every word, or you may prefer to (or only have time to) skim-read and devote the remainder of your time to question practice. Wherever you fall in the spectrum, you will find the BPP Study Text meets your needs in designing and following your personal Study Plan.

To tie in with the other components of the BPP Effective Study Package to ensure you have the best possible chance of passing the exam (see page (vi))

The BPP Effective Study Package

Recommended period of use	Elements of the BPP Effective Study Package
From the outset and throughout	**Learning to learn accountancy** Read this invaluable book as you begin your studies and refer to it as you work through the various elements of the BPP Effective Study Package. It will help you to acquire knowledge, practice and revise, efficiently and effectively.
Three to twelve months before the exam	**Study Text and i-Learn** Use the Study Text to acquire knowledge, understanding, skills and the ability to apply techniques. Use BPP's **i-Learn** product to reinforce your learning.
Throughout	**Virtual Campus** Study, practice, revise and take advantage of other useful resources with BPP's fully interactive e-learning site with comprehensive tutor support.
Throughout	**MCQ cards and i-Pass** Revise your knowledge and ability to apply techniques, as well as practising this key exam question format, with 150 multiple choice questions. **i-Pass**, our computer-based testing package, provides objective test questions in a variety of formats and is ideal for self-assessment.
One to six months before the exam	**Practice & Revision Kit** Try the numerous examination-format questions, for which there are realistic suggested solutions prepared by BPP's own authors. Then attempt the two mock exams.
From three months before the exam until the last minute	**Passcards** Work through these short, memorable notes which are focused on what is most likely to come up in the exam you will be sitting.
One to six months before the exam	**Success Tapes** These audio tapes cover the vital elements of your syllabus in less than 90 minutes per subject. Each tape also contains exam hints to help you fine tune your strategy.

HELP YOURSELF STUDY FOR YOUR ACCA EXAMS

Exams for professional bodies such as ACCA are very different from those you have taken at college or university. You will be under **greater time pressure before** the exam – as you may be combining your study with work as well as in the exam room. There are many different ways of learning and so the BPP Study Text offers you a number of different tools to help you through. Here are some hints and tips: they are not plucked out of the air, but **based on research and experience**. (You don't need to know that long-term memory is in the same part of the brain as emotions and feelings – but it's a fact anyway.)

The right approach

1 The right attitude

Believe in yourself	Yes, there is a lot to learn. Yes, it is a challenge. But thousands have succeeded before and you can too.
Remember why you're doing it	Studying might seem a grind at times, but you are doing it for a reason: to advance your career.

2 The right focus

Read through the Syllabus and Study guide	These tell you what you are expected to know and are supplemented by exam focus points in the text.
Study the Exam Paper section	Past exam papers are likely to be a reasonable guide of what you should expect in the exam.

3 The right method

The big picture	You need to grasp the detail – but keeping in mind how everything fits into the big picture will help you understand better. • The **Introduction** of each chapter puts the material in context. • The **Syllabus content**, **Study guide** and **Exam focus points** show you what you need to **grasp**.
In your own words	To absorb the information (and to practise your written communication skills), it helps **put it into your own words.** • **Take notes.** • Answer the **questions** in each chapter. You will practise your written communication skills, which become increasingly important as you progress through your ACCA exams. • Draw **mind maps**. We have an example for the whole syllabus. • Try 'teaching' to a colleague or friend.

Help Yourself Study for your ACCA Exams

Give yourself cues to jog your memory	The BPP Study Text uses **bold text** to **highlight key points** and **icons** to identify key features, such as **Exam focus points** and **Key terms.** • Try **colour coding** with a highlighter pen. • Write **key points** on cards.

4 The right review

Review, review, review	It is a **fact** that regularly reviewing a topic in summary form can **fix it in your memory**. Because **review** is so important, the BPP Study Text helps you to do so in many ways. • **Chapter roundups** summarise the key points in each chapter. Use them to recap each study session. • The **Quick quiz** is another review tool to ensure that you have grasped the essentials. • Go through the **Examples** in each chapter a second or third time.

Developing your personal Study Plan

The BPP *Learning to Learn Accountancy* book emphasises the need to prepare (and use) a study plan. Planning and sticking to the plan are key elements of learning success.

There are four steps you should work through.

Step 1. How do you learn?

First you need to be aware of your style of learning. The BPP Learning to Learn Accountancy book commits a chapter to this **self-discovery**. What types of intelligence do you display when learning? You might be advised to brush up on certain study skills before launching into this Study Text.

Help Yourself Study for your ACCA Exams

> BPP's **Learning to Learn Accountancy** book helps you to identify what intelligences you show more strongly and then details how you can tailor your study process to your preferences. It also includes handy hints on how to develop intelligences you exhibit less strongly, but which might be needed as you study accountancy.

Are you a **theorist** or are you more **practical**? If you would rather get to grips with a theory before trying to apply it in practice, you should follow the study sequence on page (x). If the reverse is true (you need to know why you are learning theory before you do so), you might be advised to flick through Study Text chapters and look at questions, case studies and examples (Steps 7, 8 and 9 in the **suggested study sequence**) before reading through the detailed theory.

Step 2. How much time do you have?

Work out the time you have available per week, given the following.

- The standard you have set yourself
- The time you need to set aside later for work on the Practice & Revision Kit and Passcards
- The other exam(s) you are sitting
- Very importantly, practical matters such as work, travel, exercise, sleep and social life

Note your time available in box A. A [Hours]

Step 3. Allocate your time

- Take the time you have available per week for this Study Text shown in box A, multiply it by the number of weeks available and insert the result in box B.   B [ ]

- Divide the figure in Box B by the number of chapters in this text and insert the result in box C.   C [ ]

Remember that this is only a rough guide. Some of the chapters in this book are longer and more complicated than others, and you will find some subjects easier to understand than others.

Step 4. Implement

Set about studying each chapter in the time shown in box C, following the key study steps in the order suggested by your particular learning style.

This is your personal **Study Plan**. You should try and combine it with the study sequence outlined below. You may want to modify the sequence a little (as has been suggested above) to adapt it to your **personal style**.

BPP's *Learning to Learn Accountancy* gives further guidance on developing a study plan and deciding when and where to study.

Help Yourself Study for your ACCA Exams

Suggested study sequence

Tackle the chapters in the order you find them in the Study Text. Taking into account your individual learning style, you could follow this sequence.

Key study steps	Activity
Step 1 **Topic list**	Each numbered topic is a numbered section in the chapter.
Step 2 **Introduction**	This gives you the **big picture** in terms of the **context** of the chapter. The content is referenced to the **Study Guide**, and **Exam Guidance** shows how the topic is likely to be examined. In other words, it sets your **objectives for study.**
Step 3 **Knowledge brought forward boxes**	In these we highlight information and techniques that it is assumed you have 'brought forward' with you from your earlier studies. If there are topics which have changed recently due to legislation for example, these topics are explained in more detail.
Step 4 **Explanations**	Proceed methodically through the chapter, reading each section thoroughly and making sure you understand.
Step 5 **Key terms and Exam focus points**	• **Key terms** can often earn you *easy marks* if you state them clearly and correctly in an appropriate exam answer (and they are indexed at the back of the text). • **Exam focus points** give you a good idea of how we think the examiner intends to examine certain topics.
Step 6 **Note taking**	Take brief notes if you wish, avoiding the temptation to copy out too much.
Step 7 **Examples**	Follow each through to its solution very carefully.
Step 8 **Case examples**	Study each one, and try to add flesh to them from your own experience – they are designed to show how the topics you are studying come alive (and often come unstuck) in the real world.
Step 9 **Questions**	Make a very good attempt at each one.
Step 10 **Answers**	Check yours against ours, and make sure you understand any discrepancies.
Step 11 **Chapter roundup**	Work through it very carefully, to make sure you have grasped the major points it is highlighting.
Step 12 **Quick quiz**	When you are happy that you have covered the chapter, use the **Quick quiz** to check how much you have remembered of the topics covered.
Step 13 **Question(s) in the Question bank**	Either at this point, or later when you are thinking about revising, make a full attempt at the **Question(s)** suggested at the very end of the chapter. You can find these at the end of the Study Text, along with the **Answers** so you can see how you did. We highlight those that are introductory, and those which are of the standard you would expect to find in an exam.

Short of time: *Skim study technique?*

You may find you simply do not have the time available to follow all the key study steps for each chapter, however you adapt them for your particular learning style. If this is the case, follow the **skim study** technique below (the icons in the Study Text will help you to do this).

- Study the chapters in the order you find them in the Study Text.
- For each chapter:
    - Follow the key study steps 1-3, and then skim-read through step 4. Jump to step 11, and then go back to step 5.
    - Follow through steps 7 and 8, and prepare outline answers to questions (steps 9/10).
    - Try the Quick Quiz (step 12), following up any items you can't answer, then do a plan for the Question (step 13), comparing it against our answers.
    - You should probably still follow step 6 (note-taking), although you may decide simply to rely on the BPP Passcards for this.

Moving on...

However you study, when you are ready to embark on the practice and revision phase of the BPP Effective Study Package, you should still refer back to this Study Text, both as a source of **reference** (you should find the list of key terms and the index particularly helpful for this) and as a **refresher** (the Chapter Roundups and Quick Quizzes help you here).

And remember to keep careful hold of this Study Text – you will find it invaluable in your work.

More advice on Study Skills can be found in the BPP **Learning to Learn Accountancy** book

Syllabus

SYLLABUS

Aim

To develop knowledge and understanding of the techniques used to prepare year-end financial statements, including necessary underlying records, and the interpretation of financial statements for incorporated enterprises, partnerships and sole traders.

Objectives

On completion of this paper students should be able to:

- describe the role and function of external financial reports and identify their users
- explain the accounting concepts and conventions present in generally accepted accounting principles
- record and summarise accounting data
- maintain records relating to fixed asset acquisition and disposal
- prepare basic financial statements for sole traders, partnerships, incorporated enterprises and simple groups
- appraise financial performance and the position of an organisation through the calculation and review of basic ratios
- demonstrate the skills expected in Part 1

Position of the paper in the overall syllabus

No prior knowledge is required before commencing study for Paper 1.1. There is some connection with Paper 1.2 *Financial Information for Management* in the areas of performance management and data recording. There are no links with Paper 1.3 *Managing People*.

The basic financial accounting in Paper 1.1 is developed in Paper 2.5 *Financial Reporting* and Paper 3.6 *Advanced Corporate Reporting*. Knowledge from Paper 1.1 provides the background to Paper 2.6 *Audit and Internal Review*.

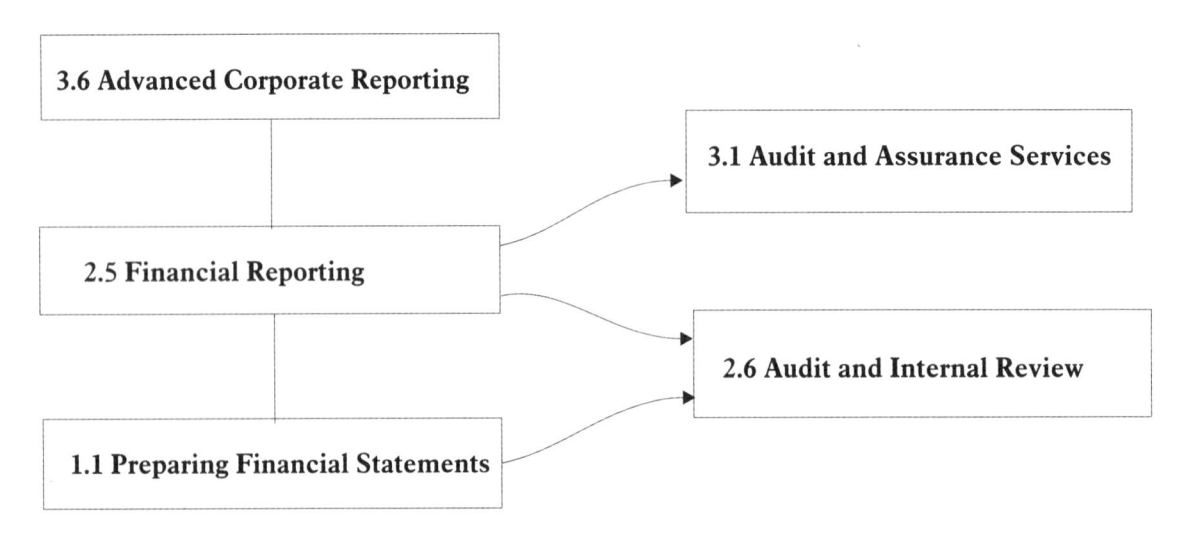

Syllabus content

1 General framework

(a) Types of business entity - limited companies, partnerships and sole traders.

(b) Forms of capital and capital structure in incorporated entities.

(c) The role of the Financial Reporting Council, the Financial Reporting Review Panel, Accounting Standards Board (ASB) and the Urgent Issues Task Force.

(d) Application of Financial Reporting Standards (FRSs) and Statements of Standard Accounting Practice (SSAPs) to the preparation and presentation of financial statements.

(e) The ASB's Statement of Principles for Financial Reporting (chapters 1, 2 and 3 only).

2 Accounting concepts and principles

(a) Basic accounting concepts and principles as stated in the ASB's Statement of Principles for Financial Reporting.

(b) Other accounting concepts

   (i) Historical cost
   (ii) Money measurement
   (iii) Entity
   (iv) Dual aspect
   (v) Time interval.

3 Double-entry bookkeeping and accounting systems

(a) Double-entry bookkeeping and accounting systems

   (i) Form and content of accounting records (manual and computerised)
   (ii) Books of original entry, including journals
   (iii) Sales and purchase ledgers
   (iv) Cash book
   (v) General ledger
   (vi) Trial balance
   (vii) Accruals, prepayments and adjustments
   (viii) Assets registers
   (ix) Petty cash.

(b) Confirming and correcting mechanisms

   (i) Control accounts
   (ii) Bank reconciliations
   (iii) Suspense accounts and the correction of errors.

(c) General principles of the operation of a value added tax.

(d) Computerised accounting systems.

4 Accounting treatments

(a) Fixed assets, tangible and intangible

Syllabus

(i) Distinction between capital and revenue expenditure
(ii) Accounting for acquisitions and disposals

(iii) Depreciation - definition, reasons for and methods, including straight line, reducing balance and sum of digits

(iv) Research and development

(v) Elementary treatment of goodwill.

(b) Current assets

(i) Stock (excluding long-term contracts)
(ii) Debtors, including accounting for bad and doubtful debts
(iii) Cash.

(c) Current liabilities and accruals

(d) Shareholders' equity

(e) Post balance sheet events

(f) Contingencies

5 Financial statements

(a) Objectives of financial statements

(b) Users and their information needs

(c) Key features of financial statements

(i) Balance sheet
(ii) Profit and loss account
(iii) Cash flow statement
(iv) Notes to the financial statements (examined to a limited extent - see d (iii) below).

(d) Preparation of financial statements for:

(i) Sole traders, including incomplete records techniques

(ii) Partnerships

(iii) Limited companies, including profit and loss accounts and balance sheets for internal purposes and for external purposes in accordance with Companies Act 1985 formats and preparation of basic cash flow statements for limited liability companies (excluding group cash flow statements). The following notes to the financial statements will be examinable and no others:

- Statement of movements in reserves
- Fixed assets
- Exceptional and extraordinary items
- Post balance sheet events
- Contingent liabilities and contingent assets
- Research and development expenditure

(iv) Groups of companies - preparation of a basic consolidated balance sheet for a company with one subsidiary.

6 Interpretation

(a) Ratio analysis of accounting information and basic interpretation.

Excluded topics

The syllabus content outlines the area for assessment. No areas of knowledge are specifically excluded from the syllabus.

Key areas of the syllabus

The objective of Paper 1.1, *Preparing Financial Statements*, is to ensure that candidates have the necessary basic accounting knowledge and skill to progress to the more advanced work of Paper 2.5 *Financial Reporting*. The two main skills required are:

- the ability to prepare basic financial statements and the underlying accounting records on which they are based.
- an understanding of the principles on which accounting is based.

The key topic areas are as follows:

- preparation of financial statements for limited companies for internal purposes or for publication
- preparation of financial statements for partnerships and sole traders (including incomplete records)
- basic group accounts - consolidated balance sheet for a company with one subsidiary
- basic bookkeeping and accounting procedures
- accounting conventions and concepts
- interpretation of financial statements
- cash flow statements
- accounting standards - SSAPs 9, 13 and 17 plus FRSs 1, 3 and the relevant sections of FRSs 12, 15 and 18.

Study Guide

Paper 1.1(U)

Preparing Financial Statements
(United Kingdom)

Study Guide

1 INTRODUCTION TO ACCOUNTING

Syllabus reference 1a, b, c, d, e, 5a and b

- Define accounting - recording, analysing and summarising transaction data.
- Explain types of business entity
  - sole trader
  - partnership
  - limited company
- Explain users of financial statements and accounting information.
- Explain the main elements of financial statements:
  - balance sheet
  - profit and loss account
- Explain the purpose of each of the main statements.
- Explain the nature, principles and scope of accounting.
- Identify the desirable qualities of accounting information and the usefulness of each (See also Session 14).
- Explain the regulatory system:
  - Financial Reporting Council, Financial Reporting Review Panel, Accounting Standards Board, Urgent Issues Task Force, Companies legislation.
- Explain the difference between capital and revenue items.

2 BASIC BALANCE SHEET AND PROFIT AND LOSS ACCOUNT

Syllabus reference 2a, b, 5c i and ii

- Explain how the balance sheet equation and business entity convention underlie the balance sheet.
- Define assets and liabilities.
- Explain how and why assets and liabilities are disclosed in the balance sheet.
- Draft a simple balance sheet in vertical format.
- Explain the matching convention and how it applies to revenue and expenses.
- Explain how and why revenue and expenses are disclosed in the trading and profit and loss account.
- Illustrate how the balance sheet and trading and profit and loss account are interrelated.
- Draft a simple trading and profit and loss account in vertical format.
- Explain the significance of gross profit and the gross profit as a percentage of sales.

3-4 BOOKKEEPING PRINCIPLES

Syllabus reference 3a and c

- Identify the main data sources and records in an accounting system.
- Explain the functions of each data source and record.
- Explain the concept of double entry and the duality concept.
- Outline the form of accounting records in a typical manual system.
- Outline the form of accounting records in a typical computerised system.
- Explain debit and credit.
- Distinguish between asset, liability, revenue and expense accounts.
- Explain the meaning of the balance on each type of account.
- Illustrate how to balance a ledger account.

- Record cash transactions in ledger accounts.
- Record credit sale and purchase transactions in ledger accounts.
- Explain the division of the ledger into sections.
- Record credit sales and purchase transactions using day books.
- Explain sales and purchases returns and their recording.
- Explain the general principles of the operation of value added tax and the consequent accounting entries.
- Explain the need for a record of petty cash transactions.
- Illustrate the typical format of the petty cash book.
- Explain the importance of using the imprest system to control petty cash.
- Extract the ledger balances into a trial balance.
- Prepare a simple profit and loss account and balance sheet from a trial balance.
- Explain and illustrate the process of closing the ledger accounts in the accounting records when the financial statements have been completed.

5 THE JOURNAL; LEDGER CONTROL ACCOUNTS; BANK RECONCILIATIONS

Syllabus reference 3b

- Explain the uses of the journal.
- Illustrate the use of the journal and the posting of journal entries into ledger accounts.
- Explain the types of error which may occur in bookkeeping systems, identifying those which can and those which cannot be detected by preparing a trial balance.
- Illustrate the use of the journal in correcting errors, including the use of a suspense account.
- Explain the preparation of statements correcting the profit for errors discovered.
- Explain the nature and purpose of control accounts for the sales and purchases ledgers.
- Explain how control accounts relate to the double entry system.
- Construct and agree a ledger control account from given information.
- Explain the purpose of bank reconciliation statements and the need for entries in the cash book when reconciling.
- Draft a bank reconciliation statement.

6 COMPUTERISED ACCOUNTING SYSTEMS

Syllabus reference 3d

- Compare manual and computerised accounting systems.
- Identify the advantages and disadvantages of computerised systems.
- Describe the main elements of a computerised accounting system.
- Describe typical data processing work.
- Explain the use of integrated accounting packages.
- Explain the nature and use of micro-computers.
- Explain other business uses of computers.
- Explain the nature and purpose of spreadsheets.
- Explain the nature and purpose of database systems.

7 THE FINANCIAL STATEMENTS OF A SOLE TRADER 1; STOCK, ACCRUALS AND PREPAYMENTS

Syllabus reference 5d i, 4b i

- Revise the format of the trading and profit and loss account and balance sheet from Sessions 1 and 2.
- Explain the need for adjustments for stock in preparing financial statements.

Study Guide

- Illustrate trading accounts with opening and closing stock.
- Explain how opening and closing stock are recorded in the stock account.
- Discuss alternative methods of valuing stock.
- Explain the provisions of SSAP 9 Stocks and Long-Term Contracts (excluding long-term contracts).
- Explain the use of continuous and period end stock records.
- Explain the need for adjustments for accruals and prepayments in preparing financial statements.
- Illustrate the process of adjusting for accruals and prepayments in preparing financial statements, emphasising the effects in both the profit and loss account and the balance sheet.
- Prepare financial statements for a sole trader including adjustments for stock, accruals and prepayments.
- Explain how to calculate the value of closing stock from given movements in stock levels, using FIFO (first in fist out), LIFO (last in first out) and AVCO (average cost).

8 THE FINANCIAL STATEMENTS OF A SOLE TRADER 2; DEPRECIATION AND BAD AND DOUBTFUL DEBTS

Syllabus reference 4a i to iii; 4b ii

- Revise the difference between fixed assets and current assets.
- Define and explain the purpose of depreciation as stated in FRS 15 Tangible Fixed Assets.
- Explain the advantages, disadvantages and calculation of the straight line, reducing balance and sum of digits methods of depreciation.
- Explain the relevance of consistency and subjectivity in accounting for depreciation.
- Explain how depreciation is presented in the profit and loss account and balance sheet.
- Explain how depreciation expense and accumulated depreciation are recorded in ledger accounts.
- Explain the inevitability of bad debts in most businesses.
- Illustrate the bookkeeping entries to write off a bad debt and the effect on the profit and loss account and balance sheet.
- Illustrate the bookkeeping entries to record bad debts recovered.
- Explain the difference between writing off a bad debt and making a provision for a doubtful debt.
- Explain and illustrate the bookkeeping entries to create and adjust a provision for doubtful debts.
- Illustrate how to include movements in the provision for doubtful debts in the profit and loss account and how the closing balance of the provision may appear in the balance sheet.
- Prepare a set of financial statements for a sole trader from a trial balance, after allowing for accruals and prepayments, depreciation and bad and doubtful debts.

9-10 INCOMPLETE RECORDS

Syllabus reference 5d i

- Explain techniques used in incomplete record situations:
  - Calculation of opening capital
  - Use of ledger total accounts to calculate missing figures.
  - Use of cash and/or bank summaries
  - Use of given gross profit percentage to calculate missing figures.

- Explain the calculation of profit or loss as the difference between opening and closing net assets.

11 REVISE ALL WORK TO DATE

12-13 PARTNERSHIP ACCOUNTS

Syllabus reference 5d ii

- Define the circumstances creating a partnership.
- Explain the advantages and disadvantages of operating as a partnership, compared with operating as a sole trader or limited liability company.
- Explain the typical contents of a partnership agreement, including profit-sharing terms.
- Explain the accounting differences between partnerships and sole traders:
    - Capital accounts
    - Current accounts
    - Division of profits
- Explain how to record partners' shares of profits/losses and their drawings in the accounting records and financial statements.
- Explain how to account for guaranteed minimum profit share.

- Explain how to account for interest on drawings.
- Draft the profit and loss account, including division of profit, and balance sheet of a partnership from a given trial balance.

Note: Other aspects of partnership (admission and retirement of partners, amalgamation and dissolution) are *not* examinable.

14 ACCOUNTING CONCEPTS AND CONVENTIONS; THE ASB'S 'STATEMENT OF PRINCIPLES FOR FINANCIAL REPORTING' (THE STATEMENT)

Syllabus reference 1d and e; 2a and b; 5a and b

- Explain the need for an agreed conceptual framework for financial accounting.
- Explain the importance of the following accounting conventions (not mentioned in the Statement).
    - Business entity
    - Money measurement
    - Duality
    - Historical cost
    - Realisation
    - Time interval
- Revise the users of financial statements from Session 1.
- Explain the qualitative characteristics of financial statements as described in chapter 3 of the Statement (Revision from Session 1).

15 ACCOUNTING FOR LIMITED COMPANIES 1 - BASICS

Syllabus reference 5d iii; 4d

Note: The inclusion of an introductory coverage of company accounts at this point is to enable students to practise the work so far on financial statements using questions on limited companies, and also to facilitate understanding of reserves referred to in the next Session.

- Explain the legal and other differences between a sole trader and a limited company.
- Explain the advantages and disadvantages of operation as a limited company rather than as a sole trader.
- Explain the capital structure of a limited company including:
    - Authorised share capital
    - Issued share capital
    - Called up share capital
    - Paid up share capital
    - Ordinary shares
    - Preference shares
    - Deferred shares
    - Debentures.
- Explain the nature of reserves and the difference between capital and revenue reserves.
- Explain the share premium account.

Study Guide

- Explain the other reserves which may appear in a company balance sheet.
- Explain why the heading 'profit and loss account' appears in a company balance sheet.
- Explain the recording of dividends paid and proposed in ledger accounts and the financial statements.
- Explain the nature of corporation tax on company profits and illustrate the ledger account required to record it.
- Explain how corporation tax appears in the profit and loss account and balance sheet of a company.
- Draft a profit and loss account and balance sheet for a company for internal purposes.

16 RECORDING AND PRESENTATION OF TRANSACTIONS IN FIXED ASSETS; LIABILITIES AND PROVISIONS

Syllabus reference 4a i to iii; 4b and c

- Explain and illustrate the ledger entries to record the acquisition and disposal of fixed assets, using separate accounts for fixed asset cost and accumulated depreciation.
- Explain and illustrate the inclusion of profits or losses on disposal in the profit and loss account.
- Explain that the upward revaluation of an asset cannot constitute a gain which may appear in the profit and loss account.
- Explain how to record the revaluation of a fixed asset in ledger accounts and the effect in the balance sheet.
- Explain why, after an upward revaluation, depreciation must be based on the revised figure, referring to the requirements of FRS 15 Tangible Fixed Assets.
- Explain the adjustments necessary if changes are made in the estimated useful life and/or residual value of a fixed asset.
- Explain how fixed asset balances and movements are disclosed in company financial statements in accordance with FRS 15 Tangible Fixed Assets and the Companies Acts.
- Define and give examples of liabilities.
- Explain the distinction between current and long-term liabilities.
- Explain the difference between liabilities and provisions.

17 GOODWILL, RESEARCH AND DEVELOPMENT

Syllabus reference 4a iv and v

- Define goodwill
- Explain the factors leading to the creation of non-purchased goodwill.
- Explain the difference between purchased and non-purchased goodwill.
- Explain why non-purchased goodwill is not normally recognised in financial statements.
- Explain how purchased goodwill arises and is reflected in financial statements.
- Explain the need to amortise purchased goodwill.
- Define 'research' and 'development'.
- Classify expenditure as research or development.
- Calculate amounts to be capitalised as development expenditure from given information.
- Disclose research and development expenditure in the financial statements in accordance with SSAP 13.

18 POST BALANCE SHEET EVENTS AND CONTINGENCIES

Syllabus reference 4e and f

- Define a post balance sheet event in accordance with SSAP 17 Accounting for Post Balance Sheet Events.
- Distinguish between adjusting and non-adjusting events and explain the methods of including them in financial statements.
- Classify events as adjusting or non-adjusting from a given list.
- Draft notes to company financial statements including requisite details of post balance sheet events.
- Define 'contingent liability' and 'contingent asset' in accordance with FRS 12 Provisions, Contingent Liabilities and Contingent Assets.
- Explain the different ways of accounting for contingent liabilities and contingent assets according to their degree of probability.
- Draft notes to company financial statements including requisite details of contingent liabilities and contingent assets.

19, 20 AND 21 ACCOUNTING FOR LIMITED COMPANIES 2 - ADVANCED

Syllabus reference 5d iii

- Revise the work of Session 15 and the preparation of financial statements for limited companies for internal purposes including the treatment of corporation tax and dividends, including proposed dividends.
- Revise the work of Session 15 on company capital structure, including equity shares, preference shares and debentures.
- Outline the advantages and disadvantages of raising finance by borrowing rather than by the issue of ordinary or preference shares.
- Define and illustrate gearing (leverage).
- Define a bonus (capitalisation) issue and its advantages and disadvantages.
- Record a bonus (capitalisation) issue in ledger accounts and show the effect in the balance sheet.
- Define a rights issue and its advantages and disadvantages.
- Record a rights issue in ledger accounts and show the effect in the balance sheet.

- Revise the definition of reserves and the different types of reserves.
- Explain the need for regulation of companies in legislation and accounting standards.
- Explain the provisions of legislation and accounting standards governing financial statements (excluding group aspects).
  - Companies Act 1985 including the standard formats for company financial statements.
  - FRS 3 Reporting Financial Performance, including provisions relating to the profit and loss account, the statement of recognised gains and losses and the note of historical cost profits and losses.
- Explain the notes to financial statements required for the syllabus.
  - Statement of movements in reserves.
  - Details of fixed assets.
  - Details of post balance sheet events.

- Details of contingent liabilities and contingent assets (see Session 18).
- Details of research and development expenditure.

• Prepare financial statements for publication complying with relevant accounting standards and legislation as detailed above.

22 REVISE ALL WORK TO DATE

23 CASH FLOW STATEMENTS

Syllabus reference 5c iii and 5d

• Explain the difference between profit and cash flow.

• Explain the need for management to control cash flow.

• Explain the value to users of financial statements of a cash flow statement.

• Explain the provisions of FRS 1 Cash Flow Statements and the standard format therein (excluding group aspects).

• Explain the inward and outward flows of cash in a typical company.

• Explain how to calculate the figures needed for the cash flow statement

including among others:
  - Cash flows from operating activities (indirect method)
  - Cash flows from investing activities (purchases, sales and depreciation of fixed assets).

• Explain how to calculate cash flow from operating activities using the direct method.

• Review of information to be derived from users from the cash flow statement (see also Sessions 25-26).

• Prepare cash flow statements from given balance sheets with or without a profit and loss account.

24 BASIC CONSOLIDATED ACCOUNTS

Syllabus reference 5d iv

• Define parent company, subsidiary company and group.

• Explain the provisions of FRS 2 Accounting for Subsidiary Undertakings and the Companies Acts defining which companies must be consolidated.

• Prepare a consolidated balance sheet for a parent with one wholly-owned subsidiary (no goodwill arising).

• Explain how to calculate the retained profit balance for the consolidated balance sheet.

• Explain how other reserves (share premium account and revaluation reserve) are dealt with on consolidation.

• Introduce the concept of goodwill on acquisition and illustrate the effect on the consolidated balance sheet.

• Explain the need to amortise goodwill and illustrate in the workings.

• Explain a methodical approach to calculating the necessary figures for the consolidated balance sheet.

• Introduce the concept of minority interests in subsidiaries and illustrate the effect on the consolidated balance sheet.

• Explain how the calculation of the minority interest is made in the workings.

25-26 INTERPRETATION OF FINANCIAL STATEMENTS

Syllabus reference 6

• Revise users of financial statements and their information needs.

- Explain the advantages and disadvantages of interpretation based on financial statements.
- Explain the factors forming the environment in which the business operates.
- Explain the uses of ratio analysis.
- Explain the main ratios to be used in interpreting financial statements to appraise:
  - Profitability
  - Liquidity
  - Working capital efficiency
  - Financial risk
  - Performance from an investor's point of view.
- Explain the working capital cycle (or cash operating cycle).
- Explain normal levels of certain ratios.
- Explain how to formulate comments on movements in ratios between one period and another or on differences between ratios for different businesses.
- Explain the factors which may distort ratios, leading to unreliable conclusions.
- Prepare and comment on a comprehensive range of ratios for a business.

27 THE THEORETICAL AND OPERATIONAL ADEQUACY OF FINANCIAL REPORTING

Syllabus reference 2a and b

- Revise the qualitative characteristics of financial information from Sessions 1 and 14.
- Explain the advantages and disadvantages of historical cost accounting (HCA) in times of changing prices.
- Explain in principle the main alternatives to HCA:
  - Current purchasing power accounting (CPP)
  - Current cost accounting (CCA)

  Note: computational questions on CPP and CCA will not be set.
- Revise the roles of the ASB in raising standards of financial reporting by setting accounting standards.

28 REVISION

The Exam Paper

THE PAPER BASED EXAMINATION

The examination is a **three hour paper** divided into **two sections**.

Section A will comprise twenty five multiple choice questions (MCQs) which will cover the whole of the syllabus. Each MCQ is worth two marks.

Section B will comprise five compulsory questions. The questions will cover the preparation of financial statements, the underlying accounting records, relevant accounting standards and interpretation of accounts. Marks awarded can vary from 8 to 12 marks per question.

There will be an element of computation but candidates should be aware that their knowledge will also be tested by means of discursive questions.

		Number of Marks
Section A:	25 compulsory multiple choice questions (2 marks each)	50
Section B:	5 compulsory questions	50
		100

Additional information

Candidates need to be aware that questions involving knowledge of new examinable regulations will not be set until at least six months after the last day of the month in which the regulation was issued.

The Study Guide provides more detailed guidance on the syllabus. Examinable documents are listed in the 'Exam Notes' section of the *Students' Newsletter*.

Analysis of past papers

The analysis below shows the topics which were examined in all sittings of the current syllabus so far and in the Pilot Paper.

June 2003

Section A

Twenty five multiple choice questions

Section B

2 Partnership accounts (12 marks)
3 Company cash flow statement (9 marks)
4 Incomplete records (9 marks)
5 Ratio analysis: calculation and comment (9 marks)
6 Definitions: reserves (including examples); bonus issue; rights issue (11 marks)

December 2002

Section A

Twenty five multiple choice questions

Section B

2 Prepare company profit and loss account for publication (12 marks)
3 Journal entries to correct errors; suspense account (9 marks)
4 Consolidated balance sheet (11 marks)
5 Depreciation policies (8 marks)
6 Advising directors as to whether items need to be disclosed in the accounts and the effects of disclosure (10 marks)

The Exam Paper

June 2002

Section A

Twenty five multiple choice questions

Section B

2 Limited company's cash flow statement (10 marks)
3 Fixed assets: ledger accounting and cash flows (9 marks)
4 Limited company balance sheet using CA 1985 format (11 marks)
5 Define and explain: going concern, accruals, substance over form and historical costs (10 marks)
6 Ratio analysis: calculation of set ratios and explaining the results (10 marks)

Note: For exams prior to June 2002, Section B questions were awarded 10 marks each

December 2001

Section A

Twenty five multiple choice questions

Section B

2 Limited company's profit and loss account
3 Incomplete records : sales, purchases and closing stock
4 Consolidated balance sheet
5 *Statement of Principles* : materiality, prudence, comparability
6 Overtrading : accounting ratios and proposals to rectify position

Pilot paper

Section A

Twenty five multiple choice questions

Section B

2 Accounting concepts: materiality; substance over form; and money measurement
3 Ratio analysis
4 Cash flow statement
5 FRS 12, SSAP 17 and SSAP 9
6 Preparation of company balance sheet

The Exam Paper

THE COMPUTER BASED EXAMINATION

ACCA offers computer based examinations (CBE) for Paper 1.1 (in addition to the conventional paper based examinations). Initially CBE was available only on disk, but from 31 October 2002 online examinations are also available. From 31 December 2003, the disk system will cease and CBE will then only be available online.

Computer based examinations must be taken at ACCA Approved Computer Examination Centres.

How does CBE work?

- The exam can be taken any time, not just in June and December
- Questions are displayed on a monitor
- Candidates enter their answer directly onto the computer
- Candidates have three hours to complete the examination
- When the candidate has completed their examination, the computer automatically marks the file containing the candidate's answers
- Candidates are provided with a certificate showing their results before leaving the examination room
- The Approved Assessment Centre returns the examination disk to the ACCA (as proof of the candidate's performance)

Paper 1.1 CBE

You will have three hours in which to answer the questions, which are worth a total of 100 marks. All questions are objective test questions of the following types.

- Multiple choice (choose one answer from four)
- Multiple response 1 (select more than one answer from a number of options by clicking tick boxes)
- Multiple response 2 (choose one option from a number of drop-down menus)
- Number entry (enter a numerical answer to the question)

Visit the ACCA website for further information.

OXFORD BROOKES BSc (Hons) IN APPLIED ACCOUNTING

The standard required of candidates completing Part 2 is that required in the final year of a UK degree. Students completing Parts 1 and 2 will have satisfied the examination requirement for an honours degree in Applied Accounting, awarded by Oxford Brookes University.

To achieve the degree, you must also submit two pieces of work based on a **Research and Analysis Project.**

- A 5,000 word **Report** on your chosen topic, which demonstrates that you have acquired the necessary research, analytical and IT skills.
- A 1,500 word **Key Skills Statement**, indicating how you have developed your interpersonal and communication skills.

BPP was selected by the ACCA and Oxford Brookes University to produce the official text *Success in your Research and Analysis Project* to support students in this task. The book pays particular attention to key skills not covered in the professional examinations.

> AN ORDER FORM FOR THE NEW SYLLABUS MATERIAL, INCLUDING THE OXFORD BROOKES PROJECT TEXT, CAN BE FOUND AT THE END OF THIS STUDY TEXT.

OXFORD INSTITUTE OF INTERNATIONAL FINANCE MBA

The Oxford Institute of International Finance (OXIIF), a joint venture between the ACCA and Oxford Brookes University, offers an MBA for finance professionals.

For this MBA, credits are awarded for your ACCA studies, and entry to the MBA course is available to those who have completed their ACCA professional stage studies. The MBA was launched in 2002 and has attracted participants from all over the world.

The qualification features an introductory module (*Markets, Management and Strategy*). Other modules include *Global Business Strategy, Managing Self Development,* and *Organisational Change & Transformation.*

Research Methods are also taught, as they underpin the **research dissertation**.

The MBA programme is delivered through the use of targeted paper study materials, developed by BPP, and taught over the Internet by OXIIF personnel using BPP's virtual campus software.

For further information, please see the Oxford Institute's website: www.oxfordinstitute.org.

Syllabus mindmap

SYLLABUS MINDMAP

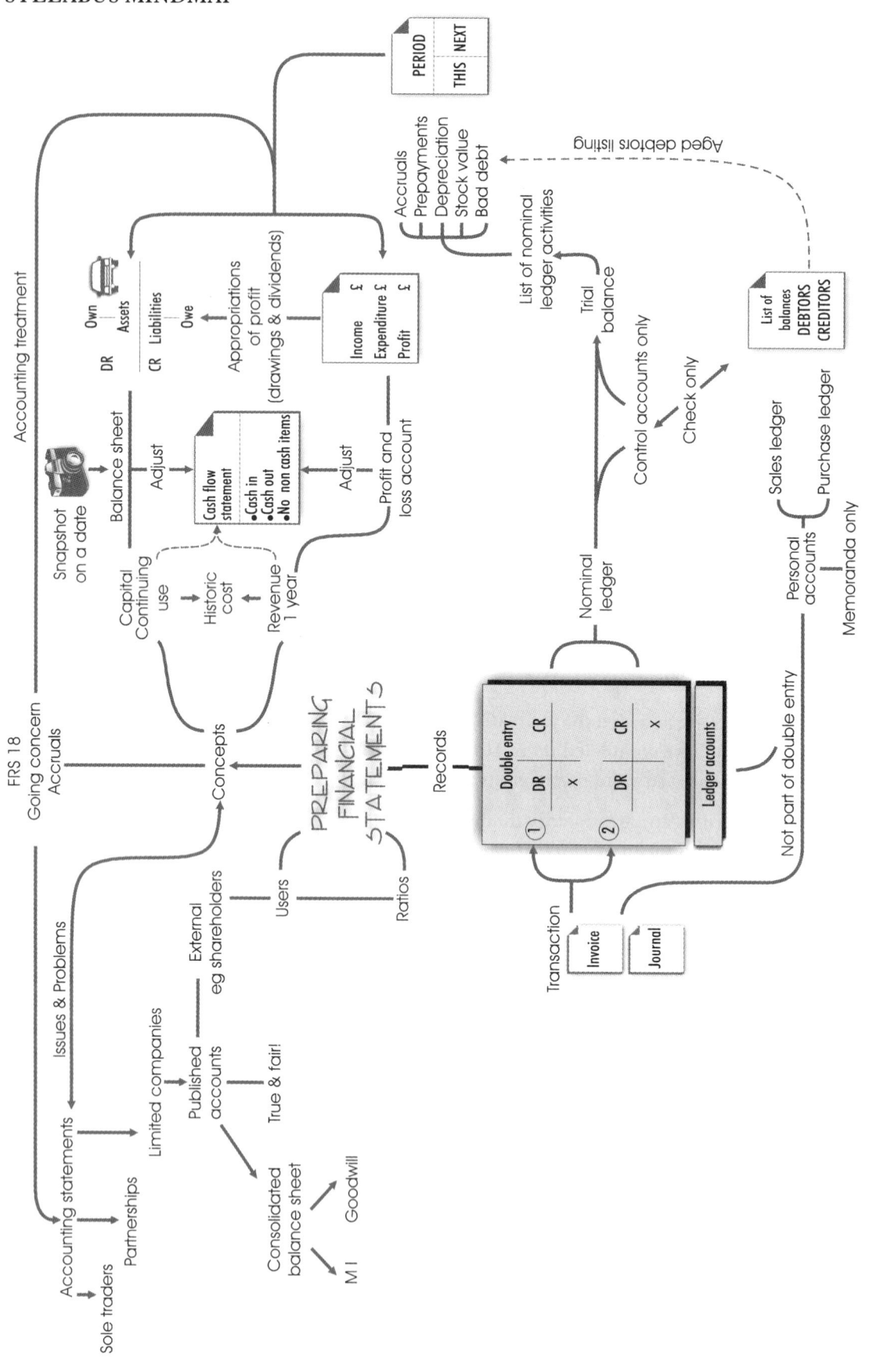

Part A
General framework

Chapter 1

INTRODUCTION TO ACCOUNTING

	Topic list	Syllabus reference
1	The purpose of accounting information	1 (a), 1(c), 5(a) – (b)
2	The main financial statements	1(a) – (e), 5(a)
3	Nature, principles and scope of accounting	1(a) - (e), 5(a)-(b)
4	Qualities of good accounting information	1(d), 5(a)
5	The regulatory system	1(c) – (e)
6	Capital and revenue expenditure	4(a)

Introduction

Paper 1.1 takes you from a standing start, through the 'nuts and bolts' of basic bookkeeping to a broader appreciation of the usefulness and limitations of accounting. As you work systematically through this Study Text, try to relate the knowledge you acquire to your practical experience at work.

Remember – accounting is an interactive subject: you only get good at it through doing it. Do not 'skip' any of the questions!

Before you learn how to prepare accounts it is important to understand why they are prepared. Sections 1 - 3 of this chapter introduce some basic ideas about accounts and give an indication of their purpose.

Now that you know what accounting information is for, you need to consider what makes accounting information useful. Section 4 of this chapter deals with the qualities which such information should have.

We touch on the standard setting process in section 5. This is covered in more detail in Chapter 24.

An important distinction is introduced: the distinction between capital and revenue expenditure. It is very important that you understand this distinction before moving on to the bookkeeping topics in Part C of the Study Text.

Study guide

Section 1 – Introduction to accounting

- Define accounting - recording, analysing and summarising transaction data.
- Explain types of business entity
    - sole trader
    - partnership
    - limited company
- Explain users of financial statements and accounting information.

Part A: General framework

- Explain the main elements of financial statements:
    - balance sheet
    - profit and loss account
- Explain the purpose of each of the main statements.
- Explain the nature, principles and scope of accounting.
- Identify the desirable qualities of accounting information and the usefulness of each.
- Explain the regulatory system:
    - Financial Reporting Council, Financial Reporting Review Panel, Accounting Standards Board, Urgent Issues Task Force, Companies legislation.
- Explain the difference between capital and revenue items.

Exam guide

As stated above, this chapter forms the foundation of your Paper 1.1 studies. You may have to answer MCQs on this general area. Also the needs of the users of financial accounting statements can (for example) form part of a question in section B of the exam.

1 THE PURPOSE OF ACCOUNTING INFORMATION

What is accounting?

> **KEY TERM**
>
> Accounting is a way of recording, analysing and summarising transactions of a business.

1.1 The transactions are recorded in 'books of prime entry' (see Chapter 4).

1.2 The transactions are then analysed and posted to the ledgers (see Chapter 5).

1.3 Finally the transactions are summarised in the financial statements (see Chapter 6).

What is a business?

1.4 There are a number of different ways of looking at a business. Some ideas are listed below.

- A business is a **commercial or industrial concern** which exists to deal in the manufacture, re-sale or supply of goods and services.
- A business is an **organisation which uses economic resources** to create goods or services which customers will buy.
- A business is an **organisation providing jobs** for people.
- A business **invests money in resources** (for example it buys buildings, machinery and so on, it pays employees) in order to make even more money for its owners.

1.5 This last definition introduces the important idea of profit. Business enterprises vary in character, size and complexity. They range from very small businesses (the local shopkeeper or plumber) to very large ones (ICI). But the objective of earning profit is common to all of them.

1: Introduction to accounting

> **KEY TERM**
>
> **Profit** is the excess of income over expenditure. When expenditure exceeds income, the business is running at a loss.

1.6 One of the jobs of an accountant is to measure income, expenditure and profit. It is not such a straightforward problem as it may seem and in later chapters we will look at some of the theoretical and practical difficulties involved.

Types of business entity

1.7 There are three main types of business entity.

- Sole traders
- Partnerships
- Limited companies

1.8 Sole traders are people who work for themselves. Examples include the local shopkeeper, a plumber and a hairdresser. Note that sole traders can employ people, the term 'sole trader' refers to the **ownership** of the business.

1.9 Partnerships occur when two or more sole traders decide to share the risks and rewards of a business together. Examples include an accountancy practice, a medical practice and a legal practice.

1.10 Limited companies are incorporated to take advantage of 'limited liability' for their owners (shareholders). This means that, while sole traders and partners are personally responsible for the amounts owed by their businesses, the shareholders of a limited company are only responsible for the amount to be paid for their shares.

1.11 Limited companies are dealt with in more detail in Chapter 19.

The need for accounts

1.12 Why do businesses need to produce accounts? If a business is being run efficiently, why should it have to go through all the bother of accounting procedures in order to produce financial information?

1.13 A business should produce information about its activities because there are various groups of people who want or need to know that information. This sounds rather vague: to make it clearer, we should look more closely at the classes of people who might need information about a business. We need also to think about what information in particular is of interest to the members of each class.

1.14 Large businesses are usually of interest to a greater variety of people than small businesses, so we will consider the case of a large public company whose shares can be purchased and sold on the Stock Exchange.

Users of financial statements and accounting information

1.15 The people who might be interested in financial information about a large public company may be classified as follows.

Part A: General framework

(a) **Managers of the company**. These are people appointed by the company's owners to supervise the day-to-day activities of the company. They need information about the company's financial situation as it is currently and as it is expected to be in the future. This is to enable them to manage the business efficiently and to take effective control and planning decisions.

(b) **Shareholders of the company**, ie the company's owners. These will want to assess how effectively management is performing its stewardship function. They will want to know how profitably management is running the company's operations and how much profit they can afford to withdraw from the business for their own use.

(c) **Trade contacts**, including suppliers who provide goods to the company on credit and customers who purchase the goods or services provided by the company. **Suppliers** will want to know about the company's ability to pay its debts; **customers** need to know that the company is a secure source of supply and is in no danger of having to close down.

(d) **Providers of finance to the company**. These might include a bank which permits the company to operate an overdraft, or provides longer-term finance by granting a loan. The bank will want to ensure that the company is able to keep up with interest payments, and eventually to repay the amounts advanced.

(e) **The Inland Revenue**, who will want to know about business profits in order to assess the tax payable by the company, and also the **Customs and Excise**.

(f) **Employees of the company**. These should have a right to information about the company's financial situation, because their future careers and the size of their wages and salaries depend on it.

(g) **Financial analysts and advisers**, who need information for their clients or audience. For example, stockbrokers will need information to advise investors in stocks and shares; credit agencies will want information to advise potential suppliers of goods to the company; and journalists need information for their reading public.

(h) **Government and their agencies.** Governments and their agencies are interested in the allocation of resources and therefore in the activities of enterprises. They also require information in order to provide a basis for national statistics.

(i) **The public**. Enterprises affect members of the public in a variety of ways. For example, enterprises may make a substantial contribution to a local economy by providing employment and using local suppliers. Another important factor is the effect of an enterprise on the environment, for example as regards pollution.

1.16 Accounting information is organised into financial statements to satisfy the **information needs** of these different groups. Not all will be equally satisfied.

1.17 **Managers** of a business need the most information, to help them take their planning and control decisions; and they obviously have 'special' access to information about the business, because they can get people to give them the types of statements they want. When managers want a large amount of information about the costs and profitability of individual products, or different parts of their business, they can arrange to obtain it through a system of cost and management accounting.

1: Introduction to accounting

Question 1

It is easy to see how 'internal' people get hold of accounting information. A manager, for example, can just go along to the accounts department and ask the staff there to prepare whatever accounting statements he needs. But external users of accounts cannot do this. How, in practice, can a business contact or a financial analyst access accounting information about a company?

Answer

The answer is that limited companies (though not other forms of business such as partnerships) are required to make certain accounting information public. They do so by sending copies of the required information to the Registrar of Companies at Companies House. The information filed at Companies House is available, at a fee, to any member of the public who asks for it. Other sources include financial comment in the press and company brochures.

1.18 In addition to management information, financial statements are prepared and perhaps published for the benefit of other user groups.

(a) The **law** provides for the provision of some information. The Companies Acts require every company to publish accounting information for its shareholders; and companies must also file a copy of their accounts with the Registrar of Companies, so that any member of the public who so wishes can go and look at them.

(b) The **Inland Revenue** authorities will receive the information they need to make tax assessments.

(c) A **bank** might demand a forecast of a company's expected future cash flows as a pre-condition of granting an overdraft.

(d) The **professional accountancy bodies** have been jointly responsible for issuing **accounting standards** and some standards require companies to publish certain additional information. Accountants, as members of these professional bodies, are placed under a strong obligation to ensure that company accounts conform to the requirements of the standards.

(e) Some companies provide, voluntarily, specially prepared financial information for issue to their employees. These statements are known as **employee reports**.

Exam focus point

You may be asked about what information would be needed by managers, employees and shareholders, and how far their needs would be met by a company's published financial statements.

Non-commercial undertakings

1.19 It is not only businesses that need to prepare accounts. **Charities and clubs**, for example, prepare financial statements every year. Accounts also need to be prepared for **government** (public sector organisations).

1.20 **Section summary**

A **business** exists to make a **profit**.

Accounts are prepared so that owners, managers, lenders and other interested parties can see how the business is doing.

Part A: General framework

2 THE MAIN FINANCIAL STATEMENTS

2.1 The two main financial statements are the balance sheet and the profit and loss account.

> **KEY TERM**
>
> The **balance sheet** is simply a list of all the assets owned and all the liabilities owed by a business as at a particular date. It is a snapshot of the financial position of the business at a particular moment.

2.2 Assets and liabilities are explained in detail in Chapter 2. However, due to the nature of double entry bookkeeping, total assets will always equal total liabilities.

2.3 The amounts that the owners have invested in the business are amounts that the business owes to its owners, ie liabilities. These liabilities have a special name, they are called **capital**.

> **KEY TERM**
>
> A **profit and loss account** is a record of income generated and expenditure incurred over a given period. The profit and loss account shows whether the business has had more income than expenditure (a profit) or vice versa (a loss).

2.4 The period chosen will depend on the purpose for which the statement is produced. The profit and loss account which forms part of the published annual accounts of a **limited company** will be made up for the period of a **year**, commencing from the date of the previous year's accounts. On the other hand, **management** might want to keep a closer eye on a company's profitability by making up **quarterly or monthly** profit and loss accounts.

Purpose of financial statements

2.5 Both the balance sheet and the profit and loss account are **summaries of accumulated data**. For example, the profit and loss account shows a figure for income earned from selling goods to customers. This is the total amount of income earned from all the individual sales made during the period. One of the jobs of an accountant is to devise methods of recording such individual transactions and eventually to produce summarised financial statements from them.

2.6 The balance sheet and the profit and loss account form the basis of the accounts of most businesses. For limited companies, other information by way of statements and notes may be required by law and/or accounting standards. For example, a **cash flow statement** may be required. These are considered in detail later in this Study Text.

Non-financial statements

2.7 Limited companies are required by law to produce certain non-financial statements. These will be considered in detail in your later studies. For now a brief outline knowledge is all that is required.

(a) The **directors' report** provides further information about the company and its operations. Examples of areas covered include the company's principal activities, likely future developments, health and safety of employees and employment of disabled persons.

(b) The **auditors' report** is an independent report on the company's financial statements.

2.8 Most large companies include a **chairman's report** on their published financial statements, although they are not required to by law. The chairman's review usually appears as the first item in the annual report and is not subject to any regulations regarding its content. The chairman is therefore free to say exactly what he wishes. His comments will generally cover the following areas: an assessment of the year's results; an examination of factors influencing those results, eg the economic and political climate or the effect of strikes; a reference to major developments, eg takeovers or new products; capital expenditure plans; and an assessment of future prospects.

2.9 The chairman's message will usually convey a fair amount of **optimism,** even if the financial facts published later in the report make depressing reading. A strong point in favour of the chairman's review is that it is readable and readily comprehensible to the layman. A major drawback is that, with regard to future prospects, it is based on **opinion** rather than fact. It is useful background material.

2.10 Many large companies also include a glossy review of the business, which may include photographs, interviews, bar charts and other diagrams. This is essentially a public relations exercise.

Question 2

Most organisations produce accounting information of some sort. Try to get examples of the different information your employer produces, especially the annual accounts. Otherwise try the website of one of the major companies on the Internet eg ICI, Shell. Look through the information carefully. As you work through this Study Text, more and more of it will become understandable.

---

3 NATURE, PRINCIPLES AND SCOPE OF ACCOUNTING

3.1 You may have a wide understanding of what accounting is about. Your job may be in one area or type of accounting, but you must understand the breadth of work which an accountant undertakes.

Management accounting

3.2 So far in this chapter we have dealt with *financial* accounts. Financial accounting is mainly a method of reporting the results and financial position of a business. It is not primarily concerned with providing information towards the more efficient conduct of the business. Although financial accounts are of interest to management, their principal function is to satisfy the information needs of persons not involved in the day-to-day running of the business.

3.3 This is particularly clear in the context of the published accounts of limited companies. **Accounting Standards** (and company law) prescribe that a company should **produce accounts to be presented to the shareholders**. There are usually detailed regulations on what the accounts must contain and this enables shareholders to assess how well the directors (or management board) have run the company. Also there are certain outsiders who need information about a company: suppliers, customers, employees, tax authorities, the general public. Their information needs are satisfied, wholly or in part, by the company's published financial statements.

Part A: General framework

3.4 **The information needs of management go far beyond those of other account users.** Managers have the responsibility of planning and controlling the resources of the business. To do this they need much more detailed information than the financial statements disclose.

> **KEY TERM**
>
> **Management (or cost) accounting** is a management information system which analyses data to provide information as a basis for managerial action. The concern of a management accountant is to present accounting information in the form most helpful to management.

3.5 It is important that you understand this distinction between management accounting and financial accounting. The accounting statements drawn up by a management accountant are often prepared and presented very differently from those of the financial accountant; for example, they do not need to comply with company law or accounting standards. You should bear in mind the different reasons for preparing management and financial accounts, and the different people to whom they are addressed.

Financial management

3.6 Financial management is a separate discipline from both management accounting and financial accounting, although in a small organisation the three roles may be carried out by the same person.

3.7 The financial manager is responsible for raising finance and controlling financial resources, including the following decisions.

(a) Should the firm borrow from a bank or raise funds by issuing shares?
(b) How much should be paid as a dividend?
(c) Should the firm spend money on new machinery?
(d) How much credit should be given to customers?
(e) How much discount should be given to customers who pay early?

3.8 The subject of financial management will be considered in your more advanced studies.

Auditing

3.9 The annual accounts of a limited company must generally be **audited** by a person independent of the company. In practice, this often means that the members of the company appoint a firm of registered auditors to investigate the financial statements and report as to whether or not they show a true and fair view of the company's results for the year and its financial position at the end of the year.

3.10 When the auditors have completed their work they must prepare a **report** explaining the work that they have done and the **opinion** they have formed.

3.11 In simple cases they will be able to report that they have carried out their work in accordance with the Auditing Standards and that, in their opinion, the accounts show a true and fair view and are properly prepared in accordance with company legislation. This is described as an **unqualified** (or 'clean') audit report.

3.12 Sometimes the auditors may disagree with management on a point in the accounts. If they are unable to persuade the management to change the accounts, and if the item at issue is large or otherwise important, it is the auditors' duty to prepare a **qualified report**, setting out the matter(s) on which they disagree with the management.

3.13 The financial statements to which the auditors refer in their report comprise the following.

- The profit and loss account
- The balance sheet
- The cash flow statement
- Supporting notes

3.14 The auditors' report is included as a part of the company's published accounts. It is addressed to the members of the company (not to the management).

Internal audit

3.15 **Internal auditors are employees of the company whose duties are fixed by management** and who report on the effectiveness of internal control systems.

Question 3

They say that America is run by lawyers and Britain is run by accountants, but what do accountants do in your organisation or country? Before moving on to the next section, think of any accountants you know and the kind of jobs they do.

---

4 QUALITIES OF GOOD ACCOUNTING INFORMATION

4.1 Below are some features that accounting information should have if it is to be useful.

(a) **Relevance**. The information provided should satisfy the needs of information users. In the case of company accounts, clearly a wide range of information will be needed to satisfy a wide range of users.

(b) **Comprehensibility**. Information may be difficult to understand because it is skimpy or incomplete; but too much detail is also a defect which can cause difficulties of understanding.

(c) **Reliability**. Information will be more reliable if it is independently verified. The law requires that the accounts published by limited companies should be verified by auditors, who must be independent of the company and must hold an approved qualification.

(d) **Completeness**. A company's accounts should present a rounded picture of its economic activities.

(e) **Objectivity**. Information should be as objective as possible. This is particularly the case where conflicting interests operate and an unbiased presentation of information is needed. In the context of preparing accounts, where many decisions must be based on judgement rather than objective facts, this problem often arises. Management are often inclined to paint a rosy picture of a company's profitability to make their own performance look impressive. By contrast, auditors responsible for verifying the accounts are inclined to take a more prudent view so that they cannot be held liable by, say, a supplier misled into granting credit to a shaky company.

Part A: General framework

(f) **Timeliness**. The usefulness of information is reduced if it does not appear until long after the period to which it relates, or if it is produced at unreasonably long intervals. What constitutes a long interval depends on the circumstances: management of a company may need very frequent (perhaps daily) information on cash flows to run the business efficiently; but shareholders are normally content to see accounts produced annually.

(g) **Comparability**. Information should be produced on a consistent basis so that valid comparisons can be made with information from previous periods and with information produced by other sources (for example the accounts of similar companies operating in the same line of business).

5 THE REGULATORY SYSTEM

Introduction

5.1 Although new to the subject, you may be aware from your reading that there have been considerable upheavals in financial reporting, mainly in response to criticism. The details of the regulatory framework of accounting and the technical aspects of the changes made will be covered later in this text and in your more advanced studies. The purpose of this section is to give a **general picture** of some of the factors which have shaped financial accounting. We will concentrate on the accounts of limited companies because this is the type of organisation whose accounts are most closely regulated by statute or otherwise.

5.2 The following factors can be identified.

- Company law
- Accounting concepts and individual judgement
- Accounting standards
- The European Union
- Other international influences
- Generally accepted accounting practice (GAAP)

Company law

5.3 Limited companies are required by law (the Companies Act 1985 or CA 1985) to prepare and publish accounts annually. The form and content of the accounts are regulated primarily by CA 1985, but must also comply with accounting standards.

Accounting concepts and individual judgement

5.4 Financial statements are prepared on the basis of a number of fundamental accounting concepts (or accounting principles as they are called in the Companies Act 1985). Many figures in financial statements are derived from the application of judgement in putting those concepts into practice.

5.5 It is clear that different people exercising their judgement on the same facts can arrive at very different conclusions.

1: Introduction to accounting

Case example

Suppose, for example, that an accountancy training firm has an excellent *reputation* amongst students and employers. How would you value this? The firm may have relatively little in the form of assets which you can touch, perhaps a building, desks and chairs. If you simply drew up a balance sheet showing the cost of the assets owned, the business would not seem to be worth much, yet its income earning potential might be high. This is true of many service organisations where the people are among the most valuable assets.

5.6 Other examples of areas where the judgement of different people may differ are as follows.

- Valuation of buildings in times of rising property prices.
- Research and development. Is it right to treat this only as an expense? In a sense it is an investment to generate future revenue.
- Accounting for inflation.
- Brands such as 'Jaffa Cakes' or 'Walkman'. Are they assets in the same way that a fork lift truck is an asset?

5.7 Working from the same data, different groups of people would produce very different financial statements. If the exercise of judgement is completely unfettered any comparability between the accounts of different organisations will disappear. This will be all the more significant in cases where deliberate manipulation occurs in order to present accounts in the most favourable light.

Accounting standards

5.8 In an attempt to deal with some of the subjectivity, and to achieve comparability between different organisations, **accounting standards** were developed.

The old regime

5.9 Between 1970 and 1990 the standards (Statements of Standard Accounting Practice or SSAPs) were devised by the **Accounting Standards Committee**. However, it was felt that these standards were too much concerned with detailed rules in which companies found it all too easy to find loopholes.

The current regime

5.10 The Accounting Standards Committee was replaced in 1990 by the **Financial Reporting Council**. Its subsidiary the **Accounting Standards Board** (ASB), issues standards 'concerned with principles rather than fine details'. Its standards are called Financial Reporting Standards (FRSs). However it adopted all existing SSAPs and some of these are still relevant although most have been replaced by FRSs. It is supported in its aim by the Urgent Issues Task Force and the Review Panel.

5.11 The **Urgent Issues Task Force (UITF)** is an offshoot of the ASB. Its function is to tackle urgent matters not covered by existing standards and for which, given the urgency, the normal standard setting process would not be practicable.

Part A: General framework

5.12 The **Financial Reporting Review Panel** (FRRP) is concerned with the examination and questioning of departures from accounting standards by large companies.

5.13 The standard setting process and its development will be considered in more detail in Chapter 24.

Accounting Standards and the law

5.14 The Companies Act 1985 requires companies to include a note to the accounts stating that the accounts have been prepared in accordance with **applicable accounting standards** or, alternatively, giving details of material departures from those standards, with reasons. The Review Panel and the Secretary of State for Trade and Industry have the power to apply to the court for revision of the accounts where non-compliance is not justified.

5.15 These provisions mean that accounting standards now have the force of law, whereas previously they had no legal standing in statute. In June 1993, Mary Arden QC, in a legal opinion contained in the ASB's *Foreword to Accounting Standards*, stated that courts are more likely than ever to rule that compliance with accounting standards is necessary for accountants to give a 'true and fair' view.

Question 4

Without looking:

(a) Why do we need accounting standards?
(b) Who produces them?
(c) Who looks into departures from accounting standards?
(d) Do they have the force of law?

Answer

(a) See paragraphs 5.7 and 5.8
(b) The ASB
(c) The FRRP
(d) Yes

The European Union

5.16 Since the United Kingdom became a member of the European Union (EU) it has been obliged to comply with legal requirements decided on by the EU. It does this by enacting UK laws to implement EU directives. For example, the Companies Act 1989 was enacted in part to implement the provisions of the seventh and eighth directives, which deal with consolidated accounts and auditors. Although your syllabus does not require you to be an expert on EU procedure, you should be aware that the form and content of company accounts can be influenced by international developments.

Other international influences

5.17 One important influence on financial accounting is the **International Accounting Standards Committee** (IASC). The IASC was set up in 1973 to work for the improvement and harmonisation of financial reporting. Its members are the professional accounting bodies. The structure of the IASC was reorganised in May 2000.

5.18 The objectives of the IASC are:

(a) To **develop**, in the public interest, a single set of high quality, understandable and enforceable **global accounting standards** that require high quality, transparent and comparable information in financial statements and other financial reporting to help participants in the world's capital markets and other users make economic decisions.

(b) To promote the use and **rigorous application** of those standards.

(c) To bring about **convergence of national accounting standards** and International Accounting Standards to high quality solutions.

The use and application of International Accounting Standards (IASs)

5.19 IASs have helped both to improve and to harmonise financial reporting around the world. The standards are used:

- As national requirements, often after a national process
- As the basis for all or some national requirements
- As an international benchmark for those countries which develop their own requirements
- By regulatory authorities for domestic and foreign companies
- By companies themselves

5.20 The EU have announced that IASs must be used by all listed companies in member states for their consolidated financial statements by 2005.

Generally Accepted Accounting Practice (GAAP)

5.21 This term has sprung up in recent years and signifies all the rules, from whatever source, which govern accounting.

> **KEY TERM**
>
> **GAAP** is a set of rules governing accounting. The rules may derive from:
>
> - Company law (mainly CA 1985)
> - Accounting standards
> - International accounting standards and statutory requirements in other countries (particularly the US)
> - Stock Exchange requirements

5.22 GAAP will be considered in more detail in Chapter 24.

True and fair view

5.23 Company law requires that:

- The balance sheet must give a **true and fair view of the state of affairs** of the company as at the end of the financial year.
- The profit and loss account must give a **true and fair view of the profit or loss** of the company for the financial year.

Part A: General framework

True and fair 'override'

> **KEY TERM**
>
> **True and fair view** is not defined in company law or accounting standards. For practical purposes, it can be taken to mean accurate and not misleading.

5.24 The Companies Act 1985 states that the directors may depart from any of its provisions if these are inconsistent with the requirement to give a true and fair view. This is commonly referred to as the 'true and fair override'. It has been treated as an important loophole in the law and has been the cause of much argument, and dissatisfaction within the accounting profession.

Question 5

List the forces that have shaped financial accounting, stating the effect of each.

Answer

(a) **Company law** requires companies to prepare accounts and regulates their form and content.

(b) **Accounting concepts** are applied by individuals using their **subjective judgement**.

(c) **Accounting standards** help to eliminate subjectivity.

(d) The **European Union** issues directives on accounting matters which we must apply.

(e) **International Accounting Standards** aim to harmonise accounting round the world.

(f) **GAAP** is a collection of rules from various sources, governing accounting.

6 CAPITAL AND REVENUE EXPENDITURE

6.1 In the next part of this Study Text you will study the mechanics of preparing financial statements. In order to tackle this subject you need to be familiar with an important distinction, the distinction between **capital and revenue expenditure**.

> **KEY TERMS**
>
> **Capital expenditure** is expenditure which results in the acquisition of fixed assets, or an improvement in their earning capacity.
>
> (a) Capital expenditure is not charged as an expense in the profit and loss account, although a depreciation charge will usually be made to write off the capital expenditure gradually over time. Depreciation charges are expenses in the profit and loss account.
>
> (b) Capital expenditure on fixed assets results in the appearance of a fixed asset in the balance sheet of the business.
>
> **Revenue expenditure** is expenditure which is incurred for either of the following reasons.
>
> (a) For the purpose of the trade of the business. This includes expenditure classified as selling and distribution expenses, administration expenses and finance charges.
>
> (b) To maintain the existing earning capacity of fixed assets.

6.2 Revenue expenditure is charged to the profit and loss account of a period, if it relates to the trading activity and sales of that particular period. For example, a business buys ten widgets for £200 (£20 each) and sells eight of them during an accounting period. It has two widgets left at the end of the period. The full £200 is revenue expenditure but only £160 is a cost of goods sold during the period. The remaining £40 (cost of two units) will be included in the balance sheet as a current asset valued at £40.

6.3 A business purchases a building for £30,000. It then adds an extension to the building at a cost of £10,000. The building needs to have a few broken windows mended, its floors polished and some missing roof tiles replaced. These cleaning and maintenance jobs cost £900.

In this example, the original purchase (£30,000) and the cost of the extension (£10,000) are capital expenditure, because they are incurred to acquire and then improve a fixed asset. The other costs of £900 are revenue expenditure, because these merely maintain the building and thus the 'earning capacity' of the building.

Capital income and revenue income

6.4 **Capital income** is the proceeds from the sale of non-trading assets (ie proceeds from the sale of fixed assets, including fixed asset investments). The profits (or losses) from the sale of fixed assets are included in the profit and loss account of a business, for the accounting period in which the sale takes place.

6.5 **Revenue income** is income derived from the following sources.

   (a) The sale of trading assets
   (b) Interest and dividends received from investments held by the business

Capital transactions

6.6 The categorisation of capital and revenue items given above does not mention raising additional capital from the owner(s) of the business, or raising and repaying loans. These are transactions which:

   (a) Add to the cash assets of the business, thereby creating a corresponding liability (capital or loan).
   (b) When a loan is repaid, reduce the liabilities (loan) and the assets (cash) of the business.

None of these transactions would be reported through the profit and loss account.

Why is the distinction between capital and revenue items important?

6.7 Revenue expenditure results from the purchase of goods and services that will:

   (a) Be used fully in the accounting period in which they are purchased, and so be a cost or expense in the trading, profit and loss account.
   (b) Result in a current asset as at the end of the accounting period because the goods or services have not yet been consumed or made use of. The current asset would be shown in the balance sheet and is not yet a cost or expense in the trading, profit and loss account.

6.8 Capital expenditure results in the **purchase or improvement** of fixed assets, which are assets that will provide benefits to the business in more than one accounting period, and which are not acquired with a view to being resold in the normal course of trade. The cost

Part A: General framework

of purchased fixed assets is not charged in full to the trading, profit and loss account of the period in which the purchase occurs. Instead, the fixed asset is gradually depreciated over a number of accounting periods.

6.9 Since revenue items and capital items are accounted for in different ways, the correct and consistent calculation of profit for any accounting period depends on the correct and consistent classification of items as revenue or capital.

6.10 This may seem rather confusing at the moment, but things will become clearer in the next few chapters. In the meantime just get used to the terminology. These words appear in the accounts standards themselves, as we will see.

Question 6

State whether each of the following items should be classified as 'capital' or 'revenue' expenditure or income for the purpose of preparing the trading, profit and loss account and the balance sheet of the business.

(a) The purchase of leasehold premises.
(b) The annual depreciation of leasehold premises.
(c) Solicitors' fees in connection with the purchase of leasehold premises.
(d) The costs of adding extra storage capacity to a mainframe computer used by the business.
(e) Computer repairs and maintenance costs.
(f) Profit on the sale of an office building.
(g) Revenue from sales by credit card.
(h) The cost of new machinery.
(i) Customs duty charged on the machinery when imported into the country.
(j) The 'carriage' costs of transporting the new machinery from the supplier's factory to the premises of the business purchasing the machinery.
(k) The cost of installing the new machinery in the premises of the business.
(l) The wages of the machine operators.

Answer

(a) Capital expenditure.
(b) Depreciation of a fixed asset is a revenue expenditure.
(c) The legal fees associated with the purchase of a property may be added to the purchase price and classified as capital expenditure. The cost of the leasehold premises in the balance sheet of the business will then include the legal fees.
(d) Capital expenditure (enhancing an existing fixed asset).
(e) Revenue expenditure.
(f) Capital income (net of the costs of sale).
(g) Revenue income.
(h) Capital expenditure.
(i) If customs duties are borne by the purchaser of the fixed asset, they may be added to the cost of the machinery and classified as capital expenditure.
(j) Similarly, if carriage costs are paid for by the purchaser of the fixed asset, they may be included in the cost of the fixed asset and classified as capital expenditure.
(k) Installation costs of a fixed asset are also added to the fixed asset's cost and classified as capital expenditure.
(l) Revenue expenditure.

Chapter roundup

- Accounting is a way of recording, analysing and summarising transactions.
- Businesses of whatever size or nature exist to make a profit.
- An **asset** is something which a business owns. A **liability** is something which a business owes.
- There are various groups of people who need information about the activities of a business. You should be fully aware of these different **user groups** and their varying needs.
- The main financial statements of a business are the **balance sheet** and the **profit and loss account**.
    - The balance sheet is a 'snapshot' of the business position at a given point in time.
    - The profit and loss account is a record of income and expenditure over a period
- Limited companies also produce certain **non-financial statements**. The main ones are:
    - The directors' report
    - The auditors' report
    - The chairman's report
- You should be able to identify the qualities of **good accounting information**.
- You should also be able to outline the factors which have shaped the **development** of **financial accounting**. These are:
    - Company law
    - Accounting concepts and individual judgement
    - Accounting standards
    - The EU and other international influences
    - Generally accepted accounting practice (GAAP)
- Many figures in financial statements are derived from the application of judgement in applying fundamental accounting concepts. This can lead to **subjectivity**.
- In an attempt to eliminate subjectivity and to achieve comparability, the **Accounting Standards Committee** issued **Statements of Standard Accounting Practice** (SSAPs).
- SSAPs were felt to be too narrow and prescriptive. The replacement Accounting Standards Board issued **Financial Reporting Standards** (FRSs) which are supposed to be more broadly based.
- You should be aware of the role played by **GAAP**, the **EU** and **International Accounting Standards**.
- Financial statements are required by law to 'give a **true and fair view'**. This is not defined.
- **Capital expenditure** is expenditure which results in the acquisition of fixed assets.
- **Revenue expenditure** is expenditure incurred for the purpose of the trade of the business or for maintenance of fixed assets.

Part A: General framework

Quick quiz

1. What is the fundamental objective of company annual reports?
2. Identify seven user groups who need accounting information.
3. What are the two main financial statements drawn up by accountants?
4. What are the qualities of useful accounting information?
5. Which of the following factors have not influenced financial accounting?

    A   National legislation
    B   Economic factors
    C   Accounting standards
    D   GAAP

6. What are the objectives of the International Accounting Standards Committee?
7. What does GAAP stand for?
8. What is meant by a 'true and fair' view?
9. Which of the following is an item of capital expenditure?

    A   Cost of goods sold
    B   Purchase of a machine
    C   Repairs to a machine
    D   Wages cost

Answers to quick quiz

1. To provide information about the financial position, performance and changes in financial position of an enterprise that is useful to a wide range of users in making economic decisions.
2. See paragraph 1.15.
3. The profit and loss account and the balance sheet.
4. See paragraph 4.1.
5. B. Economic factors do not influence the development of financial accounting; all the others do (see paragraph 5.2).
6. See paragraph 5.18.
7. Generally accepted accounting principles.
8. See paragraphs 5.23 to 5.24.
9. B. This results in the acquisition of a fixed asset. All the others are revenue expenditure.

Now try the question below from the Exam Question Bank

Question to try	Level	Marks	Time
1	Full exam	10	18 mins

Part B
Accounting concepts and principles

Chapter 2

THE ACCOUNTING AND BUSINESS EQUATIONS

Topic list	Syllabus reference
1 Assets and liabilities and the business entity	2(a) – (b)
2 The accounting equation (or balance sheet equation)	2(a) – (b)
3 The business equation	2(a) – (b)

Introduction

Part A of this Study Text gave you a broad overview of accounting information and the uses to which it can be put. Part B should provide you with an understanding of the mechanics of preparing financial accounts.

This chapter introduces two concepts which it is important for you to grasp: the **accounting equation** and the **business equation**. You may already realise that a balance sheet has to balance. You are about to learn why!

Do not rush this chapter. Without an understanding of these essential points you will find it impossible to master more complex aspects later in your studies.

Study guide

Section 2 – Basic balance sheet and profit and loss account

- Explain how the balance sheet equation and business entity convention underlie the balance sheet.
- Define assets and liabilities.
- Explain the matching convention and how it applies to revenue and expenses.

Exam guide

Another 'foundation' chapter. The odd MCQ may come up, but this is more likely to be examined as fundamental knowledge behind a more detailed question in Section B.

1 ASSETS AND LIABILITIES AND THE BUSINESS ENTITY

> **KEY TERM**
>
> An **asset** is something valuable which a business owns or has the use of.

1.1 Examples of assets are factories, office buildings, warehouses, delivery vans, lorries, plant and machinery, computer equipment, office furniture, cash and also goods held in store

Part B: Accounting concepts and principles

awaiting sale to customers, and raw materials and components held in store by a manufacturing business for use in production.

1.2 Some assets are held and used in operations for a long time. An office building might be occupied by administrative staff for years. A machine might have a productive life of many years before it wears out.

1.3 Other assets are held for only a short time. The owner of a newsagent shop, for example, will have to sell his newspapers on the same day that he gets them, and weekly newspapers and monthly magazines also have a short shelf life. The more quickly a business can sell the goods it has in store, the more profit it is likely to make, provided, of course, that the goods are sold at a higher price than it cost the business to acquire them.

KEY TERM

A **liability** is something which is owed to somebody else. 'Liabilities' is the accounting term for the debts of a business.

1.4 Some examples of liabilities are given below.

- A **bank loan** or bank *overdraft*. The liability is the amount which must eventually be repaid to the bank.

- **Amounts owed to suppliers** for goods purchased but not yet paid for. For example, a boatbuilder might buy some timber on credit from a timber merchant, which means that the boatbuilder does not have to pay for the timber until some time after it has been delivered. Until the boatbuilder pays what he owes, the timber merchant will be his creditor for the amount owed.

- **Taxation** owed to the government. A business pays tax on its profits but there is a gap in time between when a company declares its profits and becomes liable to pay tax and the time when the tax bill must eventually be paid.

- **Amounts invested in a business by its shareholders or owners**. This is explained in detail in paragraph 1.12 below.

The business as a separate entity

1.5 So far we have spoken of assets and liabilities 'of a business'. But can an intangible entity such as a business own assets in its own name, or have liabilities in its own name? There are two aspects to this question: the **strict legal position** and the **convention adopted by accountants**.

1.6 Many businesses are carried on in the form of **limited companies**. The owners of a limited company are its shareholders, who may be few in number (as with a small, family-owned company) or very numerous (for example in the case of a large public company whose shares are quoted on the Stock Exchange).

1.7 The law recognises a company as a legal entity, quite separate from its owners. A company may, in its own name, acquire assets, incur debts, and enter into contracts. If a company's assets became insufficient to meet its liabilities, the company as a separate entity might become 'bankrupt'. However the owners of the company could not usually be required to pay the debts from their own private resources: the debts are not debts of the shareholders, but of the company.

2: The accounting and business equations

1.8 The case is different, in **law**, when a business is carried on not by a company, but by an individual (a sole trader) or by a group of individuals (a partnership).

Case example

Suppose that Fiona Middleton sets herself up in business as a hairdresser trading under the business name 'Hair by Fiona'. The law now recognises no distinction between Fiona Middleton, the individual, and the business known as 'Hair by Fiona'. Any debts of the business which cannot be met from business assets must be met from Fiona's private resources.

1.9 However, in **accounting** a business is treated as a **separate entity from its owner(s)**. This applies whether or not the business is recognised in law as a separate entity, ie it applies whether the business is carried on by a company, a sole trader or a partnership. This is known as the **entity concept**.

> **KEY TERM**
>
> **Entity concept**: A business is a separate entity from its owner.

1.10 At first sight this seems illogical and unrealistic; students often have difficulty in understanding it. Nevertheless, it is an idea which you must try to appreciate. It is the basis of a fundamental rule of accounting, which is that the assets and liabilities of a business must always be equal. We will look at this rule in more detail in a later chapter, but a simple example may clarify the idea of a business as a separate entity from its owners.

1.11 EXAMPLE: THE BUSINESS AS A SEPARATE ENTITY

On 1 July 20X6, Courtney Spice decided to open up a stall in the market, to sell herbs and spices. She had saved up some money in her building society account, and had £2,500 to put into her business.

1.12 When the business is set up, an accountant's picture can be drawn of what it **owns** and what it **owes**.

The business begins by owning the cash that Courtney has put into it, £2,500. But does it owe anything? The answer is yes.

The business is a separate entity in accounting terms. It has obtained its assets, in this example cash, from its owner, Courtney Spice. It therefore owes this amount of money to its owner. If Courtney changed her mind and decided not to go into business after all, the business would be dissolved by the 'repayment' of the cash by the business to Courtney.

The amount owed by a business to its owners is often known as **capital**.

2 THE ACCOUNTING EQUATION (OR BALANCE SHEET EQUATION)

2.1 We will start by showing how to account for a business's transactions from the time that trading first begins. We will use an example to illustrate the 'accounting equation', ie the rule that the assets of a business will at all times equal its liabilities. This is also known as **the balance sheet equation**.

2.2 EXAMPLE: THE ACCOUNTING EQUATION

Let us go back to example 1.11 above. The business began by owning the cash that Courtney put into it, £2,500. The business is a separate entity in accounting terms and so it owes the money to Courtney as **capital**.

> **KEY TERM**
>
> In accounting, **capital** is an investment of money (funds) with the intention of earning a return. A business proprietor invests capital with the intention of earning profit. As long as that money is invested, accountants will treat the capital as money owed to the proprietor by the business.

2.3 When Courtney Spice sets up her business:

Capital invested	=	£2,500
Cash	=	£2,500

Capital invested is a form of liability, because it is an amount owed by the business to its owner(s). Adapting this to the idea that liabilities and assets are always equal amounts, we can state the accounting equation as follows.

| *Assets* | = | *Capital* | + | *Liabilities* |

For Courtney Spice, as at 1 July 20X6:

£2,500 (cash)	=	£2,500	+	£0

2.4 EXAMPLE CONTINUED

Courtney Spice uses some of the money invested to purchase a market stall from Noel Jarvis, who is retiring from his fruit and vegetables business. The cost of the stall is £1,800.

She also purchases some herbs and spices from a trader in the Albert Square wholesale market, at a cost of £650.

This leaves £50 in cash, after paying for the stall and goods for resale, out of the original £2,500. Courtney kept £30 in the bank and drew out £20 in small change to use as a float. She was now ready for her first day of market trading on 3 July 20X6.

2.5 The assets and liabilities of the business have now altered, and at 3 July, before trading begins, the state of her business is as follows.

Assets	£	=	*Capital*	+	*Liabilities*
Stall	1,800	=	£2,500	+	£0
Herbs and spices	650				
Cash at bank	30				
Cash in hand	20				
	2,500				

The stall and the herbs and spices are physical items, but they must be given a money value. This money value is usually what they cost the business (called **historical cost** in accounting terms).

Profit introduced into the accounting equation

2.6 Let us now suppose that on 3 July Courtney has a very successful day. She is able to sell all of her herbs and spices, for £900. All of her sales are for cash.

Since Courtney has sold goods costing £650 to earn revenue of £900, we can say that she has **earned a profit of £250 on the day's trading.**

Profits belong to the owners of a business. In this case, the £250 belongs to Courtney Spice. However, so long as the business retains the profits, and does not pay anything out to its owners, the **retained profits** are accounted for as an addition to the proprietor's capital.

Assets	£	=	*Capital*	£	+	*Liabilities*
Stall	1,800		Original investment	2,500		
Herbs and spices	0					
Cash in hand and at bank (30+20+900)	950		Retained profit	250		
	2,750	=		2,750	+	£0

2.7 We can re-arrange the accounting equation to help us to calculate the capital balance.

| Assets – liabilities | = | Capital, which is the same as |
| Net assets | = | Capital |

2.8 At the beginning and then at the end of 3 July 20X6 Courtney Spice's financial position was as follows.

		Net Assets	*Capital*
(a)	At the beginning of the day:	£(2,500 – 0) = £2,500 =	£2,500
(b)	At the end of the day:	£(2,750 – 0) = £2,750 =	£2,750

There has been an increase of £250 in net assets, which is the amount of profits earned during the day.

Drawings

> **KEY TERM**
>
> **Drawings** are amounts of money taken out of a business by its owner.

2.9 Since Courtney Spice has made a profit of £250 from her first day's work, she might well feel fully justified in drawing some of the profits out of the business. After all, business owners, like everyone else, need income for living expenses. We will suppose that Courtney decides to pay herself £180, in 'wages'.

2.10 The payment of £180 is probably regarded by Courtney as a fair reward for her day's work, and she might think of the sum as being in the nature of wages. However, the £180 is not an expense to be deducted before the figure of net profit is arrived at. In other words, it would be incorrect to calculate the net profit earned by the business as follows.

	£
Profit on sale of herbs and spices etc	250
Less 'wages' paid to Courtney	180
Net profit earned by business (incorrect)	70

Part B: Accounting concepts and principles

2.11 This is because any amounts paid by a business to its proprietor are treated by accountants as withdrawals of profit (the usual term is **appropriations of profit**), and not as expenses incurred by the business. In the case of Courtney's business, the true position is that the net profit earned is the £250 surplus on sale of flowers.

	£
Net profit earned by business	250
Less profit withdrawn by Courtney	180
Net profit retained in the business	70

2.12 Profits are capital as long as they are retained in the business. Once they are **appropriated**, the business suffers a reduction in capital.

2.13 The drawings are taken in cash, and so the business loses £180 of its cash assets. After the drawings have been made, the accounting equation would be restated.

(a)
Assets		£	=	Capital		£	+	Liabilities
Stall		1,800		Original investment		2,500		
Herbs and spices		0		Retained profit		70		
Cash (950-180)		770						
		2,570				2,570	+	£0

(b) Alternatively   Net assets   Capital
                     £(2,570 – 0)   =   £2,570

The increase in net assets since trading operations began is now only £(2,570 – 2,500) = £70, which is the amount of the retained profits.

Question 1

Fill in the missing words. (Don't cheat!)

Capital = ... less ....

Answer

Look back to paragraph 2.7.

3 THE BUSINESS EQUATION

3.1 The business equation gives a definition of profits earned. The preceding example has attempted to show that the amount of profit earned can be related to the increase in the net assets of the business, and the drawings of profits by the proprietor.

FORMULA TO LEARN

The **business equation** is:

$$P = I + D - C_i$$

Where

- P represents profit
- I represents the increase in net assets, after drawings have been taken out by the proprietor
- D represents drawings

C_i represents the amount of extra capital introduced into the business during the period. This is a negative figure in the equation, because when a business is given new capital, perhaps in the form of extra money paid in by the proprietor himself, there will be an increase in the net assets of the business without any profits being earned. This means, say, that if a proprietor puts an extra £5,000 into his business the profit from the transaction, according to the business equation would be P = £5,000 + 0 – £5,000 = £0.

3.2 In our example of Courtney Spice's business on 3 July 20X6, after drawings have been taken:

Profit = £70 + £180 – £0
= £250

3.3 EXAMPLE CONTINUED

The next market day is on 10 July, and Courtney gets ready by purchasing more herbs and spices for cash, at a cost of £740. She was not feeling well, however, because of a heavy cold, and so she decided to accept the offer of help for the day from her cousin Bianca. Bianca would be paid a wage of £40 at the end of the day.

Trading on 10 July was again very brisk, and Courtney and Bianca sold all their goods for £1,100 cash. Courtney paid Bianca her wage of £40 and drew out £200 for herself.

Required

(a) State the accounting equation before trading began on 10 July.

(b) State the accounting equation at the end of 10 July, after paying Bianca:

    (i) But before drawings are taken out.
    (ii) After drawings have been made.

(c) State the business equation to compute profits earned on 10 July.

You are reminded that the accounting equation for the business at the end of transactions for 3 July is given in Paragraph 2.13 (a).

3.4 SOLUTION

(a) After the purchase of the goods for £740.

Assets	£	=	Capital	+	Liabilities
Stall	1,800				
Goods	740				
Cash (770 – 740)	30				
	2,570	=	£2,570	+	£0

(b) (i) On 10 July, all the goods are sold for £1,100 cash, and Bianca is paid £40. The profit for the day is £320.

	£	£
Sales		1,100
Less cost of goods sold	740	
Bianca's wage	40	
		780
Profit		320

Part B: Accounting concepts and principles

	Assets		=	*Capital*		+	*Liabilities*
		£			£		
	Stall	1,800		At beginning of 10 July	2,570		
	Goods	0		Profits earned on 10 July	320		
	Cash						
	(30+ 1,100 – 40)	1,090					
		2,890	=		2,890	+	£0

(ii) After Courtney has taken drawings of £200 in cash, retained profits will be only £(320 - 200) = £120.

	Assets		=	*Capital*		+	*Liabilities*
		£			£		
	Stall	1,800		At beginning of 10 July	2,570		
	Goods	0		Retained profits for 10 July	120		
	Cash						
	(1,090 – 200)	890					
		2,690			2,690	+	£0

(c) The increase in net assets on 10 July, after drawings have been taken, is as follows.

	£
Net assets at end of 10 July	2,690
Net assets at beginning of 10 July	2,570
Increase in net assets	120

The business equation is:

$$P = I + D - C_i$$
$$= £120 + £200 - £0$$
$$= £320$$

This confirms the calculation of profit made in b(i).

Tutorial note

It is very important that you understand the principles described so far. Do not read on until you are confident that you understand the solution to this example.

Creditors and debtors

KEY TERM

A **creditor** is a person to whom a business owes money.

3.5 A **trade creditor** is a person to whom a business owes money for debts incurred in the course of trading operations. In an examination question, this term might refer to debts still outstanding which arise from the purchase from suppliers of materials, components or goods for resale.

3.6 A business does not always pay immediately for goods or services it buys. It is a common business practice to make purchases on credit, with a promise to pay within 30 days, or two months or three months of the date of the bill or 'invoice' for the goods. For example, if A buys goods costing £2,000 on credit from B, B might send A an invoice for £2,000, dated say

2: The accounting and business equations

1 March, with credit terms that payment must be made within 30 days. If A then delays payment until 31 March, B will be a creditor of A between 1 and 31 March, for £2,000.

3.7 A creditor is a **liability** of a business.

> **KEY TERM**
>
> Just as a business might buy goods on credit, so too might it sell goods to customers on credit. A customer who buys goods without paying cash for them straight away is a **debtor**.

3.8 For example, suppose that C sells goods on credit to D for £6,000 on terms that the debt must be settled within two months of the invoice date 1 October. If D does not pay the £6,000 until 30 November, D will be a debtor of C for £6,000 from 1 October until 30 November.

3.9 A debtor is an asset of a business. When the debt is finally paid, the debtor 'disappears' as an asset, to be replaced by 'cash at bank and in hand'.

3.10 EXAMPLE CONTINUED

The example of Courtney Spice's market stall will be continued further, by looking at the consequences of the following transactions in the week to 17 July 20X6. (See Paragraph 2.4 (b)(ii) for the situation as at the end of 10 July.)

(a) Courtney Spice realises that she is going to need more money in the business and so she makes the following arrangements.

　(i) She invests immediately a further £250 of her own capital.

　(ii) She persuades her Uncle Felix to lend her £500 immediately. Uncle Felix tells her that she can repay the loan whenever she likes, but in the meantime, she must pay him interest of £5 per week each week at the end of the market day. They agree that it will probably be quite a long time before the loan is eventually repaid.

(b) She is very pleased with the progress of her business, and decides that she can afford to buy a second hand van to pick up herbs and spices from her supplier and bring them to her stall in the market. She finds a car dealer, Laurie Loader, who agrees to sell her a van on credit for £700. Courtney agrees to pay for the van after 30 days' trial use.

(c) During the week before the next market day (which is on 17 July), Courtney's Uncle Grant telephones her to ask whether she would be interested in selling him some spice racks and herb chopping boards as presents for his friends. Courtney tells him that she will look for a supplier. After some investigations, she buys what Uncle Grant has asked for, paying £300 in cash to the supplier. Uncle Grant accepts delivery of the goods and agrees to pay £350 to Courtney for them, but he asks if she can wait until the end of the month for payment. Courtney agrees.

(d) The next market day approaches, and Courtney buys herbs and spices costing £800. Of these purchases £750 are paid in cash, with the remaining £50 on seven days' credit. Courtney decides to use Bianca's services again as an assistant on market day, at an agreed wage of £40.

Part B: Accounting concepts and principles

(e) For the third market day running, on 17 July, Courtney succeeds in selling all her goods earning revenue of £1,250 (all in cash). She decides to take out drawings of £240 for her week's work. She also pays Bianca £40 in cash. She decides to make the interest payment to her Uncle Felix the next time she sees him.

(f) We shall ignore any van expenses for the week, for the sake of relative simplicity.

Required

(a) State the accounting equation:

  (i) After Courtney and Uncle Felix have put more money into the business and after the purchase of the van.

  (ii) After the sale of goods to Uncle Grant.

  (iii) After the purchase of goods for the weekly market.

  (iv) At the end of the day's trading on 17 July, and after drawings have been appropriated out of profit.

(b) State the business equation showing profit earned during the week ended 17 July.

Question 2

Before you look through the solution, can you state the formula for the business equation?

3.11 SOLUTION

There are a number of different transactions to account for here. This solution deals with them one at a time in chronological order. (In practice, it would be possible to do one set of calculations which combines the results of all the transactions, but we shall defer such 'shortcut' methods until later.)

(a) (i) *The addition of Courtney's extra capital and Uncle Felix's loan*

An investment analyst might define the loan of Uncle Felix as a capital investment on the grounds that it will probably be for the long term. Uncle Felix is not the owner of the business, however, even though he has made an investment of a loan in it. He would only become an owner if Courtney offered him a partnership in the business, and she has not done so. To the business, Uncle Felix is a long-term creditor, and it is more appropriate to define his investment as a liability of the business and not as business capital.

The accounting equation after £(250 + 500) = £750 cash is put into the business will be:

Assets		= *Capital*		+ *Liabilities*	
	£		£		£
Stall	1,800	As at end of 10 July	2,690	Loan	500
Goods	0	Additional capital put in	250		
Cash (890+750)	1,640				
	3,440 =		2,940 +		500

The purchase of the van (cost £700) is on credit.

Assets		= Capital		+ Liabilities	
	£		£		£
Stall	1,800	As at end of 10 July	2,690	Loan	500
Van	700	Additional capital	250	Creditor	700
Cash	1,640				
	4,140 =		2,940 +		1,200

(ii) *The sale of goods to Uncle Grant on credit (£350) which cost the business £300 (cash paid)*

Assets		= Capital		+ Liabilities	
	£		£		£
Stall	1,800	As at end of 10 July	2,690	Loan	500
Van	700	Additional capital	250	Creditor	700
Debtors	350	Profit on sale to			
Cash (1,640 – 300)	1,340	Uncle Grant	50		
	4,190 =		2,990 +		1,200

(iii) *After the purchase of goods for the weekly market (£750 paid in cash and £50 of purchases on credit)*

Assets		= Capital		+ Liabilities	
	£		£		£
Stall	1,800	As at end of 10 July	2,690	Loan	500
Van	700			Creditor for van	700
Goods	800	Additional capital	250	Creditor for goods	50
Debtors	350	Profit on sale to			
Cash (1,340 – 750)	590	Uncle Grant	50		
	4,240 =		2,990 +		1,250

(iv) *After market trading on 17 July*

Sales of goods costing £800 earned revenues of £1,250. Bianca's wages were £40 (paid), Uncle Felix's interest charge is £5 (not paid yet) and drawings out of profits were £240 (paid). The profit for 17 July may be calculated as follows, taking the full £5 of interest as a cost on that day.

	£	£
Sales		1,250
Cost of goods sold	800	
Wages	40	
Interest	5	
		845
Profit earned on 17 July		405
Profit on sale of goods to Uncle Grant		50
Profit for the week		455
Drawings appropriated out of profits		240
Retained profit		215

Part B: Accounting concepts and principles

	Assets		=	Capital		+	Liabilities	
		£			£			£
	Stall	1,800		As at end of 10 July	2,690		Loan	500
	Van	700		Additional capital	250		Creditor for van	700
	Stocks	0					Creditor for goods	50
	Debtors	350						
	Cash (590 + 1,250 – 40 – 240)	1,560		Profits retained	215		Creditor for interest payment	5
		4,410	=		3,155	+		1,255

(b) The increase in the net assets of the business during the week was as follows.

	£
Net assets as at the end of 17 July £(4,410 – 1,255)	3,155
Net assets as at the end of 10 July (Paragraph 3.4(b)(ii))	2,690
Increase in net assets	465

The business equation for the week ended 17 July is as follows.

(Remember that extra capital of £250 was invested by the proprietor.)

$$P = I + D - C_i$$
$$= £465 + £240 - £250$$
$$= £455$$

This confirms the calculation of profit above in (a)(iv).

3.12 In the example above, we have 'matched' the income earned with the expenses incurred in earning it. So in part (a)(iv), we included all the costs of the goods sold of £800, even though £50 had not yet been paid in cash. Also the interest of £5 was deducted from income, even though it had not yet been paid. This is known as the **matching convention**.

Question 3

Calculate the profit for the year ended 31 December 20X1 from the following information.

	1 January 20X1		31 December 20X1	
	£	£	£	£
Assets				
Property	20,000		20,000	
Machinery	6,000		9,000	
Debtors	4,000		8,000	
Cash	1,000		1,500	
		31,000		38,500
Liabilities				
Overdraft	6,000		9,000	
Creditors	5,000		3,000	
		(11,000)		(12,000)
Net assets		20,000		26,500

Drawings during the year	£4,500
Additional capital introduced by the proprietor during the year	£5,000

Answer

The increase in net assets during the year was £(26,500 - 20,000) = £6,500.

$$P = I + D - C_i$$
$$= £6,500 + £4,500 - £5,000$$
$$= £6,000$$

Chapter roundup

- An **asset** is something which a business owns.
- A **liability** is something which a business owes.
- A business is a **separate entity** from its owner (for accounting purposes).
- The **accounting equation** and the **business equation** are useful introductory concepts in accounting for the following reasons.
  - The *accounting equation* emphasises the equality between assets and liabilities (including capital as a liability).
  - The *business equation* emphasises the inter-relationship between profits, net assets, appropriations of profit (drawings) and new capital investment.
- You should now be aware, for example, that when business transactions are accounted for, it should be possible to do two things as follows.
  - **Restate the assets and liabilities** of the business after the transactions have taken place.
  - **State the profit or loss**, if any, arising as a result of the transactions.
- The **matching convention** requires that income earned is matched with the expenses incurred in earning it.
- In practice, the accounting equation and business equation are rarely used to state assets and liabilities and profit.
  - The assets and liabilities of a business at any moment in time are shown in a **balance sheet**. This is very similar to the accounting equation.
  - The profit (or loss) earned by a business during a given period of time is shown in a **trading, profit and loss account**.

  These will be described in the next chapter.

Part B: Accounting concepts and principles

Quick quiz

1. In what sense can a proprietor's capital be regarded as a liability of the business.
2. What is the accounting equation?
3. What are drawings?
4. What is the business equation?
5. Distinguish between a debtor and a creditor.
6. Which ONE of the following is an asset?

    A The owner's capital
    B Van
    C An account payable
    D A bank overdraft

7. Which ONE of the following is a liability?

    A Cash
    B An account receivable
    C An account payable
    D Van

Answers to quick quiz

1. Due to the business entity concept, a business is treated as being separate from its owner(s). Therefore the capital invested in a business is strictly owed by the business to its owner(s) and so is treated as a liability.
2. Assets = Capital + Liabilities.
3. Amounts of profit withdrawn by the owner in cash and not retained in the business.
4. $P = I + D - C_i$
5. A debtor is an amount owed by a customer to the business eg on a credit sale.
   A creditor is an amount owed by the business to a supplier eg on a credit purchase.
6. B The van is an asset, all the others are liabilities.
7. C An account payable is a liability, all the others are assets.

Now try the question below from the Exam Question Bank.

Question to try	Level	Marks	Time
2	Full exam	10	18 mins

Chapter 3

AN INTRODUCTION TO FINANCIAL STATEMENTS

Topic list	Syllabus reference
1 The balance sheet	2(a), 5(c)(i)
2 The trading, profit and loss account	2(a), 5(c)(ii)

Introduction

In Chapter 2 you were introduced to the idea of the accounting equation. If you understand this, you should now have little difficulty in getting to grips with the balance sheet. You should already have some idea of what is meant by the profit and loss account. In this chapter you will see this in more detail.

There is a fair amount to learn before you will be able to prepare these statements yourself, although you will be surprised how quickly you will be in that enviable position.

It is important to introduce the financial statements now so you can see what you are aiming at. Keep them in your mind as you tackle the 'nuts and bolts' of ledger accounting in the next few chapters.

Study guide

Section 2 – Basic balance sheet and profit and loss account

- Explain how and why assets and liabilities are disclosed in the balance sheet.
- Draft a simple balance sheet in vertical format.
- Explain how and why revenue and expenses are disclosed in the trading and profit and loss account.
- Illustrate how the balance sheet and trading and profit and loss account are interrelated.
- Draft a simple trading and profit and loss account in vertical format.
- Explain the significance of gross profit and the gross profit as a percentage of sales.

Exam guide

You need to learn the concepts and ideas in this chapter. They will be developed later to enable you to answer full exam questions; either by MCQs in Part A or by preparing accounts in Part B.

Part B: Accounting concepts and principles

1 THE BALANCE SHEET

> **KEY TERM**
>
> A **balance sheet** is a statement of the liabilities, capital and assets of a business at a given moment in time. It is like a 'snapshot' photograph, since it captures on paper a still image, frozen at a single moment in time, of something which is dynamic and continually changing. Typically, a balance sheet is prepared to show the liabilities, capital and assets as at the end of the accounting period to which the financial accounts relate.

1.1 A balance sheet is, therefore, very similar to the accounting equation. In fact, there are only two differences between a balance sheet and an accounting equation.

- The manner or format in which the liabilities and assets are presented
- The extra detail which is usually contained in a balance sheet

1.2 The details shown in a balance sheet will not be described in full in this chapter. Instead we will make a start in this chapter and add more detail in later chapters as we go on to look at other ideas and methods in accounting.

1.3 A balance sheet is divided into two halves, with *either*:

(a) **Capital** in one half and **net assets** in the other; *or*
(b) **Capital and liabilities** in one half and **assets** in the other.

> **KEY TERM**
>
> Net assets = assets minus liabilities.

1.4 In other words, a balance sheet might be presented in either of two ways.

(a) *Either*

NAME OF BUSINESS
BALANCE SHEET AS AT (DATE)

	£
Assets	X
Less liabilities	X
Net assets	X
Capital	X

(b) *Or*

NAME OF BUSINESS
BALANCE SHEET AS AT (DATE)

	£		£
Assets (item by item)	X	Capital	X
	X	Liabilities (item by item)	X
	X		X

Method (a) shows capital on its own, and nets off liabilities against assets in the other half, whereas method (b) puts capital and liabilities on the same side of the balance sheet. This Study Text uses method (a), as this is the method used in practice for limited company accounts.

3: An introduction to financial statements

1.5 In either form of presentation, **the total value in one half of the balance sheet will equal the total value in the other half**. You should readily understand this from the accounting equation.

1.6 Since each half of the balance sheet has an equal value, one side balances the other. However, the equal value of the two halves is not the origin of the term balance sheet. A balance sheet is so called because it is a statement of the outstanding balances on the ledger accounts for the capital, liabilities and assets of the business, at a given moment in time. Ledger accounts are described in a later chapter.

1.7 Capital, liabilities and assets are usually shown in some detail in a balance sheet. The following paragraphs describe the sort of detail we might expect to find.

Capital (sole trader)

1.8 The proprietor's capital might well be analysed into its component parts.

	£	£
Capital as at the beginning of the accounting period (ie capital 'brought forward')		X
Add additional capital introduced during the period		X
		X
Add profit earned during the period	X	
Less drawings	(X)	
Retained profit for the period		X
Capital as at the end of the accounting period (ie capital 'carried forward')		X

> **KEY TERMS**
>
> **Brought forward** means 'brought forward from the previous period', and **carried forward** means 'carried forward to the next period'. The carried forward amount at the end of one period is also the brought forward amount of the next period. The word 'down' is sometimes used instead of 'forward'.

Liabilities

1.9 The various liabilities should be itemised separately. In addition, a distinction is made between **current liabilities** and **long-term liabilities**.

Current liabilities

> **KEY TERM**
>
> **Current liabilities** are debts of the business that must be paid within a fairly short period of time.

1.10 By convention, a 'fairly short period of time' has come to be accepted as one year. In the accounts of limited companies, the Companies Act 1985 requires use of the term 'creditors: amounts falling due within one year' rather than 'current liabilities' although they mean the same thing.

Examples of current liabilities are

(a) **Loans** repayable within one year.

Part B: Accounting concepts and principles

(b) A **bank overdraft**, as this is usually repayable on demand.

(c) **Trade creditors**.

(d) **Bills of exchange** which are payable by the business.

(e) **Taxation payable**.

(f) **Accrued charges**.

Accrued charges are expenses for which no invoice has yet been received, or for which the date of payment by standing order has not yet arrived. An example of accrued charges is the cost of gas or electricity used. If a business ends its accounting year on 31 December, but does not expect its next quarterly gas bill until the end of January, there will be two months of accrued gas charges, ie charges for which no invoice has been received and no debt is yet 'officially' payable, to record in the balance sheet as a liability. Accruals will be described more fully in a later chapter.

Long-term liabilities

> **KEY TERM**
>
> A **long-term liability** is a debt which is not payable within the 'short term' and so any liability which is not current must be long-term.

1.11 Just as 'short-term' by convention means one year or less, 'long-term' means more than one year. In the accounts of limited companies, the Companies Act 1985 requires use of the term: 'Creditors: amounts falling due after more than one year'.

1.12 Examples of long-term liabilities are:

(a) **Loans** which are not repayable for more than one year, such as a bank loan, or a loan from an individual to a business

(b) A **mortgage loan**, which is a loan specifically secured against a freehold property. (If the business fails to repay the loan, the lender then has 'first claim' on the property, and is entitled to repayment from the proceeds from the enforced sale of the property.)

(c) **Debentures** or debenture loans. These are common with limited companies. Debentures are securities issued by a company at a fixed rate of interest. They are repayable on agreed terms by a specified date in the future. Holders of debentures are therefore lenders of money to a company. Their interests, including security for the loan, are protected by the terms of a trust deed

Assets

1.13 Assets in the balance sheet are divided into two groups.

(a) Fixed assets:
   (i) Tangible fixed assets
   (ii) Intangible fixed assets
   (iii) Investments (long term)

(b) Current assets

3: An introduction to financial statements

Fixed assets

1.14 A fixed asset is **an asset acquired for continuing use within the business**, with a view to earning income or making profits from its use, either directly or indirectly. A fixed asset is not acquired for sale to a customer.

- In a manufacturing industry, a production machine would be a fixed asset, because it makes goods which are then sold.

- In a service industry, equipment used by employees giving service to customers would be classed as fixed assets (eg the equipment used in a garage, and furniture in a hotel).

- Less obviously, factory premises, office furniture, computer equipment, company cars, delivery vans or pallets in a warehouse are all fixed assets.

1.15 To be classed as a fixed asset in the balance sheet of a business, an item must satisfy two further conditions.

(a) It must be **used by the business**. For example, the proprietor's own house would not normally appear on the business balance sheet.

(b) The asset must have a **'life' in use of more than one year** (strictly, more than one 'accounting period' which might be more or less than one year).

KEY TERMS

A **tangible** fixed asset is a physical asset, ie one that can be touched. It has a real, 'solid' existence. All of the examples of fixed assets mentioned above are tangible.

An **intangible** fixed asset is an asset which does not have a physical existence. It cannot be 'touched'. An example is a patent which protects an idea. Intangible assets will be discussed in more detail in a later chapter.

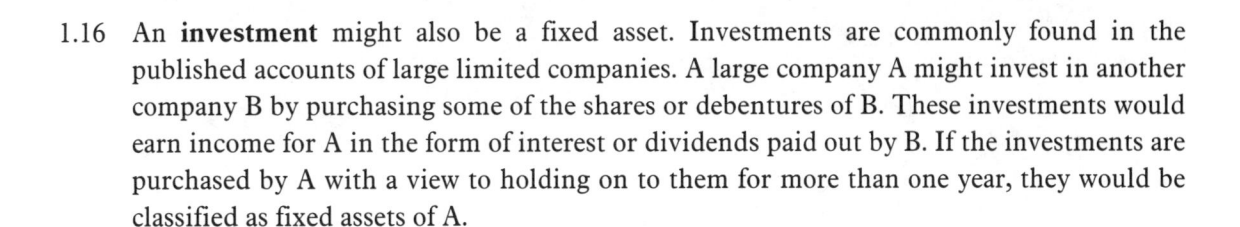

1.16 An **investment** might also be a fixed asset. Investments are commonly found in the published accounts of large limited companies. A large company A might invest in another company B by purchasing some of the shares or debentures of B. These investments would earn income for A in the form of interest or dividends paid out by B. If the investments are purchased by A with a view to holding on to them for more than one year, they would be classified as fixed assets of A.

In this chapter, we shall restrict our attention to tangible fixed assets.

Fixed assets and depreciation

1.17 Fixed assets might be held and used by a business for a number of years, but they wear out or lose their usefulness in the course of time. Every tangible fixed asset has a limited life. The only exception is land held freehold or on a very long leasehold.

1.18 The accounts of a business try to recognise that the cost of a fixed asset is gradually consumed as the asset wears out. This is done by gradually writing off the asset's cost in the profit and loss account over several accounting periods. For example, in the case of a machine costing £1,000 and expected to wear out after ten years, it might be appropriate to reduce the balance sheet value by £100 each year. This process is known as **depreciation**. It will be defined more closely in a later chapter.

Part B: Accounting concepts and principles

1.19 If a balance sheet were drawn up four years, say, after the asset was purchased, the amount of depreciation which would have accumulated would be 4 × £100 = £400. The machine would then appear in the balance sheet as follows.

	£
Machine at original cost	1,000
Less accumulated depreciation	400
Net book value*	600

* ie the value of the asset in the books of account, net of depreciation. After ten years the asset would be fully depreciated and would appear in the balance sheet with a net book value of zero.

Question 1

Depreciation is discussed in detail in a later chapter. However here is a little test which brings in the concept of **residual value**. A business buys a car for £10,000. It expects to keep the car for three years and then to trade it in at an estimated value of £3,400. How much depreciation should be accounted for in each year of the car's use?

Answer

The point to note is that the car has a residual value of £3,400. So it would be inappropriate to write off the whole £10,000 in the three years. The aim is to account for only the loss in value over the three years ie £6,600 (£10,000 - £3,400). So depreciation may be £2,200 each year (3 × £2,200 = £6,600).

Current assets

KEY TERM

Current assets are either:

(a) items owned by the business with the intention of turning them into cash within one year; or

(b) cash, including money in the bank, owned by the business.

These assets are 'current' in the sense that they are continually flowing through the business.

1.20 The definition in (a) above needs explaining further. Let us suppose that a trader David Wickes, runs a business selling motor cars, and purchases a showroom which he stocks with cars for sale. We will also suppose that he obtains the cars from a manufacturer, and pays for them in cash on delivery.

(a) If he sells a car in a cash sale, the goods are immediately converted into cash. The cash might then be used to buy more cars for re-sale.

(b) If he sells a car in a credit sale, the car will be given to the customer, who then becomes a debtor of the business. Eventually, the debtor will pay what he owes, and David Wickes will receive cash. Once again, the cash might then be used to buy more cars for sale.

1.21 Current assets can be identified in this example as follows.

(a) The cars (goods) held in stock for re-sale are current assets, because David Wickes intends to sell them within one year, in the normal course of trade.

3: An introduction to financial statements

(b) Any debtors are current assets, if they are expected to pay what they owe within one year.

(c) Cash is a current asset.

1.22 The transactions described above could be shown as a **cash cycle.**

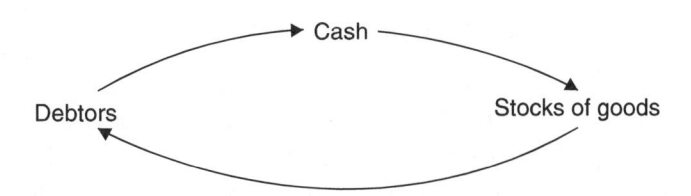

```
        → Cash →
      ↗          ↘
  Debtors ←——— Stocks of goods
```

1.23 Cash is used to buy goods which are sold. Sales on credit create debtors, but eventually cash is earned from the sales. Some, perhaps most, of the cash will then be used to replenish stocks.

1.24 The main items of current assets are therefore:

- Stocks
- Debtors
- Cash

Question 2

This exercise should ensure you understand asset classification. Cover up the grid in the solution. You should then decide which of the following assets falls into the 'fixed' category and which should be treated as 'current'.

ASSET	BUSINESS	CURRENT OR FIXED
VAN	DELIVERY FIRM	
MACHINE	MANUFACTURING COMPANY	
CAR	CAR TRADER	
INVESTMENT	ANY	

Answer

ASSET	BUSINESS	CURRENT OR FIXED
VAN	DELIVERY FIRM	FIXED
MACHINE	MANUFACTURING COMPANY	FIXED
CAR	CAR TRADER	CURRENT
INVESTMENT	ANY	EITHER*

* The classification of the investment will depend on the purpose for which it is held. If the intention is to make a long-term investment it will be a fixed asset, but if it is a short term way of investing spare cash it will be a current asset.

1.25 It is important to realise that cars are current assets of David Wickes because he is in the business of buying and selling them, ie he is a car trader. If he also has a car which he keeps and uses for business purposes, this car would be a fixed asset.

Part B: Accounting concepts and principles

> **IMPORTANT!**
>
> The distinction between a fixed asset and a current asset is not what the asset is physically, but for what purpose it is obtained and used by the business.

1.26 There are some other categories of current assets.

(a) **Short-term investments**. These are stocks and shares of other businesses, currently owned, but with the intention of selling them in the near future. For example, if a business has a lot of spare cash for a short time, its managers might decide to 'have a flutter' on the stock exchange, and buy shares in, say, Marks and Spencer, ICI or GEC. The shares will later be sold when the business needs the cash again. If share prices rise in the meantime, the business will make a profit from its short-term investment.

(b) **Prepayments**. These are amounts of money already paid by the business for benefits which have not yet been enjoyed but will be enjoyed within the next accounting period. Suppose, for example, that a business pays an annual insurance premium of £240 to insure its premises against fire and theft, and that the premium is payable annually in advance on 1 December. Now, if the business has an accounting year end of 31 December it will pay £240 on 1 December, but only enjoy one month's insurance cover by the end of the year. The remaining 11 months' cover (£220 cost, at £20 per month) will be enjoyed in the next year. The prepayment of £220 would therefore be shown in the balance sheet of the business, at 31 December, as a current asset.

A prepayment might be thought of as a form of debtor. In the example above, at 31 December the insurance company still owes the business 11 months' worth of insurance cover.

Trade debtors and other debtors

1.27 Although it is convenient to think of debtors as customers who buy goods on credit, it is more accurate to say that a debtor is anyone who owes the business money. Continuing the example of an insurance policy, if a business makes an insurance claim for fire damage, the insurance company would be a debtor for the money payable on the claim.

1.28 A distinction can be made between two groups of debtors.

- **Trade debtors**, ie customers who still owe money for goods or services bought on credit in the course of the trading activities of the business.
- **Other debtors**, ie anyone else owing money to the business.

Question 3

Shop fixtures and fittings are *fixed assets*. Or are they? Can you think of circumstances where they would be current assets?

Answer

If a supplier or manufacturer of shop fittings had some fittings in stock.

1.29 EXAMPLE: BALANCE SHEET PREPARATION

We shall now look at how the various types of assets and liabilities are shown in the balance sheet of a business. You might like to attempt to prepare a balance sheet yourself before reading the solution which follows.

Question 4

You are required to prepare a balance sheet for the Ted Hills Hardware Store as at 31 December 20X6, given the information below.

	£
Capital as at 1 January 20X6	47,600
Profit for the year to 31 December 20X6	8,000
Freehold premises, net book value at 31 December 20X6	50,000
Motor vehicles, net book value at 31 December 20X6	9,000
Fixtures and fittings, net book value at 31 December 20X6	8,000
Long-term loan (mortgage)	25,000
Bank overdraft*	2,000
Goods held in stock for resale	16,000
Debtors	500
Cash in hand*	100
Creditors	1,200
Taxation payable	3,500
Drawings	4,000
Accrued costs of rent	600
Prepayment of insurance	300

* A shop might have cash in its cash registers, but an overdraft at the bank.

Answer

TED HILLS BALANCE SHEET
AS AT 31 DECEMBER 20X6

	£	£
Fixed assets at net book value		
Freehold premises		50,000
Fixtures and fittings		8,000
Motor vehicles		9,000
		67,000
Current assets		
Stocks	16,000	
Debtors	500	
Prepayment	300	
Cash	100	
	16,900	
Current liabilities		
Bank overdraft	2,000	
Creditors	1,200	
Taxation payable	3,500	
Accrued costs	600	
	7,300	
Net current assets		9,600
		76,600
Long-term liabilities		
Loan		(25,000)
		51,600
Capital		
Capital as at 1 January 20X6		47,600
Profit for the year		8,000
		55,600
Less drawings		(4,000)
		51,600

Part B: Accounting concepts and principles

The order of items in the balance sheet

1.30 By convention, a balance sheet lists liabilities and assets in a particular order. This order is not compulsory, nor will you find that it is used all the time; however, you should try to get into the habit of using the conventional order of items yourself.

1.31 The format most commonly used is the vertical balance sheet format, shown above. As you will appreciate, there is no hard and fast rule about the order of items in a vertical balance sheet, except that the Companies Act 1985 requires net assets above and capital below to be used for the published accounts of most limited companies. This format is therefore one in particular you should try to familiarise yourself with and use as a matter of habit.

Order of items within categories: points to note

1.32 (a) **Fixed assets** are listed in a descending order of 'length of useful life'. Property has a longer life than fixtures and fittings, which in turn perhaps have a longer life than motor vehicles. This is why the fixed assets are listed in the order shown above.

(b) **Current assets** are listed in descending order of the length of time it might be before the asset will be converted into cash. Broadly speaking, stocks will convert into debtors, and debtors will convert into cash, and so stock, debtors and cash will be listed in that order. Prepayments, because they are similar to debtors, should be listed after debtors and before cash.

Working capital, or net current assets

> **KEY TERM**
>
> The **working capital** of a business is the difference between its current assets and current liabilities, ie working capital is the amount of net current assets.

1.33 In the balance sheet above, the Ted Hills Hardware shop has net current assets of £(16,900 − 7,300) = £9,600. This is a figure which is shown separately when a balance sheet is prepared in a vertical format.

2 THE TRADING, PROFIT AND LOSS ACCOUNT

2.1 The profit and loss account has already been mentioned several times as a statement in which revenues and expenditure are compared to arrive at a figure of profit or loss. Many businesses try to distinguish between a **gross profit** earned on trading, and a net profit. They prepare a statement called a **trading, profit and loss account.**

- In the first part of the statement (the **trading account**) revenue from selling goods is compared with direct costs of acquiring or producing the goods sold to arrive at a gross profit figure.

- From this, deductions are made in the second half of the statement (the **profit and loss account**) in respect of indirect costs (overheads).

FORMULA TO LEARN

Gross profit = sales less cost of sales.

Net profit = gross profit less expenses.

2.2 The trading, profit and loss account is a statement showing in detail how the profit (or loss) of a period has been made. The owners and managers of a business obviously want to know how much profit or loss has been made, but there is only a limited information value in the profit figure alone. In order to exercise financial control effectively, managers need to know how much income has been earned, what various items of costs have been, and whether the performance of sales or the control of costs appears to be satisfactory. This is the basic reason for preparing the trading, profit and loss account.

2.3 We have briefly mentioned the **matching convention** before. The profit and loss account has to **match the revenue earned to the costs of earning that revenue.** This is the reason why prepayments and accrued expenses have to be brought into the financial statements. Prepayments are deducted from expenses and are included the balance sheet, because they relate to future periods. Similarly accrued expenses are added to expenses and shown in the balance sheet, because they relate to the current period.

2.4 The two parts of the statement may be examined in more detail.

(a) The **trading account**. This shows the **gross profit** for the accounting period. Gross profit is the difference between:

(i) The value of sales (excluding value added tax)
(ii) The purchase cost or production cost of the goods sold.

In the retail business, the cost of the goods sold is their purchase cost from the suppliers. In a manufacturing business, the production cost of goods sold is the cost of raw materials in the finished goods, plus the cost of the labour required to make the goods, and often plus an amount of production 'overhead' costs.

(b) The **profit and loss account**. This shows the **net profit** of the business. The net profit is:

(i) The gross profit
(ii) Plus any other income from sources other than the sale of goods
(iii) Minus other expenses of the business which are not included in the cost of goods sold.

2.5 Gross profit is a highly significant figure in the income statements. It represents the profit made from the sale of goods or services. It can be represented as a percentage of sales, called the gross profit margin.

FORMULA TO LEARN

Gross profit margin = $\dfrac{\text{Gross profit}}{\text{Sales}} \times 100\%$

Part B: Accounting concepts and principles

2.6 The gross profit margin will be looked at in more detail later in this Study Text. However it is a very important ratio, as it can be used to compare the results of different periods to see how well the costs of sales are being controlled as sales increase. It can also be used to compare the results of different businesses in the same industry.

Detail in the profit and loss account

2.7 **Income from other sources** will include:

(a) Dividends or interest received from investments

(b) Profits on the sale of fixed assets

(c) Bad debts written off in a previous accounting period which were unexpectedly paid in the current period (see Paragraph 2.8(a)(vii) below)

2.8 Other business expenses that will appear in the profit and loss account are as follows.

(a) **Selling and distribution expenses**. These are expenses associated with the process of selling and delivering goods to customers. They include the following items.

   (i) The salaries of a sales director and sales management.

   (ii) The salaries and commissions of salesmen.

   (iii) The travelling and entertainment expenses of salesmen.

   (iv) Marketing costs (eg advertising and sales promotion expenses).

   (v) The costs of running and maintaining delivery vans.

   (vi) Discounts allowed to customers for early payment of their debt. For example, a business might sell goods to a customer for £100 and offer a discount of 5% for payment in cash. If the customer takes the discount, the accounts of the business would not record the sales value at £95; they would instead record sales at the full £100, with a cost for discounts allowed of £5. Discounts are described more fully in a later chapter.

   (vii) Bad debts written off. Sometimes debtors fail to pay what they owe, and a business might have to decide at some stage of chasing after payment that there is now no prospect of ever being paid. The debt has to be written off as 'bad'. The amount of the debt written off is charged as an expense in the profit and loss account. Bad debts will be described more fully in a later chapter.

(b) **Administration expenses**. These are the expenses of providing management and administration for the business. They include:

   (i) The salaries of directors, management and office staff
   (ii) Rent and rates
   (iii) Insurance
   (iv) Telephone and postage
   (v) Printing and stationery
   (vi) Heating and lighting

(c) **Finance expenses**. These include, for example:

   (i) Interest on a loan
   (ii) Bank overdraft interest

As far as possible, you should try to group items of expenses (selling and distribution, administration and finance) but this is not something that you should worry about unnecessarily at this stage.

2.9 EXAMPLE: TRADING, PROFIT AND LOSS ACCOUNT

On 1 June 20X5, Jock Heiss commenced trading as an ice cream salesman, selling ice creams from a van which he drove around the streets of his town.

(a) He rented the van at a cost of £1,000 for three months. Running expenses for the van averaged £300 per month.

(b) He hired a part time helper at a cost of £100 per month.

(c) He borrowed £2,000 from his bank, and the interest cost of the loan was £25 per month.

(d) His main business was to sell ice cream to customers in the street, but he also did some special catering arrangements for business customers, supplying ice creams for office parties. Sales to these customers were usually on credit.

(e) For the three months to 31 August 20X5, his total sales were:

   (i) cash sales £8,900;
   (ii) credit sales £1,100.

(f) He purchased his ice cream from a local manufacturer, Floors Ltd. The cost of purchases in the three months to 31 August 20X5 was £6,200, and at 31 August he had sold every item of stock. He still owed £700 to Floors Ltd for unpaid purchases on credit.

(g) One of his credit sale customers has gone bankrupt, owing Jock £250. Jock has decided to write off the debt in full, with no prospect of getting any of the money owed.

(h) He used his own home for his office work. Telephone and postage expenses for the three months to 31 August were £150.

(i) During the period he paid himself £300 per month.

Required

Prepare a trading, profit and loss account for the three months 1 June to 31 August 20X5.

2.10 SOLUTION

JOCK HEISS
TRADING, PROFIT AND LOSS ACCOUNT
FOR THE THREE MONTHS ENDED 31 AUGUST 20X5

	£	£
Sales		10,000
Less cost of sales ⎱ Trading a/c		6,200
Gross profit ⎰		3,800
Wages	300	
Van rental	1,000	
Van expenses ⎱	900	
Bad debt written off ⎰ Profit and loss a/c	250	
Telephone and postage	150	
Interest charges	75	
		2,675
Net profit (transferred to the balance sheet)		1,125

Part B: Accounting concepts and principles

Relationship between the profit and loss account and the balance sheet

- The net profit is the profit for the period, and it is transferred to the balance sheet of the business as part of the proprietor's capital.

- Drawings are appropriations of profit and not expenses. They must not be included in the profit and loss account. In this example, the payments that Jock Heiss makes to himself (£900) are drawings. They are included in the capital account on the balance sheet.

- The cost of sales is £6,200, even though £700 of the costs have not yet been paid for. Floors Ltd is a trade creditor for £700 in the balance sheet. This is an example of the matching concept.

2.11 EXAMPLE: GROSS PROFIT MARGIN

In the above example, the gross profit margin of Jock Heiss for the three months to 31 August 20X5 is:

$$\frac{3,800}{10,000} \times 100\% = 38\%$$

This can be compared to the gross profit margin for future trading periods to see whether the margin is maintained or improved. If the margin starts to fall, then Jock will need to examine his control of the costs of sales.

Chapter roundup

- This chapter introduced in broad outline the characteristics of the **balance sheet** and the **trading, profit and loss account**. In the next chapters, we shall go on to consider in detail some of the techniques and principles applied to prepare the trading, profit and loss account.

- A **balance sheet** is a statement of the **financial position** of a business at a given moment in time.

- A **trading, profit and loss account** is a financial statement showing in detail **how the profit or loss of a period has been made**.

- A distinction is made in the balance sheet between **long-term liabilities** and **current liabilities**, and between **fixed assets** and **current assets**.

- 'Current' means 'within one year'. **Current assets** are expected to be converted into cash within one year. **Current liabilities** are debts which are payable within one year.

- **Fixed assets** are those acquired for long-term use within the business. They are normally valued at cost less depreciation.

- The **profit and loss account** consists of two parts.
    - A **trading account** shows **gross profit** from the sale of goods or services
    - A **profit and loss account** shows the **net profit** (ie gross profit less expenses)

- The **profit and loss account** is prepared under the **matching convention**.

- The **gross profit margin** is a means of comparing the cost control between one period and the next.

3: An introduction to financial statements

Quick quiz

1. What are the component parts of the item 'proprietor's capital' in a balance sheet?
2. What are 'accrued charges'?
3. Which ONE of the following is a long-term liability?

    A A bank overdraft
    B A bank loan repayable within a year
    C A mortgage repayable in five year's time
    D A trade creditor

4. What is depreciation?
5. What are the main items in current assets in a balance sheet?
6. What are prepayments?
7. What is the difference between gross profit and net profit?
8. Which of the following expenses is included in cost of sales?

    A Sales people's salaries
    B Management salaries
    C Overdraft interest
    D Cost of raw material

9. A business has sales of £100,000, cost of sales of £60,000 and expenses of £20,000. Which of the following statements is true?

    A The gross profit margin is 60%
    B The gross profit margin is 40%
    C The gross profit margin is 20%
    D The gross profit margin is 80%

Answers to quick quiz

1. See paragraph 1.8.
2. Expenses already incurred by the business, which have not yet been billed.
3. C The mortgage is repayable in over a year's time and, therefore, is a long-term liability. The bank overdraft is repayable on demand, a trade creditor is usually paid within a year and the bank loan is repayable within one year, so these are all current liabilities.
4. Depreciation is a means of allocating the cost of an asset over the period of its useful life. (This is another example of the matching concept.)
5.
    - Stock
    - Debtors
    - Cash
6. Expenses already paid for by the business but which will be used, or the benefits enjoyed, in the next period of trading.
7. Net profit = gross profit less expenses plus non-trading income.
8. D The others are examples of selling expenses (A), administration expenses (B) and finance expenses (C).
9. B Gross profit margin = $\dfrac{\text{Gross profit}}{\text{Sales}} \times 100\% = \dfrac{(100{,}000 - 60{,}000)}{100{,}000} \times 100\% = 40\%$

Now try the question below from the Exam Question Bank

Question to try	Level	Marks	Time
3	Full exam	10	18 mins

Part C
Double entry bookkeeping and accounting treatments

Chapter 4

SOURCES, RECORDS AND THE BOOKS OF PRIME ENTRY

Topic list	Syllabus reference
1 The role of source documents	3(a)
2 The need for books of prime entry	3(a)
3 Sales and purchase day books	3(a)
4 Cash books	3(a)

Introduction

From your studies of the first three chapters you should have grasped some important points about the nature and purpose of accounting.

- Most organisations exist to provide products and services in the ultimate hope of making a surplus or **profit** for their owners, which they do by receiving payment in money for goods and services provided.

- The role of the accounting system is to **record** these monetary effects and create information about them.

You should also, by now, understand the basic principles underlying the balance sheet and profit and loss account and have an idea of what they look like.

In **part C** we turn our attention to the process by which a business transaction works its way through to the financial statements.

It is usual to record a business transaction on a **document**. Such documents include invoices, orders, credit notes and goods received notes, all of which will be discussed in Section 1 of this chapter. In terms of the accounting system these are known as **source documents**. The information on them is processed by the system by, for example, aggregating (adding together) or classifying.

Records of source documents are kept in **books of prime entry**, which, as the name suggests, are the first stage at which a business transaction enters into the accounting system. The various types of books of prime entry are discussed in Sections 2 to 4.

In the next chapter we consider what happens to transactions after the books of prime entry stage.

Study guide

Sections 3 and 4 – Bookkeeping principles

- Identify the main data sources and records in an accounting system.
- Explain the functions of each data source and record.
- Outline the form of accounting records in a typical manual system.
- Outline the form of accounting records in a typical computerised system.
- Record credit sales and purchase transactions using day books.

Part C: Double entry bookkeeping and accounting treatments

- Explain sales and purchase returns and their recording.
- Explain the need for a record of petty cash transactions.
- Illustrate the typical format of the petty cash book.
- Explain the importance of using the imprest system to control petty cash.

Exam guide

We are starting to move towards more examinable areas. The most likely area for books of prime entry to come up is MCQs. However you could be asked to write up a cash book or the day books as part of a Section B question.

1 THE ROLE OF SOURCE DOCUMENTS

1.1 Whenever a business transaction takes place, involving sales or purchases, receiving or paying money, or owing or being owed money, it is usual for the transaction to be recorded on a **document**. These documents are the source of all the information recorded by a business.

1.2 Documents used to record the business transactions in the 'books of account' of the business **include** the following. You will meet other examples as you work through this Text.

- **Sales order**. A customer writes out an order or signs an order for goods or services he wishes to buy.
- **Purchase order**. A business makes an order from another business for the purchase of goods or services, such as material supplies.
- **Invoices** and **credit notes**. These are discussed further below.
- **Remittance advices**. A customer sends this with a payment.
- **Cheque stubs**. A business's record of payments it has made.
- **Petty cash vouchers**. A claim for reimbursement out of petty cash.

The invoice

> **KEY TERM**
>
> An **invoice** relates to a sales order or a purchase order.
>
> - When a business sells goods or services on credit to a customer, it sends out an invoice. The details on the invoice should match up with the details on the sales order. The invoice is a request for the customer to pay what he owes.
> - When a business buys goods or services on credit it receives an invoice from the supplier. The details on the invoice should match up with the details on the purchase order.

1.3 The invoice is primarily a **demand for payment**, but it is used for other purposes as well, as we shall see. Because it has several uses, an invoice is often produced on multi-part stationery, or photocopied, or carbon-copied. The top copy will go to the customer and other copies will be used by various people within the business.

4: Sources, records and the books of prime entry

What does an invoice show?

1.4 Most invoices are numbered, so that the business can keep track of all the invoices it sends out. Information usually shown on an invoice includes the following.

(a) Name and address of the seller and the purchaser

(b) Date of the sale

(c) Description of what is being sold

(d) Quantity and unit price of what has been sold (eg 20 pairs of shoes at £25 a pair)

(e) Details of trade discount, if any (eg 10% reduction in cost if buying over 100 pairs of shoes). We shall look at discounts in a later chapter

(f) Total amount of the invoice including (in the UK) any details of VAT

(g) Sometimes, the date by which payment is due, and other terms of sale

The credit note

1.5 Student Supplies Ltd sent out an invoice to the county council for 450 rulers delivered to the local primary school. The typist accidentally typed in a total of £162.10, instead of £62.10. The county council has been *overcharged* by £100. What is Student Supplies to do?

1.6 Alternatively, suppose that when the primary school received the rulers, it found that they had all been broken in the post and that it was going to send them back. Although the county council has received an invoice for £62.10, it has no intention of paying it, because the rulers were useless. Again, what is Student Supplies to do?

1.7 The answer is that the supplier (in this case, Student Supplies) sends out a **credit note**. A credit note is sometimes printed in red to distinguish it from an invoice. Otherwise, it will be made out in much the same way as an invoice, but with less detail and 'Credit Note Number' instead of 'Invoice Number'.

> **KEY TERM**
>
> A **credit note** is a document relating to returned goods or refunds when a customer has been overcharged. It can be regarded as a 'negative invoice'.

1.8 Other documents sometimes used in connection with sales and purchases are:

- Debit notes
- Goods received notes

1.9 A **debit note** might be issued instead of raising an invoice to **adjust an invoice** already issued. This is also commonly achieved by issuing a revised invoice after raising a credit or debit note purely for internal purposes (ie to keep the records straight).

1.10 More commonly, a debit note is issued to a supplier as a means of formally requesting a credit note.

1.11 **Goods received notes** (GRNs) are filled in to record a receipt of goods, most commonly in a warehouse. They may be used in addition to suppliers' advice notes. Often the accounts department will require sight of the relevant GRN before paying a supplier's invoice. Even

Part C: Double entry bookkeeping and accounting treatments

where GRNs are not routinely used, the details of a consignment from a supplier which arrives without an advice note must always be recorded.

Question 1

Fill in the blank.

'Student Supplies Ltd sends out a .... to a credit customer in order to correct an error where a customer has been overcharged on an ....

Answer

Credit note; invoice.

2 THE NEED FOR BOOKS OF PRIME ENTRY

2.1 We have seen that in the course of business, source documents are created. The details on these source documents need to be summarised, as otherwise the business might forget to ask for some money, or forget to pay some, or even accidentally pay something twice. In other words, it needs to keep records of source documents - of transactions - so that it can keep tabs on what is going on. Such records are made in **books of prime entry**.

> **KEY TERM**
>
> **Books of prime entry** are books in which we first record transactions. They are sometimes called books of **original entry**.

2.2 The main books of prime entry which we need to look at are as follows.

(a) Sales day book
(b) Purchase day book
(c) Sales returns day book
(d) Purchases returns day book
(e) Journal (described in the next chapter)
(f) Cash book
(g) Petty cash book

2.3 It is worth bearing in mind that, for convenience, this chapter describes books of prime entry as if they are actual books. Nowadays, books of prime entry are often not books at all, but rather files hidden in the memory of a computer. However, the principles remain the same whether they are manual or computerised.

3 SALES AND PURCHASE DAY BOOKS

The sales day book

> **KEY TERM**
>
> The **sales day book** is the book of prime entry for credit sales.

3.1 The **sales day book** is used to keep a list of all invoices sent out to customers each day. An extract from a sales day book might look like this.

4: Sources, records and the books of prime entry

SALES DAY BOOK

Date 20X0	Invoice	Customer	Sales ledger folio	Total amount invoiced £
Jan 10	247	Jones & Co	SL14	105.00
	248	Smith Ltd	SL 8	86.40
	249	Alex & Co	SL 6	31.80
	250	Enor College	SL 9	1,264.60
				1,487.80

3.2 The column called 'sales ledger folio' is a reference to the sales ledger. It means, for example, that the sale to Jones & Co for £105 is also recorded on page 14 of the sales ledger.

3.3 Most businesses 'analyse' their sales. For example, suppose that the business sells boots and shoes, and that the sale to Smith was entirely boots, the sale to Alex was entirely shoes, and the other two sales were a mixture of both.

3.4 Then the sales day book might look like this.

SALES DAY BOOK

Date 20X0	Invoice	Customer	Sales ledger folio	Total amount invoiced £	Boot sales £	Shoe sales £
Jan 10	247	Jones & Co	SL 14	105.00	60.00	45.00
	248	Smith Ltd	SL 8	86.40	86.40	
	249	Alex & Co	SL 6	31.80		31.80
	250	Enor College	SL 9	1,264.60	800.30	464.30
				1,487.80	946.70	541.10

3.5 This sort of analysis gives the managers of the business useful information which helps them to decide how best to run the business.

The purchase day book

3.6 A business also keeps a record in the purchase day book of all the invoices it receives.

KEY TERM

The **purchase day book** is the book of prime entry for credit purchases.

3.7 An extract from a purchase day book might look like this.

PURCHASE DAY BOOK

Date 20X8	Supplier	Purchase ledger folio	Total amount invoiced £	Purchases £	Electricity etc £
Mar 15	Cook & Co	PL 31	315.00	315.00	
	W Butler	PL 46	29.40	29.40	
	EEB	PL 42	116.80		116.80
	Show Fair Ltd	PL 12	100.00	100.00	
			561.20	444.40	116.80

Part C: Double entry bookkeeping and accounting treatments

3.8 Points to note:

(a) The 'purchase ledger folio' is a reference to the purchase ledger just as the sales ledger folio was to the sales ledger. Again, we will see the purpose of this in the next chapter.

(b) There is no 'invoice number' column, because the purchase day book records other people's invoices, which have all sorts of different numbers.

(c) Like the sales day book, the purchase day book analyses the invoices which have been sent in. In this example, three of the invoices related to goods which the business intends to re-sell (called simply 'purchases') and the fourth invoice was an electricity bill.

The sales returns day book

3.9 When customers return goods for some reason, the returns are recorded in the sales return day book. An extract from the sales returns day book might look like this:

SALES RETURNS DAY BOOK

Date 20X8	Customer and goods	Sales ledger folio	Amount £
30 April	Owen Plenty 3 pairs 'Texas' boots	SL 82	135.00

> **KEY TERM**
>
> The **sales returns day book** is the book of prime entry for goods returned by the customers.

3.10 Not all sales returns day books analyse what goods were returned, but it makes sense to keep as complete a record as possible.

The purchase returns day book

3.11 There are no prizes for guessing that the purchase returns day book is kept to record goods which the business sends back to its suppliers. The business might expect a cash refund from the supplier. In the meantime, however, it might issue a debit note to the supplier, indicating the amount by which the business expects its total debt to the supplier to be reduced.

3.12 An extract from the purchase returns day book might look like this:

PURCHASE RETURNS DAY BOOK

Date 20X8	Supplier and goods	Purchase ledger folio	Amount £
29 April	Boxes Ltd 300 cardboard boxes	PL 123	46.60

KEY TERM

The **purchase returns day book** is the book of prime entry for goods returned to suppliers.

4 CASH BOOKS

The cash book

4.1 The cash book is also a day book, which is used to keep a cumulative record of money received and money paid out by the business. The cash book deals with money paid into and out of the business **bank account**. This could be money received on the business premises in notes, coins and cheques. There are also receipts and payments made by bank transfer, standing order, direct debit and, in the case of bank interest and charges, directly by the bank.

4.2 Some cash, in notes and coins, is usually kept on the business premises in order to make occasional payments for odd items of expense. This cash is usually accounted for separately in a **petty cash book** (which we will look at shortly).

4.3 One part of the cash book is used to record receipts of cash, and another part is used to record payments. The best way to see how the cash book works is to follow through an example.

KEY TERM

The **cash book** is the book of prime entry for cash and bank receipts and payments.

4.4 EXAMPLE: CASH BOOK

At the beginning of 1 September, Robin Plenty had £900 in the bank. During 1 September 20X7, Robin Plenty had the following receipts and payments.

(a) Cash sale - receipt of £80
(b) Payment from credit customer Hay £400 less discount allowed £20
(c) Payment from credit customer Been £720
(d) Payment from credit customer Seed £150 less discount allowed £10
(e) Cheque received for cash to provide a short-term loan from Len Dinger £1,800
(f) Second cash sale - receipts of £150
(g) Cash received for sale of machine £200
(h) Payment to supplier Kew £120
(i) Payment to supplier Hare £310
(j) Payment of telephone bill £400
(k) Payment of gas bill £280
(l) £100 in cash withdrawn from bank for petty cash
(m) Payment of £1,500 to Hess for new plant and machinery

If you look through these transactions, you will see that seven of them are receipts and six of them are payments.

Part C: Double entry bookkeeping and accounting treatments

The receipts part of the cash book for 1 September would look like this.

CASH BOOK (RECEIPTS)

Date 20X7	Narrative	Folio	Total £
1 Sept	Balance b/d*		900
	Cash sale		80
	Debtor: Hay		380
	Debtor: Been		720
	Debtor: Seed		140
	Loan: Len Dinger		1,800
	Cash sale		150
	Sale of fixed asset		200
			4,370
2 Sept	Balance b/d*		1,660

* 'b/d' = brought down (ie brought forward)

4.5 Points to note:

(a) There is space on the right hand side of the cash book so that the receipts can be analysed under various headings - for example, 'receipts from debtors', 'cash sales' and 'other receipts'.

(b) The cash received in the day amounted to £3,470. Added to the £900 at the start of the day, this comes to £4,370. But this is not, of course, the amount to be carried forward to the next day, because first we have to subtract all the payments made during 1 September.

4.6 The payments part of the cash book for 1 September would look like this.

CASH BOOK (PAYMENTS)

Date 20X7	Narrative	Folio	Total £
1 Sept	Creditor: Kew		120
	Creditor: Hare		310
	Telephone		400
	Gas bill		280
	Petty cash		100
	Machinery purchase		1,500
	Balance c/d		1,660
			4,370

4.7 As you can see, this is very similar to the receipts part of the cash book. But note the following.

(a) The analysis on the right would be under headings like 'payments to creditors', 'payments into petty cash', 'wages' and 'other payments'.

(b) Payments during 1 September totalled £2,710. We know that the total of receipts was £4,370. That means that there is a balance of £4,370 − £2,710 = £1,660 to be 'carried down' to the start of the next day. As you can see this 'balance carried down' is noted at the end of the payments column, so that the receipts and payments totals show the same figure of £4,370 at the end of 1 September. And if you look to the receipts part of this example, you can see that £1,660 has been brought down ready for the next day.

4: Sources, records and the books of prime entry

4.8 With analysis columns completed, the cash book given in the examples above might look as follows.

CASH BOOK (RECEIPTS)

Date	Narrative	Folio	Total £	Debtors £	Cash sales £	Other £
20X7						
1 Sept	Balance b/d		900			
	Cash sale		80		80	
	Debtor - Hay		380	380		
	Debtor - Been		720	720		
	Debtor - Seed		140	140		
	Loan - Len Dinger		1,800			1,800
	Cash sale		150		150	
	Sale of fixed asset		200			200
			4,370	1,240	230	2,000

CASH BOOK (PAYMENTS)

Date	Narrative	Folio	Total £	Creditors £	Petty cash £	Wages £	Other £
20X7							
1 Sept	Creditor - Kew		120	120			
	Creditor - Hare		310	310			
	Telephone		400				400
	Gas bill		280				280
	Petty cash		100		100		
	Machinery purchase		1,500				1,500
	Balance c/d		1,660				
			4,370	430	100	-	2,180

Bank statements

4.9 Weekly or monthly, a business will receive a **bank statement**. Bank statements should be used to check that the amount shown as a balance in the cash book agrees with the amount on the bank statement, and that no cash has 'gone missing'. This agreement or 'reconciliation' of the cash book with a statement is the subject of a later chapter.

Petty cash book

4.10 Most businesses keep a small amount of cash on the premises to make occasional small payments in cash - eg to pay the milkman, to buy a few postage stamps, to pay the office cleaner, to pay for some bus or taxi fares etc. This is often called the cash float or **petty cash** account. The cash float can also be the resting place for occasional small receipts, such as cash paid by a visitor to make a phone call, or take some photocopies etc.

4.11 Although the amounts involved are small, petty cash transactions still need to be recorded; otherwise the cash float could be abused for personal expenses or even stolen.

4.12 There are usually more payments than receipts, and petty cash must be 'topped up' from time to time with cash from the business bank account. A typical layout follows.

Part C: Double entry bookkeeping and accounting treatments

PETTY CASH BOOK

Receipts £	Date 20X7	Narrative	Total £	Milk £	Postage £	Travel £	Other £
250	1 Sept	Bal b/d					
		Milk bill	25	25			
		Postage stamps	5		5		
		Taxi fare	10			10	
		Flowers for sick staff	15				15
		Bal c/d	195				
250			250	25	5	10	15

KEY TERM

A **petty cash book** is a cash book for small payments.

4.13 Under what is called the **imprest system**, the amount of money in petty cash is kept at an agreed sum or 'float' (say £100). Expense items are recorded on vouchers as they occur, so that at any time:

	£
Cash still held in petty cash	X
Plus voucher payments	X
Must equal the agreed sum or float	X

The total float is made up regularly (to £100, or whatever the agreed sum is) by means of a cash payment from the bank account into petty cash. The amount of the 'top-up' into petty cash will be the total of the voucher payments since the previous top-up.

KEY TERM

The **imprest system** is a system where a refund is made of total cash paid out in a period.

Exam focus point

Although questions requiring large-scale recording of routine trading transactions will not be set in the exam, it is important that you understand these basics and how they lead on to ledger accounting and double-entry bookkeeping. These processes are developed in the next chapter.

Question 2

State which books of prime entry the following transactions would be entered into.

(a) Your business pays A Brown (a supplier) £450.00.
(b) You send D Smith (a customer) an invoice for £650.
(c) Your accounts manager asks you for £12 urgently in order to buy some envelopes.
(d) You receive an invoice from A Brown for £300.
(e) You pay D Smith £500.
(f) F Jones (a customer) returns goods to the value of £250.
(g) You return goods to J Green to the value of £504.
(h) F Jones pays you £500.

4: Sources, records and the books of prime entry

Answer

(a) Cash book
(b) Sales day book
(c) Petty cash book
(d) Purchases day book
(e) Cash book
(f) Sales returns day book
(g) Purchase returns day book
(h) Cash book

4.14 Another book of prime entry is the **journal** which is considered in the next chapter.

Chapter roundup

- Business transactions are recorded on **source documents**. These include the following.
  - Sales orders
  - Purchase orders
  - Invoices
  - Credit notes
- These transactions are recorded in **books of prime entry** of which there are seven.
  - Sales day book
  - Sales returns day book
  - Purchase day book
  - Purchase returns day book
  - Cash book
  - Petty cash book
  - Journal
- Most businesses keep **petty cash** on the premises which is topped up from the main bank account. Under the **imprest system** the petty cash is kept at an agreed sum.
- You should be aware of which transactions go in a given book of prime entry.

Quick quiz

1. Name four pieces of information normally shown on an invoice.
2. Name the seven books of prime or original entry.
3. What information is summarised in the sales day book?
4. What is the purchase returns day book used to record?

   A Supplier's invoices
   B Customer's invoices
   C Details of goods returned to suppliers
   D Details of goods returned by customers

5. What is the difference between the cash book and the petty cash book?

6. Petty cash is controlled under and imprest system. The imprest amount is £100. During a period, payments totalling £53 have been made. How much needs to be reimbursed at the end of the period to restore petty cash to the imprest account?

   A £100
   B £53
   C £47
   D £50

Part C: Double entry bookkeeping and accounting treatments

Answers to quick quiz

1   **Four** from the following

- Invoice number
- Seller's name and address
- Purchaser's name and address
- Date of sale
- Description of goods or services
- Quantity and unit price
- Trade discount (if any)
- Total amount, including value added tax (if any)
- Any special terms

2   See paragraph 2.2.

3   Credit sales invoices, analysed into sales of different products.

4   C.

5   The cash book records amounts paid into or out of the bank account. The petty cash book records payments of small amounts of cash.

6   B   Under the imprest system, a reimbursement is made of the amount of the vouchers (or payments made) for the period.

Now try the question below from the Exam Question Bank

Question to try	Level	Marks	Time
4	Full exam	10	18 mins

Chapter 5

LEDGER ACCOUNTING AND DOUBLE ENTRY

Topic list	Syllabus reference
1 Why do we need ledger accounts?	3(a)
2 The nominal ledger	3(a)
3 Double entry bookkeeping	2(b), 3(a)
4 The journal	3(a), 3(b)
5 Day book analysis	3(a)
6 The imprest system	3(a)
7 The sales and purchase ledgers	3(a)
8 Accounting for value added tax	3(c)

Introduction

In the previous chapter we saw how to organise transactions into lists. It is not easy, however, to see how a business is doing from the information scattered throughout the books of prime entry. The lists need to be summarised. This is **ledger accounting**.

The summary is produced in the nominal ledger by a process you may have heard of known as **double entry bookkeeping**. This is the cornerstone of accounts preparation and is surprisingly simple.

Study guide

Sections 3 and 4 – Bookkeeping principles

- Explain the concept of double entry and the duality concept.
- Explain debit and credit.
- Distinguish between asset, liability, revenue and expense accounts.
- Explain the meaning of the balance on each type of account.
- Illustrate how to balance a ledger account.
- Record cash transactions in ledger accounts.
- Record credit sale and purchase transactions in ledger accounts.
- Explain the division of the ledger into sections.
- Explain the general principles of the operation of value added tax and the consequent accounting entries.

Part C: Double entry bookkeeping and accounting treatments

Section 5 – The journal; ledger control accounts; bank reconciliations

- Explain the uses of the journal.
- Illustrate the use of the journal and the posting of journal entries into ledger accounts.

Exam guide

Learn the journal format. It is likely that you will have to produce journals in the exam.

---

1 WHY DO WE NEED LEDGER ACCOUNTS?

1.1 In earlier chapters we saw how a profit and loss account and balance sheet are presented. We have also seen, by means of the accounting equation and the business equation, that it would be possible to prepare a statement of the affairs of a business at any time we like, and that a profit and loss account and a balance sheet could be drawn up on any date, relating to any period of time.

1.2 A business is continually making transactions eg buying and selling and we would not want to prepare a profit and loss account and a balance sheet on completion of every individual transaction. To do so would be a time-consuming and cumbersome administrative task.

1.3 It is common sense that a business should keep a record of the transactions that it makes, the assets it acquires and liabilities it incurs. When the time comes to prepare a profit and loss account and a balance sheet, the relevant information can be taken from those records.

1.4 The **records of transactions, assets and liabilities** should be:

(a) In **chronological order**, and **dated** so that transactions can be related to a particular period of time.

(b) Built up in **cumulative totals**. For example, a business may build up the total of its sales:

(i) Day by day (eg total sales on Monday, total sales on Tuesday)
(ii) Week by week
(iii) Month by month
(iv) Year by year

1.5 We have already seen the first step in this process, which is to list all the transactions in various books of prime entry. Now we must turn our attention to the method used to summarise these records: **ledger accounting** and **double entry**.

2 THE NOMINAL LEDGER

KEY TERM

The **nominal ledger** is an accounting record which summarises the financial affairs of a business.

2.1 The nominal ledger is sometimes called the '**general ledger**'.

2.2 It contains details of assets, liabilities and capital, income and expenditure and so profit and loss. It consists of a large number of different accounts, each account having its own purpose or 'name' and an identity or code.

2.3 There may be various subdivisions, whether for convenience, ease of handling, confidentiality, security, or to meet the needs of computer software design. For example, the ledger may be split alphabetically, with different clerks responsible for sections A-F, G-M, N-R and S-Z. This can help to stop fraud, as there would have to be collusion between the different section clerks.

2.4 Examples of accounts in the nominal ledger include the following.

(a) Plant and machinery at cost (fixed asset)
(b) Motor vehicles at cost (fixed asset)
(c) Plant and machinery, provision for depreciation (liability)
(d) Motor vehicles, provision for depreciation (liability)
(e) Proprietor's capital (liability)
(f) Stocks - raw materials (current asset)
(g) Stocks - finished goods (current asset)
(h) Total debtors (current asset)
(i) Total creditors (current liability)
(j) Wages and salaries (expense item)
(k) Rent and rates (expense item)
(l) Advertising expenses (expense item)
(m) Bank charges (expense item)
(n) Motor expenses (expense item)
(o) Telephone expenses (expense item)
(p) Sales (income or revenue item)
(q) Total cash or bank overdraft (current asset or liability)

2.5 In the financial statements, the revenue and expenditure accounts will help to form the profit and loss account; while the asset and liability accounts go into the balance sheet.

The format of a ledger account

2.6 If a ledger account were to be kept in an actual book rather than as a computer record, it might look like this:

ADVERTISING EXPENSES

Date	Narrative	Folio	£	Date	Narrative	Folio	£
20X6							
15 April	JFK Agency for quarter to 31 March	PL 348	2,500				

2.7 There are two sides to the account, and an account heading on top, and so it is convenient to think in terms of 'T' accounts.

(a) On top of the account is its name.
(b) There is a left hand side, or **debit side**.
(c) There is a right hand side, or **credit side**.

Part C: Double entry bookkeeping and accounting treatments

	NAME OF ACCOUNT		
DEBIT SIDE	£	CREDIT SIDE	£

3 DOUBLE ENTRY BOOKKEEPING

Dual effect (duality concept)

3.1 **Double entry bookkeeping** is the method used to transfer our weekly/monthly totals from our books of prime entry into the nominal ledger.

3.2 Central to this process is the idea that every transaction has two effects, the **dual effect**. This feature is not something peculiar to businesses. If you were to purchase a car for £1,000 cash for instance, you would be affected in two ways.

(a) You own a car worth £1,000.
(b) You have £1,000 less cash.

If instead you got a bank loan to make the purchase:

(a) You own a car worth £1,000.
(b) You owe the bank £1,000.

A month later if you pay a garage £50 to have the exhaust replaced:

(a) You have £50 less cash.
(b) You have incurred a repairs expense of £50.

3.3 **Ledger accounts**, with their debit and credit side, are kept in a way which allows the two-sided nature of business transactions to be recorded. This system of accounting is known as the '**double entry**' system of bookkeeping, so called because **every transaction is recorded twice** in the accounts.

The rules of double entry bookkeeping

3.4 The basic rule which must always be observed is that **every financial transaction gives rise to two accounting entries, one a debit and the other a credit**. The total value of debit entries in the nominal ledger is therefore always equal at any time to the total value of credit entries. Which account receives the credit entry and which receives the debit depends on the nature of the transaction.

> **KEY TERMS**
>
> - An **increase** in an **expense** (eg a purchase of stationery) or an **increase in an asset** (eg a purchase of office furniture) is a **debit**.
>
> - An **increase** in **income** (eg a sale) or an **increase in a liability** (eg buying goods on credit) is a **credit**.
>
> - A **decrease** in an **asset** (eg making a cash payment) is a **credit**.
>
> - A **decrease** in a **liability** (eg paying a creditor) is a **debit**.

5: Ledger accounting and double entry

3.5 This can be illustrated by the 'T' accounts below.

ASSET		LIABILITY	
DEBIT	CREDIT	DEBIT	CREDIT
Increase	Decrease	Decrease	Increase

CAPITAL	
DEBIT	CREDIT
Decrease	Increase

Income increases profit, which increases capital, so:

INCOME		EXPENSES	
DEBIT	CREDIT	DEBIT	CREDIT
Decrease	Increase	Increase	Decrease

Have a go at the question below before you learn about this topic in detail.

Question 1

Complete the following table relating to the transactions of a bookshop. (The first two are done for you.)

(a) Purchase of books on credit

    (i)   creditors increase   CREDIT   creditors   (increase in liability)
    (ii) purchases expense increases   DEBIT   purchases   (item of expense)

(b) Purchase of cash register

    (i)   own a cash register   DEBIT   cash register   (increase in asset)
    (ii) cash at bank decreases   CREDIT   cash at bank   (decrease in asset)

(c) Payment received from a debtor

    (i)   debtors decrease
    (ii) cash at bank increases

(d) Purchase of van

    (i)   own a van
    (ii) cash at bank decreases

Answer

(c) Payment received from a debtor

    (i)   debtors decrease   CREDIT   debtors   (decrease in asset)
    (ii) cash at bank increases   DEBIT   cash at bank (increase in asset)

(d) Purchase of van

    (i)   own a van   DEBIT   van   (increases in asset)
    (ii) cash at bank decreases   CREDIT   cash at bank (decrease in asset)

3.6 How did you get on? Students coming to the subject for the first time often have difficulty in knowing where to begin. A good starting point is the cash account, ie the nominal ledger

Part C: Double entry bookkeeping and accounting treatments

account in which receipts and payments of cash are recorded. The rule to remember about the cash account is as follows.

(a) A cash **payment** is a **credit** entry in the cash account. Here the **asset is decreasing**. Cash may be paid out, for example, to pay an expense (such as rates) or to purchase an asset (such as a machine). The matching debit entry is therefore made in the appropriate expense account or asset account.

(b) A cash **receipt** is a **debit** entry in the cash account. Here the **asset is increasing**. Cash might be received, for example, by a retailer who makes a cash sale. The credit entry would then be made in the sales account.

KEY TERM

Double entry bookkeeping is the method by which a business records financial transactions. An account is maintained for every supplier, customer, asset, liability, and income and expense. Every transaction is recorded twice so that for every *debit* there is an equal, corresponding *credit*.

3.7 EXAMPLE: DOUBLE ENTRY FOR CASH TRANSACTIONS

In the cash book of a business, the following transactions have been recorded.

(a) A cash sale (ie a receipt) of £2
(b) Payment of a rent bill totalling £150
(c) Buying some goods for cash at £100
(d) Buying some shelves for cash at £200

3.8 How would these four transactions be posted to the ledger accounts? For that matter, which ledger accounts should they be posted to? Don't forget that each transaction will be posted twice, in accordance with the rule of double entry.

3.9 SOLUTION

(a) The two sides of the transaction are:
    (i) Cash is received (debit entry in the cash account).
    (ii) Sales increase by £2 (credit entry in the sales account).

CASH ACCOUNT

	£		£
Sales a/c	2		

SALES ACCOUNT

	£		£
		Cash a/c	2

(Note how the entry in the cash account is cross-referenced to the sales account and vice-versa. This enables a person looking at one of the accounts to trace where the other half of the double entry can be found.)

(b) The two sides of the transaction are:

(i) Cash is paid (credit entry in the cash account).
(ii) Rent expense increases by £150 (debit entry in the rent account).

CASH ACCOUNT

	£		£
		Rent a/c	150

RENT ACCOUNT

	£		£
Cash a/c	150		

(c) The two sides of the transaction are:
(i) Cash is paid (credit entry in the cash account).
(ii) Purchases increase by £100 (debit entry in the purchases account).

CASH ACCOUNT

	£		£
		Purchases a/c	100

PURCHASES ACCOUNT

	£		£
Cash a/c	100		

(d) The two sides of the transaction are:
(i) Cash is paid (credit entry in the cash account).
(ii) Assets - in this case, shelves - increase by £200 (debit entry in shelves account).

CASH ACCOUNT

	£		£
		Shelves a/c	200

SHELVES (ASSET) ACCOUNT

	£		£
Cash a/c	200		

3.10 If all four of these transactions related to the same business, the cash account of that business would end up looking as follows.

CASH ACCOUNT

	£		£
Sales a/c	2	Rent a/c	150
		Purchases a/c	100
		Shelves a/c	200

Credit transactions

3.11 Not all transactions are settled immediately in cash. A business might purchase goods or fixed assets from its suppliers on credit terms, so that the suppliers would be creditors of the business until settlement was made in cash. Equally, the business might grant credit terms

Part C: Double entry bookkeeping and accounting treatments

to its customers who would then be debtors of the business. Clearly no entries can be made in the cash book when a credit transaction occurs, because initially no cash has been received or paid. Where then can the details of the transactions be entered?

3.12 The solution to this problem is to use **debtors and creditors accounts**. When a business acquires goods or services on credit, the credit entry is made in an account designated 'creditors' instead of in the cash account. The debit entry is made in the appropriate expense or asset account, exactly as in the case of cash transactions. Similarly, when a sale is made to a credit customer the entries made are a debit to the total debtors account (instead of cash account) and a credit to sales account.

3.13 EXAMPLE: CREDIT TRANSACTIONS

Recorded in the sales day book and the purchase day book are the following transactions.

(a) The business sells goods on credit to a customer Mr A for £2,000.
(b) The business buys goods on credit from a supplier B Ltd for £100.

How and where are these transactions posted in the ledger accounts?

3.14 SOLUTION

(a)

DEBTORS ACCOUNT

	£		£
Sales a/c	2,000		

SALES ACCOUNT

	£		£
		Debtors account	2,000

(b)

CREDITORS ACCOUNT

	£		£
		Purchases a/c	100

PURCHASES ACCOUNT

	£		£
Creditors a/c	100		

When cash is paid to creditors or by debtors

3.15 What happens when a credit transaction is eventually settled in cash? Suppose that, in the example above, the business paid £100 to B Ltd one month after the goods were acquired. The two sides of this new transaction are:

(a) Cash is paid (credit entry in the cash account)
(b) The amount owing to creditors is reduced (debit entry in the creditors account).

5: Ledger accounting and double entry

CASH ACCOUNT

	£		£
		Creditors a/c (B Ltd)	100

CREDITORS ACCOUNT

	£		£
Cash a/c	100		

3.16 If we now bring together the two parts of this example, the original purchase of goods on credit and the eventual settlement in cash, we find that the accounts appear as follows.

CASH ACCOUNT

	£		£
		Creditors a/c	100

PURCHASES ACCOUNT

	£		£
Creditors a/c	100		

CREDITORS ACCOUNT

	£		£
Cash a/c	100	Purchases a/c	100

3.17 The two entries in the creditors account cancel each other out, indicating that no money is owing to creditors any more. We are left with a credit entry of £100 in the cash account and a debit entry of £100 in the purchases account. These are exactly the entries which would have been made to record a *cash* purchase of £100 (compare example above). This is what we would expect: after the business has paid off its creditors it is in exactly the position of a business which has made cash purchases of £100, and the accounting records reflect this similarity.

3.18 Similar reasoning applies when a customer settles his debt. In the example above when Mr A pays his debt of £2,000 the two sides of the transaction are:

(a) Cash is received (debit entry in the cash account)
(b) The amount owed by debtors is reduced (credit entry in the debtors account).

CASH ACCOUNT

	£		£
Debtors a/c	2,000		

DEBTORS ACCOUNT

	£		£
		Cash a/c	2,000

3.19 The accounts recording this sale to, and payment by, Mr A now appear as follows.

Part C: Double entry bookkeeping and accounting treatments

CASH ACCOUNT

	£		£
Debtors a/c	2,000		

SALES ACCOUNT

	£		£
		Debtors a/c	2,000

DEBTORS ACCOUNT

	£		£
Sales a/c	2,000	Cash a/c	2,000

3.20 The two entries in the debtors account cancel each other out; while the entries in the cash account and sales account reflect the same position as if the sale had been made for cash (see above).

3.21 Now try the following questions.

Question 2

See if you can identify the debit and credit entries in the following transactions.

(a) Bought a machine on credit from A, cost £8,000.
(b) Bought goods on credit from B, cost £500.
(c) Sold goods on credit to C, value £1,200.
(d) Paid D (a creditor) £300.
(e) Collected £180 from E, a debtor.
(f) Paid wages £4,000.
(g) Received rent bill of £700 from landlord G.
(h) Paid rent of £700 to landlord G.
(i) Paid insurance premium £90.

Answer

			£	£
(a)	DEBIT	Machine account (fixed asset)	8,000	
	CREDIT	Creditors (A)		8,000
(b)	DEBIT	Purchases account	500	
	CREDIT	Creditors (B)		500
(c)	DEBIT	Debtors (C)	1,200	
	CREDIT	Sales		1,200
(d)	DEBIT	Creditors (D)	300	
	CREDIT	Cash		300
(e)	DEBIT	Cash	180	
	CREDIT	Debtors (E)		180
(f)	DEBIT	Wages account	4,000	
	CREDIT	Cash		4,000
(g)	DEBIT	Rent account	700	
	CREDIT	Creditors (G)		700
(h)	DEBIT	Creditors (G)	700	
	CREDIT	Cash		700
(i)	DEBIT	Insurance costs	90	
	CREDIT	Cash		90

5: Ledger accounting and double entry

Question 3

See now whether you can record the ledger entries for the following transactions. Ron Knuckle set up a business selling keep fit equipment, trading under the name of Buy Your Biceps Shop. He put £7,000 of his own money into a business bank account (transaction A) and in his first period of trading, the following transactions occurred.

		£
Transaction		
B	Paid rent of shop for the period	3,500
C	Purchased equipment (stocks) on credit	5,000
D	Raised loan from bank	1,000
E	Purchase of shop fittings (for cash)	2,000
F	Sales of equipment: cash	10,000
G	Sales of equipment: on credit	2,500
H	Payments to trade creditors	5,000
I	Payments from debtors	2,500
J	Interest on loan (paid)	100
K	Other expenses (all paid in cash)	1,900
L	Drawings	1,500

All stocks purchased during the period was sold, and so there were no closing stocks of equipment.

Try to do as much of this exercise as you can by yourself before reading the solution.

Answer

Clearly, there should be an account for cash, debtors, creditors, purchases, a shop fittings account, sales, a loan account and a proprietor's capital account. It is also useful to keep a separate **drawings account** until the end of each accounting period. Other accounts should be set up as they seem appropriate and in this exercise, accounts for rent, bank interest and other expenses would seem appropriate.

It has been suggested to you that the cash account is a good place to start, if possible. You should notice that cash transactions include the initial input of capital by Ron Knuckle, subsequent drawings, the payment of rent, the loan from the bank, the interest, some cash sales and cash purchases, and payments to creditors and by debtors. (The transactions are identified below by their reference, to help you to find them.)

CASH

	£		£
Capital - Ron Knuckle (A)	7,000	Rent (B)	3,500
Bank loan (D)	1,000	Shop fittings (E)	2,000
Sales (F)	10,000	Trade creditors (H)	5,000
Debtors (I)	2,500	Bank loan interest (J)	100
		Incidental expenses (K)	1,900
		Drawings (L)	1,500
			14,000
		Balancing figure - the amount of cash left over after payments have been made	
			6,500
	20,500		20,500

CAPITAL (RON KNUCKLE)

	£		£
		Cash (A)	7,000

BANK LOAN

	£		£
		Cash (D)	1,000

77

Part C: Double entry bookkeeping and accounting treatments

PURCHASES

	£		£
Trade creditors (C)	5,000		

TRADE CREDITORS

	£		£
Cash (H)	5,000	Purchases (C)	5,000

RENT

	£		£
Cash (B)	3,500		

FIXED ASSETS

	£		£
Cash (E)	2,000		

SALES

	£		£
		Cash (F)	10,000
		Debtors (G)	2,500
			12,500

DEBTORS

	£		£
Sales (G)	2,500	Cash (I)	2,500

BANK LOAN INTEREST

	£		£
Cash (J)	100		

OTHER EXPENSES

	£		£
Cash (K)	1,900		

DRAWINGS ACCOUNT

	£		£
Cash (L)	1,500		

(a) If you want to make sure that this solution is complete, you should go through the transactions A to L and tick off each of them twice in the ledger accounts, once as a debit and once as a credit. When you have finished, all transactions in the 'T' account should be ticked, with only totals left over.

(b) In fact, there is an easier way to check that the solution to this sort of problem does 'balance' properly, which we will meet in the next chapter.

(c) On asset and liability accounts, the debit or credit balance represents the amount of the asset or liability outstanding at the period end. For example, on the cash account, debits exceed credits by £6,500 and so there is a debit balance of cash in hand of £6,500. On the capital account, there is a credit balance of £7,000 and so the business owes Ron £7,000.

(d) The balances on the revenue and expenses accounts represent the total of each revenue or expense for the period. For example, sales for the period total £12,500.

4 THE JOURNAL

4.1 You should remember that one of the books of prime entry from the previous chapter was the **journal**.

> **KEY TERM**
>
> The **journal** keeps a record of unusual movement between accounts. It is used to record any double entries made which do not arise from the other books of prime entry. For example, journal entries are made when errors are discovered and need to be corrected.

4.2 Whatever type of transaction is being recorded, the **format of a journal entry** is:

Date	Folio	Debit	Credit
		£	£
Account to be debited		X	
Account to be credited			X
(Narrative to explain the transaction)			

(Remember: in due course, the ledger accounts will be written up to include the transactions listed in the journal.)

4.3 A **narrative explanation** must accompany each journal entry. It is required for audit and control, to indicate the purpose and authority of every transaction which is not first recorded in a book of prime entry.

> **Exam focus point**
>
> An examination question might ask you to 'journalise' transactions which would not in practice be recorded in the journal at all. If you are faced with such a problem, you should simply record the debit and credit entries for every transaction you can recognise, giving some supporting narrative to each transaction.

4.4 EXAMPLES: JOURNAL ENTRIES

The following is a summary of the transactions of 'Hair by Fiona' hairdressing business of which Fiona is the sole proprietor.

1 January	Put in cash of £2,000 as capital
	Purchased brushes and combs for cash £50
	Purchased hair driers from Gilroy Ltd on credit £150
30 January	Paid three months rent to 31 March £300
	Collected and paid in takings £600
31 January	Gave Mrs Sullivan a perm, highlights etc on credit £80

Show the transactions by means of journal entries.

Part C: Double entry bookkeeping and accounting treatments

4.5 SOLUTION

JOURNAL

				£	£
1 January	DEBIT	Cash		2,000	
	CREDIT	Fiona Middleton - capital account			2,000
	Initial capital introduced				
1 January	DEBIT	Brushes and combs account		50	
	CREDIT	Cash			50
	The purchase for cash of brushes and combs as fixed assets				

				£	£
1 January	DEBIT	Hair dryer account		150	
	CREDIT	Sundry creditors account *			150
	The purchase on credit of hair driers as fixed assets				
30 January	DEBIT	Rent account		300	
	CREDIT	Cash			300
	The payment of rent to 31 March				
30 January	DEBIT	Cash		600	
	CREDIT	Sales (or takings account)			600
	Cash takings				
31 January	DEBIT	Debtors account		80	
	CREDIT	Sales account (or takings account)			80
	The provision of a hair-do on credit				

* *Note.* Creditors who have supplied fixed assets are included amongst sundry creditors, as distinct from creditors who have supplied raw materials or goods for resale, who are trade creditors. It is quite common to have separate 'total creditors' accounts, one for trade creditors and another for sundry other creditors.

The correction of errors

4.6 The journal is most commonly used to record corrections to errors that have been made in writing up the nominal ledger accounts. Errors corrected by the journal must be **capable of correction by means of a double entry** in the ledger accounts. In other words the error must not have caused total debits and total credits to be unequal. Special rules, covered in a later chapter, apply when errors are made which break the rule of double entry.

4.7 There are several types of error which can occur. They are looked at in detail in Chapter 13 along with the method of using journal entries to correct them.

5 DAY BOOK ANALYSIS

5.1 In the previous chapter, we used the following example of four transactions entered into the sales day book.

SALES DAY BOOK

Date 20X0	Invoice	Customer	Sales ledger folios	Total amount invoiced £	Boot sales £	Shoe sales £
Jan 10	247	Jones & Co	SL 14	105.00	60.00	45.00
	248	Smith Ltd	SL 8	86.40	86.40	
	249	Alex & Co	SL 6	31.80		31.80
	250	Enor College	SL 9	1,264.60	800.30	464.30
				1,487.80	946.70	541.10

5.2 We have already seen that in theory these transactions are posted to the ledger accounts as follows.

DEBIT	Total debtors account	£1,487.80	
CREDIT	Sales account		£1,487.80

5.3 However a total sales account is not very informative, particularly if the business sells lots of different products. So, using our example, the business might open up a 'sale of shoes' account and a 'sale of boots' account, then at the end of the day, the ledger account postings are:

		£	£
DEBIT	Debtors account	1,487.80	
CREDIT	Sale of shoes account		541.10
	Sale of boots account		946.70

5.4 That is why the analysis of sales is kept. Exactly the same reasoning lies behind the analyses kept in other books of prime entry.

6 THE IMPREST SYSTEM

6.1 In the last chapter, we saw how the petty cash book was used to operate the imprest system for petty cash. It is now time to see how the **double entry** works in the imprest system.

6.2 Suppose a business starts off a cash float on 1.3.20X7 with £250. This will be a payment from cash at bank to petty cash, ie:

DEBIT	Petty cash	£250	
CREDIT	Cash at bank		£250

6.3 Suppose further that five payments were made out of petty cash during March 20X7. The petty cash book might look as follows.

Receipts £	Date	Narrative	Total £	Payments Postage £	Travel £
250.00	1.3.X7	Cash			
	2.3.X7	Stamps	12.00	12.00	
	8.3.X7	Stamps	10.00	10.00	
	19.3.X7	Travel	16.00		16.00
	23.3.X7	Travel	5.00		5.00
	28.3.X7	Stamps	11.50	11.50	
250.00			54.50	33.50	21.00

6.4 At the end of each month (or at any other suitable interval) the total credits in the petty cash book are **posted** to ledger accounts. For March 20X7, £33.50 would be debited to postage account, and £21.00 to travel account. The total expenditure of £54.50 is credited to the petty cash account. The cash float would need to be topped up by a payment of £54.50 from the main cash book, ie:

		£	£
DEBIT	Petty cash	54.50	
CREDIT	Cash		54.50

Part C: Double entry bookkeeping and accounting treatments

6.5 So the rules of double entry have been satisfied, and the petty cash book for the month of March 20X7 will look like this.

Receipts £	Date	Narrative	Total £	Payments Postage £	Travel £
250.00	1.3.X7	Cash			
	2.3.X7	Stamps	12.00	12.00	
	8.3.X7	Stamps	10.00	10.00	
	19.3.X7	Travel	16.00		16.00
	23.3.X7	Travel	5.00		5.00
	28.3.X7	Stamps	11.50	11.50	
	31.3.X7	Balance c/d	195.50		
250.00			250.00	33.50	21.00
195.50	1.4.X7	Balance b/d			
54.50	1.4.X7	Cash			

6.6 As you can see, the cash float is back up to £250 on 1.4.X7, ready for more payments to be made.

Question 4

Summit Glazing operates an imprest petty cash system. The imprest amount is £150.00. At the end of the period the totals of the four analysis columns in the petty cash book were as follows.

	£
Column 1	23.12
Column 2	6.74
Column 3	12.90
Column 4	28.50

How much cash is required to restore the imprest amount?

Answer

£71.26. This is the total amount of cash that has been used.

7 THE SALES AND PURCHASE LEDGERS

Impersonal accounts and personal accounts

7.1 The accounts in the nominal ledger (ledger accounts) relate to types of income, expense, asset, liability - rent, rates, sales, debtors, creditors etc - rather than to the person to whom the money is paid or from whom it is received. They are therefore called **impersonal** accounts. However, there is also a need for **personal** accounts, most commonly for debtors and creditors, and these are contained in the sales ledger and purchase ledger.

POINT TO NOTE

Personal accounts include details of transactions which have already been summarised in ledger accounts (eg sales invoices are recorded in sales and total debtors, payments to creditors in the cash and creditors accounts). The personal accounts do not therefore form part of the double entry system, as otherwise transactions would be recorded twice over (ie two debits and two credits for each transaction). They are **memorandum accounts only**.

The sales ledger

7.2 The sales day book provides a chronological record of invoices sent out by a business to credit customers. For many businesses, this might involve very large numbers of invoices per day or per week. The same customer might appear in several different places in the sales day book, for purchases he has made on credit at different times. So at any point in time, a customer may owe money on several unpaid invoices.

7.3 In addition to keeping a chronological record of invoices, a business should also keep a record of how much money each individual credit customer owes, and what this total debt consists of. The need for a **personal account for each customer** is a practical one.

(a) A customer might telephone, and ask how much he currently owes. Staff must be able to tell him.

(b) It is a common practice to send out statements to credit customers at the end of each month, showing how much they still owe, and itemising new invoices sent out and payments received during the month.

(c) The managers of the business will want to keep a check on the credit position of an individual customer, and to ensure that no customer is exceeding his credit limit by purchasing more goods.

(d) Most important is the need to match payments received against debts owed. If a customer makes a payment, the business must be able to set off the payment against the customer's debt and establish how much he still owes on balance.

KEY TERM

The **sales ledger** is a ledger for customers' personal accounts.

7.4 Sales ledger accounts are written up as follows.

(a) When entries are made in the sales day book (invoices sent out), they are subsequently also made in the **debit side** of the relevant customer account in the sales ledger.

(b) Similarly, when entries are made in the cash book (payments received), or in the sales returns day book, they are also made in the **credit side** of the relevant customer account.

7.5 Each customer account is given a reference or code number, and it is that reference which is the 'sales ledger folio' in the **sales day book**. We say that amounts are **posted** from the sales day book to the sales ledger.

7.6 Here is an example of how a sales ledger account is laid out.

ENOR COLLEGE

A/c no: SL 9

		£		£
Balance b/f		250.00		
10.1.X0	Sales - SDB 48			
	(invoice no 250)	1,264.60	Balance c/d	1,514.60
		1,514.60		1,514.60
11.1.X0	Balance b/d	1,514.60		

Part C: Double entry bookkeeping and accounting treatments

7.7 The debit side of this personal account, then, shows amounts owed by Enor College. When Enor pays some of the money it owes it will be entered into the cash book (receipts) and subsequently 'posted' to the credit side of the personal account. For example, if the college paid £250 on 10.1.20X0, it would appear as follows.

ENOR COLLEGE

A/c no: SL 9

		£			£
	Balance b/f	250.00	10.1.X0	Cash	250.00
10.1.X0	Sales - SDB 48				
	(invoice no 250)	1,264.60		Balance c/d	1,264.60
		1,514.60			1,514.60
11.1.X0	Balance b/d	1,264.60			

7.8 The opening balance owed by Enor College on 11.1.X0 is now £1,264.60 instead of £1,514.60, because of the £250 receipt which came in on 10.1.X0.

The purchase ledger (bought ledger)

7.9 The purchase ledger, like the sales ledger, consists of a number of personal accounts. These are separate accounts for **each individual supplier**, and they enable a business to keep a continuous record of how much it owes each supplier at any time.

> **KEY TERM**
>
> The **purchase ledger** is a ledger for suppliers' personal accounts.

7.10 After entries are made in the purchase day book, cash book, or purchase returns day book - ie after entries are made in the books of prime entry - they are also made in the relevant supplier account in the purchase ledger. Again we say that the entries in the purchase day book are **posted** to the suppliers' personal accounts in the purchase ledger.

7.11 Here is an example of how a purchase ledger account is laid out.

COOK & CO

A/c no: SL 31

	£		£
Balance c/d	515.00	Balance b/f	200.00
		15 Mar 20X8	
		Invoice received	
		PDB 37	315.00
	515.00		515.00
		16 March 20X8	
		Balance b/d	515.00

7.12 The credit side of this personal account, then, shows amounts owing to Cook & Co. If the business paid Cook & Co some money, it would be entered into the cash book (payments) and subsequently be posted to the debit side of the personal account. For example, if the business paid Cook & Co £100 on 15 March 20X8, it would appear as follows:

5: Ledger accounting and double entry

COOK & CO

A/c no: SL 31

		£			£
15.3.X8	Cash	100.00		Balance b/f	200.00
			15.3.X8	Invoice received	
	Balance c/d	415.00		PDB 37	315.00
		515.00			515.00
			16.3.X8	Balance b/d	415.00

7.13 The opening balance owed to Cook & Co on 16.3.X8 is now £415.00 instead of £515.00 because of the £100 payment made during 15.3.X8.

8 ACCOUNTING FOR VALUE ADDED TAX

> **KEY TERM**
>
> **Value added tax** is an indirect tax levied on the sale of goods and services. It is administered by Customs and Excise rather than the Inland Revenue.

8.1 Most of the work of collecting the tax falls on VAT-registered businesses and they remit the tax they collect to the authorities.

8.2 VAT is a cumulative tax, collected at various stages of a product's life. In the illustrative example below, a manufacturer of a television buys materials and components and then sells the television to a wholesaler, who in turn sells it to a retailer, who then sells it to a customer. It is assumed that the rate for VAT is 17.5% on all items. All the other figures are for illustration only.

				Price net of VAT £	VAT 17.5% £	Total price £
(a)	(i)		Manufacturer purchases raw materials and components	40	7	47
	(ii)		Manufacturer sells the completed television to a wholesaler	200	35	235
			The manufacturer hands over to Customs and Excise in VAT		28	
(b)	(i)		Wholesaler purchases television for	200	35	235
	(ii)		Wholesaler sells television to a retailer	320	56	376
			Wholesaler hands over to Customs and Excise in VAT		21	
(c)	(i)		Retailer purchases television for	320	56	376
	(ii)		Retailer sells television	480	84	564
			Retailer hands over to Customs and Excise in VAT		28	
(d)			Customer purchases television for	480	84	564

8.3 The total tax of £84 is borne by the ultimate consumer. However, the tax is handed over to the authorities in stages. If we assume that the VAT of £7 on the initial supplies to the manufacturer is paid by the supplier, Customs and Excise would collect the VAT as follows.

	£
Supplier of materials and components	7
Manufacturer	28
Wholesaler	21
Retailer	28
Total VAT paid	84

Input and output VAT

8.4 The example in Paragraphs 8.2 and 8.3 assumes that the supplier, manufacturer, wholesaler and retailer are all VAT-registered traders.

A VAT-registered trader must carry out the following tasks.

(a) Charge VAT on the goods and services sold at the rate prescribed by the government.

(b) Pay VAT on goods and services purchased from other businesses.

(c) Pay to Customs and Excise the difference between the VAT collected on sales and the VAT paid to suppliers for purchases. Payments are made at quarterly intervals.

8.5 VAT charged on goods and services sold by a business is referred to as **output VAT**. VAT paid on goods and services 'bought in' by a business is referred to as **input VAT**.

(a) If output VAT exceeds input VAT, the business pays the difference in tax to the authorities.

(b) If output VAT is less than input VAT in a period, Customs and Excise will refund the difference to the business.

Irrecoverable VAT

8.6 There are some circumstances in which traders are not allowed to reclaim VAT paid on their inputs. In these cases the trader must bear the cost of VAT and account for it accordingly. Three such cases need to be considered.

(a) Non-registered persons
(b) Registered persons carrying on exempted activities
(c) Non-deductible inputs

Non-registered persons

8.7 Traders whose sales (outputs) are below a certain minimum level need not register for VAT. Non-registered persons will pay VAT on their inputs and, because they are not registered, they cannot reclaim it. The VAT paid will effectively increase the cost of their P & L expenses and the cost of any fixed assets they may purchase. Non-registered persons do not charge VAT on their outputs.

Registered persons carrying on exempted activities

8.8 All outputs of registered traders are either taxable or exempt. Taxable outputs are charged to VAT at zero per cent (zero-rated items) or at 17.5% (standard-rated items). Some items are charged at the lower rate of 5% (eg domestic fuel), but this has limited application in business accounts.

5: Ledger accounting and double entry

8.9 Traders carrying on exempt activities (such as banks) cannot reclaim VAT paid on their inputs, even though they may be VAT-registered. Some traders and companies carry on a mixture of taxable and exempt activities. Such traders need to apportion the VAT paid on inputs. Only VAT relating to taxable outputs may be reclaimed.

Non-deductible inputs

8.10 There are a few special cases where the input tax is not deductible even for a taxable person with taxable outputs. These are as follows.

(a) VAT on motor cars is never reclaimable unless a car is acquired new for resale, ie by a car dealer. VAT on a car used wholly for business purposes is reclaimable. However, company cars usually have some private use, so you should assume that the VAT is not reclaimable unless told otherwise. VAT on accessories such as car radios is deductible if ordered on a separate purchase order and fitted after delivery. The VAT charged when a car is hired is reclaimable if all use is business use. If there is some non-business use and the leasing company reclaimed VAT, the hirer can only reclaim 50% of the VAT on the hire charge.

(b) VAT on business entertaining is not deductible other than VAT on entertaining staff.

(c) VAT on expenses incurred on domestic accommodation for directors.

(d) VAT on non-business items passed through the business accounts with limited relief where the goods are used partly in the business.

(e) VAT which does not relate to the making of supplies in the course of a business.

> **Exam focus point**
> Where VAT is not recoverable, for any of the reasons described above, it must be regarded as part of the cost of the items purchased and included in the P & L charge or in the balance sheet as appropriate

Accounting for VAT

8.11 A business does not make any profit out of the VAT it charges. It therefore follows that its sales should not include VAT. For example, if a business sells goods for £600 + VAT £105, ie for £705 total price, the sales account should only record the £600 excluding VAT. The accounting entries to record the sale would be as follows.

DEBIT	Cash or trade debtors	£705	
CREDIT	Sales		£600
CREDIT	VAT creditor (output VAT)		£105

8.12 The cost of purchases in the profit and loss account may or may not include the 'input' VAT paid, depending on whether or not the input VAT is recoverable.

(a) If input VAT is recoverable, the cost of purchases should exclude the VAT and be recorded net of tax. For example, if a business purchases goods on credit for £400 + VAT £70, the transaction would be recorded as follows.

DEBIT	Purchases	£400	
DEBIT	VAT creditor (input VAT recoverable)	£70	
CREDIT	Trade creditors		£470

Part C: Double entry bookkeeping and accounting treatments

(b) If the input VAT is not recoverable, the cost of purchases must include the tax, because it is the business itself which must bear the cost of the tax.

8.13 The table below summarises the treatment of VAT in the profit and loss account.

	Purchases	Sales
Profit and Loss Account	Irrecoverable input VAT: include Recoverable input VAT: exclude	Exclude VAT

VAT in the sales day book, purchase day book and cash book

8.14 When a business makes a credit sale the total amount invoiced, including VAT, will be recorded in the sales day book. The analysis columns will then separate the VAT from the sales income of the business as follows.

Date	Total	Sales income	VAT
	£	£	£
A Detter and Sons	235	200	35

8.15 When a business is invoiced by a supplier the total amount payable, including VAT, will be recorded in the purchase day book. The analysis columns will then separate the recoverable input VAT from the net purchase cost to the business as follows.

Date	Total	Purchase	VAT
	£	£	£
A Splier (Merchants)	188	160	28

8.16 When debtors pay what they owe, or creditors are paid, there is **no need to show** the VAT in an analysis column of the cash book, because input and output VAT arise when the sale is made, not when the debt is settled.

8.17 However, VAT charged on **cash sales** or VAT paid on **cash purchases** will be analysed in a separate column of the cash book. This is because output VAT has just arisen from the cash sale and must be credited to the VAT creditor in the ledger accounts. Similarly input VAT paid on cash purchases, having just arisen, must be debited to the VAT creditor.

8.18 For example, the receipts side of a cash book might be written up as follows.

Date	Narrative	Folio	Total	Sales ledger (debtors)	Cash sales	Output VAT on cash sales
			£	£	£	£
	A Detter & Sons		235	235		
	Owen Ltd		660	660		
	Cash sales		329		280	49
	Newgate Merchants		184	184		
	Cash sales		94		80	14
			1,502	1,079	360	63

The payments side of a cash book might be written up as follows.

5: Ledger accounting and double entry

Date	Narrative	Folio	Total	Purchase ledger (creditors)	Cash purchases and sundry items	Input VAT on cash purchases
			£	£	£	£
	A Splier (Merchants)		188	188		
	Telephone bill paid		141		120	21
	Cash purchase of stationery		47		40	7
	VAT paid to Customs and Excise		1,400		1,400	
			1,776	188	1,560	28

Question 5

Are trade debtors and trade creditors shown in the accounts inclusive of VAT or exclusive of VAT?

Answer

Inclusive of VAT, as the accounts have to reflect the total amount due to the creditor or due from the debtor.

Exam focus point

A small element of VAT is quite likely in questions. It is worth spending a bit of time ensuring that you understand the logic behind the way VAT is accounted for, rather than trying to learn the rules by rote. This will ensure that even if you forget the rules, you will be able to work out what should be done.

Creditor for VAT

8.19 The VAT paid to the authorities each quarter is the difference between recoverable input VAT on purchases and output VAT on sales. For example, if a business is invoiced for input VAT of £8,000 and charges VAT of £15,000 on its credit sales and VAT of £2,000 on its cash sales, the VAT creditor account would be as follows.

VAT CREDITOR

	£		£
Creditors (input VAT)	8,000	Debtors (output VAT invoiced)	15,000
Cash (payment to authorities)	9,000	Cash (output VAT on cash sales)	2,000
	17,000		17,000

8.20 Payments to the authorities do not coincide with the end of the accounting period of a business, and so at the balance sheet date there will be a balance on the VAT creditor account. If this balance is for an amount payable to the authorities, the outstanding creditor for VAT will appear as a current liability in the balance sheet.

8.21 Occasionally, a business will be owed money back by the authorities, and in such a situation, the VAT refund owed by the authorities would be a current asset in the balance sheet.

Chapter roundup

- **Double entry bookkeeping** is based on the idea that each transaction has an equal but opposite effect.

- Every accounting event must be entered in ledger accounts both as a debit and as an equal but opposite credit. The principal accounts are contained in a ledger called the **nominal ledger**.

- Some accounts in the nominal ledger represent the total of very many smaller balances. For example, the **debtors account** represents all the balances owed by individual customers of the business, while the **creditors account** represents all amounts owed by the business to its suppliers.

- **Debits and credits** are defined as follows.
    - Debit
        - Increase in asset
        - Decrease in liability
        - Increase in expense
    - Credit
        - Increase in liability
        - Decrease in asset
        - Increase in income

- To keep track of individual customer and supplier balances, it is common to maintain **personal accounts** (called the **sales ledger** and the **purchase ledger** respectively). Each account in these ledgers represents the balance owed by or to an individual customer or supplier. These **personal accounts** are kept purely for reference and are therefore known as **memorandum records**. They do *not* normally form part of the double entry system.

- VAT is an indirect tax levied on the sale of goods and services.

- Output VAT is charged on the sales made by a business. Input VAT is paid by a business on its purchases.

- The difference between input VAT and output VAT is paid to or reclaimed from Customs and Excise.

- If input VAT is recoverable it is excluded from the cost of purchases in the profit and loss account. VAT charged on sales to customers is also excluded from the profit and loss account.

- An outstanding creditor for VAT will appear as a current liability in the balance sheet.

- Some inputs are described as non-deductible, for example, cars unless they are bought for resale by a person trading in cars. Exam questions may try to catch you out with this.

Quick quiz

1. Give six examples of nominal ledger accounts.
2. What is the double entry to record a cash sale of £50?
3. What is the double entry to record a purchase of office chairs for £1,000?
4. What is the double entry to record a credit sale of £500 + VAT £87.50?
5. Name one reason for making a journal entry.
6. Individual customer accounts are kept in which ledger?

    A General ledger
    B Debtors account
    C Sales ledger
    D Nominal ledger

Answers to quick quiz

1. See paragraph 2.4.

2.
		£	£
DEBIT	Cash a/c	50	
CREDIT	Sales a/c		50

3.
		£	£
DEBIT	Fixed assets a/c	1,000	
CREDIT	Cash a/c		1,000

4.
		£	£
DEBIT	Debtors a/c	587.50	
CREDIT	Sales a/c		500
	VAT a/c		87.50

5. Most commonly to correct an error, although it can be used to make any entry that is not recorded in a book of prime entry (eg prepayments, accrued expenses, depreciation).

6. C The sales ledger contains the individual customer accounts. The general ledger (A) and nominal ledger (D) are different names for the same ledger. This contains the debtors account (B) which is the **total** of all the individual customer accounts.

Now try the questions below from the Exam Question Bank

Question to try	Level	Marks	Time
5	Full exam	10	18 mins
6	Full exam	10	18 mins

Chapter 6

FROM TRIAL BALANCE TO FINANCIAL STATEMENTS

Topic list	Syllabus reference
1 The trial balance	3(a)
2 The trading, profit and loss account	5(c)
3 The balance sheet	5(c)
4 Balancing accounts; preparing financial statements	3(a), 5(c)

Introduction

In the previous chapter you learned the principles of double entry and how to post to the ledger accounts. The next step in our progress towards the financial statements is the **trial balance**.

Before transferring the relevant balances at the year end to the profit and loss account and putting closing balances carried forward into the balance sheet, it is usual to test the accuracy of double entry bookkeeping records by preparing a trial balance. This is done by taking all the balances on every account. Because of the self-balancing nature of the system of double entry the **total of the debit balances will be exactly equal to the total of the credit balances.**

In very straightforward circumstances, where no complications arise and where the records are complete, it is possible to prepare accounts directly from a trial balance. This is covered in Section 4.

Study guide

Sections 3 and 4 – Bookkeeping principles

- Extract the ledger balances into a trial balance.
- Prepare a simple profit and loss account and balance sheet from a trial balance.
- Explain and illustrate the process of closing the ledger accounts in the accounting records when the financial statements have been completed.

Exam guide

Exam questions at all levels in financial accounting sometimes involve preparation of final accounts from trial balance. Last but not least, you may end up having to do it in 'real life'.

1   THE TRIAL BALANCE

1.1   Imagine that an examination question has given you a list of transactions, and has asked you to post them to the relevant ledger accounts. You do it as quickly as possible and find that you have a little time left over at the end of the examination. How do you check that you have posted all the debit and credit entries properly?

There is no foolproof method, but a technique which shows up the more obvious mistakes is to prepare a **trial balance.**

6: From trial balance to financial statements

> **KEY TERM**
>
> A **trial balance** is a list of ledger balances shown in debit and credit columns.

The first step

1.2 Before you draw up a trial balance, you must have a collection of ledger accounts. For the sake of convenience, we will use the accounts of Ron Knuckle, which we drew up in the previous chapter.

CASH

	£		£
Capital - Ron Knuckle (A)	7,000	Rent	3,500
Bank loan	1,000	Shop fittings	2,000
Sales	10,000	Trade creditors	5,000
Debtors	2,500	Bank loan interest	100
		Incidental expenses	1,900
		Drawings	1,500
			14,000
		Balancing figure - the amount of cash left over after payments have been made	6,500
	20,500		20,500

CAPITAL (RON KNUCKLE)

	£		£
		Cash	7,000

BANK LOAN

	£		£
		Cash	1,000

PURCHASES

	£		£
Trade creditors	5,000		

TRADE CREDITORS

	£		£
Cash	5,000	Purchases	5,000

RENT

	£		£
Cash	3,500		

SHOP FITTINGS

	£		£
Cash	2,000		

Part C: Double entry bookkeeping and accounting treatments

SALES

	£		£
		Cash	10,000
		Debtors	2,500
			12,500

DEBTORS

	£		£
Sales	2,500	Cash	2,500

BANK LOAN INTEREST

	£		£
Cash	100		

OTHER EXPENSES

	£		£
Cash	1,900		

DRAWINGS ACCOUNT

	£		£
Cash	1,500		

1.3 The next step is to close or 'balance off' each account.

Balancing ledger accounts

1.4 At the end of an accounting period, a **balance is struck** on each account in turn. This means that all the debits on the account are totalled and so are all the credits. **If the total debits exceed the total credits there is said to be a debit balance on the account; if the credits exceed the debits then the account has a credit balance.**

1.5 In our simple example, there is very little balancing to do.

   (a) Both the trade creditors account and the debtors account balance off to zero.
   (b) The cash account has a debit balance of £6,500.
   (c) The total on the sales account is £12,500, which is a credit balance.

   Otherwise, the accounts have only one entry each, so there is no totalling to do to arrive at the balance on each account.

Collecting the balances

1.6 If the basic principle of double entry has been correctly applied throughout the period it will be found that the credit balances equal the debit balances in total. This can be illustrated by collecting together the balances on Ron Knuckle's accounts.

6: From trial balance to financial statements

	Debit £	Credit £
Cash	6,500	
Capital		7,000
Bank loan		1,000
Purchases	5,000	
Trade creditors	-	-
Rent	3,500	
Shop fittings	2,000	
Sales		12,500
Debtors	-	-
Bank loan interest	100	
Other expenses	1,900	
Drawings	1,500	
	20,500	20,500

1.7 This list of balances is called the **trial balance**. It does not matter in what order the various accounts are listed. It is just a method used to test the accuracy of the double entry bookkeeping.

What if the trial balance shows unequal debit and credit balances?

1.8 If the two columns of the trial balance are not equal, there must be an error in recording the transactions in the accounts. A trial balance, however, will not disclose the following types of errors.

(a) The **complete omission** of a transaction, because neither a debit nor a credit is made.

(b) The posting of a debit or credit to the correct side of the ledger, but to a **wrong account**.

(c) **Compensating errors** (eg an error of £100 is exactly cancelled by another £100 error elsewhere).

(d) **Errors of principle**, eg cash received from debtors being debited to the debtors account and credited to cash instead of the other way round.

1.9 EXAMPLE: TRIAL BALANCE

As at 30.3.20X7, your business has the following balances on its ledger accounts.

Accounts	Balance £
Bank loan	12,000
Cash	11,700
Capital	13,000
Rates	1,880
Trade creditors	11,200
Purchases	12,400
Sales	14,600
Sundry creditors	1,620
Debtors	12,000
Bank loan interest	1,400
Other expenses	11,020
Vehicles	2,020

During the year the business made the following transactions.

(a) Bought materials for £1,000, half for cash and half on credit.

Part C: Double entry bookkeeping and accounting treatments

    (b) Made £1,040 sales, £800 of which was for credit.
    (c) Paid wages to shop assistants of £260 in cash.

You are required to draw up a trial balance showing the balances as at the end of 31.3.X7.

1.10 SOLUTION

First it is necessary to put the original balances into a trial balance - ie decide which are debit and which are credit balances.

Account	Dr £	Cr £
Bank loan		12,000
Cash	11,700	
Capital		13,000
Rates	1,880	
Trade creditors		11,200
Purchases	12,400	
Sales		14,600
Sundry creditors		1,620
Debtors	12,000	
Bank loan interest	1,400	
Other expenses	11,020	
Vehicles	2,020	
	52,420	52,420

1.11 Now we must take account of the effects of the three transactions which took place on 31.3.X7.

			£	£
(a)	DEBIT	Purchases	1,000	
	CREDIT	Cash		500
		Trade creditors		500
(b)	DEBIT	Cash	240	
		Debtors	800	
	CREDIT	Sales		1,040
(c)	DEBIT	Other expenses	260	
	CREDIT	Cash		260

1.12 When these figures are included in the trial balance, it becomes:

Account	Dr £	Cr £
Bank loan		12,000
Cash (11,700 + 240 – 500 – 260)	11,180	
Capital		13,000
Rates	1,880	
Trade creditors		11,700
Purchases	13,400	
Sales		15,640
Sundry creditors		1,620
Debtors	12,800	
Bank loan interest	1,400	
Other expenses	11,280	
Vehicles	2,020	
	53,960	53,960

1.13 Before moving on, try this question to make sure you have understood the basics.

Question 1

Here is a list of balances. Arrange them into debit and credit columns as in a trial balance.

LIST OF BALANCES AS AT 31 JULY 20X2

	£
Cash	215
Bank	96
Capital	250
Rent	30
Carriage	23
B Jackson	130
G Mitchell	186
D Wickes	64
D Cotton	129
C Beale	26
Purchases	459
Sales	348

Answer

TRIAL BALANCE AS AT 31 JULY 20X2

	Dr £	Cr £
Cash	215	
Bank	96	
Capital		250
Rent	30	
Carriage	23	
B Jackson		130
G Mitchell		186
D Wickes		64
D Cotton	129	
C Beale	26	
Purchases	459	
Sales		348
	978	978

---

2 THE TRADING, PROFIT AND LOSS ACCOUNT

2.1 The first step in the process of preparing the financial statements is to open up another ledger account, called the **trading, profit and loss account**. In it a business summarises its results for the period by gathering together all the ledger account balances relating to income and expenses. This account is still part of the double entry system, so the basic rule of double entry still applies: every debit must have an equal and opposite credit entry.

2.2 This trading, profit and loss account we have opened up is **not** the financial statement we are aiming for, even though it has the same name. The difference between the two is not very great, because they contain the same information. However, the financial statement lays it out differently and may be much less detailed.

2.3 So what do we do with this new ledger account? The first step is to look through the ledger accounts and identify which ones relate to income and expenses. In the case of Ron Knuckle, the income and expense accounts consist of purchases, rent, sales, bank loan interest, and other expenses.

Part C: Double entry bookkeeping and accounting treatments

2.4 The balances on these accounts are transferred to the new trading, profit and loss account. For example, the balance on the purchases account is £5,000 DR. To balance this to zero, we write in £5,000 CR. But to comply with the rule of double entry, there has to be a debit entry somewhere, so we write £5,000 DR in the trading, profit and loss account. Now the balance on the purchases account has been moved to the trading, profit and loss account.

2.5 If we do the same thing with all the income and expense accounts of Ron Knuckle, the result is as follows.

PURCHASES

	£		£
Trade creditors	5,000	Trading, P & L a/c	5,000

RENT

	£		£
Cash	3,500	Trading, P & L a/c	3,500

SALES

	£		£
Trading, P & L a/c	12,500	Cash	10,000
		Debtors	2,500
	12,500		12,500

BANK LOAN INTEREST

	£		£
Cash	100	Trading, P & L a/c	100

OTHER EXPENSES

	£		£
Cash	1,900	Trading, P & L a/c	1,900

TRADING, PROFIT AND LOSS ACCOUNT

	£		£
Purchases	5,000	Sales	12,500
Rent	3,500		
Bank loan interest	100		
Other expenses	1,900		

(Note that the trading, profit and loss account has not yet been balanced off but we will return to that later.)

2.6 If you look at the items we have gathered together in the trading, profit and loss account, they should strike a chord in your memory. They are the same items that we need to draw up the trading, profit and loss account in the form of a financial statement. With a little rearrangement they could be presented as follows.

6: From trial balance to financial statements

RON KNUCKLE: TRADING, PROFIT AND LOSS ACCOUNT

	£	£
Sales		12,500
Cost of sales (= purchases in this case)		(5,000)
Gross profit		7,500
Expenses		
Rent	3,500	
Bank loan interest	100	
Other expenses	1,900	
		(5,500)
Net profit		2,000

3 THE BALANCE SHEET

3.1 Look back at the ledger accounts of Ron Knuckle. Now that we have dealt with those relating to income and expenses, which ones are left? The answer is that we still have to find out what to do with cash, capital, bank loan, trade creditors, shop fittings, debtors and the drawings account.

3.2 Are these the only ledger accounts left? No: don't forget there is still the last one we opened up, called the **trading, profit and loss account**. The balance on this account represents the profit earned by the business, and if you go through the arithmetic, you will find that it has a credit balance - a profit - of £2,000. (Not surprisingly, this is the figure that is shown in the trading profit and loss account financial statement.)

3.3 These remaining accounts must also be balanced and ruled off, but since they represent assets and liabilities of the business (not income and expenses) their balances are not transferred to the trading profit and loss account. Instead they are **carried forward** in the books of the business. This means that they become opening balances for the next accounting period and indicate the value of the assets and liabilities at the end of one period and the beginning of the next.

3.4 The conventional method of ruling off a ledger account at the end of an accounting period is illustrated by the bank loan account in Ron Knuckle's books.

BANK LOAN ACCOUNT

	£		£
Balance carried forward (c/f)	1,000	Cash (D)	1,000
		Balance brought forward (b/f)	1,000

3.5 Ron Knuckle therefore begins the new accounting period with a credit balance of £1,000 on this account. A **credit balance brought forward** denotes a **liability**. An **asset** would be represented by a **debit balance brought forward**.

3.6 One further point is worth noting before we move on to complete this example. You will remember that a proprietor's capital comprises any cash introduced by him, plus any profits made by the business, less any drawings made by him. At the stage we have now reached these three elements are contained in different ledger accounts: cash introduced of £7,000 appears in the capital account; drawings of £1,500 appear in the drawings account; and the profit made by the business is represented by the £2,000 credit balance on the trading profit and loss account. It is convenient to gather together all these amounts into one **capital account**, in the same way as we earlier gathered together income and expense accounts into one trading and profit and loss account.

Part C: Double entry bookkeeping and accounting treatments

3.7 If we go ahead and gather the three amounts together, the results are as follows.

DRAWINGS

	£		£
Cash	1,500	Capital a/c	1,500

TRADING, PROFIT AND LOSS ACCOUNT

	£		£
Purchases	5,000	Sales	12,500
Rent	3,500		
Bank loan interest	100		
Other expenses	1,900		
Capital a/c	2,000		
	12,500		12,500

CAPITAL

	£		£
Drawings	1,500	Cash	7,000
Balance c/f	7,500	Trading, P & L a/c	2,000
	9,000		9,000
		Balance b/f	7,500

3.8 A re-arrangement of these balances will complete Ron Knuckle's simple balance sheet:

RON KNUCKLE
BALANCE SHEET AT END OF FIRST TRADING PERIOD

	£
Fixed assets	
Shop fittings	2,000
Current assets	
Cash	6,500
Total assets	8,500
Liabilities	
Bank loan	(1,000)
Net assets	7,500
Proprietor's capital	7,500

3.9 When a balance sheet is drawn up for an accounting period which is not the first one, then it ought to show the capital at the start of the accounting period and the capital at the end of the accounting period. This will be illustrated in Question 2.

4 BALANCING ACCOUNTS; PREPARING FINANCIAL STATEMENTS

4.1 The question which follows is **by far the most important in this text so far**. It uses all the accounting steps from entering up ledger accounts to preparing the financial statements, and is set out in a style which you might well find in an examination. It is very important that you try the question by yourself: if you do not, you will be missing out a vital part of this text.

Question 2

A business is established with capital of £2,000, and this amount is paid into a business bank account by the proprietor. During the first year's trading, the following transactions occurred:

6: From trial balance to financial statements

	£
Purchases of goods for resale, on credit	4,300
Payments to trade creditors	3,600
Sales, all on credit	5,800
Payments from debtors	3,200
Fixed assets purchased for cash	1,500
Other expenses, all paid in cash	900

The bank has provided an overdraft facility of up to £3,000.

Prepare the ledger accounts, a trading, profit and loss account for the year and a balance sheet as at the end of the year.

Answer

The first thing to do is to open ledger accounts so that the transactions can be entered up. The relevant accounts which we need for this example are: cash; capital; trade creditors; purchases; fixed assets; sales and debtors; other expenses.

The next step is to work out the double entry bookkeeping for each transaction. Normally you would write them straight into the accounts, but to make this example easier to follow, they are first listed below.

(a)	Establishing business (£2,000)	DR Cash;	CR Capital
(b)	Purchases (£4,300)	DR Purchases;	CR Creditors
(c)	Payments to creditors (£3,600)	DR Creditors;	CR Cash
(d)	Sales (£5,800)	DR Debtors;	CR Sales
(e)	Payments by debtors (£3,200)	DR Cash;	CR Debtors
(f)	Fixed assets (£1,500)	DR Fixed assets;	CR Cash
(g)	Other (cash) expenses (£900)	DR Other expenses;	CR Cash

So far, the ledger accounts will look like this.

CASH

	£		£
Capital	2,000	Creditors	3,600
		Fixed assets	1,500
Debtors	3,200	Other expenses	900

CAPITAL

	£		£
		Cash	2,000

CREDITORS

	£		£
Cash	3,600	Purchases	4,300

PURCHASES

	£		£
Creditors	4,300		

FIXED ASSETS

	£		£
Cash	1,500		

SALES

	£		£
		Debtors	5,800

101

Part C: Double entry bookkeeping and accounting treatments

DEBTORS

	£		£
Sales	5,800	Cash	3,200

OTHER EXPENSES

	£		£
Cash	900		

The next thing to do is to balance all these accounts. It is at this stage that you could, if you wanted to, draw up a trial balance to make sure the double entries are accurate. There is not very much point in this simple example, but if you did draw up a trial balance, it would look like this.

	Dr £	Cr £
Cash		800
Capital		2,000
Creditors		700
Purchases	4,300	
Fixed assets	1,500	
Sales		5,800
Debtors	2,600	
Other expenses	900	
	9,300	9,300

After balancing the accounts, the trading, profit and loss account should be opened. Into it should be transferred all the balances relating to income and expenses (ie purchases, other expenses, and sales). At this point, the ledger accounts will be:

CASH

	£		£
Capital	2,000	Trade creditors	3,600
Debtors	3,200	Fixed assets	1,500
Balance c/f	800	Other expenses	900
	6,000		6,000
		Balance b/f	800*

* A credit balance b/f means that this cash item is a liability, not an asset. This indicates a bank overdraft of £800, with cash income of £5,200 falling short of payments of £6,000 by this amount.

CAPITAL

	£		£
Balance c/f	2,600	Cash	2,000
		P & L a/c	600
	2,600		2,600

TRADE CREDITORS

	£		£
Cash	3,600	Stores (purchases)	4,300
Balance c/f	700		
	4,300		4,300
		Balance b/f	700

PURCHASES ACCOUNT

	£		£
Trade creditors	4,300	Trading a/c	4,300

FIXED ASSETS

	£		£
Cash	1,500	Balance c/f	1,500
Balance b/f	1,500		

SALES

	£		£
Trading a/c	5,800	Debtors	5,800

DEBTORS

	£		£
Sales	5,800	Cash	3,200
		Balance c/f	2,600
	5,800		5,800
Balance b/f	2,600		

OTHER EXPENSES

	£		£
Cash	900	P & L a/c	900

TRADING, PROFIT AND LOSS ACCOUNT

	£		£
Purchases account	4,300	Sales	5,800
Gross profit c/f	1,500		
	5,800		5,800
Other expenses	900	Gross profit b/f	1,500
Net profit (transferred to capital account)	600		
	1,500		1,500

So the trading, profit and loss account financial statement will be:

TRADING, PROFIT AND LOSS ACCOUNT
FOR THE ACCOUNTING PERIOD

	£
Sales	5,800
Cost of sales (purchases)	(4,300)
Gross profit	1,500
Expenses	900
Net profit	600

Part C: Double entry bookkeeping and accounting treatments

Listing and then rearranging the balances on the ledger accounts gives the balance sheet as:

BALANCE SHEET AS AT THE END OF THE PERIOD

	£	£
Fixed assets		1,500
Current assets		
Debtors	2,600	
Current liabilities		
Bank overdraft	800	
Trade creditors	700	
	1,500	
Net current assets		1,100
		2,600
Capital		
At start of period		2,000
Net profit for period		600
At end of period		2,600

Exam focus point

In an examination you need not spell out your answer in quite such detail. The detail is given here to help you to work through the example properly, and you may wish to do things this way yourself until you get more practised in accounting techniques and are confident enough to take short cuts.

Chapter roundup

- At suitable intervals, the entries in each ledger accounts are totalled and a balance is struck. Balances are usually collected in a **trial balance** which is then used as a basis for preparing a profit and loss account and a balance sheet.

- A trial balance can be used to **test the accuracy** of the double entry accounting records. It works by listing the balances on ledger accounts, some of which will be debits and some credits, to see if they balance off to zero.

- A **profit and loss ledger account** is opened up to gather all items relating to income and expenses. When rearranged, the items make up the **profit and loss account** financial statement.

- The balances on all remaining ledger accounts (including the profit and loss account) can be listed and rearranged to form the **balance sheet**.

Quick quiz

1   What is the purpose of a trial balance?

2   Give four circumstances in which a trial balances might balance although some of the balances are wrong.

3   In a period, sales are £140,000, purchases £75,000 and other expenses £25,000. What is the figure for net profit to be transferred to the capital account?

    A   £40,000
    B   £65,000
    C   £75,000
    D   £140,000

4   What is the difference between balancing off an expense account and balancing off a liability account?

Answers to quick quiz

1. To test the accuracy of the double entry bookkeeping.
2. See paragraph 1.8.
3. A

TRADING, PROFIT & LOSS ACCOUNT

	£		£
Purchases	75,000	Sales	140,000
Gross profit c/d	65,000		
	140,000		140,000
Other expenses	25,000	Gross profit b/d	65,000
Net profit – to capital a/c	40,000		
	65,000		65,000

4. When an expense account is balanced off, the balance is transferred to the trading, profit and loss account. When a liability account is balanced off, the balance is carried forward to the next trading period.

Now try the questions below from the Exam Question Bank

Question to try	Level	Marks	Time
7	Introductory	n/a	27 mins
8	Introductory	n/a	27 mins
9	Introductory	n/a	36 mins

Chapter 7

THE COST OF GOODS SOLD, ACCRUALS AND PREPAYMENTS

Topic list	Syllabus reference
1 Cost of goods sold	3(a), 4(b)
2 Accruals and prepayments	3(a), 4(b)-(c)

Introduction

So far we have calculated profit as follows.

	£
Sales	X
Less cost of goods sold	(X)
Gross profit	X
Less expenses	(X)
Net profit	X

However, the figures for 'cost of sales' and 'expenses' may not always be simple. Some adjustments may need to be made.

Section 1 of this chapter deals with the adjustments which may need to be made to the **cost of goods sold**. Section 2 deals with the adjustments which may need to be made to the **expenses**.

Study guide

Section 7 – The financial statements of a sole trader 1; stock, accruals and prepayments

- Revise the format of the trading, profit and loss account and balance sheet from Sections 1 and 2.
- Explain the need for adjustments for stock in preparing financial statements.
- Illustrate trading accounts with opening and closing stock.
- Explain the need for adjustments for accruals and prepayments in preparing financial statements.
- Illustrate the process of adjusting for accruals and prepayments in preparing financial statements, emphasising the effects in both the profit and loss account and the balance sheet.
- Prepare financial statements for a sole trader including adjustments for stock, accruals and prepayments.

Exam guide

You will need to make these adjustments in at least one of the questions in Section B. MCQs are often set on accruals and prepayments.

7: The cost of goods sold, accruals and prepayments

1 COST OF GOODS SOLD

Unsold goods in stock at the end of an accounting period

1.1 Goods might be unsold at the end of an accounting period and so still be **held in stock** at the end of the period. The purchase cost of these goods should not be included therefore in the cost of sales of the period.

1.2 EXAMPLE: CLOSING STOCK

Perry P Louis, trading as the Umbrella Shop, ends his financial year on 30 September each year. On 1 October 20X4 he had no goods in stock. During the year to 30 September 20X5, he purchased 30,000 umbrellas costing £60,000 from umbrella wholesalers and suppliers. He resold the umbrellas for £5 each, and sales for the year amounted to £100,000 (20,000 umbrellas). At 30 September there were 10,000 unsold umbrellas left in stock, valued at £2 each.

What was Perry P Louis's gross profit for the year?

1.3 SOLUTION

Perry P Louis purchased 30,000 umbrellas, but only sold 20,000. Purchase costs of £60,000 and sales of £100,000 do not represent the same quantity of goods.

The gross profit for the year should be calculated by 'matching' the sales value of the 20,000 umbrellas sold with the cost of those 20,000 umbrellas. The cost of sales in this example is therefore the cost of purchases minus the cost of goods in stock at the year end.

	£	£
Sales (20,000 units)		100,000
Purchases (30,000 units)	60,000	
Less closing stock (10,000 units @ £2)	20,000	
Cost of sales (20,000 units)		40,000
Gross profit		60,000

1.4 EXAMPLE CONTINUED

The Umbrella Shop's next accounting year runs from 1 October 20X5 to 30 September 20X6. During the course of this year, Perry P Louis purchased 40,000 umbrellas at a total cost of £95,000. During the year he sold 45,000 umbrellas for £230,000. At 30 September 20X6 he had 5,000 umbrellas left in stock, which had cost £12,000.

What was his gross profit for the year?

1.5 SOLUTION

In this accounting year, he purchased 40,000 umbrellas to add to the 10,000 he already had in stock at the start of the year. He sold 45,000, leaving 5,000 umbrellas in stock at the year end. Once again, gross profit should be calculated by matching the value of 45,000 units of sales with the cost of those 45,000 units.

The cost of sales is the value of the 10,000 umbrellas in stock at the beginning of the year, plus the cost of the 40,000 umbrellas purchased, less the value of the 5,000 umbrellas in stock at the year end.

Part C: Double entry bookkeeping and accounting treatments

	£	£
Sales (45,000 units)		230,000
Opening stock (10,000 units) *	20,000	
Add purchases (40,000 units)	95,000	
	115,000	
Less closing stock (5,000 units)	12,000	
Cost of sales (45,000 units)		103,000
Gross profit		127,000

*Taken from the closing stock value of the previous accounting year, see paragraph 1.3.

The cost of goods sold

1.6 The cost of goods sold is found by applying the following formula.

> **FORMULA TO LEARN**
>
> | | £ |
> |---|---:|
> | Opening stock value | X |
> | Add cost of purchases (or, in the case of a manufacturing company, the cost of production) | X |
> | | X |
> | Less closing stock value | (X) |
> | Equals cost of goods sold | X |

In other words, to match 'sales' and the 'cost of goods sold', it is necessary to adjust the cost of goods manufactured or purchased to allow for increases or reduction in stock levels during the period.

1.7 Hopefully you will agree that the 'formula' above is logical. You should learn it, because it is fundamental among the principles of accounting.

Test your knowledge of the formula with the following example.

1.8 EXAMPLE: COST OF GOODS SOLD AND VARIATIONS IN STOCK LEVELS

On 1 January 20X6, the Grand Union Food Stores had goods in stock valued at £6,000. During 20X6 its proprietor, who ran the shop, purchased supplies costing £50,000. Sales turnover for the year to 31 December 20X6 amounted to £80,000. The cost of goods in stock at 31 December 20X6 was £12,500.

Calculate the gross profit for the year.

1.9 SOLUTION

GRAND UNION FOOD STORES
TRADING ACCOUNT FOR THE YEAR ENDED 31 DECEMBER 20X6

	£	£
Sales		80,000
Opening stocks	6,000	
Add purchases	50,000	
	56,000	
Less closing stocks	12,500	
Cost of goods sold		43,500
Gross profit		36,500

The cost of carriage inwards and outwards

1.10 'Carriage' refers to the **cost of transporting purchased goods** from the supplier to the premises of the business which has bought them. Someone has to pay for these delivery costs: sometimes the supplier pays, and sometimes the purchaser pays. When the purchaser pays, the cost to the purchaser is carriage inwards (**into** the business). When the supplier pays, the cost to the supplier is known as carriage outwards (**out of** the business).

1.11 The **cost of carriage inwards** is usually added to the **cost of purchases**, and is therefore included in the **trading account**.

The **cost of carriage outwards** is a **selling and distribution expense** in the **profit and loss account**.

1.12 EXAMPLE: CARRIAGE INWARDS AND CARRIAGE OUTWARDS

Gwyn Tring, trading as Clickety Clocks, imports and resells cuckoo clocks and grandfather clocks. He must pay for the costs of delivering the clocks from his supplier in Switzerland to his shop in Wales.

He resells the clocks to other traders throughout the country, paying the costs of carriage for the consignments from his business premises to his customers.

On 1 July 20X5, he had clocks in stock valued at £17,000. During the year to 30 June 20X6 he purchased more clocks at a cost of £75,000. Carriage inwards amounted to £2,000. Sales for the year were £162,100. Other expenses of the business amounted to £56,000 excluding carriage outwards which cost £2,500. Gwyn Tring took drawings of £20,000 from the business during the course of the year. The value of the goods in stock at the year end was £15,400.

Required

Prepare the trading, profit and loss account of Clickety Clocks for the year ended 30 June 20X6.

1.13 SOLUTION

CLICKETY CLOCKS
TRADING, PROFIT AND LOSS ACCOUNT FOR THE YEAR ENDED 30 JUNE 20X6

	£	£
Sales		162,100
Opening stock	17,000	
Purchases	75,000	
Carriage inwards	2,000	
	94,000	
Less closing stock	15,400	
Cost of goods sold		78,600
Gross profit		83,500
Carriage outwards	2,500	
Other expenses	56,000	
		58,500
Net profit (transferred to balance sheet)		25,000

Goods written off or written down

1.14 A trader might be unable to sell all the goods that he purchases, because a number of things might happen to the goods before they can be sold. For example:

(a) Goods might be lost or stolen.

(b) Goods might be damaged, and so become worthless. Such damaged goods might be thrown away.

(c) Goods might become obsolete or out of fashion. These might have to be thrown away, or possibly sold off at a very low price in a clearance sale.

1.15 When goods are **lost, stolen or thrown away** as worthless, the business will make a loss on those goods because their '**sales value' will be nil**.

Similarly, when goods lose value because they have become **obsolete** or out of fashion, the business will **make a loss** if their clearance sales value is less than their cost. For example, if goods which originally cost £500 are now obsolete and could only be sold for £150, the business would suffer a loss of £350.

1.16 If, at the end of an accounting period, a business still has goods in stock which are either worthless or worth less than their original cost, the value of the stocks should be **written down** to:

(a) Nothing, if they are worthless.
(b) Or their net realisable value, if this is less than their original cost.

This means that the loss will be reported as soon as the loss is foreseen, even if the goods have not yet been thrown away or sold off at a cheap price. This is an application of another concept - the prudence concept - which we will look at in a later chapter.

1.17 The costs of stock written off or written down should not usually cause any problems in calculating the gross profit of a business, because the cost of goods sold will include the cost of stocks written off or written down, as the following example shows.

7: The cost of goods sold, accruals and prepayments

1.18 EXAMPLE: STOCKS WRITTEN OFF AND WRITTEN DOWN

Lucas Wagg, trading as Fairlock Fashions, ends his financial year on 31 March. At 1 April 20X5 he had goods in stock valued at £8,800. During the year to 31 March 20X6, he purchased goods costing £48,000. Fashion goods which cost £2,100 were still held in stock at 31 March 20X6, and Lucas Wagg believes that these could only now be sold at a sale price of £400. The goods still held in stock at 31 March 20X6 (including the fashion goods) had an original purchase cost of £7,600. Sales for the year were £81,400.

Required

Calculate the gross profit of Fairlock Fashions for the year ended 31 March 20X6.

1.19 SOLUTION

Initial calculation of closing stock values:

STOCK COUNT

	At cost £	Realisable value £	Amount written down £
Fashion goods	2,100	400	1,700
Other goods (balancing figure)	5,500	5,500	
	7,600	5,900	1,700

FAIRLOCK FASHIONS
TRADING ACCOUNT FOR THE YEAR ENDED 31 MARCH 20X6

	£	£
Sales		81,400
Value of opening stock	8,800	
Purchases	48,000	
	56,800	
Less closing stock	5,900	
Cost of goods sold		50,900
Gross profit		30,500

Question 1

Gross profit for 20X7 can be calculated from

A   purchases for 20X7, plus stock at 31 December 20X7, less stock at 1 January 20X7
B   purchases for 20X7, less stock at 31 December 20X7, plus stock at 1 January 20X7
C   cost of goods sold during 20X7, plus sales during 20X7
D   net profit for 20X7, plus expenses for 20X7

Answer

The answer is given with Question 2, so you won't see it before you've thought about it for yourself!

---

2 ACCRUALS AND PREPAYMENTS

Introduction

2.1   It has already been stated that the gross profit for a period should be calculated by **matching** sales and the cost of goods sold. In the same way, the net profit for a period should be calculated by charging the expenses which relate to that period. For example, in preparing the profit and loss account of a business for a period of, say, six months, it would

Part C: Double entry bookkeeping and accounting treatments

be appropriate to charge six months' expenses for rent and rates, insurance costs and telephone costs etc.

2.2 Expenses might not be paid for during the period to which they relate. For example, if a business rents a shop for £20,000 per annum, it might pay the full annual rent on, say, 1 April each year. Now if we were to calculate the profit of the business for the first six months of the year 20X7, the correct charge for rent in the profit and loss account would be £10,000 even though the rent payment would be £20,000 in that period. Similarly, the rent charge in a profit and loss account for the business in the second six months of the year would be £10,000, even though no rent payment would be made in that six month period.

KEY TERMS

Accruals or accrued expenses are expenses which are charged against the profit for a particular period, even though they have not yet been paid for.

Prepayments are payments which have been made in one accounting period, but should not be charged against profit until a later period, because they relate to that later period.

2.3 Accruals and prepayments might seem difficult at first, but the following examples might help to clarify the principle involved, that expenses should be matched against the period to which they relate.

2.4 EXAMPLE: ACCRUALS

Horace Goodrunning, trading as Goodrunning Motor Spares, ends his financial year on 28 February each year. His telephone was installed on 1 April 20X6 and he receives his telephone account quarterly at the end of each quarter. He pays it promptly as soon as it is received. On the basis of the following data, you are required to calculate the telephone expense to be charged to the profit and loss account for the year ended 28 February 20X7.

Goodrunning Motor Spares - telephone expense for the three months ended:

	£
30.6.20X6	23.50
30.9.20X6	27.20
31.12.20X6	33.40
31.3.20X7	36.00

2.5 SOLUTION

The telephone expenses for the year ended 28 February 20X7 are:

	£
1 March - 31 March 20X6 (no telephone)	0.00
1 April - 30 June 20X6	23.50
1 July - 30 September 20X6	27.20
1 October - 31 December 20X6	33.40
1 January - 28 February 20X7 (two months)	24.00
	108.10

The charge for the period 1 January - 28 February 20X7 is two-thirds of the quarterly charge received on 31 March. As at 28 February 20X7, no telephone bill has been received for the quarter, because it is not due for another month. However, it would be inappropriate to ignore the telephone expenses for January and February, and so an accrued charge of £24 should be made, being two-thirds of the quarter's bill of £36.

The accrued charge will also appear in the balance sheet of the business as at 28 February 20X7, as a current liability.

Question 2

Ratsnuffer is a business dealing in pest control. Its owner, Roy Dent, employs a team of eight who were paid £12,000 per annum each in the year to 31 December 20X5. At the start of 20X6 he raised salaries by 10% to £13,200 per annum each.

On 1 July 20X6, he hired a trainee at a salary of £8,400 per annum.

He pays his work force on the first working day of every month, one month in arrears, so that his employees receive their salary for January on the first working day in February, etc.

Required

(a) Calculate the cost of salaries which would be charged in the profit and loss account of Ratsnuffer for the year ended 31 December 20X6.
(b) Calculate the amount actually paid in salaries during the year (ie the amount of cash received by the work force).
(c) State the amount of accrued charges for salaries which would appear in the balance sheet of Ratsnuffer as at 31 December 20X6.

Answer

(a) *Salaries cost in the profit and loss account*

	£
Cost of 8 employees for a full year at £13,200 each	105,600
Cost of trainee for a half year	4,200
	109,800

(b) *Salaries actually paid in 20X6*

	£
December 20X5 salaries paid in January (8 employees × £1,000 per month)	8,000
Salaries of 8 employees for January - November 20X6 paid in February – December (8 employees × £1,100 per month × 11 months)	96,800
Salaries of trainee (for July - November paid in August - December 20X6: 5 months × £700 per month)	3,500
Salaries actually paid	108,300

(c) *Accrued salaries costs as at 31 December 20X6*
(ie costs charged in the P & L account, but not yet paid)

	£
8 employees x 1 month x £1,100 per month	8,800
1 trainee x 1 month x £700 per month	700
	9,500

(d) *Summary*

	£
Accrued wages costs as at 31 December 20X5	8,000
Add salaries cost for 20X6 (P & L account)	109,800
	117,800
Less salaries paid	108,300
Equals accrued wages costs as at 31 December 20X6	9,500

Note. The answer to Question 1 is D. Remember that net profit = gross profit less expenses.

2.6 EXAMPLE: PREPAYMENTS

The Square Wheels Garage pays fire insurance annually in advance on 1 June each year. The firm's financial year end is 28 February. From the following record of insurance payments you are required to calculate the charge to profit and loss for the financial year to 28 February 20X8.

Part C: Double entry bookkeeping and accounting treatments

		Insurance paid
		£
1.6.20X6		600
1.6.20X7		700

2.7 Insurance cost for:

	£
(a) The 3 months, 1 March - 31 May 20X7 (3/12 × £600)	150
(b) The 9 months, 1 June 20X7 - 28 February 20X8 (9/12 × £700)	525
Insurance cost for the year, charged to the P & L account	675

At 28 February 20X8 there is a prepayment for fire insurance, covering the period 1 March - 31 May 20X8. This insurance premium was paid on 1 June 20X7, but only nine months worth of the full annual cost is chargeable to the accounting period ended 28 February 20X8. The prepayment of (3/12 × £700) £175 as at 28 February 20X8 will appear as a current asset in the balance sheet of the Square Wheels Garage as at that date.

In the same way, there was a prepayment of (3/12 × £600) £150 in the balance sheet one year earlier as at 28 February 20X7.

Summary	£
Prepaid insurance premiums as at 28 February 20X7	150
Add insurance premiums paid 1 June 20X7	700
	850
Less insurance costs charged to the P & L account for the year ended 28 February 20X8	675
Equals prepaid insurance premiums as at 28 February 20X8	175

Question 3

The Batley Print Shop rents a photocopying machine from a supplier for which it makes a quarterly payment as follows:

(a) three months rental in advance;
(b) a further charge of 2 pence per copy made during the quarter just ended.

The rental agreement began on 1 August 20X4 and the first six quarterly bills were as follows.

Bills dated and received	*Rental*	*Costs of copies taken*	*Total*
	£	£	£
1 August 20X4	2,100	0	2,100
1 November 20X4	2,100	1,500	3,600
1 February 20X5	2,100	1,400	3,500
1 May 20X5	2,100	1,800	3,900
1 August 20X5	2,700	1,650	4,350
1 November 20X5	2,700	1,950	4,650

The bills are paid promptly, as soon as they are received.

(a) Calculate the charge for photocopying expenses for the year to 31 August 20X4 and the amount of prepayments and/or accrued charges as at that date.

(b) Calculate the charge for photocopying expenses for the following year to 31 August 20X5, and the amount of prepayments and/or accrued charges as at that date.

Answer

(a) *Year to 31 August 20X4*

	£
One months' rental (1/3 × £2,100) *	700
Accrued copying charges (1/3 × £1,500) **	500
Photocopying expense (P & L account)	1,200

* From the quarterly bill dated 1 August 20X4
** From the quarterly bill dated 1 November 20X4

7: The cost of goods sold, accruals and prepayments

There is a prepayment for 2 months' rental (£1,400) as at 31 August 20X4.

(b) *Year to 31 August 20X5*

	£	£
Rental from 1 September 20X4 - 31 July 20X5 (11 months at £2,100 per quarter or £700 per month)		7,700
Rental from 1 August - 31 August 20X5 (1/3 × £2,700)		900
Rental charge for the year		8,600
Copying charges:		
1 September - 31 October 20X4 (2/3 × £1,500)	1,000	
1 November 20X4 - 31 January 20X5	1,400	
1 February - 30 April 20X5	1,800	
1 May - 31 July 20X5	1,650	
Accrued charges for August 20X5 (1/3 × £1,950)	650	
		6,500
Total photocopying expenses (P & L account)		15,100

There is a prepayment for 2 months' rental (£1,800) as at 31 August 20X5.

Summary of year 1 September 20X4 - 31 August 20X5

	Rental charges £	Copying costs £
Prepayments as at 31.8.20X4	1,400	
Accrued charges as at 31.8.20X4		(500)
Bills received during the year		
1 November 20X4	2,100	1,500
1 February 20X5	2,100	1,400
1 May 20X5	2,100	1,800
1 August 20X5	2,700	1,650
Prepayment as at 31.8.20X5	(1,800)	
Accrued charges as at 31.8.20X5		650
Charge to the P & L account for the year	8,600	6,500
Balance sheet items as at 31 August 20X5		
Prepaid rental (current asset)	1,800	
Accrued copying charges (current liability)		650

Exam focus point
The MCQs in Section A will almost undoubtedly test your understanding of accruals and prepayments.

2.8 FURTHER EXAMPLE: ACCRUALS

Suppose that Willie Woggle opens a shop on 1 May 20X6 to sell hiking and camping equipment. The rent of the shop is £12,000 per annum, payable quarterly in arrears (with the first payment on 31 July 20X6). Willie decides that his accounting period should end on 31 December each year.

2.9 The rent account as at 31 December 20X6 will record only two rental payments (on 31 July and 31 October) and there will be two months' accrued rental expenses for November and December 20X6, (£2,000) since the next rental payment is not due until 31 January 20X7.

The charge to the P & L account for the period to 31 December 20X6 will be for 8 months' rent (May-December inclusive) and so it follows that the total rental cost should be £8,000.

2.10 So far, the rent account appears as follows.

Part C: Double entry bookkeeping and accounting treatments

RENT ACCOUNT

20X6		£	20X6		£
31 July	Cash	3,000			
31 Oct	Cash	3,000	31 Dec	P & L account	8,000

2.11 To complete the picture, the accruals of £2,000 have to be put in, not only to balance the account, but also to have an opening balance of £2,000 ready for next year. So the accrued rent of £2,000 is debited to the rent account as a balance to be carried down, and credited to the rent account as a balance brought down.

RENT ACCOUNT

20X6		£	20X6		£
31 July	Cash *	3,000			
31 Oct	Cash *	3,000			
31 Dec	Balance c/f (accruals)	2,000	31 Dec	P & L account	8,000
		8,000			8,000
			20X7		
			1 Jan	Balance b/f	2,000

* The corresponding credit entry would be cash if rent is paid without the need for an invoice - eg with payment by standing order or direct debit at the bank. If there is always an invoice where rent becomes payable, the double entry would be:

| DEBIT | Rent account | £2,000 | |
| CREDIT | Creditors | | £2,000 |

Then when the rent is paid, the ledger entries would be:

| DEBIT | Creditors | £2,000 | |
| CREDIT | Cash | | £2,000 |

2.12 The rent account for the **next** year to 31 December 20X7, assuming no increase in rent in that year, would be as follows.

RENT ACCOUNT

20X7		£	20X7		£
31 Jan	Cash	3,000	1 Jan	Balance b/f	2,000
30 Apr	Cash	3,000			
31 Jul	Cash	3,000			
31 Oct	Cash	3,000			
31 Dec	Balance c/f (accruals)	2,000	31 Dec	P & L account	12,000
		14,000			14,000
			20X8		
			1 Jan	Balance b/f	2,000

2.13 Here you will see that, for a full year, a full twelve months' rental charges are taken as an expense to the P & L account.

2.14 FURTHER EXAMPLE: PREPAYMENTS

Terry Trunk commences business as a landscape gardener on 1 September 20X5. He immediately decides to join his local trade association, the Confederation of Luton Gardeners, for which the annual membership subscription is £180, payable annually in advance. He paid this amount on 1 September. Terry decides that his account period should end on 30 June each year.

2.15 In the first period to 30 June 20X6 (10 months), a full year's membership will have been paid, but only ten twelfths of the subscription should be charged to the period (ie 10/12 × £180 = £150). There is a prepayment of two months of membership subscription - ie 2/12 × £180 = £30.

2.16 The prepayment is recognised in the ledger account for subscriptions. This is done by using the balance carried down/brought down technique.

CREDIT	Subscriptions account with prepayment as a balance c/f		£30
DEBIT	Subscriptions account with the same balance b/f	£30	

The remaining expenses in the subscriptions account should then be taken to the P & L account. The balance on the account will appear as a current asset (prepaid subscriptions) in the balance sheet as at 30 June 20X6.

SUBSCRIPTIONS ACCOUNT

			£				£
20X5				*20X6*			
1 Sept	Cash		180	30 Jun	P & L account		150
				30 Jun	Balance c/f (prepayment)		30
			180				180
20X6							
1 Jul	Balance b/f		30				

2.17 The subscription account for the next year, assuming no increase in the annual charge and that Terry Trunk remains a member of the association, will be:

SUBSCRIPTIONS ACCOUNT

			£				£
20X6				*20X7*			
1 Jul	Balance b/f		30	30 Jun	P & L account		180
1 Sep	Cash		180	30 Jun	Balance c/f (prepayment)		30
			210				210
20X67							
1 Jul	Balance b/f		30				

2.18 Again, we see here for a full accounting year, the charge to the P & L account is for a full year's subscriptions.

Part C: Double entry bookkeeping and accounting treatments

Question 4

The Umbrella Shop has the following trial balance as at 30 September 20X8.

	£	£
Sales		156,000
Purchases	65,000	
Land & buildings – net book value at 30.9.X8	125,000	
Plant & machinery – net book value at 30.9.X8	75,000	
Stock at 1.10.X7	10,000	
Cash at bank	12,000	
Trade debtors	54,000	
Trade creditors		40,000
Selling expenses	10,000	
Cash in hand	2,000	
Administration expenses	15,000	
Finance expenses	5,000	
Carriage inwards	1,000	
Carriage outwards	2,000	
Capital account at 1.10.X7		180,000
	376,000	376,000

The following information is available:

(a) Closing stock at 30.9.X8 is £13,000, after writing off damaged goods of £2,000.

(b) Included in administration expenses is machinery rental of £6,000 covering the year to 31 December 20X8.

(c) A late invoice for £12,000 covering rent for the year ended 30 June 20X9 has not been included in the trial balance.

Prepare a trading, profit and loss account and balance sheet for the year ended 30 September 20X8. (*Tutorial note:* This will provide useful revision of the forms of the profit and loss account and balance sheet. If necessary refer back to Chapter 6 of this Study Text).

Answer

THE UMBRELLA SHOP
TRADING, PROFIT AND LOSS ACCOUNT FOR THE YEAR END 30 SEPTEMBER 20X8

	£	£
Sales		156,000
Opening stock	10,000	
Purchases	65,000	
Carriage inwards	1,000	
	76,000	
Closing stock (W1)	13,000	
Cost of goods sold		63,000
Gross profit		93,000
Selling expenses	10,000	
Carriage outwards	2,000	
Administration expenses (W2)	16,500	
Finance expenses	5,000	33,500
Net profit for the period		59,500

7: The cost of goods sold, accruals and prepayments

THE UMBRELLA SHOP
BALANCE SHEET AS AT 30 SEPTEMBER 20X8

	£	£
Fixed assets		
Land & buildings		125,000
Plant & machinery		75,000
		200,000
Current assets		
Stock (W1)	13,000	
Trade debtors	54,000	
Prepayments (W4)	1,500	
Cash at bank and in hand	14,000	
	82,500	
Current liabilities	40,000	
Trade creditor	3,000	
Accruals (W3)	43,000	
Net current assets		39,500
		239,500
Capital		
Proprietor's capital		
Balance brought forward		180,000
Profit for the period		59,500
Balance carried forward		239,500

Workings

1   **Closing stock**

   As the figure of £13,000 is **after** writing off damaged goods, no further adjustments are necessary. Remember that you are effectively crediting closing stock to the trading account of the profit and loss account and the corresponding debit is to the balance sheet.

2   **Administration expenses**

	£
Per trial balance	15,000
Add: accrual (W3)	3,000
	18,000
Less: prepayment (W4)	(1,500)
	16,500

3   **Accrual**

	£
Rent for year to 30 June 20X9	12,000
Accrual for period to 30 September 20X8 ($^3/_{12}$ × £12,000)	3,000

4   **Prepayment**

	£
Machinery rental for the year to 31 December 20X8	6,000
Prepayment for period 1 October to 31 December 20X8 ($^3/_{12}$ × £6,000)	1,500

Part C: Double entry bookkeeping and accounting treatments

Chapter roundup

- This chapter has illustrated how the amount of profit is calculated when:
  - There are opening or closing stocks of goods in hand.
  - There is carriage inwards and/or carriage outwards.
  - Stocks are written off or written down in value.
  - There are accrued charges.
  - There are prepayments of expenses.

- The **cost of goods** sold is calculated as follows:

	£
Opening stock	X
Plus purchases	X
	X
Less closing stock	(X)
	X

- **Accrued expenses** are expenses which relate to an accounting period but have not yet been paid for. They are a **charge against the profit** for the period and they are shown in the balance sheet as at the end of the period as a current liability.

- **Prepayments** are expenses which have already been paid but relate to a future accounting period. They are **not charged against the profit** of the current period, and they are shown in the balance sheet at the end of the period as a **current asset**.

Quick quiz

1. How is the cost of goods sold calculated?

2. Distinguish between carriage inwards and carriage outwards.

3. The cost of goods sold is £14,000. The purchases for the period are £14,000, carriage inwards is £1,000, carriage outwards is £1,500 and closing stock is £13,000. What was the opening stock figure?

    A £10,500
    B £11,500
    C £12,000
    D £13,000

4. Give three reasons why goods purchased might have to be written off.

5. If a business has paid rates of £1,000 for the year to 31 March 20X9, what is the prepayment in the accounts for the year to 31 December 20X8?

6. Define an accrual.

Answers to quick quiz

1 See formula to learn in paragraph 1.6.

2 Carriage inwards is paid on goods coming **into** the business and is added to the cost of purchases.

   Carriage outwards is paid on goods going **out of** the business to customers and is charged to selling expenses.

3 C

	£
Opening stock value (balancing figure)	12,000
Add: purchases (incl carriage inwards)	15,000
	27,000
Less: closing stock	(13,000)
Cost of goods sold	14,000

   If you picked A, then you wrongly included carriage outwards in cost of goods sold. If you chose B, then you used the carriage outwards instead of the carriage inwards figure in your calculations. With D, you ignored carriage inwards and outwards altogether!

4
- Goods are stolen or lost
- Goods are damaged
- Goods are obsolete

5 $3/12 \times £1,000 = £250$

6 Expenses charged against profit for a period, even though they have not yet been paid or invoiced.

Now try the questions below from the Exam Question Bank

Question to try	Level	Marks	Time
10	Introductory	n/a	36 mins
11	Introductory	n/a	45 mins

Chapter 8

DISCOUNTS, BAD DEBTS AND PROVISIONS

Topic list	Syllabus reference
1 Discounts	3(a)
2 Bad debts	4(b)
3 Provisions for doubtful debts	4(b)
4 Accounting for bad and doubtful debts	4(b)

Introduction

In this chapter we move closer to our goal of preparing the financial statements. We look at two types of adjustment which need to be made in respect of credit sales and purchases:

- Discounts
- Bad and doubtful debts

Study guide

Section 8 – The financial statements of a sole trader 2: Depreciation and bad and doubtful debts

- Explain the inevitability of bad debts in most businesses.
- Illustrate the bookkeeping entries to write off a bad debt and the effect on the profit and loss account and balance sheet.
- Illustrate the bookkeeping entries to record bad debts recovered.
- Explain the difference between writing off a bad debt and making a provision for a doubtful debt.
- Explain and illustrate the bookkeeping entries to create and adjust a provision for doubtful debts.
- Illustrate how to include movements in the provision for doubtful debts in the profit and loss account and how the closing balance of the provision may appear in the balance sheet.

Exam guide

You will always get an exam question involving final accounts preparation. Such questions will nearly always involve an adjustment for discounts, bad and doubtful debts or both.

1 DISCOUNTS

Types of discount

1.1 A discount is a reduction in the price of goods below the amount at which those goods would normally be sold to other customers of the supplier. A distinction must be made between:

- **Trade discount**
- **Cash discount**, or **settlement discount**.

> **KEY TERM**
>
> **Trade discount** is a reduction in the cost of goods owing to the nature of the trading transaction. It usually results from buying goods in bulk.

1.2 **Examples of trade discount**

(a) A customer might be quoted a price of £1 per unit for a particular item, but a lower price of, say, 95 pence per unit if the item is bought in quantities of, say, 100 units or more at a time.

(b) An important customer or a regular customer might be offered a discount on all the goods he buys, regardless of the size of each individual order, because the total volume of his purchases over time is so large.

> **KEY TERM**
>
> **Cash discount** is a reduction in the amount payable to the supplier, in return for immediate payment in cash, rather than purchase on credit.

1.3 For example, a supplier might charge £1,000 for goods, but offer a discount of, say, 5% if the goods are paid for immediately in cash.

> **KEY TERM**
>
> **Settlement discount** is similar to cash discount. It is a discount on the price of the goods purchased for credit customers who pay their debts promptly.

1.4 For example, a supplier might charge £1,000 to a credit customer for goods purchased, but offer a discount of, say, 5% for payment within so many days of the invoice date.

Accounting for trade discounts

1.5 A trade discount is a reduction in the amount of money demanded from a customer.

(a) If a trade discount is received by a business for goods purchased from a supplier, the amount of money demanded from the business by the supplier will be net of discount (ie it will be the normal sales value less the discount).

(b) Similarly, if a trade discount is given by a business for goods sold to a customer, the amount of money demanded by the business will be after deduction of the discount.

Part C: Double entry bookkeeping and accounting treatments

1.6 Trade discounts should therefore be accounted for as follows.

   (a) **Trade discounts received** should be deducted from the gross cost of purchases. In other words, the cost of purchases in the trading account will be stated at gross cost minus discount (ie it will be stated at the invoiced amount).

   (b) **Trade discounts allowed** should be deducted from the gross sales price, so that sales for the period will be reported in the trading account at their invoice value.

Cash discounts and settlement discounts received

1.7 When a business is given the opportunity to take advantage of a cash discount or a settlement discount for prompt payment, the decision as to whether or not to take the discount is a matter of financing policy, not of trading policy.

1.8 EXAMPLE: CASH AND SETTLEMENT DISCOUNTS RECEIVED

Suppose that A buys goods from B, on the understanding that A will be allowed a period of credit before having to pay for the goods. The terms of the transaction might be as follows.

   (a) Date of sale: 1 July 20X6

   (b) Credit period allowed: 30 days

   (c) Invoice price of the goods: £2,000 (the invoice will be issued at this price when the goods are delivered)

   (d) Cash discount offered: 4% discount for prompt payment

1.9 A has the choice between:

   (a) Holding on to his money for 30 days and then paying the full £2,000.
   (b) Paying £2,000 less 4% - ie £1,920 now.

   This is a financing decision about whether it is worthwhile for A to save £80 by paying its debts sooner, or whether it can employ its cash more usefully for 30 days, and pay the debt at the latest acceptable moment.

1.10 If A decides to take the cash discount, he will pay £1,920, instead of the invoiced amount £2,000. The cash discount received (£80) will be accounted for in the books of A as follows.

   (a) In the trading account, the cost of purchases will be at the invoiced price (or 'full trade' price) of £2,000. When the invoice for £2,000 is received by A, it will be recorded in his books of account at that price, and the subsequent financing decision about accepting the cash discount is ignored.

   (b) In the profit and loss account, the cash discount received is shown as though it were income received. There is no expense in the P & L account from which the cash discount can be deducted, and so there is no alternative other than to show the discount received as income.

1.11 In our example, we would have:

	£
Cost of purchase from B by A (trading account)	2,000
Discount received (income in the P & L account)	(80)
Net cost	1,920

Settlement discounts received are accounted for in exactly the same way as cash discounts received.

Question 1

Soft Supplies Ltd recently purchased from Hard Imports Ltd 10 printers originally priced at £200 each. A 10% trade discount was negotiated together with a 5% cash discount if payment was made within 14 days. Calculate the following.

(a) The total of the trade discount
(b) The total of the cash discount

Answer

(a) £200 (£200 × 10 × 10%)
(b) £90 (£200 × 10 × 90% × 5%)

Cash discounts and settlement discounts allowed

1.12 The same principle is applied in accounting for cash discounts or settlement discounts allowed to customers. Goods are sold at a trade price, and the offer of a discount on that price is a matter of financing policy for the business and not a matter of trading policy.

1.13 EXAMPLE: CASH DISCOUNTS AND SETTLEMENT DISCOUNTS ALLOWED

X sells goods to Y at a price of £5,000. Y is allowed 60 days' credit before payment, but is also offered a settlement discount of 2% for payment within 10 days of the invoice date.

X will issue an invoice to Y for £5,000 when the goods are sold. X has no idea whether or not Y will take advantage of the discount. In trading terms, and in terms of the amount charged in the invoice to Y, Y is a debtor for £5,000.

1.14 If Y subsequently decides to take the discount, he will pay £5,000 less 2% - ie £4,900 - ten days later. The discount allowed (£100) will be accounted for by X as follows:

(a) in the trading account, sales will be valued at their full invoice price, £5,000;
(b) in the profit and loss account, the discount allowed will be shown as an expense.

1.15 In our example, we would have:

	£
Sales (trading account)	5,000
Discounts allowed (P & L account)	(100)
Net sales	4,900

Cash discounts allowed are accounted for in exactly the same way as settlement discounts allowed.

Question 2

You are required to prepare the trading, profit and loss account of Seesaw Timber Merchants for the year ended 31 March 20X6, given the following information.

Part C: Double entry bookkeeping and accounting treatments

	£
Goods in stock, 1 April 20X5	18,000
Purchases at gross cost	120,000
Trade discounts received	4,000
Cash and settlement discounts received	1,500
Goods in stock, 31 March 20X6	25,000
Cash sales	34,000
Credit sales at invoice price	150,000
Cash and settlement discounts allowed	8,000
Selling expenses	32,000
Administrative expenses	40,000
Drawings by proprietor, Tim Burr	22,000

Answer

SEESAW TIMBER MERCHANTS
TRADING, PROFIT AND LOSS ACCOUNT
FOR THE YEAR ENDED 31 MARCH 20X6

	£	£
Sales (note 1)		184,000
Opening stocks	18,000	
Purchases (note 2)	116,000	
	134,000	
Less closing stocks	25,000	
Cost of goods sold		109,000
Gross profit		75,000
Discounts received		1,500
		76,500
Expenses		
Selling expenses	32,000	
Administrative expenses	40,000	
Discounts allowed	8,000	
		80,000
Net loss transferred to balance sheet		(3,500)

Notes
1. £(34,000 + 150,000)
2. £(120,000 – 4,000)
3. Drawings are not an expense, but an appropriation of profit.

2 BAD DEBTS

2.1 Customers who buy goods on credit might fail to pay for them, perhaps out of dishonesty or perhaps because they have gone bankrupt and cannot pay. Customers in another country might be prevented from paying by the unexpected introduction of foreign exchange control restrictions by their country's government during the credit period.

For one reason or another, a business might decide to give up expecting payment and to write the debt off as a 'lost cause'.

> **KEY TERM**
>
> A **bad debt** is a debt which is not expected to be repaid.

Writing off bad debts

2.2 When a business decides that a particular debt is unlikely ever to be repaid, the amount of the debt should be '**written off**' as an expense in the profit and loss account.

2.3 For example, if Alfred's Mini-Cab Service sends an invoice for £300 to a customer who subsequently does a 'moonlight flit' from his office premises, never to be seen or heard of again, the debt of £300 must be written off. It might seem sensible to record the business transaction as:

Sales £(300 – 300) = £0.

2.4 However, bad debts written off are accounted for as follows.

(a) **Sales** are shown at their invoice value in the **trading account**. The sale has been made, and gross profit should be earned. The subsequent failure to collect the debt is a separate matter, which is reported in the P & L account.

(b) **Bad debts** written off are shown as an **expense in the profit and loss account**.

2.5 In our example of Alfred's Mini-Cab Service:

	£
Sale (in the trading account)	300
Bad debt written off (expense in the P & L account)	300
Net profit on this transaction	0

2.6 Obviously, when a debt is written off, the value of the debtor as a current asset falls to zero. If the debt is expected to be uncollectable, its '**net realisable value**' is nil, and so it has a zero balance sheet value.

Bad debts written off and subsequently paid

2.7 A bad debt which has been written off might occasionally be unexpectedly paid. The only accounting problem to consider is when a debt written off as bad in one accounting period is subsequently paid in a later accounting period. The amount recovered should be recorded as additional **income** in the profit and loss account of the period in which the payment is received.

2.8 For example, a trading, profit and loss account for the Blacksmith's Forge for the year to 31 December 20X5 could be prepared as shown below from the following information.

	£
Stocks of goods in hand, 1 January 20X5	6,000
Purchases of goods	122,000
Stocks of goods in hand, 31 December 20X5	8,000
Cash sales	100,000
Credit sales	70,000
Discounts allowed	1,200
Discounts received	5,000
Bad debts written off	9,000
Debts paid in 20X5 which were previously written off as bad in 20X4 (ie bad debts recovered)	2,000
Other expenses	31,800

Part C: Double entry bookkeeping and accounting treatments

BLACKSMITH'S FORGE
TRADING, PROFIT AND LOSS ACCOUNT FOR THE YEAR ENDED 31.12.20X5

	£	£
Sales		170,000
Opening stock	6,000	
Purchases	122,000	
	128,000	
Less closing stock	8,000	
Cost of goods sold		120,000
Gross profit		50,000
Add: discounts received		5,000
debts paid, previously written off as bad		2,000
		57,000
Expenses		
Discounts allowed	1,200	
Bad debts written off	9,000	
Other expenses	31,800	
		42,000
Net profit		15,000

3 PROVISIONS FOR DOUBTFUL DEBTS

3.1 When bad debts are written off, specific debts owed to the business are identified as unlikely ever to be collected.

However, because of the risks involved in selling goods on credit, it might be accepted that a certain percentage of outstanding debts at any time are unlikely to be collected. But although it might be estimated that, say, 5% of debts will turn out bad, the business will not know until later which specific debts are bad.

3.2 A business commences operations on 1 July 20X4, and in the twelve months to 30 June 20X5 makes sales of £300,000 (all on credit) and writes off bad debts amounting to £6,000. Cash received from customers during the year is £244,000, so that at 30 June 20X5, the business has outstanding debtors of £50,000.

	£
Credit sales during the year	300,000
Add debtors at 1 July 20X4	0
Total debts owed to the business	300,000
Less cash received from credit customers	244,000
	56,000
Less bad debts written off	6,000
Debtors outstanding at 30 June 20X5	50,000

Now, some of these outstanding debts might turn out to be bad. The business does not know on 30 June 20X5 which specific debts in the total £50,000 owed will be bad, but it might guess (from experience perhaps) that 5% of debts will eventually be found to be bad.

3.3 When a business expects bad debts amongst its current debtors, but does not yet know which specific debts will be bad, it can make a **general provision for doubtful debts**.

KEY TERM

A **general provision for doubtful debts** is an estimate of the percentage of debts which are not expected to be paid.

8: Discounts, bad debts and provisions

3.4 A 'provision' is a 'providing for' and so a provision for doubtful debts provides for future bad debts, as a prudent precaution by the business. The business will be more likely to avoid claiming profits which subsequently fail to materialise because some debts turn out to be bad.

(a) When a provision is first made, the amount of this initial provision is charged as an expense in the profit and loss account of the business, for the period in which the provision is created.

(b) When a provision already exists, but is subsequently increased in size, the amount of the **increase** in provision is charged as an **expense** in the profit and loss account, for the period in which the increased provision is made.

(c) When a provision already exists, but is subsequently reduced in size, the amount of the **decrease** in provision is recorded as an item of **'income'** in the profit and loss account, for the period in which the reduction in provision is made.

> **Exam focus point**
> In an exam you will often be required, as part of a longer question, to calculate the increase or decrease in the provision for doubtful debts. In addition, there is likely to be an MCQ on this topic.

3.5 The balance sheet, as well as the profit and loss account of a business, must be adjusted to show a provision for doubtful debts.

> **IMPORTANT!**
> The value of debtors in the balance sheet must be shown after deducting the provision for doubtful debts.

This is because the net realisable value of all the debtors of the business is estimated to be less than their 'sales value'. After all, this is the reason for making the provision in the first place. The net realisable value of debtors is the total value of debtors minus the provision for doubtful debts. Such a provision is an example of the **prudence concept**, discussed in detail in Chapter 14.

3.6 In the example above (in paragraph 3.2) the newly created provision for doubtful debts at 30 June 20X5 will be 5% of £50,000 = £2,500. This means that although total debtors are £50,000, eventual payment of only £47,500 is expected.

(a) In the P & L account, the newly created provision of £2,500 will be shown as an expense.

(b) In the balance sheet, debtors will be shown as:

	£
Total debtors at 30 June 20X5	50,000
Less provision for doubtful debts	2,500
	47,500

3.7 EXAMPLE: PROVISION FOR DOUBTFUL DEBTS

Corin Flakes owns and runs the Aerobic Health Foods Shop in Dundee. He commenced trading on 1 January 20X1, selling health foods to customers, most of whom make use of a credit facility that Corin offers. (Customers are allowed to purchase up to £200 of goods on credit but must repay a certain proportion of their outstanding debt every month.)

Part C: Double entry bookkeeping and accounting treatments

This credit system gives rise to a large number of bad debts, and Corin Flake's results for his first three years of operations are as follows.

Year to 31 December 20X1
Gross profit	£27,000
Bad debts written off	£8,000
Debts owed by customers as at 31 December 20X1	£40,000
Provision for doubtful debts	2½% of outstanding debtors
Other expenses	£20,000

Year to 31 December 20X2
Gross profit	£45,000
Bad debts written off	£10,000
Debts owed by customers as at 31 December 20X2	£50,000
Provision for doubtful debts	2½% of outstanding debtors
Other expenses	£28,750

Year to 31 December 20X3
Gross profit	£60,000
Bad debts written off	£11,000
Debts owed by customers as at 31 December 20X3	£30,000
Provision for doubtful debts	3% of outstanding debtors
Other expenses	£32,850

Required

For each of these three years, prepare the profit and loss account of the business, and state the value of debtors appearing in the balance sheet as at 31 December.

3.8 SOLUTION

AEROBIC HEALTH FOOD SHOP
PROFIT AND LOSS ACCOUNTS FOR THE YEARS ENDED 31 DECEMBER

	20X1 £	20X1 £	20X2 £	20X2 £	20X3 £	20X3 £
Gross profit		27,000		45,000		60,000
Sundry income : reduction in provision for doubtful debts*						350
						60,350
Expenses:						
Bad debts written off	8,000		10,000		11,000	
Increase in provision for doubtful debts*	1,000		250		-	
Other expenses	20,000		28,750		32,850	
		29,000		39,000		43,850
Net(loss)/profit		(2,000)		6,000		16,500

*At 1 January 20X1 when Corin began trading the provision for doubtful debts was nil. At 31 December 20X1 the provision required was 2½% of £40,000 = £1,000. The increase in the provision is therefore £1,000. At 31 December 20X2 the provision required was 2½% of £50,000 = £1,250. The 20X1 provision must therefore be increased by £250. At 31 December 20X3 the provision required is 3% × £30,000 = £900. The 20X2 provision is therefore reduced by £350.

8: Discounts, bad debts and provisions

VALUE OF DEBTORS IN THE BALANCE SHEET

	As at 31.12.20X1 £	As at 31.12.20X2 £	As at 31.12.20X3 £
Total value of debtors	40,000	50,000	30,000
Less provision for doubtful debts	1,000	1,250	900
Balance sheet value	39,000	48,750	29,100

You should now try to use what you have learned to attempt a solution to the following exercise, which involves preparing a trading, profit and loss account and balance sheet.

Question 3

The financial affairs of Newbegin Tools prior to the commencement of trading were as follows.

NEWBEGIN TOOLS
BALANCE SHEET AS AT 1 AUGUST 20X5

	£	£
Fixed assets		
Motor vehicle	2,000	
Shop fittings	3,000	
		5,000
Current assets		
Stocks	12,000	
Cash	1,000	
	13,000	
Current liabilities		
Bank overdraft	2,000	
Trade creditors	4,000	
	6,000	
Net current assets		7,000
		12,000
Financed by		
Capital		12,000

At the end of six months the business had made the following transactions.

(a) Goods were purchased on credit at a gross amount of £10,000.

(b) Trade discount received was 2% on this gross amount and there was a settlement discount received of 5% on settling debts to suppliers of £8,000. These were the only payments to suppliers in the period.

(c) Closing stocks of goods were valued at £5,450.

(d) Cash sales and credit sales together totalled £27,250.

(e) Outstanding debtors' balances at 31 January 20X6 amounted to £3,250 of which £250 were to be written off.

(f) A further provision for doubtful debts is to be made amounting to 2% of the remaining outstanding debtors.

(g) Cash payments were made in respect of the following expenses.

			£
(i)	Stationery, postage and wrapping		500
(ii)	Telephone charges		200
(iii)	Electricity		600
(iv)	Cleaning and refreshments		150

(h) Cash drawings by the proprietor, Alf Newbegin, amounted to £6,000.

(i) The outstanding overdraft balance as at 1 August 20X5 was paid off. Interest charges and bank charges on the overdraft amounted to £40.

Alf Newbegin knew the balance of cash on hand at 31 January 20X6 but he wanted to know if the business had made a profit for the six months that it had been trading, and so he asked his friend, Harry Oldhand, if he could tell him.

Part C: Double entry bookkeeping and accounting treatments

Prepare the trading, profit and loss account of Newbegin Tools for the six months to 31 January 20X6 and a balance sheet as at that date.

Answer

The trading, profit and loss account should be fairly straightforward.

NEWBEGIN TOOLS
TRADING AND PROFIT AND LOSS ACCOUNT
FOR THE SIX MONTHS ENDED 31 JANUARY 20X6

	£	£
Sales		27,250
Opening stocks	12,000	
Purchases (note (a))	9,800	
	21,800	
Less closing stocks	5,450	
Cost of goods sold		16,350
Gross profit		10,900
Discounts received (note (b))		400
		11,300
Electricity (note (c))	600	
Stationery, postage and wrapping	500	
Bad debts written off	250	
Provision for doubtful debts (note (d))	60	
Telephone charges	200	
Cleaning and refreshments	150	
Interest and bank charges	40	
		1,800
Net profit		9,500

Notes

(a) Purchases at cost £10,000 less 2% trade discount.

(b) 5% of £8,000 = £400

(c) Expenses are grouped into sales and distribution expenses (here assumed to be electricity, stationery and postage, bad debts and provision for doubtful debts) administration expenses (here assumed to be telephone charges and cleaning) and finance charges.

(d) 2% of £3,000 = £60.

The preparation of a balance sheet is not so easy, because we must calculate the value of creditors and cash in hand.

(a) *Creditors as at 31 January 20X6*

The amount owing to creditors is the sum of the amount owing at the beginning of the period, plus the cost of purchases during the period (net of all discounts), less the payments already made for purchases. (What is still owed is the total amount of costs incurred less payments already made.)

	£
Creditors as at 1 August 20X5	4,000
Add purchases during the period, net of trade discount	9,800
	13,800
Less settlement discounts received	(400)
	13,400
Less payments to creditors during the period*	(7,600)
	5,800

* £8,000 less cash discount of £400.

(b) *Cash at bank and in hand at 31 January 20X6*

This too requires a fairly lengthy calculation. You need to identify cash payments received and cash payments made.

8: Discounts, bad debts and provisions

			£
(i)		*Cash received from sales*	
		Total sales in the period	27,250
		Add debtors as at 1 August 20X5	0
			27,250
		Less unpaid debts as at 31 January 20X6	3,250
		Cash received	24,000

			£
(ii)		*Cash paid*	
		Trade creditors (see (a))	7,600
		Stationery, postage and wrapping	500
		Telephone charges	200
		Electricity	600
		Cleaning and refreshments	150
		Bank charges and interest	40
		Bank overdraft repaid	2,000
		Drawings by proprietor	6,000
			17,090

Note. It is easy to forget some of these payments, especially drawings.

		£
(iii)	Cash in hand at 1 August 20X5	1,000
	Cash received in the period	24,000
		25,000
	Cash paid in the period	(17,090)
	Cash at bank and in hand as at 31 January 20X6	7,910

(c) When bad debts are written off, the value of outstanding debtors must be reduced by the amount written off. This is because the debtors are no longer expected to pay, and it would be misleading and absurd to show them in the balance sheet as current assets of the business for which cash payment is expected within one year. Debtors in the balance sheet will be valued at £3,000 less the provision for doubtful debts of £60 - ie at £2,940.

(d) Fixed assets should be depreciated. However, in this exercise depreciation has been ignored.

NEWBEGIN TOOLS
BALANCE SHEET AS AT 31 JANUARY 20X6

	£	£
Fixed assets		
Motor vehicles	2,000	
Shop fittings	3,000	
		5,000
Current assets		
Stocks	5,450	
Debtors	2,940	
Cash	7,910	
		16,300
		21,300
Current liabilities		
Trade creditors		(5,800)
		15,500
Capital		
Capital at 1 August 20X5		12,000
Net profit for the period		9,500
		21,500
Less drawings		6,000
Capital at 31 January 20X6		15,500

The bank overdraft has now been repaid and is therefore not shown.

Part C: Double entry bookkeeping and accounting treatments

4 ACCOUNTING FOR BAD AND DOUBTFUL DEBTS

Bad debts written off: ledger accounting entries

4.1 For bad debts written off, there is a bad debts account. The double-entry bookkeeping is fairly straightforward, but there are two separate transactions to record.

(a) When it is decided that a particular debt will not be paid, the customer is no longer called an outstanding debtor, and becomes a bad debt. We therefore:

DEBIT   Bad debts account (expense)
CREDIT   Debtors account

(b) At the end of the accounting period, the balance on the bad debts account is transferred to the P & L ledger account (like all other expense accounts):

DEBIT   P & L account
CREDIT   Bad debts account.

4.2 Where a bad debt is subsequently recovered in the same accounting period, you simply reverse the entries in (a) above and so there will be no need to carry out the entries in (b) above.

DEBIT   Debtors account
CREDIT   Bad debts account (expense)

4.3 However, where a bad debt is subsequently recovered in a later accounting period the accounting entries will be as follows.

DEBIT   Debtors account
CREDIT   Bad debts recovered (income in the P & L a/c)

4.4 EXAMPLE: BAD DEBTS WRITTEN OFF

At 1 October 20X5 a business had total outstanding debts of £8,600. During the year to 30 September 20X6:

(a) Credit sales amounted to £44,000.

(b) Payments from various debtors amounted to £49,000.

(c) Two debts, for £180 and £420, were declared bad and the customers are no longer purchasing goods from the company. These are to be written off.

Required

Prepare the debtors account and the bad debts account for the year.

4.5 SOLUTION

DEBTORS

	£		£
Opening balance b/f	8,600	Cash	49,000
Sales	44,000	Bad debts	180
		Bad debts	420
		Closing balance c/f	3,000
	52,600		52,600
Opening balance b/f	3,000		

8: Discounts, bad debts and provisions

BAD DEBTS

	£		£
Debtors	180	P & L a/c: bad debts written off	600
Debtors	420		
	600		600

4.6 In the sales ledger, personal accounts of the customers whose debts are bad will be taken off the ledger. The business should then take steps to ensure that it does not sell goods on credit to those customers again.

Provision for doubtful debts: ledger accounting entries

4.7 A provision for doubtful debts is rather different. A business might know from past experience that, say 2% of debtors' balances are unlikely to be collected. It would then be considered prudent to make a general provision of 2%. It may be that no particular customers are regarded as suspect and so it is not possible to write off any individual customer balances as bad debts. The procedure is then to leave the total debtors balances completely untouched, but to open up a provision account by the following entries:

DEBIT   Doubtful debts account (expense)
CREDIT   Provision for doubtful debts

> **IMPORTANT!**
> When preparing a balance sheet, the credit balance on the provision account is deducted from the total debit balances in the debtors ledger.

4.8 **In subsequent years, adjustments may be needed to the amount of the provision**. The procedure to be followed then is as follows.

(a) Calculate the new provision required.

(b) Compare it with the existing balance on the provision account (ie the balance b/f from the previous accounting period).

(c) Calculate increase or decrease required.

  (i) If a higher provision is required now:

   CREDIT   Provision for doubtful debts
   DEBIT   P & L account

   with the amount of the increase.

  (ii) If a lower provision is needed now than before:

   DEBIT   Provision for doubtful debts
   CREDIT   P & L account

   with the amount of the decrease.

4.9 **EXAMPLE: ACCOUNTING ENTRIES FOR PROVISION FOR DOUBTFUL DEBTS**

Alex Gullible has total debtors' balances outstanding at 31 December 20X2 of £28,000. He believes that about 1% of these balances will not be collected and wishes to make an appropriate provision. Before now, he has not made any provision for doubtful debts at all.

On 31 December 20X3 his debtors balances amount to £40,000. His experience during the year has convinced him that a provision of 5% should be made.

Part C: Double entry bookkeeping and accounting treatments

What accounting entries should Alex make on 31 December 20X2 and 31 December 20X3, and what figures for debtors will appear in his balance sheets as at those dates?

4.10 SOLUTION

At 31 December 20X2

Provision required = 1% × £28,000
= £280

Alex will make the following entries:

DEBIT	P & L account (doubtful debts)	£280	
CREDIT	Provision for doubtful debts		£280

In the balance sheet debtors will appear as follows under current assets.

	£
Sales ledger balances	28,000
Less provision for doubtful debts	280
	27,720

At 31 December 20X3

Following the procedure described above, Alex will calculate as follows.

	£
Provision required now (5% × £40,000)	2,000
Existing provision	(280)
∴ Additional provision required	1,720

He will make the following entries:

DEBIT	P & L account (doubtful debts)	£1,720	
CREDIT	Provision for doubtful debts		£1,720

The provision account will by now appear as follows.

PROVISION FOR DOUBTFUL DEBTS

20X2		£	20X2		£
31 Dec	Balance c/f	280	31 Dec	P & L account	280
20X3			20X3		
31 Dec	Balance c/f	2,000	1 Jan	Balance b/f	280
			31 Dec	P & L account	1,720
		2,000			2,000
			20X4		
			1 Jan	Balance b/f	2,000

For the balance sheet debtors will be valued as follows.

	£
Sales ledger balances	40,000
Less provision for doubtful debts	2,000
	38,000

4.11 In practice, it is unnecessary to show the total debtors balances and the provision as separate items in the balance sheet. A balance sheet would normally show only the net figure (£27,720 in 20X2, £38,000 in 20X3). **If you do show the net figure show the set off of the provision as a working.**

4.12 Now try the following question on provision for doubtful debts for yourself.

8: Discounts, bad debts and provisions

Question 4

Horace Goodrunning fears that his business will suffer an increase in defaulting debtors in the future and so he decides to make a provision for doubtful debts of 2% of outstanding debtors at the balance sheet date from 28 February 20X6. On 28 February 20X8, Horace decides that the provision has been over-estimated and he reduces it to 1% of outstanding debtors. Outstanding debtors balances at the various balance sheet dates are as follows.

	£
28.2.20X6	15,200
28.2.20X7	17,100
28.2.20X8	21,400

You are required to show extracts from the following accounts for each of the three years above.

(a) Debtors
(b) Provision for doubtful debts
(c) Profit and loss

Show how debtors would appear in the balance sheet at the end of each year.

Answer

The entries for the three years are denoted by (a), (b) and (c) in each account.

DEBTORS (EXTRACT)

			£
(a)	28.2.20X6	Balance	15,200
(b)	28.2.20X7	Balance	17,100
(c)	28.2.20X8	Balance	21,400

PROVISION FOR DOUBTFUL DEBTS

				£				£
(a)	28.2.20X6	Balance c/f (2% of 15,200)		304	28.2.20X6	Profit and loss		304
				304				304
(b)	28.2.20X7	Balance c/f (2% of 17,100)		342	1.3.20X6	Balance b/f		304
					28.2.20X7	Profit and loss (note (i))		38
				342				342
(c)	28.2.20X8	Profit and loss (note (ii))		128	1.3.20X7	Balance b/f		342
	28.2.20X8	Balance c/f (1% of 21,400)		214				
				342				342
					1.3.20X8	Balance b/f		214

PROFIT AND LOSS (EXTRACT)

		£			£
28.2.20X6	Provision for doubtful debts	304			
28.2.20X7	Provision for doubtful debts	38			
			28.2.20X8	Provision for doubtful debts	128

Notes

(i) The increase in the provision is £(342 - 304) = £38
(ii) The decrease in the provision is £(342 - 214) = £128

We calculate the net debtors figure for inclusion in the balance sheet as follows.

	20X6	20X7	20X8
	£	£	£
Current assets			
Debtors	15,200	17,100	21,400
Less provision for doubtful debts	304	342	214
	14,896	16,758	21,186

Part C: Double entry bookkeeping and accounting treatments

Chapter roundup

- In this chapter, the following terms were defined.
    - **Trade discount** is a reduction in the catalogue price of an article, given by a wholesaler or manufacturer to a retailer. It is often given in return for bulk purchase orders.
    - **Cash discount** is a reduction in the amount payable for the purchase of goods or services in return for payment in cash rather than taking credit.
    - **Settlement discount** is a reduction in the amount payable for the purchase of goods or services in return for prompt payment within an agreed credit period.
    - **Bad debts** are specific debts owed to a business which it decides are never going to be paid.
    - **Doubtful debts** are debts which might become bad in the future but are not yet bad.
    - A **provision** is an amount written off to provide for depreciation or the fall in value of an asset, or to provide for any known liability of uncertain value. The amount is written off by:
        - charging the amount of the extra provision as an expense in the P & L account, and also
        - reducing the value of the asset in the balance sheet by the amount of the provision.
- We looked at the accounting treatment of each of these items.
    - **Trade discounts received** are deducted from the cost of purchases.
    - **Cash and settlement discounts received** are included as 'other income' of the period in the profit and loss account. Similarly, cash and settlement discounts allowed are shown as expenses in the profit and loss account.
    - **Bad debts written off** are an expense in the profit and loss account.
- An *increase* in the **provision for doubtful debts** is an expense in the profit and loss account whereas a decrease in the provision for doubtful debts is shown as 'other income' in the P & L account.
- **Debtors** are valued in the balance sheet **after deducting any provision** for doubtful debts.

Quick quiz

1 A bad debt arises in which of the following situations?

   A A debtor pays part of the account
   B An invoice is in dispute
   C The debtor goes bankrupt
   D The invoice is not yet due for payment

2 A provision for doubtful debt of 2% is required. Trade debtors at the period end are £200,000 and the provision for doubtful debt brought forward from the previous period is £2,000. What movements are required this year?

   A Increase by £4,000
   B Decrease by £4,000
   C Increase by £2,000
   D Decrease by £2,000

3 If a doubtful debts provision is increased, what is the effect on the P&L a/c?

4 What is the double entry to record a bad debt written off?

8: Discounts, bad debts and provisions

Answers to quick quiz

1. C
2. C 2% of £200,000 = £4,000. Therefore the provision needs to be increased by £2,000.
3. The increase in the provision is charged as an expense in the P&L a/c.
4. DEBIT   Bad debts account (expenses)
   CREDIT Trade debtors

Now try the questions below from the Exam Question Bank

Question to try	Level	Marks	Time
12	Introductory	n/a	27 mins
13	Introductory	n/a	27 mins

Chapter 9

ACCOUNTING FOR STOCKS

Topic list	Syllabus reference
1 Accounting for opening and closing stocks	4(b)
2 Stocktaking	4(b)
3 Valuing stocks	4(b)
4 Statutory regulations and SSAP 9 requirements	4(b)

Introduction

Stock is one of the most important assets in a company's balance sheet. As we have seen, it also affects the profit and loss account.

So far you have come across stock in the preparation of a simple balance sheet and in the calculation of the cost of goods sold. This chapter explores the **difficulties of valuing stock**.

This is the first time (although by no means the last) that you will be required to consider the impact of the relevant accounting standard and statutory rules on the valuation and presentation of an item in the accounts.

Study guide

Section 7 – The financial statements of a sole trader 1; stocks, accruals and prepayments

- Explain how opening and closing stock are recorded in the stock account.
- Discuss alternative methods of valuing stock.
- Explain the provisions of SSAP 9 Stocks and Long-Term Contracts (excluding long-term contracts).
- Explain the use of continuous and period end stock records.
- Explain how to calculate the value of closing stock from given movements in stock levels, using FIFO (first in fist out), LIFO (last in first out) and AVCO (average cost).

Exam guide

SSAP 9 is likely to form the whole or part of a question in Part B. MCQs often deal with opening and closing stocks.

1   ACCOUNTING FOR OPENING AND CLOSING STOCKS

1.1   In an earlier chapter, we saw that in order to calculate **gross profit** it is necessary to work out the **cost of goods sold,** and in order to calculate the cost of goods sold it is necessary to have values for the **opening stock** (ie stock in hand at the beginning of the accounting period) and **closing stock** (ie stock in hand at the end of the accounting period).

1.2   You should remember, in fact, that the trading part of a profit and loss account includes:

9: Accounting for stocks

	£
Opening stock	X
Plus purchases	X
Less closing stock	(X)
Equals cost of goods sold	X

1.3 However, just writing down this formula hides three basic problems.

(a) How do you manage to get a **precise count** of stock in hand at any one time?

(b) Even once it has been counted, how do you **value** the stock?

(c) Assuming the stock is given a value, how does the **double entry** bookkeeping for stock work?

1.4 The purpose of this chapter is to answer all three of these questions. In order to make the presentation a little easier to follow, it is convenient to take the last one first.

Ledger accounting for stocks

1.5 It has already been shown that purchases are introduced to the trading account by means of the double entry:

DEBIT	Trading account	£X	
CREDIT	Purchases account		£X

1.6 But what about opening and closing stocks? How are their values accounted for in the double entry bookkeeping system? The answer is that a **stock account** must be kept. This stock account is only ever used at the end of an accounting period, when the business counts up and values the stock in hand, in a stocktake.

(a) When a stock-take is made, the business will have a value for its closing stock, and the double entry is:

DEBIT	Stock account (closing stock value)	£X	
CREDIT	Trading account		£X

However, rather than show the closing stock as a 'plus' value in the trading account (eg by adding it to sales) it is usual to show it as a 'minus' figure in arriving at cost of sales. This is illustrated in paragraph 1.2 above. The debit balance on stock account represents an asset, which will be shown as part of current assets in the balance sheet.

(b) Closing stock at the end of one period becomes opening stock at the start of the next period. The stock account remains unchanged until the end of the next period, when the value of opening stock is taken to the trading account; ie

DEBIT	Trading account	£X	
CREDIT	Stock account (value of opening stock)		£X

1.7 Partly as an example of how this ledger accounting for stocks works, and partly as revision of ledger accounting in general, try the following question. It is an example from an earlier part of this text which has had a closing stocks figure included.

Question 1

A business is established with capital of £2,000 and this amount is paid into a business bank account by the proprietor. During the first year's trading, the following transactions occurred.

Part C: Double entry bookkeeping and accounting treatments

	£
Purchases of goods for resale, on credit	4,300
Payments to trade creditors	3,600
Sales, all on credit	4,000
Payments from debtors	3,200
Fixed assets purchased for cash	1,500
Other expenses, all paid in cash	900

The bank has provided an overdraft facility of up to £3,000.

All 'other expenses' relate to the current year.

Closing stocks of goods are valued at £1,800. (Because this is the first year of the business, there are no opening stocks.)

Ignore depreciation and drawings.

Required

Prepare the ledger accounts, a trading, profit and loss account for the year and a balance sheet as at the end of the year.

Answer

CASH

	£		£
Capital	2,000	Trade creditors	3,600
Debtors	3,200	Fixed assets	1,500
Balance c/f	800	Other expenses	900
	6,000		6,000
		Balance b/f	800

CAPITAL

	£		£
Balance c/f	2,600	Cash	2,000
		P & L a/c	600
	2,600		2,600
		Balance b/f	2,600

TRADE CREDITORS

	£		£
Cash	3,600	Purchases	4,300
Balance c/f	700		
	4,300		4,300
		Balance b/f	700

PURCHASES ACCOUNT

	£		£
Trade creditors	4,300	Trading a/c	4,300

FIXED ASSETS

	£		£
Cash	1,500	Balance c/f	1,500
Balance b/f	1,500		

SALES

	£		£
Trading a/c	4,000	Debtors	4,000

DEBTORS

	£		£
Sales	4,000	Cash	3,200
		Balance c/f	800
	4,000		4,000
Balance b/f	800		

OTHER EXPENSES

	£		£
Cash	900	P & L a/c	900

TRADING, PROFIT AND LOSS ACCOUNT

	£		£
Purchases account	4,300	Sales	4,000
Gross profit c/f	1,500	Closing stock (stock account)	1,800
	5,800		5,800
Other expenses	900	Gross profit b/f	1,500
Net profit (transferred to capital account)	600		
	1,500		1,500

STOCK ACCOUNT

	£		£
Trading account (closing stock)	1,800	Balance c/f (balance sheet)	1,800

BALANCE SHEET AS AT THE END OF THE PERIOD

	£	£
Fixed assets		1,500
Current assets		
Goods in stock	1,800	
Debtors	800	
	2,600	
Current liabilities		
Bank overdraft	800	
Trade creditors	700	
	1,500	
Net current assets		1,100
		2,600
Capital		
At start of period		2,000
Profit for period		600
		2,600

1.8 So if we can establish the value of stocks on hand, the above paragraphs and exercise show us how to account for that value. That takes care of one of the problems noted in the introduction of this chapter. But now another of those problems becomes apparent - how do we establish the value of stocks on hand? The first step must be to establish **how much stock is held**.

2 STOCKTAKING

2.1 Business trading is a continuous activity, but accounting statements must be drawn up at a particular date. In preparing a balance sheet it is necessary to '**freeze**' the activity of a

Part C: Double entry bookkeeping and accounting treatments

business so as to determine its assets and liabilities at a given moment. This includes establishing the quantities of stocks on hand, which can create problems.

2.2 A business buys stocks continually during its trading operations and either sells the goods onwards to customers or incorporates them as raw materials in manufactured products. This constant movement of stocks makes it difficult to establish what exactly is held at any precise moment.

2.3 In simple cases, when a business holds easily counted and relatively small amounts of stock, quantities of stocks on hand at the balance sheet date can be determined by physically counting them in a **stocktake**.

2.4 The continuous nature of trading activity may cause a problem in that stock movements will not necessarily cease during the time that the physical stocktake is in progress. Two possible solutions are:

(a) to **close down** the business while the count takes place; or
(b) to keep **detailed records** of stock movements during the course of the stocktake.

2.5 **Closing down** the business for a short period for a stocktake (eg over a weekend or at Christmas) is considerably **easier** than trying to keep detailed records of stock movements during a stocktake. So most businesses prefer that method unless they happen to keep detailed records of stock movements anyway (for example, because they wish to keep strict control on stock movements).

2.6 In more complicated cases, where a business holds considerable quantities of varied stock, an alternative approach to establishing stock quantities is to maintain **continuous stock records**. This means that a card is kept for every item of stock, showing receipts and issues from the stores, and a running total. A few stock items are counted each day to make sure their record cards are correct - this is called a 'continuous' stocktake because it is spread out over the year rather than completed in one stocktake at a designated time.

2.7 One obstacle is overcome once a business has established how much stock is on hand. But another of the problems noted in the introduction immediately raises its head. What **value** should the business place on those stocks?

3 VALUING STOCKS

The basic rule

3.1 There are **several methods** which, in theory, might be used for the valuation of stock items.

(a) Stocks might be valued at their **expected selling price**.

(b) Stocks might be valued at their expected selling price, less any costs still to be incurred in getting them ready for sale and then selling them. This amount is referred to as the **net realisable value** (NRV) of the stocks.

(c) Stocks might be valued at their **historical cost** (ie the cost at which they were originally bought).

(d) Stocks might be valued at the amount it would cost to replace them. This amount is referred to as the **current replacement cost** of stocks.

3.2 Current replacement costs are not used in the type of accounts dealt with in this syllabus. They will be considered again briefly in Chapter 25.

Selling price

3.3 The use of selling prices in stock valuation is **ruled out** because this would create a profit for the business before the stock has been sold.

3.4 A simple example might help to explain this. Suppose that a trader buys two items of stock, each costing £100. He can sell them for £140 each, but in the accounting period we shall consider, he has only sold one of them. The other is closing stock in hand.

3.5 Since only one item has been sold, you might think it is common sense that profit ought to be £40. But if closing stock is valued at selling price, profit would be £80 - ie profit would be taken on the closing stock as well.

	£	£
Sales		140
Opening stock	-	
Purchases (2 × 100)	200	
	200	
Less closing stock (at selling price)	140	
Cost of sale		60
Profit		80

This would contradict the accounting concept of prudence - ie to claim a profit before the item has actually been sold. We will look at the prudence concept in more detail in a later chapter.

NRV

3.6 The same objection **usually** applies to the use of NRV in stock valuation. Say that the item purchased for £100 requires £5 of further expenditure in getting it ready for sale and then selling it (eg £5 of processing costs and distribution costs). If its expected selling price is £140, its NRV is £(140-5) = £135. To value it at £135 in the balance sheet would still be to anticipate a £35 profit.

3.7 We are left with **historical cost** as the normal basis of stock valuation. **The only time when historical cost is not used is in the exceptional cases where the prudence concept requires a lower value to be used.**

3.8 Staying with the example in paragraph 3.6, suppose that the market in this kind of product suddenly slumps and the item's expected selling price is only £90. The item's NRV is then £(90 – 5) = £85 and the business has in effect made a loss of £15 (£100 – £85). The prudence concept requires that losses should be recognised as soon as they are foreseen. This can be achieved by valuing the stock item in the balance sheet at its NRV of £85.

Lower of cost and NRV

3.9 The argument developed above suggests that the rule to follow is that stocks should be valued at cost, or if lower, net realisable value. The accounting treatment of stock is governed by an accounting standard, SSAP 9 *Stocks and long-term contracts*. SSAP 9 states that **stock should be valued at the lower of cost and net realisable value**. This is an important rule and one which you should learn by heart.

> **RULE TO LEARN**
>
> Stocks should be valued at the lower of cost and net realisable value.

Part C: Double entry bookkeeping and accounting treatments

Applying the basic valuation rule

3.10 If a business has many stock items on hand the comparison of cost and NRV should theoretically be carried out for each item separately. It is not sufficient to compare the total cost of all stock items with their total NRV. An example will show why.

3.11 Suppose a company has four items of stock on hand at the end of its accounting period. Their cost and NRVs are as follows:

Stock item	Cost £	NRV £	Lower of cost/NRV £
1	27	32	27
2	14	8	8
3	43	55	43
4	29	40	29
	113	135	107

3.12 It would be incorrect to compare total costs (£113) with total NRV (£135) and to state stocks at £113 in the balance sheet. The company can foresee a loss of £6 on item 2 and this should be recognised. If the four items are taken together in total the loss on item 2 is masked by the anticipated profits on the other items. By performing the cost/NRV comparison for each item separately the prudent valuation of £107 can be derived. This is the value which should appear in the balance sheet.

3.13 However, for a company with large amounts of stock this procedure may be impracticable. In this case it is acceptable to group similar items into categories and perform the comparison of cost and NRV category by category, rather than item by item.

Question 2

From the following figures, calculate the figure for stock valuation:

(a) Category by category
(b) Item by item

Stock at 31 December 20X7

Item	Categories	Cost	Net realisable value
1	A	560	660
2	A	880	740
3	A	780	960
4	B	340	500
5	B	420	620
6	C	800	700
7	C	1,720	1,200
8	D	1,140	1,320
9	D	1,540	1,980

Answer

(a) Category by category:

			£
A	Lower of (560 + 880 + 780) or (660 + 740 + 960)		
	ie 2,220 or 2,360		2,220
B	Lower of (340 + 420) or (500 + 620)		
	ie 760 or 1,120		760
C	Lower of (860 + 1,720) or (700 + 1,200)		
	ie 2,520 or 1,900		1,900
D	Lower of (1,140 + 1,540) or (1,320 + 1,980)		
	ie 2,680 or 3,300		2,680
			7,560

(b) Item by item: 560 + 740 + 780 + 340 + 420 + 700 + 1,200 + 1,140 + 1,540 = £7,420

3.14 So have we now solved the problem of how a business should value its stocks? It seems that all the business has to do is to choose the lower of cost and net realisable value. This is true as far as it goes, but there is one further problem, perhaps not so easy to foresee: for a given item of stock, **what was** the **cost**?

Determining the purchase cost

3.15 Stock may be **raw materials** or components bought from suppliers, **finished goods** which have been made by the business but not yet sold, or work in the process of production, but only part-completed (this type of stock is called **work in progress** or WIP). It will simplify matters, however, if we think about the historical cost of purchased raw materials and components, which ought to be their purchase price.

3.16 A business may be continually purchasing consignments of a particular component. As each consignment is received from suppliers they are stored in the appropriate bin or on the appropriate shelf or pallet, where they will be mingled with previous consignments. When the storekeeper issues components to production he will simply pull out from the bin the nearest components to hand, which may have arrived in the latest consignment or in an earlier consignment or in several different consignments. Our concern is to devise a pricing technique, a rule of thumb which we can use to attribute a cost to each of the components issued from stores.

3.17 There are several techniques which are used in practice.

> **KEY TERMS**
>
> (a) **FIFO (first in, first out)**. Using this technique, we assume that components are used in the order in which they are received from suppliers. The components issued are deemed to have formed part of the oldest consignment still unused and are costed accordingly.
>
> (b) **LIFO (last in, first out)**. This involves the opposite assumption, that components issued to production originally formed part of the most recent delivery, while older consignments lie in the bin undisturbed.
>
> (c) **Average cost**. As purchase prices change with each new consignment, the average price of components in the bin is constantly changed. Each component in the bin at any moment is assumed to have been purchased at the average price of all components in the bin at that moment.

3.18 Any or all of these methods might provide a suitable basis for valuing stocks. But it is worth mentioning here that if you are preparing **financial accounts** you would normally expect to use FIFO or average costs for the balance sheet valuation of stock. **SSAP 9 specifically discourages the use of LIFO costs**. Nevertheless, you should know about all of the methods so that you can discuss the differences between them. You should note furthermore that terms such as LIFO and FIFO refer to **pricing techniques** only. The actual components can be used in any order.

3.19 To illustrate the various pricing methods, the following transactions will be used in each case:

Part C: Double entry bookkeeping and accounting treatments

TRANSACTIONS DURING MAY 20X3

	Quantity Units	Unit cost £	Total cost £	Market value per unit on date of transactions £
Opening balance 1 May	100	2.00	200	
Receipts 3 May	400	2.10	840	2.11
Issues 4 May	200			2.11
Receipts 9 May	300	2.12	636	2.15
Issues 11 May	400			2.20
Receipts 18 May	100	2.40	240	2.35
Issues 20 May	100			2.35
Closing balance 31 May	200			2.38
			1,916	

Receipts mean goods are received into store and issues represent the issue of goods from store.

The problem is to put a valuation on:

(a) The issues of materials
(b) The closing stock

How would issues and closing stock be valued using:

(a) FIFO?
(b) LIFO?
(c) Average cost?

FIFO (first in, first out)

3.20 FIFO assumes that materials are **issued out of stock in the order in which they were delivered into stock**, ie issues are priced at the cost of the earliest delivery remaining in stock.

The cost of issues and closing stock value in the example, using FIFO would be as follows (note that o/s stands for opening stock).

Date of issue	Quantity Units	Value issued £	Cost of issues £ £
4 May	200	100 o/s at £2	200
		100 at £2.10	210
			410
11 May	400	300 at £2.10	630
		100 at £2.12	212
			842
20 May	100	100 at £2.12	212
			1,464
Closing stock value	200	100 at £2.12	212
		100 at £2.40	240
			452
			1,916

Note that the cost of materials issued plus the value of closing stock equals the cost of purchases plus the value of opening stock (£1,916).

9: Accounting for stocks

LIFO (last in, first out)

3.21 LIFO assumes that materials are **issued out of stock in the reverse order to which they were delivered**, ie most recent deliveries are issued before earlier ones, and are priced accordingly.

3.22 The following table shows a method of calculating the cost of issues and the closing stock value under the LIFO method.

		Opening stock in units	Purchases in units 3 May	9 May	18 May
Issues		100	400	300	100
4 May			(200)		
11 May			(100)	(300)	
20 May					(100)
Closing stock		100	100	-	-

				£	£
Issues	4 May	200 @ £2.10			420
	11 May	300 @ £2.12		636	
		100 @ £2.10		210	
					846
	20 May	100 @ £2.40			240
Cost of materials issued					1,506
		100 @ £2.00		200	
Closing stock valuation:		100 @ £2.10		220	
					410
					1,916

Again, note that the cost of materials issued plus the value of closing stock equals the cost of purchases plus the value of opening stock (£1,916).

Average cost

3.23 There are various ways in which average costs may be used in pricing stock issues. The most common (cumulative weighted average pricing) is illustrated below.

3.24 The **cumulative weighted average pricing method** calculates a weighted average price for all units in stock. Issues are priced at this average cost, and the balance of stock remaining would have the same unit valuation.

A new weighted average price is calculated whenever a new delivery of materials into store is received. This is the key feature of cumulative weighted average pricing.

3.25 In our example, issue costs and closing stock values would be as follows.

Part C: Double entry bookkeeping and accounting treatments

Date	Received Units	Issued Units	Balance Units	Total stock value £	Unit cost £	Price of issue £
Opening stock			100	200	2.00	
3 May	400			840	2.10	
			500	1,040	2.08 ★	
4 May		200		(416)	2.08 ★★	416
			300	624	2.08	
9 May	300			636	2.12	
			600	1,260	2.10 ★	
11 May		400		(840)	2.10 ★★	840
			200	420	2.10	
18 May	100			240	2.40	
			300	660	2.20 ★	
20 May		100		(220)	2.20 ★★	220
						1,476
Closing stock value			200	440	2.20	440
						1,916

★ A new unit cost of stock is calculated whenever a new receipt of materials occurs.

★★ Whenever stocks are issued, the unit value of the items issued is the current weighted average cost per unit at the time of the issue.

For this method too, the cost of materials issued plus the value of closing stock equals the cost of purchases plus the value of opening stock (£1,916).

Stock valuations and profit

3.26 In the previous descriptions of FIFO, LIFO and average cost, the example used raw materials as an illustration. Each method of valuation produced different costs both of closing stocks and also of material issues. Since raw material costs affect the cost of production, and the cost of production works through eventually into the cost of sales, it follows that different methods of stock valuation will provide different profit figures. An example may help to illustrate this point.

3.27 EXAMPLE: STOCK VALUATIONS AND PROFIT

On 1 November 20X2 a company held 300 units of finished goods item No 9639 in stock. These were valued at £12 each. During November 20X2 three batches of finished goods were received into store from the production department as follows:

Date	Units received	Production cost per unit
10 November	400	£12.50
20 November	400	£14
25 November	400	£15

Goods sold out of stock during November were as follows:

Date	Units sold	Sale price per unit
14 November	500	£20
21 November	500	£20
28 November	100	£20

What was the profit from selling stock item 9639 in November 20X2, applying the following principles of stock valuation:

(a) FIFO
(b) LIFO
(c) Cumulative weighted average costing?

Ignore administration, sales and distribution costs.

3.28 SOLUTION

(a) FIFO

		Issue cost Total £	Closing stock £
Date	Issue costs		
14 November	300 units × £12 plus		
	200 units × £12.50	6,100	
21 November	200 units × £12.50 plus		
	300 units × £14	6,700	
28 November	100 units × £14	1,400	
Closing stock	400 units × £15		6,000
		14,200	6,000

(b) LIFO

14 November	400 units × £12.50 plus		
	100 units × £12	6,200	
21 November	400 units × £14 plus		
	100 units × £12	6,800	
28 November	100 units × £15	1,500	
Closing stock	300 units × £15 plus		
	100 units × £12		5,700
		14,500	5,700

(c) Cumulative weighted average costs:

			Unit cost £	Balance in stock £	Total cost of issues £	Closing stock £
1 November	Opening stock	300	12.000	3,600		
10 November		400	12.500	5,000		
		700	12.286	8,600		
14 November		500	12.286	6,143	6,143	
		200	12.286	2,457		
20 November		400	14.000	5,600		
		600	13.428	8,057		
21 November		500	13.428	6,714	6,714	
		100	13.428	1,343		
25 November		400	15.000	6,000		
		500	14.686	7,343		
28 November		100	14.686	1,469	1,469	
30 November		400	14.686	5,874	14,326	5,874

Part C: Double entry bookkeeping and accounting treatments

Summary: profit

	FIFO £	LIFO £	Weighted average £
Opening stock	3,600	3,600	3,600
Cost of production	16,600	16,600	16,600
	20,200	20,200	20,200
Closing stock	6,000	5,700	5,874
Cost of sales	14,200	14,500	14,326
Sales (1,100 × £20)	22,000	22,000	22,000
Profit	7,800	7,500	7,674

3.29 Different stock valuations have produced different cost of sales figures, and therefore different profits. In our example opening stock values are the same, therefore the difference in the amount of profit under each method is the same as the difference in the valuations of closing stock.

3.30 The profit differences are only temporary. In our example, the opening stock in December 20X2 will be £6,000, £5,700 or £5,874, depending on the stock valuation used. Different opening stock values will affect the cost of sales and profits in December, so that in the long run inequalities in costs of sales each month will even themselves out.

Exam focus point
If you have to work out the closing stock value using one of the above rules you must set out your schedule neatly and clearly.

9: Accounting for stocks

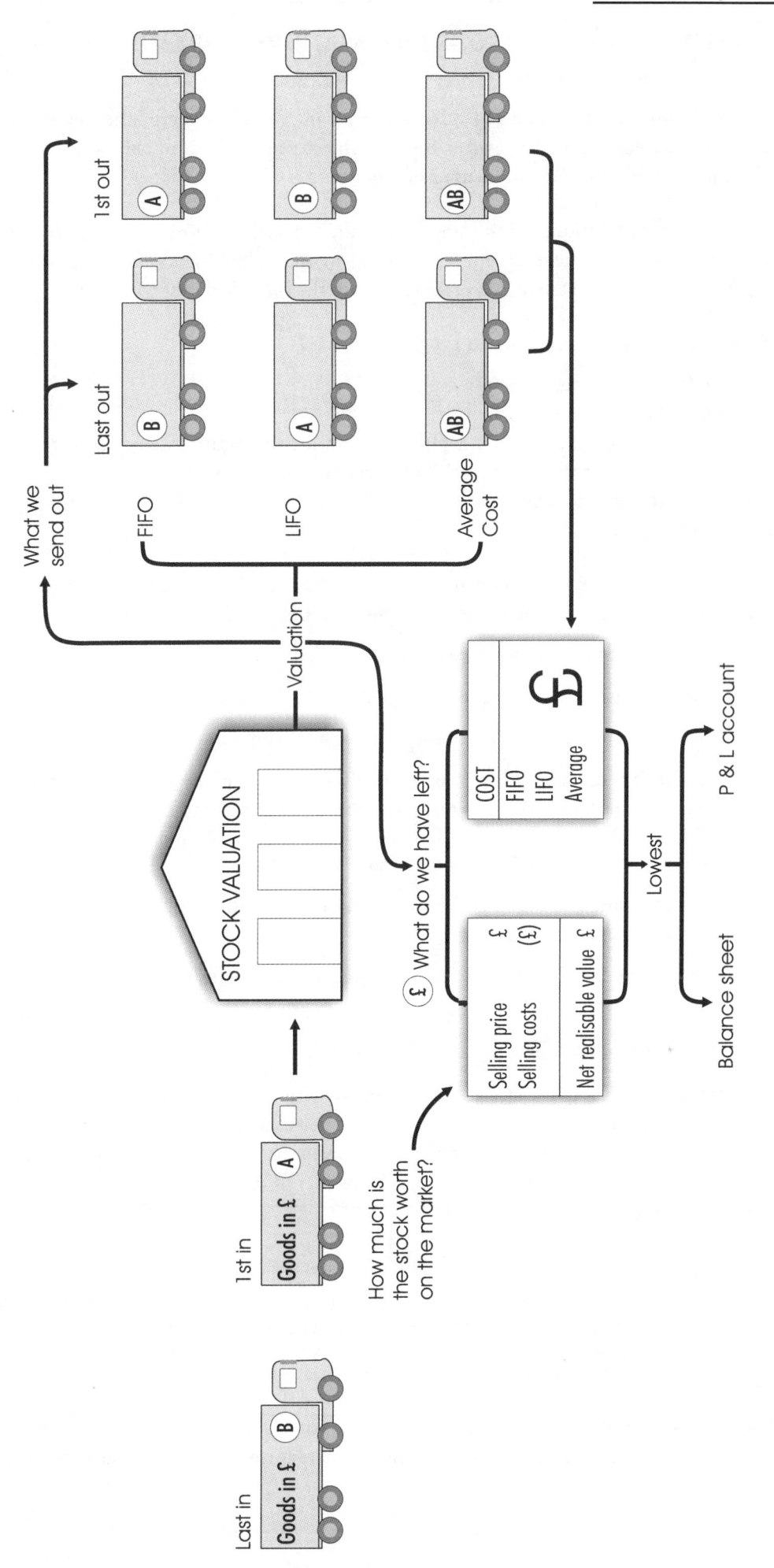

Part C: Double entry bookkeeping and accounting treatments

4 STATUTORY REGULATIONS AND SSAP 9 REQUIREMENTS Pilot paper, December 2002

4.1 In most businesses the value put on stock is an important factor in the determination of profit. Stock valuation is, however, a highly subjective exercise and consequently there is a wide variety of different methods used in practice.

4.2 The **statutory regulations** (now embodied in the CA 1985) and SSAP 9 requirements have been developed to achieve greater uniformity in the valuation methods used and in the disclosure in financial statements prepared under the historical cost convention.

4.3 SSAP 9 defines stocks and work in progress as:

(a) Goods or other assets purchased for resale
(b) Consumable stores
(c) Raw materials and components purchased for incorporation into products for sale
(d) Products and services in intermediate stages of completion
(e) Long-term contract balances
(f) Finished goods

4.4 In published accounts, the Companies Act 1985 requires that these stock categories should be grouped and disclosed under the following headings:

(a) Raw materials and consumables (ie (c) and (b) above)

(b) Work in progress (ie (d) and (e) above)

(c) Finished goods and goods for resale (ie (f) and (a) above)

(d) Payments on account. This is presumably intended to cover the case of a company which has paid for stock items but not yet received them into stock

4.5 A distinction is also made in SSAP 9 between:

(a) Stocks and work in progress other than long-term contract work in progress
(b) Long-term contract work in progress.

Long-term contracts are outside the scope of your Paper 1.1 studies.

Determination of the cost of stock

4.6 To determine profit, **costs should be matched with related revenues**. Since the cost of unsold stock and work in progress at the end of an accounting period has been incurred in the expectation of future sales revenue, it is appropriate to carry these costs forward in the balance sheet, and to charge them against the profits of the period in which the future sales revenue is eventually earned.

4.7 However, as the explanatory note to SSAP 9 expresses it:

'If there is no reasonable expectation of sufficient future revenue to cover cost incurred (eg as a result of deterioration, obsolescence or a change in demand) the irrecoverable cost should be charged to revenue in the year under review. Thus stocks normally need to be stated at cost, or, if lower, at net realisable value.'

4.8 The **comparison** of cost and net realisable value should be made **separately** for **each** item of stock, but if this is impracticable, **similar categories** of stock item can be grouped together.

9: Accounting for stocks

4.9 This valuation principle has now been given legislative backing by the CA 1985, which requires that the amount to be included in the balance sheet in respect of any current asset (including stocks) is the lower of its purchase price or production cost, and its net realisable value. However, the CA 1985 (under its alternative accounting rules) allows stocks to be stated at their **current cost**. If historical costs are used in determining purchase price or production cost, the difference between the historical cost and the current cost valuations must be stated.

4.10 The SSAP 9 definition of NRV is as follows.

'Net realisable value: the actual or estimated selling price (net of trade but before settlement discounts) less:

(a) All further costs to completion.
(b) All costs to be incurred in marketing, selling and distributing.'

4.11 The cost of stocks is harder to determine. SSAP 9 states:

'Cost is .... that expenditure which has been incurred in the normal course of business in bringing the product or service to its present location and condition. This expenditure should include, in addition to the cost of purchase, such costs of conversion as are appropriate to that location and condition.

Cost of purchase comprises purchase price including import duties, transport and handling costs and any other directly attributable costs, less trade discounts, rebates and subsidies.

Cost of conversion comprises:

(a) Costs which are specifically attributable to units of production, eg direct labour, direct expenses and sub-contracted work.
(b) Production overheads.
(c) Other overheads, if any, attributable in the particular circumstances of the business to bringing the product or service to its present location and condition.'

4.12 The CA 1985 also allows (but, unlike SSAP 9, does not require) the inclusion of production overheads in the valuation of stock.

4.13 The CA 1985 additionally permits the inclusion of interest payable on capital borrowed to finance the production of the asset, to the extent that it accrues in respect of the period of production. Any interest so included must be disclosed in a note to the accounts. Such capitalisation of interest would also be an allowable addition to cost under SSAP 9 if it fell within the scope of part (c) quoted above.

4.14 Two further points to note concern the determination of cost of purchase (purchase price in CA 1985 terminology) and attributable production overhead.

4.15 SSAP 9 states the following general principle regarding **cost of purchase**:

'The methods used in allocating costs to stocks need to be selected with a view to providing the fairest possible approximation to the expenditure actually incurred.'

4.16 Appendix 1 to SSAP 9 mentions the following specific methods which may satisfy the general principle.

(a) Job costing
(b) Batch costing
(c) Process costing
(d) Standard costing
(e) Unit cost
(f) Average cost

Part C: Double entry bookkeeping and accounting treatments

(g) FIFO

4.17 The appendix also states that methods such as base stock and LIFO do not generally satisfy the principle, though it is worth noting that LIFO is, with FIFO and weighted average price, one of the methods specifically permitted by the CA 1985. The Act merely requires that the chosen method should be one which, in the directors' opinion, is appropriate to the company.

4.18 When **allocating production overheads to the valuation of stock** care must be taken to exclude all abnormal overheads such as exceptional spoilage, idle capacity and other losses which are avoidable under normal conditions. Refer again to the SSAP 9 definition of cost quoted in paragraph 4.11 above which allows only 'expenditure incurred in the normal course of business'.

4.19 The appendix to SSAP 9 provides practical guidelines on the valuation of stocks and work in progress. A detailed discussion of these is outside the scope of Paper 1.1 syllabus. It is relevant to note, however, that in the UK, the **Inland Revenue** accepts FIFO, average cost and (in the case of many retailing companies) 'selling price less normal gross profit margin' as stock valuation methods in arriving at taxable profit. It **does not accept LIFO**.

Question 3

Hudson Ltd specialises in retailing one product. The firm purchases its stock from a regional wholesaler and sells through a catalogue. Details of Hudson Ltd's purchases and sales for the three month period 1 January to 31 March 20X7 are as follows.

Purchases

Date	Quantity in units	Price per unit £
14 January	280	24
30 January	160	24
15 February	300	25
3 March	150	26
29 March	240	26

Sales

Date	Quantity in units	Price per unit £
22 January	170	60
4 February	140	60
18 February	90	63
26 February	70	64
4 March	110	64
19 March	200	66
30 March	80	66

Note: Hudson Ltd had no stock in hand at 1 January 20X7.

Required

(a) Record the company's stock movements for the period 1 January to 31 March by the preparation of a stores card applying:

    (i) First In First Out principles
    (ii) Last In First Out principles

(b) Prepare the firm's trading account for the three month period applying:

    (i) First In First Out principles
    (ii) Last In First Out principles

9: Accounting for stocks

(c) Note how SSAP 9 affects the valuation of a company's stock in trade.

Answer

(a) (i) FIFO

		Quantity		Movement	
		Move-ment	Balance	Unit cost £	Total value £
14 Jan	Receipt	280	280	24	6,720
22 Jan	Issue	(170)	110	24	(4,080)
30 Jan	Receipt	160	270	24	3,840
4 Feb	Issue	(140)	130	24	(3,360)
15 Feb	Receipt	300	430	25	7,500
18 Feb	Issue	(90)	340	24	(2,160)
26 Feb	Issue	(70)	270	40 24 / 30 25	(1,710)
3 Mar	Receipt	150	420	26	3,900
4 Mar	Issue	(110)	310	25	(2,750)
19 Mar	Issue	(200)	110	160 25 / 40 26	(5,040)
29 Mar	Receipt	240	350	26	6,240
30 Mar	Issue	(80)	270	26	(2,080)
		Total receipts			28,200
		Total issues			21,180
					7,020

(ii) LIFO

		Quantity		Movement	
		Move-ment	Balance	Unit cost £	Total value £
14 Jan	Receipt	280	280	24	6,720
22 Jan	Issue	(170)	110	24	(4,080)
30 Jan	Receipt	160	270	24	3,840
4 Feb	Issue	(140)	130	24	(3,360)
15 Feb	Receipt	300	430	25	7,500
18 Feb	Issue	(90)	340	25	(2,250)
26 Feb	Issue	(70)	270	25	(1,750)
3 Mar	Receipt	150	420	26	3,900
4 Mar	Issue	(110)	310	26	(2,860)
19 Mar	Issue	(200)	110	20 24 / 140 25 / 40 26	(5,020)
29 Mar	Receipt	240	350	26	6,240
30 Mar	Issue	(80)	270	26	(2,080)
		Total receipts			28,200
		Total issues			(21,400)
					6,800

Part C: Double entry bookkeeping and accounting treatments

(b) HUDSON
TRADING ACCOUNT FOR THE 3 MONTH PERIOD TO 31 MARCH 20X7

	FIFO		LIFO	
	£	£	£	£
Sales		54,270		54,270
Opening stock	-		-	
Purchases	28,200		28,200	
	28,200		28,200	
Closing stock	7,020		6,800	
Cost of sales		21,180		21,400
Gross profit		33,090		32,870

Workings: sales 1 Jan to 31 Mar X5

	Units	Selling price £	Sales value £
22 Jan	170	60	10,200
4 Feb	140	60	8,400
18 Feb	90	63	5,670
26 Feb	70	64	4,480
4 Mar	110	64	7,040
19 Mar	200	66	13,200
30 Mar	80	66	5,280
			54,270

(c) SSAP 9 states that stocks should be stated at the lower of cost and net realisable value. Cost is defined as the expenditure which has been incurred in the normal course of business in bringing the product or service to its present location and condition. Net realisable value is the actual or estimated selling price less all further costs to be incurred in realising the stock.

Chapter roundup

- The quantity of stocks held at the year end is established by means of a physical count of stock in an annual **stocktaking** exercise, or by a 'continuous' stocktake.

- The value of these stocks is then calculated, taking the **lower of cost and net realisable value** for each separate item or group of stock items.

- In order to value the stocks, some rule of thumb must be adopted. The possibilities include **FIFO, LIFO, and average costs**. But remember that in **financial accounts FIFO** or **average cost** should normally be used.

- **NRV** is the selling price less all costs to completion and less selling costs.

- **Cost** comprises purchase costs and costs of conversion.

- The value of closing stocks is accounted for in the nominal ledger by debiting a stock account and crediting the trading account at the end of an accounting period. The stock will therefore always have a debit balance at the end of a period, and this balance will be shown in the balance sheet as a **current asset** for stocks.

- **Opening stocks** brought forward in the stock account are transferred to the **trading account**, and so at the end of the accounting year, the balance on the stock account ceases to be the opening stock value b/f, and becomes instead the closing stock value c/f.

- The **Companies Act 1985** requires that the balance sheet should show stocks subdivided as follows.

    Stocks
    Raw materials and consumables
    Work in progress
    Finished goods and goods for resale
    Payments on account.

9: Accounting for stocks

Quick quiz

1   When is a stock account used?

2   How is closing stock incorporated in to the financial statements?

3   What is 'continuous' stocktaking?

4   An item of stock was purchased for £10. However, due to a fall in demand, its selling price will be only £8. In addition further costs will be incurred prior to sale of £1. What is the net realisable value?

    A   £7
    B   £8
    C   £10
    D   £11

5   Why is stock not valued at expected selling price?

6   Give three methods of pricing a stock item at historical cost.

7   What is included in the cost of purchase of stocks according to SSAP 9?

8   What are the most likely situations when the NRV of stocks falls below cost?

Answers to quick quiz

1   Only at the end of an accounting period.

2   DEBIT: Stock in hand (balance sheet)
    CREDIT: Closing stock (trading account)

3   A card is kept for every item of stock. It shows receipts and issues, with a running total. A few stock items are counted each day to test that the cards are correct.

4   A   Net realisable value is selling price (£8) less further costs to sale (£1), ie £7.

5   Mainly because this would result in the business taking a profit before the goods have been sold.

6
- FIFO
- LIFO
- Average cost

7   Purchase price **plus** import duties, **plus** transport costs, **plus** any other directly attributable costs **less** trade discount.

8
- Increase in costs or a fall in selling price
- Physical deterioration of stock
- Obsolescence
- Marketing strategy
- Errors in production or purchasing

Now try the question below from the Exam Question Bank

Question to try	Level	Marks	Time
14	Introductory	n/a	36 mins

Chapter 10

FIXED ASSETS - DEPRECIATION, DISPOSAL AND REVALUATION

Topic list	Syllabus reference
1 Depreciation	4(a)
2 Fixed asset disposals	4(a)
3 Fixed assets: statutory requirements	4(a), 5(c), 5(d)
4 FRS 15 Tangible fixed assets	4(a), 5(c), 5(d)
5 Revaluations	4(a)
6 The fixed assets register	3(a)
7 Preparation of final accounts for a sole trader	5(d)

Introduction

You should by now be familiar with the distinction between **fixed and current assets**, a fixed asset being one bought for ongoing use in the business. If you are unsure of this, look back to Chapter 3 to refresh your memory.

Fixed assets might be held and used by a business for a number of years, but they wear out or lose their usefulness in the course of time. Nearly every tangible fixed asset has a **limited** life. The process by which this is recognised in the accounts is **depreciation**, and this is discussed in Section 1.

Section 2 deals with **disposals** of fixed assets. A profit may arise on the sale of a fixed asset if too much depreciation has been charged.

Section 3 deals with the statutory requirements relating to fixed assets. Fixed assets are the subject of a *financial reporting standard* (FRS 15), which you will need to know for your exam. The standard is fairly straightforward and is discussed in Section 4.

Occasionally, particularly in the case of land or buildings, the market value of a fixed asset will rise with time. The asset may then be **revalued**. The accounting treatment of revaluations and the effect on depreciation are considered in Section 5.

Section 6 looks at how organisations record their fixed assets.

You are now ready to prepare the accounts of a sole trader! Section 7 shows you how.

Study guide

Section 8 – The financial statements of a sole trader 2; depreciation and bad and doubtful debts

- Revise the difference between fixed assets and current assets.
- Define and explain the purpose of depreciation as stated in FRS 15 *Tangible fixed assets*.
- Explain the advantages, disadvantages and calculation of the straight line, reducing balance and sum of digits methods of depreciation.

- Explain the relevance of consistency and subjectivity in accounting for depreciation.
- Explain how depreciation is presented in the profit and loss account and balance sheet.
- Explain how depreciation expense and accumulated depreciation are recorded in ledger accounts.
- Prepare a set of financial statements for a sole trader from a trial balance, after allowing for accruals and prepayments, depreciation and bad and doubtful debts.

Section 16 – Recording and presentation of transactions in fixed assets; liabilities and provisions

- Explain and illustrate the ledger entries to record the acquisition and disposal of fixed assets, using separate accounts for fixed asset cost and accumulated depreciation.
- Explain and illustrate the inclusion of profits or losses on disposal in the profit and loss account.
- Explain that the upward revaluation of an asset cannot constitute a gain which may appear in the profit and loss account.
- Explain how to record the revaluation of a fixed asset in ledger accounts and the effect in the balance sheet.
- Explain why, after an upward revaluation, depreciation must be based on the revised figure, referring to the requirements of FRS 15 *Tangible fixed assets*.
- Explain the adjustments necessary if changes are made in the estimated useful life and/or residual value of a fixed asset.
- Explain how fixed asset balances and movements are disclosed in company financial statements in accordance with FRS 15 *Tangible fixed assets* and the Companies Acts.

Exam guide

This is a key subject area. You will need to calculate depreciation and perhaps the profit or loss on disposal of a fixed asset when you are preparing accounts. You also need to understand the main points of FRS 15 *Tangible fixed assets* well enough to write about them for, say, 10 marks in the exam.

1 DEPRECIATION   June 2002, December 2002

1.1 This section is a detailed look at depreciation and how it is calculated. Depreciation is also discussed in section 4 when we will see how FRS 15 affects the use of depreciation.

1.2 A fixed asset is acquired for use within a business with a view to earning profits. Its life extends over more than one accounting period, and so it earns profits over more than one period. In contrast, a current asset is used and replaced many times within the period eg stock is sold and replaced, debtors increase with sales and decrease with payments received.

1.3 With the exception of land held on freehold or very long leasehold, every fixed asset eventually wears out over time. Machines, cars and other vehicles, fixtures and fittings, and even buildings do not last for ever. When a business acquires a fixed asset, it will have some idea about how long its useful life will be, and it might decide:

(a) To keep on using the fixed asset until it becomes completely worn out, useless, and worthless.

(b) To sell off the fixed asset at the end of its useful life, either by selling it as a second-hand item or as scrap.

1.4 Since a fixed asset has a cost, and a limited useful life, and its value eventually declines, it follows that a charge should be made in the trading, profit and loss account to reflect the use that is made of the asset by the business. This charge is called **depreciation**.

161

Part C: Double entry bookkeeping and accounting treatments

Definition of depreciation

1.5 Suppose that a business buys a machine for £40,000. Its expected life is four years, and at the end of that time it is expected to be worthless.

1.6 Since the fixed asset is used to make profits for four years, it would be reasonable to charge the cost of the asset over those four years (perhaps by charging £10,000 per annum) so that at the end of the four years the total cost of £40,000 would have been charged against profits.

1.7 Indeed, one way of defining depreciation is to describe it as **a means of spreading the cost of a fixed asset over its useful life**, and so matching the cost against the full period during which it earns profits for the business. Depreciation charges are an example of the application of the accruals (or matching) concept to calculate profits.

1.8 Depreciation has two important aspects.
   (a) Depreciation is a **measure of the wearing out** or depletion of a fixed asset through use, time or obsolescence.
   (b) Depreciation charges should be **spread fairly** over a fixed asset's life, and so allocated to the accounting periods which are expected to benefit (ie make profits) from the asset's use.

The total charge for depreciation: the depreciable amount

1.9 The total amount to be charged over the life of a fixed asset ('the depreciable amount') is usually its cost less any expected 'residual' sales value or disposal value at the end of the asset's life.
   (a) A fixed asset costing £20,000, which has an expected life of five years and an expected residual value of nil, should be depreciated by £20,000 in total over the five year period.
   (b) A fixed asset costing £20,000, which has an expected life of five years and an expected residual value of £3,000, should be depreciated by £17,000 in total over the five years.

Depreciation in the accounts of a business

1.10 When a fixed asset is depreciated, two things must be accounted for.
   (a) The **charge for depreciation** is a **cost or expense** of the accounting period. Depreciation is an expense in the profit and loss account.
   (b) At the same time, the fixed asset is wearing out and diminishing in value. So the value of the fixed asset in the balance sheet must be reduced by the amount of depreciation charged. The balance sheet value of the fixed asset will be its '**net book value**', which is the value after depreciation in the books of account of the business.

1.11 The amount of depreciation will build up (or 'accumulate') over time, as more depreciation is charged in each successive accounting period. This accumulated depreciation is a 'provision' because it provides for the fall in value in use of the fixed asset. The term 'provision for depreciation' means the 'accumulated depreciation' of a fixed asset.

10: Fixed assets - depreciation, disposal and revaluation

1.12 For example, if a fixed asset costing £40,000 has an expected life of four years and an estimated residual value of nil, it might be depreciated by £10,000 per annum.

	Depreciation charge for the year (P & L a/c) (A) £	Accumulated depreciation at end of year (B) £	Cost of the asset (C) £	Net book value at end of year (C-B) £
At beginning of its life	-	-	40,000	40,000
Year 1	10,000	10,000	40,000	30,000
Year 2	10,000	20,000	40,000	20,000
Year 3	10,000	30,000	40,000	10,000
Year 4	10,000	40,000	40,000	0

1.13 So each year, £10,000 depreciation is charged as an expense in the profit and loss account. Also each year, the net book value (NBV) recorded in the balance sheet reduces by £10,000 until the NBV reaches the residual value (nil in this case).

Methods of depreciation

1.14 There are several different methods of depreciation. Of these, the ones you need to know about are:

- Straight line method
- Reducing balance method
- Sum of the digits method

The straight line method

1.15 This is the most commonly used method of all. The total depreciable amount is charged in equal instalments to each accounting period over the expected useful life of the asset. So the net book value of the fixed asset declines at a steady rate, or in a 'straight line' over time.

1.16 The annual depreciation charge is calculated as:

$$\frac{\text{Cost of asset minus residual value}}{\text{Expected useful life of the asset}}$$

1.17 EXAMPLE: STRAIGHT LINE DEPRECIATION

(a) A fixed asset costing £20,000 with an estimated life of 10 years and no residual value would be depreciated at the rate of:

$$\frac{£20,000}{10 \text{ years}} = £2,000 \text{ per annum}$$

(b) A fixed asset costing £60,000 has an estimated life of 5 years and a residual value of £7,000. The annual depreciation charge using the straight line method would be:

$$\frac{£(60,000 - 7,000)}{5 \text{ years}} = £10,600 \text{ per annum}$$

The net book value of the fixed asset would be:

Part C: Double entry bookkeeping and accounting treatments

	After 1 year £	After 2 years £	After 3 years £	After 4 years £	After 5 years £
Cost of the asset	60,000	60,000	60,000	60,000	60,000
Accumulated depreciation	10,600	21,200	31,800	42,400	53,000
Net book value	49,400	38,800	28,200	17,600	7,000 *

* ie its estimated residual value.

1.18 Since the depreciation charge per annum is the same amount every year with the straight line method, it is often convenient to state that depreciation is charged at the rate of x per cent per annum on the cost of the asset. In the example in paragraph 1.17(a) above, the depreciation charge per annum is 10% of cost (ie 10% of £20,000 = £2,000).

Examination questions often describe straight line depreciation in this way.

1.19 The straight line method of depreciation is a fair allocation of the total depreciable amount between the different accounting periods, provided the business enjoys equal benefits from the use of the asset in every period throughout its life.

Assets acquired in the middle of an accounting period

1.20 A business can purchase new fixed assets at any time during the course of an accounting period. So it might seem fair to charge a reduced amount for depreciation in the period when the purchase occurs.

1.21 EXAMPLE: ASSETS ACQUIRED IN THE MIDDLE OF AN ACCOUNTING PERIOD

A business which has an accounting year which runs from 1 January to 31 December purchases a new fixed asset on 1 April 20X1, at a cost of £24,000. The expected life of the asset is 4 years, and its residual value is nil. What should be the depreciation charge for 20X1?

1.22 SOLUTION

The annual depreciation charge will be $\dfrac{24,000}{4 \text{ years}}$ = £6,000 per annum

However, since the asset was acquired on 1 April 20X1, the business has only benefited from the use of the asset for 9 months instead of a full 12 months. It would therefore seem fair to charge depreciation in 20X1 of only

$\dfrac{9}{12} \times £6,000 = £4,500$

> **Exam focus point**
> If an examination question gives you the purchase or disposal date of a fixed asset, part way through an accounting period, you should assume that depreciation is calculated as a 'part-year' amount, unless told to the contrary in the question. However, you will only be given such a problem when the straight line method of depreciation is used.

1.23 In practice, many businesses ignore the niceties of part-year depreciation, and charge a full year's depreciation on fixed assets in the year of their purchase and/or disposal, regardless of the time of year they were acquired.

The reducing balance method

1.24 The **reducing balance method** of depreciation calculates the depreciation charge as a fixed percentage of the net book value of the asset, as at the end of the accounting period.

1.25 For example, a business purchases a fixed asset at a cost of £10,000. Its expected useful life is 3 years and its estimated residual value is £2,160. The business wishes to use the reducing balance method to depreciate the asset, and calculates that the rate of depreciation should be 40% of the reducing balance (NBV) of the asset. (The method of deciding that 40% is a suitable annual percentage is a problem of mathematics, not financial accounting, and is not described here.)

The total depreciable amount is £(10,000 − 2,160) = £7,840.

The depreciation charge per annum and the net book value of the asset as at the end of each year will be as follows:

	NBV £	Accumulated depreciation £	
Asset at cost	10,000		
Depreciation in year 1 (40% × £10,000)	4,000	4,000	
Net book value at end of year 1	6,000		
Depreciation in year 2 (40% × £6,000)	2,400	6,400	(4,000 + 2,400)
Net book value at end of year 2	3,600		
Depreciation in year 3 (40% × £3,600)	1,440	7,840	(6,400 + 1,440)
Net book value at end of year 3	2,160		

1.26 With the reducing balance method, the annual charge for depreciation is higher in the earlier years of the asset's life, and lower in the later years. In the example above, the annual charges for years 1, 2 and 3 are £4,000, £2,400 and £1,440 respectively. The reducing balance method, therefore, is used when it is considered fair to allocate a greater proportion of the total depreciable amount to the earlier years and a lower proportion to later years, on the assumption that the benefits obtained by the business from using the asset decline over time.

Exam focus point
It is likely that one of the above two methods will be tested in the exam rather than the sum of the digits method.

Sum of the digits method

1.27 This is a variant of the reducing balance method, based on the estimated useful life of an asset. If an asset has an estimated useful life of five years, then the digits 1, 2, 3, 4 and 5 are added together, giving a total of 15. Depreciation of 5/15, 4/15, 3/15, and so on, of the depreciable amount is charged in the respective years.

Part C: Double entry bookkeeping and accounting treatments

1.28 EXAMPLE: SUM OF THE DIGITS METHOD

A van cost £20,000 and is expected to be sold for £4,000 after four years. Calculate the depreciation to be provided in each of the years 1 to 4 using the sum of the digits method.

1.29 SOLUTION

Sum of digits = 1+2+3+4 = 10. Depreciable amount = £20,000 – £4,000 = £16,000

		£
Year 1	Cost	20,000
	Depreciation at 4/10 of £16,000	6,400
	Net book value	13,600
Year 2	Depreciation at 3/10 of £16,000	4,800
	Net book value	8,800
Year 3	Depreciation at 2/10 of £16,000	3,200
	Net book value	5,600
Year 4	Depreciation at 1/10 of £16,000	1,600
	Net book value	4,000*

*The residual value

Revaluation method

1.30 This is used when depreciation is charged on a value other than cost, ie a revalued amount. Revaluations are dealt with in Section 5 of this chapter.

Applying a depreciation method consistently

1.31 It is up to the business concerned to decide which method of depreciation to apply to its fixed assets. Once that decision has been made, however, it should not be changed - the chosen method of depreciation should be applied **consistently from year to year**. This is an instance of the consistency concept, which we will look at later in Chapter 14.

1.32 Similarly, it is up to the business to decide what a sensible life span for a fixed asset should be. Again, once that life span has been chosen, it should not be changed unless something unexpected happens to the fixed asset.

1.33 It is permissible for a business to depreciate different categories of fixed assets in different ways. For example, if a business owns three cars, then each car would normally be depreciated in the same way (eg by the straight line method); but another category of fixed asset, say, photocopiers, can be depreciated using a different method (eg by the sum of digits method).

Question 1

A lorry bought for a business cost £17,000. It is expected to last for five years and then be sold for scrap for £2,000.

Required

Work out the depreciation to be charged each year under:

(a) The straight line method
(b) The reducing balance method (using a rate of 35%)
(c) The sum of digits method.

10: Fixed assets - depreciation, disposal and revaluation

Answer

(a) Under the straight line method, depreciation for each of the five years is: $\frac{£17,000 - £2,000}{5}$ = £3,000 pa (5 × £3,000 = £15,000).

(b) Under the reducing balance method, depreciation for each of the five years is:

Year	Depreciation		
1	35% × £17,000	=	£5,950
2	35% × (£17,000 – £5,950) = 35% × £11,050	=	£3,868
3	35% × (£11,050 – £3,868) = 35% × £7,182	=	£2,514
4	35% × (£7,182 – £2,514) = 35% × £4,668	=	£1,634
5	Balance to bring book value down to £2,000 = £4,668 – £1,634 – £2,000	=	£1,034
			£15,000

(c) The sum of digits is 5+4+3+2+1=15 and the depreciable amount is £15,000 (£17,000 – £2,000).

Year		Depreciation (£)
1	5/15 x £15,000	5,000
2	4/15 x £15,000	4,000
3	3/15 x £15,000	3,000
4	2/15 x £15,000	2,000
5	1/15 x £15,000	1,000
		15,000

A fall in the value of a fixed asset

1.34 When the 'market' value of a fixed asset falls so that it is worth less than the amount of its net book value, and the fall in value is expected to be **permanent**, the asset should be **written down to its new low market value**. The charge in the profit and loss account for the permanent diminution in the value of the asset during the accounting period should then be:

	£
Net book value at the beginning of the period	X
Less: new reduced value	(X)
Equals: the charge for the diminution in the asset's value in the period.	X

1.35 EXAMPLE: FALL IN ASSET VALUE

A business purchased a leasehold property on 1 January 20X1 at a cost of £100,000. The lease has a 20 year life. After 5 years' use, on 1 January 20X6, the business decides that since property prices have fallen sharply, the leasehold is now worth only £60,000, and that the value of the asset should be reduced in the accounts of the business.

The leasehold was being depreciated at the rate of 5% per annum on cost.

1.36 Before the asset is reduced in value, the annual depreciation charge is:

$\frac{£100,000}{20 \text{ years}}$ = £5,000 per annum (= 5% of £100,000)

After 5 years, the accumulated depreciation would be £25,000, and the net book value of the leasehold £75,000, which is £15,000 more than the new asset value. This £15,000 should be written off as a charge for depreciation or fall in the asset's value in year 5, so that the total charge in year 5 is:

	£
Net book value of the leasehold after 4 years (£100,000 - 20,000)	80,000
Revised asset value at end of year 5	60,000
Charge against profit in year 5	20,000

An alternative method of calculation is:

	£
'Normal' depreciation charge per annum	5,000
Further fall in value, from net book value at end of year 5 to revised value	15,000
Charge against profit in year 5	20,000

1.37 The leasehold has a further 15 years to run, and its value is now £60,000. From year 6 to year 20, the annual charge for depreciation will be:

$$\frac{£60,000}{15 \text{ years}} = £4,000 \text{ per annum}$$

Change in expected life of an asset

1.38 The depreciation charge on a fixed asset depends not only on the cost (or value) of the asset and its estimated residual value, but also on its **estimated useful life**.

1.39 A business purchased a fixed asset costing £12,000 with an estimated life of four years and no residual value. If it used the straight line method of depreciation, it would make an annual provision of 25% of £12,000 = £3,000.

Now what would happen if the business decided after two years that the useful life of the asset has been underestimated, and it still had five more years in use to come (making its total life seven years)?

For the first two years, the asset was depreciated by £3,000 per annum, so that its net book value after two years is £(12,000 – 6,000) = £6,000. If the remaining life of the asset is now revised to five more years, the remaining amount to be depreciated (£6,000) is spread over the remaining life, giving an annual depreciation charge for the final five years of:

$$\frac{\text{Net book value at time of life readjustment, minus residual value}}{\text{New estimate of remaining useful life}}$$

$$= \frac{£6,000}{5 \text{ years}} = £1,200 \text{ per annum}$$

FORMULA TO LEARN

$$\text{New depreciation} = \frac{\text{NBV less residual value}}{\text{Revised useful life}}$$

1.40 The same formula is used if there is a **revision of residual value**.

1.41 In the example in paragraph 1.39, the business also decides that the fixed asset will have a residual value of £1,000 at the end of the five years. The new depreciation is calculated as follows:

$$\text{New depreciation} = \frac{\text{NBV less new residual value}}{\text{Revised useful life}}$$

$$= \frac{£6,000 - £1,000}{5}$$

$$= £1,000 \text{ per annum}$$

Depreciation is not a cash expense

1.42 Depreciation spreads the cost of a fixed asset (less its estimated residual value) over the asset's life. The cash payment for the fixed asset will be made when, or soon after, the asset is purchased. Therefore, annual depreciation of the asset in subsequent years is **not a cash expense**.

1.43 For example, a business purchased some shop fittings for £6,000 on 1 July 20X5 and paid for them in cash on that date.

Subsequently, depreciation may be charged at £600 pa for ten years. So each year £600 is deducted from profits and the net book value of the fittings goes down, but no actual cash is being paid. The cash was all paid on 1 July 20X5. So annual depreciation is not a cash expense, but rather an allocation of the original cost to later years.

Provision for depreciation

> **KEY TERM**
>
> A **provision for depreciation** is the amount written off for the wearing out of fixed assets.

1.44 There are two basic aspects of the provision for depreciation to remember:

(a) A depreciation charge (provision) is made in the profit and loss account in each accounting period for every depreciable fixed asset. Nearly all fixed assets are depreciable, the most important exceptions being freehold land and long-term investments.

(b) The total accumulated depreciation on a fixed asset builds up as the asset gets older. Unlike a provision for doubtful debts, therefore, the total provision for depreciation is always getting larger, until the fixed asset is fully depreciated.

1.45 If you understand these points, the similarity in the accounting treatment of the provision for doubtful debts and the provision for depreciation may become apparent to you.

1.46 The ledger accounting entries for the provision for depreciation are as follows.

(a) There is a provision for depreciation account for each separate category of fixed assets, for example, plant and machinery, land and buildings, fixtures and fittings.

Part C: Double entry bookkeeping and accounting treatments

(b) The depreciation charge for an accounting period is a charge against profit. It is an increase in the provision for depreciation and is accounted for as follows:
DEBIT   P & L account (depreciation expense)
CREDIT   Provision for depreciation account
with the depreciation charge for the period.

(c) The balance on the provision for depreciation account is the **total accumulated depreciation**. This is always a credit balance brought forward in the ledger account for depreciation.

(d) The fixed asset accounts are unaffected by depreciation. Fixed assets are recorded in these accounts at cost (or, if they are revalued, at their revalued amount).

(e) In the balance sheet of the business, the total balance on the provision for depreciation account (ie accumulated depreciation) is set against the value of fixed asset accounts (ie fixed assets at cost or revalued amount) to derive the net book value of the fixed assets.

1.47 EXAMPLE: PROVISION FOR DEPRECIATION

Brian Box set up his own computer software business on 1 March 20X6. He purchased a computer system on credit from a manufacturer, at a cost of £16,000. The system has an expected life of three years and a residual value of £2,500. Using the straight line method of depreciation, the fixed asset account, provision for depreciation account and P & L account (extract) and balance sheet (extract) would be as follows, for each of the next three years ended 28 February 20X7, 20X8 and 20X9.

FIXED ASSET - COMPUTER EQUIPMENT

	Date		£	Date		£
(a)	1.3.X6	Creditor	16,000	28.2.X7	Balance c/f	16,000
(b)	1.3.X7	Balance b/f	16,000	28.2.X8	Balance c/f	16,000
(c)	1.3.X8	Balance b/f	16,000	28.2.X9	Balance c/f	16,000
(d)	1.3.X9	Balance b/f	16,000			

In theory, the fixed asset has completed its expected useful life. However, until it is sold off or scrapped, the asset will still appear in the balance sheet at cost (less accumulated depreciation) and it should remain in the ledger account for computer equipment until it is eventually disposed of.

PROVISION FOR DEPRECIATION

	Date		£	Date		£
(a)	28.2.X7	Balance c/f	4,500	28.2.X7	P & L account	4,500
(b)	28.2.X8	Balance c/f	9,000	1.3.X7	Balance b/f	4,500
				28.2.X8	P & L account	4,500
			9,000			9,000
(c)	28.2.X9	Balance c/f	13,500	1.3.X8	Balance b/f	9,000
				28.2.X9	P & L account	4,500
			13,500			13,500
				1 Mar 20X9 Balance b/f		13,500

The annual depreciation charge is $\dfrac{(£16{,}000 - 2{,}500)}{3 \text{ years}} = £4{,}500 \text{ pa}$

At the end of three years, the asset is fully depreciated down to its residual value. If it continues to be used by Brian Box, it will not be depreciated any further (unless its estimated residual value is reduced).

P & L ACCOUNT (EXTRACT)

		Date		£
(a)		28 Feb 20X7	Provision for depreciation	4,500
(b)		28 Feb 20X8	Provision for depreciation	4,500
(c)		28 Feb 20X9	Provision for depreciation	4,500

BALANCE SHEET (EXTRACT) AS AT 28 FEBRUARY

	20X7	20X8	20X9
	£	£	£
Computer equipment at cost	16,000	16,000	16,000
Less accumulated depreciation	4,500	9,000	13,500
Net book value	11,500	7,000	2,500

1.48 EXAMPLE: PROVISION FOR DEPRECIATION WITH ASSETS ACQUIRED PART-WAY THROUGH THE YEAR

Brian Box prospers in his computer software business, and before long he purchases a car for himself, and later for his chief assistant Bill Ockhead. Relevant data is as follows:

	Date of purchase	Cost	Estimated life	Estimated residual value
Brian Box car	1 June 20X6	£20,000	3 years	£2,000
Bill Ockhead car	1 June 20X7	£8,000	3 years	£2,000

The straight line method of depreciation is to be used.

Prepare the motor vehicles account and provision for depreciation of motor vehicle account for the years to 28 February 20X7 and 20X8. (You should allow for the part-year's use of a car in computing the annual charge for depreciation.)

Calculate the net book value of the motor vehicles as at 28 February 20X8.

1.49 SOLUTION

(a) (i) Brian Box car Annual depreciation $\frac{£(20,000 - 2,000)}{3 \text{ years}} =$ £6,000 pa

Monthly depreciation £500
Depreciation 1 June-20X6 - 28 February 20X7 (9 months) £4,500
1 March 20X7 - 28 February 20X8 £6,000

(ii) Bill Ockhead car Annual depreciation $\frac{£(8,000 - 2,000)}{3 \text{ years}} =$ £2,000 pa

Depreciation 1 June 20X7 - 28 February 20X8 (9 months) £1,500

Part C: Double entry bookkeeping and accounting treatments

(b)

MOTOR VEHICLES

Date		£	Date		£
1 Jun 20X6	Creditors (or cash) (car purchase)	20,000	28 Feb 20X7	Balance c/f	20,000
1 Mar 20X7	Balance b/f	20,000			
1 Jun 20X7	Creditors (or cash) (car purchase)	8,000	28 Feb 20X8	Balance c/f	28,000
		28,000			28,000
1 Mar 20X8	Balance b/f	28,000			

PROVISION FOR DEPRECIATION OF MOTOR VEHICLES

Date		£	Date		£
28 Feb 20X7	Balance c/f	4,500	28 Feb 20X7	P & L account	4,500
			1 Mar 20X7	Balance b/f	4,500
28 Feb 20X8	Balance c/f	12,000	28 Feb 20X8	P & L account (6,000+1,500)	7,500
		12,000			12,000
			1 March 20X8	Balance b/f	12,000

BALANCE SHEET (WORKINGS) AS AT 28 FEBRUARY 20X8

	Brian Box car £	£	Bill Ockhead car £	£	Total £
Asset at cost		20,000		8,000	28,000
Accumulated depreciation:					
Year to:					
28 Feb 20X7	4,500		-		
28 Feb 20X8	6,000		1,500		
		10,500		1,500	12,000
Net book value		9,500		6,500	16,000

1.50 In practice the provision for depreciation account is usually known as the **accumulated depreciation** account.

2 FIXED ASSET DISPOSALS

June 2002

The disposal of fixed assets

2.1 Fixed assets are not purchased by a business with the intention of reselling them in the normal course of trade. However, they might be sold off at some stage, eg when their useful life is over. A business may sell off a fixed asset long before its useful life has ended, eg to get more a more up to date model.

2.2 Whenever a business sells something, it makes a profit or a loss. So when fixed assets are disposed of, there is a profit or loss on disposal. This is a **capital gain** or a **capital loss**.

2.3 These gains or losses are reported in the profit and loss account of the business (and not as a trading profit in the trading account). They are commonly referred to as '**profit on disposal of fixed assets**' or '**loss on disposal**'.

2.4 Examination questions on the disposal of fixed assets usually ask for ledger accounts to be prepared, showing the entries in the accounts to record the disposal. But before we look at the ledger accounting for disposing of assets, we had better look at the principles behind calculating the profit (or loss) on disposing of assets.

10: Fixed assets - depreciation, disposal and revaluation

The principles behind calculating the profit or loss on disposal

2.5 The profit or loss on the disposal of a fixed asset is the difference between:

(a) The net book value of the asset at the time of its sale.
(b) Its net sale price, which is the price minus any costs of making the sale.

A profit is made when the sale price exceeds the net book value, and a loss is made when the sale price is less than the net book value.

2.6 EXAMPLE: DISPOSAL OF A FIXED ASSET

A business purchased a fixed asset on 1 January 20X1 for £25,000. It had an estimated life of six years and an estimated residual value of £7,000. The asset was eventually sold after three years on 1 January 20X4 to another trader who paid £17,500 for it.

What was the profit or loss on disposal, assuming that the business uses the straight line method for depreciation?

2.7 SOLUTION

$$\text{Annual depreciation} = \frac{£(25,000 - 7,000)}{6 \text{ years}}$$

$$= £3,000 \text{ per annum}$$

	£
Cost of asset	25,000
Less accumulated depreciation (three years)	9,000
Net book value at date of disposal	16,000
Sale price	17,500
Profit on disposal	1,500

This profit will be shown in the profit and loss account of the business, where it will be an item of other income added to the gross profit brought down from the trading account, as shown below.

	£
Gross profit	30,000
Profit on disposal of fixed assets	1,500
	31,500
Expenses	21,500
Net profit	10,000

2.8 SECOND EXAMPLE: DISPOSAL OF A FIXED ASSET

A business purchased a machine on 1 July 20X1 at a cost of £35,000. The machine had an estimated residual value of £3,000 and a life of eight years. The machine was sold for £18,600 on 31 December 20X4, the last day of the accounting year of the business. To make the sale, the business had to incur dismantling costs and costs of transporting the machine to the buyer's premises. These amounted to £1,200.

The business uses the straight line method of depreciation. What was the profit or loss on disposal of the machine?

2.9 SOLUTION

$$\text{Annual depreciation} \quad \frac{£(35,000 - 3,000)}{8 \text{ years}} = £4,000 \text{ per annum}$$

Part C: Double entry bookkeeping and accounting treatments

It is assumed that in 20X1 only one-half year's depreciation was charged, because the asset was purchased six months into the year.

	£	£
Fixed asset at cost		35,000
Depreciation in 20X1 (6 months)	2,000	
20X2, 20X3 and 20X4 (3 years)	12,000	
Accumulated depreciation		14,000
Net book value at date of disposal		21,000
Sale price	18,600	
Costs incurred in making the sale	(1,200)	
Net sale price		17,400
Loss on disposal		(3,600)

This loss will be shown as an expense in the profit and loss account of the business. It is a capital loss, not a trading loss, and it should not therefore be shown in the trading account.

Profit and loss account (extract)

		£
Gross profit		30,000
Expenses	21,500	
Loss on sale of fixed assets	3,600	25,100
Net profit		4,900

The disposal of fixed assets: ledger accounting entries

2.10 A profit on disposal is an item of 'other income' in the P & L account, and a loss on disposal is an item of expense in the P & L account.

2.11 It is customary in ledger accounting to record the disposal of fixed assets in a **disposal of fixed assets** account.

   (a) The profit or loss on disposal is the difference between:

   (i) The sale price of the asset (if any).
   (ii) The net book value of the asset at the time of sale.

   (b) The relevant items which must appear in the disposal of fixed assets account are therefore:

   (i) The value of the asset (at cost, or revalued amount*).
   (ii) The accumulated depreciation up to the date of sale.
   (iii) The sale price of the asset.

   *To simplify the explanation of the rules, we will assume now that the fixed assets disposed of are valued at cost.

   (c) The ledger accounting entries are:

   (i) DEBIT   Disposal of fixed asset account
       CREDIT Fixed asset account

   With the cost of the asset disposed of.

   (ii) DEBIT   Provision for depreciation account (or accumulated depreciation account)
        CREDIT Disposal of fixed asset account

   With the accumulated depreciation on the asset as at the date of sale.

   (iii) DEBIT   Debtor account or cash book
         CREDIT Disposal of fixed asset account

   With the sale price of the asset. The sale is therefore not recorded in a sales account, but in the disposal of fixed asset account itself.

(iv) The balance on the disposal account is the profit or loss on disposal and the corresponding double entry is recorded in the P & L account itself.

> **Exam focus point**
>
> Calculation of profit or loss on disposal is likely to come up in an exam.

2.12 EXAMPLE: DISPOSAL OF ASSETS: LEDGER ACCOUNTING ENTRIES

A business has £110,000 worth of machinery at cost. Its policy is to make a provision for depreciation at 20% per annum straight line. The total provision now stands at £70,000. The business now sells for £19,000 a machine which it purchased exactly two years ago for £30,000.

Show the relevant ledger entries.

2.13 SOLUTION

PLANT AND MACHINERY ACCOUNT

	£		£
Balance b/f	110,000	Plant disposals account	30,000
		Balance c/f	80,000
	110,000		110,000
Balance b/f	80,000		

PLANT AND MACHINERY ACCUMULATED DEPRECIATION

	£		£
Plant disposals (20% of £30,000 for 2 years)	12,000	Balance b/f	70,000
Balance c/f	58,000		
	70,000		70,000
		Balance b/f	58,000

PLANT DISPOSALS

	£		£
Plant and machinery account	30,000	Accumulated depreciation	12,000
Profit and loss a/c (profit on sale)	1,000	Cash	19,000
	31,000		31,000

Check:

	£
Asset at cost	30,000
Accumulated depreciation at time of sale	12,000
Net book value at time of sale	18,000
Sale price	19,000
Profit on sale	1,000

2.14 EXAMPLE CONTINUED

Taking the example above assume that, instead of the machine being sold for £19,000, it was exchanged for a new machine costing £60,000, a credit of £19,000 being received upon exchange. In other words £19,000 is the trade-in price of the old machine. Now what are the relevant ledger account entries?

Part C: Double entry bookkeeping and accounting treatments

2.15 SOLUTION

PLANT AND MACHINERY ACCOUNT

	£		£
Balance b/f	110,000	Plant disposal	30,000
Cash (60,000 - 19,000)	41,000	Balance c/f	140,000
Plant disposals	19,000		
	170,000		170,000
Balance b/f	140,000		

The new asset is recorded in the fixed asset account at cost £(41,000 + 19,000) = £60,000.

PLANT AND MACHINERY ACCUMULATED DEPRECIATION

	£		£
Plant disposals (20% of £30,000 for 2 years)	12,000	Balance b/f	70,000
Balance c/f	58,000		
	70,000		70,000
		Balance b/f	58,000

PLANT DISPOSALS

	£		£
Plant and machinery	30,000	Accumulate depreciation	12,000
Profit transferred to P & L	1,000	Plant and machinery	19,000
	31,000		31,000

Question 2

A business purchased two widget-making machines on 1 January 20X5 at a cost of £15,000 each. Each had an estimated life of five years and a nil residual value. The straight line method of depreciation is used.

Owing to an unforeseen slump in market demand for widgets, the business decided to reduce its output of widgets, and switch to making other products instead. On 31 March 20X7, one widget-making machine was sold (on credit) to a buyer for £8,000.

Later in the year, however, it was decided to abandon production of widgets altogether, and the second machine was sold on 1 December 20X7 for £2,500 cash.

Prepare the machinery account, provision for depreciation of machinery account and disposal of machinery account for the accounting year to 31 December 20X7.

Answer

MACHINERY ACCOUNT

		£			£
20X7			20X7		
1 Jan	Balance b/f	30,000	31 Mar	Disposal of machinery account	15,000
			1 Dec	Disposal of machinery account	15,000
		30,000			30,000

10: Fixed assets - depreciation, disposal and revaluation

PROVISION FOR DEPRECIATION OF MACHINERY

20X7		£	20X7		£
31 Mar	Disposal of machinery account*	6,750	1 Jan	Balance b/f	12,000
1 Dec	Disposal of machinery account**	8,750	31 Dec	P & L account***	3,500
		15,500			15,500

* Depreciation at date of disposal £6,000 + £750
** Depreciation at date of disposal £6,000 + £2,750
*** Depreciation charge for the year = £750 + £2,750

DISPOSAL OF MACHINERY

20X7		£	20X7		£
31 Mar	Machinery account	15,000	31 Mar	Debtor account (sale price)	8,000
			31 Mar	Provision for depreciation	6,750
1 Dec	Machinery	15,000	1 Dec	Cash (sale price)	2,500
			1 Dec	Provision for depreciation	8,750
			31 Dec	P & L account (loss on disposal)	4,000
		30,000			30,000

You should be able to calculate that there was a loss on the first disposal of £250, and on the second disposal of £3,750, giving a total loss of £4,000.

Workings

1. At 1 January 20X7, accumulated depreciation on the machines will be

    2 machines × 2 years × $\frac{£15,000}{5}$ per machine pa = £12,000,

    or £6,000 per machine

2. Monthly depreciation is $\frac{£3,000}{12}$ = £250 per machine per month

3. The machines are disposed of in 20X7.

    (a) On 31 March - after 3 months of the year.
    Depreciation for the year on the machine = 3 months × £250 = £750.

    (b) On 1 December - after 11 months of the year.
    Depreciation for the year on the machine = 11 months × £250 = £2,750

3 FIXED ASSETS: STATUTORY REQUIREMENTS

3.1 This section acts as an introduction to the Companies Act requirements for all fixed assets.

Statutory provisions relating to all fixed assets

3.2 The standard balance sheet format of CA 1985 divides fixed assets into three categories:

(a) **Intangible assets**
(b) **Tangible assets**
(c) **Investments**

3.3 Companies Act requirements in regard to fixed assets may be considered under two headings.

Part C: Double entry bookkeeping and accounting treatments

(a) **Valuation:** the amounts at which fixed assets should be stated in the balance sheet.

(b) **Disclosure:** the information which should be disclosed in the accounts as to valuation of fixed assets and as to movements on fixed asset accounts during the year.

Valuation of fixed assets

3.4 Where an asset is **purchased**, its cost is simply the **purchase price plus any expenses incidental to its acquisition.**

3.5 Where an asset is **produced by a company for its own use**, its 'production cost' **must** include the cost of **raw materials, consumables** and **other attributable direct costs** (such as labour). Production cost may additionally include a reasonable proportion of indirect costs, together with the interest on any capital borrowed to finance production of the asset.

3.6 The 'cost' of any fixed asset having a limited economic life, whether purchase price or production cost, must be reduced by provisions for depreciation calculated to write off the cost, less any residual value, systematically over the period of the asset's useful life. This very general requirement is supplemented by the more detailed provisions of FRS 15 *Tangible fixed assets*.

3.7 Provision for a permanent reduction in value (now called impairment) of a fixed asset must be made in the profit and loss account and the asset should be disclosed at the reduced amount in the balance sheet. Any such provision should be disclosed on the face of the profit and loss account or by way of note. Where a provision becomes no longer necessary, because the conditions giving rise to it have altered, it should be written back, and again disclosure should be made.

Fixed assets valuation: alternative accounting rules

3.8 Although the Companies Act 1985 maintains historical cost principles as the normal basis for the preparation of accounts, **alternative bases** allowing for revaluations and current cost accounting are permitted provided that:

(a) The **items affected** and the **basis of valuation** are **disclosed** in a note to the accounts.

(b) The **historical cost** in the current and previous years is **separately disclosed** in the balance sheet or in a note to the accounts. Alternatively, the difference between the revalued amount and historical cost may be disclosed.

> **KEY TERM**
>
> Using the **alternative accounting rules** the appropriate value of any fixed asset (its current cost or market value), rather than its purchase price or production cost, may be included in the balance sheet.

3.9 Where appropriate, depreciation may be provided on the basis of the new valuation(s), such depreciation being referred to in the Companies Act 1985 as the 'adjusted amount' of depreciation. For profit and loss account purposes it is acceptable under the Companies Act to calculate (and disclose) depreciation in respect of any such fixed asset on the basis of historical cost. If the 'historical cost amount' rather than the 'adjusted amount' of depreciation were to be used in the profit and loss account, the difference between the two would be shown separately in the profit and loss account or in a note to the accounts.

(However, FRS 15 (see below) specifically states that depreciation must be charged on the revalued amount and that the *whole* charge must be taken to the profit and loss account.)

Revaluation reserve

3.10 Where the value of any fixed asset is determined by using the alternative accounting rules the amount of profit or loss arising must be credited or (as the case may be) debited to a separate reserve, the revaluation reserve. The calculation of the relevant amounts should be based on the written down values of the assets prior to revaluation.

3.11 The revaluation reserve must be reduced to the extent that the amounts standing to the credit of the reserves are, in the opinion of the directors of the company, no longer necessary for the purposes of the accounting policies adopted by the company. However, an amount may only be transferred from the reserve to the profit and loss account if either:

(a) The amount in question was previously charged to that account
(b) It represents realised profit (for example on disposal of a fixed asset).

The **only other** transfer possible from the revaluation reserve is on capitalisation, that is, when a bonus issue is made.

3.12 The amount of a revaluation reserve must be shown under a separate sub-heading on the balance sheet. However, the reserve need not necessarily be called a 'revaluation reserve'.

Fixed assets: disclosure

3.13 Notes to the accounts must show, for each class of fixed assets, an analysis of the movements on both costs and depreciation provisions.

3.14 The following format (with notional figures) is commonly used to disclose fixed assets movements.

Part C: Double entry bookkeeping and accounting treatments

	Total £	Land and buildings £	Plant and machinery £
Cost or valuation			
At 1 January 20X4	50,000	40,000	10,000
Revaluation surplus	12,000	12,000	–
Additions in year	4,000	–	4,000
Disposals in year	(1,000)	–	(1,000)
At 31 December 20X4	65,000	52,000	13,000
Depreciation			
At 1 January 20X4	16,000	10,000	6,000
Charge for year	4,000	1,000	3,000
Elimination on revaluation	–	(10,000)	–
Eliminated on disposals	(500)	–	(500)
At 31 December 20X4	9,500	1,000	8,500
Net book value			
At 31 December 20X4	55,500	51,000	4,500
At 1 January 20X4	34,000	30,000	4,000

3.15 Where any fixed assets of a company (other than listed investments) are included in the accounts at an alternative accounting valuation, the following information must also be given.

(a) The years (so far as they are known to the directors) in which the assets were severally valued and the several values

(b) In the case of assets that have been valued during the financial period, the names of the persons who valued them or particulars of their qualifications for doing so and (whichever is stated) the bases of valuation used by them.

3.16 A note to the accounts must classify land and buildings under the headings of:

(a) Freehold property

(b) Leasehold property, distinguishing between:

(i) Long leaseholds, in which the unexpired term of the lease at the balance sheet date is not less than 50 years.

(ii) Short leaseholds which are all leaseholds other than long leaseholds.

4 FRS 15 TANGIBLE FIXED ASSETS

4.1 FRS 15 *Tangible fixed assets* was published in February 1999. It goes into a lot more detail than the Companies Act.

Objective

4.2 FRS 15 deals with accounting for the initial measurement, valuation and depreciation of tangible fixed assets. It also sets out the information that should be disclosed to enable readers to understand the impact of the accounting policies adopted in relation to these issues.

10: Fixed assets - depreciation, disposal and revaluation

Initial measurement

4.3 A tangible fixed asset should **initially be measured at cost**.

> **KEY TERM**
>
> **Cost** is purchase price and any costs directly attributable to bringing the asset into working condition for its intended use.

4.4 Examples of directly attributable costs are:

- **Acquisition costs**, eg stamp duty, import duties
- Cost of **site preparation** and clearance
- Initial **delivery and handling** costs
- **Installation** costs
- **Professional fees** eg legal fees
- The estimated cost of **dismantling and removing** the asset and restoring the site, to the extent that it is recognised as a provision under FRS 12 *Provisions, contingent liabilities and contingent assets* (discussed in Chapter 16).

4.5 Any abnormal costs, such as those arising from design error, industrial disputes or idle capacity are not directly attributable costs and therefore should not be capitalised as part of the cost of the asset.

Finance costs

4.6 The **capitalisation of finance costs**, including interest, is **optional**. However, if an entity does capitalise finance costs they must do so **consistently**.

4.7 All finance costs that are **directly attributable** to the construction of a tangible fixed asset should be capitalised as part of the cost of the asset.

> **KEY TERM**
>
> **Directly attributable finance costs** are those that would have been avoided if there had been no expenditure on the asset.

4.8 If finance costs are capitalised, capitalisation should start when:

- Finance costs are being incurred
- Expenditure on the asset is being incurred
- Activities necessary to get the asset ready for use are in progress

4.9 Capitalisation of finance costs should cease when the asset is ready for use.

Subsequent expenditure

4.10 Subsequent expenditure on a tangible fixed asset should only be capitalised in the following three circumstances.

Part C: Double entry bookkeeping and accounting treatments

(a) It enhances the economic benefits over and above those previously estimated. An example might be modifications made to a piece of machinery that increases its capacity or useful life.

(b) A component of an asset that has been treated separately for depreciation purposes (because it has a substantially different useful economic life from the rest of the asset) has been restored or replaced.

(c) It relates to a major inspection or overhaul that restores economic benefits that have been consumed and reflected in the depreciation charge.

Question 3

Can you think of examples for (b) and (c) above?

Answer

(b) A factory building may require a new roof every 10 years, whereas the factory itself may have a useful economic life of 50 years. In this case the roof will be treated as a separate asset and depreciated over 10 years and the expenditure incurred in replacing the roof will be accounted for as an addition and the carrying amount of the replaced asset removed from the balance sheet.

(c) An aircraft may be required by law to be overhauled every three years. Unless the overhaul is carried out the aircraft will not be licensed to fly. The entity will reflect the need to overhaul the aircraft by depreciating an amount equivalent to the estimated cost of the overhaul over the three year period. The cost of the overhaul will then be capitalised because it restores the economic value of the aircraft.

Valuation

4.11 FRS 15 supplements and clarifies the rules on revaluation of fixed assets which the Companies Act allows. Revaluation is discussed in the next section.

Depreciation

4.12 As noted earlier, the Companies Act 1985 requires that all fixed assets having a limited economic life should be depreciated. FRS 15 gives a useful discussion of the purpose of depreciation and supplements the statutory requirements in important ways.

> **KEY TERM**
>
> **Depreciation** is defined in FRS 15 as the measure of the cost or revalued amount of the economic benefits of the tangible fixed asset that have been consumed during the period. Consumption includes the wearing out, using up or other reduction in the useful economic life of a tangible fixed asset, whether arising from use, effluxion of time or obsolescence through either changes in technology or demand for the goods and services produced by the asset.

4.13 This definition covers the amortisation of assets with a pre-determined life, such as a leasehold, and the depletion of wasting assets such as mines.

4.14 The need to depreciate fixed assets arises from the accruals concept. If money is expended in purchasing an asset then the amount expended must at some time be charged against profits. If the asset is one which contributes to an enterprise's revenue over a number of accounting periods it would be inappropriate to charge any single period (for example the period in which the asset was acquired) with the whole of the expenditure. Instead, some method must be found of spreading the cost of the asset over its useful economic life.

4.15 This view of depreciation as a process of **allocation** of the cost of an asset over several accounting periods is the view adopted by FRS 15. It is worth mentioning here two common **misconceptions** about the purpose and effects of depreciation.

(a) It is sometimes thought that the net book value (NBV) of an asset is equal to its net realisable value and that the object of charging depreciation is to reflect the fall in value of an asset over its life. This misconception is the basis of a common, but incorrect, argument which says that freehold properties (say) need not be depreciated in times when property values are rising. It is true that historical cost balance sheets often give a misleading impression when a property's NBV is much below its market value, but in such a case it is open to a business to incorporate a revaluation into its books, or even to prepare its accounts on the current cost convention. This is a separate problem from that of allocating the property's cost over successive accounting periods.

(b) Another misconception is that depreciation is provided so that an asset can be replaced at the end of its useful life. This is not the case.

(i) If there is no intention of replacing the asset, it could then be argued that there is no need to provide for any depreciation at all.

(ii) If prices are rising, the replacement cost of the asset will exceed the amount of depreciation provided.

4.16 FRS 15 contains **no detailed guidance** on the calculation of depreciation or the suitability of the various depreciation methods, merely stating the following two **general principles**.

> 'The depreciable amount of a tangible fixed asset should be allocated on a **systematic** basis over its useful economic life. The depreciation method used should reflect as fairly as possible the pattern in which the asset's economic benefits are consumed by the entity. The depreciation charge for each period should be recognised as an expense in the profit and loss account unless it is permitted to be included in the carrying amount of another asset.'

> 'A variety of methods can be used to allocate the depreciable amount of a tangible fixed asset on a systematic basis over its useful economic life. The method chosen should result in a **depreciation charge throughout the asset's useful** economic life and not just towards the end of its useful economic life or when the asset is falling in value.'

We will therefore consider first the factors affecting depreciation and then proceed to an analysis of the main depreciation methods available.

Factors affecting depreciation

4.17 FRS 15 states that the following factors need to be considered in determining the useful economic life, residual value and depreciation method of an asset.

(a) The **expected usage** of the asset by the entity, assessed by reference to the asset's expected capacity or physical output

(b) The **expected physical deterioration** of the asset through use or effluxion of time; this will depend upon the repair and maintenance programme of the entity both when the asset is in use and when it is idle

Part C: Double entry bookkeeping and accounting treatments

(c) **Economic or technological obsolescence**, for example arising from changes or improvements in production, or a change in the market demand for the product or service output of that asset

(d) **Legal or similar limits** on the use of the asset, such as the expiry dates of related leases

4.18 If it becomes clear that the **original estimate** of an asset's useful life was **incorrect**, it should be **revised**. Normally, no adjustment should be made in respect of the depreciation charged in previous years; instead the remaining net book value of the asset should be depreciated over the new estimate of its remaining useful life. If future results could be materially distorted, the adjustment to accumulated depreciation should be recognised in the accounts in accordance with FRS 3 (usually as an exceptional item). FRS 3 is discussed in a later chapter of this Study Text.

Methods of depreciation

4.19 The **cost of an asset less its residual value is known as the depreciable amount** of the asset. For example, if plant has a five year expected life and the anticipated capital costs are:

	£
Purchase cost	19,000
Delivery	1,500
Installation by own employees	2,700
	23,200

while the residual value at the end of the fifth year is expected to be £3,200, the depreciable amount would be £20,000. Any repair and maintenance costs incurred during the period are written off as running costs in the year in which they are incurred.

4.20 However, if major improvements are made to an asset, thereby increasing its expected life, the depreciable amount should be adjusted. For example, if at the beginning of year 3, £11,000 was spent on technological improvements to the plant so prolonging its expected life by three years (with a residual value of £1,200 at the end of the eighth year), the depreciable amount would be adjusted.

	£
Original depreciable amount	20,000
Less amount already depreciated (say 2 × £4,000)	8,000
	12,000
Add fall in residual value £(3,200 – 1,200)	2,000
	14,000
Add further capital expenditure	11,000
New depreciable amount	25,000

The new depreciable amount would be written off over the remaining useful life of the asset, 6 years.

4.21 There are a number of different methods of calculating the depreciation charge for an accounting period, each giving a different result. The most common are:

- Straight line method
- Reducing balance method
- Sum of digits method
- Machine hour method
- Revaluation

4.22 The **straight line method** is the simplest and the most commonly used in practice. The **reducing balance** and **sum of digits** methods are accelerated methods which lead to a higher charge in earlier years. Since repair and maintenance costs tend to increase as assets grow older these methods lead to a more even allocation of total fixed asset costs (depreciation plus maintenance).

4.23 The **machine hour method** is suited to assets which depreciate primarily through use rather than through passing of time. Such assets might include mines and quarries, which are subject to gradual exhaustion of the minerals that they contain, and also delivery lorries, which may be argued to depreciate in accordance with the number of miles travelled.

4.24 Neither the CA nor FRS 15 prescribes which method should be used. **Management must exercise its judgement.** Furthermore, FRS 15 states:

> 'The useful economic life of a tangible fixed asset should be **reviewed at the end of each reporting period** and revised if expectations are significantly different from previous estimates. If a useful economic life is revised, the carrying amount of the tangible fixed asset at the date of revision should be **depreciated over the revised remaining useful economic life.**'

4.25 FRS 15 also states that a **change from one method** of providing depreciation **to another** is permissible only on the grounds that the new method will give a **fairer presentation** of the results and of the financial position. Such a change does **not**, however, constitute a **change of accounting policy**; the carrying amount of the tangible fixed asset is depreciated using the revised method over the remaining useful economic life, beginning in the period in which the change is made.

4.26 Tangible fixed assets other than non depreciable land, should be **reviewed for impairment** at the end of the reporting period where:

- No depreciation is charged on the grounds that it would immaterial
- The estimated remaining useful economic life exceeds 50 years.

The review should be in accordance with FRS 11 *Impairment of fixed assets and goodwill* (this is not within the scope of Paper 1.1).

4.27 Many companies carry fixed assets in their balance sheets at revalued amounts, particularly in the case of freehold buildings. When this is done, the **depreciation charge** should be calculated **on the basis of the revalued amount** (not the original cost), in spite of the alternative accounting rules in CA 1985.

4.28 Where the tangible fixed asset comprises two or more major components with substantially different useful economic lives, each component should be accounted for separately for depreciation purposes and depreciated over its individual useful economic life.

4.29 You still need to charge depreciation if there is subsequent expenditure on a tangible fixed asset that maintains or enhances the previously assessed standard of performance of the asset.

Disclosure requirements of FRS 15

4.30 The following information should be disclosed separately in the financial statements for each class of tangible fixed assets.

Part C: Double entry bookkeeping and accounting treatments

(a) The depreciation methods used

(b) The useful economic lives or the depreciation rates used

(c) Total depreciation charged for the period

(d) Where material, the financial effect of a change during the period in either the estimate of useful economic lives or the estimate of residual values

(e) The cost or revalued amount at the beginning of the financial period and at the balance sheet date

(f) The cumulative amount of provisions for depreciation or impairment at the beginning of the financial period and at the balance sheet date

(g) A reconciliation of the movements, separately disclosing additions, disposals, revaluations, transfers, depreciation, impairment losses, and reversals of past impairment losses written back in the financial period

(h) The net carrying amount at the beginning of the financial period and at the balance sheet date

4.31 Where there has been a change in the depreciation method used, the effect, if material, should be disclosed in the period of change. The reason for the change should also be disclosed.

Question 4

The Furrow Manufacturing Company has recently purchased a machine for £256,000 and expects to use it for three years at the end of which period it will be sold as scrap for £4,000.

REQUIREMENTS:

(a) Calculate in respect of each of the three years the annual depreciation charge using each of the following methods:

(i) Straight line
(ii) Reducing balance (at 75% per annum).

(b) Suppose that the Furrow Manufacturing Company adopted the reducing balance method and depreciated the machine for one year; then at the end of the following year the company decided to change from the reducing balance method to the straight line method. Indicate how the machine should appear in the balance sheet at the end of its second year (including any notes relating thereto) assuming that all the original estimates had proved accurate, and bearing in mind the requirements of FRS 15.

Answer

(a) The depreciable amount of the machine is £(256,000 – 4,000) = £252,000

(i) The annual depreciation charge $\dfrac{£252,000}{3} = £84,000$

(ii) The annual depreciation charge is as follows.

		NBV £'000	Charge for year £'000
Year 1:	cost	256	
	depreciation (75%)	(192)	192
	net book value	64	
Year 2:	depreciation (75%)	(48)	48
	net book value	16	
Year 3:	depreciation (75%)	(12)	12
	net book value	4	
			252

(b) FRS 15 states that if the depreciation method is changed it is unnecessary to adjust amounts charged in previous years. Instead, the new method is simply applied to the unamortised cost of the asset over its remaining useful life.

At the end of year 1, the machine's net book value (after one year's depreciation on the reducing balance method) is £64,000 (see part (a)). For year 2, it is decided to use the straight line method over the remaining two years of useful life. The charge for depreciation in year 2 will therefore be £30,000 ((£64,000 − £4,000) ÷ 2) and the asset's net book value at the end of year 2 will be £34,000.

FURROW MANUFACTURING COMPANY
BALANCE SHEET AT END OF YEAR 2 (EXTRACT)

		£
Fixed assets		
Tangible assets		
Plant and machinery: cost		256,000
depreciation		(222,000)
		34,000

Question 5

Annette Book is the financial controller of a medium-sized publishing company. The managing director, Eddie Torial, is a man of sound literary judgement and marketing instinct, but has no accountancy training. Annette has received from him the following note.

'I understand that we have to provide "depreciation" on all our fixed assets except land. This is going to come out of our profit, so there has to be a reason for it. Could you answer the following questions?'

(a) Why do we provide depreciation?

(b) What exactly is net book value? (I think I know roughly what it is.)

(c) Why do we sometimes use the reducing balance method and not the straight line method?

Required

Write Annette's reply to Eddie, addressing each of the above queries.

Answer

To: Eddie Torial
Managing Director
From: Annette Book
Date: 5 March 1997
Subject: Depreciation

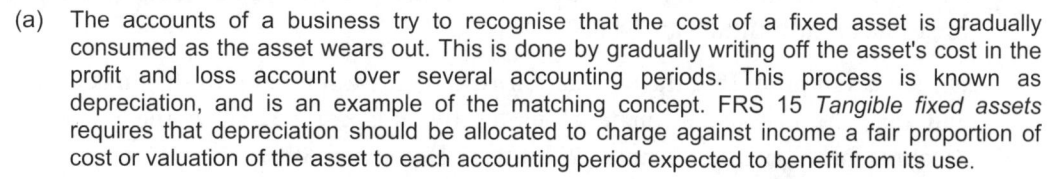

(a) The accounts of a business try to recognise that the cost of a fixed asset is gradually consumed as the asset wears out. This is done by gradually writing off the asset's cost in the profit and loss account over several accounting periods. This process is known as depreciation, and is an example of the matching concept. FRS 15 *Tangible fixed assets* requires that depreciation should be allocated to charge against income a fair proportion of cost or valuation of the asset to each accounting period expected to benefit from its use.

With regard to the matching principle, it is fair that the profits should be reduced by the depreciation charge; this is not an arbitrary exercise. Depreciation is not, as is sometime supposed, an attempt to set aside funds to purchase new fixed assets when required. Depreciation is not generally provided on freehold land because it does not 'wear out' (unless it is held for mining etc).

(b) In simple terms the net book value of an asset is the cost of an asset less the 'accumulated depreciation', that is all depreciation charged so far. It should be emphasised that the main purpose of charging depreciation is to ensure that profits are fairly reported. Thus depreciation is concerned with the profit and loss account rather than the balance sheet. In consequence the net book value figure in the balance sheet can be quite arbitrary. In particular, it does not necessarily bear any relation to the market value of an asset and is of little use for planning and decision making.

An obvious example of the disparity between net book value and market value is found in the case of buildings, which may be worth more than ten times as much as their net book value.

Part C: Double entry bookkeeping and accounting treatments

(c) The reducing balance method of depreciation is used instead of the straight line method when it is considered fair to allocate a greater proportion of the total depreciable amount to the earlier years and a lower proportion to the later years on the assumption that the benefits obtained by the business from using the asset decline over time.

In favour of this method it may be argued that it links the depreciation charge to the costs of maintaining and running the asset. In the early years these costs are low and the depreciation charge is high, while in later years this is reversed.

5 REVALUATIONS

5.1 For freehold property which is in operational use, the principle laid down in FRS 15 is that since **buildings have a finite useful life**, a part of their **cost must be charged against profit each year,** in order to be consistent with the accruals concept.

5.2 Although **freehold land does not normally require a provision for depreciation** (unless it is subject to depletion, for example where mineral resources are extracted) **buildings on that land have a limited life** which may be affected by technological and environmental changes. **Buildings should therefore be depreciated.**

5.3 Where there is a freehold property this means that the land element in its cost will not be depreciated, but the building element of cost must be depreciated.

5.4 As previously discussed, a property's NBV may be well below its market value. A business may, therefore, decide to revalue the property to its market value. When a property is revalued, depreciation should be charged to write off the new valuation over the estimated remaining useful life of the building (see paragraph 4.27).

5.5 The gain on revaluation can not go to the profit and loss account, as it has not been realised. Therefore the 'gain' is transferred to a revaluation reserve (see paragraphs 3.10 to 3.12).

5.6 EXAMPLE: REVALUATION OF A FREEHOLD BUILDING

A freehold building is purchased on 1 January 20X4 for £20,000. Its estimated useful life is 20 years and it is depreciated at the rate of £1,000 per annum in each of the years ending 31 December 20X4 and 20X5. On 1 January 20X6 a professional valuer estimates the value of the building at £54,000.

On the assumption that the revaluation is to be incorporated into the books of account, and that the original estimate of useful life was correct, show the relevant ledger accounts for the period 1 January 20X4 to 31 December 20X6.

5.7 SOLUTION

FREEHOLD BUILDING AT COST

			£			£
1.1.X4	Purchase		20,000	31.12.X4 Balance c/d		20,000
1.1.X5	Balance b/d		20,000	31.12.X5 Balance c/d		20,000
1.1.X6	Balance b/d		20,000			
	Revaluation		34,000	31.12.X6 Balance c/d		54,000
			54,000			54,000

DEPRECIATION ON FREEHOLD BUILDINGS

		£			£
31.12.X4 Balance c/d		1,000	31.12.X4 P & L account		1,000
			1.1.X5 Balance b/d		1,000

10: Fixed assets - depreciation, disposal and revaluation

		£			£
31.12.X5	Balance c/d	2,000	31.12.X5	P & L account	1,000
		2,000			2,000
1.1.X6	Revaluation	2,000	1.1.X6	Balance b/d	2,000
			31.12.X6	P & L account	
31.12.X6	Balance c/d	3,000		(£54,000/18 years)	3,000
		5,000			5,000

REVALUATION RESERVE

		£			£
			1.1.X6	Freehold building	34,000
31.12.X6	Balance c/d	36,000		Dep'n on freehold	2,000
		36,000			36,000

Note that the revaluation surplus is the difference between valuation (£54,000) and net book value at the time of revaluation (£20,000 – £2,000 = £18,000). The revalued amount, £54,000, must then be depreciated over the asset's remaining estimated useful life of 18 years, ie £3,000 per annum.

Balance sheet as at 31.12.X6 (extracts)
(a) Revaluation

	£
Fixed assets	
Freehold buildings – valuation	54,000
– accumulated depreciation	(3,000)
– NBV	51,000
Capital and reserves	
Revaluation reserves	36,000

(b) If revaluation had not taken place

	£
Fixed assets	
Freehold buildings – cost	20,000
– accumulated depreciation (3 years)	(3,000)
– NBV	17,000

Note that the balance sheet under (a) is effectively £15,000 (£51,000 - £36,000), compared to £17,000 under (b). This difference of £2,000 is due to the increased depreciation after the revaluation (old rate of depreciation £1,000 pa, new rate £3,000 pa).

FRS 15 rules

5.8 An entity may adopt a policy of **revaluing tangible fixed assets**. Where this policy is adopted **it must be applied consistently** to all assets of the same class.

> **KEY TERM**
>
> A **class of fixed assets** is 'a category of tangible fixed assets having a similar nature, function or use in the business of an entity'. (FRS 15)

5.9 Where an asset is revalued its carrying amount should be its **current value** as at the balance sheet date, current value being the **lower of replacement cost and recoverable amount**.

5.10 To achieve the above, the standard states that a **full valuation** should be carried out **at least every five years** with an **interim valuation in year 3**. If it is likely that there has been a material change in value, interim valuations in years 1, 2 and 4 should also be carried out.

Part C: Double entry bookkeeping and accounting treatments

5.11 A full valuation should be conducted by either a **qualified external valuer** or a **qualified internal valuer**, provided that the valuation has been subject to review by a qualified external valuer. An interim valuation may be carried out by either an external or internal valuer.

5.12 For certain types of assets (other than properties) eg company cars, there may be an active second hand market for the asset or appropriate indices may exist, so that the directors can establish the asset's value with reasonable reliability and therefore avoid the need to use the services of a qualified valuer.

Valuation basis

5.13 The following valuation bases should be used for properties that are not impaired.

(a) **Specialised properties** should be valued on the basis of **depreciated replacement cost**.

Specialised properties are those which, due to their specialised nature, are rarely, if ever, sold on the open market for single occupation for a continuation of their existing use, except as part of a sale of the business in occupation. Eg oil refineries, chemical works, power stations, or schools, colleges and universities where there is no competing market demand from other organisations using these types of property in the locality.

(b) **Non-specialised properties** should be valued on the basis of **existing use value** (EUV).

(c) **Properties surplus** to an entity's requirements should be valued on the basis of **open market value** (OMV).

5.14 Where there is an indication of impairment, an impairment review should be carried out in accordance with FRS 11. (FRS 11 is outside the scope of the Paper 1.1 syllabus.) The asset should be recorded at the lower of revalued amount (as above) and recoverable amount.

5.15 Tangible fixed assets other than properties should be valued using market value or, if not obtainable, depreciated replacement cost.

> **Exam focus point**
> For your exam, you should be able to discuss the FRS 15 rules. Practically, you only need to know how to treat revaluations in the ledger accounts, how to set up a revaluation reserve and how to calculate revised depreciation.

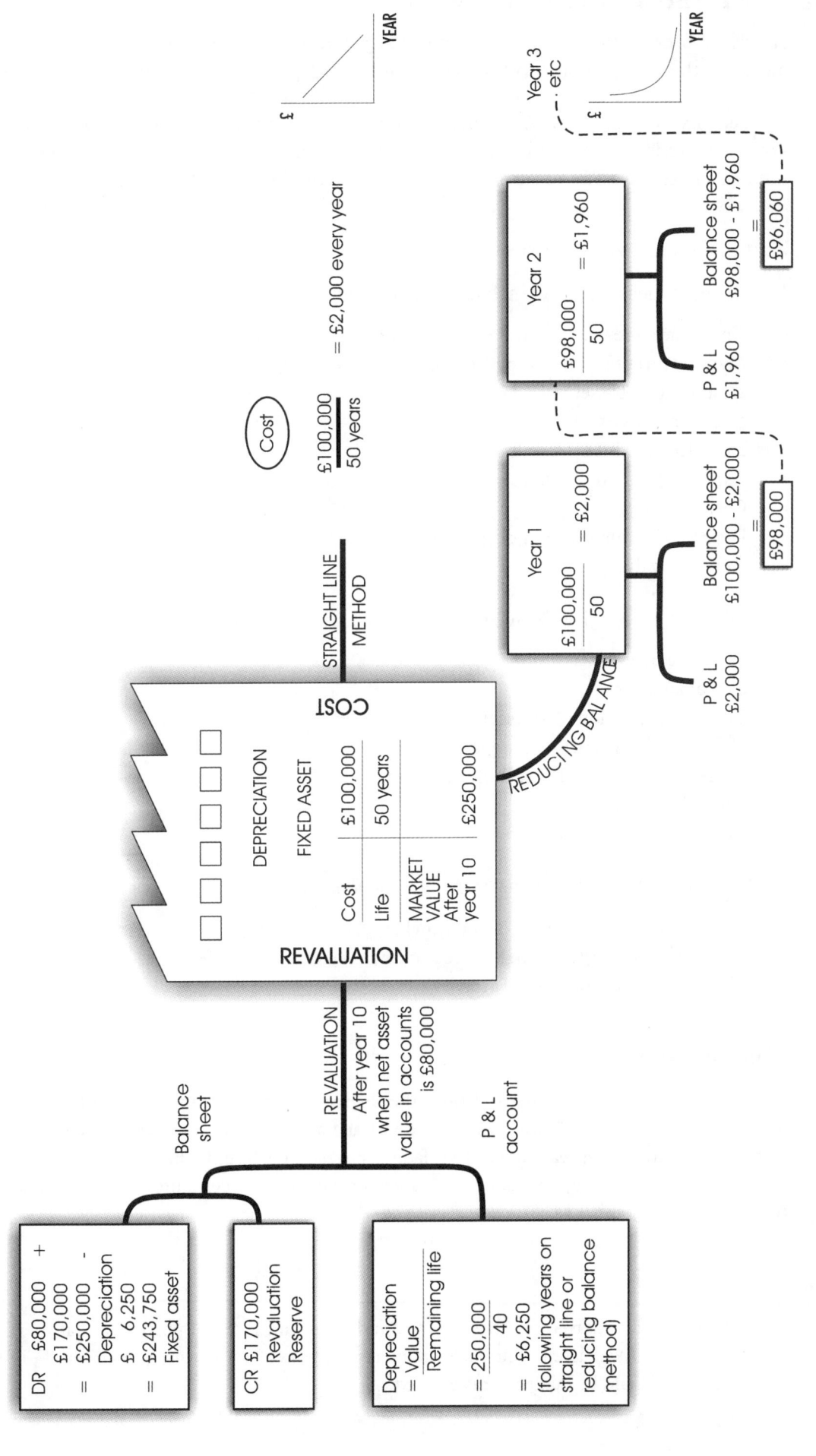

10: Fixed assets - depreciation, disposal and revaluation

FIXED ASSET

Cost	£100,000
Life	50 years
MARKET VALUE After year 10	£250,000

DEPRECIATION

COST

STRAIGHT LINE METHOD

$$\frac{£100,000}{50 \text{ years}} = £2,000 \text{ every year}$$

Year 1
$$\frac{£100,000}{50} = £2,000$$

- P & L £2,000
- Balance sheet £100,000 − £2,000 = £98,000

Year 2
$$\frac{£98,000}{50} = £1,960$$

- P & L £1,960
- Balance sheet £98,000 − £1,960 = £96,060

Year 3 etc

REDUCING BALANCE

REVALUATION

After year 10 when net asset value in accounts is £80,000

Balance sheet

DR £80,000 +
£170,000
= £250,000 −
Depreciation
£ 6,250
= £243,750
Fixed asset

CR £170,000 Revaluation Reserve

P & L account

Depreciation
= Value / Remaining life
= 250,000 / 40
= £6,250
(following years on straight line or reducing balance method)

191

Part C: Double entry bookkeeping and accounting treatments

6 THE FIXED ASSETS REGISTER

6.1 Nearly all organisations keep a fixed assets register. This is a listing of all fixed assets owned by the organisation, broken down perhaps by department, location or asset type.

6.2 A fixed assets register is maintained primarily for internal purposes. It shows an organisation's investment in capital equipment. A fixed asset register is also part of the **internal control system**. Fixed assets registers are sometimes called **real accounts.**

Data kept in a fixed assets register

6.3 Details about each fixed asset include the following.

- The internal reference number (for physical identification purposes)
- Manufacturer's serial number (for maintenance purposes)
- Description of asset
- Location of asset
- Department which 'owns' asset
- Purchase date (for calculation of depreciation)
- Cost
- Depreciation method and estimated useful life (for calculation of depreciation)
- Net book value (or written down value)

6.4 The following events give rise to entries in a fixed asset register.

- Purchase of an asset
- Sale of an asset
- Loss or destruction of an asset
- Transfer of assets between departments
- Revision of estimated useful life of an asset
- Scrapping of an asset
- Revaluation of an asset

6.5 'Outputs' from a fixed assets register include the following.

- Reconciliations of NBV to the nominal ledger
- Depreciation charges posted to the nominal ledger
- Physical verification/audit purposes

Layout of fixed assets register

6.6 The layout of a fixed assets register (and the degree of detail included) depends on the organisation in question. With a hand written fixed asset register, the details are usually recorded in columns spread across two facing pages. The column headings reflect the details outlined in paragraph 6.3 above. For the layout of a computerised fixed asset register, see paragraph 6.14.

Control

6.7 It is important, for external reporting (ie the audit) and for internal purposes, that there are controls over fixed assets. The fixed assets register has already been mentioned. Four further points should be made in this context.

10: Fixed assets - depreciation, disposal and revaluation

(a) **Purchase** of fixed assets must be authorised and must only be made by a responsible official. The purchaser should obtain several quotations. The person authorising the expenditure should not be the person using the asset.

(b) Procedures should exist and be enforced for **disposal** of fixed assets to ensure that the sales proceeds are not misappropriated.

(c) The fixed assets register must reconcile with the nominal ledger.

(d) The fixed assets register must reconcile with the physical presence of capital items.

The fixed assets register and the nominal ledger

6.8 The fixed assets register is not part of the double entry and is there for **memorandum** and **control** purposes.

6.9 The fixed assets register must be reconciled to the nominal ledger to make sure that all additions, disposals and depreciation charges have been posted. For example, the total of all the 'cost' figures in the register for motor vehicles should equal the balance on the 'motor vehicles cost' account in the nominal ledger. The same goes for accumulated depreciation.

The fixed assets register and the physical assets

6.10 It is possible that the fixed assets register may not reconcile with the fixed assets actually present. This may be for the following reasons.

- Asset has been stolen or damaged, which has not been noticed or recorded
- Excessive wear and tear or obsolescence has not been recorded
- New assets not yet recorded in the register because it has not been kept up to date
- Errors made in entering details in the register
- Improvement and modifications have not been recorded in the register

6.11 Therefore it is important that the company physically inspects all the items in the fixed assets register and keeps the fixed assets register up to date.

The nature of the inspection will vary between organisations. A large company could inspect 25% of assets by value each year, aiming to cover all categories every five years. A small company may inspect all its fixed assets very quickly, although this 'inspection' may not be formally recorded.

Dealing with discrepancies

6.12 As mentioned in 6.10 above, some assets may require an adjustment in their expected life due to excessive wear and tear or damage. The proper person must authorise any change to estimates of the life of an asset. The accounts department will need a copy of the authorised changes to make the right adjustments in the journal, the register and the ledger.

6.13 When discrepancies are discovered, it may be possible to resolve them by updating the fixed assets register and/or nominal ledger. It may not be possible for the person who discovers the discrepancy to resolve it himself. For example, if a fixed asset has to be revalued downwards due to wear and tear or obsolescence, it should be authorised by his superior.

Part C: Double entry bookkeeping and accounting treatments

> **Exam focus point**
>
> An examination question may ask for adjustment of the nominal ledger where it does not reconcile with the fixed assets register.

6.14 EXAMPLE: EXTRACT FROM A COMPUTERISED FIXED ASSETS REGISTER

Most fixed assets registers will be computerised. Below is an extract from a fixed asset register showing one item as it might appear when the details are printed out.

FASSET HOLDINGS PLC

Asset Code: 938		Next depreciation: 539.36
A	Description:	1 × Seisha Laser printer YCA40809
B	Date of purchase:	25/05/X6
C	Cost:	1618.25
D	Accumulated depreciation:	584.35
E	Depreciation %:	33.33%
F	Depreciation type:	straight line
G	Date of disposal:	NOT SET
H	Sale proceeds:	0.00
I	Accumulated depreciation amount:	55Q O/EQPT DEP CHARGE
J	Depreciation expense account:	34F DEPN O/EQPT
K	Depreciation period:	standard
L	Comments:	electronic office
M	Residual value:	0.00
N	Cost account:	65C O/E ADDITIONS

7 PREPARATION OF FINAL ACCOUNTS FOR A SOLE TRADER

7.1 You have already had practice at preparing a profit and loss account and balance sheet from a simple trial balance. Now see if you can do the same thing but at a more advanced level, taking account of adjustments for depreciation, stock, accruals, prepayments and bad and doubtful debts. Have a go at the following question.

Question 6

The following trial balance was extracted from the ledger of Kevin Webster, a sole trader, as at 31 May 20X1, the end of his financial year.

KEVIN WEBSTER
TRIAL BALANCE AS AT 31 MAY 20X1

	Dr £	Cr £
Property, at cost	120,000	
Equipment, at cost	80,000	
Provisions for depreciation (as at 1 June 20X0)		
- on property		20,000
- on equipment		38,000
Purchases	250,000	
Sales		402,200
Stock, as at 1 June 20X0	50,000	
Discounts allowed	18,000	
Discounts received		4,800
Returns out		15,000
Wages and salaries	58,800	
Bad debts	4,600	
Loan interest	5,100	
Other operating expenses	17,700	
Trade creditors		36,000
Trade debtors	38,000	
Cash on hand	300	
Bank	1,300	
Drawings	24,000	
Provision for doubtful debts		500
17% long-term loan		30,000
Capital, as at 1 June 20X0		121,300
	667,800	667,800

The following additional information as at 31 May 20X1 is available.

(a) Stock as at the close of business has been valued at cost at £42,000.
(b) Wages and salaries need to be accrued by £800.
(c) Other operating expenses are prepaid by £300.
(d) The provision for doubtful debts is to be adjusted so that it is 2% of trade debtors.
(e) Depreciation for the year ended 31 May 20X1 has still to be provided for as follows:
   Property: 1.5% per annum using the straight line method
   Equipment: 25% per annum using the reducing balance method

Required

Prepare Kevin Webster's profit & loss account for the year ended 31 May 20X1 and his balance sheet as at that date.

Part C: Double entry bookkeeping and accounting treatments

Answer

KEVIN WEBSTER
PROFIT AND LOSS ACCOUNT
FOR THE YEAR ENDED 31 MAY 20X1

	£	£
Sales		402,200
Cost of sales		
Opening stock	50,000	
Purchases	250,000	
Purchases returns	(15,000)	
	285,000	
Closing stock	42,000	
		243,000
Gross profit		159,200
Other income: discounts received		4,800
		164,000
Expenses		
Wages and salaries (£58,800 + £800)	59,600	
Discounts allowed	18,000	
Bad debts (W1)	4,860	
Loan interest	5,100	
Depreciation (W2)	12,300	
Other operating expenses (£17,700 – £300)	17,400	
		117,260
Net profit for the year		46,740

KEVIN WEBSTER
BALANCE SHEET AS AT 31 MAY 20X1

	£	£
Fixed assets		
Property: cost	120,000	
accumulated depreciation (W2)	21,800	
		98,200
Equipment: cost	80,000	
accumulated depreciation (W2)	48,500	
		31,500
		129,700
Current assets		
Stock	42,000	
Trade debtors		
(less provision: £38,000 less 2%)	37,240	
Prepayments	300	
Bank	1,300	
Cash in hand	300	
	81,140	
Current liabilities		
Trade creditors	36,000	
Accruals	800	
	36,800	
Net current assets		44,340
		174,040
Long-term liabilities		
17% loan		30,000
		144,040

Capital

	£
Capital	
Balance at 1 June 20X0	121,300
Net profit for the year	46,740
Drawings	(24,000)
Balance at 31 May 20X1	144,040

Workings

1   *Provision for doubtful debts*

	£
Previous provision	500
New provision (2% × 38,000)	760
Increase	260
Per trial balance	4,600
P + L a/c	4,860

2   *Depreciation*

	£
Property	
Opening provision	20,000
Provision for the year (1.5% × 120,000)	1,800
Closing provision	21,800
Equipment	
Opening provision	38,000
Provision for the year (25% × 42,000)	10,500
Closing provision	48,500
Change to P+L (1,800 + 10,500)	12,300

Tips for final accounts questions

The examination paper will contain a compulsory question involving preparation of final accounts.

- Such a question may involve a sole trader, which is the type of organisation you have dealt with so far.
- Alternatively, you may have to prepare the final accounts of a limited liability company or a partnership and the accounts may have to be prepared from incomplete records, all topics you will cover later in this Study Text.

Whatever form the final accounts question takes, you should bear in mind the following tips.

- **Annotate the trial balance**. If you are given a trial balance, note the final destination of each item, for example:

  T = Trading account

  P+L = Profit and loss account

  B/S = Balance sheet

- **Show workings clearly**. The workings should be clearly referenced to the final accounts and should enable the marker to follow through your calculations. This is particularly important because if, as often happens under time pressure, you make minor arithmetical mistakes; you will not be heavily penalised if the marker can see that you have used the right method.

- **Present a clear, logical layout of financial accounts**. Allow plenty of space, better too much than too little. For example if you have to do a profit and loss account and balance sheet you should allow at least one page for the profit and loss account, one for the balance sheet and one or more for your workings. Underline any totals for columns and figures, and if you make a mistake, cross it out neatly and clearly. **You do not have time to wait for correcting fluid to dry.**

Part C: Double entry bookkeeping and accounting treatments

Chapter roundup

- This has been a long chapter with a lot to take in, so do not be surprised if it has taken you longer than you expected to work through it. Now that you have finally reached the end, you should understand the following points.

- The cost of a fixed asset, less its estimated residual value, is allocated fairly between accounting periods by means of **depreciation**. The provision for depreciation is both:
  - Charged against profit
  - Deducted from the value of the fixed asset in the balance sheet.

- There are several different methods of depreciation, but the **straight line method** and the **reducing balance method** are most commonly used in practice. You also need to know how to use the **sum of the digits method** of depreciation. Every method described in this chapter allocates the total depreciable amount between accounting periods, although in different ways.

- When a fixed asset is **revalued**, depreciation is charged on the residual amount.

- When a fixed asset is sold, there is likely to be a **profit or loss on disposal**. This is the difference between the net sale price of the asset and its net book value at the time of disposal.

- You should also know how to handle the double entry bookkeeping for providing for depreciation, and for the disposal of fixed assets.

- A number of accounting regulations on the valuation and disclosure of fixed assets are contained in the Companies Act 1985. In the case of tangible fixed assets, these regulations are supplemented by the provisions of FRS 15 on tangible fixed assets.

- Most organisations keep a fixed assets register. This is a listing of all fixed assets owned by the organisation broken down perhaps by department, location or asset type. This must be kept up to date.

- Discrepancies between the fixed assets register and the physical assets or the nominal ledger must be investigated and either resolved or referred to the appropriate person.

Quick quiz

1. Which of the following statements regarding fixed asset accounting is correct?

   A All fixed assets should be revalued each year.
   B Fixed assets may be revalued at the discretion of management. Once revaluation has occurred it must be repeated regularly for all fixed assets in a class.
   C Management can choose which fixed assets in a class of fixed assets should be revalued.
   D Fixed assets should be revalued to reflect rising prices.

2. Which of the following statements regarding depreciation is correct?

   A All fixed assets must be depreciated.
   B Straight line depreciation is usually the most appropriate method of depreciation.
   C A change in the chosen depreciation method is a change in accounting policy which should be disclosed.
   D Depreciation charges must be based upon the depreciable amount.

3. What is an asset's net book value?

4. Give three common depreciation methods.

> 5 A fixed asset (cost £10,000, depreciation £7,500) is given in part exchange for a new asset costing £20,500. The agreed trade-in value was £3,500. The profit and loss account will include?
>
>   A   A loss on disposal £1,000
>
>   B   A profit on disposal £1,000
>
>   C   A loss on purchase of a new asset £3,500
>
>   D   A profit on disposal £3,500
>
> 6 What details about a fixed asset might be included in an assets register?
>
> 7 Why might the assets register not reconcile with the fixed assets accounts?

Answers to quick quiz

1   B   Correct.
    A   Fixed assets may be revalued, there is no requirement to do so in FRS 15.
    C   Incorrect, all fixed assets in a class must be revalued.
    D   Incorrect, fixed assets may be reduced in value as well as being increased.

2   D   Correct.
    A   Incorrect, some fixed assets are not depreciated eg land.
    B   Incorrect, management should choose the most appropriate method.
    C   Incorrect, a method change is not a change in accounting policy.

3   Its cost less accumulated depreciation.

4   Straight-line, reducing balance and sum of the digits.

5   B

	£
Net book value at disposal	2,500
Trade-in allowance	3,500
Profit	1,000

6
- Date of purchase
- Description
- Original cost
- Depreciation rate and method
- Accumulated depreciation to date
- Date and amount of any revaluation

7
- Asset stolen or damaged
- Obsolete
- New assets, not yet recorded in the register
- Improvements not yet recorded in the register
- Errors in the register

Now try the questions below from the Exam Question Bank

Number	Level	Marks	Time
15	Introductory	n/a	45 mins
16	Introductory	n/a	54 mins

Chapter 11

BANK RECONCILIATIONS

Topic list	Syllabus reference
1 Bank statement and cash book	3(b)
2 The bank reconciliation	3(b)
3 Worked examples	3(b)

Introduction

It is very likely that you will have had to do a bank reconciliation at work. If not, you will probably have done one on your own bank account without even being aware of it.

The first two sections of this chapter explain why we need a bank reconciliation, and the sort of differences that need to be reconciled. The third section takes you through some examples of increasing complexity.

Study guide

Section 5 – The journal; ledger control accounts; bank reconciliations

- Explain the purpose of bank reconciliation statements and the need for entries in the cash book when reconciling.
- Draft a bank reconciliation statement.

Exam guide

Bank reconciliations test your understanding of double entry. They will feature in MCQs and occasionally, a written question.

1 BANK STATEMENT AND CASH BOOK

1.1 The cash book of a business is the record of **how much cash the business believes** that it **has in the bank**. In the same way, you yourself might keep a private record of how much money you think you have in your own personal account at your bank, perhaps by making a note in your cheque book of income received and the cheques you write. If you do keep such a record you will probably agree that when your bank sends you a bank statement from time to time the amount it shows as being the balance in your account is rarely exactly the amount that you have calculated for yourself as being your current balance.

1.2 Why might your own estimate of your bank balance be different from the amount shown on your bank statement? There are three common explanations.

    (a) **Error**. Errors in calculation, or recording income and payments, are more likely to have been made by you than by the bank, but it is conceivable that the bank has made a mistake too.

(b) **Bank charges or bank interest**. The bank might deduct charges for interest on an overdraft or for its services, which you are not informed about until you receive the bank statement.

(c) **Time differences**

   (i) There might be some cheques that you have received and paid into the bank, but which have not yet been '**cleared**' and added to your account. So although your own records show that some cash has been added to your account, it has not yet been acknowledged by the bank - although it will be in a very short time when the cheque is eventually cleared.

   (ii) Similarly, you might have made some payments by cheque, and reduced the balance in your account accordingly in the record that you keep, but the person who receives the cheque might not bank it for a while. Even when it is banked, it takes a day or two for the banks to process it and for the money to be deducted from your account.

1.3 If you do keep a personal record of your cash position at the bank, and if you do check your periodic bank statements against what you think you should have in your account, you are doing exactly the same thing that the bookkeepers of a business do when they make a bank reconciliation.

> **KEY TERM**
>
> A **bank reconciliation** is a comparison of a bank statement (sent monthly, weekly or even daily by the bank) with the cash book. Differences between the balance on the bank statement and the balance in the cash book will be errors or timing differences, and they should be identified and satisfactorily explained.

2 THE BANK RECONCILIATION

The bank statement

2.1 It is a common practice for a business to issue a monthly statement to each credit customer, itemising:

(a) The **balance** he owed on his account at the **beginning** of the month
(b) **New debts** incurred by the customer during the month
(c) **Payments** made by him during the month
(d) The **balance** he owes on his account at the **end** of the month.

In the same way, a bank statement is sent by a bank to its short-term debtors and creditors - ie customers with bank overdrafts and customers with money in their account - itemising the balance on the account at the beginning of the period, receipts into the account and payments from the account during the period, and the balance at the end of the period.

2.2 However, remember that if a customer has money in his account, the bank owes him that money, and the customer is therefore a **creditor** of the bank (hence the phrase 'to be in credit' means to have money in your account). If a business has £8,000 cash in the bank, it will have a debit balance in its own cash book, but the bank statement will show a credit balance of £8,000. (**Think of sales and purchases: in the customer's books, the supplier is a creditor; in the supplier's books, the customer is a debtor.**)

Part C: Double entry bookkeeping and accounting treatments

Why is a bank reconciliation necessary?

2.3 A bank reconciliation is needed to identify and account for the differences between the cash book and the bank statement.

Question 1

These differences fall into three categories. What are they?

Answer

Error, bank charges or interest, time differences

What to look for when doing a bank reconciliation

2.4 The cash book and bank statement will rarely agree at a given date. If you are doing a bank reconciliation, you may have to look for the following items.

(a) **Corrections and adjustments to the cash book:**

   (i) Payments made into the account or from the account by way of standing order, which have not yet been entered in the cash book.

   (ii) Dividends received (on investments held by the business), paid direct into the bank account but not yet entered in the cash book.

   (iii) Bank interest and bank charges, not yet entered in the cash book.

(b) **Items reconciling the correct cash book balance to the bank statement:**

   (i) Cheques drawn (ie paid) by the business and credited in the cash book, which have not yet been presented to the bank, or 'cleared' and so do not yet appear on the bank statement.

   (ii) Cheques received by the business, paid into the bank and debited in the cash book, but which have not yet been cleared and entered in the account by the bank, and so do not yet appear on the bank statement.

3 WORKED EXAMPLES

3.1 EXAMPLE: BANK RECONCILIATION

At 30 September 20X6, the balance in the cash book of Wordsworth Ltd was £805.15 debit. A bank statement on 30 September 20X6 showed Wordsworth Ltd to be in credit by £1,112.30.

On investigation of the difference between the two sums, it was established that:

(a) The cash book had been undercast by £90.00 on the debit side*.
(b) Cheques paid in not yet credited by the bank amounted to £208.20.
(c) Cheques drawn not yet presented to the bank amounted to £425.35.

* Note. 'Casting' is an accountant's term for adding up.

Required

(a) Show the correction to the cash book.

(b) Prepare a statement reconciling the balance per bank statement to the balance per cash book.

3.2 SOLUTION

(a)

	£
Cash book balance brought forward	805.15
Add	
Correction of undercast	90.00
Corrected balance	895.15

(b)

	£	£
Balance per bank statement		1,112.30
Add		
Cheques paid in, recorded in the cash book, but not yet credited to the account by the bank	208.20	
Less		
Cheques paid by the company but not yet presented to the company's bank for settlement	425.35	
		(217.15)
Balance per cash book		895.15

Question 2

On 31 January 20X8 a company's cash book showed a credit balance of £150 on its current account which did not agree with the bank statement balance. In performing the reconciliation the following points come to light.

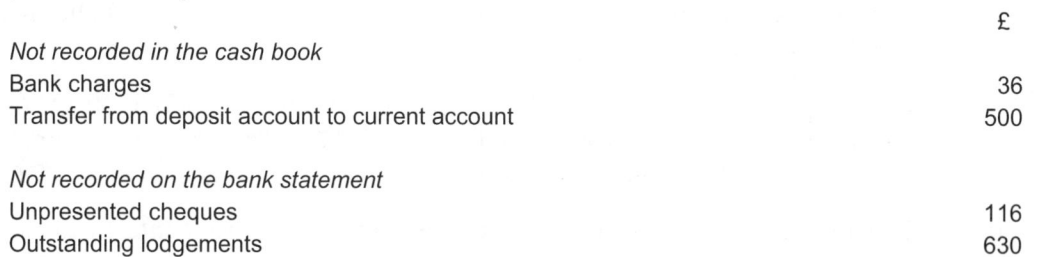

	£
Not recorded in the cash book	
Bank charges	36
Transfer from deposit account to current account	500
Not recorded on the bank statement	
Unpresented cheques	116
Outstanding lodgements	630

It was also discovered that the bank had debited the company's account with a cheque for £400 in error. What was the original balance on the bank statement?

Answer

CASH ACCOUNT

	£		£
		Balance b/f	150
Transfer from deposit a/c	500	Charges	36
		Balance c/f	314
	500		500

	£
Balance per cash book	314
Add unpresented cheques	116
Less uncleared lodgements	(630)
Less error by bank	(400)
Balance per bank statement	(600)

Note that on the bank statement Dr is overdrawn

Question 3

A company's bank statement shows £715 direct debits and £353 investment income not recorded in the cash book. The bank statement does not show a customer's cheque for £875 entered in the cash

Part C: Double entry bookkeeping and accounting treatments

book on the last day of the accounting period. If the cash book shows a credit balance of £610 what balance appears on the bank statement?

Answer

	£	£
Balance per cash book		(610)
Items on statement, not in cash book		
Direct debits	(715)	
Investment income	353	
		(362)
Corrected balance per cash book		(972)
Item in cash book not on statement:		
Customer's cheque		(875)
Balance per bank statement		(1,847)

3.3 EXAMPLE: MORE COMPLICATED BANK RECONCILIATION

On 30 June 20X0, Cook's cash book showed that he had an overdraft of £300 on his current account at the bank. A bank statement as at the end of June 20X0 showed that Cook was in credit with the bank by £65.

On checking the cash book with the bank statement you find the following.

(a) Cheques drawn, amounting to £500, had been entered in the cash book but had not been presented.

(b) Cheques received, amounting to £400, had been entered in the cash book, but had not been credited by the bank.

(c) On instructions from Cook the bank had transferred interest received on his deposit account amounting to £60 to his current account, recording the transfer on 5 July 20X0. This amount had, however, been credited in the cash book as on 30 June 20X0.

(d) Bank charges of £35 shown in the bank statement had not been entered in the cash book.

(e) The payments side of the cash book had been undercast by £10.

(f) Dividends received amounting to £200 had been paid direct to the bank and not entered in the cash book.

(g) A cheque for £50 drawn on deposit account had been shown in the cash book as drawn on current account.

(h) A cheque issued to Jones for £25 was replaced when out of date. It was entered again in the cash book, no other entry being made. Both cheques were included in the total of unpresented cheques shown above.

Required

(a) Indicate the appropriate adjustments in the cash book.

(b) Prepare a statement reconciling the amended balance with that shown in the bank statement.

3.4 SOLUTION

(a) The errors to correct are given in notes (c) (e) (f) (g) and (h) of the problem. Bank charges (note (d)) also call for an adjustment.

11: Bank reconciliations

CASH BOOK

		£			£
20X0			20X0		
Jun 30	Bank interest - reversal of incorrect entry (c)	60	Jun 30	Balance brought down	300
	Bank interest account (c)(Note 1)	60		Bank charges (d)	35
	Dividends paid direct to bank (f)	200		Correction of undercast (e)	10
	Cheque drawn on deposit account written back (g)	50		Balance carried down	50
	Cheque issued to Jones Cancelled (h) (Note 2)	25			
		395			395

Notes

1 Item (c) is rather complicated. The transfer of interest from the deposit to the current account was presumably given as an instruction to the bank on or before 30 June 20X0. Since the correct entry is to debit the current account (and credit the deposit account) the correction in the cash book should be to debit the current account with $2 \times £60 = £120$ - ie to cancel out the incorrect credit entry in the cash book and then to make the correct debit entry. However, the bank does not record the transfer until 5 July, and so it will not appear in the bank statement.

2 Item (h). Two cheques have been paid to Jones, but one is now cancelled. Since the cash book is credited whenever a cheque is paid, it should be debited whenever a cheque is cancelled. The amount of cheques paid but not yet presented should be reduced by the amount of the cancelled cheque.

(b) BANK RECONCILIATION STATEMENT AT 30 JUNE 20X0

	£	£
Balance per bank statement		65
Add: outstanding lodgements		
(ie cheques paid in but not yet credited) (b)	400	
deposit interest not yet credited (c)	60	
		460
		525
Less: unpresented cheques (a)	500	
less cheque to Jones cancelled (h)	(25)	
		475
Balance per corrected cash book		50

Exam focus point

Notice that in preparing a bank reconciliation it is good practice to begin with the balance shown by the bank statement and end with the balance shown by the cash book. It is this corrected cash book balance which will appear in the balance sheet as 'cash at bank'. But examination questions sometimes ask for the reverse order: as always, read the question carefully.

Question 4

From the information given below relating to PWW Ltd you are required:

(a) To make such additional entries in the cash at bank account of PWW Ltd as you consider necessary to show the correct balance at 31 October 20X2.

(b) To prepare a statement reconciling the correct balance in the cash at bank account as shown in (a) above with the balance at 31 October 20X2 that is shown on the bank statement from Z Bank plc.

Part C: Double entry bookkeeping and accounting treatments

CASH AT BANK ACCOUNT IN THE LEDGER OF PWW LIMITED

20X2 October		£	20X2 October		£
1	Balance b/f	274	1	Wages	3,146
8	Q Manufacturing	3,443	1	Petty Cash	55
8	R Cement	1,146	8	Wages	3,106
11	S Limited	638	8	Petty Cash	39
11	T & Sons	512	15	Wages	3,029
11	U & Co	4,174	15	Petty Cash	78
15	V plc	1,426	22	A & Sons	929
15	W Electrical	887	22	B Limited	134
22	X and Associates	1,202	22	C & Company	77
26	Y Limited	2,875	22	D & E	263
26	Z Limited	982	22	F Limited	1,782
29	ABC plc	1,003	22	G Associates	230
29	DEE Corporation	722	22	Wages	3,217
29	GHI Limited	2,461	22	Petty Cash	91
31	Balance c/f	14	25	H & Partners	26
			26	J Sons & Co Ltd	868
			26	K & Co	107
			26	L, M & N	666
			28	O Limited	112
			29	Wages	3,191
			29	Petty Cash	52
			29	P & Sons	561
		21,759			21,759

11: Bank reconciliations

Z BANK PLC - STATEMENT OF ACCOUNT WITH PWW LIMITED

20X2 October		Payments £	Receipts £		Balance £
1					1,135
1	cheque	55			
1	cheque	3,146			
1	cheque	421		O/D	2,487
2	cheque	73			
2	cheque	155		O/D	2,715
6	cheque	212		O/D	2,927
8	sundry credit		4,589		
8	cheque	3,106			
8	cheque	39		O/D	1,483
11	sundry credit		5,324		3,841
15	sundry credit		2,313		
15	cheque	78			
15	cheque	3,029			3,047
22	sundry credit		1,202		
22	cheque	3,217			
22	cheque	91			941
25	cheque	1,782			
25	cheque	134		O/D	975
26	cheque	929			
26	sundry credit		3,857		
26	cheque	230			1,723
27	cheque	263			
27	cheque	77			1,383
29	sundry credit		4,186		
29	cheque	52			
29	cheque	3,191			
29	cheque	26			
29	dividends on investments		2,728		
29	cheque	666			4,362
31	bank charges	936			3,426

Answer

(a)

CASH BOOK

		£				£
31 Oct	Dividends received	2,728	31 Oct	Unadjusted balance b/f (overdraft)		14
			31 Oct	Bank charges		936
			31 Oct	Adjusted balance c/f		1,778
		2,728				2,728

(b) **BANK RECONCILIATION STATEMENT AT 31 OCTOBER 20X2**

	£	£
Corrected balance as per cash book		1,778
Cheques paid out but not yet presented	1,648	
Cheques paid in but not yet cleared by bank	0	
		1,648
Balance as per bank statement		3,426

Part C: Double entry bookkeeping and accounting treatments

Workings

1	Payments shown on bank statement but not in cash book* £(421 + 73 + 155 + 212)	£861

* Presumably recorded in cash book before 1 October 20X2 but not yet presented for payment as at 30 September 20X2

2	Payments in the cash book and on the bank statement £(3,146 + 55 + 3,106 + 39 + 78 + 3,029 + 3,217 + 91 + 1,782 + 134 + 929 + 230 + 263 + 77 + 52 + 3,191 + 26 + 666)	£20,111
3	Payments in the cash book but not on the bank statement = Total payments in cash book £21,759 minus £20,111 =	£1,648

			£
(Alternatively	J & Sons		868
	K & Co		107
	O Ltd		112
	P & Sons		561
			1,648)

4	Bank charges, not in the cash book	£936
5	Receipts recorded by bank statement but not in cash book: dividends on investments	£2,728
6	Receipts in the cash book and also bank statement (8 Oct £4,589; 11 Oct £5,324; 15 Oct £2,313; 22 Oct £1,202; 26 Oct £3,857; 29 Oct £4,186)	£21,471
7	Receipts recorded in cash book but not bank statement	None

Chapter roundup

- In theory, the entries appearing on a business's **bank statement** should be exactly the same as those in the business **cash book**. The balance shown by the bank statement as on a particular date should be the same as the cash book balance at the same date.

- It is common (and a very important financial control) to check this at regular intervals, say weekly or monthly. Invariably it will be found that the picture shown by the bank statement differs from that shown by the cash book. There are three reasons for this.

  - **Errors**. Entries on the bank statement may be incorrect, but more commonly, errors may be found in the cash book.
  - **Omissions**. Items may appear on the bank statement which have not yet been entered in the cash book. These may include bank changes and payments made by direct debit.
  - **Timing differences**. Cheques are entered in the cash book as soon as they are written, but there may be a delay before the payee receives them and a further delay while they are processed through the bank clearing system.

- When these discrepancies are noticed, appropriate adjustments must be made. Errors must be corrected; omissions from the cash book must be made good. The balance in the cash book will then be correct and up to date.

- Any remaining difference between the cash book balance and the statement balance should then be explained as the result of identifiable timing differences.

11: Bank reconciliations

Quick quiz

1. Name four common reasons for differences between the cash book and the bank statements.
2. Show the standard layout of a bank reconciliation.
3. A bank statement shows a balance of £1,200 in credit. An examination of the statement shows a £500 cheque paid in per the cash book but not yet on the bank statement and a £1,250 cheque paid out but not yet on the statement. In addition the cash book shows deposit interest received of £50 but this is not yet on the statement. What is the balance per the cash book?

   A £1,900 overdrawn
   B £500 overdrawn
   C £1,900 in hand
   D £500 in hand

Answers to quick quiz

1. See paragraph 2.4.

2.
	£	£
Balance per bank statement		X
Add: outstanding lodgements	X	
deposit interest not yet credited	X	X
		X
Less: unpresented cheques		(X)
Balance per corrected cash book		X

3. D
	£	£
Balance per bank statement		1,200
Add: outstanding lodgements	500	
deposit interest not yet credited	50	550
		1,750
Less: unpresented cheques		(1,250)
Balance per cash book		500

Now try the questions below in the Exam Question Bank

Question to try	Level	Marks	Time
17	Full exam	10	18 mins
18	Full exam	10	18 mins

Chapter 12

CONTROL ACCOUNTS

Topic list	Syllabus reference
1 What are control accounts?	3(b)
2 The operation of control accounts	3(b)
3 The purpose of control accounts	3(b)

Introduction

So far in this text we have assumed that the bookkeeping and double entry (and subsequent preparation of financial accounts) has been carried out by a business without any mistakes. This is not likely to be the case in real life: even the bookkeeper of a very small business with hardly any accounting entries to make will be prone to human error.

If a debit is written as £123 and the corresponding credit as £321, then the books of the business are immediately out of balance by £198.

Once an error has been detected, it has to be corrected. In addition, a business is likely to have late adjustments to make to the figures in its accounts (eg depreciation; bad debt provision). A business needs to have some method available for making these corrections or adjustments.

In this chapter and in Chapter 13 we explain how errors can be detected, what kinds of error might exist, and how to post corrections and adjustments to produce final accounts.

Study guide

Section 5 – The journal; ledger control accounts; bank reconciliations

- Explain the nature and purpose of control accounts for the sales and purchases ledgers.
- Explain how control accounts relate to the double entry system.
- Construct and agree a ledger control account from given information.

Exam guide

As with bank reconciliations, control accounts are a good measure of how well you have grasped the concepts of double entry. Be prepared to tackle a question in section B of the exam.

1 WHAT ARE CONTROL ACCOUNTS?

KEY TERMS

A **control account** is an account in the nominal ledger in which a record is kept of the total value of a number of similar but individual items. Control accounts are used chiefly for debtors and creditors.

12: Control accounts

> - A **debtors control account** is an account in which records are kept of transactions involving all debtors in total. The balance on the debtors control account at any time will be the total amount due to the business at that time from its debtors.
> - A **creditors control account** is an account in which records are kept of transactions involving all creditors in total, and the balance on this account at any time will be the total amount owed by the business at that time to its creditors.

1.1 Although control accounts are used mainly in accounting for debtors and creditors, they can also be kept for other items, such as stocks of goods, wages and salaries. The first important idea to remember, however, is that a control account is an account which keeps a total record for a collective item (eg debtors) which in reality consists of many individual items (eg individual debtors).

1.2 A control account is an (impersonal) ledger account which will appear in the nominal ledger. Before we look at the reasons for having control accounts, we will first look at how they are made up.

Control accounts and personal accounts

1.3 The personal accounts of individual debtors are kept in the sales ledger, and the amount owed by each debtor will be a balance on his personal account. The amount owed by all the debtors together will be a balance on the debtors control account.

1.4 At any time the balance on the debtors control account should be equal to the sum of the individual balances on the personal accounts in the sales ledger.

1.5 For example, if a business has three debtors, A Arnold who owes £80, B Bagshaw who owes £310 and C Cloning who owes £200, the debit balances on the various accounts would be:

Sales ledger (personal accounts)

	£
A Arnold	80
B Bagshaw	310
C Cloning	200

Nominal ledger - debtors control account   590

1.6 What has happened here is that the three entries of £80, £310 and £200 were first entered into the sales day book. They were also recorded in the three personal accounts of Arnold, Bagshaw and Cloning in the sales ledger - but remember that this **is not part** of the double entry system (see Chapter 5).

1.7 Later, the **total** of £590 is posted from the sales day book into the debtors (control) account. It is fairly obvious that if you add up all the debit figures on the personal accounts, they also should total £590.

2 THE OPERATION OF CONTROL ACCOUNTS

2.1 EXAMPLE: ACCOUNTING FOR DEBTORS

You might still be uncertain why we need to have control accounts at all. Before turning our attention to this question, it will be useful first of all to see how transactions involving debtors are accounted for by means of an illustrative example. Folio numbers are shown in

Part C: Double entry bookkeeping and accounting treatments

the accounts to illustrate the cross-referencing that is needed, and in the example folio numbers beginning:

(a) SDB, refer to a page in the sales day book
(b) SL, refer to a particular account in the sales ledger
(c) NL, refer to a particular account in the nominal ledger
(d) CB, refer to a page in the cash book.

2.2 At 1 July 20X2, the Outer Business Company had no debtors at all. During July, the following transactions affecting credit sales and customers occurred.

(a) July 3: invoiced A Arnold for the sale on credit of hardware goods: £100

(b) July 11: invoiced B Bagshaw for the sale on credit of electrical goods: £150

(c) July 15: invoiced C Cloning for the sale on credit of hardware goods: £250

(d) July 10: received payment from A Arnold of £90, in settlement of his debt in full, having taken a permitted discount of £10 for payment within seven days

(e) July 18: received a payment of £72 from B Bagshaw in part settlement of £80 of his debt. A discount of £8 was allowed for payment within seven days of invoice

(f) July 28: received a payment of £120 from C Cloning, who was unable to claim any discount.

Account numbers are as follows:

SL 4	Personal account: A Arnold
SL 9	Personal account: B Bagshaw
SL 13	Personal account: C Cloning
NL 6	Debtors control account
NL 7	Discounts allowed
NL 21	Sales: hardware
NL 22	Sales: electrical
NL 1	Cash control account

2.3 The accounting entries, suitably dated, would be as follows.

SALES DAY BOOK   SDB 35

Date 20X2	Name	Folio	Total £	Hardware £	Electrical £
July 3	A Arnold	SL 4 Dr	100.00	100.00	
11	B Bagshaw	SL 9 Dr	150.00		150.00
15	C Cloning	SL13 Dr	250.00	250.00	
			500.00	350.00	150.00
			NL 6 Dr	NL 21 Cr	NL 22 Cr

Note. The personal accounts in the sales ledger are debited on the day the invoices are sent out. The double entry in the ledger accounts might be made at the end of each day, week or month; here it is made at the end of the month, by posting from the sales day book as follows.

			£	£
DEBIT	NL 6	Debtors control account	500	
CREDIT	NL 21	Sales: hardware		350
	NL 22	Sales: electrical		150

12: Control accounts

CASH BOOK EXTRACT
RECEIPTS CASH BOOK - JULY 20X2

CB 23

Date 20X2	Narrative	Folio	Total £	Discount £	Debtors £
July 10	A Arnold	SL 4 Cr	90.00	10.00	100.00
18	B Bagshaw	SL 9 Cr	72.00	8.00	80.00
28	C Cloning	SL 13 Cr	120.00	-	120.00
			282.00	18.00	300.00
			NL 1 Dr	NL 7 Dr	NL 6 Cr

The personal accounts in the sales ledger are memorandum accounts, because they are not a part of the double entry system.

MEMORANDUM SALES LEDGER
ARNOLD

A/c no: SL 4

Date 20X2	Narrative	Folio	£	Date 20X2	Narrative	Folio	£
July 3	Sales	SDB 35	100.00	July 10	Cash	CB 23	90.00
					Discount	CB 23	10.00
			100.00				100.00

B BAGSHAW

A/c no: SL 9

Date 20X2	Narrative	Folio	£	Date 20X2	Narrative	Folio	£
July 11	Sales	SDB 35	150.00	July 18	Cash	CB 23	72.00
					Discount	CB 23	8.00
				July 31	Balance	c/d	70.00
			150.00				150.00
Aug 1	Balance	b/d	70.00				

C CLONING

A/c no: SL 13

Date 20X2	Narrative	Folio	£	Date 20X2	Narrative	Folio	£
July 15	Sales	SDB 35	250.00	July 28	Cash	CB 23	120.00
				July 31	Balance	c/d	130.00
			250.00				250.00
Aug 1	Balance	b/d	130.00				

In the nominal ledger, the accounting entries can be made from the books of prime entry to the ledger accounts, in this example at the end of the month.

NOMINAL LEDGER (EXTRACT)
TOTAL DEBTORS (SALES LEDGER CONTROL ACCOUNT)

A/c no: NL 6

Date 20X2	Narrative	Folio	£	Date 20X2	Narrative	Folio	£
July 31	Sales	SDB 35	500.00	July 31	Cash and discount	CB 23	300.00
				July 31	Balance	c/d	200.00
			500.00				500.00
Aug 1	Balance	b/d	200.00				

Note. At 31 July the closing balance on the debtors control account (£200) is the same as the total of the individual balances on the personal accounts in the sales ledger (£0 + £70 + £130).

Part C: Double entry bookkeeping and accounting treatments

DISCOUNT ALLOWED — A/c no: NL 7

Date 20X2	Narrative	Folio	£	Date	Narrative	Folio	£
July 31	Debtors	CB 23	18.00				

CASH CONTROL ACCOUNT — A/c no: NL 1

Date 20X2	Narrative	Folio	£	Date	Narrative	Folio	£
July 31	Cash received	CB 23	282.00				

SALES - HARDWARE — A/c no: NL 21

Date	Narrative	Folio	£	Date 20X2	Narrative	Folio	£
				July 31	Debtors	SDB 35	350.00

SALES - ELECTRICAL — A/c no: NL 22

Date	Narrative	Folio	£	Date 20X2	Narrative	Folio	£
				July 31	Debtors	SDB 35	150.00

2.4 If we took the balance on the accounts shown in this example as at 31 July 20X2 the trial balance (insofar as it is appropriate to call these limited extracts by this name) would be as follows.

TRIAL BALANCE

	Debit £	Credit £
Cash (all receipts)	282	
Debtors	200	
Discount allowed	18	
Sales: hardware		350
Sales: electrical		150
	500	500

The trial balance is shown here to emphasise the point that a trial balance **includes** the balances on control accounts, but **excludes** the balances on the personal accounts in the sales ledger and purchase ledger.

Accounting for creditors

2.5 If you were able to follow the example above dealing with the debtors control account, you should have no difficulty in dealing with similar examples relating to purchases/creditors. If necessary refer back to revise the entries made in the purchase day book and purchase ledger personal accounts.

Entries in control accounts

2.6 Typical entries in the control accounts are listed below. Folio reference Jnl indicates that the transaction is first lodged in the journal before posting to the control account and other accounts indicated. References SRDB and PRDB are to sales returns and purchase returns day books.

12: Control accounts

SALES LEDGER (DEBTORS) CONTROL

	Folio	£		Folio	£
Opening debit balances	b/f	7,000	Opening credit balances		
Sales	SDB	52,390	(if any)	b/f	200
Dishonoured bills or	Jnl	1,000	Cash received	CB	52,250
cheques			Discounts allowed	CB	1,250
Cash paid to clear credit			Returns inwards from		
balances	CB	110	debtors	SRDB	800
Closing credit balances	c/f	120	Bad debts	Jnl	300
			Closing debit balances	c/f	5,820
		60,620			60,620
Debit balances b/f		5,820	Credit balances b/f		120

Note. Opening credit balances are unusual in the debtors control account. They represent debtors to whom the business owes money, probably as a result of the over payment of debts or for advance payments of debts for which no invoices have yet been sent.

BOUGHT LEDGER (CREDITORS) CONTROL

	Folio	£		Folio	£
Opening debit balances			Opening credit balances	b/f	8,300
(if any)	b/f	70	Purchases and other		
Cash paid	CB	29,840	expenses	PDB	31,000
Discounts received	CB	30	Cash received clearing		
Returns outwards to	PRDB		debit balances	CB	20
suppliers		60	Closing debit balances		
Closing credit balances	c/f	9,400	(if any)	c/f	80
		39,400			39,400
Debit balances	b/f	80	Credit balances	b/f	9,400

Note. Opening debit balances in the creditors control account would represent suppliers who owe the business money, perhaps because debts have been overpaid or because debts have been prepaid before the supplier has sent an invoice.

2.7 Posting from the journal to the memorandum sales or bought ledgers and to the nominal ledger may be effected as in the following example, where C Cloning has returned goods with a sales value of £50.

Journal entry	Folio	Dr £	Cr £
Sales	NL 21	50	
To debtors' control	NL 6		50
To C Cloning (memorandum)	SL 13	-	50

Return of electrical goods inwards.

Question 1

A creditors control account contains the following entries:

	£
Bank	79,500
Credit purchases	83,200
Discounts received	3,750
Contra with debtors control account	4,000
Balance c/f at 31 December 20X8	12,920

There are no other entries in the account. What was the opening balance brought forward at 1 January 20X8?

215

Part C: Double entry bookkeeping and accounting treatments

Answer

	£	£
Amounts due to creditors at 1 January (balancing figure)		16,970
Purchases in year		83,200
		100,170
Less: cash paid to creditors in year	79,500	
Discounts received	3,750	
Contra with debtors control	4,000	
		87,250
Amounts still unpaid at 31 December		12,920

Question 2

The total of the balances in a company's sales ledger is £800 more than the debit balance on its debtors control account. Which one of the following errors could by itself account for the discrepancy?

- A   The sales day book has been undercast by £800
- B   Settlement discounts totalling £800 have been omitted from the nominal ledger
- C   One sales ledger account with a credit balance of £800 has been treated as a debit balance
- D   The cash receipts book has been undercast by £800

Answer

A   The total of sales invoices in the day book is debited to the control account. If the total is understated by £800, the debits in the control account will also be understated by £800. Options B and D would have the opposite effect: credit entries in the control account would be understated. Option C would lead to a discrepancy of 2 × £800 = £1,600.

2.8   It may help you to see how the debtors ledger and debtors (control) account are used set out in flowchart form.

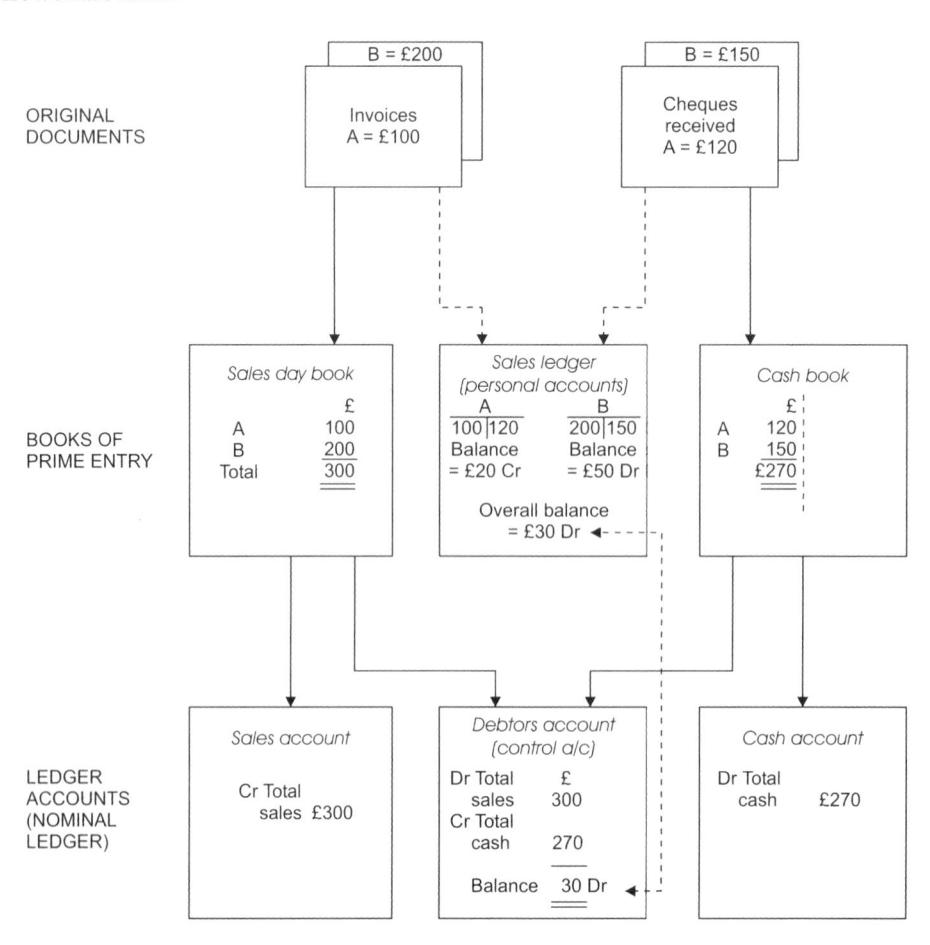

12: Control accounts

> **POINTS TO NOTE**
>
> - The debtors ledger is not part of the double entry system (it is not used to post the ledger accounts).
>
> - Nevertheless, the total balance on the debtors ledger (ie all the personal account balances added up) should equal the balance on the debtors account (the debtors control account).

2.9 See now whether you can do the following question yourself.

Question 3

On examining the books of Exports Ltd, you ascertain that on 1 October 20X8 the debtors' ledger balances were £8,024 debit and £57 credit, and the creditors' ledger balances on the same date £6,235 credit and £105 debit.

For the year ended 30 September 20X9 the following particulars are available.

	£
Sales	63,728
Purchases	39,974
Cash received from debtors	55,212
Cash paid to creditors	37,307
Discount received	1,475
Discount allowed	2,328
Returns inwards	1,002
Returns outwards	535
Bad debts written off	326
Cash received in respect of debit balances in creditors' ledger	105
Amount due from customer as shown by debtors' ledger, offset against amount due to the same firm as shown by creditors' ledger (settlement by contra)	434
Cash received in respect of debt written off as bad in a previous period	94
Allowances to customers on goods damaged in transit	212

On 30 September 20X9 there were no credit balances in the debtors' ledger except those outstanding on 1 October 20X8, and no debit balances in the creditors' ledger.

You are required to write up the following accounts recording the above transactions bringing down the balances as on 30 September 20X9:

(a) debtors control account; and
(b) creditors control account.

Answer

(a)

DEBTORS CONTROL ACCOUNT

20X8		£	20X8		£
Oct 1	Balances b/f	8,024	Oct 1	Balances b/f	57
20X9			20X9		
Sept 30	Sales	63,728	Sept 30	Cash received from debtors	55,212
	Balances c/f	57		Discount allowed	2,328
				Returns	1,002
				Bad debts written off	326
				Transfer creditors control account	434
				Allowances on goods damaged	212
				Balances c/f	12,238
		71,809			71,809

217

Part C: Double entry bookkeeping and accounting treatments

(b)

CREDITORS CONTROL ACCOUNT

		£			£
20X8			20X8		
Oct 1	Balances b/f	105	Oct 1	Balances b/f	6,235
20X9			20X9		
Sept 30	Cash paid to creditors	37,307	Sept 30	Purchases	39,974
	Discount received	1,475		Cash	105
	Returns outwards	535			
	Transfer debtors control account	434			
	Balances c/f	6,458			
		46,314			46,314

Note. The double entry in respect of cash received for the bad debt written off in a previous period is:

| DEBIT | Cash | £94 | |
| CREDIT | Profit and loss account | | £94 |

3 THE PURPOSE OF CONTROL ACCOUNTS

Reasons for having control accounts

3.1 The reasons for having control accounts are as follows.

(a) They provide a **check on the accuracy** of entries made in the personal accounts in the sales ledger and purchase ledger. It is very easy to make a mistake in posting entries, because there might be hundreds of entries to make. Figures might get transposed. Some entries might be omitted altogether, so that an invoice or a payment transaction does not appear in a personal account as it should. By comparing:

- The total balance on the debtors control account with the total of individual balances on the personal accounts in the sales ledger
- The total balance on the creditors control account with the total of individual balances on the personal accounts in the purchase ledger

It is possible to identify the fact that errors have been made.

(b) The control accounts could also assist in the **location of errors**, where postings to the control accounts are made daily or weekly, or even monthly. If a clerk fails to record an invoice or a payment in a personal account, or makes a transposition error, it would be a formidable task to locate the error or errors at the end of a year, say, given the hundreds or thousands of transactions during the year. By using the control account, a comparison with the individual balances in the sales or purchase ledger can be made for every week or day of the month, and the error found much more quickly than if control accounts did not exist.

(c) Where there is a separation of clerical (bookkeeping) duties, the control account provides an **internal check**. The person posting entries to the control accounts will act as a check on a different person whose job it is to post entries to the sales and purchase ledger accounts.

(d) To provide debtors' and creditors' balances more quickly for producing a trial balance or balance sheet. A single balance on a control account is obviously **extracted more simply and quickly** than many individual balances in the sales or purchase ledger. This means also that the number of accounts in the double entry bookkeeping system can be kept down to a manageable size, since the personal accounts are memorandum accounts only and the control accounts instead provide the accounts required for a double entry system.

3.2 However, particularly in computerised systems, it may be feasible to use sales and purchase ledgers without the need for operating separate control accounts. In such a system, the sales or purchase ledger printouts produced by the computer constitute the list of individual balances as well as providing a total balance which represents the control account balance.

> **Exam focus point**
> You may be asked to explain the purpose of control accounts. However, the most likely type of question is a **control account reconciliation**. This is covered below.

Balancing and agreeing control accounts with sales and purchase (bought) ledgers

3.3 The control accounts should be **balanced regularly** (at least monthly), and the balance on the account agreed with the sum of the individual debtors' or creditors' balances extracted from the sales or bought ledgers respectively. It is one of the sad facts of an accountant's life that more often than not the balance on the control account does not agree with the sum of balances extracted, for one or more of the following reasons.

(a) An **incorrect amount** may be **posted** to the control account because of a miscast of the total in the book of prime entry (ie adding up incorrectly the total value of invoices or payments). The nominal ledger debit and credit postings will then balance, but the control account balance will not agree with the sum of individual balances extracted from the (memorandum) sales ledger or purchase ledger. A journal entry must then be made in the nominal ledger to correct the control account and the corresponding sales or expense account.

(b) A **transposition** error may occur in posting an individual's balance from the book of prime entry to the memorandum ledger, eg the sale to C Cloning of £250 might be posted to his account as £520. This means that the sum of balances extracted from the memorandum ledger must be corrected. No accounting entry would be required to do this, except to alter the figure in C Cloning's account.

(c) A transaction may be recorded in the control account and not in the memorandum ledger, or vice versa. This requires an entry in the ledger that has been **missed out** which means a double posting if the control account has to be corrected, and a single posting if it is the individual's balance in the memorandum ledger that is at fault.

(d) The sum of balances extracted from the memorandum ledger may be **incorrectly extracted** or **miscast**. This would involve simply correcting the total of the balances.

Example: agreeing control account balances with the sales and bought ledgers

3.4 Reconciling the control account balance with the sum of the balances extracted from the (memorandum) sales ledger or bought ledger should be done in two stages.

(a) Correct the total of the balances extracted from the memorandum ledger. (The errors must be located first of course.)

Part C: Double entry bookkeeping and accounting treatments

	£	£
Sales ledger total		
Original total extracted		15,320
Add difference arising from transposition error (£95 written as £59)		36
		15,356
Less		
Credit balance of £60 extracted as a debit balance (£60 × 2)	120	
Overcast of list of balances	90	
		210
		15,146

(b) Bring down the balance before adjustments on the control account, and adjust or post the account with correcting entries.

DEBTORS CONTROL

	£		£
Balance before adjustments	15,091	Petty cash - posting omitted	10
		Returns inwards - individual posting omitted from control account	35
Undercast of total invoices issued in sales day book	100	Balance c/f (now in agreement with the corrected total of individual balances in (a))	15,146
	15,191		15,191
Balance b/f	15,146		

Chapter roundup

- The two most important **control accounts** are those for **debtors** and **creditors**. They are part of the double entry system.

- Cash books and day books are totalled periodically (say once a month) and the appropriate **totals are posted** to the control accounts.

- The individual entries in cash and day books will have been entered one by one in the appropriate **personal accounts** contained in the sales ledger and purchase ledger. These personal accounts are not part of the double entry system: they are memorandum only.

- At suitable intervals the balances on personal accounts are extracted from the ledgers, listed and totalled. The total of the outstanding balances can then be **reconciled** to the balance on the appropriate control account and any errors located and corrected.

Quick quiz

1   Name five accounting items for which control accounts may be used in the nominal ledger.

2   Give four reasons why a debtors control account is needed as well as a sales ledger.

3   During a period, A Ltd has the following transactions on debtors control account. Sales £125,000, cash received £50,000, discounts allowed £2,000. The balance carried forward is £95,000. What was the opening balance at the beginning of the period?

   A   £22,000 debit
   B   £22,000 credit
   C   £26,000 debit
   D   £20,000 debit

Answers to quick quiz

1. Debtors, creditors, stock, wages and salaries, cash.

2. See paragraph 3.1.

3. A

Debtors control			
	£		£
Bal b/f (bal figure)	22,000	Cash	50,000
Sales	125,000	Discounts allowed	2,000
		Bal c/f	95,000
	147,000		147,000

Now try the question below from the Exam Question Bank

Question to try	Level	Marks	Time
19	Full exam	10	18 mins

Chapter 13

CORRECTION OF ERRORS

Topic list	Syllabus reference
1 Types of error in accounting	3(b)
2 The correction of errors	3(b)

Introduction

This chapter continues the subject of errors in accounts. You have already learned about errors which arise in the context of the cash book or the sales and purchase ledgers and debtors and creditors control accounts. Here we deal with errors that may be corrected by means of the journal or a suspense account.

By the end of this chapter you should be able to prepare a set of final accounts for a sole trader from a trial balance after incorporating adjustments to profit for errors.

Study guide

Section 5 - The journal; ledger control accounts; bank reconciliations

- Explain the uses of the journal.
- Illustrate the use of the journal and the posting of journal entries into ledger accounts.
- Explain the types of error which may occur in bookkeeping systems, identifying those which can and those which cannot be detected by preparing a trial balance.
- Illustrate the use of the journal in correcting errors, including the use of a suspense account.
- Explain the preparation of statements correcting the profit for errors discovered.

Exam guide

Errors are more likely to be the subject of a MCQ in Section A. However the correction of errors could be included as part of a larger question in Section B.

1 TYPES OF ERROR IN ACCOUNTING

1.1 It is not really possible to draw up a complete list of all the errors which might be made by bookkeepers and accountants. Even if you tried, it is more than likely that as soon as you finished, someone would commit a completely new error that you had never even dreamed of! However, it is possible to describe five **types of error** which cover most of the errors which might occur. They are as follows.

- Errors of **transposition**
- Errors of **omission**
- Errors of **principle**
- Errors of **commission**
- **Compensating** errors

13: Correction of errors

Some of these we have already looked at in the context of the cash book, sales and purchase ledgers and debtors and creditors control accounts.

1.2 Once an error has been detected, it needs to be put right.

(a) If the correction **involves a double entry** in the ledger accounts, then it is done by using a **journal entry** in the journal.

(b) When the error **breaks the rule of double entry**, then it is corrected by the use of a **suspense account** as well as a journal entry.

1.3 In this chapter we will:

(a) Look at the five common types of error
(b) Review journal entries (which we briefly looked at earlier in this text)
(c) Define a **suspense account**, and describe how it is used.

Errors of transposition

> **KEY TERM**
>
> An **error of transposition** is when two digits in an amount are accidentally recorded the wrong way round.

1.4 For example, suppose that a sale is recorded in the sales account as £6,843, but it has been incorrectly recorded in the total debtors account as £6,483. The error is the transposition of the 4 and the 8. The consequence is that total debits will not be equal to total credits. *Note: Differences arising from transposition errors are always divisible by 9. If you have a difference that is a multiple of 9, this might be an indication that you should be looking for a transposition error. For example, £6,843 – £6,483 = £360; £360 ÷ 9 = 40.*

Errors of omission

> **KEY TERM**
>
> An **error of omission** means failing to record a transaction at all, or making a debit or credit entry, but not the corresponding double entry.

1.5 Here are two examples.

(a) If a business receives an invoice from a supplier for £250, the transaction might be omitted from the books entirely. As a result, both the total debits and the total credits of the business will be out by £250.

(b) If a business receives an invoice from a supplier for £300, the purchase ledger control account might be credited, but the debit entry in the purchases account might be omitted. In this case, the total credits would not equal total debits (because total debits are £300 less than they ought to be).

Part C: Double entry bookkeeping and accounting treatments

Errors of principle

> **KEY TERM**
>
> An **error of principle** involves making a double entry in the belief that the transaction is being entered in the correct accounts, but subsequently finding out that the accounting entry breaks the 'rules' of an accounting principle or concept.

1.6 A typical example of such an error is to treat certain revenue expenditure incorrectly as capital expenditure.

(a) For example, repairs to a machine costing £150 should be treated as revenue expenditure, and debited to a repairs account. If, instead, the repair costs are added to the cost of the fixed asset (capital expenditure) an error of principle would have occurred. As a result, although total debits still equal total credits, the repairs account is £150 less than it should be and the cost of the fixed asset is £150 greater than it should be.

(b) Similarly, suppose that the proprietor of the business sometimes takes cash out of the till for his personal use and during a certain year these drawings amount to £280. The book-keeper states that he has reduced cash sales by £280 so that the cash book could be made to balance. This would be an error of principle, and the result of it would be that the drawings account is understated by £280, and so is the total value of sales in the sales account.

Errors of commission

> **KEY TERM**
>
> **Errors of commission** are where the bookkeeper makes a mistake in carrying out his or her task of recording transactions in the accounts.

1.7 Here are two common errors of commission.

(a) **Putting a debit entry or a credit entry in the wrong account**. For example, if telephone expenses of £540 are debited to the electricity expenses account, an error of commission would have occurred. The result is that although total debits and total credits balance, telephone expenses are understated by £540 and electricity expenses are overstated by the same amount.

(b) **Errors of casting (adding up)**. Suppose for example that the total daily credit sales in the sales day book of a business should add up to £28,425, but are incorrectly added up as £28,825. The total sales in the sales day book are then used to credit total sales and debit total debtors in the ledger accounts, so that total debits and total credits are still equal, although incorrect.

Compensating errors

> **KEY TERM**
>
> **Compensating errors** are errors which are, coincidentally, equal and opposite to one another.

1.8 For example, two transposition errors of £540 might occur in extracting ledger balances, one on each side of the double entry. In the administration expenses account, £2,282 might be written instead of £2,822, while in the sundry income account, £8,391 might be written instead of £8,931. Both the debits and the credits would be £540 too low, and the mistake would not be apparent when the trial balance is cast. Consequently, compensating errors hide the fact that there are errors in the trial balance.

2 THE CORRECTION OF ERRORS   December 2002

Journal entries

2.1 Some errors can be corrected by **journal entries**. To remind you, the format of a journal entry is:

Date	*Folio*	*Debit*	*Credit*
		£	£
Account to be debited		X	
Account to be credited			X
(Narrative to explain the transaction)			

> **Exam focus point**
>
> As already indicated, you are often required in an exam to present answers in the form of journal entries. The December 2002 exam included a nine mark question on journal entries to correct errors and writing up a suspense account.

2.2 The journal requires a debit and an equal credit entry for each 'transaction' - ie for each correction. This means that if total debits equal total credits before a journal entry is made then they will still be equal after the journal entry is made. This would be the case if, for example, the original error was a debit wrongly posted as a credit or vice versa.

2.3 Similarly, if total debits and total credits are unequal before a journal entry is made, then they will still be unequal (by the same amount) after it is made.

2.4 For example, a bookkeeper accidentally posts a bill for £40 to the rates account instead of to the electricity account. A trial balance is drawn up, and total debits are £40,000 and total credits are £40,000. A journal entry is made to correct the misposting error as follows.

1.7.20X7

DEBIT	Electricity account	£40	
CREDIT	Rates account		£40

To correct a misposting of £40 from the rates account to electricity account.

2.5 After the journal has been posted, total debits will still be £40,000 and total credits will be £40,000. Total debits and totals credits are still equal.

Part C: Double entry bookkeeping and accounting treatments

2.6 Now suppose that, because of some error which has not yet been detected, total debits were originally £40,000 but total credits were £39,900. If the same journal correcting the £40 is put through, total debits will remain £40,000 and total credits will remain £39,900. Total debits were different by £100 *before* the journal, and they are still different by £100 *after* the journal.

2.7 This means that journals can only be used to correct errors which require both a credit and (an equal) debit adjustment.

2.8 EXAMPLE: JOURNAL ENTRIES

Listed below are five errors which were used as examples earlier in this chapter. Write out the journal entries which would correct these errors.

(a) A business receives an invoice for £250 from a supplier which was omitted from the books entirely.

(b) Repairs worth £150 were incorrectly debited to the fixed asset (machinery) account instead of the repairs account.

(c) The bookkeeper of a business reduces cash sales by £280 because he was not sure what the £280 represented. In fact, it was drawings.

(d) Telephone expenses of £540 are incorrectly debited to the electricity account.

(e) A page in the sales day book has been added up to £28,425 instead of £28,825.

2.9 SOLUTION

(a) DEBIT   Purchases   £250
    CREDIT Creditors   £250

   A transaction previously omitted.

(b) DEBIT   Repairs account   £150
    CREDIT Fixed asset (machinery) a/c   £150

   The correction of an error of principle. Repairs costs incorrectly added to fixed asset costs.

(c) DEBIT   Drawings account   £280
    CREDIT Sales   £280

   An error of principle, in which sales were reduced to compensate for cash drawings not accounted for.

(d) DEBIT   Telephone expenses   £540
    CREDIT Electricity expenses   £540

   Correction of an error of commission. Telephone expenses wrongly charged to the electricity account.

(e) DEBIT   Debtors   £400
    CREDIT Sales   £400

   The correction of a casting error in the sales day book.
   (£28,825 − £28,425 = £400)

Use of journal entries in examinations

2.10 Occasionally an examination question might ask you to 'journalise' a transaction (ie write it out in the form of a journal entry), even though the transaction is perfectly normal and nothing to do with an error. This is just the examiner's way of finding out whether you know your debits and credits. For example:

Question: A business sells £500 of goods on credit. Journalise the transaction.

Answer:

DEBIT	Debtors	£500	
CREDIT	Sales		£500

Goods to the value of £500 sold on credit.

2.11 No error has occurred here, just a normal credit sale of £500. By asking you to put it in the form of a journal, the examiner can see that you understand the double-entry bookkeeping.

Suspense accounts

KEY TERM

A **suspense account** is an account showing a balance equal to the difference in a trial balance.

2.12 A suspense account is a **temporary** account which can be opened for a number of reasons. The most common reasons are as follows.

(a) A trial balance is drawn up which does not balance (ie total debits do not equal total credits).

(b) The bookkeeper of a business knows where to post the credit side of a transaction, but does not know where to post the debit (or vice versa). For example, a cash payment might be made and must obviously be credited to cash. But the bookkeeper may not know what the payment is for, and so will not know which account to debit.

2.13 In both these cases, a temporary suspense account is opened up until the problem is sorted out. The next few paragraphs explain exactly how this works.

Use of suspense account: when the trial balance does not balance

2.14 When an error has occurred which results in an imbalance between total debits and total credits in the ledger accounts, the first step is to open a suspense account. For example, suppose an accountant draws up a trial balance and finds that, for some reason he cannot immediately discover, total debits exceed total credits by £162.

2.15 He knows that there is an error somewhere, but for the time being he opens a suspense account and enters a credit of £162 in it. This serves two purposes.

(a) Because the suspense account now exists, the accountant will not forget that there is an error (of £162) to be sorted out.

(b) Now that there is a credit of £162 in the suspense account, the trial balance balances.

2.16 When the cause of the £162 discrepancy is tracked down, it is corrected by means of a journal entry. For example, suppose it turned out that the accountant had accidentally failed to make a credit of £162 to purchases. The journal entry would be:

DEBIT	Suspense a/c	£162	
CREDIT	Purchases		£162

To close off suspense a/c and correct error.

Part C: Double entry bookkeeping and accounting treatments

2.17 Whenever an error occurs which results in total debits not being equal to total credits, the first step an accountant makes is to open up a suspense account. Three more examples are given below.

2.18 EXAMPLE: TRANSPOSITION ERROR

The bookkeeper of Mixem Gladly Ltd made a transposition error when entering an amount for sales in the sales account. Instead of entering the correct amount of £37,453.60 he entered £37,543.60, transposing the 4 and 5. The debtors were posted correctly, and so when total debits and credits on the ledger accounts were compared, it was found that credits exceeded debits by £(37,543.60 – 37,453.60) = £90.

2.19 The initial step is to equalise the total debits and credits by posting a debit of £90 to a suspense account.

2.20 When the cause of the error is discovered, the double entry to correct it should be logged in the journal as:

DEBIT	Sales	£90	
CREDIT	Suspense a/c		£90

To close off suspense a/c and correct transposition error.

2.21 EXAMPLE: ERROR OF OMISSION

When Guttersnipe Builders paid the monthly salary cheques to its office staff, the payment of £5,250 was correctly entered in the cash account, but the bookkeeper omitted to debit the office salaries account. As a consequence, the total debit and credit balances on the ledger accounts were not equal, and credits exceeded debits by £5,250.

2.22 The initial step in correcting the situation is to debit £5,250 to a suspense account, to equalise the total debits and total credits.

2.23 When the cause of the error is discovered, the double entry to correct it should be logged in the journal as:

DEBIT	Office salaries account	£5,250	
CREDIT	Suspense account		£5,250

To close off suspense account and correct error of omission.

2.24 EXAMPLE: ERROR OF COMMISSION

A bookkeeper might make a mistake by entering what should be a debit entry as a credit, or vice versa. For example, suppose that a credit customer pays £460 of the £660 he owes to Ashdown Tree Felling Contractors, but Ashdown's bookkeeper has debited £460 on the debtors account in the nominal ledger by mistake instead of crediting the payment received.

2.25 The total debit balances in Ashdown's ledger accounts would now exceed the total credits by 2 × £460 = £920. The initial step in correcting the error would be to make a credit entry of £920 in a suspense account. When the cause of the error is discovered, it should be corrected as follows.

DEBIT	Suspense account	£920	
CREDIT	Debtors		£920

To close off suspense account and correct error of commission.

13: Correction of errors

2.26 In the debtors account in the nominal ledger, the correction would appear therefore as follows.

DEBTORS ACCOUNT

	£		£
Balance b/f	660	Suspense account: error corrected	920
Payment incorrectly debited	460	Balance c/f	200
	1,120		1,120

Use of suspense account: not knowing where to post a transaction

2.27 Another use of suspense accounts occurs when a bookkeeper does not know in which account to post one side of a transaction. Until the mystery is sorted out, the credit entry can be recorded in a suspense account. A typical example is when the business receives cash through the post from a source which cannot be determined. The double entry in the accounts would be a debit in the cash book, and a credit to a suspense account.

2.28 EXAMPLE: NOT KNOWING WHERE TO POST A TRANSACTION

Windfall Garments received a cheque in the post for £620. The name on the cheque is R J Beasley Esq, but Windfall Garments have no idea who this person is, nor why he should be sending £620. The bookkeeper decides to open a suspense account, so that the double entry for the transaction is:

DEBIT	Cash	£620	
CREDIT	Suspense account		£620

2.29 Eventually, it transpires that the cheque was in payment for a debt owed by the Haute Couture Corner Shop and paid out of the proprietor's personal bank account. The suspense account can now be cleared, as follows.

DEBIT	Suspense account	£620	
CREDIT	Debtors		£620

Question 1

You are assisting the accountant, of Beavis Ltd in preparing the accounts for the year ended 31 December 20X7. You draw up a trial balance and you notice that the credit side is greater than the debit side by £11,482.29. You enter this difference in a suspense account.

On investigation, the following errors and omissions are found to have occurred.

(a) An invoice for £3,217.20 for general insurance has been posted to cash but not to the ledger account.

(b) A customer went into liquidation just before the year end, owing Justin & West £1,425.53. The amount was taken off debtors but the corresponding entry to expense the bad debt has not been made.

(c) A cheque paid for purchases has been posted to the purchases account as £4,196.29, when the cheque was made out for £4,916.29.

(d) A van was purchased during the year for £3,059.78, but this amount was credited to the motor vehicles account.

Required

(a) Show the journal required to clear the suspense account.
(b) Show the suspense account in ledger account form.

Part C: Double entry bookkeeping and accounting treatments

Answer

(a) *Journal*

		£	£
DEBIT	Insurance	3,217.20	
	Bad debt expense	1,425.53	
	Purchases (£4,916.29 – £4,196.29)	720.00	
	Motor vehicles (£3,059.78 × 2)	6,119.56	
CREDIT	Suspense account		11,482.29

(b) *In ledger account form*

SUSPENSE ACCOUNT

	£		£
Balance b/f	11,482.29	Insurance	3,217.20
		Bad debt expense	1,425.53
		Purchases	720.00
Payment incorrectly debited		Motor vehicles	6,119.56
	11,482.29		11,482.29

Suspense accounts might contain several items

2.30 If more than one error or unidentifiable posting to a ledger account arises during an accounting period, they will all be merged together in the same suspense account. Indeed, until the causes of the errors are discovered, the bookkeepers are unlikely to know exactly how many errors there are. An examination question might give you a balance on a suspense account, together with enough information to make the necessary corrections, leaving a nil balance on the suspense account and correct balances on various other accounts. In practice, of course, finding these errors is far from easy!

Suspense accounts are temporary

2.31 It must be stressed that a suspense account can only be temporary. Postings to a suspense account are only made when the bookkeeper doesn't know yet what to do, or when an error has occurred. Mysteries must be solved, and errors must be corrected. Under no circumstances should there still be a suspense account when it comes to preparing the balance sheet of a business. The suspense account must be cleared and all the correcting entries made before the final accounts are drawn up.

Question 2

At the year end of T Down & Co, an imbalance in the trial balance was revealed which resulted in the creation of a suspense account with a credit balance of £1,040.

Investigations revealed the following errors.

(i) A sale of goods on credit for £1,000 had been omitted from the sales account.

(ii) Delivery and installation costs of £240 on a new item of plant had been recorded as a revenue expense.

(iii) Cash discount of £150 on paying a creditor, JW, had been taken, even though the payment was made outside the time limit.

(iv) Stock of stationery at the end of the period of £240 had been ignored.

(v) A purchase of raw materials of £350 had been recorded in the purchases account as £850.

(vi) The purchase returns day book included a sales credit note for £230 which had been entered correctly in the account of the debtor concerned, but included with purchase returns in the nominal ledger.

13: Correction of errors

Required

(a) Prepare journal entries to correct *each* of the above errors. Narratives are *not* required.

(b) Open a suspense account and show the corrections to be made.

(c) Prior to the discovery of the errors, T Down & Co's gross profit for the year was calculated at £35,750 and the net profit for the year at £18,500.

Calculate the revised gross and net profit figures after the correction of the errors.

Answer

(a)

				Dr £	Cr £
(i)		DEBIT	Suspense a/c	1,000	
		CREDIT	Sales		1,000
(ii)		DEBIT	Plant	240	
		CREDIT	Delivery cost		240
(iii)		DEBIT	Cash discount received	150	
		CREDIT	JW a/c		150
(iv)		DEBIT	Stock of stationery	240	
		CREDIT	Stationery expense		240
(v)		DEBIT	Suspense a/c	500	
		CREDIT	Purchases		500
(vi)		DEBIT	Purchase returns	230	
		DEBIT	Sales returns	230	
		CREDIT	Suspense a/c		460

(b)

SUSPENSE A/C

		£		£
(i)	Sales	1,000	End of year balance	1,040
(v)	Purchases	500	(vi) Purchase returns/sales returns	460
		1,500		1,500

(c)

	£
Gross profit originally reported	35,750
Sales omitted	1,000
Plant costs wrongly allocated	240
Incorrect recording of purchases	500
Sales credit note wrongly allocated	(460)
Adjusted gross profit	37,030

	£
Net profit originally reported	18,500
Adjustments to gross profit £(37,030 – 35,750)	1,280
Cash discount incorrectly taken	(150)
Stationery stock	240
Adjusted net profit	19,870

Note. It has been assumed that the delivery and installation costs on plant have been included in purchases.

Part C: Double entry bookkeeping and accounting treatments

Chapter roundup

- There are five **types of error**.
    - Errors of transposition
    - Errors of omission
    - Errors of principle
    - Errors of commission
    - Compensating errors

- Errors which leave total debits and total credits on the ledger accounts in balance can be corrected by using **journal entries**. Otherwise, a suspense account has to be opened first (and a journal entry used later to record the correction of the error, clearing the suspense account in the process).

- **Suspense accounts**, as well as being used to correct some errors, are also opened when it is not known immediately where to post an amount. When the mystery is solved, the suspense account is closed and the amount correctly posted using a journal entry.

- **Suspense accounts are only temporary**. None should exist when it comes to drawing up the financial statements at the end of the accounting period.

Quick quiz

1. List five types of error made in accounting.
2. What is the format of a journal entry?
3. Explain what a suspense account is.
4. What must be done with a suspense account before preparing a balance sheet?
5. Sales returns of £460 have inadvertently been posted to the purchase returns, although the correct entry has been made to the debtors control. A suspense account needs to be set up for how much?

    A £460 debit
    B £460 credit
    C £920 debit
    D £920 credit

Answers to quick quiz

1. Transposition, omission, principle, commission and compensating errors.
2. See paragraph 2.1.
3. An account showing a balance equal to the difference on a trial balance.
4. All errors must be identified and the suspense account cleared to nil.
5. C The sales returns of £460 will have to be credited to debtors and also £460 has been credited to purchase returns. Therefore the trial balance needs a debit of 2 × £460 = £920 to balance.

Now try the question below from the Exam Question Bank

Question to try	Level	Marks	Time
20	Introductory	n/a	36 mins

Part D
Accounting conventions and standards

Chapter 14

ACCOUNTING CONVENTIONS

Chapter topic list	Syllabus reference
1 Background	1(d), 2(a)
2 Fundamental accounting concepts	1(d), 2(a)
3 Other important concepts and conventions	2(b)
4 Accounting policies	1(d), 2(a)
5 The ASB's Statement	1(e), 2(a)

Introduction

The purpose of this part of the text is to encourage you to think more deeply about the **assumptions** on which financial accounts are prepared.

This chapter deals with the accounting conventions which lie behind accounts preparation and which you may have absorbed subconsciously in the preceding chapters on bookkeeping.

In Chapters 15 and 16 you will see how conventions and assumptions are **put into practice** with regard to certain items which are the subject of accounting standards.

Study guide

Section 14 - Accounting concepts and conventions; The ASB's 'Statement of Principles for Financial Reporting' (The Statement)

- Explain the need for an agreed conceptual framework for financial accounting.

- Explain the importance of the following accounting conventions (not mentioned in the Statement).

    - Business entity
    - Money measurement
    - Duality
    - Historical cost
    - Realisation
    - Time interval

- Revise the users of financial statements from Session 1.

- Explain the qualitative characteristics of financial statements as described in Chapter 3 of the Statement (Revision from Section 1).

Exam guide

You may be asked to discuss accounting concepts and to give examples to back up your arguments. Practise written questions on this subject as it is useful to develop your written work in preparation for the exam.

Part D: Accounting conventions and standards

1 BACKGROUND

1.1 Accounting practice has developed gradually over a matter of centuries. Many of its procedures are operated automatically by people who have never questioned whether alternative methods exist which are just as valid. However, the procedures in common use imply the acceptance of certain **concepts** which are by no means self-evident; nor are they the only possible **concepts**. These concepts could be used to build up an accounting framework.

1.2 Our next step is to look at some of the more important concepts which are taken for granted in preparing accounts. Originally, a statement of standard accounting practice (SSAP 2 *Disclosure of accounting policies*) described four concepts as *fundamental accounting concepts*: they were **going concern, prudence, accruals** and **consistency**. These four are also identified as fundamental by the Companies Act 1985, which adds a fifth to the list (the **separate valuation** principle).

1.3 In December 2000 FRS 18 *Accounting policies* replaced SSAP 2. FRS 18 emphasises the importance of **going concern** and **accruals** calling them the **bedrock** of financial statements. **Prudence** and **consistency** have been relegated to '**desirable**' elements of financial statements.

> **Exam focus point**
>
> You still need to learn the concepts of prudence and consistency, just put them into the correct context; going concern and accruals are **more** important concepts.

1.4 In this chapter we shall single out the following concepts for discussion.

(a) The **going concern** concept
(b) The **accruals** or matching concept
(c) The **prudence** concept
(d) The **consistency** concept
(e) The **entity** concept
(f) The **money measurement** concept
(g) The **separate valuation** principle
(h) The **materiality** concept
(i) The **historical cost** convention
(j) The **stable monetary** unit
(k) The **objectivity** concept
(l) The **realisation** concept
(m) The **duality** concept
(n) **Substance over form**
(o) The **time interval** concept

2 FUNDAMENTAL ACCOUNTING CONCEPTS   June 2002

2.1 Below are discussed the two fundamental accounting concepts as identified by FRS 18 *Accounting policies*.

14: Accounting conventions

The going concern concept

June 2002

> **KEY TERM**
>
> The **going concern concept** implies that the business will continue in operational existence for the foreseeable future, and that there is no intention to put the company into liquidation or to make drastic cutbacks to the scale of operations.

2.2 FRS 18 states that the financial statements **must** be prepared under the going concern basis unless the entity is being (or is going to be) liquidated or if it has ceased (or is about to cease) trading. The directors of a company must also disclose any significant doubts about the company's future if and when they arise.

2.3 The main significance of the going concern concept is that the assets of the business should not be valued at their 'break-up' value, which is the amount that they would sell for if they were sold off piecemeal and the business were thus broken up.

2.4 EXAMPLE: GOING CONCERN CONCEPT

Emma acquires a T-shirt making machine at a cost of £60,000. The asset has an estimated life of six years, and it is normal to write off the cost of the asset to the profit and loss account over this time. In this case a depreciation cost of £10,000 per annum will be charged.

2.5 Using the going concern concept, it is presumed that the business will continue its operations and so the asset will live out its full six years in use. A depreciation charge of £10,000 will be made each year, and the value of the asset in the balance sheet will be its cost less the accumulated amount of depreciation charged to date. After one year, the **net book value** of the asset would therefore be £(60,000 – 10,000) = £50,000, after two years it would be £40,000, after three years £30,000 etc, until it has been written down to a value of 0 after 6 years.

2.6 Now suppose that this asset has no other operational use outside the business, and in a forced sale it would only sell for scrap. After one year of operation, its scrap value is, say, £8,000.

2.7 The net book value of the asset, applying the going concern concept, is £50,000 after one year, but its immediate sell-off value only £8,000. It might be argued that the asset is over-valued at £50,000 and that it should be written down to its break-up value (ie shown at £8,000 in the balance sheet and the balance of its cost treated as an expense). However, provided that the going concern concept is valid so that the asset continues to be used and not sold, it is appropriate accounting practice to value the asset at its net book value.

Question 1

Now try this example yourself.

A retailer commences business on 1 January and buys a stock of 20 washing machines, each costing £100. During the year he sells 17 machines at £150 each. How should the remaining machines be valued at 31 December if:

(a) He is forced to close down his business at the end of the year and the remaining machines will realise only £60 each in a forced sale?

Part D: Accounting conventions and standards

(b) He intends to continue his business into the next year?

Answer

(a) If the business is to be closed down, the remaining three machines must be valued at the amount they will realise in a forced sale, ie 3 × £60 = £180.

(b) If the business is regarded as a going concern, the stock unsold at 31 December will be carried forward into the following year, when the cost of the three machines will be matched against the eventual sale proceeds in computing that year's profits. The three machines will therefore appear in the balance sheet at 31 December at cost, 3 × £100 = £300.

The accruals concept or matching concept   June 2002

2.8 FRS 18 also stipulates that financial statements must be prepared under the accruals concept. This concept is a cornerstone of present day financial statements, so work through this section carefully so that you understand how it is applied during the preparation of accounts.

> **KEY TERM**
>
> The **accruals concept** states that revenue and costs must be recognised as they are earned or incurred, not as money is received or paid. They must be matched with one another so far as their relationship can be established or justifiably assumed, and dealt with in the profit and loss account of the period to which they relate.

2.9 If Emma makes 20 T-shirts at a cost of £100 and sells them for £200, she makes a profit of £100.

2.10 However, if Emma had only sold eighteen T-shirts, it would have been incorrect to charge her profit and loss account with the cost of twenty T-shirts, as she still has two T-shirts in stock. If she intends to sell them in June she is likely to make a profit on the sale. Therefore, only the purchase cost of eighteen T-shirts (£90) should be matched with her sales revenue, leaving her with a profit of £90.

Her balance sheet would therefore look like this.

	£
Assets	
Stock (at cost, ie 2 × £5)	10
Debtors (18 × £10)	180
	190
Liabilities	
Creditors	100
	90
Proprietor's capital (profit for the period)	90

2.11 Suppose, Emma had decided to give up selling T-shirts, then the going concern concept would no longer apply and the value of the two T-shirts in the balance sheet would be a break-up valuation rather than cost. Similarly, if the two unsold T-shirts were now unlikely to be sold at more than their cost of £5 each (say, because of damage or a fall in demand) then they should be recorded on the balance sheet at their **net realisable value** (ie the likely eventual sales price less any expenses incurred to make them saleable, eg paint) rather than cost. This shows the application of the prudence concept (see section 3 for details).

2.12 In this example, the concepts of going concern and matching are linked. As the business is assumed to be a going concern, it is possible to carry forward the cost of the unsold T-shirts as a charge against profits of the next period.

The accruals concept defined

2.13 Essentially, the accruals concept states that, in computing profit, revenue earned must be matched against the expenditure incurred in earning it.

2.14 The Companies Act 1985 gives legal recognition to the accruals concept, stating that: 'All income and charges relating to the financial year to which the accounts relate shall be taken into account, without regard to the date of receipt or payment.' This has the effect, as we have seen, of requiring businesses to take credit for sales and purchases when made, rather than when paid for, and also to carry unsold stock forward in the balance sheet rather than to deduct its cost from profit for the period.

3 OTHER IMPORTANT CONCEPTS AND CONVENTIONS
Pilot paper, December 2001, June 2002

The prudence concept December 2001

> **KEY TERM**
>
> The **prudence concept** states that where alternative procedures, or alternative valuations, are possible, the one selected should be the one which gives the most cautious presentation of the business's financial position or results.

3.1 The importance of **prudence** has diminished over time. Prudence is a **desirable quality** of financial statements but **not** a bedrock. The key reason for this change of perspective is that some firms have been over pessimistic and **over stated provisions** in times of high profits in order to 'profit-smooth'.

3.2 You should bear this in mind as you read through the explanation of prudence. On the one hand assets and profits should not be overstated, but a balance must be achieved to prevent the material overstatement of liabilities or losses.

3.3 You may have wondered why the three washing machines in Question 1 were stated in the balance sheet at their cost (£100 each) rather than their selling price (£150 each). This is simply an aspect of the prudence concept: to value the machines at £150 would be to anticipate making a profit before the profit had been realised.

3.4 The other aspect of the prudence concept is that where a **loss** is foreseen, it **should** be anticipated and taken into account immediately. If a business purchases stock for £1,200 but because of a sudden slump in the market only £900 is likely to be realised when the stock is sold the prudence concept dictates that the stock should be valued at £900. It is not enough to wait until the stock is sold, and then recognise the £300 loss; it must be recognised as soon as it is foreseen.

3.5 A profit can be considered to be a **realised profit** when it is in the form of:

- Cash.

Part D: Accounting conventions and standards

- Another asset which has a reasonably certain cash value. This includes amounts owing from debtors, provided that there is a reasonable certainty that the debtors will eventually pay up what they owe.

3.6 SSAP 2 described the prudence concept as follows.

> 'Revenue and profits are not anticipated, but are recognised by inclusion in the profit and loss account only when realised in the form either of cash or of other assets the ultimate cash realisation of which can be assessed with reasonable certainty; provision is made for all known . . . expenses and losses whether the amount of these is known with certainty or is a best estimate in the light of the information available.'

3.7 EXAMPLES: PRUDENCE CONCEPT

Some examples might help to explain the application of the prudence concept.

(a) A company begins trading on 1 January 20X5 and sells goods worth £100,000 during the year to 31 December. At 31 December there are debts outstanding of £15,000. Of these, the company is now doubtful whether £6,000 will ever be paid.

The company should make a **provision for doubtful debts** of £6,000. Sales for 20X5 will be shown in the profit and loss account at their full value of £100,000, but the provision for doubtful debts would be a charge of £6,000. Because there is some uncertainty that the sales will be realised in the form of cash, the prudence concept dictates that the £6,000 should not be included in the profit for the year.

(b) Samson Feeble trades as a carpenter. He has undertaken to make a range of kitchen furniture for a customer at an agreed price of £1,000. At the end of Samson's accounting year the job is unfinished (being two thirds complete) and the following data has been assembled:

	£
Costs incurred in making the furniture to date	800
Further estimated costs to completion of the job	400
Total cost	1,200

The incomplete job represents **work in progress** at the end of the year which is an asset, like stock. Its cost to date is £800, but by the time the job is completed Samson will have made a loss of £200.

The full £200 loss should be charged against profits of the current year. The value of work in progress at the year end should be its **net realisable value**, which is lower than its cost. The net realisable value can be calculated in either of two ways:

	(i) £		(ii) £
Eventual sales value	1,000	Work in progress at cost	800
Less further costs to completion in order to make the sale	400	Less loss foreseen	200
Net realisable value	600		600

14: Accounting conventions

> **Exam focus point**
>
> You should be prepared for an occasional question which tests your ability to recognise a situation which calls for some consideration of the prudence concept. There is no hard-and-fast rule about what 'prudence' is in any particular situation. However, the types of situation in which you might need to discuss prudence and how it should affect the accounts (trading, profit and loss account or balance sheet) are:
>
> - Deciding when revenue should be 'realised' and brought into the trading, profit and loss account (and so deciding when profits are realised)
> - Deciding how to put a value to assets in the balance sheet

3.8 Attempt your own brief solution to the following question.

Question 2

It is generally agreed that sales revenue should only be 'realised' and so 'recognised' in the trading, profit and loss account when:

(a) The sale transaction is for a specific quantity of goods at a known price, so that the sales value of the transaction is known for certain.

(b) The sale transaction has been completed, or else it is certain that it will be completed (eg in the case of long-term contract work, when the job is well under way but not yet completed by the end of an accounting period).

(c) The *critical event* in the sale transaction has occurred. The critical event is the event after which:
   (i) It becomes virtually certain that cash will eventually be received from the customer.
   (ii) Cash is actually received.

Usually, revenue is 'recognised':

(a) When a cash sale is made.

(b) The customer promises to pay on or before a specified future date, and the debt is legally enforceable.

The prudence concept is applied here in the sense that revenue should not be anticipated, and included in the trading, profit and loss account, before it is reasonably certain to 'happen'.

Required

Given that prudence is the main consideration, discuss under what circumstances, if any, revenue might be recognised at the following stages of a sale.

(a) Goods have been acquired by the business which it confidently expects to resell very quickly.
(b) A customer places a firm order for goods.
(c) Goods are delivered to the customer.
(d) The customer is invoiced for goods.
(e) The customer pays for the goods.
(f) The customer's cheque in payment for the goods has been cleared by the bank.

Answer

(a) A sale must never be recognised before the goods have even been ordered by a customer. There is no certainty about the value of the sale, nor when it will take place, even if it is virtually certain that goods will be sold.

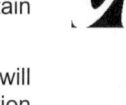

(b) A sale must never be recognised when the customer places an order. Even though the order will be for a specific quantity of goods at a specific price, it is not yet certain that the sale transaction will go through. The customer may cancel the order, the supplier might be unable to deliver the goods as ordered or it may be decided that the customer is not a good credit risk.

(c) A sale will be recognised when delivery of the goods is made only when:
   (i) The sale is for cash, and so the cash is received at the same time.
   (ii) The sale is on credit and the customer accepts delivery (eg by signing a delivery note).

(d) The critical event for a credit sale is usually the despatch of an invoice to the customer. There is then a legally enforceable debt, payable on specified terms, for a completed sale transaction.

Part D: Accounting conventions and standards

(e) The critical event for a cash sale is when delivery takes place and when cash is received; both take place at the same time.

It would be too cautious or 'prudent' to await cash payment for a credit sale transaction before recognising the sale, unless the customer is a high credit risk and there is a serious doubt about his ability or intention to pay.

(f) It would again be over-cautious to wait for clearance of the customer's cheques before recognising sales revenue. Such a precaution would only be justified in cases where there is a very high risk of the bank refusing to honour the cheque.

The consistency concept   December 2001

3.9 Accounting is not an exact science. There are many areas in which judgement must be exercised in attributing money values to items appearing in accounts. Over the years certain procedures and principles have come to be recognised as good accounting practice, but within these limits there are often various acceptable methods of accounting for similar items.

> **KEY TERM**
>
> The **consistency concept** states that similar items should be accorded similar accounting treatments.

3.10 The consistency concept states that in preparing accounts consistency should be observed in two respects.

(a) Similar items within a single set of accounts should be given similar accounting treatment.

(b) The same treatment should be applied from one period to another in accounting for similar items. This enables valid comparisons to be made from one period to the next (sometimes called the **comparability** concept).

3.11 Consistency has been sidelined to a certain extent by FRS 18. FRS 18 is more concerned with the **reliability** of the financial statements. The preparers of financial statements must consider which accounting policy is most appropriate and then apply this policy to give a true and fair view. Changing an accounting policy may contradict the consistency concept. In the next section we look at accounting policies in more detail.

The entity concept

3.12 This concept has already been discussed in Chapter 2. Briefly, the concept is that accountants regard a business as a separate entity, distinct from its owners or managers. The concept applies whether the business is a limited company (and so recognised in law as a separate entity) or a sole proprietorship or partnership (in which case the business is not separately recognised by the law.

The money measurement concept   Pilot paper

> **KEY TERM**
>
> The **money measurement concept** states that accounts will only deal with those items to which a monetary value can be attributed.

3.13 For example, in the balance sheet of a business monetary values can be attributed to such assets as machinery (eg the original cost of the machinery; or the amount it would cost to replace the machinery) and stocks of goods (eg the original cost of the goods, or, theoretically, the price at which the goods are likely to be sold).

3.14 The money measurement concept introduces limitations to the subject-matter of accounts. A business may have intangible assets such as the flair of a good manager or the loyalty of its workforce. These may be important enough to give it a clear superiority over an otherwise identical business, but because they cannot be evaluated in monetary terms they do not appear anywhere in the accounts.

The separate valuation principle

> **KEY TERM**
>
> The **separate valuation principle** states that, in determining the amount to be attributed to an asset or liability in the balance sheet, each component item of the asset or liability must be determined separately.

3.15 These separate valuations must then be aggregated to arrive at the balance sheet figure. For example, if a company's stock comprises 50 separate items, a valuation must (in theory) be arrived at for each item separately; the 50 figures must then be aggregated and the total is the stock figure which should appear in the balance sheet.

The materiality concept   Pilot paper, December 2001

> **KEY TERM**
>
> The **materiality concept**. Only items material in amount or in their nature will affect the true and fair view given by a set of accounts.

3.16 An error which is too trivial to affect anyone's understanding of the accounts is referred to as **immaterial**. In preparing accounts it is important to assess what is material and what is not, so that time and money are not wasted in the pursuit of excessive detail.

3.17 Determining whether or not an item is material is a **very subjective exercise**. There is no absolute measure of materiality. It is common to apply a convenient rule of thumb (for example to define material items as those with a value greater than 5% of the net profit disclosed by the accounts). However some items disclosed in accounts are regarded as particularly sensitive and even a very small misstatement of such an item would be regarded as material. An example in the accounts of a limited company might be the amount of remuneration paid to directors of the company.

3.18 The assessment of an item as material or immaterial may affect its treatment in the accounts. For example, the profit and loss account of a business will show the expenses incurred by the business grouped under suitable captions (heating and lighting expenses, rent and rates expenses etc); but in the case of very small expenses it may be appropriate to lump them together under a caption such as 'sundry expenses', because a more detailed breakdown would be inappropriate for such immaterial amounts.

Part D: Accounting conventions and standards

> **IMPORTANT!**
>
> In assessing whether or not an item is material, it is not only the amount of the item which needs to be considered. The context is also important.

3.19 EXAMPLE: MATERIALITY

(a) If a balance sheet shows fixed assets of £2 million and stocks of £30,000 an error of £20,000 in the depreciation calculations might not be regarded as material, whereas an error of £20,000 in the stock valuation probably would be. In other words, the total of which the erroneous item forms part must be considered.

(b) If a business has a bank loan of £50,000 and a £55,000 balance on bank deposit account, it might well be regarded as a material misstatement if these two amounts were displayed on the balance sheet as 'cash at bank £5,000'. In other words, incorrect presentation may amount to material misstatement even if there is no monetary error.

Question 3

Would you capitalise the following items in the accounts of a company?

(a) A box file
(b) A computer
(c) A small plastic display stand

Answer

(a) No. You would write it off to the profit and loss account as an expense.

(b) Yes. You would capitalise the computer and charge depreciation on it.

(c) Your answer depends on the size of the company and whether writing off the item has a material effect on its profits. A larger organisation might well write this item off under the heading of advertising expenses, while a small one would capitalise it and depreciate it over time. This is because the item would be material to the small company but not to the large company.

The historical cost convention   June 2002

3.20 A basic principle of accounting (some writers include it in the list of fundamental accounting concepts) is that resources are normally stated in accounts at historical cost, ie at the amount which the business paid to acquire them. An important advantage of this procedure is that the objectivity of accounts is maximised: there is usually objective, documentary evidence to prove the amount paid to purchase an asset or pay an expense.

> **KEY TERM**
>
> **Historical cost** means transactions are recorded at the cost when they occurred.

3.21 In general, accountants prefer to deal with costs, rather than with 'values'. This is because valuations tend to be subjective and to vary according to what the valuation is for. For example, suppose that a company acquires a machine to manufacture its products. The machine has an expected useful life of four years. At the end of two years the company is preparing a balance sheet and has to decide what monetary amount to attribute to the asset.

3.22 Numerous possibilities might be considered:

- The original cost (historical cost) of the machine
- Half of the historical cost, on the ground that half of its useful life has expired
- The amount the machine might fetch on the secondhand market
- The amount it would cost to replace the machine with an identical machine
- The amount it would cost to replace the machine with a more modern machine incorporating the technological advances of the previous two years
- The machine's economic value, ie the amount of the profits it is expected to generate for the company during its remaining life

3.23 All of these valuations have something to commend them, but the great advantage of the first two is that they are based on a figure (the machine's historical cost) which is objectively verifiable. The subjective judgement involved in the other valuations, particularly the last, is so great as to lessen the reliability of any accounts in which they are used.

Stable monetary unit

3.24 The financial statements must be expressed in terms of a monetary unit (eg in the UK the £). It is assumed that the value of this unit remains constant.

3.25 In practice, of course, the value of the unit is not usually constant and comparisons between the accounts of the current year and those of previous years may be misleading.

Objectivity (neutrality)

3.26 An accountant must show objectivity in his work. This means he should try to strip his answers of any personal opinion or prejudice and should be as precise and as detailed as the situation warrants. The result of this should be that any number of accountants will give the same answer independently of each other.

> **KEY TERM**
>
> **Objectivity** means that accountants must be free from bias. They must adopt a neutral stance when analysing accounting data.

3.27 In practice, objectivity is difficult. Two accountants faced with the same accounting data may come to different conclusions as to the correct treatment. It was to combat subjectivity that accounting standards were developed.

The realisation concept

> **KEY TERM**
>
> The **realisation concept** means that revenue and profits are recognised when realised.

3.28 In the words of SSAP 2 (now replaced by FRS 18):

Part D: Accounting conventions and standards

'revenue and profits are not anticipated but are recognised by inclusion in the profit and loss account only when realised in the form either of cash or of other assets the ultimate cash realisation of which can be assessed with reasonable certainty; provision is made for all known liabilities (expenses and losses) whether the amount of these is known with certainty or is a best estimate in the light of the information available.'

3.29 There are some **exceptions** to the rule, notably for land and buildings. With dramatic rises in property prices in the past, it has been a common practice to **revalue land** and **buildings** periodically to a current value, to avoid having a misleading balance sheet. Even if the sale of the property is not contemplated, such revaluations create an unrealised profit:

DEBIT   Land and buildings account
CREDIT   Reserves account.

This profit is sometimes known as a holding gain, because it is a profit which arises in the course of holding the asset as a result of its increase in value above cost.

3.30 In spite of such exceptions, however, the realisation principle has long been accepted by all practising accountants and has now been given statutory recognition in the Companies Act 1985 which states that only profits realised at the balance sheet date should be included in the profit and loss account.

3.31 Unfortunately the Companies Act 1985 does not provide a definition of realised profits and losses except to say that they are 'such profits or losses of a company as fall to be treated as realised in accordance with principles generally accepted at the time when the accounts are prepared, with respect to the determination for accounting purposes of realised profits' (s 262 (3) CA 1985). One aspect of the problem is the question **At what point in the business cycle should revenue be recognised as earned?**

Revenue recognition

3.32 Accruals accounting is based on the matching of costs with the revenue they generate. It is crucially important under this convention that we can establish the point at which revenue may be recognised so that the correct treatment can be applied to the related costs. For example, the costs of producing an item of finished goods should be carried as an asset in the balance sheet until such time as it is sold; they should then be written off as a charge to the trading account.

3.33 Which of these two treatments should be applied cannot be decided until it is clear at what moment the sale of the item takes place. The decision has a direct impact on profit since under the prudence concept it would be unacceptable to recognise the profit on sale until a sale had taken place in accordance with the criteria of revenue recognition.

3.34 Revenue is generally recognised as earned at the point of sale, because at that point four criteria will generally have been met.

(a) The product or service has been provided to the buyer.

(b) The buyer has recognised his liability to pay for the goods or services provided. The converse of this is that the seller has recognised that ownership of goods has passed from himself to the buyer.

(c) The buyer has indicated his willingness to hand over cash or other assets in settlement of his liability.

(d) The monetary value of the goods or services has been established.

3.35 At earlier points in the business cycle there will not in general be firm evidence that the above criteria will be met. Until work on a product is complete, there is a risk that some flaw in the manufacturing process will necessitate its writing off; even when the product is complete there is no guarantee that it will find a buyer.

3.36 At later points in the business cycle, for example when cash is received for the sale, the recognition of revenue may occur in a period later than that in which the related costs were charged. Revenue recognition would then depend on fortuitous circumstances, such as the cash flow of a company's debtors, and might fluctuate misleadingly from one period to another.

3.37 However, there are times when revenue is recognised at other times than at the completion of a sale.

Sale on hire purchase

- Title to goods provided on hire purchase terms does not pass until the last payment is made, at which point the sale is complete. To defer the recognition of revenue until that point, however, would be to distort the nature of the revenue earned.

- The profits of an HP retailer in effect represent the interest charged on finance provided and such interest arises over the course of the HP agreement rather than at its completion. Revenue in this case is recognised when each instalment of cash is received.

The duality concept

3.38 Every transaction has two effects. This convention underpins double entry bookkeeping, and you have seen it at work in your studies from Chapter 5 onwards.

Substance over form   Pilot paper, June 2002

> **KEY TERM**
>
> **Substance over form** means that transactions should be accounted for and presented in accordance with their economic substance, not their legal form.

3.39 An example of substance over form is that of assets acquired on hire purchase. Legally the purchaser does not own the asset until the final instalment has been paid. However, the accounting treatment is to record a fixed asset in the accounts at the start of the hire purchase agreement. The substance of the transaction is that the business owns the asset. The same could be said of fixed assets acquired under long-term leases.

The time interval concept (periodicity concept)

3.40 The activities of an entity are conveniently split up into blocks of time, be these days, months, quarters or years. The activities continue to occur but the intervals are placed so as to record activities between two points in time. The time intervals under consideration are usually of equal length to facilitate comparison, but this does not need to be the case (consider months: February is usually three days shorter than August).

Part D: Accounting conventions and standards

4 ACCOUNTING POLICIES

4.1 FRS 18 *Accounting policies* was introduced in December 2000 to update SSAP 2. The introduction of the *Statement of Principles* in the previous year had seen a **framework** brought to the standard setting process and a change of **emphasis** in the preparation and regulation of financial statements.

4.2 Under FRS 18 there is a distinction between **accounting policies** and **accounting estimates**.

> **KEY TERM**
>
> An **accounting policy** is concerned with the
>
> - Recognition
> - Selection of measurement base and
> - Presentation
>
> of assets, liabilities, gains and losses of an entity.

> **KEY TERM**
>
> An **accounting estimate** is the method used to establish the monetary value of assets, liabilities, gains and losses using the measurement base selected by the accounting policy.

Accounting policies

4.3 The **most appropriate** accounting policy should be selected in order to give a 'true and fair' view. Two points should be noted about this approach.

- Accounting policies **must conform** to the relevant accounting standards. They can be changed only where a standard **allows** choice.
- Accounting policies should not be chopped and changed on an ad hoc basis. A **balance** must be struck to achieve **consistency** and **reliability**.

Accounting estimates

4.4 Accounting estimates involve the use of judgement when applying an accounting policy. The following paragraph gives examples of accounting estimates. The point to note is that a change in accounting estimate does not constitute a change in accounting policy.

4.5 EXAMPLES: ACCOUNTING ESTIMATES

(a) *Depreciation of fixed assets*

   (i) Fixed assets may be depreciated by a number of different methods (by the straight line method, reducing balance method, sum-of-the-digits method, etc).

   (ii) Some fixed assets such as land might not be depreciated at all, because they are not used up.

14: Accounting conventions

(iii) Each method provides a different estimate of depreciation.

(iv) There remains the more subjective problem of deciding what the expected life of an asset should be, and what its residual value might be, and there is no accounting basis which can rule over this exercise of judgement.

(b) *Research and development expenditure*

(i) Research expenditure is charged against profit in the period it is incurred. However, development expenditure can be deferred until a later period when the benefits of the development are obtained by the entity.

(ii) Thus if a company spends £10,000 in 20X5 on developing a new product which is not sold on the market until 20X6, there is a choice of:

(1) Charging £10,000 against profits in 20X5

(2) Recording some (or all) of the £10,000 as an asset at the end of 20X5, and charging it against profits in 20X6 (and even 20X7 or later years).

It depends whether the expenditure is pure research or meets certain conditions so that it can be deferred as development costs (see Chapter 15).

(iii) There are only two ways of accounting for R & D expenditure. However, there is scope for subjective management decisions about how much of the expenditure should be deferred until later years, and over how many years the costs should be spread.

5 THE ASB'S STATEMENT December 2001

The search for a conceptual framework

> **KEY TERM**
>
> A **conceptual framework**, is a statement of generally accepted theoretical principles which form the frame of reference for financial reporting. These theoretical principles provide the basis for the development of new reporting standards and the evaluation of those already in existence.

5.1 The financial reporting process is concerned with providing information that is useful in the business and economic decision-making process. Therefore a conceptual framework will form the theoretical basis for determining which events should be accounted for, how they should be measured and how they should be communicated to the user.

5.2 Although it is theoretical in nature, a conceptual framework for financial reporting has highly practical final aims.

5.3 The need for a conceptual framework is demonstrated by the way UK standards have developed over recent years. Standards were produced in a haphazard and fire-fighting approach. Had an agreed framework existed, the old ASC could have acted as an architect or designer, rather than a fire-fighter, building accounting rules on the foundation of sound, agreed basic principles.

5.4 The lack of a conceptual framework also meant that fundamental principles were tackled more than once in different standards, thereby producing contradictions and inconsistencies in basic concepts, such as those of prudence and matching. This led to ambiguity and it has affected the true and fair concept of financial reporting.

Part D: Accounting conventions and standards

5.5 Another problem with the lack of a conceptual framework has become apparent in the USA. The large number of highly detailed standards produced by the Financial Accounting Standards Board (FASB) has created a financial reporting environment governed by specific rules rather than general principles. This would be avoided if a cohesive set of principles were in place.

5.6 A conceptual framework would also bolster the standard setters against political pressure from various 'lobby groups' and interested parties. Such pressure would only prevail if it was acceptable under the conceptual framework.

5.7 Towards the end of its existence, the ASC recognised the IASC's *Framework* on the preparation and presentation of financial statements, as a set of guidelines to help it develop proposals for new standards and revisions to existing standards. This represented a significant shift from the previous approach of developing SSAPs in a haphazard manner as working solutions to practical problems.

5.8 The *Framework* deals with:

   (a) The objective of financial statements.

   (b) The qualitative characteristics that determine the usefulness of information in financial statements.

   (c) The definition, recognition and measurement of the elements from which financial statements are constructed.

   (d) Concepts of capital and capital maintenance.

   The IASC believes that further international harmonisation of accounting methods can best be promoted by focusing on these four topics since they will then lead to producing financial statements that meet the common needs of most users.

5.9 The ASB has gone further than the ASC in that it has already incorporated the IASC's *Framework* into its *Statement of Principles*.

5.10 Another publication which has a bearing on the area of a conceptual framework is Professor David Solomons' 1989 discussion paper, *Guidelines for Financial Reporting Standards*. The Solomons report deals with:

   (a) The purpose of financial reporting
   (b) Financial statements and their elements
   (c) The qualitative characteristics of accounting information
   (d) Recognition and measurement
   (e) The choice of a general purpose accounting model

   The report thus followed the same route as the IASC's *Framework*.

Advantages and disadvantages of a conceptual framework

5.11 The advantages arising from using a conceptual framework may be summarised as follows.

   (a) SSAPs were being developed on a 'patchwork quality' basis where a particular accounting problem was recognised by the ASC as having emerged, and resources were then channelled into standardising accounting practice in that area, without regard to whether that particular issue was necessarily the most important issue remaining at that time without standardisation.

(b) As stated earlier, the development of certain SSAPs (for example SSAP 13) has been subject to considerable political interference from interested parties. Where there is a conflict of interest between user groups on which policies to choose, policies deriving from a conceptual framework will be less open to criticism that the ASC buckled to external pressure.

(c) Some SSAPs seem to concentrate on the income statement (profit and loss account), some to concentrate on the valuation of net assets (balance sheet). There was no cohesive approach to the financial statements as a whole.

5.12 A counter-argument to supporters of a conceptual framework might be as follows.

(a) Financial statements are intended for a variety of users, and it is not certain that a single conceptual framework can be devised which will suit all users.

(b) Given the diversity of user requirements, there may be a need for a variety of accounting Standards, each produced for a different purpose (and with different concepts as a basis).

(c) It is not clear that a conceptual framework will make the task of preparing and then implementing standards any easier than it is now.

ASB Statement of Principles

5.13 The Accounting Standards Board (ASB) published (in November 1995) an exposure draft of its *Statement of Principles for Financial Reporting*. In March 1999, the text was substantially revised with particular attention being given to the clarity of expression. The *Statement of Principles* was then finalised in December 1999. The statement consists of eight chapters.

(1) The objective of financial statements
(2) The reporting entity
(3) The qualitative characteristics of financial information
(4) The elements of financial statements
(5) Recognition in financial statements
(6) Measurement in financial statements
(7) Presentation of financial information
(8) Accounting for interests in other entities

What is examinable

5.14 The up-to-date Study Guide includes the following as examinable.

- The objectives of financial statements as defined in Chapter 1 of the *Statement of Principles*
- The reporting entity as defined in Chapter 2 of the *Statement of Principles*
- The qualitative characteristics of financial statements in Chapter 3 of the *Statement of Principles*

Exam focus point

A detailed knowledge of Chapters 4 to 8 of the *Statement of Principles* is not examinable, but students should be aware of their general principles.

Part D: Accounting conventions and standards

Purpose of the *Statement of Principles*

5.15 The following are the main reasons why the Accounting Standards Board (ASB) developed the *Statement of Principles*.

(a) To assist the ASB by providing a basis for reducing the number of alternative accounting treatments permitted by accounting standards and company law

(b) To provide a framework for the future development of accounting standards

(c) To assist auditors in forming an opinion as to whether financial statements conform with accounting standards

(d) To assist users of accounts in interpreting the information contained in them

(e) To provide guidance in applying accounting standards

(f) To give guidance on areas which are not yet covered by accounting standards

(g) To inform interested parties of the approach taken by the ASB in formulating accounting standards

The role of the *Statement* can thus be summed up as being to provide **consistency, clarity and information**.

Chapter 1 The objective of financial statements

5.16 The main points raised here are as follows.

(a) The objective of financial statements is to provide information about the **financial position, performance** and **financial adaptability** of an enterprise that is useful to a wide range of users for assessing the stewardship of management and for making economic decisions.

(b) It is acknowledged that while all not all the information needs of users can be met by financial statements, there are needs that are common to all users. Financial statements that meet the needs of providers of risk capital to the enterprise will also meet most of the needs of other users that financial statements can satisfy.

Users of financial statements other than investors include the following.

(i) Employees
(ii) Lenders
(iii) Suppliers and other creditors
(iv) Customers
(v) Government and their agencies
(vi) The public

(c) The limitations of financial statements are emphasised as well as the strengths.

(d) All of the components of financial statements (balance sheet, profit and loss account, cash flow statement) are interrelated because they reflect different aspects of the same transactions.

(e) The exposure draft emphasises the ways financial statements provide information about the financial position of an enterprise. The main elements which affect the position of the company are:

(i) The economic resources it controls
(ii) Its financial structure
(iii) Its liquidity and solvency

14: Accounting conventions

(iv) Its capacity to adapt to changes in the environment in which it operates (called **financial adaptability**)

The exposure draft discusses the importance of each of these elements and how they are disclosed in the financial statements.

Question 4

Consider the information needs of the users of financial information listed above, including shareholders. (You have covered this in Chapter 1, but see if you can remember them.)

Answer

(a) *Shareholders*

    (i) Information is required to help make a decision about buying or selling shares, taking up a rights issue and voting at the Annual General Meeting (AGM).

    (ii) The shareholder must have information about the level of dividend, past, present and future and any changes in share price.

    (iii) The shareholders will also need to know whether the management has been running the company efficiently.

    (iv) As well as the position indicated by the profit and loss account, balance sheet and earnings per share (EPS), the shareholders will want to know about the liquidity position of the company, the company's future prospects, and how the company's shares compare with those of its competitors.

(b) *Employees* need information about the security of employment and future prospects for jobs in the company, and to help with collective pay bargaining.

(c) *Lenders* need information to help them decide whether to lend to a company. They will also need to check that the value of any security remains adequate, that the interest repayments are secure, that the cash is available for redemption at the appropriate time and that any financial restrictions (such as maximum debt/equity ratios) have not been breached. Investors will need information about loans which are traded on the stock market to decide whether to buy or sell them.

(d) *Suppliers* need to know whether the company will be a good customer and pay its debts.

(e) *Customers* need to know whether the company will be able to continue producing and supplying goods.

(f) *Government's* interest in a company may be one of creditor or customer, as well as being specifically concerned with compliance with tax and company law, ability to pay tax and the general contribution of the company to the economy.

(g) The *public* at large would wish to have information for all the reasons mentioned above, but it could be suggested that it would be impossible to provide general purpose accounting information which was specifically designed for the needs of the public.

Chapter 2 The reporting entity

5.17 This chapter makes the point that it is important that entities that ought to prepare financial statements, in fact do so. The entity must be a cohesive economic unit. It has a determinable boundary and is held to account for all the things it can control.

Chapter 3 Qualitative characteristics of financial information

5.18 A diagrammatic representation is shown below.

(a) Qualitative characteristics that relate to **content** are **relevance** and **reliability**.

(b) Qualitative characteristics that relate to **presentation** are **comparability** and **understandability**.

The diagram shown here is reasonably explanatory.

Part D: Accounting conventions and standards

```
                          What makes financial information useful?
                                            |
    ┌───────────┬──────────────┬──────────────┬──────────────┐
Threshold   MATERIALITY ─────────────────────────────── Giving information that is not
quality                                                  material may impair the
                                                         usefulness of the other
                                                         information given

 RELEVANCE        RELIABILITY           COMPARABILITY   UNDERSTANDABILITY

Information that  Information that is a complete   Similarities and    The significance
has the ability   and faithful representation      differences can be  of the information
to influence                                       discerned and       can be perceived
decisions                                          evaluated

Predictive  Confirmatory  Free from   Faithful      Neutral Complete Prudence   Consistency Disclosure  Users'     Aggregation
value       value         material    representation                                                    abilities  and
                          error                                                                                    classification
```

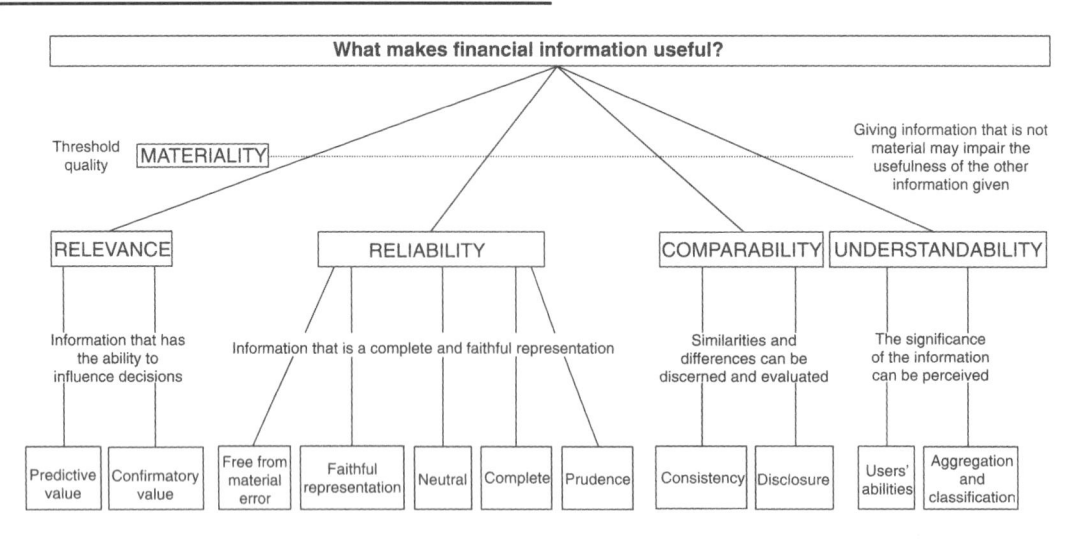

Chapter 4 Elements of financial statements

5.19 The elements of financial statements are listed. They are:

 (a) Assets
 (b) Liabilities
 (c) Ownership interest
 (d) Gains
 (e) Losses
 (f) Contributions from owners
 (g) Distributions to owners

5.20 Any item that does not fall within one of the definitions of elements should not be included in financial statements. The definitions are as follows.

 (a) **Assets** are rights or other access to future economic benefits controlled by an entity as a result of past transactions or events.

 (b) **Liabilities** are obligations of an entity to transfer economic benefits as a result of past transactions or events.

 (c) **Ownership interest** is the residual amount found by deducting all of the entity's liabilities from all of the entity's assets.

 (d) **Gains** are increases in ownership interest, other than those relating to contributions from owners.

 (e) **Losses** are decreases in ownership interest, other than those relating to distributions to owners.

 (f) **Contributions from owners** are increases in ownership interest resulting from investments made by owners in their capacity as owners.

 (g) **Distributions to owners** are decreases in ownership interest resulting from transfers made to owners in their capacity as owners.

Question 5

Consider the following situations. In each case, do we have an asset or liability within the definitions given by the *Statement of Principles?* Give reasons for your answer.

 (a) Pat Ltd has purchased a patent for £20,000. The patent gives the company sole use of a particular manufacturing process which will save £3,000 a year for the next five years.

(b) Baldwin Ltd paid Don Brennan £10,000 to set up a car repair shop, on condition that priority treatment is given to cars from the company's fleet.

(c) Deals on Wheels Ltd provides a warranty with every car sold.

(d) Monty Ltd has signed a contract with a human resources consultant. The terms of the contract are that the consultant is to stay for six months and be paid £3,000 per month.

(e) Rachmann Ltd owns a building which for many years it had let out to students. The building has been declared unsafe by the local council. Not only is it unfit for human habitation, but on more than one occasion slates have fallen off the roof, nearly killing passers-by. To rectify all the damage would cost £300,000; to eliminate the danger to the public would cost £200,000. The building could then be sold for £100,000.

Answer

(a) This is an asset, albeit an intangible one. There is a past event, control and future economic benefit (through cost savings).

(b) This cannot be classified as an asset. Baldwin Ltd has no control over the car repair shop and it is difficult to argue that there are 'future economic benefits'.

(c) This is a liability; the business has taken on an obligation. It would be recognised when the warranty is issued rather than when a claim is made.

(d) As a firm financial commitment, this has all the appearance of a liability. However, as the consultant has not done any work yet, there has been no past event which could give rise to a liability. Similarly, because there has been no past event there is no asset.

(e) The situation is not clear cut. It could be argued that there is a liability, depending on the whether the potential danger to the public arising from the building creates a legal obligation to do the repairs. If there is such a liability, it might be possible to set off the sale proceeds of £100,000 against the cost of essential repairs of £200,000, giving a net obligation to transfer economic benefits of £100,000.

The building is clearly not an asset, because although there is control and there has been a past event, there is no expected access to economic benefit.

Chapter 5 Recognition in financial statements

5.21 This chapter explains what is meant by recognition and discusses the three stages of recognition of assets and liabilities.

(a) Initial recognition
(b) Subsequent remeasurement
(c) Derecognition

5.22 The chapter goes on to describe the criteria which determine each of these stages.

Chapter 6 Measurement in financial statements

5.23 This chapter, with its emphasis on current values, is fairly radical and controversial. The following approach is taken.

(a) Initially, when an asset is purchased or a liability incurred, the asset/liability is recorded at the transaction cost, that is historical cost, which at that time is equal to current replacement cost.

(b) An asset/liability may subsequently be 'remeasured'. In a historical cost system, this can involve writing down an asset to its recoverable amount. For a liability, the corresponding treatment would be amendment of the monetary amount to the amount ultimately expected to be paid.

(c) Such re-measurements will, however, only be recognised if there is sufficient evidence that the monetary amount of the asset/liability has changed and the new amount can be reliably measured.

Part D: Accounting conventions and standards

Question 6

Why might historical cost be considered less relevant to users of accounting statements?

Answer

In times of high inflation, an historic cost only a year old may be hopelessly inadequate to express the current value of an asset.

Chapter 7 Presentation of financial information

5.24 Aspects of this chapter have also given rise to some controversy. The chapter begins by making the general point that financial information is presented in the form of a structured set of financial statements comprising primary statements and supporting notes and, in some cases, supplementary information.

Components of financial statements

5.25 The primary financial statements are as follows.

(a) Profit and loss account
(b) Statement of total recognised gains and losses
(c) Balance sheet
(d) Cash flow statement

(a) and (b) are the 'statements of financial performance'.

5.26 The notes to the financial statements 'amplify and explore' the primary statements; together they form an 'integrated whole'. Disclosure in the notes does not correct or justify non-disclosure or misrepresentation in the primary financial statements.

5.27 'Supplementary information' embraces voluntary disclosures and information which is too subjective for disclosure in the primary financial statement and the notes.

Chapter 8 Accounting for interests in other entities

5.28 Financial statements need to reflect the effect on the reporting entity's financial performance and financial position of its interests in other entities. This involves various measurement, presentation and consolidation issues which are dealt with in this chapter of the *Statement*.

Summary

5.29 The *Statement of Principles* does not have direct effect. It is not an accounting standard with which companies have to comply. Having said that, it is influential and persuasive, especially where there is no specific standard dealing with an issue. The statement should help structure new statements and create a coherent framework, this in turn will prevent controversy and help enhance the reputation of the accounting profession.

Chapter roundup

- In preparing financial statements, certain **fundamental concepts** are adopted as a framework.
- Two such concepts are identified by FRS 18 *Accounting policies* as the bedrock of accounting.
    - The **going concern concept**. Unless there is evidence to the contrary, it is assumed that a business will continue to trade normally for the foreseeable future.
    - The **accruals or matching concept**. Revenue earned must be matched against expenditure incurred in earning it.
- A number of other concepts may be regarded as fundamental.
    - The **prudence concept**. Where alternative accounting procedures are acceptable, choose the one which gives the less optimistic view of profitability and asset values.
    - The **consistency concept**. Similar items should be accorded similar accounting treatments.
    - The **entity concept**. A business is an entity distinct from its owner(s).
    - The **money measurement concept**. Accounts only deal with items to which monetary values can be attributed.
    - The **separate valuation principle**. Each component of an asset or liability must be valued separately.
    - The **materiality concept**. Only items material in amount or in their nature will affect the true and fair view given by a set of accounts.
    - The **historical cost convention**. Transactions are recorded at the cost when they occurred.
    - The **stable monetary unit**. The value of the unit in which accounting statements are prepared does not change.
    - **Objectivity**. Accountants must be free from bias.
    - The **realisation concept**. Revenue and profits are recognised when realised.
    - **Duality**. Every transaction has two effects.
    - **Substance over form**. Transactions must be presented and accounted for in accordance with their substance and financial reality and not merely with their legal form.
- **Accounting policies** are selected from the choices provided by accounting standards to provide a true and fair view.
- Accounting estimates are the application of judgement to allocate monetary values using the criteria provided by an accounting policy.
- Whereas in the past accounting standards were produced on an *ad hoc* basis, in recent years attempts have been made to develop a **conceptual framework** of accounting, on which future accounting standards should be based.
- The ASB's **Statement of Principles** should provide the backbone of the conceptual framework in the UK.
- Key elements in the *Statement* are as follows.
    - Financial statements should give financial information useful for assessing stewardship of management and for making economic decisions.
    - Financial information should be relevant, reliable, comparable and understandable.
    - Assets and liabilities have conceptual priority over the profit and loss account.
    - Accounts should move towards current cost valuations.
    - Statement of total recognised gains and losses is for assets held for the business to continue trading.

Part D: Accounting conventions and standards

Quick quiz

1. Which FRS deals with accounting assumptions?
2. Which of the following assumptions are included in FRS 18?
   - A Money measurement
   - B Objectivity
   - C Going concern
   - D Business entity
3. Define 'going concern'.
4. What is meant by the prudence concept?
5. Only items which have a monetary value can be included in accounts. Which accounting concept is this?
   - A Historical cost
   - B Money measurement
   - C Realisation
   - D Business entity
6. Suggest four possible values which might be attributed to an asset in the balance sheet of a business.
7. Generally, when should revenue be recognised?
8. What are the chapters of the *Statement of Principles*?
9. How does the *Statement* define 'gains' and 'losses'?

Answers to quick quiz

1. FRS 18 *Accounting policies*.
2. C Only going concern is included in FRS 18, the others are assumptions and concepts generally used in accountancy, but not mentioned in FRS 18.
3. The assumption that a business will continue in operation for the foreseeable future, without going into liquidation or materially scaling down its operations.
4. Prudence means to be cautious when exercising judgement. In particular profits should not be recognised until realised, but a loss should be recognised as soon as it is foreseen.
5. B This is the definition of the money measurement concept.
6. Any four of the following.
   - Historical cost
   - Historical cost depreciated over its useful life
   - The amount it would fetch if sold secondhand
   - Replacement cost of an identical machine
   - Replacement cost of the latest machine
   - Economic value
7. At the point of sale.
8. See paragraph 5.13.
9. See paragraph 5.20.

Now try the question below from the Exam Question Bank

Question to try	Level	Marks	Time
21	Full exam	10	18 mins

Chapter 15

INTANGIBLE FIXED ASSETS

Topic list	Syllabus reference
1 Goodwill	4(a)
2 Research and development costs	4(a), 5(c), 5(d)

Introduction

Intangible fixed assets are fixed assets which have a value to the business because they have been paid for, but which do not have any physical substance. The most significant of such intangible assets are **goodwill** and **deferred development costs**.

The concept of goodwill might be familiar to you already, from common everyday knowledge. It is discussed in Section 1 of this chapter.

In many companies, especially those which produce food or 'scientific' products such as medicines or 'high technology' products, the expenditure on **research and development** is considerable. When R & D is a large item of cost its accounting treatment may have a significant influence on the profits of a business and its balance sheet valuation. Because of this attempts have been made to standardise the treatment, and these are discussed in Section 2 of this chapter.

Study guide

Section 17 - Goodwill, research and development

- Define goodwill.
- Explain the factors leading to the creation of non-purchased goodwill.
- Explain the difference between purchased and non-purchased goodwill.
- Explain why non-purchased goodwill is not normally recognised in financial statements.
- Explain how purchased goodwill arises and is reflected in financial statements.
- Explain the need to amortise purchased goodwill.
- Define 'research' and 'development'.
- Classify expenditure as research or development.
- Calculate amounts to be capitalised as development expenditure from given information.
- Disclose research and development expenditure in the financial statements in accordance with SSAP 13.

Exam guide

Goodwill also comes up in consolidations. You must be able to calculate it and discuss its treatment. Research and development could come up as part of a written question in Section B. It is not enough just to quote SECTOR though. Apply the rules in your answer to show you understand them.

Part D: Accounting conventions and standards

1 GOODWILL

> **KEY TERM**
>
> If a business has **goodwill** it means that the value of the business as a going concern is greater than the value of its separate tangible assets.

1.1 Goodwill is created by good relationships between a business and its customers, for example:

(a) By building up a reputation (by word of mouth perhaps) for high quality products or high standards of service.

(b) By responding promptly and helpfully to queries and complaints from customers.

(c) Through the personality of the staff and their attitudes to customers.

1.2 The value of goodwill to a business might be extremely significant. However, **goodwill is not usually valued** in the accounts of a business at all, and we should not normally expect to find an amount for goodwill in its balance sheet.

1.3 For example, the welcoming smile of the bar staff may contribute more to a pub's profits than the fact that a new electronic cash register has recently been acquired; even so, whereas the cash register will be recorded in the accounts as a fixed asset, the value of staff would be ignored for accounting purposes.

1.4 On reflection, this omission of goodwill from the accounts of a business might be easy to understand.

(a) The goodwill is inherent in the business but it has not been paid for, and it does not have an 'objective' value. We can guess at what such goodwill is worth, but such guesswork would be a matter of individual opinion, and not based on hard facts.

(b) Goodwill changes from day to day. One act of bad customer relations might damage goodwill and one act of good relations might improve it. Staff with a favourable personality might retire or leave to find another job, to be replaced by staff who need time to find their feet in the job, etc. Since goodwill is continually changing in value, it cannot realistically be recorded in the accounts of the business.

Purchased goodwill

1.5 There is one exception to the general rule that goodwill has no objective valuation. This is when a business is sold. People wishing to set up in business have a choice of how to do it - they can either buy their own fixed assets and stock and set up their business from scratch, or they can buy up an existing business from a proprietor willing to sell it.

1.6 When a buyer purchases an existing business, he will have to purchase not only its fixed assets and stocks (and perhaps take over its creditors and debtors too) but also the goodwill of the business.

1.7 **EXAMPLE: GOODWILL**

Tony Tycoon agrees to purchase the business of Clive Dunwell for £30,000. Clive's business has net fixed assets valued at £14,000 and net current assets of £11,000, all of which are taken over by Tony. Tony will be paying more for the business than its tangible assets are

15: Intangible fixed assets

worth, because he is purchasing the goodwill of the business too. The balance sheet of Tony's business when it begins operations will be:

TONY TYCOON
BALANCE SHEET AS AT THE START OF BUSINESS

	£
Intangible fixed asset: goodwill	5,000
Tangible fixed assets: net book value	14,000
Net current assets	11,000
Net assets	30,000
Capital	30,000

1.8 Purchased goodwill is shown in this balance sheet because it has been **paid for**. It has no tangible substance, you can not touch it, and so it is an **intangible** fixed asset.

> **KEY TERM**
>
> **Purchased goodwill** has been defined as 'the excess of the price paid for a business over the fair market value of the individual assets and liabilities acquired'.

Question 1

To make sure that you understand goodwill, try a solution to the following quick exercise.

Toad goes into business with £10,000 capital and agrees to buy Thrush's shoe-repair shop in the centre of a busy town for £6,500. Thrush's recent accounts show net assets of £3,500, which Toad values at £4,000.

Required

Prepare the balance sheet of Toad's business:

(a) Before he purchases Thrush's business.
(b) After the purchase.

Answer

(a) Toad's balance sheet before the purchase is:

	£
Cash	10,000
Proprietor's interest	10,000

(b) Thrush's valuation of the assets to be acquired is irrelevant to Toad who sees the situation thus:

	£
Consideration (cash to be paid)	6,500
Less net assets acquired (at Toad's valuation)	4,000
Difference (= goodwill)	2,500

Toad must credit his cash book with the £6,500 paid. He can only debit sundry assets with £4,000. A further debit of £2,500 is thus an accounting necessity and he must open up a goodwill account.

Toad's balance sheet immediately after the transfer would therefore be:

	£
Goodwill	2,500
Sundry assets	4,000
Cash (£10,000 - £6,500)	3,500
	10,000
Proprietor's interest	10,000

Part D: Accounting conventions and standards

(Normally one would have more detail as to the breakdown of the sundry assets into fixed assets, current assets etc, but this is not relevant to the illustration. The main point is that the sundry assets acquired are tangible whereas the goodwill is not.)

This exercise highlights the difference between 'internally generated' goodwill, which (as in Thrush's case above) is not shown in the books and 'purchased' goodwill, which is. The purchased goodwill in this case is simply Thrush's internally generated goodwill, which has changed hands, bought by Toad at a price shown in Toad's accounts.

The accounting treatment of purchased goodwill

1.9 Once purchased goodwill appears in the accounts of a business, we must decide what to do with it. Purchased goodwill is basically a premium paid for the acquisition of a business as a going concern: indeed, it is often referred to as a 'premium on acquisition'. When a purchaser agrees to pay such a premium for goodwill, he does so because he believes that the true value of the business is worth more to him than the value of its tangible assets.

1.10 One major reason why he might think so, is that the business will earn good profits over the next few years and so he will pay a premium now in the expectation of getting his money back later. He pays for the goodwill at the time of purchase, and the value of the goodwill will eventually wear off.

1.11 Goodwill, it was suggested earlier, is a continually changing thing. A business cannot last forever on its past reputation; it must create new goodwill as time goes on. Even goodwill created by a favourable location might suddenly disappear - for example, a newsagent's shop by a bus stop will lose its location value if the bus route is axed.

1.12 Since goodwill erodes it would be inadvisable to keep purchased goodwill indefinitely in the accounts of a business.

1.13 The treatment of goodwill is the subject of an accounting standard, FRS 10 *Goodwill and intangible assets*. The FRS requires that goodwill should be **capitalised** and shown in the balance sheet as an **intangible fixed asset**. It is then **amortised over its expected economic life**. (There is a presumption that this does not exceed 20 years, although it may be longer than this in limited cases.)

1.14 **Amortisation** is the name for depreciation in the case of **intangible** fixed assets.

1.15 The gradual 'write-off' approach is based on the idea that goodwill has a limited life and is a cost to be offset against future profits. Consistent with this approach is the fact that if goodwill is presumed to last longer than 20 years, an annual **impairment review** must be carried out to make sure that the presumption is still appropriate.

Exam focus point

You do not need to know about FRS 10 in any detail for your exam. You only need to know the treatment of purchased goodwill and about amortisation.

How is the value of purchased goodwill decided?

1.16 When a business is sold, there is likely to be some purchased goodwill in the buying price. How is the amount of this purchased goodwill decided?

1.17 This is not really a problem for accountants, who must simply record the goodwill in the accounts of the new business. The value of the goodwill is a matter for the purchaser and seller to agree upon in fixing the purchase/sale price.

1.18 No matter how goodwill is calculated within the total agreed purchase price, the goodwill shown by the purchaser **in his accounts** will be **the difference between the purchase consideration and his own valuation of the tangible net assets acquired.**

1.19 A values his tangible net assets at £40,000, and goodwill is agreed at £21,000. B pays £61,000 for the business, but values the tangible net assets at only £38,000. The goodwill in **B's books** will be £61,000 – £38,000 = £23,000.

2 RESEARCH AND DEVELOPMENT COSTS

2.1 Large companies may spend significant amounts of money on **research and development** (R & D) activities. These amounts must be credited to cash and debited to an account for research and development expenditure. The accounting problem is how to treat the debit balance on R & D account at the balance sheet date.

2.2 There are two possibilities.

(a) The debit balance may be classified as an **expense** and transferred to the profit and loss account. This is referred to as 'writing off' the expenditure.

(b) The debit balance may be classified as an **asset** and included in the balance sheet. This is referred to as 'capitalising' or 'carrying forward' or 'deferring' the expenditure.

2.3 The argument for writing off R & D expenditure is that it is an expense just like rates or wages and its accounting treatment should be the same.

2.4 The argument for carrying forward R & D expenditure is based on the accruals concept. If R & D activity eventually leads to new or improved products which generate revenue, the costs should be carried forward to be matched against that revenue in future accounting periods.

2.5 Like goodwill, R & D expenditure is the subject of an accounting standard, SSAP 13 *Accounting for research and development*. SSAP 13 defines research and development expenditure as falling into one or more of the following categories.

(a) **Pure research** is original research to obtain new scientific or technical knowledge or understanding. There is no clear commercial end in view and such research work does not have a practical application. Companies and other business entities might carry out this type of research in the hope that it will provide new knowledge which can subsequently be exploited.

(b) **Applied research** is original research work which also seeks to obtain new scientific or technical knowledge, but which has a specific practical aim or application (eg research on improvements in the effectiveness of medicines). Applied research may develop from 'pioneering' pure research, but many companies have full-time research teams working on applied research projects.

(c) **Development** is the use of existing scientific and technical knowledge to produce new (or substantially improved) products or systems, prior to starting commercial production operations.

Part D: Accounting conventions and standards

How do we distinguish these categories?

2.6 The dividing line between each of these categories will often be indistinct in practice, and some expenditure might be classified as research or as development. It may be even more difficult to distinguish development costs from production costs. For example, if a prototype model of a new product is developed and then sold to a customer, the costs of the prototype will include both development and production expenditure.

2.7 SSAP 13 states that although there may be practical difficulties in isolating research costs and development costs, there is a difference of principle in the method of accounting for each type of expenditure.

   (a) (i) Expenditure on pure and applied research is usually a continuing operation which is necessary to ensure a company's survival.

   (ii) One accounting period does not gain more than any other from such work, and it is therefore appropriate that **research costs** should be **written off** as they are incurred (ie in the year of expenditure).

   (iii) This conforms with CA 1985, which seems not to envisage the capitalisation of research expenditure in any circumstances.

   (b) (i) The development of new and improved products is different, because development expenditure is incurred with a particular commercial aim in view and in the reasonable expectation of earning profits or reducing costs.

   (ii) In these circumstances it is appropriate that **development costs** should be **deferred (capitalised) and matched against the future revenues**.

> **Exam focus point**
>
> If you are in a hurry, or revising, just read the SECTOR mnemonic below.

2.8 SSAP 13 attempts to restrict indiscriminate deferrals of development expenditure and states that development costs may only be deferred to future periods, when the following criteria are met.

   (a) There must be a clearly defined development project, and the related expenditure on this project is separately identifiable.

   (b) The expected outcome of the project must have been assessed, and there should be reasonable certainty that it is both

   (i) Technically feasible

   (ii) Commercially viable, having regard to market conditions, competition, public opinion and consumer and environmental legislation

   (c) The eventual profits from the developed product or system should reasonably be expected to cover the past and future development costs.

   (d) The company should have adequate resources to complete the development project.

   If *any* of these conditions are not satisfied the development costs should be written off in the year of expenditure.

2.9 The following mnemonic may be helpful. Remember: SECTOR.

> | | |
> |---|---|
> | **S** | Separately defined project |
> | **E** | Expenditure separately identifiable |
> | **C** | Commercially viable |
> | **T** | Technically feasible |
> | **O** | Overall profit expected |
> | **R** | Resources exist to complete project |

2.10 Where development expenditure is deferred to future periods, its **amortisation should begin with the commencement of production**, and should then be written off over the period in which the product is expected to be sold. Deferred development expenditure should be reviewed at the end of every accounting period. If the conditions which justified the deferral of the expenditure no longer apply or are considered doubtful, the deferred expenditure, to the extent that it is now considered to be irrecoverable, should be written off.

2.11 Development expenditure once written off can now be reinstated, if the uncertainties which had led to its being written off no longer apply. This was not permitted by the original SSAP 13, but it has been amended because the CA 1985 does permit the reinstatement of costs previously written off.

2.12 EXAMPLES OF R & D ITEMS

Examples given by SSAP 13 (revised) of activities that would normally be **included** in R & D are:

(a) Experimental, theoretical or other work aimed at the discovery of new knowledge or the advancement of existing knowledge.

(b) Searching for applications of that knowledge.

(c) Formulation and design of possible applications for such work.

(d) Testing in search for, or evaluation of, product, service or process alternatives.

(e) Design, construction and testing of pre-production prototypes and models and development batches.

(f) Design of products, services, processes or systems involving new technology or substantially improving those already produced or installed.

(g) Construction and operation of pilot plants.

2.13 EXAMPLES OF NON R & D ITEMS

Examples of activities that would normally be **excluded** from research and development include:

(a) Testing and analysis either of equipment or product for purposes of quality or quantity control.

(b) Periodic alterations to existing products, services or processes even though these may represent some improvement.

(c) Operational research not tied to a specific research and development activity.

Part D: Accounting conventions and standards

(d) Cost of corrective action in connection with break-downs during commercial production.

(e) Legal and administrative work in connection with patent applications, records and litigation and the sale or licensing of patents.

(f) Activity, including design and construction engineering, relating to the construction, relocation, rearrangement or start-up of facilities or equipment other than facilities or equipment whose sole use is for a particular research and development project.

(g) Market research.

Under the revised SSAP 13, a company can still defer the expenditure under the accruals concept (if it is prudent so to do) but it must be disclosed entirely separately from deferred development expenditure.

2.14 EXAMPLES OF ITEMS EXCLUDED FROM SSAP 13

The above provisions of SSAP 13 do not extend to the following cases.

(a) Expenditure on tangible fixed assets acquired or constructed to provide facilities for research and/or development activities should be capitalised and depreciated over their useful lives in the usual way. However, the depreciation may be capitalised as part of deferred development expenditure if the development work for which the assets are used meets the criteria given above.

(b) Expenditure incurred in locating mineral deposits in extractive industries is outside the scope of SSAP 13.

(c) Expenditure incurred where there is a firm contract to:

(i) Carry out development work on behalf of third parties on such terms that the related expenditure is to be fully reimbursed.

(ii) Develop and manufacture at an agreed price which has been calculated to reimburse expenditure on development as well as on manufacture.

Is not to be treated as deferred development expenditure.

Any such expenditure which has not been reimbursed at the balance sheet date should be included in work in progress.

Question 2

(a) Tank Top Ltd has purchased a tank for £50,000. The purpose of the tank is to investigate the possibility of growing food under water. What would be the appropriate accounting treatment for this item as per SSAP 13?

(b) Applying the accounting concepts of accruals, prudence and consistency to the requirements of SSAP 13, discuss whether there is any conflict between these concepts and SSAP 13.

Answer

(a) SSAP 13 states that expenditure on tangible fixed assets acquired or constructed to provide facilities for research and/or development activities should be capitalised and depreciated over their useful lives in the usual way. The depreciation may be capitalised as part of deferred development expenditure if the development work for which the assets are used meets the criteria given in the SSAP. However, since the tank is for pure research, this does not apply.

(b) The argument for carrying forward development expenditure is based on the accruals concept. If R&D activity eventually leads to new or improved products which generate revenue, the costs should be carried forward to be matched against that revenue in future accounting periods.

However, it could be argued that SSAP 13 conflicts with the prudence concept. Research and development projects have considerable risk. For prudence to prevail, all such costs should be expensed rather than capitalised in advance of the known success of the project. SSAP 13 is, however, prudent in defining the criteria for capitalisation very narrowly.

15: Intangible fixed assets

There is a clear conflict between SSAP 13 and the consistency concept in that companies have a choice between immediate write off and capitalisation. While some consistency is achieved through the requirement to apply the policy of deferral (if adopted) to all development projects that meet the criteria, it is certainly possible for a company to change from a policy of writing off to one of deferral. It is also apparent that different companies may treat the same type of expenditure in different ways. Possibly the choice of treatment may be influenced by the wish to present the results in a favourable light, rather than to give a true and fair view.

Exam focus point

A detailed question is likely to be set on SSAP 13 for Paper 1.1 because it is not likely to be re-examined in depth in Paper 2.5. Be prepared for a question that 'makes you think'.

Disclosure requirements

2.15 The Companies Act 1985 does not require disclosure of the total amount of R & D expenditure during an accounting period, but SSAP 13 (revised) requires that all large companies (defined below) should disclose this total, distinguishing between current year expenditure and amortisation of deferred development expenditure.

2.16 SSAP 13 (revised) requires the following companies to disclose R & D expenditure.

   (a) All public companies

   (b) All special category companies (ie banking and insurance companies)

   (c) All holding companies with a plc or special category company as a subsidiary

   (d) All companies who satisfy the criteria, multiplied by 10, for defining a medium-sized company

This means that, currently, a private company will be exempted if it is not itself (and does not control) a special category company and it meets two of the following criteria:

- turnover ≤ £112 million
- total assets (*before* deduction of current or long-term liabilities) ≤ £56 million
- ≤ 2,500 employees

2.17 Where deferred development costs are included in a company's balance sheet the following information must be given in the notes to the accounts:

   (a) Movements on deferred development expenditure, and the amount brought forward and carried forward at the beginning and end of the period.

   (b) The accounting policy used to account for R & D expenditure should be clearly explained.

Question 3

Y Ltd is a research company which specialises in developing new materials and manufacturing processes for the furniture industry. The company receives payments from a variety of manufacturers, which pay for the right to use the company's patented fabrics and processes.

Research and development costs for the year ended 30 September 20X5 can be analysed as follows.

Part D: Accounting conventions and standards

	£
Expenditure on continuing research projects	1,420,000
Amortisation of development expenditure capitalised in earlier years	240,000

New projects started during the year:

Project A — 280,000

New flame-proof padding. Expected to cost a total of £800,000 to develop. Expected total revenue £2,000,000 once work completed - probably late 20X6

Project B — 150,000

New colour-fast dye. Expected to cost a total of £3,000,000 to complete. Future revenues are likely to exceed £5,000,000. The completion date is uncertain because external funding will have to be obtained before research work can be completed.

Project C — 110,000

Investigation of new adhesive recently developed in aerospace industry. If this proves effective then Y Ltd may well generate significant income because it will be used in place of existing adhesives.

2,200,000

The company has a policy of capitalising all development expenditure where permitted by SSAP 13.

Explain how the three research projects A, B and C will be dealt with in Y Ltd's profit and loss account and balance sheet.

In each case, explain your proposed treatment in terms of SSAP 13 and, where relevant, in terms of the fundamental accounting assumptions of going concern and accruals, and the prudence concept.

Answer

Project A

This project meets the SECTOR criteria for SSAP 13 for development expenditure to be recognised as an asset. These are as follows.

(a) The product or process is clearly defined and the costs attributable to the product or process can be separately identified and measured reliably.

(b) The project is commercially feasible.

(c) The technical feasibility of the product or process can be demonstrated.

(d) An overall profit is expected.

(e) Adequate resources exist, or their availability can be demonstrated, to complete the project and market or use the product or process.

The capitalisation development costs in a company which is a going concern means that these are accrued in order that they can be matched against the income they are expected to generate.

Hence the costs of £280,000 incurred to date should be transferred from research and development costs to capitalised development expenditure and carried forward until revenues are generated; they should then be matched with those revenues.

Project B

Whilst this project meets most of the criteria discussed above which would enable the costs to be carried forward it fails on the requirements that 'adequate resources exist, or their availability can be demonstrated, to complete the project.

Hence it would be prudent to write off these costs. Once funding is obtained the situation can then be reassessed and these and future costs may be capitalised. In this case the prudence concept overrides the accruals assumption.

Project C

This is a research project according to SSAP 13, ie original and planned investigation undertaken with the prospect of gaining new scientific or technical knowledge or understanding.

15: Intangible fixed assets

There is no certainty as to its ultimate success or commercial viability and therefore it cannot be considered to be a development project. SSAP 13 therefore requires that costs be written off as incurred. Once again, prudence overrides the accruals assumption.

Chapter roundup

- **Intangible fixed assets** are those which have a value to the business but which do not have any physical substance. The most significant intangible assets are goodwill and deferred development expenditure.

- If a business has **goodwill**, it means that the value of the business as a going concern is greater than the value of its separate tangible assets.
    - The valuation of goodwill is extremely subjective and fluctuates constantly.
    - For this reason, goodwill is not normally shown as an asset in the balance sheet.

- The exception to this rule is **purchased goodwill,** when someone purchases a business as a going concern. In this case the purchaser and vendor will fix an agreed price which includes an element in respect of goodwill. The way in which goodwill is then valued is not an accounting problem, but a matter of agreement between the two parties.

- Purchased goodwill may then either be immediately written off as an expense in the profit and loss account, or be retained in the balance sheet as an intangible asset. If it is retained in the balance sheet, it must be **amortised** over its estimated useful economic life.

- Expenditure on **research** activities must always be **written off** in the period in which it is incurred.

- Expenditure on **development** activities may also be written off in the same way. But if the criteria laid down by SSAP 13 are satisfied, such expenditure *may* be **capitalised** as an intangible asset. It must then be amortised, beginning from the time when the development project is brought into commercial production.

Quick quiz

1. Why is it unusual to record goodwill as an asset in the accounts?
2. What is purchased goodwill?
3. What method of accounting for purchased goodwill is permitted by FRS 10?
4. How is the amount of purchased goodwill calculated?
5. What is the required accounting treatment for expenditure on research?
6. In what circumstances may development costs be recognised as an asset?
7. When can a write down of capitalised development costs be reversed?

Part D: Accounting conventions and standards

Answers to quick quiz

1. Because goodwill can not be measured accurately and changes from day to day.
2. When someone purchases a business, they may pay more than the net tangible assets are worth to reflect the 'goodwill' built up by the previous owner. This is purchased goodwill.
3. To write off goodwill over its expected economic life (not exceeding 20 years).
4. The purchaser deducts his valuation of the net tangible assets acquired from the price he paid to arrive at the goodwill figure.
5. It is an expense in the period it was incurred.
6. Apply the SECTOR criteria (see paragraph 2.9).
7. If the events that led to the write off cease to exist and there is persuasive evidence that the new circumstances will persist for the foreseeable future.

Now try the question below from the Exam Question Bank

Question to try	Level	Marks	Time
22	Full exam	10	18 mins

Chapter 16

PROVISIONS, CONTINGENCIES AND POST BALANCE SHEET EVENTS

Topic list		Syllabus reference
1	Timing and disclosure	1(d)
2	SSAP 17 *Accounting for post balance sheet events*	4(e), 5(c), 5(d)
3	FRS 12 *Provisions, contingent liabilities and contingent assets*	4(f), 5(c), 5(d)

Introduction

As in the previous chapter you are required here to consider accounting issues which are the subject of standards.

You will see in SSAP 17 and FRS 12 the application of the accounting concept of prudence, which you learnt about in Chapter 14. These accounting standards are important for your auditing studies later and must be thoroughly learnt. They are more straightforward in theory than in practice.

Study guide

Section 18 - Post balance sheet events and contingencies

- Define a post balance sheet event in accordance with SSAP 17 Accounting for Post Balance Sheet Events.
- Distinguish between adjusting and non-adjusting events and explain the methods of including them in financial statements.
- Classify events as adjusting or non-adjusting from a given list.
- Draft notes to company financial statements including requisite details of post balance sheet events.
- Define 'contingent liability' and 'contingent asset' in accordance with FRS 12 Provisions, Contingent Liabilities and Contingent Assets.
- Explain the different ways of accounting for contingent liabilities and contingent assets according to their degree of probability.
- Draft notes to company financial statements including requisite details of contingent liabilities and contingent assets.

Exam guide

These are important areas which are likely to come up regularly. Learn them and be confident you can decide upon the correct accounting treatment for a given situation, but more importantly that you can explain your decision.

Part D: Accounting conventions and standards

1 TIMING AND DISCLOSURE

1.1 The financial statements are significant indicators of a company's success or failure. It is important, therefore, that they include all the information necessary for an understanding of the company's position.

1.2 SSAP 17 *Accounting for post balance sheet events* and FRS 12 *Provisions, contingent liabilities and contingent assets* both require the provision of additional information in order to facilitate such an understanding. SSAP 17 deals with events *after* the balance sheet date which may affect the position at the balance sheet date. FRS 12 deals with matters which are **uncertain** at the balance sheet date.

2 SSAP 17 ACCOUNTING FOR POST BALANCE SHEET EVENTS Pilot paper, December 2002

2.1 SSAP 17 defines post balance sheet events as follows.

> **KEY TERM**
>
> '**Post balance sheet events** are those events, both favourable and unfavourable, which occur between the balance sheet date and the date on which the financial statements are approved by the board of directors.'

2.2 SSAP 17 also explains the rationale behind the proposed accounting treatment of such events.

> 'Events arising after the balance sheet date need to be reflected in financial statements if they provide additional evidence of conditions that existed at the balance sheet date and materially affect the amounts to be included.'

2.3 Even events which do not provide such evidence may need to be disclosed if a true appreciation is to be made of a company's state of affairs and profit or loss.

> 'To prevent financial statements from being misleading, disclosure needs to be made by way of notes of other material events arising after the balance sheet date which provide evidence of conditions not existing at the balance sheet date. Disclosure is required where this information is necessary for a proper understanding of the financial position.'

2.4 The circumstances described above correspond to the distinction made in SSAP 17 between 'adjusting events' and 'non-adjusting events'.

Adjusting events

2.5 SSAP 17 defines adjusting events as follows.

> **KEY TERM**
>
> '**Adjusting events** are post balance sheet events which provide additional evidence of conditions existing at the balance sheet date. They include events which because of statutory or conventional requirements are reflected in financial statements.'

2.6 The second sentence of this definition refers to such events as:

(a) Resolutions relating to proposed dividends and amounts appropriated to reserves.

(b) The effects of changes in taxation rates.

(c) The declaration, by subsidiaries or associated companies, of dividends relating to periods prior to the balance sheet date of the holding company.

2.7 EXAMPLES OF ADJUSTING EVENTS

An appendix to SSAP 17 cites a number of post balance sheet events which normally should be classified as adjusting events. They include:

(a) The subsequent determination of the purchase price or of sale proceeds of assets purchased or sold before the year end.

(b) The valuation of a property which provides evidence of a permanent diminution in value.

(c) The receipt of a copy of the financial statements or other information in respect of an unlisted company which provides evidence of a permanent diminution in the value of a long-term investment.

(d) The receipt of proceeds of sale or other evidence after the balance sheet date concerning the net realisable value of stock.

(e) The receipt of evidence that the previous estimate of accrued profit on a long term contract was materially inaccurate.

(f) The renegotiation of amounts owing by debtors, or the insolvency of a debtor.

(g) Amounts received or receivable in respect of insurance claims which were in the course of negotiation at the balance sheet date.

(h) The discovery of errors or frauds which show that the financial statements were incorrect.

2.8 Some events occurring after the balance sheet date, such as a deterioration in the company's operating results and in its financial position, may indicate a need to consider whether it is appropriate to use the going concern concept in the preparation of financial statements. Consequently such events may fall to be treated as adjusting events.

Non-adjusting events

2.9 SSAP 17 states:

> **KEY TERM**
>
> '**Non-adjusting events** are events which arise after the balance sheet date and concern conditions which did not exist at that time. Consequently they do not result in changes in amounts in financial statements. They may, however, be of such materiality that their disclosure is required by way of notes to ensure that financial statements are not misleading.'

2.10 EXAMPLES OF NON-ADJUSTING EVENTS

Again, a number of examples are given in the appendix including the following.

Part D: Accounting conventions and standards

   (a) Issues of shares and debentures

   (b) Purchases and sales of fixed assets and investments

   (c) Losses of fixed assets or stocks as a result of a catastrophe such as fire or flood

   (d) Opening new trading activities or extending existing trading activities

   (e) Closing a significant part of the trading activities if this was not anticipated at the year end

   (f) Decline in the value of property and investments held as fixed assets, if it can be demonstrated that the decline occurred after the year end

   (g) Government action, such as nationalisation

   (h) Strikes and other labour disputes

2.11 In exceptional circumstances, to accord with the prudence concept, an adverse event which would normally be classified as non-adjusting may need to be reclassified as adjusting. In such circumstances full disclosure of the adjustment would be required.

'Window dressing'

2.12 Although 'window dressing' is not a precise term, and SSAP 17 does not attempt to define it, disclosure is required of the reversal or maturity after the year end of transactions entered into before the year end, the substance of which was primarily to **alter the appearance** of the company's balance sheet. Any 'window dressing' which may encompass fraud is, of course, unlawful and unacceptable.

Disclosure requirements

2.13 Financial statements should be prepared on the basis of **conditions existing** at the **balance sheet** date and should also disclose the date on which they were approved by the board of directors (so that users can establish the duration of the 'post balance sheet events period'). The standard is not intended to apply to events occurring after the date of board approval, but recommends that if such events are material the directors should consider publishing the relevant information so that users of financial statements are not misled.

2.14 SSAP 17 states that a material post balance sheet event requires **changes** in the amounts to be included in financial statements where:

   (a) It is an **adjusting event**.

   (b) It indicates that application of the **going concern** concept to the whole or a material part of the company is **not appropriate**.

   Separate disclosure of adjusting events is not normally required as they do no more than provide additional evidence in support of items in financial statements. However in exceptional circumstances, where a non-adjusting event is reclassified as an adjusting event, full disclosure of the adjustment is required.

2.15 The CA 1985 requires that all liabilities and losses which have arisen or are likely to arise in respect of the financial year to which the accounts relate (or a previous financial year) shall be taken into account, including those that only become apparent between the balance sheet date and the date on which it is signed on behalf of the board of directors.

16: Provisions, contingencies and post balance sheet events

The Act therefore gives some statutory enforcement to the provisions in SSAP 17 in respect of adjusting post balance sheet events, but refers to 'liabilities and losses' only, and not to 'gains'.

2.16 SSAP 17 also requires that a material post balance sheet event should be **disclosed** where:

(a) It is a **non-adjusting event** of such materiality that its non-disclosure would affect the ability of the users of financial statements to reach a proper understanding of the financial position.

(b) It is the reversal or maturity after the year end of a transaction entered into before the year end, the substance of which was primarily to alter the appearance of the company's balance sheet.

2.17 In delaying whether a non-adjusting event is material enough to need disclosure, consider whether the users of financial statements would be misled if the disclosure was omitted.

2.18 In respect of each post balance sheet event which is required to be disclosed the following information should also be given:

(a) The nature of the event.

(b) An estimate of the financial effect, or a statement that it is not practicable to make such an estimate. (*Note*. The estimate of the financial effect should be disclosed before taking account of taxation and the taxation implications should be explained where necessary for a proper understanding of the financial position.)

2.19 The CA 1985 requires that the directors' report should contain particulars of any important events affecting the company (or its subsidiaries) which have occurred since the end of the year.

2.20 Although this gives some statutory backing to the provisions of SSAP 17 in respect of non-adjusting post balance sheet events, it suggests the information be given in the directors' report rather than the notes to the accounts (as required by SSAP 17).

2.21 The following diagram summarises the key points you need to know about SSAP 17 *Accounting for post balance sheet events*.

Part D: Accounting conventions and standards

```
┌─────────────────────────────────────────┐
│ POST BALANCE SHEET EVENTS occur         │
│ between the balance sheet date and the  │
│ date on which the financial statements  │
│ are approved by the board of directors. │
└─────────────────────────────────────────┘
         │                    │
┌────────────────────┐  ┌────────────────────┐
│ ADJUSTING EVENTS   │  │ NON-ADJUSTING      │
│ Provide additional │  │ EVENTS             │
│ evidence of        │  │ Concern conditions │
│ conditions existing│  │ which did not exist│
│ at the balance     │  │ at the balance     │
│ sheet date.        │  │ sheet date.        │
└────────────────────┘  └────────────────────┘
         │                    │
┌────────────────────┐  ┌────────────────────┐
│ STANDARD ACCOUNTING│  │ STANDARD ACCOUNTING│
│ Change the figures │  │ Disclose a post    │
│ in the financial   │  │ balance sheet event│
│ statements if the  │  │ in a note if it is │
│ post balance sheet │  │ material and either│
│ event is material  │  │ it's a non-adjust- │
│ and either it's an │  │ ing event or it was│
│ adjusting event or │  │ window dressing.   │
│ the going concern  │  │                    │
│ concept is no      │  │                    │
│ longer appropriate.│  │                    │
└────────────────────┘  └────────────────────┘
         │                    │
┌─────────────────────────────────────────┐
│ EVENTS AFTER THE DATE OF APPROVAL OF    │
│ THE ACCOUNTS                            │
│ The directors should consider publishing│
│ these if material.                      │
└─────────────────────────────────────────┘
```

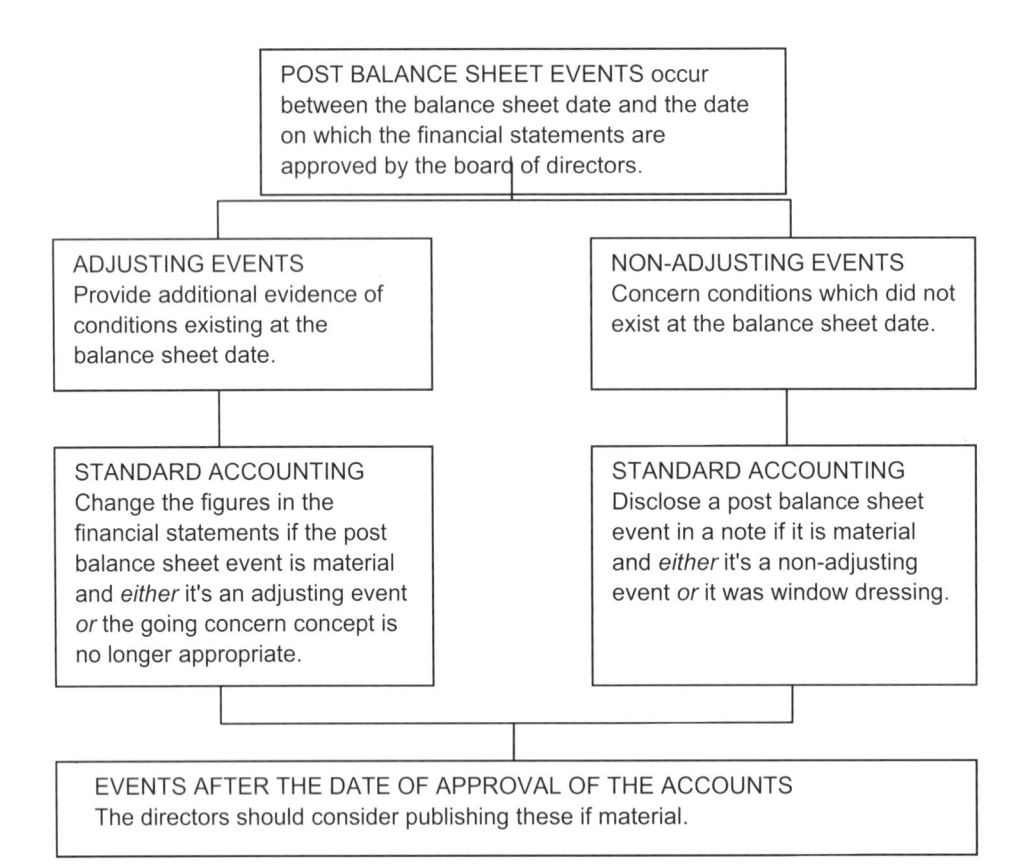

Question 1

State whether the following post balance sheet events are adjusting or non-adjusting:

(a) Purchase of an investment
(b) A change in the rate of corporation tax, applicable to the previous year
(c) An increase in pension benefits
(d) Losses due to fire
(e) A bad debt suddenly being paid
(f) The receipt of proceeds of sales or other evidence concerning the net realisable value of stock
(g) A sudden decline in the value of property held as a fixed asset
(h) A merger

Answer

(b), (e) and (f) are adjusting; the others are non-adjusting.

Question 2

In the case of item (g) in Question 1 above, the following additional information is available. A factory held as a fixed asset with a NBV of £500,000 in the balance sheet. Due to the sudden abandonment of the local council's redevelopment plans in the Northwich area, the market value of the property has fallen to £250,000. Draft a note to the company financial statements.

Answer

Note: Post balance sheet event

After the balance sheet date, the local council abandoned its redevelopment plans for the Northwich area. The company has a factory in that area and the market value of that property has now fallen to £250,000. The factory is shown in the accounts with a net book value of £500,000 at the balance sheet date.

Tutorial note: When drafting these type of notes give all the information that is available in the question.

16: Provisions, contingencies and post balance sheet events

> **Exam focus point**
>
> As with SSAP 13, the Paper 2.5 examiner is not likely to set detailed questions on SSAP 17. It is therefore ripe for a Paper 1.1 question.

3 FRS 12 PROVISIONS, CONTINGENT LIABILITIES AND CONTINGENT ASSETS
Pilot paper, December 2002

3.1 As we have seen with regard to post balance sheet events, financial statements must include **all the information necessary for an understanding of the company's financial position**. Provisions, contingent liabilities and contingent assets are 'uncertainties' that must be accounted for consistently if are to achieve this understanding.

3.2 FRS 12 *Provisions, contingent liabilities and contingent assets* aims to ensure that appropriate **recognition** and **measurement** are applied to provisions, contingent liabilities and contingent assets and that **sufficient information** is disclosed in the **notes** to the financial statements to enable users to understand their nature, timing and amount.

Provisions

3.3 You will be familiar with provisions for depreciation and doubtful debts from your earlier studies. The sorts of provisions addressed by FRS 12 are, however, rather different.

3.4 Before FRS 12, there was no accounting standard dealing with provisions. Companies wanting to show their results in the most favourable light used to make large **'one off' provisions** in years where a high level of underlying profits was generated. These provisions, often known as **'big bath'** provisions, were then available to shield expenditure in future years when perhaps the underlying profits were not as good.

3.5 In other words, **provisions were used for profit smoothing**. Profit smoothing is misleading.

> **POINT TO NOTE**
>
> The key aim of FRS 12 is to ensure that **provisions are made only where there are valid grounds for them.**

3.6 FRS 12 views a provision as a **liability**.

> **KEY TERMS**
>
> A **provision** is a **liability** of uncertain timing or amount.
>
> A **liability** is an obligation of an entity to transfer economic benefits as a result of past transactions or events. (FRS 12)

3.7 The FRS distinguishes provisions from other liabilities such as trade creditors and accruals. This is on the basis that for a provision there is **uncertainty** about the timing or amount of the future expenditure. Whilst uncertainty is clearly present in the case of certain accruals the uncertainty is generally much less than for provisions.

Part D: Accounting conventions and standards

Recognition

3.8 FRS 12 states that a provision should be **recognised** as a liability in the financial statements when:

- An entity has a **present obligation** (legal or constructive) as a result of a past event
- It is probable that a **transfer of economic benefits** will be required to settle the obligation
- A **reliable estimate** can be made of the obligation

Meaning of obligation

3.9 It is fairly clear what a legal obligation is. However, you may not know what a **constructive obligation** is.

KEY TERM

FRS 12 defines a **constructive obligation** as

'An obligation that derives from an entity's actions where:

- By an established pattern of past practice, published policies or a sufficiently specific current statement the entity has indicated to other parties that it will accept certain responsibilities.
- As a result, the entity has created a valid expectation on the part of those other parties that it will discharge those responsibilities.

Question 3

In which of the following circumstances might a provision be recognised?

(a) On 13 December 20X9 the board of an entity decided to close down a division. The accounting date of the company is 31 December. Before 31 December 20X9 the decision was not communicated to any of those affected and no other steps were taken to implement the decision.

(b) The board agreed a detailed closure plan on 20 December 20X9 and details were given to customers and employees.

(c) A company is obliged to incur clean up costs for environmental damage (that has already been caused).

(d) A company intends to carry out future expenditure to operate in a particular way in the future.

Answer

(a) No provision would be recognised as the decision has not been communicated.

(b) A provision would be made in the 20X9 financial statements.

(c) A provision for such costs is appropriate.

(d) No present obligation exists and under FRS 12 no provision would be appropriate. This is because the entity could avoid the future expenditure by its future actions, maybe by changing its method of operation.

16: Provisions, contingencies and post balance sheet events

Probable transfer of economic benefits

3.10 For the purpose of the FRS, a transfer of economic benefits is regarded as '**probable**' if the event is **more likely than not** to occur. This appears to indicate a probability of more than 50%. However, the standard makes it clear that where there is a number of similar obligations the probability should be based on considering all the obligations, rather than one single item.

3.11 EXAMPLE: TRANSFER OF ECONOMIC BENEFITS

If a company has entered into a warranty obligation then the probability of transfer of economic benefits may well be extremely small in respect of one specific item. However, when considering all the warranties, the probability of some transfer of economic benefits is quite likely to be much higher. If there is a **greater than 50% probability** of some transfer of economic benefits then a **provision** should be made for the **expected amount**.

Measurement of provisions

> **POINT TO NOTE**
>
> The amount recognised as a provision should be the best estimate of the expenditure required to settle the present obligation at the balance sheet date.

3.12 The estimates will be determined by the **judgement** of the entity's management supplemented by the experience of similar transactions.

3.13 Allowance is made for **uncertainty**.

3.14 Where the effect of the **time value of money** is material, the amount of a provision should be the **present value** of the expenditure required to settle the obligation. An appropriate **discount** rate should be used.

Provisions for restructuring

3.15 One of the main purposes of FRS 12 was to target abuses of provisions for restructuring. Accordingly, FRS 12 lays down **strict criteria** to determine when such a provision can be made.

> **KEY TERM**
>
> FRS 12 defines a **restructuring** as:
>
> A programme that is planned and is controlled by management and materially changes either:
>
> - The scope of a business undertaken by an entity
> - The manner in which that business is conducted.

3.16 The FRS gives the following **examples** of events that may fall under the definition of restructuring.

- The **sale or termination** of a line of business

Part D: Accounting conventions and standards

- The **closure of business locations** in a country or region or the **relocation** of business activities from one country region to another
- **Changes in management structure**, for example, the elimination of a layer of management
- **Fundamental reorganisations** that have a material effect on the **nature and focus** of the entity's operations

3.17 The question is whether or not an entity has an obligation - legal or constructive - at the balance sheet date.

- An entity must have a **detailed formal plan** for the restructuring.
- It must have **raised a valid expectation** in those affected that it will carry out the restructuring by starting to implement that plan or announcing its main features to those affected by it

POINT TO NOTE

A mere management decision is not normally sufficient. Management decisions may sometimes trigger off recognition, but only if earlier events such as negotiations with employee representatives and other interested parties have been concluded subject only to management approval.

3.18 Where the restructuring involves the **sale of an operation** then FRS 12 states that no obligation arises until the entity has entered into a **binding sale agreement**. This is because until this has occurred the entity will be able to change its mind and withdraw from the sale even if its intentions have been announced publicly.

Costs to be included within a restructuring provision

3.19 The FRS states that a restructuring provision should include only the **direct expenditures** arising from the restructuring, which are those that are both:

- **Necessarily entailed** by the restructuring
- Not associated with the **ongoing activities** of the entity.

3.20 The following costs should specifically **not** be included within a restructuring provision.

- **Retraining** or relocating continuing staff
- **Marketing**
- **Investment in new systems** and distribution networks

Disclosure

3.21 Disclosures for provisions fall into two parts.

- Disclosure of details of the **change in carrying value** of a provision from the beginning to the end of the year
- Disclosure of the **background** to the making of the provision and the uncertainties affecting its outcome

Contingent liabilities

3.22 Now you understand provisions it will be easier to understand contingent assets and liabilities.

> **KEY TERM**
>
> FRS 12 defines a **contingent liability** as:
>
> - A possible obligation that arises from past events and whose existence will be confirmed only by the occurrence or non-occurrence of one or more uncertain future events not wholly within the entity's control; or
> - A present obligation that arises from past events but is not recognised because:
>   - It is not probable that a transfer of economic benefits will be required to settle the obligation
>   - Or the amount of the obligation cannot be measured with sufficient reliability.

3.23 As a rule of thumb, probable means more than 50% likely. **If an obligation is probable, it is not a contingent liability** - instead, a **provision is needed**.

Treatment of contingent liabilities

3.24 Contingent liabilities **should not be recognised in financial statements** but they **should be disclosed**. The required disclosures are:

- A brief description of the nature of the contingent liability
- An estimate of its financial effect
- An indication of the uncertainties that exist
- The possibility of any reimbursement

Contingent assets

> **KEY TERM**
>
> FRS 12 defines a **contingent asset** as:
>
> A possible asset that arises from past events and whose existence will be confirmed by the occurrence of one or more uncertain future events not wholly within the entity's control.

3.25 **A contingent asset must not be recognised**. Only when the realisation of the related economic benefits is **virtually certain** should recognition take place. At that point, **the asset is no longer a contingent asset!**

3.26 Before trying Question 4, study the flow chart, taken from FRS 12, which is a good summary of the requirements of the standard.

Part D: Accounting conventions and standards

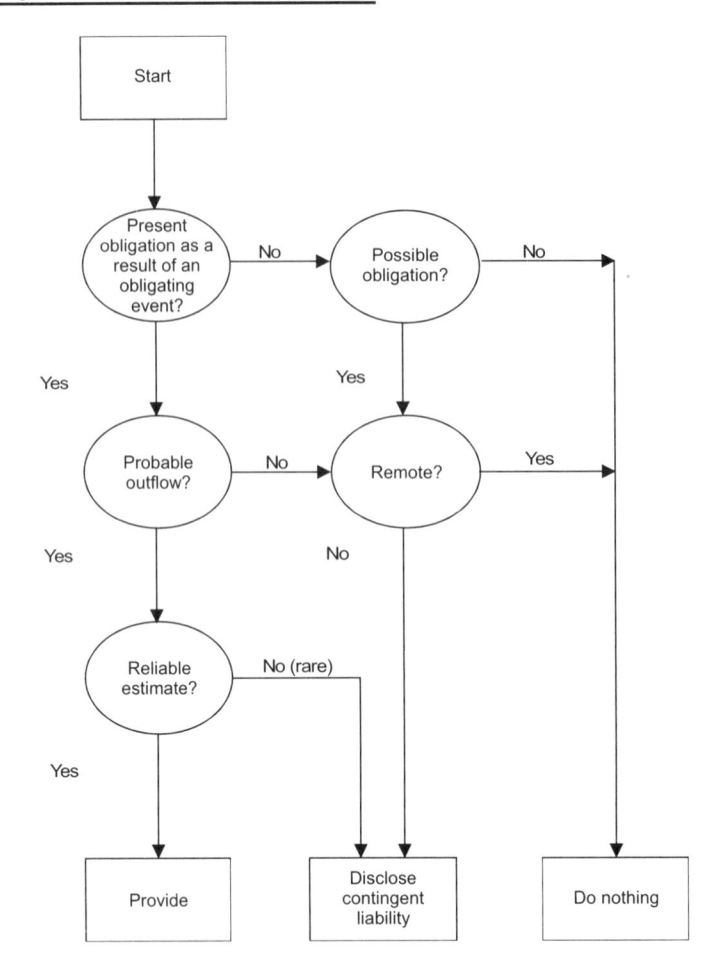

[Flowchart: Start → Present obligation as a result of an obligating event?
- No → Possible obligation?
  - No → Do nothing
  - Yes → Remote?
    - Yes → Do nothing
    - No → Disclose contingent liability
- Yes → Probable outflow?
  - No → Remote? (joins above)
  - Yes → Reliable estimate?
    - No (rare) → Disclose contingent liability
    - Yes → Provide]

Question 4

During 20X9 Smack Ltd gives a guarantee of certain borrowings of Pony Ltd, whose financial condition at that time is sound. During 20Y0, the financial condition of Pony Ltd deteriorates and at 30 June 20Y0 Pony Ltd files for protection from its creditors.

What accounting treatment is required:

(a) At 31 December 20X9?

(b) At 31 December 20Y0?

Answer

(a) At 31 December 20X9

There is a present obligation as a result of a past obligating event. The obligating event is the giving of the guarantee, which gives rise to a legal obligation. However, at 31 December 20X9 no transfer of economic benefits is probable in settlement of the obligation.

No provision is recognised. The guarantee is disclosed as a contingent liability unless the probability of any transfer is regarded as remote.

(b) At 31 December 20Y0

As above, there is a present obligation as a result of a past obligating event, namely the giving of the guarantee.

At 31 December 20Y0 it is probable that a transfer of economic events will be required to settle the obligation. A provision is therefore recognised for the best estimate of the obligation.

16: Provisions, contingencies and post balance sheet events

> **Exam focus point**
>
> You will certainly be given **practical examples** in the exam. So you must be able to apply the theory to a given situation.

Question 5

From Question 4(a), draft the note to the financial statements as at 31 December 20X9. Assume that Pony Ltd is a subsidiary of Smack Ltd and that the bank borrowings of Pony Ltd at 31 December 20X9 were £2 million.

Answer

Note: Contingent liability

The company has given a guarantee to the bankers of Pony Ltd, a subsidiary of the company. This guarantee is in respect of borrowings totalling £2 million as at 31 December 20X9. However, Pony Ltd's financial condition is sound and the company does not foresee any payments becoming due under this guarantee at the current time.

Chapter roundup

- SSAP 17 *Accounting for post balance sheet events* amplifies the CA 1985 requirement to take account of post balance sheet liabilities and losses by distinguishing between **adjusting events** and **non-adjusting events** and giving examples.

- The SSAP also requires disclosure of **window dressing** transactions.

- Where an otherwise non-adjusting event indicates that the going concern concept is no longer appropriate then the accounts may have to be restated on a break-up basis.

- You should be able to define and discuss all these terms and apply them to practical examples.

- Under FRS 12 a **provision** should be recognised
    - When an entity has a **present obligation**, legal or constructive
    - It is probable that a **transfer of economic benefits** will be required to settle It
    - A **reliable estimate** can be made of its amount

- An entity **should not recognise a contingent asset or liability** but they **should be disclosed by way of notes to the financial statements.**

Quick quiz

1. When does an event occurring after the balance sheet date require changes to the financial statements?
2. What treatment is required for dividends declared after the balance sheet date?
3. What disclosure is required when it is not possible to estimate the financial effect of an event not requiring adjustment?
4. How does FRS 12 define a contingent liability?
5. When should a contingent liability be recognised?

Answers to quick quiz

1 Assets and liabilities should be adjusted for events occurring after the balance sheet date when these provide additional evidence for estimates existing at the balance sheet date.

2 Dividends relating to the period covered by the financial statements, but declared after the balance sheet date, should be adjusted for in the accounts.

3 A statement of the nature of the event and the fact that a financial estimate of the event can not be made.

4 See Key Term in paragraph 3.22.

5 They should **never** be recognised, but disclosed by way of note.

Now try the question below from the Exam Question Bank

Question to try	Level	Marks	Time
23	Introductory	n/a	36 mins

Part E
Financial statements

Chapter 17

INCOMPLETE RECORDS

Topic list	Syllabus reference
1 Incomplete records questions	5(d)
2 The opening balance sheet	5(d)
3 Credit sales and debtors	5(d)
4 Purchases and trade creditors	5(d)
5 Establishing cost of sales	5(d)
6 Stolen goods or goods destroyed	5(d)
7 The cash book	5(d)
8 Accruals and prepayments	5(d)
9 Drawings	5(d)
10 Dealing with incomplete records problems in the examination	5(d)

Introduction

So far in your work on preparing the final accounts for a sole trader we have assumed that a full set of records are kept. In practice many sole traders do not keep a full set of records and you must apply certain techniques to arrive at the necessary figures.

Incomplete records questions are a very good test of your understanding of the way in which a set of accounts is built up.

Limited companies are obliged by law to keep proper accounting records. They will be considered in Chapter 19.

Study guide

Sections 9 and 10 - Incomplete records

- Explain techniques used in incomplete record situations:
    - Calculation of opening capital
    - Use of ledger total accounts to calculate missing figures.
    - Use of cash and/or bank summaries
    - Use of given gross profit percentage to calculate missing figures.

- Explain the calculation of profit or loss as the difference between opening and closing net assets.

Exam guide

Incomplete record questions will feature in Section A and sometimes in Section B. Learn the tricks presented in this chapter and you should be able to tackle anything the examiner throws at you. Make sure you understand the difference between **margin** and **mark-up**.

Part E: Financial statements

1 INCOMPLETE RECORDS QUESTIONS December 2001, June 2003

1.1 Incomplete records problems occur when a business does not have a full set of accounting records, either because:

- The proprietor of the business does not keep a full set of accounts
- Some of the business accounts are accidentally lost or destroyed.

1.2 The problem for the accountant is to prepare a set of year-end accounts for the business; ie a trading, profit and loss account, and a balance sheet. Since the business does not have a full set of records, preparing the final accounts is not a simple matter of closing off accounts and transferring balances. The task of preparing the final accounts involves:

(a) Establishing the **cost of purchases** and **other expenses**

(b) Establishing the **total amount of sales**

(c) Establishing the amount of **creditors, accruals, debtors** and **prepayments** at the end of the year

1.3 Examination questions often take incomplete records problems a stage further, by introducing an 'incident' - such as fire or burglary - which leaves the owner of the business uncertain about how much stock has been destroyed or stolen.

1.4 The great merit of incomplete records problems is that they focus attention on the relationship between cash received and paid, sales and debtors, purchases and creditors, and stocks, as well as calling for the preparation of final accounts from basic principles.

1.5 To understand what incomplete records are about, it will obviously be useful now to look at what exactly might be incomplete. The items we shall consider in turn are:

(a) The opening balance sheet
(b) Credit sales and debtors
(c) Purchases and trade creditors
(d) Purchases, stocks and the cost of sales
(e) Stolen goods or goods destroyed
(f) The cash book
(g) Accruals and prepayments
(h) Drawings

Exam focus point

Incomplete records questions are a good test of whether you have a really thorough grasp of double entry. Examiners are fond of them. With practice they become easier and can be very satisfying!

2 THE OPENING BALANCE SHEET

2.1 In practice there should not be any missing item in the opening balance sheet of the business, because it should be available from the preparation of the previous year's final accounts. However, an examination problem might provide information about the assets and liabilities of the business at the beginning of the period under review, but then leave the balancing figure - ie the proprietor's business capital - unspecified.

17: Incomplete records

2.2 EXAMPLE: OPENING BALANCE SHEET

Suppose a business has the following assets and liabilities as at 1 January 20X3.

	£
Fixtures and fittings at cost	7,000
Provision for depreciation, fixtures and fittings	4,000
Motor vehicles at cost	12,000
Provision for depreciation, motor vehicles	6,800
Stock in trade	4,500
Trade debtors	5,200
Cash at bank and in hand	1,230
Trade creditors	3,700
Prepayment	450
Accrued rent	2,000

You are required to prepare a balance sheet for the business, inserting a balancing figure for proprietor's capital.

2.3 SOLUTION

Balance sheet as at 1 January 20X3

	£	£
Fixed assets		
Fixtures and fittings at cost	7,000	
Less accumulated depreciation	4,000	
		3,000
Motor vehicles at cost	12,000	
Less accumulated depreciation	6,800	
		5,200
		8,200
Current assets		
Stock in trade	4,500	
Trade debtors	5,200	
Prepayment	450	
Cash	1,230	
	11,380	
Current liabilities		
Trade creditors	3,700	
Accrual	2,000	
	5,700	
Net current assets		5,680
		13,880
Proprietor's capital as at 1 January 20X3 (balancing figure)		13,880

3 CREDIT SALES AND DEBTORS

3.1 If a business does not keep a record of its sales on credit, the value of these sales can be derived from the opening balance of trade debtors, the closing balance of trade debtors, and the payments received from trade debtors during the period.

Part E: Financial statements

> **FORMULA TO LEARN**
>
> Credit sales are:
> | | £ |
> |---|---|
> | Payments received from trade debtors | X |
> | Plus closing balance of trade debtors (since these represent sales in the current period for which cash payment has not yet been received) | X |
> | Less opening balance of trade debtors (unless these become bad debts, they will pay what they owe in the current period for sales in a previous period) | (X) |
> | | X |

3.2 For example, suppose that a business had trade debtors of £1,750 on 1 April 20X4 and trade debtors of £3,140 on 31 March 20X5. If payments received from trade debtors during the year to 31 March 20X5 were £28,490, and if there are no bad debts, then credit sales for the period would be:

	£
Cash received from debtors	28,490
Plus closing debtors	3,140
Less opening debtors	(1,750)
Credit sales	29,880

If there are bad debts during the period, the value of sales will be increased by the amount of bad debts written off, no matter whether they relate to opening debtors or credit sales during the current period.

3.3 The same calculation could be made in a T account, with credit sales being the balancing figure to complete the account.

DEBTORS

	£		£
Opening balance b/f	1,750	Cash received	28,490
Credit sales (balancing fig)	29,880	Closing balance c/f	3,140
	31,630		31,630

You should recognise that this is, in fact, the debtors control account.

3.4 The same interrelationship between credit sales, cash from debtors, and opening and closing debtors balances can be used to derive a missing figure for cash from debtors, or opening or closing debtors, given the values for the three other items. For example, if we know that opening debtors are £6,700, closing debtors are £3,200 and credit sales for the period are £69,400, then cash received from debtors during the period would be as follows.

DEBTORS

	£		£
Opening balance	6,700	Cash received (balancing figure)	72,900
Sales (on credit)	69,400	Closing balance c/f	3,200
	76,100		76,100

4 PURCHASES AND TRADE CREDITORS

4.1 A similar relationship exists between purchases of stock during a period, the opening and closing balances for trade creditors, and amounts paid to trade creditors during the period.

17: Incomplete records

> **FORMULA TO LEARN**
>
> If we wish to calculate an unknown amount for purchases, the amount would be derived as follows:
>
> | | £ |
> |---|---|
> | Payments to trade creditors during the period | X |
> | Plus closing balance of trade creditors | X |
> | (since these represent purchases in the current period for which payment has not yet been made) | |
> | Less opening balance of trade creditors | (X) |
> | (these relate to purchases in a previous period) | |
> | Purchases during the period | X |

4.2 For example, suppose that a business had trade creditors of £3,728 on 1 October 20X5 and trade creditors of £2,645 on 30 September 20X6. If payments to trade creditors during the year to 30 September 20X6 were £31,479, then purchases during the year would be:

	£
Payments to trade creditors	31,479
Plus closing balance of trade creditors	2,645
Less opening balance of trade creditors	(3,728)
Purchases	30,396

4.3 The same calculation could be made in a T account, with purchases being the balancing figure to complete the account.

CREDITORS

	£		£
Cash payments	31,479	Opening balance b/f	3,728
Closing balance c/f	2,645	Purchases (balancing figure)	30,396
	34,124		34,124

Once again, you should recognise that this is the creditors control account.

Question 1

Mr Harmon does not keep full accounting records, but the following information is available in respect of his accounting year ended 31 December 20X9.

	£
Cash purchases in year	3,900
Cash paid for goods supplied on credit	27,850
Creditors at 1 January 20X9	970
Creditors at 31 December 20X9	720

In his trading account for 20X9, what will be Harmon's figure for purchases?

Answer

CREDITORS

	£		£
Cash payments	31,750	Opening balance b/f	970
Closing balance c/f	720	Purchases (balancing figure)	31,500
	32,470		32,470

Alternatively, you could prepare the creditors control account to just include credit purchases and then add on the cash purchases, as a separate calculation.

Part E: Financial statements

5 ESTABLISHING COST OF SALES

5.1 When the value of purchases is not known, a different approach might be required to find out what they were, depending on the nature of the information given to you.

5.2 One approach would be to use information about the cost of sales, and opening and closing stocks, in other words, to use the trading account rather than the trade creditors account to find the cost of purchases.

FORMULA TO LEARN

		£
Since	Opening stocks	X
	Plus purchases	X
	Less closing stocks	(X)
	Equals the cost of goods sold	X
Then	The cost of goods sold	X
	Plus closing stocks	X
	Less opening stocks	(X)
	Equals purchases	X

5.3 The stock in trade of a business on 1 July 20X6 has a balance sheet value of £8,400, and a stock taking exercise at 30 June 20X7 showed stock to be valued at £9,350. Sales for the year to 30 June 20X7 are £80,000, and the business makes a gross profit of $33^1/3$% on cost for all the items that it sells. What were the purchases during the year?

5.4 You should remember that sales – cost of sales = gross profit. In the example we are told that gross profit is $33_{1/3}$% **on cost**. So cost of sales is 100% and sales must be $133_{1/3}$% ($133_{1/3}$% - 100% = $33_{1/3}$%)

	£
Sales ($133^1/3$%)	80,000
Cost of sales (100%)	60,000
Gross profit ($33^1/3$%)	20,000

	£
Cost of goods sold	60,000
Plus closing stock	9,350
Less opening stocks	(8,400)
Purchases	60,950

5.5 The above example illustrates **markup**. We are told that the business makes a gross profit of $33^1/_3$% on **cost**. From this we were able to deduce that cost of sales were 100% and sales $133^1/_3$%. In other words, the business has a markup of $33^1/_3$% on cost.

5.6 Another way of calculating cost of sales uses gross profit **margin**. Suppose that we were told that the sales were £80,000 and the business had a gross profit margin of $33^1/_3$%. This means that sales are 100% and so cost of sales are $66^2/_3$%.

	£
Sales (100%)	80,000
Cost of Sales ($66^2/_3$%)	53,333
Gross profit ($33^1/_3$%)	26,667

17: Incomplete records

> **IMPORTANT!**
>
> **Markup** means that cost of sales is the 100% figure.
>
> **Margin** means that sales is the 100% figure.

Question 2

Harry has budgeted sales for the coming year of £175,000. He achieves a constant gross mark-up of 40% on cost. He plans to reduce his stock level by £13,000 over the year.

What will Harry's purchases be for the year?

Answer

Cost of sales = 100/140 × £175,000
            = £125,000

Since the stock level is being allowed to fall, it means that purchases will be £13,000 less than £125,000.

6 STOLEN GOODS OR GOODS DESTROYED

6.1 A similar type of calculation might be required to derive the value of goods stolen or destroyed. When an unknown quantity of goods is lost, whether they are stolen, destroyed in a fire, or lost in any other way such that the quantity lost cannot be counted, then the cost of the goods lost is the difference between:

(a) The **cost of goods sold**

(b) **Opening stock of the goods** (at cost) plus **purchases** less **closing stock of the goods** (at cost)

In theory (a) and (b) should be the same. However, if (b) is a larger amount than (a), it follows that the difference must be the cost of the goods purchased and neither sold nor remaining in stock - ie the cost of the goods lost.

6.2 EXAMPLE: COST OF GOODS DESTROYED

Orlean Flames is a shop which sells fashion clothes. On 1 January 20X5, it had stock in trade which cost £7,345. During the 9 months to 30 September 20X5, the business purchased goods from suppliers costing £106,420. Sales during the same period were £154,000. The shop makes a gross profit markup of 40% on cost for everything it sells. On 30 September 20X5, there was a fire in the shop which destroyed most of the stock in it. Only a small amount of stock, known to have cost £350, was undamaged and still fit for sale.

How much stock was lost in the fire?

6.3 SOLUTION

(a)

	£
Sales (140%)	154,000
Gross profit (40%)	44,000
Cost of goods sold (100%)	110,000

Part E: Financial statements

(b)
	£
Opening stock, at cost	7,345
Plus purchases	106,420
	113,765
Less closing stock, at cost	350
Equals cost of goods sold and goods lost	113,415

(c)
	£
Cost of goods sold and lost	113,415
Cost of goods sold	110,000
Cost of goods lost	3,415

6.4 EXAMPLE: COST OF GOODS STOLEN

Beau Gullard runs a jewellery shop in the High Street. On 1 January 20X9, his stock in trade, at cost, amounted to £4,700 and his trade creditors were £3,950.

During the six months to 30 June 20X9, sales were £42,000. Beau Gullard makes a gross profit margin of $33^{1}/_{3}\%$ on the sales value of everything he sells.

On 30 June, there was a burglary at the shop, and all the stock was stolen.

In trying to establish how much stock had been taken, Beau Gullard was only able to say that:

(a) He knew from his bank statements that he had paid £28,400 to creditors in the 6 month period to 30 June 20X9.

(b) He currently owed creditors £5,550.

Required

(a) Calculate the amount of stock stolen.
(b) Prepare a trading account for the 6 months to 30 June 20X9.

6.5 SOLUTION

Step 1. The first 'unknown' is the amount of purchases during the period. This is established by the method previously described in Section 4.

CREDITORS

	£		£
Payments to creditors	28,400	Opening balance b/f	3,950
Closing balance c/f	5,550	Purchases (balancing figure)	30,000
	33,950		33,950

Step 2. The cost of goods sold is also unknown, but this can be established from the gross profit margin and the sales for the period.

		£
Sales	(100%)	42,000
Gross profit	($33^{1}/_{3}\%$)	14,000
Cost of goods sold	($66^{2}/_{3}\%$)	28,000

294

Step 3. The cost of the goods stolen is:

	£
Opening stock at cost	4,700
Purchases	30,000
	34,700
Less closing stock (after burglary)	0
Cost of goods sold and goods stolen	34,700
Cost of goods sold (see Step 2 above)	28,000
Cost of goods stolen	6,700

Step 4. The cost of the goods stolen will not be a charge in the trading account, and so the trading account for the period is as follows:

BEAU GULLARD
TRADING ACCOUNT FOR THE SIX MONTHS TO 30 JUNE 20X9

	£	£
Sales		42,000
Less cost of goods sold		
Opening stock	4,700	
Purchases	30,000	
	34,700	
Less stock stolen	6,700	
		28,000
Gross profit		14,000

Accounting for stock destroyed, stolen or otherwise lost

6.6 When stock is stolen, destroyed or otherwise lost, the loss must be accounted for somehow. The procedure was described briefly in the earlier chapter on accounting for stocks. Since the loss is not a trading loss, the cost of the goods lost is not included in the trading account, as the previous example showed. The accounting double entry is therefore

DEBIT	See below
CREDIT	Trading account (although instead of showing the cost of the loss as a credit, it is usually shown as a deduction on the debit side of the trading account, which is the same as a 'plus' on the credit side).

6.7 The account that is to be debited is one of two possibilities, depending on whether or not the lost goods were insured against the loss.

(a) If the lost goods were not insured, the business must bear the loss, and the loss is shown in the P & L account: ie

DEBIT	Profit and loss
CREDIT	Trading account

(b) If the lost goods were insured, the business will not suffer a loss, because the insurance will pay back the cost of the lost goods. This means that there is no charge at all in the P&L account, and the appropriate double entry is:

DEBIT	Insurance claim account (debtor account)
CREDIT	Trading account

with the cost of the loss. The insurance claim will then be a current asset, and shown in the balance sheet of the business as such. When the claim is paid, the account is then closed by

DEBIT	Cash
CREDIT	Insurance claim account

Part E: Financial statements

7 THE CASH BOOK

7.1 The construction of a cash book, largely from bank statements showing receipts and payments of a business during a given period, is often an important feature of incomplete records problems.

> **Exam focus point**
>
> In an examination, the purpose of an incomplete records question is largely to test the understanding of candidates about how various items of receipts or payments relate to the preparation of a final set of accounts for a business.

7.2 We have already seen in this chapter that information about cash receipts or payments might be needed to establish:

(a) The amount of purchases during a period
(b) The amount of credit sales during a period

Other items of receipts or payments might be relevant to establishing:

(a) The amount of cash sales
(b) The amount of certain expenses in the P & L account
(c) The amount of drawings by the business proprietor

7.3 It might therefore be helpful, if a business does not keep a cash book day-to-day, to construct a cash book at the end of an accounting period. A business which typically might not keep a day-to-day cash book is a shop, where:

(a) Many sales, if not all sales, are cash sales (ie with payment by notes and coins, cheques, or credit cards at the time of sale).

(b) Some payments are made in notes and coins out of the till rather than by payment out of the business bank account by cheque.

7.4 Where there appears to be a sizeable volume of receipts and payments in cash (ie notes and coins), then it is also helpful to construct a two column cash book.

> **KEY TERM**
>
> A **two column cash book** is a cash book with one column for receipts and payments, and one column for money paid into and out of the business bank account.

An example will illustrate the technique and the purpose of a two column cash book.

7.5 EXAMPLE: TWO COLUMN CASH BOOK

Jonathan Slugg owns and runs a shop selling fishing tackle, making a gross profit of 25% on the cost of everything he sells. He does not keep a cash book.

On 1 January 20X7 the balance sheet of his business was as follows.

	£	£
Net fixed assets		20,000
Stock	10,000	
Cash in the bank	3,000	
Cash in the till	200	
	13,200	
Trade creditors	1,200	
		12,000
		32,000
Proprietor's capital		32,000

In the year to 31 December 20X7:

(a) There were no sales on credit
(b) £41,750 in receipts were banked
(c) The bank statements of the period show the payments:

			£
(i)	To trade creditors		36,000
(ii)	Sundry expenses		5,600
(iii)	In drawings		4,400

(d) Payments were also made in cash out of the till:

			£
(i)	To trade creditors		800
(ii)	Sundry expenses		1,500
(iii)	In drawings		3,700

At 31 December 20X7, the business had cash in the till of £450 and trade creditors of £1,400. The cash balance in the bank was not known and the value of closing stock has not yet been calculated. There were no accruals or prepayments. No further fixed assets were purchased during the year. The depreciation charge for the year is £900.

Required

(a) Prepare a two column cash book for the period.

(b) Prepare the trading, profit and loss account for the year to 31 December 20X7 and the balance sheet as at 31 December 20X7.

7.6 DISCUSSION AND SOLUTION

A two column cash book is completed as follows.

Step 1. Enter the opening cash balances.

Step 2. Enter the information given about cash payments (and any cash receipts, if there had been any such items given in the problem).

Step 3. The cash receipts banked are a 'contra' entry, being both a debit (bank column) and a credit (cash in hand column) in the same account.

Step 4. Enter the closing cash in hand (cash in the bank at the end of the period is not known).

Part E: Financial statements

CASH BOOK

	Cash in hand £	Bank £		Cash in hand £	Bank £
Balance b/f	200	3,000	Trade creditors	800	36,000
Cash receipts banked		41,750	Sundry expenses	1,500	5,600
			Drawings	3,700	4,400
Sales*	48,000		Cash receipts banked	41,750	
			Balance c/f		450
Balance c/f		*1,250			
	48,200	46,000		48,200	46,000

* Balancing figure

Step 5. The closing balance of money in the bank is a balancing figure. Notice that this is a credit balance ie an overdraft.

Step 6. Since all sales are for cash, a balancing figure that can be entered in the cash book is sales, in the cash in hand (debit) column.

7.7 It is important to notice that since not all receipts from cash sales are banked, the value of cash sales during the period is:

	£
Receipts banked	41,750
Plus expenses and drawings paid out of the till in cash £(800 + 1,500 + 3,700)	6,000
Plus any cash stolen (here there is none)	0
Plus the closing balance of cash in hand	450
	48,200
Less the opening balance of cash in hand	(200)
Equals cash sales	48,000

7.8 The cash book constructed in this way has enabled us to establish both the closing balance for cash in the bank and also the volume of cash sales. The trading, profit and loss account and the balance sheet can also be prepared, once a value for purchases has been calculated.

CREDITORS

	£		£
Cash book:		Balance b/f	1,200
Payments from bank	36,000	Purchases (balancing figure)	37,000
Cash book:			
Payments in cash	800		
Balance c/f	1,400		
	38,200		38,200

The gross profit markup of 25% on cost indicates that the cost of the goods sold is £38,400, ie:

	£
Sales (125%)	48,000
Gross profit (25%)	9,600
Cost of goods sold (100%) ($^{100}/_{125}$ x £48,000)	38,400

The closing stock amount is now a balancing figure in the trading account.

JONATHAN SLUGG
TRADING, PROFIT AND LOSS ACCOUNT
FOR THE YEAR ENDED 31 DECEMBER 20X7

	£	£
Sales		48,000
Less cost of goods sold		
Opening stock	10,000	
Purchases	37,000	
	47,000	
Less closing stock (balancing figure)	8,600	
		38,400
Gross profit (25/125 × £48,000)		9,600
Expenses		
Sundry £(1,500 + 5,600)	7,100	
Depreciation	900	
		8,000
Net profit		1,600

JONATHAN SLUGG
BALANCE SHEET AS AT 31 DECEMBER 20X7

	£	£
Net fixed assets £(20,000 − 900)		19,100
Stock	8,600	
Cash in the till	450	
	9,050	
Bank overdraft	1,250	
Trade creditors	1,400	
	2,650	
Net current assets		6,400
		25,500
Proprietor's capital		
Balance b/f		32,000
Net profit for the year		1,600
		33,600
Drawings £(3,700 + 4,400)		(8,100)
Balance c/f		25,500

Theft of cash from the till

7.9 When cash is stolen from the till, the amount stolen will be a credit entry in the cash book, and a debit in either the P&L account or insurance claim account, depending on whether the business is insured. The missing figure for cash sales, if this has to be calculated, must not ignore cash received but later stolen - see above.

8 ACCRUALS AND PREPAYMENTS

8.1 Where there is an accrued expense or a prepayment, the charge to be made in the P&L account for the item concerned should be found from the opening balance b/f, the closing balance c/f, and cash payments for the item during the period. The charge in the P&L account is perhaps most easily found as the balancing figure in a T account.

8.2 For example, on 1 April 20X6 a business had prepaid rent of £700 which relates to the next accounting period. During the year to 31 March 20X7 it pays £9,300 in rent, and at 31 March 20X7 the prepayment of rent is £1,000. The cost of rent in the P&L account for the year to 31 March 20X7 would be the balancing figure in the following T account. (Remember that a prepayment is a current asset, and so is a debit balance b/f.)

Part E: Financial statements

RENT

	£		£
Prepayment: balance b/f	700	P & L account (balancing figure)	9,000
Cash	9,300	Prepayment: balance c/f	1,000
	10,000		10,000
Balance b/f	1,000		

8.3 Similarly, if a business has accrued telephone expenses as at 1 July 20X6 of £850, pays £6,720 in telephone bills during the year to 30 June 20X7, and has accrued telephone expenses of £1,140 as at 30 June 20X7, then the telephone expense to be shown in the P&L account for the year to 30 June 20X7 is the balancing figure in the following T account. (Remember that an accrual is a current liability, and so is a credit balance b/f.)

TELEPHONE EXPENSES

	£		£
Cash	6,720	Balance b/f (accrual)	850
Balance c/f (accrual)	1,140	P&L a/c (balancing figure)	7,010
	7,860		7,860
		Balance b/f	1,140

9 DRAWINGS

9.1 Drawings would normally represent no particular problem at all in preparing a set of final accounts from incomplete records, but it is not unusual for examination questions to introduce a situation in which:

(a) The business owner pays income into his bank account which has nothing whatever to do with the business operations. For example, the owner might pay dividend income, or other income from investments into the bank, from stocks and shares which he owns personally, separate from the business itself. (In other words, there are no investments in the business balance sheet, and so income from investments cannot possibly be income of the business).

(b) The business owner pays money out of the business bank account for items which are not business expenses, such as life insurance premiums or a payment for his family's holidays etc.

9.2 Where such **personal items of receipts or payments** are made:

(a) Receipts should be set off against drawings. For example, if a business owner receives £600 in dividend income and pays it into his business bank account, although the dividends are from investments not owned by the business, then the accounting entry is:

DEBIT   Cash
CREDIT Drawings

(b) Payments should be charged to drawings; ie

DEBIT   Drawings
CREDIT Cash

Drawings: beware of the wording in an examination question

9.3 You should note that:

(a) If a question states that a proprietor's drawings during a given year are 'approximately £40 per week' then you should assume that drawings for the year are £40 × 52 weeks = £2,080.

(b) However, if a question states that drawings in the year are 'between £35 and £45 per week', do not assume that the drawings average £40 per week and so amount to £2,080 for the year. You could not be certain that the actual drawings did average £40, and so you should treat the drawings figure as a missing item that needs to be calculated.

10 DEALING WITH INCOMPLETE RECORDS PROBLEMS IN THE EXAMINATION

10.1 A suggested approach to dealing with incomplete records problems brings together the various points described so far in this chapter. The nature of the 'incompleteness' in the records will vary from problem to problem, but the approach, suitably applied, should be successful in arriving at the final accounts whatever the particular characteristics of the problem might be.

10.2 The approach is as follows.

Step 1. If possible, and if it is not already known, establish the opening balance sheet and the proprietor's interest.

Step 2. Open up four accounts.

- **Trading account** (if you wish, leave space underneath for entering the P&L account later)
- A **cash book**, with two columns if cash sales are significant and there are payments in cash out of the till
- A **debtors account**
- A **creditors account**

Step 3. Enter the opening balances in these accounts.

Step 4. Work through the information you are given line by line; and each item should be entered into the appropriate account if it is relevant to one or more of these four accounts.

You should also try to recognise each item as a 'P&L account income or expense item' or a 'closing balance sheet item'.

It may be necessary to calculate an amount for drawings and an amount for fixed asset depreciation.

Step 5. Look for the balancing figures in your accounts. In particular you might be looking for a value for credit sales, cash sales, purchases, the cost of goods sold, the cost of goods stolen or destroyed, or the closing bank balance. Calculate these missing figures, and make any necessary double entry (eg to the trading account from the creditors account for purchases, to the trading account from the cash book for cash sales, and to the trading account from the debtors account for credit sales).

Step 6. Now complete the P&L account and balance sheet. Working T accounts might be needed where there are accruals or prepayments.

Part E: Financial statements

> **Exam focus point**
>
> Although the following examples deal with a long computational question, remember that any of the individual techniques can be examined in a MCQ. In particular a MCQ may ask for the computation of profit given opening and closing net assets. In this case use the business equation: $P = I + D - Ci$ (see Chapter 2).

10.3 An example will illustrate this approach.

10.4 EXAMPLE: AN INCOMPLETE RECORDS PROBLEM

John Snow is the sole distribution agent in the Branton area for Diamond floor tiles. Under an agreement with the manufacturers, John Snow purchases the Diamond floor tiles at a trade discount of 20% off list price and annually in May receives an agency commission of 1% of his purchases for the year ended on the previous 31 March.

For several years, John Snow has obtained a gross profit of 40% on all sales. In a burglary in January 20X1 John Snow lost stock costing £4,000 as well as many of his accounting records. However, after careful investigations, the following information has been obtained covering the year ended 31 March 20X1.

(a) Assets and liabilities at 31 March 20X0 were as follows:

		£
Buildings:	at cost	10,000
	provision for depreciation	6,000
Motor vehicles:	at cost	5,000
	provision for depreciation	2,000
Stock: at cost		3,200
Trade debtors (for sales)		6,300
Agency commission due		300
Prepayments (trade expenses)		120
Balance at bank		4,310
Trade creditors		4,200
Accrued vehicle expenses		230

(b) John Snow has been notified that he will receive an agency commission of £440 on 1 May 20X1.

(c) Stock, at cost, at 31 March 20X1 was valued at an amount £3,000 more than a year previously.

(d) In October 20X0 stock costing £1,000 was damaged by dampness and had to be scrapped as worthless.

(e) Trade creditors at 31 March 20X1 related entirely to goods received whose list prices totalled £9,500.

(f) Discounts allowed amounted to £1,620 whilst discounts received were £1,200.

(g) Trade expenses prepaid at 31 March 20X1 totalled £80.

(h) Vehicle expenses for the year ended 31 March 20X1 amounted to £7,020.

(i) Trade debtors (for sales) at 31 March 20X1 were £6,700.

(j) All receipts are passed through the bank account.

(k) Depreciation is provided annually at the following rates.

Buildings 5% on cost
Motor vehicles 20% on cost.

(l) Commissions received are paid directly to the bank account.

(m) In addition to the payments for purchases, the bank payments were:

	£
Vehicle expenses	6,720
Drawings	4,300
Trade expenses	7,360

(n) John Snow is not insured against loss of stock owing to burglary or damage to stock caused by damp.

Required

Prepare John Snow's trading and profit and loss account for the year ended 31 March 20X1 and a balance sheet on that date.

10.5 DISCUSSION AND SOLUTION

This is an incomplete records problem because we are told that John Snow has lost many of his accounting records. In particular we do not know sales for the year, purchases during the year, or all the cash receipts and payments.

10.6 The first step is to find the opening balance sheet, if possible. In this case, it is. The proprietor's capital is the balancing figure.

JOHN SNOW
BALANCE SHEET AS AT 31 MARCH 20X0

	Cost £	Dep'n £	NBV £
Fixed assets			
Buildings	10,000	6,000	4,000
Motor vehicles	5,000	2,000	3,000
	15,000	8,000	7,000
Current assets			
Stock		3,200	
Trade debtors		6,300	
Commission due		300	
Prepayments		120	
Balance at bank		4,310	
		14,230	
Current liabilities			
Trade creditors		4,200	
Accrued expenses		230	
		4,430	
			9,800
			16,800
Proprietor's capital as at 31 March 20X0			16,800

10.7 The next step is to open up a trading account, cash book, debtors account and creditors account and to insert the opening balances, if known. Cash sales and payments in cash are not a feature of the problem, and so a single column cash book is sufficient.

10.8 The problem should then be read line by line, identifying any transactions affecting those accounts.

Part E: Financial statements

TRADING ACCOUNT

	£	£
Sales (note (f))		60,000
Opening stock	3,200	
Purchases (note (a))	44,000	
	47,200	
Less: damaged stock written off (note (c))	(1,000)	
stock stolen (note (e))	(4,000)	
	42,200	
Less closing stock (note (b))	6,200	
Cost of goods sold		36,000
Gross profit (note (f))		24,000

CASH BOOK

	£		£
Opening balance	4,310	Trade creditors	
Trade debtors (see below)	57,980	(see creditors a/c)	39,400
Agency commission (note (g))	300	Trade expenses	7,360
		Vehicle expenses	6,720
		Drawings	4,300
		Balance c/f	4,810
	62,590		62,590

TRADE DEBTORS

	£		£
Opening balance b/f	6,300	Discounts allowed (note (d))	1,620
Sales (note (f))	60,000	Cash received (balancing figure)	57,980
		Closing balance c/f	6,700
	66,300		66,300

TRADE CREDITORS

	£		£
Discounts received (note (d))	1,200	Opening balance b/f	4,200
Cash paid (balancing figure)	39,400	Purchases (note (a))	44,000
Closing balance c/f (note (i))	7,600		
	48,200		48,200

VEHICLE EXPENSES

	£		£
Cash	6,720	Accrual b/f	230
Accrual c/f (balancing figure)	530	P & L account	7,020
	7,250		7,250

10.9 The trading account is complete already, but now the P&L account and balance sheet can be prepared. Remember not to forget items such as the stock losses, commission earned on purchases, discounts allowed and discounts received.

JOHN SNOW - TRADING, PROFIT AND LOSS ACCOUNT
FOR THE YEAR ENDED 31 MARCH 20X1

	£	£
Sales (note (f))		60,000
Opening stock	3,200	
Purchases (note (a))	44,000	
	47,200	
Less: damaged stock written off (note (c))	(1,000)	
stock stolen	(4,000)	
	42,200	
Less closing stock (note (b))	6,200	
Cost of goods sold		36,000
Gross profit (note (f))		24,000
Add: commission on purchases		440
discounts received		1,200
		25,640
Expenses		
Trade expenses (note (h))	7,400	
Stock damaged	1,000	
Stock stolen	4,000	
Vehicle expenses	7,020	
Discounts allowed	1,620	
Depreciation		
Buildings	500	
Motor vehicles	1,000	
		22,540
Net profit (to capital account)		3,100

JOHN SNOW
BALANCE SHEET AS AT 31 MARCH 20X1

	Cost £	Dep'n £	NBV £
Fixed assets			
Buildings	10,000	6,500	3,500
Motor vehicles	5,000	3,000	2,000
	15,000	9,500	5,500
Current assets			
Stock		6,200	
Trade debtors		6,700	
Commission due		440	
Prepayments (trade expenses)		80	
Balance at bank		4,810	
		18,230	
Current liabilities			
Trade creditors		7,600	
Accrued expenses		530	
		8,130	
			10,100
			15,600
Proprietor's capital			
As at 31 March 20X0			16,800
Net profit for year to 31 March 20X1		3,100	
Less drawings		(4,300)	
Retained deficit			(1,200)
As at 31 March 20X1			15,600

Notes

(a) The agency commission due on 1 May 20X1 indicates that purchases for the year to 31 March 20X1 were

100%/1% × £440 = £44,000

Part E: Financial statements

(b) Closing stock at cost on 31 March 20X1 was £(3,200 + 3,000) = £6,200.

(c) Stock scrapped (£1,000) is accounted for by:
CREDIT   Trading account
DEBIT   P&L account

(d) Discounts allowed are accounted for by:
DEBIT   Discounts allowed account
CREDIT   Debtors

Similarly, discounts received are:
DEBIT   Creditors
CREDIT   Discounts received

Note. Discounts received represents settlement discounts, not *trade* discounts, which are not usually accounted for as they are given automatically at source.

(e) Stocks lost in the burglary are accounted for by:
CREDIT   Trading account
DEBIT   P&L account

(f) The trade discount of 20% has already been deducted in arriving at the value of the purchases. The gross profit is 40% on sales, so with cost of sales = £36,000

		£
Cost	(60%)	36,000
Profit	(40%)	24,000
Sales	(100%)	60,000

(It is assumed that trade expenses are not included in the trading account, and so should be ignored in this calculation.)

(g) The agency commission of £300 due on 1 May 20X0 would have been paid to John Snow at that date.

(h) The P&L account expenditure for trade expenses and closing balance on vehicle expenses account are as follows:

TRADE EXPENSES

	£		£
Prepayment b/f	120	P&L account (balancing figure)	7,400
Cash	7,360	Prepayment c/f	80
	7,480		7,480

(i) Trade creditors at the year end are £9,500 less 20% trade discount, ie £7,600 (80 × £9,500).

Exam focus point

Incomplete records questions in the exam will only be for sole traders (not partnerships). Also, as the average question in Part B is worth around 10 marks, you will only have to calculate **some** of these missing figures.

However, you need to practice doing questions with different missing figures, as you do not know which missing figures will be examined eg it could be sales and purchases, or cash sales and stolen stock. Therefore you need to get as much practice as possible on all types of incomplete records questions. Make sure that you make a good attempt at the questions in the exam question bank.

Using a debtors account to calculate both cash sales and credit sales

10.10 A final point which needs to be considered is how a missing value can be found for cash sales and credit sales, when a business has both, but takings banked by the business are not divided between takings from cash sales and takings from credit sales.

10.11 EXAMPLE: USING A DEBTORS ACCOUNT

A business had, on 1 January 20X8, trade debtors of £2,000, cash in the bank of £3,000, and cash in hand of £300.

During the year to 31 December 20X8 the business banked £95,000 in takings.

It also paid out the following expenses in cash from the till:

Drawings	£1,200
Sundry expenses	£800

On 29 August 20X8 a thief broke into the shop and stole £400 from the till.

At 31 December 20X8 trade debtors amounted to £3,500, cash in the bank £2,500 and cash in the till £150.

What was the value of sales during the year?

10.12 SOLUTION

If we tried to prepare a debtors account and a two column cash book, we would have insufficient information, in particular about whether the takings which were banked related to cash sales or credit sales.

DEBTORS

	£		£
Balance b/f	2,000	Payments from debtors (credit sales)	Unknown
Credit sales	Unknown		
		Balance c/f	3,500

CASH BOOK

	Cash £	Bank £		Cash £	Bank £
Balance b/f	300	3,000	Drawings	1,200	
			Sundry expenses	800	
Debtors-payments		Unknown	Cash stolen	400	
Cash sales	Unknown		Balance c/f	150	2,500

All we do know is that the combined sums from debtors and cash takings banked is £95,000.

The value of sales can be found instead by using the debtors account, which should be used to record cash takings banked as well as payments by debtors. The balancing figure in the debtors account will then be a combination of credit sales and some cash sales. The cash book only needs to be a single column.

DEBTORS

	£		£
Balance b/f	2,000	Cash banked	95,000
Sales-to trading account	96,500	Balance c/f	3,500
	98,500		98,500

Part E: Financial statements

CASH (EXTRACT)

	£		£
Balance in hand b/f	300	Payments in cash:	
Balance in bank b/f	3,000	Drawings	1,200
Debtors a/c	95,000	Expenses	800
		Other payments	?
		Cash stolen	400
		Balance in hand c/f	150
		Balance in bank c/f	2,500

The remaining 'undiscovered' amount of cash sales is now found as follows.

	£	£
Payments in cash out of the till		
Drawings	1,200	
Expenses	800	
		2,000
Cash stolen		400
Closing balance of cash in hand		150
		2,550
Less opening balance of cash in hand		(300)
Further cash sales		2,250

(This calculation is similar to the one described above for calculating cash sales.)

Total sales for the year are:

	£
From debtors account	96,500
From cash book	2,250
Total sales	98,750

Question 3

Mary Grimes, retail fruit and vegetable merchant, does not keep a full set of accounting records. However, the following information has been produced from the business's records.

(a) Summary of the bank account for the year ended 31 August 20X8

	£		£
1 Sept 20X7 balance brought forward	1,970	Payment to suppliers	72,000
		Purchase of motor van (E471 KBR)	13,000
Receipts from trade debtors	96,000	Rent and rates	2,600
Sale of private yacht	20,000	Wages	15,100
Sale of motor van (A123 BWA)	2,100	Motor vehicle expenses	3,350
		Postages and stationery	1,360
		Drawings	9,200
		Repairs and renewals	650
		Insurances	800
		31 August 20X8 balance c/fwd	2,010
	120,070		120,070
1 Sept 20X8 balance b/fwd	2,010		

(b) Assets and liabilities, other than balance at bank as at:

17: Incomplete records

		1 Sept 20X7 £	31 Aug 20X8 £
Trade creditors		4,700	2,590
Trade debtors		7,320	9,500
Rent and rates accruals		200	260
Motor vans:			
A123 BWA:	At cost	10,000	-
	Provision for depreciation	8,000	-
E471 KBR:	At cost	-	13,000
	Provision for depreciation	-	To be determined
Stock in trade		4,900	5,900
Insurance prepaid		160	200

(c) All receipts are banked and all payments are made from the business bank account.

(d) A trade debt of £300 owing by John Blunt and included in the trade debtors at 31 August 20X8 (see (b) above), is to be written off as a bad debt.

(e) It is Mary Grimes' policy to provide depreciation at the rate of 20% on the cost of motor vans held at the end of each financial year; no depreciation is provided in the year of sale or disposal of a motor van.

(f) Discounts received during the year ended 31 August 20X8 from trade creditors amounted to £1,100.

Required

(a) Prepare Mary Grimes' trading and profit and loss account for the year ended 31 August 20X8.

(b) Prepare Mary Grimes' balance sheet as at 31 August 20X8.

Answer

(a) TRADING AND PROFIT AND LOSS ACCOUNT
FOR THE YEAR ENDED 31 AUGUST 20X8

	£	£
Sales (W1)		98,180
Opening stock	4,900	
Purchases (W2)	70,990	
	75,890	
Less closing stock	5,900	
		69,990
Gross profit		28,190
Discounts received		1,100
Profit on sale of motor vehicle £2,100 - £(10,000 - 8,000)		100
		29,390
Rent and rates (W3)	2,660	
Wages	15,100	
Motor vehicle expenses	3,350	
Postages and stationery	1,360	
Repairs and renewals	650	
Insurances (W4)	760	
Bad debt	300	
Depreciation of van (20% × £13,000)	2,600	
		26,780
		2,610

Part E: Financial statements

(b) BALANCE SHEET AS AT 31 AUGUST 20X8

	£	£
Fixed assets		
Motor van: cost	13,000	
depreciation	2,600	
		10,400
Current assets		
Stock	5,900	
Debtors (£9,500 - £300 bad debt)	9,200	
Prepayment	200	
Cash at bank	2,010	
	17,310	
Current liabilities		
Creditors	2,590	
Accrual	260	
	2,850	
Net current assets		14,460
		24,860
Capital account		
Balance at 1 September 20X7 (W5)		11,450
Additional capital: proceeds on sale of yacht		20,000
Net profit for the year	2,610	
Less drawings	9,200	
Retained loss for the year		(6,590)
Balance at 31 August 20X8		24,860

Workings

1   Sales

	£
Cash received from customers	96,000
Add debtors balances at 31 August 20X8	9,500
	105,500
Less debtors balances at 1 September 20X7	7,320
Sales in year	98,180

2   Purchases

	£	£
Payments to suppliers		72,000
Add: creditors balances at 31 August 20X8	2,590	
discounts granted by creditors	1,100	
		3,690
		75,690
Less creditors balances at 1 September 20X7		4,700
		70,990

3   Rent and rates

	£
Cash paid in year	2,600
Add accrual at 31 August 20X8	260
	2,860
Less accrual at 1 September 20X7	200
Charge for the year	2,660

4   Insurances

	£
Cash paid in year	800
Add prepayment at 1 September 20X7	160
	960
Less prepayment at 31 August 20X8	200
	760

Workings 1-4 could also be presented in ledger account format as follows.

17: Incomplete records

TOTAL DEBTORS

	£		£
Balance b/f	7,320	Bank	96,000
∴ Sales	98,180	Balance c/f	9,500
	105,500		105,500

TOTAL CREDITORS

	£		£
Bank	72,000	Balance b/f	4,700
Discounts received	1,100	∴ Purchases	70,990
Balance c/f	2,590		
	75,690		75,690

RENT AND RATES

	£		£
Bank	2,600	Balance b/f	200
Balance c/f	260	∴ P & L charge	2,660
	2,860		2,860

INSURANCES

	£		£
Balance b/f	160	∴ P & L charge	760
Bank	800	Balance c/f	200
	960		960

5 *Capital at 1 September 20X7*

	£	£
Assets		
Bank balance		1,970
Debtors		7,320
Motor van £(10,000 − 8,000)		2,000
Stock		4,900
Prepayment		160
		16,350
Liabilities		
Trade creditors	4,700	
Accrual	200	
		4,900
		11,450

Part E: Financial statements

Chapter roundup

- **Incomplete records** questions may test your ability to prepare accounts in the following situations.
    - A trader does not maintain a ledger and therefore has no continuous double entry record of transactions.
    - Accounting records are destroyed by accident, such as fire.
    - Some essential figure is unknown and must be calculated as a balancing figure. This may occur as a result of stock being damaged or destroyed, or because of misappropriation of assets.
- The approach to incomplete records questions is to build up the information given so as to complete the necessary double entry. This may involve reconstructing **control accounts** for:
    - Cash and bank (often in columnar format)
    - Debtors and creditors
- Where stock, sales or purchases is the unknown figure it will be necessary to use information on **gross profit percentages** so as to construct a trading account in which the unknown figure can be inserted as a balance.

Quick quiz

1. In the absence of a sales account or sales day book, how can a figure of sales for the year be computed?
2. In the absence of a purchase account or purchases day book, how can a figure of purchases for the year be computed?
3. What is the difference between 'mark-up' and 'margin'?
4. What is the accounting double entry to record the loss of stock by fire or burglary?
5. In what circumstances is a two-column cash book useful?
6. If a business proprietor pays his personal income into the business bank account, what is the accounting double entry to record the transaction?

Answers to quick quiz

1. By using the debtors control account to calculate sales as a balancing figure.
2. By using the creditors control account to calculate purchases as a balancing figure.
3. - Mark-up is the profit as a percentage of cost.
   - Margin is the profit as a percentage of sales.
4. DEBIT P & L a/c
   CREDIT Trading a/c

   Assuming that the goods were not insured.
5. Where a large amount of receipts and payments are made in cash.
6. DEBIT Cash
   CREDIT Drawings

Now try the questions below from the Exam Question Bank

Question to try	Level	Marks	Time
24	Introductory	n/a	36 mins
25	Introductory	n/a	45 mins
26	Introductory	n/a	45 mins

Chapter 18

PARTNERSHIP ACCOUNTS

	Topic list	Syllabus reference
1	The characteristics of partnerships	5(d)
2	Preparing partnership accounts	5(d)

Introduction

So far we have considered businesses owned by one person: sole traders. Now we will consider how we can account for businesses owned by more than one person. This chapter will examine how we can account for partnerships and the next chapter will examine how we can account for companies.

Study guide

Section 12 and 13 - Partnership accounts

- Define the circumstances creating a partnership.

- Explain the advantages and disadvantages of operating as a partnership, compared with operating as a sole trader or limited liability company.

- Explain the typical contents of a partnership agreement, including profit-sharing terms.

- Explain the accounting differences between partnerships and sole traders:
    - Capital accounts
    - Current accounts
    - Division of profits

- Explain how to record partners' shares of profits/losses and their drawings in the accounting records and financial statements.

- Explain how to account for guaranteed minimum profit share.

- Explain how to account for interest on drawings.

- Draft the profit and loss account, including division of profit, and balance sheet of a partnership from a given trial balance.

Note: Other aspects of partnership (admission and retirement of partners, amalgamation and dissolution) are **not** examinable.

Exam guide

This section is straightforward. Learn how to prepare partnership accounts and also the advantages and disadvantages of trading as a partnership.

1 THE CHARACTERISTICS OF PARTNERSHIPS

1.1 Try this question to get you thinking.

18: Partnership accounts

Question 1

Try to think of reasons why a business should be conducted as a partnership, rather than:

(a) As a sole trader
(b) As a company

Answer

(a) The main problems with trading as a sole trader is the limitation on resources it implies. As the business grows, there will be a need for:

  (i) Additional capital. Although some capital may be provided by a bank, it would not be desirable to have the business entirely dependent on borrowing.

  (ii) Additional expertise. A sole trader technically competent in his own field may not have, for example, the financial skills that would be needed in a larger business.

  (iii) Additional management time. Once a business grows to a certain point, it becomes impossible for one person to look after all aspects of it without help.

(b) The main disadvantage of incorporating is the regulatory burden faced by limited companies. In addition, there are certain 'businesses' which are not allowed to enjoy limited liability; you may have read about the Lloyd's 'names' who face personal bankruptcy because the option of limited liability was not available to them.

There are also tax factors to consider, but these are beyond the scope of this book.

KEY TERM

Partnership is defined by the Partnership Act 1890 as the relationship which exists between persons carrying on a business in common with a view of profit.

1.2 In other words, a partnership is an arrangement between two or more individuals in which they undertake to share the risks and rewards of a joint business operation.

1.3 It is usual for a partnership to be established formally by means of a **partnership agreement**. However, if individuals act as though they are in partnership even if no written agreement exists, then it will be presumed in law that a partnership does exist and that its terms of agreement are the same as those laid down in the Partnership Act 1890.

The partnership agreement

1.4 The partnership agreement is a written agreement in which the terms of the partnership are set out, and in particular the financial arrangements as between partners. The items it should cover include the following.

(a) **Capital**. Each partner puts in a share of the business capital. If there is to be an agreement on how much each partner should put in and keep in the business, as a minimum fixed amount, this should be stated.

(b) **Profit-sharing ratio**. Partners can agree to share profits in any way they choose. For example, if there are three partners in a business, they might agree to share profits equally but on the other hand, if one partner does a greater share of the work, or has more experience and ability, or puts in more capital, the ratio of profit sharing might be different.

(c) **Interest on capital**. Partners might agree to pay themselves interest on the capital they put into the business. If they do so, the agreement will state what rate of interest is to be applied.

Part E: Financial statements

(d) **Partners' salaries**. Partners might also agree to pay themselves salaries. These are not salaries in the same way that an employee of the business will be paid a wage or salary, because partners' salaries are an appropriation of profit, and not an expense in the profit and loss account of the business. The purpose of paying salaries is to give each partner a satisfactory basic income before the residual profits are shared out.

(e) **Drawings**. Partners may draw out their share of profits from the business. However, they might agree to put a limit on how much they should draw out in any period. If so, this limit should be specified in the partnership agreement. To encourage partners to delay taking drawings out of the business until the financial year has ended, the agreement might also be that partners should be charged interest on their drawings during the year.

(f) **Guaranteed minimum profit shares**. Some partnership agreements may guarantee a minimum share of profits for one or more partners. This would mean that a partner was entitled to a stipulated amount from the profits. If the amount allocated by the **profit-sharing ratio** is lower than this, then the partner would receive the guaranteed minimum profit share and the remainder of the profits would be a shared between the other partners according to the partnership agreement. Occasionally, one partner will guarantee another partner's minimum profit share. In this case that partner will make up the difference between the profit-sharing ratio and the minimum guaranteed amount.

Even in loss making situations, the partner is entitled to the guaranteed minimum profit share.

1.5 In the absence of a formal agreement between the partners, certain rules laid down by the **Partnership Act 1890** are presumed to apply instead.

(a) Residual profits are shared equally between the partners

(b) There are no partners' salaries

(c) Partners receive no interest on the capital they invest in the business

(d) Partners are entitled to interest of 5% per annum on any loans they advance to the business in excess of their agreed capital.

Exam focus point

Don't forget that these terms only apply in the absence of any agreement to the contrary. In tackling examination questions you should look first of all for the details of a specific partnership agreement; only if none are given should you apply the provisions of the Partnership Act 1890.

1.6 EXAMPLE: PARTNERS' SALARIES AND PROFIT-SHARING

Suppose Bill and Ben are partners sharing profit in the ratio 2:1 and that they agree to pay themselves a salary of £10,000 each. If profits before deducting salaries are £26,000, how much income would each partner receive?

1.7 SOLUTION

First, the two salaries are deducted from profit, leaving £6,000 (£26,000 – £20,000).

18: Partnership accounts

1.8 This £6,000 has to be distributed between Bill and Ben in the ratio 2:1. In other words, Bill will receive twice as much as Ben. You can probably work this out in your head and see that Bill will get £4,000 and Ben £2,000, but we had better see how this is calculated properly.

1.9 Add the 'parts' of the ratio together. For our example, 2 + 1 = 3. Divide this total into whatever it is that has to be shared out. In our example, £6,000 ÷ 3 = £2,000. Each 'part' is worth £2,000, so Bill receives 2 × £2,000 = £4,000 and Ben will receive 1 × £2,000 = £2,000.

1.10 So the final answer to the question is that Bill receives his salary plus £4,000 and Ben his salary plus £2,000. This could be laid out as follows:

	Bill	Ben	Total
	£	£	£
Salary	10,000	10,000	20,000
Share of residual profits (ratio 2:1)	4,000	2,000	6,000
	14,000	12,000	26,000

Question 2

Suppose Tom, Dick and Harry want to share out £150 in the ratio 7:3:5. How much would each get?

Answer

The sum of the ratio 'parts' is 7 + 3 + 5 = 15. Each part is therefore worth £150 ÷ 15 = £10. So the £150 would be shared as follows:

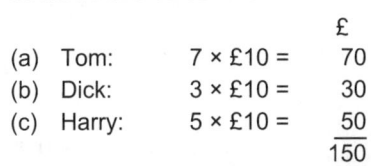

			£
(a)	Tom:	7 × £10 =	70
(b)	Dick:	3 × £10 =	30
(c)	Harry:	5 × £10 =	50
			150

Advantages and disadvantages of trading as a partnership

1.11 Operating as a partnership entails certain advantages and disadvantages when compared with both sole traders and limited companies.

Partnership v sole trader

1.12 The advantages of operating as a partnership rather than as a sole trader are practical rather than legal. They include the following.

   (a) Risks are spread across a larger number of people.
   (b) The trader will have access to a wider network of contacts through the other partners.
   (c) Partners should bring to the business not only capital but skills and experience.
   (d) It may well be easier to raise finance from external sources such as banks.

1.13 Possible disadvantages include the following.

   (a) While the risk is spread over a larger number of people, so are the profits!
   (b) By bringing in more people the former sole trader dilutes control over his business.
   (c) There may be disputes between the partners.

Part E: Financial statements

Partnership v limited company

1.14 Limited companies (covered in detail in the next chapter) offer limited liability to their owners. This means that the maximum amount that an owner stands to lose in the event that the company becomes insolvent and must pay off its debts is the capital in the business. In the case of partnerships (and sole traders), liability for the debts of the business is unlimited, which means that if the business runs up debts and is unable to pay, the proprietors will become personally liable for the unpaid debts and would be required, if necessary, to sell their private possessions in order to pay for them.

1.15 Limited liability is clearly a significant incentive for a partnership to incorporate (become a company). Other advantages of incorporation are that it is easier to raise capital and that the retirement or death of one of its members does not necessitate dissolution and re-formation of the firm.

1.16 In practice, however, particularly for small firms, these advantages are more apparent than real. Banks will normally seek personal guarantees from shareholders before making loans or granting an overdraft facility and so the advantage of limited liability is lost to a small owner managed business.

1.17 In addition, a company faces a greater administrative and financial burden arising from:

(a) Compliance with the Companies Act, notably in having to prepare annual accounts and have them audited, file annual returns and keep statutory books.

(b) Compliance with SSAPs and FRSs.

(c) Formation and annual registration costs.

2 PREPARING PARTNERSHIP ACCOUNTS June 2003

How does accounting for partnerships differ from accounting for sole traders?

2.1 Partnership accounts are identical in many respects to the accounts of sole traders.

(a) The assets of a partnership are like the assets of any other business, and are accounted for in the same way. The assets side of a partnership balance sheet is no different from what has been shown in earlier chapters of this Study Text.

(b) The net profit of a partnership is calculated in the same way as the net profit of a sole trader. The only minor difference is that if a partner makes a loan to the business (as distinct from capital contribution) then interest on the loan will be an expense in the profit and loss account, in the same way as interest on any other loan from a person or organisation who is not a partner. We will return to partner loans later in the chapter.

2.2 There are two respects in which partnership accounts are different, however.

(a) The funds put into the business by each partner are shown differently.

(b) The net profit must be **appropriated** by the partners. This appropriation of profits must be shown in the partnership accounts.

> **Exam focus point**
> **Appropriation of profit** means sharing out profits in accordance with the partnership agreement.

Funds employed

2.3 When a partnership is formed, each partner puts in some capital to the business. These initial capital contributions are recorded in a series of **capital accounts**, one for each partner. (Since each partner is ultimately entitled to repayment of his capital it is clearly vital to keep a record of how much is owed to whom.) Partners do not have to put in the same amount.

> **IMPORTANT!**
>
> The balance for the capital account will always be a brought forward credit entry in the partnership accounts, because the capital contributed by proprietors is a liability of the business.

2.4 In addition to a capital account, each partner normally has:

(a) A **current account**.
(b) A **drawings account**.

> **KEY TERM**
>
> A **current account** is used to record the **profits retained in the business** by the partner.

2.5 It is therefore a sort of capital account, which increases in value when the partnership makes profits, and falls in value when the partner whose current account it is makes drawings out of the business.

2.6 The main differences between the capital and current account in accounting for partnerships are as follows.

(a) (i) The balance on the capital account remains static from year to year (with one or two exceptions).

 (ii) The current account is continually fluctuating up and down, as the partnership makes profits which are shared out between the partners, and as each partner takes out drawings.

(b) A further difference is that when the partnership agreement provides for interest on capital, partners receive interest on the balance in their capital account, but **not on the balance in their current account.**

2.7 The drawings accounts serve exactly the same purpose as the drawings account for a sole trader. Each partner's drawings are recorded in a separate account. At the end of an accounting period, each partner's drawings are cleared to his current account; ie

DEBIT   Current account of partner
CREDIT   Drawings account of partner

(If the amount of the drawings exceeds the balance on a partner's current account, the current account will show a debit balance. However, in normal circumstances, we should expect to find a credit balance on the current accounts.)

2.8 The partnership balance sheet will therefore consist of:

(a) The capital accounts of each partner.
(b) The current accounts of each partner, net of drawings.

Part E: Financial statements

This will be illustrated in an example later.

Loans by partners

2.9 In addition, it is sometimes the case that an existing or previous partner will make a loan to the partnership in which case he becomes a creditor of the partnership. On the balance sheet, such a loan is not included as partners' funds, but is shown separately as a long-term liability (unless repayable within twelve months in which case it is a current liability). This is the case whether or not the loan creditor is also an existing partner.

2.10 However, **interest on such loans will be credited to the partner's current account** (if he is an existing partner). This is administratively more convenient, especially when the partner does not particularly want to be paid the loan interest in cash immediately it becomes due. Remember:

(a) Interest on loans from a partner is accounted for as an expense in the P & L account, and not as an appropriation of profit, even though the interest is added to the current account of the partners.

(b) If there is no interest rate specified, the Partnership Act 1890 (section 24) provides for interest to be paid at 5% pa on loans by partners.

Appropriation of net profits

2.11 The net profit of a partnership is shared out between them according to the terms of their agreement. This sharing out is shown in a **profit and loss appropriation account**, which follows on from the profit and loss account itself.

The accounting entries are:

(a) DEBIT   Profit and loss account with net profit c/d
    CREDIT   Profit and loss appropriation account with net profit b/d

(b) DEBIT   Profit and loss appropriation account
    CREDIT   The current accounts of each partner

With an individual share of profits for each partner.

2.12 The way in which profit is shared out depends on the terms of the partnership agreement. The steps to take are as follows.

Step 1. Establish how much the net profit is.

Step 2. Appropriate interest on capital and salaries first. Both of these items are an appropriation of profit and are not expenses in the P & L account.

Step 3. If partners agree to pay interest on their drawings during the year

   DEBIT   Current accounts
   CREDIT   Appropriation of profit account

Step 4. **Residual profits**: the difference between net profits (plus any interest charged on drawings) and appropriations for interest on capital and salaries is the residual profit. This is shared out between partners in the profit-sharing ratio.

Step 5. Each partner's share of profits is credited to his current account.

Step 6. The balance on each partner's drawings account is debited to his current account.

2.13 In practice each partner's capital account will occupy a separate ledger account, as will his current account etc. The examples which follow in this text use the columnar form; they

18: Partnership accounts

might also ignore the breakdown of net assets employed (fixed, current assets etc) to help to clarify and simplify the illustrations.

> **Exam focus point**
> For examination purposes, it is customary to represent the details of these accounts side by side, in columnar form, to save time.

2.14 EXAMPLE: PARTNERSHIP ACCOUNTS

Locke, Niece and Munster are in partnership with an agreement to share profits in the ratio 3:2:1. They also agree that:

(a) All three should receive interest at 12% on capital.

(b) Munster should receive a salary of £6,000 per annum.

(c) Interest will be charged on drawings at the rate of 5% (charged on the end of year drawings balances).

(d) The interest rate on the loan by Locke is 5%.

The balance sheet of the partnership as at 31 December 20X5 revealed the following:

	£	£
Capital accounts		
Locke	20,000	
Niece	8,000	
Munster	6,000	
		34,000
Current accounts		
Locke	3,500	
Niece	(700)	
Munster	1,800	
		4,600
Loan account (Locke)		6,000
Capital employed to finance net fixed assets and working capital		44,600

Drawings made during the year to 31 December 20X6 were:

	£
Locke	6,000
Niece	4,000
Munster	7,000

The net profit for the year to 31 December 20X6 was £24,530 before deducting loan interest.

Required

Prepare the profit and loss appropriation account for the year to 31 December 20X6, and the partners' capital accounts, and current accounts.

2.15 SOLUTION

The interest payable by each partner on their drawings during the year is:

		£
Locke	5% of £6,000	300
Niece	5% of £4,000	200
Munster	5% of £7,000	350
		850

Part E: Financial statements

These payments are debited to the current accounts and credited to the profit and loss **appropriation** account.

2.16 The interest payable to Locke on his loan is:

5% of £6,000 = £300

2.17 We can now begin to work out the appropriation of profits.

		£	£
Net profit, less loan interest deducted in P & L a/c (£24,530 - £300)			24,230
Add interest on drawings			850
			25,080
Less Munster salary			6,000
			19,080
Less Interest on capital			
Locke	(12% of £20,000)	2,400	
Niece	(12% of £ 8,000)	960	
Munster	(12% of £ 6,000)	720	
			4,080
			15,000
Residual profits:			
Locke	(3)	7,500	
Niece	(2)	5,000	
Munster	(1)	2,500	
			15,000

2.18 Make sure you remember what the various interest figures represent and that you understand exactly what has been calculated here.

(a) The partners can take some drawings out of the business, but if they do they will be charged interest on it.

(b) The partners have capital tied up in the business (of course, otherwise there would be no business) and they have agreed to pay themselves interest on whatever capital each has put in.

(c) Once all the necessary adjustments have been made to net profit, £15,000 remains and is divided up between the partners in the ratio 3:2:1.

2.19 Now the accounts for the partnership can be prepared.

LOCKE NIECE MUNSTER
PROFIT AND LOSS APPROPRIATION ACCOUNT
FOR THE YEAR ENDED 31 DECEMBER 20X6

	£	£		£	£
			Net profit b/f		24,230
Salaries - Munster		6,000	Interest on drawings:		
Interest on capital			Current account of		
Locke	2,400		Locke	300	
Niece	960		Niece	200	
Munster	720		Munster	350	
		4,080			850
Residual profits					
Locke	7,500				
Niece	5,000				
Munster	2,500				
		15,000			
		25,080			25,080

PARTNERS' CURRENT ACCOUNTS

	Locke £	Niece £	Munster £		Locke £	Niece £	Munster £
Balance b/f		700		Balance b/f	3,500		1,800
Interest on drawings	300	200	350	Loan interest	300		
Drawings	6,000	4,000	7,000	Interest on capital	2,400	960	720
Balance c/f	7,400	1,060	3,670	Salary			6,000
				Residual profits	7,500	5,000	2,500
	13,700	5,960	11,020		13,700	5,960	11,020
				Balance b/f	7,400	1,060	3,670

PARTNERS' CAPITAL ACCOUNTS

	Locke £	Niece £	Munster £
Balance b/f	20,000	8,000	6,000

2.20 The balance sheet as at 31 December 20X6 would be:

	£	£
Capital accounts		
Locke	20,000	
Niece	8,000	
Munster	6,000	
		34,000
Current accounts		
Locke	7,400	
Niece	1,060	
Munster	3,670	
		12,130
		46,130

	£
Net assets	
As at 31 December 20X5	44,600
Added during the year (applying the business equation, this is the difference between net profits and drawings = £24,230 - £17,000)	7,230
Add loan interest added to Locke's current account and not paid out	300
As at 31 December 20X6	52,130
Less long term creditors	
Loan: Locke	(6,000)
	46,130

2.21 Again, make sure you understand what has happened here.

(a) The partners' *capital* accounts have not changed. They were brought forward at £20,000, £8,000 and £6,000, and they are just the same in the new balance sheet.

(b) The partners' *current* accounts have changed. The balances brought forward from last year's balance sheet of £3,500, (£700) and £1,800 have become £7,400, £1,060 and £3,670 in the new balance sheet. How this came about is shown in the partners' current (ledger) accounts.

(c) The events recorded in the current accounts are a reflection of how the partnership has distributed its profit, and this was shown in the profit and loss appropriation account.

Part E: Financial statements

Chapter roundup

- Accounting for a partnership is for the most part the same as accounting for a sole trader except in the following respects.
- The initial capital put into the business by each partner is shown by means of a **capital account** for each partner.
- Each partner also has a **current account** and a drawings account.
- The net profit of the partnership is **appropriated** by the partners according to some **previously agreed ratio**.
- Partners may be charged **interest on their drawings**, and may receive interest on capital. If a partner makes a **loan** to the business, he will receive interest on it in the normal way.
- Partnerships may be **terminated** either by closing down the business entirely or by disposing of the business as a going concern to a limited company.

Quick quiz

1 What is a partnership?
2 Is a partner's salary an expense of the partnership?
3 Why might a sole trader take on a partner?
4 What is the difference between a partner's capital account and a partner's current account?
5 How is profit shared between partners?
6 A,B and C are in partnership with a profit sharing ratio of 3:2:1. For the year ended 31.12.X9, the partnership profits are £18,000. What is B's share of the profits?

   A £3,000
   B £6,000
   C £9,000
   D £18,000

Answers to quick quiz

1 An arrangement between two or more individuals to carry on the risks and rewards of a business together.
2 No. It is an appropriation of profit.
3 See paragraph 1.12.
4 The capital account reflects the amount of money invested in the business by each partner. The current account reflects each partner's share of the profits less withdrawals made.
5 According to the terms of the partnership agreements. This may allow interest on capital accounts, charge interest on drawings, allow salaries and then divide the residual profits according to the profit sharing ratio.
6 B. Each 'share' is worth $\frac{£18,000}{6}$ = £3,000. B's share is, therefore, £6,000.

Now try the questions below from the Exam Question Bank

Question to try	Level	Marks	Time
27	Full exam	10	18 mins
28	Full exam	10	18 mins

Chapter 19

LIMITED COMPANIES

Topic list	Syllabus reference
1 What are limited companies?	5(d)
2 The accounting records of limited companies	5(d)
3 The capital of limited companies	1(b), 5(d)
4 The board of directors	5(d)
5 Dividends	5(d)
6 Types of share	1(b), 5(d)
7 The final accounts of limited companies: internal use	4(a)-(d), 5(c), 5(d)
8 Fixed assets	4(a), 5(d)
9 Current and long-term liabilities	4(c), 5(d)
10 Debenture loans	5(d)
11 Taxation	5(d)
12 Ledger accounts and limited companies	5(d)
13 Share capital and reserves	4(d), 5(d)
14 Example: company accounts for internal purposes	5(d)

Introduction

You are now in a position to look at the financial statements of limited companies.

At this stage you will be concerned with the preparation of limited company accounts for *internal* purposes. Such accounts do not need to follow all the requirements of the Companies Act format, but you still need to be aware of certain terms which are peculiar to company accounts.

Study guide

Section 15 - Accounting for limited companies 1 - basics

- Explain the legal and other differences between a sole trader and a limited company.
- Explain the advantages and disadvantages of operation as a limited company rather than as a sole trader.
- Explain the capital structure of a limited company including:
    - Authorised share capital
    - Issued share capital
    - Called up share capital

325

Part E: Financial statements

- Paid up share capital
- Ordinary shares
- Preference shares
- Deferred shares
- Debentures.

- Explain the nature of reserves and the difference between capital and revenue reserves.
- Explain the share premium account.
- Explain the other reserves which may appear in a company balance sheet.
- Explain why the heading 'profit and loss account' appears in a company balance sheet.
- Explain the recording of dividends paid and proposed in ledger accounts and the financial statements.
- Explain the nature of corporation tax on company profits and illustrate the ledger account required to record it.
- Explain how corporation tax appears in the profit and loss account and balance sheet of a company.
- Draft a profit and loss account and balance sheet for a company for internal purposes.

Section 16 – Recording and presentation of transactions in fixed assets; liabilities and provisions

- Define and give examples of liabilities.
- Explain the distinction between current and long-term liabilities.
- Explain the difference between liabilities and provisions.

Sections 19, 20 and 21 - Accounting for limited companies 2 - advanced

- Revise the work of Session 15 and the preparation of financial statements for limited companies for internal purposes including the treatment of corporation tax and dividends, including proposed dividends.
- Revise the work of Session 15 on company capital structure, including equity shares, preference shares and debentures.
- Outline the advantages and disadvantages of raising finance by borrowing rather than by the issue of ordinary or preference shares.
- Define and illustrate gearing (leverage).
- Define a bonus (capitalisation) issue and its advantages and disadvantages.
- Record a bonus (capitalisation) issue in ledger accounts and show the effect in the balance sheet.
- Define a rights issue and its advantages and disadvantages.
- Record a rights issue in ledger accounts and show the effect in the balance sheet.
- Revise the definition of reserves and the different types of reserves.

Exam guide

Your later financial accounting studies will be concerned almost entirely with company accounts so it is vital that you acquire a sound understanding of the basic concepts now. This is a key exam area.

1 WHAT ARE LIMITED COMPANIES?

1.1 As we should expect, the accounting rules and conventions for recording the business transactions of limited companies and then preparing their final accounts are much the same as for sole traders. For example, companies will have a cash book, sales day book, purchase day book, journal, sales ledger, purchase ledger and nominal ledger. They will also

19: Limited companies

prepare a profit and loss account annually and a balance sheet at the end of the accounting year.

1.2 There are, however, some **differences** in the accounts of limited companies, of which the following are perhaps the most significant.

(a) The **legislation** governing the activities of limited companies is very extensive. Amongst other things, the Companies Acts define certain minimum accounting records which must be maintained by companies.

(i) They specify that the **annual accounts** of a company must be filed with the Registrar of Companies and so available for public inspection

(ii) They contain detailed requirements on the **minimum information** which must be disclosed in a company's accounts. Businesses which are not limited companies (non-incorporated businesses) enjoy comparative freedom from statutory regulation.

(b) The owners of a company (its **members** or **shareholders**) may be very numerous. Their capital is shown differently from that of a sole trader; and similarly the 'appropriation account' of a company is different.

Limited liability

> **KEY TERM**
>
> **Unlimited liability** means that if the business runs up debts that it is unable to pay, the proprietors will become personally liable for the unpaid debts, and would be required, if necessary, to sell their private possessions in order to repay them.

1.3 Sole traders are generally fairly small concerns. The amount of capital involved may be modest, and the proprietor of the business usually participates in managing it. His or her liability for the debts of the business is unlimited. For example, if the business owes £40,000 which it cannot repay, the trader might have to sell his or her house to raise the money to pay off the business debts.

1.4 Limited companies offer limited liability to their owners.

> **KEY TERM**
>
> **Limited liability** means that the maximum amount that an owner stands to lose in the event that the company becomes insolvent and cannot pay off its debts, is his share of the capital in the business.

1.5 Thus limited liability is a major advantage of turning a business into a limited company. However, in practice, banks will normally seek personal guarantees from shareholders of a small owner managed company before making loans or granting an overdraft facility, and so the advantage of limited liability is lost.

1.6 There are other disadvantages too. In comparison with sole trader businesses, there is a significantly increased administrative and financial burden. This arises from:

Part E: Financial statements

    (a) Compliance with the Companies Act 1985, notably in having to prepare annual accounts and have them audited, in keeping statutory registers and having to publish accounts

    (b) Having to comply with all SSAPs and FRSs

    (c) Formation and annual registration costs

1.7 As a business grows, it needs more capital to finance its operations, and significantly more than the people currently managing the business can provide themselves. One way of obtaining more capital is to invite **investors from outside** the business to invest in the ownership or equity of the business. These new co-owners would not usually be expected to help with managing the business. To such investors, **limited liability is very attractive**.

1.8 Investments are always risky undertakings, but with limited liability the investor knows the maximum amount that he stands to lose when he puts some capital into a company.

Public and private companies

1.9 There are two classes of limited company.

    (a) **Private companies**. These have the word 'limited' at the end of their name. Being private, they cannot invite members of the public to invest in their equity (ownership).

    (b) **Public companies**. These are much fewer in number than private companies, but are generally much larger in size. They have the words 'public limited company' - shortened to PLC or plc (or the Welsh language equivalent) at the end of their name. Public limited companies can invite members of the general public to invest in their equity, and the 'shares' of these companies may be traded on The Stock Exchange.

Question 1

Limited liability means that the directors do not have to account for their mistakes. True or false?

Answer

False. But what *does* it mean? Look back to paragraph 1.4.

2 THE ACCOUNTING RECORDS OF LIMITED COMPANIES

2.1 There is a legal requirement for companies in the UK to keep **accounting records** which are sufficient to show and explain the company's transactions. The records should:

    (a) Disclose the company's current financial position at any time.

    (b) Contain:

        (i) Day-to-day entries of money received and spent.

        (ii) A record of the company's assets and liabilities.

        (iii) Where the company deals in goods:

- A statement of stocks held at the year end, and supporting stocktaking sheets.
- With the exception of retail sales, statements of goods bought and sold which identify the sellers and buyers of those goods.

(c) Enable the directors of the company to ensure that the final accounts of the company give a true and fair view of the company's profit or loss and balance sheet position.

> **Exam focus point**
>
> Theoretically, therefore, there can be no incomplete records for a limited company. However disasters can occur, eg books lost in a fire, which can result in incomplete records.
>
> For exam purposes, the syllabus states that incomplete records techniques will only be included for sole traders. Make sure that you have read the syllabus and study guide in the roman pages at the front of this Text.

Registers: the statutory books

2.2 A company must also keep a number of non-accounting registers. These include:

- Register of members
- Register of shareholders' 3 per cent interests
- Register of charges and a register of debenture holders
- Register of directors and company secretaries
- Register of directors' interests (in shares or debentures of the company)

These registers are known collectively as the **statutory books** of the company.

3 THE CAPITAL OF LIMITED COMPANIES

3.1 The proprietors' capital in a limited company consists of **share capital**. When a company is set up for the first time, it issues shares. These are paid for by investors, who then become shareholders of the company. Shares are denominated in units of 25 pence, 50 pence, £1 or whatever seems appropriate. This 'face value' of the shares is called their **nominal value**.

3.2 For example, when a company is set up with a share capital of, say, £100,000, it may be decided to issue:

(a) 100,000 shares of £1 each nominal value
(b) 200,000 shares of 50p each
(c) 400,000 shares of 25p each
(d) 250,000 shares of 40p each etc

3.3 The amount at which the shares are issued may exceed their nominal value. For example, a company might issue 100,000 £1 shares at a price of £1.20 each. Subscribers will then pay a total of £120,000. The issued share capital of the company would be shown in its accounts at nominal value, £100,000; the excess of £20,000 is described not as share capital, but **as share premium** (see Section 13).

Authorised, issued, called-up and paid-up share capital

3.4 A distinction must be made between authorised, issued, called-up and paid-up share capital.

(a) **Authorised (or nominal) capital** is the maximum amount of share capital that a company is empowered to issue. The amount of authorised share capital varies from company to company, and can change by agreement.

Part E: Financial statements

For example, a company's authorised share capital might be 5,000,000 ordinary shares of £1 each. This would then be the maximum number of shares it could issue, unless the maximum were to be changed by agreement.

(b) **Issued capital** is the nominal amount of share capital that has been issued to shareholders. The amount of issued capital cannot exceed the amount of authorised capital.

Continuing the example above, the company with authorised share capital of 5,000,000 ordinary shares of £1 might have issued 4,000,000 shares. This would leave it the option to issue 1,000,000 more shares at some time in the future.

When share capital is issued, shares are allotted to shareholders. The term 'allotted' share capital means the same thing as issued share capital.

(c) **Called-up capital**. When shares are issued or allotted, a company does not always expect to be paid the full amount for the shares at once. It might instead call up only a part of the issue price, and wait until a later time before it calls up the remainder.

For example, if a company allots 400,000 ordinary shares of £1, it might call up only, say, 75 pence per share. The issued share capital would be £400,000, but the called up share capital would only be £300,000.

(d) **Paid-up capital**. Like everyone else, investors are not always prompt or reliable payers. When capital is called up, some shareholders might delay their payment (or even default on payment). Paid-up capital is the amount of called-up capital that has been paid.

For example, if a company issues 400,000 ordinary shares of £1 each, calls up 75 pence per share, and receives payments of £290,000, we would have:

	£
Issued capital	400,000
Called-up capital	300,000
Paid-up capital	290,000
Called-up capital not paid	10,000

The balance sheet of the company would then include called up capital not paid on the assets side, as a debtor:

	£
Called-up capital not paid	10,000
Cash at bank	290,000
	300,000
Called-up share capital	
400,000 ordinary shares of £1, with 75p per share called up.	300,000

Question 2

Distinguish between authorised and issued share capital.

Answer

Look back to paragraph 3.4 (a) and (b)

4 THE BOARD OF DIRECTORS

4.1 A company can have a large number of **shareholders**, or only a few. No matter how many there are, they delegate authority for the day-to-day management of the company to its

directors, who are directly responsible to the shareholders for what they do. (In some smaller companies, the directors of the company and its shareholders are the same people.)

4.2 There must also be a company secretary. Company policy is decided at regular meetings of the board of directors.

> **IMPORTANT!**
>
> The salary of a sole trader or a partner is not a charge in the P & L account, but is an appropriation of profit. However, the salary of a director is a P & L account expense. This is because the directors are considered to be **employees** of the company, even when a director is also a shareholder of the company.

4.3 It would be wrong to give the impression that all companies are large-scale with many shareholders. The vast majority of UK companies are in fact small and family-owned.

> **Case example**
>
> There are many good reasons why a sole trader, say Alfred Newbegin Tools might choose to set up his own company (Newbegin Tools Ltd). These include limited personal liability and various tax advantages. Such a company would typically have one director (Alf) and his wife (Mabel) would be the company secretary. There would be two shareholders (Alf and Mabel) and board meetings would tend to be held during the commercial breaks on television or over breakfast. In this case it would be true to say that the providers of capital would also be running the business (as is normal with a sole trader). However Alf and Mabel as individuals would now be distinct from the business, because a company is a 'person' in its own right in the eyes of the law. Alf's salary, formerly an appropriation of profit, would now be a charge against company profits.

5 DIVIDENDS

5.1 Shareholders are entitled to a share of the profits made by the company.

> **KEY TERM**
>
> **Dividends** are appropriations of profit after tax.

5.2 A company might pay dividends in two stages during the course of their accounting year:

(a) In mid year, after the half-year financial results are known, the company might pay an **interim dividend**.

(b) At the end of the year, the company might pay a further **final dividend**.

5.3 The total dividend for the year is the sum of the interim and the final dividend. (Not all companies pay an interim dividend. Interim dividends are, however, commonly paid out by public limited companies.)

5.4 At the end of an accounting year, a company's directors may have proposed a final dividend payment, which has not yet been paid. This means that the final dividend should be appropriated out of profits and shown as a current liability in the balance sheet.

Part E: Financial statements

5.5 The terminology of dividend payments can be confusing, since they may be expressed either in the form, as 'x pence per share' or as 'y per cent'. In the latter case, the meaning is always 'y per cent of the nominal value of the shares in issue'. For example, suppose a company's issued share capital consists of 100,000 50p ordinary shares which were issued at a premium of 10p per share. The company's balance sheet would include the following:

		£
Called up share capital:	100,000 50p ordinary shares	50,000
Share premium account	(100,000 × 10p)	10,000

If the directors wish to pay a dividend of £5,000, they may propose:

(a) A dividend of 5p per share (100,000 × 5p = £5,000).
(b) A dividend of 10% (10% × £50,000 = £5,000)

Profits re-invested

5.6 Not all profits are distributed as dividends; some will be retained in the business to finance future projects. The 'market value' of the share (see below) should, all other things being equal, be increased if these projects are profitable.

Question 3

A company has authorised share capital of 1,000,000 50p ordinary shares and an issued share capital of 800,000 50p ordinary shares. If an ordinary dividend of 5% is declared, what is the amount payable to shareholders?

Answer

800,000 × 50p × 5% = £20,000.

6 TYPES OF SHARE

6.1 At this stage it is relevant to distinguish between the various types of shares most often encountered: **preference shares**, **deferred shares** and **ordinary shares**.

KEY TERM

Preference shares are shares which confer certain preferential rights on their holder.

6.2 **Preference shares** are now rather old-fashioned and are rarely issued, although they do have occasional resurgences of popularity.

6.3 They carry the right to a final dividend which is expressed as a percentage of their nominal value: eg a 6% £1 preference share carries a right to an annual dividend of 6p. Preference dividends have priority over ordinary dividends; in other words, if the directors of a company wish to pay a dividend (which they are not obliged to do) they must pay any preference dividend first. Otherwise, no ordinary dividend may be paid.

6.4 The rights attaching to preference shares are set out in the company's constitution. They may vary from company to company, but typically:

(a) Preference shareholders have a **priority right** over ordinary shareholders to a **return of their capital** if the company goes into liquidation.

(b) Preference shares do **not carry a right to vote**.

(c) If the preference shares are cumulative, it means that before a company can pay an ordinary dividend it must not only pay the current year's preference dividend, but must also make good any arrears of preference dividends unpaid in previous years.

6.5 **Deferred shares** are equity shares that will receive a dividend only after other classes of share (including ordinary shares) have received a specified rate of dividend, or will receive a dividend only after a specified time from issue.

6.6 **Ordinary shares** are by far the most common. They carry no right to a fixed dividend but are entitled to all profits left after payment of any preference dividend. Generally however, only a part of such remaining profits is distributed, the rest being kept in reserve (see below).

> **KEY TERM**
>
> **Ordinary shares** are shares which are not preferential with regard to dividend payments. Thus a holder only receives a dividend after fixed dividends have been paid to preference shareholders.

6.7 The amount of ordinary dividends fluctuates, although there is a general expectation that it will increase from year to year. Should the company be wound up, any surplus not distributed is shared between the ordinary shareholders. Ordinary shares normally carry voting rights.

6.8 Ordinary shareholders are thus the effective owners of a company. They own the 'equity' of the business, and any reserves of the business (described later) belong to them. Ordinary shareholders are sometimes referred to as equity shareholders. Preference shareholders are in many ways more like creditors (although legally they are members, not creditors).

6.9 It should be emphasised that the precise rights attached to preference, deferred and ordinary shares vary from company to company; the distinctions noted above are generalisations.

6.10 EXAMPLE: DIVIDENDS, ORDINARY SHARES AND PREFERENCE SHARES

Garden Gloves Ltd has issued 50,000 ordinary shares of 50 pence each and 20,000 7% preference shares of £1 each. Its profits after taxation for the year to 30 September 20X5 were £8,400. The board of directors has decided to pay an ordinary dividend (ie a dividend on ordinary shares) which is 50% of profits after tax and preference dividend.

Required

Show the amount in total of dividends and of retained profits, and calculate the dividend per share on ordinary shares.

6.11 SOLUTION

Profits after tax and preference dividend are called **earnings**, and an important measure of company performance is the **earnings per share**. Although not required by the problem, the earnings per share (EPS) is also shown below.

Part E: Financial statements

	£
Profit after tax	8,400
Preference dividend (7% of £1 × 20,000)	1,400
Earnings (profit after tax and preference dividend)	7,000
Earnings per share (÷ 50,000) 14 pence	
Ordinary dividend (50% of earnings)	3,500
Retained profit (also 50% of earnings)	3,500

The ordinary dividend is 7 pence per share (£3,500 ÷ 50,000 ordinary shares).

The appropriation of profit would be shown as follows:

	£	£
Profit after tax		8,400
Dividends: preference	1,400	
ordinary	3,500	
		4,900
Retained profit		3,500

The market value of shares

6.12 The nominal value of shares will be different from their market value, which is the price at which someone is prepared to purchase shares in the company from an existing shareholder. If Mr A owns 1,000 £1 shares in Z Ltd he may sell them to B for £1.60 each.

6.13 This transfer of existing shares does not affect Z Ltd's own financial position in any way and, apart from changing the register of members, Z Ltd does not have to bother with the sale by Mr A to Mr B at all. There are certainly no accounting entries to be made for the share sale.

6.14 Shares in private companies do not change hands very often, hence their market value is often hard to estimate. Public companies are usually (not always) quoted; a quoted company is one whose shares are traded on The Stock Exchange and it is the market value of the shares which is quoted.

7 THE FINAL ACCOUNTS OF LIMITED COMPANIES: INTERNAL USE
Pilot paper, December 2001

7.1 The preparation and publication of the final accounts of limited companies in the UK are governed by the Companies Act 1985 as amended by the Companies Act 1989. At this stage we are concerned with the preparation of limited company accounts for **internal use**. If you are asked to produce such a set of final accounts, you need not follow the detailed regulations laid down by the Act. However, the general format of the balance sheet and profit and loss account of a limited company is shown below, with some simplifications, in order to introduce certain assets and liabilities which we have not come across in earlier chapters of this Study Text.

7.2 TYPICAL COMPANY LIMITED BALANCE SHEET AS AT....

	£	£	£
Fixed assets			
Intangible assets			
Development costs		X	
Concessions, patents, licences, trademarks		X	
Goodwill		X	
			X
Tangible assets			
Land and buildings		X	
Plant and machinery		X	
Fixtures, fittings, tools and equipment		X	
Motor vehicles		X	
			X
Investments			X
			X
Current assets			
Stocks		X	
Debtors and prepayments		X	
Investments		X	
Cash at bank and in hand		X	
		X	
Creditors: amounts falling due within one year (ie current liabilities)			
Debenture loans (nearing their redemption date)	X		
Bank overdraft and loans	X		
Trade creditors	X		
Bills of exchange payable	X		
Taxation	X		
Accruals	X		
Proposed dividend	X		
		(X)	
Net current assets			X
Total assets less current liabilities			X
Creditors: amounts falling due after more than one year (ie long term liabilities)			
Debenture loans		X	
Taxation		X	
			(X)
			X
Capital and reserves			
Called up share capital			
Ordinary shares		X	
Preference shares		X	
			X
Reserves			
Share premium account		X	
Revaluation reserve		X	
Other reserves		X	
Profit and loss account (retained profits)		X	
			X
			X

7.3 The profit and loss account of a company might have a format roughly similar to the one below.

Part E: Financial statements

TYPICAL COMPANY LIMITED
PROFIT AND LOSS ACCOUNT FOR THE YEAR ENDED...

	£	£
Turnover		X
Cost of sales		(X)
Gross profit		X
Distribution costs	X	
Administrative expenses	X	
		(X)
		X
Other operating income	X	
Income from fixed asset investments	X	
Other interest receivable and similar income	X	
		X
		X
Interest payable		(X)
Profit before taxation		X
Tax		(X)
Profit after tax		X
Dividends: preference	X	
ordinary	X	
		(X)
Retained profit for the year		X
Profit and loss account as at the beginning of the year		X
Profit and loss account as at the end of the year		X

7.4 You may be asked to produce a set of accounts for **external use**, in which case you will have to follow the statutory format in all respects. This is covered in Chapter 24.

7.5 We will now consider some of the components in more detail in the following sections.

8 FIXED ASSETS

Intangible fixed assets

8.1 Intangible fixed assets represent amounts of money paid by a business to acquire benefits of a long-term nature. **Goodwill** and **deferred development expenditure** are two intangible assets which were discussed in detail in an earlier chapter.

8.2 If a company purchases some **patent rights**, or a concession from another business, or the right to use a trademark, the cost of the purchase can be accounted for as the purchase of an intangible fixed asset. These assets must then be **amortised** (depreciated) over their economic life.

Tangible fixed assets

8.3 As with any other type of business, tangible fixed assets are shown in the balance sheet at their net book value (ie at cost less provision for depreciation). Sometimes, a fixed asset, such as a building, might be revalued to a current market value. Depreciation would then be based on the revalued amount, and the balance sheet value of the asset would be the revalued amount less provision for depreciation on the revalued amount.

Investments

8.4 Investments are fixed assets if the company intends to hold on to them for a long time, and current assets if they are only likely to be held for a short time before being sold (eg to invest funds not needed for say six months).

9 CURRENT AND LONG-TERM LIABILITIES

9.1 The term **'creditors: amounts falling due within one year'** is used in the Companies Act 1985 as an alternative phrase meaning 'current liabilities'. You will therefore come across this term increasingly often as you progress through your accountancy studies.

9.2 The sub-headings in paragraph 7.2 show the main types of liabilities. Refer back to Chapter 16 for a definition of a liability, as opposed to a provision.

9.3 Similarly, the term **'creditors : amounts falling due after more than one year'** is the Companies Act 1985 term for long-term liabilities.

10 DEBENTURE LOANS

10.1 Limited companies may issue **debenture stock** (debentures) or loan stock. These are **long-term liabilities** described on the balance sheet as loan capital. They are different from share capital in the following ways.

(a) **Shareholders** are **members** of a company, while **providers of loan capital** are **creditors**.

(b) **Shareholders** receive **dividends** (appropriations of profit) whereas the holders of loan capital are entitled to a **fixed rate of interest** (an expense charged against revenue).

(c) Loan capital holders can take legal action against a company if their interest is not paid when due, whereas **shareholders cannot enforce the payment of dividends**.

(d) **Debentures** or loan stock are often **secured on company assets**, whereas shares are not.

10.2 The holder of loan capital is generally in a less risky position than the shareholder. He has greater security, although his income is fixed and cannot grow, unlike ordinary dividends. As remarked earlier, preference shares are in practice very similar to loan capital, not least because the preference dividend is normally fixed.

10.3 Interest is calculated on the nominal value of loan capital, regardless of its market value. If a company has £700,000 (nominal value) 12% debentures in issue, interest of £84,000 will be charged in the profit and loss account per year. Interest is usually paid half-yearly; examination questions often require an accrual to be made for interest due at the year-end.

10.4 For example, a company has £700,000 of 12% debentures in issue and pays interest on 30 June and 31 December each year. It ends its accounting year on 30 September. There would be an accrual of three months' unpaid interest (3/12 × £84,000) = £21,000 at the end of each accounting year that the debentures are still in issue.

10.5 **Advantages of raising finance by borrowing by debentures**

(a) Debenture holders are creditors, not shareholders, and so do not affect the **control** of the company.
(b) The interest rate is fixed and a known cost.

Part E: Financial statements

(c) The interest is usually allowable for offset against the company's corporation tax.

(d) If a debenture is secured as assets the interest rate will normally be lower than, say, an overdraft.

10.6 **Disadvantages of raising finance by borrowing debenture**

(a) Debenture interest **must** be paid, whereas directors do not need to pay shareholders a dividend.

(b) Dividends are appropriations of profit and do not reduce the company's corporation tax.

(c) Debenture holders can force the sale of any assets used as security, if their loan is not repaid on the due date.

10.7 Raising finance by borrowing will affect a company's **gearing**. This will be dealt with in detail in Chapter 22.

11 TAXATION

11.1 Companies pay **corporation tax** on the profits they earn. Currently (2003-2004), small companies pay tax at the rate of 19% on their taxable profits and large companies pay 30%. There are variations, but these are outside the scope of your syllabus.

11.2 Note that because a company has a separate legal personality, its tax is included in its accounts. An unincorporated business would not show income tax in its accounts, as it would not be a business expense but the personal affair of the proprietors.

11.3 **Presentation in accounts**

(a) The **charge** for corporation tax on profits for the year is shown as a **deduction** from **net profit**, before appropriations.

(b) In the balance sheet, **tax payable** to the government is generally shown as a **current liability** as it is usually due within nine months of the year end.

(c) For various reasons, the tax on profits in the P & L account and the tax payable in the balance sheet are not usually the same amount. However the reasons are outside the scope of your syllabus.

12 LEDGER ACCOUNTS AND LIMITED COMPANIES

12.1 Limited companies keep ledger accounts and the only difference from sole traders, is the nature of some of the transactions, assets and liabilities.

For example, there will be an account for each of the following items:

(a) *Taxation*

(i) Tax charged against profits will be accounted for by:

DEBIT   P & L account
CREDIT   Taxation account.

(ii) The outstanding balance on the taxation account will be a liability in the balance sheet, until eventually paid, when the accounting entry would be:

DEBIT   Taxation account
CREDIT   Cash

(b) *Dividends*

A separate account will be kept for the dividends for each different class of shares (eg preference, ordinary).

(i) Dividends declared out of profits (proposed dividends) will be accounted for by

DEBIT   P & L appropriation account
CREDIT   Dividends payable account

Dividends payable (but not yet paid) are a current liability.

(ii) When dividends are paid, we then have

DEBIT   Dividends payable account
CREDIT   Cash

(c) *Debenture loans*

Debenture loans being a long-term liability will be shown as a credit balance in a debenture loan account.

(i) Interest payable on such loans is not credited to the loan account, but is credited to a separate creditors' account for interest until it is eventually paid: ie

DEBIT   Interest account (an expense, chargeable against profits)
CREDIT   Interest payable (creditors, and a current liability until eventually paid)

(ii) When paid, the entries are

DEBIT   Interest payable
CREDIT   Cash

(d) *Share capital and reserves*

There will be a separate account for:

(i) Each different class of share capital (always a credit balance b/f).
(ii) Each different type of reserve (nearly always a credit balance b/f).

We shall now turn our attention to these items in more detail.

13 SHARE CAPITAL AND RESERVES   June 2003

13.1 The net fixed assets of a company, plus the working capital (ie current assets minus current liabilities) minus the long-term liabilities, are 'financed' by the shareholders' capital.

13.2 Shareholders' capital consists of both:

(a) The nominal value of issued capital (minus any amounts not yet called up on issued shares).

(b) Reserves.

13.3 The share capital itself might consist of both ordinary shares and preference shares. All reserves, however, are owned by the ordinary shareholders, who own the 'equity' in the company.

Called-up share capital

13.4 A company's issued share capital is its called-up share capital, provided that there are no shares in issue which have so far only been partly called up.

Part E: Financial statements

This means that if a company has issued 200,000 ordinary shares of 50 pence each, and 50,000 10% preference shares of £1 each, all fully called up, the called up share capital in the balance sheet will be

	£
200,000 ordinary shares of 50p each	100,000
50,000 10% preference shares of £1 each	50,000
	150,000

Reserves

13.5 In the case of a sole trader, the proprietor's interest = net assets of the business, and in the case of a partnership, partners' funds = net assets. For a company the equation is:

> Shareholders' funds = net assets
>
> Furthermore:
>
> Shareholders' funds = share capital and reserves

A company's share capital will remain fixed from year to year, unless new shares are issued. Reserves are difficult to define neatly since different reserves arise for different reasons, but it follows from the above that:

Reserves = net assets minus share capital

So the total amount of reserves in a company varies, according to changes in the net assets of the business.

13.6 The typical balance sheet in paragraph 7.2 lists a number of reserves, although the list is not comprehensive.

13.7 A distinction should be made between:

(a) **Statutory reserves**, which are reserves which a company is required to set up by law, eg the revaluation reserve, and which are not available for the distribution of dividends.

(b) **Non-statutory reserves**, which are reserves consisting of profits which are distributable as dividends, if the company so wishes.

Profit and loss reserve (retained profits)

13.8 The most significant **non-statutory reserve** (revenue reserve) is variously described as:

(a) Revenue reserve
(b) Retained profits
(c) Retained earnings
(d) Undistributed profits
(e) Profit and loss account
(f) Unappropriated profits

13.9 These are **profits** earned by the company and **not appropriated** by dividends, taxation or transfer to another reserve account.

13.10 Provided that a company is earning profits, this reserve generally increases from year to year, as most companies do not distribute all their profits as dividends. Dividends can be paid from it: even if a loss is made in one particular year, a dividend can be paid from previous years' retained profits.

13.11 For example, if a company makes a loss of £100,000 in one year, yet has unappropriated profits from previous years totalling £250,000, it can pay a dividend not exceeding £150,000. One reason for retaining some profit each year is to enable the company to pay dividends even when profits are low (or non-existent). Another reason is usually shortage of cash.

13.12 Very occasionally, you might come across a debit balance on the profit and loss account. This would indicate that the company has **accumulated losses**.

Other non-statutory reserves

13.13 The company directors may choose to set up other reserves. These may have a specific purpose (eg plant and machinery replacement reserve) or not (eg general reserve). The creation of these reserves usually indicates a **general intention not to distribute** the profits involved at any future date, although legally any such reserves, being non-statutory, remain available for the payment of dividends.

Appropriation of profit

13.14 Profits are transferred to these reserves by making an appropriation out of profits, usually profits for the year. Typically, you might come across the following:

	£	£
Profit after taxation		100,000
Appropriations of profit		
Dividend	60,000	
Transfer to general reserve	10,000	
		70,000
Retained profits for the year		30,000
Profit and loss reserve b/f		250,000
Profit and loss reserve c/f		280,000

The share premium account

13.15 There are a number of statutory (or **capital**) reserves. One is the revaluation reserve, which we met in Chapter 10. However, the most important one at this stage is the **share premium account**. Section 130 of the Companies Act 1985 states that 'where a company issues shares at a premium, whether for cash or otherwise, a sum equal to.... the premiums on those shares shall be transferred to the share premium account'.

13.16 By **'premium'** is meant the difference between the issue price of the share and its nominal value. When a company is first incorporated (set up) the issue price of its shares will probably be the same as their nominal value and so there would be no share premium. If the company does well the market value of its shares will increase, but not the nominal value. The price of any new shares issued will be approximately their market value.

13.17 The difference between cash received by the company and the nominal value of the new shares issued is transferred to the share premium account. For example, if X Ltd issues 1,000 £1 ordinary shares at £2.60 each the book entry will be:

		£	£
DEBIT	Cash	2,600	
CREDIT	Ordinary share capital		1,000
	Share premium account		1,600

Part E: Financial statements

13.18 A **share premium account** only comes into being when a company issues shares at a price in excess of their nominal value. The market price of the shares, once they have been issued, has no bearing at all on the company's accounts, and so if their market price goes up or down, the share premium account would remain unaltered.

> **KEY TERM**
>
> A **share premium account** is an account into which sums received as payment for shares in excess of their nominal value must be placed.

13.19 Once established, the share premium account constitutes capital of the company which cannot be paid out in dividends. The share premium account will increase in value if and when new shares are issued at a price above their nominal value.

13.20 The share premium account can be 'used' - and so decrease in value - only in certain very limited ways. One use of the share premium account, however, is to 'finance' the issue of bonus shares, which are described later in this chapter.

> **IMPORTANT!**
>
> The share premium account cannot be distributed as dividend under any circumstances.

13.21 The reason for creating statutory reserves is to **maintain the capital** of the company. This capital 'base' provides some **security for the company's creditors**, bearing in mind that the liability of shareholders is limited in the event that the company cannot repay its debts. It would be most unjust - and illegal - for a company to pay its shareholders a dividend out of its base capital when it is not even able to pay back its debts.

13.22 Another reason why statutory reserves cannot be distributed is the fact that they often represent unrealised profits. A profit does arise when assets are revalued but it is not realised into cash. It is a generally accepted accounting principle that profit can only be distributed when it is realised because an unrealised profit can disappear if the value of the revalued asset subsequently drops.

> **Exam focus point**
>
> You may be asked to explain why statutory reserves cannot be distributed.

Question 4

What are the ledger entries needed to record the issue of 200,000 £1 ordinary shares at a premium of 30p and paid for in full by cheque?

Answer

		£	£
DEBIT	Bank	260,000	
CREDIT	Share capital		200,000
CREDIT	Share premium		60,000

Distinction between reserves and provisions

> **KEY TERMS**
>
> A **reserve** is an appropriation of distributable profits for a specific purpose (eg plant replacement) while a provision is an amount charged against revenue as an expense. A provision relates either to a diminution in the value of an asset (eg doubtful debtors) or a known liability (eg audit fees), the amount of which cannot be established with any accuracy.
>
> **Provisions** (for depreciation, doubtful debts etc) are dealt with in company accounts in the same way as in the accounts of other types of business.

Bonus issues

13.23 A company may wish to increase its share capital without needing to raise additional finance by issuing new shares. For example, a profitable company might expand from modest beginnings over a number of years. Its profitability would be reflected in large balances on its reserves, while its original share capital might look like that of a much smaller business.

13.24 It is open to such a company to **re-classify some of its reserves as share capital**. This is purely a paper exercise which **raises no funds**. Any reserve may be re-classified in this way, including a share premium account or other statutory reserve. Such a re-classification **increases the capital base** of the company and gives **creditors greater protection**.

13.25 EXAMPLE: BONUS ISSUE

BUBBLES LIMITED
BALANCE SHEET (EXTRACT)

	£'000	£'000
Funds employed		
Share capital		
£1 ordinary shares (fully paid)		1,000
Reserves		
Share premium	500	
Undistributed profit	2,000	
		2,500
Shareholders' funds		3,500

Bubbles decided to make a '3 for 2' bonus issue (ie 3 new shares for every 2 already held). So shares with a nominal value of £1,500,000 need to be issued.

The double entry is	£'000	£'000
DEBIT Share premium	500	
Undistributed profit	1,000	
CREDIT Ordinary share capital		1,500

After the issue the balance sheet is as follows	£'000
Share capital	
£1 ordinary shares (fully paid)	2,500
Reserves	
Undistributed profit	1,000
Shareholders' funds	3,500

Part E: Financial statements

13.26 1,500,000 new ('bonus') shares are issued to existing shareholders, so that if Mr X previously held 20,000 shares he will now hold 50,000. The total value of his holding should theoretically remain the same however, since the net assets of the company remain unchanged and his share of those net assets remains at 2% (ie 50,000/2,500,000; previously 20,000/1,000,000).

Rights issues

13.27 A rights issue (unlike a bonus issue) is an issue of shares for cash. The 'rights' are offered to existing shareholders, who can sell them if they wish.

13.28 EXAMPLE: RIGHTS ISSUE

Bubbles Ltd (above) decides to make a rights issue, shortly after the bonus issue. The terms are '1 for 5 @ £1.20' (ie one new share for every five already held, at a price of £1.20). Assuming that all shareholders take up their rights (which they are not obliged to) the double entry is:

		£'000	£'000
DEBIT	Cash	600	
CREDIT	Ordinary share capital		500
	Share premium		100

13.29 Mr X who previously held 50,000 shares will now hold 60,000, and the value of his holding should increase (all other things being equal) because the net assets of the company will increase. The new balance sheet will show:

	£'000	£'000
Share capital		
£1 ordinary shares		3,000
Reserves		
Share premium	100	
Undistributed profit	1,000	
		1,100
Shareholders' funds		4,100

The increase in funds of £600,000 represents the cash raised from the issue of 500,000 new shares at a price of £1.20 each.

13.30 Rights issues are a popular way of **raising cash** by issuing shares and they are **cheap to administer**. In addition, **shareholders retain control** of the business as their holding is not diluted.

13.31 The disadvantages of a rights issue is that shareholders are **not obliged** to take up their rights and so the issue could fail to raise the money required. For this reason companies usually try to find a broker to 'underwrite' the issue, ie who will buy any rights not taken up by the shareholders.

14 EXAMPLE: COMPANY ACCOUNTS FOR INTERNAL PURPOSES

14.1 We can now try to draw together several of the items described in this chapter into an illustrative example. Study it carefully.

14.2 The accountant (unqualified) of Wislon Ltd has prepared the following trial balance as at 31 December 20X7.

19: Limited companies

	£'000
50p ordinary shares (fully paid)	350
7% £1 preference shares (fully paid)	100
10% debentures (secured)	200
Retained profit 1.1.X7	242
General reserve 1.1.X7	171
Freehold land and buildings 1.1.X7 (cost)	430
Plant and machinery 1.1.X7 (cost)	830
Provision for depreciation:	
Freehold buildings 1.1.X7	20
Plant and machinery 1.1.X7	222
Stock 1.1.X7	190
Sales	2,695
Purchases	2,152
Preference dividend	7
Ordinary dividend (interim)	8
Debenture interest	10
Wages and salaries	254
Light and heat	31
Sundry expenses	113
Suspense account	135
Debtors	179
Creditors	195
Cash	126

Notes

(a) Sundry expenses include £9,000 paid in respect of insurance for the year ending 1 September 20X8. Light and heat does not include an invoice of £3,000 for electricity for the three months ending 2 January 20X8, which was paid in February 20X8. Light and heat also includes £20,000 relating to salesmen's commission.

(b) The suspense account is in respect of the following items:

	£'000
Proceeds from the issue of 100,000 ordinary shares	120
Proceeds from the sale of plant	300
	420
Less consideration for the acquisition of Mary & Co	285
	135

(c) The net assets of Mary & Co were purchased on 3 March 20X7. Assets were valued as follows:

	£'000
Investments	230
Stock	34
	264

All the stock acquired was sold during 20X7. The investments were still held by Wislon at 31.12.X7.

(d) The freehold property was acquired some years ago. The buildings element of the cost was estimated at £100,000 and the estimated useful life of the assets was fifty years at the time of purchase. As at 31 December 20X7 the property is to be revalued at £800,000.

(e) The plant which was sold had cost £350,000 and had a net book value of £274,000 as on 1.1.X7. £36,000 depreciation is to be charged on plant and machinery for 20X7.

(f) The debentures have been in issue for some years. The 50p ordinary shares all rank for dividends at the end of the year.

Part E: Financial statements

(g) The directors wish to provide for:
   (i) Debenture interest due
   (ii) A final ordinary dividend of 2p per share
   (iii) A transfer to general reserve of £16,000
   (iv) Audit fees of £4,000

(h) Stock as at 31 December 20X7 was valued at £220,000 (cost).

(i) Taxation is to be ignored.

Required

Prepare the final accounts of Wislon Ltd in a form suitable for internal purposes.

Approach and suggested solution

14.3 (a) Normal adjustments are needed for accruals and prepayments (insurance, light and heat, debenture interest and audit fees). The debenture interest accrued is calculated as follows:

	£'000
Charge needed in P & L account (10% × £200,000)	20
Amount paid so far, as shown in trial balance	10
Accrual - presumably six months' interest now payable	10

	£'000
The accrued expenses shown in the balance sheet comprise:	
Debenture interest	10
Light and heat	3
Audit fee	4
	17

(b) The misposting of £20,000 to light and heat is also adjusted, by reducing the light and heat expense, but charging £20,000 to salesmen's commission.

(c) Depreciation on the freehold building is calculated as $\frac{£100,000}{50} = £2,000$.

The NBV of the freehold property is then £430,000 - £20,000 - £2,000 = £408,000 at the end of the year. When the property is revalued a reserve of £800,000 - £408,000 = £392,000 is then created.

(d) The profit on disposal of plant is calculated as proceeds £300,000 (per suspense account) less NBV £274,000, ie £26,000. The cost of the remaining plant is calculated at £830,000 – £350,000 = £480,000. The depreciation provision at the year end is:

	£'000
Balance 1.1.X7	222
Charge for 20X7	36
Less depreciation on disposals (350 – 274)	(76)
	182

(e) Goodwill arising on the purchase of Mary & Co is:

	£'000
Consideration (per suspense account)	285
Assets at valuation	264
Goodwill	21

In the absence of other instructions, this is shown as an asset on the balance sheet. The investments, being owned by Wislon at the year end, are also shown on the balance sheet, whereas Mary's stock, acquired and then sold, is added to the purchases figure for the year.

(f) The other item in the suspense account is dealt with as follows:

	£'000
Proceeds of issue of 100,000 ordinary shares	120
Less nominal value 100,000 × 50p	50
Excess of consideration over nominal value (= share premium)	70

(g) Appropriations of profit must be considered. The final ordinary dividend, shown as a current liability in the balance sheet, is

(700,000 + 100,000 ordinary shares) × 2p = £16,000

(h) The transfer to general reserve increases that reserve to £171,000 + £16,000 = £187,000.

14.4 WISLON LIMITED
TRADING AND PROFIT AND LOSS ACCOUNT
FOR THE YEAR ENDED 31 DECEMBER 20X7

	£'000	£'000	£'000
Sales			2,695
Less cost of sales			
Opening stock		190	
Purchases		2,186	
		2,376	
Less closing stock		220	
			2,156
Gross profit			539
Profit on disposal of plant			26
			565
Less expenses			
Wages, salaries and commission		274	
Sundry expenses		107	
Light and heat		14	
Depreciation: freehold buildings		2	
plant		36	
Audit fees		4	
Debenture interest		20	
			457
Net profit			108
Appropriations			
Transfer to general reserve		16	
Dividends: preference (paid)	7		
ordinary: interim (paid)	8		
final (proposed)	16		
		31	
			47
Retained profit for the year			61
Retained profit brought forward			242
Retained profit carried forward			303

Part E: Financial statements

14.5 WISLON LIMITED
BALANCE SHEET AS AT 31 DECEMBER 20X7

	Cost/val'n £'000	Dep'n £'000	£'000
Fixed assets			
Intangible assets			
Goodwill			21
Tangible assets			
Freehold property	800	-	800
Plant and machinery	480	182	298
	1,280	182	
Investments			230
			1,349
Current assets			
Stock		220	
Debtors		179	
Prepayment		6	
Cash		126	
		531	
Creditors: amounts falling due within one year			
Creditors	195		
Accrued expenses	17		
Proposed dividend	16		
		228	
Net current assets			303
Total assets less current liabilities			1,652
Creditors: amounts falling due after more than one year			
10% debentures (secured)			(200)
			1,452
Capital and reserves			
Called up share capital			
50p ordinary shares		400	
7% £1 preference shares		100	
			500
Reserves			
Share premium		70	
Revaluation reserve		392	
General reserve		187	
Profit and loss account		303	
			952
			1,452

Chapter roundup

- Limited companies have **limited liability,** which means that their members' liability in the event of insolvency is limited to the amount of capital they put in.
- You should be able to distinguish:
    - **Private companies**
    - **Public companies**
- Limited companies must keep **accounting records**.
- Limited companies have a **share capital**. Distinguish:
    - Authorised share capital
    - Issued share capital

Chapter Roundup (Continued)

- o Called up share capital
- o Paid up share capital

- **Dividends** are **appropriations of profit**.
- **Ordinary shares** are different from **preference shares**, mainly because they carry no right to a fixed dividend.
- **Revenue reserves** are available for distribution. **Capital reserves** are not.
- **Debentures** are long term liabilities, not capital. Unlike dividends, debenture interest must be paid.
- Companies pay **corporation tax** on their profits.

Quick quiz

1 What is the meaning of limited liability?
2 What is the difference between issued capital and called-up capital?
3 What are the differences between ordinary shares and preference shares?
4 What are the differences between debentures and share capital?
5 A company issues 50,000 £1 shares at a price of £1.25 per share. How much should be posted to the share premium account?

    A   £50,000

    B   £12,500

    C   £62,500

    D   £60,000

6 Distinguish between a bonus (capitalisation) issue and a rights issue.
7 Which items should be included in current assets and current liabilities?

Answers to quick quiz

1 The maximum amount that a shareholder has to pay is the amount paid on his shares.
2 Issued share capital is the nominal value of shares issued to shareholders. Called-up share capital is the amount payable to date by the shareholders.
3 Ordinary shares can be paid any or no dividend. The dividend attaching to preference shares is set from the start.
4 Debentures are long-term loans, and so debentureholders are creditors. Shareholders own the company.
5 B. (50,000 × 25p)
6 A bonus issue is financed by capitalising revenue reserves. A rights issue is paid for by the shareholders taking up the shares.
7 Current assets and liabilities are those which are due to be settled within 12 months of the balance sheet date.

Question to try	Level	Marks	Time
29	Introductory	n/a	32 mins
30	Full exam	10	18 mins
31	Introductory	n/a	45 mins

Chapter 20

CASH FLOW STATEMENTS

Topic list	Syllabus reference
1 FRS 1 *Cash flow statements*	5(c)
2 Preparing a cash flow statement	5(d)

Introduction

In the long run, a profit will result in an increase in the company's cash balance but, as Keynes observed, 'in the long run we are all dead'. In the short run, the making of a profit will not necessarily result in an increased cash balance. The observation leads us to two questions:

- What is the difference between cash and profit?
- How useful are the profit and loss account and balance sheet in demonstrating whether a company has sufficient cash to finance its operations?

The importance of the distinction between cash and profit and the scant attention paid to this by the profit and loss account has resulted in the development of cash flow statements.

Study guide

Section 23 - Cash flow statements

- Explain the difference between profit and cash flow.
- Explain the need for management to control cash flow.
- Explain the value to users of financial statements of a cash flow statement.
- Explain the provisions of FRS 1 Cash Flow Statements and the standard format therein (excluding group aspects).
- Explain the inward and outward flows of cash in a typical company.
- Explain how to calculate the figures needed for the cash flow statement including among others:
    - Cash flows from operating activities (indirect method)
    - Cash flows from investing activities (purchases, sales and depreciation of fixed assets).
- Explain how to calculate cash flow from operating activities using the direct method.
- Review of information to be derived from users from the cash flow statement (see also Sections 25-26).
- Prepare cash flow statements from given balance sheets with or without a profit and loss account.

Exam guide

This chapter adopts a systematic approach to the preparation of cash flow statements in examinations; you should learn this method and you will then be equipped for any questions in the exam itself. A **question is certain** to appear in the exam.

1 FRS 1 CASH FLOW STATEMENTS

1.1 It has been argued that 'profit' does not always give a useful or meaningful picture of a company's operations. Readers of a company's financial statements might even be **misled by a reported profit figure**.

(a) Shareholders might believe that if a company makes a profit after tax, of say, £100,000 then this is the amount which it could afford to pay as a dividend. Unless the company has sufficient cash available to stay in business and also to pay a dividend, the shareholders' expectations would be wrong.

(b) Employees might believe that if a company makes profits, it can afford to pay higher wages next year. This opinion may not be correct: the ability to pay wages depends on the availability of cash.

(c) Cash is the lifeblood of the business. Survival of a business entity depends not so much on profits as on its ability to pay its debts when they fall due. Such payments might include 'profit and loss' items such as material purchases, wages, interest and taxation etc, but also capital payments for new fixed assets and the repayment of loan capital when this falls due (for example on the redemption of debentures).

1.2 From these examples, it may be apparent that a company's performance and prospects depend not so much on the 'profits' earned in a period, but more realistically on liquidity or **cash flows**.

1.3 The great advantage of a cash flow statement is that it is unambiguous and provides information which is additional to that provided in the rest of the accounts. It also describes the cash flows of an organisation by activity and not by balance sheet classification.

1.4 EXAMPLE: CASH FLOW STATEMENT

Flail Ltd commenced trading on 1 January 20X1 with a medium-term loan of £21,000 and a share issue which raised £35,000. The company purchased fixed assets for £21,000 cash, and during the year to 31 December 20X1 entered into the following transactions.

(a) Purchases from suppliers were £19,500, of which £2,550 was unpaid at the year end.

(b) Wages and salaries amounted to £10,500, of which £750 was unpaid at the year end.

(c) Interest on the loan of £2,100 was fully paid in the year and a repayment of £5,250 was made.

(d) Sales turnover was £29,400, including £900 debtors at the year end.

(e) Interest on cash deposits at the bank amounted to £75.

(f) A dividend of £4,000 was proposed as at 31 December 20X1.

You are required to prepare a historical cash flow statement for the year ended 31 December 20X1.

Part E: Financial statements

1.5 SOLUTION

FLAIL LIMITED
STATEMENT OF CASH FLOWS FOR
THE YEAR ENDED 31 DECEMBER 20X1

	£	£
Operating activities		
Cash received from customers	28,500	
(£29,400 – £900)		
Cash paid to suppliers (£19,500 – £2,550)	(16,950)	
Cash paid to and on behalf of employees (£10,500 – £750)	(9,750)	
Cash flow from operating activities		1,800
Returns on investment and servicing of finance		
Interest paid	(2,100)	
Interest received	75	
		(2,025)
Capital expenditure		
Purchase of fixed assets	(21,000)	
Cash flow from investing activities		(21,000)
Financing		
Issue of shares	35,000	
Proceeds from medium-term loan	21,000	
Repayment of medium-term loan	(5,250)	
Cash flow from financing activities		50,750
Net increase in cash		29,525
Cash at 1 January 20X1		-
Cash at 31 December 20X1		29,525

Note that the dividend is only proposed and so there is no related cash flow in 20X1.

Question 1

The directors of Flail Ltd obtain the following information in respect of projected cash flows for the year to 31 December 20X2.

(a) Fixed asset purchases for cash will be £3,000.

(b) Further expenses will be:

　(i) Purchases from suppliers - £18,750 (£4,125 owed at the year end)
　(ii) Wages and salaries - £11,250 (£600 owed at the year end)
　(iii) Loan interest - £1,575

(c) Turnover will be £36,000 (£450 debtors at the year end).

(d) Interest on bank deposits will be £150.

(e) A further capital repayment of £5,250 will be made on the loan.

(f) A dividend of £5,000 will be proposed and last year's final dividend paid.

(g) Corporation tax of £2,300 will be paid in respect of 20X1.

Prepare the cash flow forecast for the year to 31 December 20X2.

Answer

FLAIL LIMITED
STATEMENT OF FORECAST CASH FLOWS FOR
THE YEAR ENDING 31 DECEMBER 20X2

	£	£
Operating activities		
Cash received from customers	36,450	
(£36,000 + £900 – £450)		
Cash paid to suppliers (£18,750 + £2,550 – £4,125)	(17,175)	
Cash paid to and on behalf of employees		
(£11,250 + £750 – £600)	(11,400)	
Net cash flow from operating activities		7,875
Returns on investments and servicing of finance		
Interest paid	(1,575)	
Interest received	150	
		(1,425)
Taxation		(2,300)
Capital expenditure		
Purchase of fixed assets		(3,000)
		1,150
Equity dividends paid		(4,000)
Financing		
Repayment of medium-term loan		(5,250)
Forecast net decrease in cash at 31 December 20X2		(8,100)
Cash as at 31 December 20X1		29,525
Forecast cash as at 31 December 20X2		21,425

Indirect method

1.6 Another way of arriving at net cash flows from operating activities is to start from operating profit and adjust for non-cash items, such as depreciation, debtors etc. This is known as the **indirect method**. A proforma calculation is given below.

> **FORMULA TO LEARN**
>
> | | £ |
> |---|---:|
> | Operating profit (P&L) | X |
> | Add depreciation | X |
> | Loss (profit) on sale of fixed assets | X |
> | (Increase)/decrease in stocks | (X)/X |
> | (Increase)/decrease in debtors | (X)/X |
> | Increase/(decrease) in creditors | X/(X) |
> | Net cash flow from operating activities | X |

1.7 It is important to understand why certain items are added and others subtracted. Note the following points.

(a) Depreciation is not a cash expense, but is deducted in arriving at the profit figure in the profit and loss account. It makes sense, therefore, to eliminate it by adding it back.

(b) By the same logic, a loss on a disposal of a fixed asset (arising through underprovision of depreciation) needs to be added back and a profit deducted.

(c) An increase in stocks means less cash - you have spent cash on buying stock.

(d) An increase in debtors means debtors have not paid as much, therefore less cash.

Part E: Financial statements

(e) If we pay off creditors, causing the figure to decrease, again we have less cash.

> **Exam focus point**
>
> You will probably need to use the **indirect method** in examination questions based around FRS 1 (see below).

FRS 1 *Cash flow statements* (revised)

1.8 FRS 1 sets out the structure of a cash flow statement and it also sets the minimum level of disclosure. Examination questions are likely to be computational, but some discussion and interpretation may be required.

1.9 In October 1996 the ASB issued a revised version of FRS 1 *Cash flow statements*. The revision of FRS 1 was part of a normal process of revision, but it also responded to various criticisms of the original FRS 1.

Objective

1.10 The FRS begins with the following statement.

> 'The objective of this FRS is to ensure that reporting entities falling within its scope:
>
> (a) Report their cash generation and cash absorption for a period by highlighting the significant components of cash flow in a way that facilitates comparison of the cash flow performance of different businesses.
>
> (b) Provide information that assists in the assessment of their liquidity, solvency and financial adaptability.'

Scope

1.11 The FRS applies to all financial statements intended to give a true and fair view of the financial position and profit or loss (or income and expenditure), except those of various exempt bodies in group accounts situations or where the content of the financial statement is governed by other statutes or regulatory regimes. In addition, small entities are excluded as defined by companies legislation.

Format of the cash flow statement

1.12 An example is given of the format of a cash flow statement for a single company and this is reproduced below.

1.13 A cash flow statement should list its cash flows for the period classified under the following **standard headings**:

(a) **Operating activities** (using either the direct or indirect method)
(b) **Returns on investments and servicing of finance**
(c) **Taxation**
(d) **Capital expenditure** and financial investment
(e) **Acquisitions and disposals**
(f) **Equity dividends paid**
(g) **Management of liquid resources**
(h) **Financing**

20: Cash flow statements

The last two headings can be shown in a single section provided a subtotal is given for each heading. Acquisitions and disposals are not on your syllabus; the heading is included here for completeness.

1.14 Individual categories of inflows and outflows under the standard headings should be disclosed separately either in the cash flow statements or in a note to it unless they are allowed to be shown net. Cash inflows and outflows may be shown net if they relate to the management of liquid resources or financing and the inflows and outflows:

(a) Relate in substance to a single financing transaction (unlikely to be a concern in Paper 1.1).

(b) Or are due to short maturities and high turnover occurring from rollover or reissue (for example, short-term deposits).

The requirement to show cash inflows and outflows separately does not apply to cash flows relating to operating activities.

1.15 Each cash flow should be classified according to the substance of the transaction giving rise to it.

Links to other primary statements

1.16 Because the information given by a cash flow statement is best appreciated in the context of the information given by the other primary statements, the FRS requires **two reconciliations**, between:

(a) **Operating profit and the net cash flow from operating activities**
(b) **The movement in cash in the period and the movement in net debt**.

Neither reconciliation forms part of the cash flow statement but each may be given either adjoining the statement or in a separate note.

1.17 The reconciliation in point (a) above has already been given in the formula to learn following paragraph 1.6.

1.18 The **movement in net debt** should identify the following components and reconcile these to the opening and closing balance sheet amount:

(a) The cash flows of the entity
(b) Other non-cash changes
(c) The recognition of changes in market value and exchange rate movements

Definitions

1.19 The FRS includes the following important definitions (only those of direct concern to your syllabus are included here). Note particularly the definitions of cash and liquid resources.

(a) An **active market** is a market of sufficient depth to absorb the investment held without a significant effect on the price. (This definition affects the definition of liquid resources below.)

(b) **Cash** is cash in hand and deposits repayable on demand with any qualifying financial institution, less overdrafts from any qualifying financial institution repayable on demand. Deposits are repayable on demand if they can be withdrawn at any time without notice and without penalty or if a maturity or period of notice of not more

Part E: Financial statements

than 24 hours or one working day has been agreed. Cash includes cash in hand and deposit denominated in foreign currencies.

(c) **Cash flow** is an increase or decrease in an amount of cash.

(d) **Liquid resources** are current asset investments held as readily disposable stores of value. A readily disposable investment is one that:

 (i) Is disposable by the reporting entity without curtailing or disrupting its business

 (ii) Is either:

 (1) Readily convertible into known amounts of cash at or close to its carrying amount, or

 (2) Traded in an active market.

(e) **Net debt** is the borrowings of the reporting entity less cash and liquid resources. Where cash and liquid resources exceed the borrowings of the entity reference should be to 'net funds' rather than to 'net debt'.

(f) **Overdraft** is a borrowing facility repayable on demand that is used by drawing on a current account with a qualifying financial institution.

Classification of cash flows by standard heading

1.20 The FRS looks at each of the cash flow categories in turn.

Operating activities

1.21 Cash flows from operating activities are in general the cash effects of transactions and other events relating to operating or trading activities, normally shown in the profit and loss account in arriving at operating profit. They include cash flows in respect of operating items relating to provisions, whether or not the provision was included in operating profit.

1.22 A reconciliation between the **operating profit** reported in the profit and loss account and the **net cash flow from operating activities** should be given either adjoining the cash flow statement or as a note. The reconciliation is not part of the cash flow statement: if adjoining the cash flow statement, it should be clearly labelled and kept separate. The reconciliation should disclose separately the movements in stocks, debtors and creditors related to operating activities and other differences between cash flows and profits.

> **Exam focus point**
>
> You *must* know the **reconciliation** and **format** of the cash flow statement, even if you don't know any of the other notes. When you come to revise, skip over paragraphs 1.23-1.37 and go straight to the example in paragraph 1.38.

Returns on investments and servicing of finance

1.23 These are receipts resulting from the ownership of an investment and payments to providers of finance and non-equity shareholders (eg the holders of preference shares).

1.24 Cash inflows from returns on investments and servicing of finance include:

 (a) Interest received, including any related tax recovered
 (b) Dividends received, net of any tax credits

1.25 Cash outflows from returns on investments and servicing of finance include:

(a) Interest paid (even if capitalised), including any tax deducted and paid to the relevant tax authority.

(b) Cash flows that are treated as finance costs (this will include issue costs on debt and non-equity share capital).

(c) The interest element of finance lease rental payments.

(d) Dividends paid on non-equity shares of the entity.

Taxation

1.26 These are cash flows to or from taxation authorities in respect of the reporting entity's revenue and capital profits. VAT and other sales taxes are discussed below.

(a) Taxation cash inflows include cash receipts from the relevant tax authority of tax rebates, claims or returns of overpayments.

(b) Taxation cash outflows include cash payments to the relevant tax authority of tax, including payments of advance corporation tax.

Capital expenditure and financial investment **June 2002**

1.27 These cash flows are those related to the acquisition or disposal of any fixed asset other than one required to be classified under 'acquisitions and disposals' (discussed below), and any current asset investment not included in liquid resources (also dealt with below). If no cash flows relating to financial investment fall to be included under this heading the caption may be reduced to 'capital expenditure'.

1.28 The cash inflows here include:

(a) Receipts from sales or disposals of property, plant or equipment.
(b) Receipts from the repayment of the reporting entity's loans to other entities.

1.29 Cash outflows in this category include:

(a) Payments to acquire property, plant or equipment
(b) Loans made by the reporting entity

Acquisitions and disposals

1.30 These cash flows are related to the acquisition or disposal of any trade or business, or of an investment in an entity that is either an associate, a joint venture, or a subsidiary undertaking (**these group matters are beyond the scope of your syllabus**).

(a) Cash inflows here include receipts from sales of trades or businesses.
(b) Cash outflows here include payments to acquire trades or businesses.

Equity dividends paid

1.31 The cash outflows are dividends paid on the reporting entity's equity shares, excluding any advance corporation tax.

Part E: Financial statements

Management of liquid resources

1.32 This section should include cash flows in respect of liquid resources as defined above. Each entity should explain what it includes as liquid resources and any changes in its policy. The cash flows in this section can be shown in a single section with those under 'financing' provided that separate subtotals for each are given.

1.33 Cash inflows include:

   (a) Withdrawals from short-term deposits not qualifying as cash

   (b) Inflows from disposal or redemption of any other investments held as liquid resources

1.34 Cash outflows include:

   (a) Payments into short-term deposits not qualifying as cash
   (b) Outflows to acquire any other investments held as liquid resources

Financing

1.35 Financing cash flows comprise receipts or repayments of principal from or to external providers of finance. The cash flows in this section can be shown in a single section with those under 'management of liquid resources' provided that separate subtotals for each are given.

1.36 Financing cash inflows include:

   (a) Receipts from issuing shares or other equity instruments

   (b) Receipts from issuing debentures, loans and from other long-term and short-term borrowings (other than overdrafts)

1.37 Financing cash outflows include:

   (a) Repayments of amounts borrowed (other than overdrafts)
   (b) The capital element of finance lease rental payments
   (c) Payments to reacquire or redeem the entity's shares
   (d) Payments of expenses or commission on any issue of equity shares

1.38 EXAMPLE: SINGLE COMPANY

The following example is provided by the standard for a single company.

XYZ LIMITED
CASH FLOW STATEMENT FOR THE YEAR ENDED 31 DECEMBER 1996

Reconciliation of operating profit to net cash inflow from operating activities

	£'000
Operating profit	6,022
Depreciation charges	899
Increase in stocks	(194)
Increase in debtors	(72)
Increase in creditors	234
Net cash inflow from operating activities	6,899

CASH FLOW STATEMENT

	£'000
Net cash inflow from operating activities	6,889
Returns on investments and servicing of finance (note 1)	2,999
Taxation	(2,922)
Capital expenditure (note 1)	(1,525)
	5,441
Equity dividends paid	(2,417)
	3,024
Management of liquid resources (note 1)	(450)
Financing (note 1)	57
Increase in cash	2,631

Reconciliation of net cash flow to movement in net debt (note 2)

	£'000	£'000
Increase in cash in the period	2,631	
Cash to repurchase debenture	149	
Cash used to increase liquid resources	450	
Change in net debt*		3,230
Net debt at 1.1.96		(2,903)
Net funds at 31.12.96		327

*In this example all changes in net debt are cash flows.

The reconciliation of operating profit to net cash flows from operating activities can be shown in a note.

NOTES TO THE CASH FLOW STATEMENT

1 *Gross cash flows*

	£'000	£'000
Returns on investments and servicing of finance		
Interest received	3,011	
Interest paid	(12)	
		2,999
Capital expenditure		
Payments to acquire intangible fixed assets	(71)	
Payments to acquire tangible fixed assets	(1,496)	
Receipts from sales of tangible fixed assets	42	
		(1,525)
Management of liquid resources		
Purchase of treasury bills	(650)	
Sale of treasury bills	200	
		(450)
Financing		
Issue of ordinary share capital	211	
Repurchase of debenture loan	(149)	
Expenses paid in connection with share issues	(5)	
		57

Note. These gross cash flows can be shown on the face of the cash flow statement, but it may sometimes be neater to show them as a note like this.

Part E: Financial statements

2   Analysis of changes in net debt

	As at 1 Jan 1996 £'000	Cash flows £'000	Other changes £'000	At 31 Dec 1996 £'000
Cash in hand, at bank	42	847		889
Overdrafts	(1,784)	1,784		
		2,631		
Debt due within 1 year	(149)	149	(230)	(230)
Debt due after 1 year	(1,262)		230	(1,032)
Current asset investments	250	450		700
Total	(2,903)	3,230	-	327

Question 2
Close the book for a moment and jot down the format of the cash flow statement.

2   PREPARING A CASH FLOW STATEMENT   Pilot paper, June 2002, June 2003

2.1   In essence, preparing a cash flow statement is very straightforward. You should therefore simply learn the format given above and apply the steps noted in the example below. Note that the following items are treated in a way that might seem confusing, but the treatment is logical if you think in terms of **cash**.

(a) Increase in stock is treated as **negative** (in brackets). This is because it represents a cash **outflow**; cash is being spent on stock.

(b) An increase in debtors would be treated as **negative** for the same reasons; more debtors means less cash.

(c) By contrast an increase in creditors is **positive** because cash is being retained and not used to pay off creditors. There is therefore more of it.

2.2   EXAMPLE: PREPARATION OF A CASH FLOW STATEMENT

Kane Ltd's profit and loss account for the year ended 31 December 20X2 and balance sheets at 31 December 20X1 and 31 December 20X2 were as follows.

KANE LIMITED
PROFIT AND LOSS ACCOUNT FOR THE YEAR ENDED 31 DECEMBER 20X2

	£'000	£'000
Sales		720
Raw materials consumed	70	
Staff costs	94	
Depreciation	118	
Loss on disposal	18	
		300
Operating profit		420
Interest payable		28
Profit before tax		392
Taxation		124
		268
Dividend		72
Profit retained for year		196
Balance brought forward		490
		686

20: Cash flow statements

KANE LIMITED
BALANCE SHEETS AS AT 31 DECEMBER

	20X2		20X1	
	£'000	£'000	£'000	£'000
Fixed assets				
Cost		1,596		1,560
Depreciation		318		224
		1,278		1,336
Current assets				
Stock	24		20	
Trade debtors	66		50	
Recoverable corporation tax	10		8	
Bank	48		56	
	148		134	
Current liabilities				
Trade creditors	12		6	
Taxation	102		86	
Proposed dividend	30		24	
	144		116	
Working capital		4		18
		1,282		1,354
Long-term liabilities				
Long-term loans		200		500
		1,082		854
Share capital		360		340
Share premium		36		24
Profit and loss		686		490
		1,082		854

During the year, the company paid £90,000 for a new piece of machinery.

Required

Prepare a cash flow statement for Kane Ltd for the year ended 31 December 20X2 in accordance with the requirements of FRS 1 (revised).

2.3 SOLUTION

Step 1. Set out the proforma cash flow statement with all the headings required by FRS 1 (revised). You should leave plenty of space. Ideally, use three or more sheets of paper, one for the main statement, one for the notes (particularly if you have a separate note for the gross cash flows) and one for your workings. It is obviously essential to know the formats very well.

Step 2. Complete the reconciliation of operating profit to net cash inflow as far as possible. When preparing the statement from balance sheets, you will usually have to calculate such items as depreciation, loss on sale of fixed assets and profit for the year (see Step 4).

Step 3. Calculate the figures for tax paid, dividends paid, purchase or sale of fixed assets, issue of shares and repayment of loans if these are not already given to you (as they may be). Note that you may not be given the tax charge in the profit and loss account. You will then have to assume that the tax paid in the year is last year's year-end provision and calculate the charge as the balancing figure.

Step 4. If you are not given the profit figure, open up a working for the profit and loss account. Using the opening and closing balances, the taxation charge and

Part E: Financial statements

dividends paid and proposed, you will be able to calculate profit for the year as the balancing figure to put in the statement.

Step 5. Complete Note 1, the gross cash flows, if asked for it. Alternatively, the information may go straight into the statement.

Step 6. You will now be able to complete the statement by slotting in the figures given or calculated.

Step 7. Complete Note 2, the analysis of changes in net debt, if asked.

KANE LIMITED
CASH FLOW STATEMENT FOR THE YEAR ENDED 31 DECEMBER 20X2

Reconciliation of operating profit to net cash inflow

	£'000
Operating profit	420
Depreciation charges	118
Loss on sale of tangible fixed assets	18
Increase in stocks	(4)
Increase in debtors	(16)
Increase in creditors	6
Net cash inflow from operating activities	542

CASH FLOW STATEMENT

	£'000	£'000
Net cash flows from operating activities		542
Returns on investment and servicing of finance		
Interest paid		(28)
Taxation		
Corporation tax paid (W1)		(110)
Capital expenditure		
Payments to acquire tangible fixed assets	(90)	
Receipts from sales of tangible fixed assets	12	
Net cash outflow from capital expenditure		(78)
		326
Equity dividends paid (72 – 30 + 24)		(66)
		260
Financing		
Issues of share capital (360 + 36 – 340 – 24)	32	
Long-term loans repaid (500 – 200)	(300)	
Net cash outflow from financing		(268)
Decrease in cash		(8)

NOTES TO THE CASH FLOW STATEMENT

Analysis of changes in net debt

	At 1 Jan 20X2 £'000	Cash flows £'000	At 31 Dec 20X2 £'000
Cash in hand, at bank	56	(8)	48
Debt due after 1 year	(500)	300	(200)
Total	(444)	292	(152)

Workings

1 Corporation tax paid

	£'000
Opening CT payable (86 – 8)	78
Charge for year	124
Net CT payable at 31.12.X2 (102 – 10)	(92)
Paid	110

2 Fixed asset disposals

COST

	£'000		£'000
At 1.1.X2	1,560	At 31.12.X2	1,596
Purchases	90	Disposals	54
	1,650		1,650

ACCUMULATED DEPRECIATION

	£'000		£'000
At 31.1.X2	318	At 1.1.X2	224
Depreciation on disposals	24	Charge for year	118
	342		342

	£'000
NBV of disposals	30
Net loss reported	(18)
Proceeds of disposals	12

Question 3

The summarised accounts of Rene plc for the year ended 31 December 20X8 are as follows.

RENE PLC
BALANCE SHEET AS AT 31 DECEMBER 20X8

	20X8 £'000	20X8 £'000	20X7 £'000	20X7 £'000
Fixed assets				
Tangible assets		628		514
Current assets				
Stocks	214		210	
Debtors	168		147	
Cash	7		-	
	389		357	
Creditors: amounts falling due within one year				
Trade creditors	136		121	
Tax payable	39		28	
Dividends payable	18		16	
Overdraft	-		14	
	193		179	
Net current assets		196		178
Total assets less current liabilities		824		692
Creditors: amounts falling due after more than one year				
10% debentures		(80)		(50)
		744		642
Capital and reserves				
Share capital (£1 ords)		250		200
Share premium account		70		60
Revaluation reserve		110		100
Profit and loss account		314		282
		744		642

Part E: Financial statements

RENE PLC
PROFIT AND LOSS ACCOUNT
FOR THE YEAR ENDED 31 DECEMBER 20X8

	£'000
Sales	600
Cost of sales	(319)
Gross profit	281
Other expenses (including depreciation of £42,000)	(194)
Profit before tax	87
Tax	(31)
Profit after tax	56
Dividends	(24)
Retained profit for the year	32

You are additionally informed that there have been no disposals of fixed assets during the year. New debentures were issued on 1 January 20X8. Wages for the year amounted to £86,000.

Required

Produce a cash flow statement using the direct method suitable for inclusion in the financial statements, as per FRS 1 (revised).

Answer

RENE PLC
CASH FLOW STATEMENT
FOR THE YEAR ENDED 31 DECEMBER 20X8

	£'000	£'000
Operating activities		
Cash received from customers (W1)	579	
Cash payments to suppliers (W2)	(366)	
Cash payments to and on behalf of employees	(86)	
		127
Returns on investments and servicing of finance		
Interest paid		(8)
Taxation		
UK corporation tax paid (W5)		(20)
Capital expenditure		
Purchase of tangible fixed assets (W6)	(146)	
Net cash outflow from capital expenditure		(146)
		(47)
Equity dividends paid (W4)		(22)
Financing		
Issue of share capital	60	
Issue of debentures	30	
Net cash inflow from financing		90
Increase in cash		21

NOTES TO THE CASHFLOW STATEMENT

1 *Reconciliation of operating profit to net cash inflow from operating activities*

	£'000
Operating profit (87 + 8)	95
Depreciation	42
Increase in stock	(4)
Increase in debtors	(21)
Increase in creditors	15
	127

20: Cash flow statements

2 *Reconciliation of net cash flow to movement in net debt*

	£'000
Net cash inflow for the period	21
Cash received from debenture issue	(30)
Change in net debt	(9)
Net debt at 1 January 20X8	(64)
Net debt at 31 December 20X8	(73)

3 *Analysis of changes in net debt*

	At 1 January 20X8 £'000	Cash flows £'000	At 31 December 20X8 £'000
Cash at bank	-	7	7
Overdrafts	(14)	14	-
		21	
Debt due after 1 year	(50)	(30)	(80)
Total	(64)	(9)	(73)

Workings

1 *Cash received from customers*

DEBTORS CONTROL ACCOUNT

	£'000		£'000
B/f	147	Cash received (bal)	579
Sales	600	C/f	168
	747		747

2 *Cash paid to suppliers*

CREDITORS CONTROL ACCOUNT

	£'000		£'000
Cash paid (bal)	366	B/f	121
C/f	136	Purchases (W3)	381
	502		502

3 *Purchases*

	£'000
Cost of sales	319
Opening stock	(210)
Closing stock	214
Expenses (194 – 42 – 86 – 8 debenture interest)	58
	381

4 *Dividends*

DIVIDENDS

	£'000		£'000
∴ Dividends paid	22	Balance b/f	16
Balance c/f	18	Dividend for year	24
	40		40

5 *Taxation*

TAXATION

	£'000		£'000
∴ Tax paid	20	Balance b/f	28
Balance c/f	39	Charge for year	31
	59		59

6 *Purchase of fixed assets*

	£'000
Opening fixed assets	514
Less depreciation	(42)
Add revaluation (110 – 100)	10
	482
Closing fixed assets	628
Difference = additions	146

Part E: Financial statements

The advantages of cash flow accounting

2.4 The advantages of cash flow accounting are as follows.

(a) Survival in business depends on the ability to generate cash. Cash flow accounting directs attention towards this critical issue.

(b) Cash flow is more comprehensive than 'profit' which is dependent on accounting conventions and concepts.

(c) Creditors (long and short-term) are more interested in an entity's ability to repay them than in its profitability. Whereas 'profits' might indicate that cash is likely to be available, cash flow accounting is more direct with its message.

(d) Cash flow reporting provides a better means of comparing the results of different companies than traditional profit reporting.

(e) Cash flow reporting satisfies the needs of all users better.

   (i) For management, it provides the sort of information on which decisions should be taken: (in management accounting, 'relevant costs' to a decision are future cash flows); traditional profit accounting does not help with decision-making.

   (ii) For shareholders and auditors, cash flow accounting can provide a satisfactory basis for stewardship accounting.

   (iii) As described previously, the information needs of creditors and employees will be better served by cash flow accounting.

(f) Cash flow forecasts are easier to prepare, as well as more useful, than profit forecasts.

(g) They can in some respects be audited more easily than accounts based on the accruals concept.

(h) The accruals concept is confusing, and cash flows are more easily understood.

(i) Cash flow accounting should be both retrospective, and also include a forecast for the future. This is of great information value to all users of accounting information.

(j) Forecasts can subsequently be monitored by the publication of variance statements which compare actual cash flows against the forecast.

(k) Management need to control cash flows and the cash flow statement shows exactly which activities are generating and which using cash.

Question 4

Can you think of some possible disadvantages of cash flow accounting?

Answers

The main disadvantages of cash accounting are essentially the advantages of accruals accounting (proper matching of related items). There is also the practical problem that few businesses keep historical cash flow information in the form needed to prepare a historical cash flow statement and so extra record keeping is likely to be necessary.

Chapter roundup

- **Cash flow statements** were made compulsory for companies because it was recognised that accounting profit is not the only indicator of a company's performance. FRS 1 *Cash flow statements* was revised in October 1996.

- Cash flow statements concentrate on the **sources** and **uses of cash** and are a useful indicator of a company's liquidity and solvency.

- You need to learn the **format** of the statement; setting out the format is an essential first stage in preparing the statement but it will only really sink in with more question practice.

- Remember the **step-by-step** preparation procedure and use it for all the questions you practise.

Quick quiz

1 What is the objective of FRS 1?

2 Which of the following headings is not a classification of cash flows in FRS 1?

    A   Operating activities
    B   Financial investment
    C   Administration
    D   Financing

3 What is the 'indirect method' of preparing a cash flow statement?

4 Set out the seven steps required in preparing a cash flow statement.

5 What are the advantages of cash flow accounting?

Answers to quick quiz

1 To provide information to users about the company's ability to generate cash and cash absorption.

2 C. Administration costs are a classification in the profit and loss account, not the cash flow statement.

3 The operating cash flow is arrived at by adjusting net profits (or loss) for non-cash items and changes in stock, trade debtors and trade creditors.

4 See paragraph 2.3.

5 See paragraph 2.4.

Now try the question below from the Exam Question Bank

Question to try	Level	Marks	Time
32	Full exam	10	18 mins

Chapter 21

GROUP ACCOUNTS

	Topic list	Syllabus reference
1	Definitions	5(d)
2	Exclusion of subsidiary undertakings from group accounts	5(d)
3	Exemption from the requirement to prepare group accounts	5(d)
4	Content of group accounts	5(d)
5	Cancellation and part cancellation	5(d)
6	Minority interests	5(d)
7	Goodwill arising on consolidation	5(d)
8	A technique of consolidation	5(d)
9	Summary: consolidated balance sheet	5(d)

Introduction

This is a key area in the syllabus. In order to consolidate a subsidiary's results you need to know what a subsidiary is and the various rules applicable to subsidiaries.

Study guide

Section 24 – Basic consolidated accounts

- Define parent company, subsidiary company and group.
- Explain the provisions of FRS 2 Accounting for Subsidiary Undertakings and the Companies Acts defining which companies must be consolidated.
- Prepare a consolidated balance sheet for a parent with one wholly-owned subsidiary (no goodwill arising).
- Explain how to calculate the retained profit balance for the consolidated balance sheet.
- Explain how other reserves (share premium account and revaluation reserve) are dealt with on consolidation.
- Introduce the concept of goodwill on acquisition and illustrate the effect on the consolidated balance sheet.
- Explain the need to amortise goodwill and illustrate in the workings.
- Explain a methodical approach to calculating the necessary figures for the consolidated balance sheet.
- Introduce the concept of minority interests in subsidiaries and illustrate the effect on the consolidated balance sheet.
- Explain how the calculation of the minority interest is made in the workings.

Exam guide

This subject is likely to come up as a question in Part B. One possibility will be a consolidation, the other may require you to discuss whether the company is a subsidiary or not. You can also expect a few MCQs testing areas such as minority interests.

1 DEFINITIONS

1.1 You will probably know that many large companies actually consist of several companies controlled by one central or administrative company. Together these companies are called a **group**. The controlling company, called the parent or **holding company**, will own some or all of the shares in the other companies, called subsidiary and associated companies.

1.2 There are many reasons for businesses to operate as groups; for the goodwill associated with the names of the subsidiaries, for tax or legal purposes and so forth. Company law requires that the results of a group should be presented as a whole. Unfortunately, it is not possible simply to add all the results together and this chapter and those following will teach you how to **consolidate** all the results of companies within a group.

1.3 In traditional accounting terminology, a **group of companies** consists of a **holding company** (or parent company) and one or more **subsidiary companies** which are controlled by the holding company. The CA 1989 widened this definition. (The Act amended the CA 1985 and references below are to the amended sections.) As a result, FRS 2 *Accounting for subsidiary undertakings* was published in July 1992 by the ASB, incorporating the CA 1989 changes.

Exam focus point
If you are revising, go straight to the summary at the end of this section.

1.4 There are **two** definitions of a group in company law. One uses the terms 'holding company' and 'subsidiary' and applies for general purposes. The other is wider and applies **only for accounting purposes**. It uses the terms 'parent undertaking' and 'subsidiary undertaking'. The purpose of this widening of the group for accounting purposes was to curb the practice of structuring a group in such a way that not all companies or ventures within it had to be consolidated. This is an example of off balance sheet financing and has been used extensively to make consolidated accounts look better than is actually justified.

1.5 We are only really interested in the accounting definitions of parent and subsidiary undertaking here: they automatically include 'holding companies' and 'subsidiaries' under the general definition.

Parent and subsidiary undertakings: definition

1.6 FRS 2 states that an undertaking is the **parent undertaking** of another undertaking (**a subsidiary undertaking**) if any of the following apply.

Part E: Financial statements

> **PARENT UNDERTAKING**
>
> (a) It holds a **majority of the voting rights** in the undertaking.
>
> (b) It is a **member** of the undertaking and has the right to **appoint or remove directors** holding a majority of the voting rights at meetings of the board on all, or substantially all, matters.
>
> (c) It has the right to exercise a **dominant influence** over the undertaking:
>
>   (i) By virtue of provisions contained in the undertaking's memorandum or articles
>
>   (ii) By virtue of a control contract (in writing, authorised by the memorandum or articles of the controlled undertaking, permitted by law)
>
> (d) It is a member of the undertaking and controls alone, under an agreement with other shareholders or members, a majority of the voting rights in the undertaking.
>
> (e) It has a **participating interest** in the undertaking and one of two things apply.
>
>   (i) It actually exercises a dominant influence over the undertaking.
>   (ii) It and the undertaking are managed on a unified basis.
>
> (f) A parent undertaking is also treated as the parent undertaking of the subsidiary undertakings of its subsidiary undertakings.

1.7 This replaced the previous criterion of owning a majority of equity with one of holding a majority of voting rights. Also, the board is considered to be controlled if the holding company has the right to appoint directors with a majority of the voting rights on the board (not just to appoint a simple majority of the directors, regardless of their voting rights).

Other definitions

1.8 The above definition is extremely important and you may be asked to apply it to a given situation in an exam. It depends in turn, however, on the definition of various terms which are included in Paragraph 1.6.

Participating interest

1.9 FRS 2 states that a **participating** interest is an interest held by an undertaking in the shares of another undertaking which it holds on a **long-term basis** for the purpose of securing a contribution to its activities by the exercise of control or influence arising from or related to that interest.

(a) A holding of **20% or more** of the shares of an undertaking is **presumed** to be a participating interest unless the contrary is shown.

(b) An interest in shares includes an interest which is convertible into an interest in shares, and includes an option to acquire shares or any interest which is convertible into shares.

(c) An interest held on behalf of an undertaking shall be treated as held by that undertaking (ie all group holdings must be aggregated to determine if a subsidiary exists).

1.10 A 'participating interest', like an investment in a 'subsidiary undertaking', **need not be in a company,** because an 'undertaking' means one of three things.

(a) A body corporate

(b) A partnership

(c) An unincorporated association carrying on a trade or business, with or without a view to profit

1.11 'Shares' therefore means **allotted** shares or for undertakings without share capital, the **right to share** in the **capital and profits** and the corresponding **liability to meet losses and debts on winding up.**

Dominant influence

> **KEY TERM**
>
> FRS 2 defines **dominant influence** as influence that can be exercised to achieve the operating and financial policies desired by the holder of the influence, notwithstanding the rights or influence of any other party.

1.12 The standard then distinguishes between the two different situations involving dominant influence.

(a) In the context of Paragraph 1.6(c) above, **the right to exercise a dominant influence** means that the holder has a right to give directions with respect to the operating and financial policies of another undertaking with which its directors are obliged to comply, whether or not they are for the benefit of that undertaking.

(b) **The actual exercise of dominant influence** is the exercise of an influence that achieves the result that the operating and financial policies of the undertaking influenced are set in accordance with the wishes of the holder of the influence and for the holder's benefit whether or not those wishes are explicit. The actual exercise of dominant influence is identified by its effect in practice rather than by the way in which it is exercised.

1.13 There are four other important definitions.

> (a) **Control** is the ability of an undertaking to direct the financial and operating policies of another undertaking with a view to gaining economic benefits from its activities.
>
> (b) An **interest held on a long-term basis** is an interest which is held other than exclusively with a view to subsequent resale.
>
> (c) An **interest held exclusively with a view to subsequent resale** is either:
>
> (i) An interest for which a purchaser has been identified or is being sought, and which is reasonably expected to be disposed of within approximately one year of its date of acquisition, *or*
>
> (ii) An interest that was acquired as a result of the enforcement of a security, unless the interest has become part of the continuing activities of the group or the holder acts as if it intends the interest to become so
>
> (d) **Managed on a unified basis:** two or more undertakings are managed on a unified basis if the whole of the operations of the undertakings are integrated and they are

Part E: Financial statements

> managed as a single unit. Unified management does not arise solely because one undertaking manages another.

The requirement to consolidate

1.14 FRS 2 requires a parent undertaking to prepare consolidated financial statements for its group unless it uses one of the exemptions available in the standard (see Section 2).

> **KEY TERM**
>
> **Consolidation** is defined as: 'The process of adjusting and combining financial information from the individual financial statements of a parent undertaking and its subsidiary undertaking to prepare consolidated financial statements that present financial information for the group as a single economic entity.'

1.15 **Section summary**

At this stage, it will probably be helpful to recap. An undertaking S is a subsidiary undertaking of H if:

(a) S is a **subsidiary** of H (general definition), ie H is a member of S and *either* holds or controls > 50% of the voting rights *or* controls the board; OR

(b) S is a **subsidiary** (general definition) because it is a **subsidiary of a subsidiary** of H (ie S is a sub-subsidiary); OR

(c) H has the right to exercise a **dominant influence** over S (laid down in the memorandum or articles or a control contract); OR

(d) H has a **participating interest** in S **and** either **actually** exercises a **dominant influence** over S *or* H and S are managed on a unified basis.

∴ **Special treatment: consolidate**

2 EXCLUSION OF SUBSIDIARY UNDERTAKINGS FROM GROUP ACCOUNTS

2.1 S 229 CA 1985 (as amended by the CA 1989) provides that a **subsidiary may be omitted** from the consolidated accounts of a group if any of the following apply.

(a) In the opinion of the directors, its inclusion 'is **not material** for the purpose of giving a true and fair view; but two or more undertakings may be excluded only if they are not material taken together'.

(b) There are **severe long-term restrictions** in exercising the parent company's rights.

(c) The holding is **exclusively for resale.**

(d) The information cannot be obtained 'without **disproportionate expense** or undue delay'.

2.2 If in the opinion of the directors, a subsidiary undertaking's consolidation is undesirable because the business of the holding company and subsidiary are so different that they cannot reasonably be treated as a single undertaking, then that undertaking *must* be excluded.

21: Group accounts

> 'This .... does not apply merely because some of the undertakings are industrial, some commercial and some provide services, or because they carry on industrial or commercial activities involving different products or provide different services.'

2.3 FRS 2 states that a **subsidiary must be excluded** from consolidation in the following circumstances.

(a) Severe long-term restrictions are **substantially hindering the exercise** of the **parent's rights** over the subsidiary's assets or management.

(b) The group's interest in the subsidiary undertaking is held **exclusively with a view to subsequent resale** *and* the subsidiary has **not been consolidated previously**.

(c) The subsidiary undertaking's **activities are so different** from those of other undertakings to be included in the consolidation that its inclusion would be incompatible with the obligation to give a true and fair view.

The FRS requires the circumstances in which subsidiary undertakings are to be excluded from consolidation to be interpreted **strictly**.

2.4 Where a subsidiary is excluded from group accounts, FRS 2 lays down supplementary provisions on the disclosures and accounting treatment required.

2.5 Where a subsidiary is excluded on grounds of **dissimilar activities** (which should be exceptional), the group accounts should include separate financial statements for that subsidiary including:

(a) A note of the **holding company's interest**

(b) Details of **intra-group balances**

(c) The **nature of its transactions** with the rest of the group

(d) A **reconciliation of the subsidiary's** results (as shown separately) with the value in the consolidated accounts for the 'group's investment in the subsidiary'

In the consolidated accounts, the excluded subsidiary should be accounted for by the **equity method** of accounting (as though it were an associated company). The details of equity accounting are beyond the scope of your syllabus.

2.6 Subsidiary undertakings excluded from consolidation because of **severe long-term restrictions** are to be treated as **fixed asset investments**. They are to be included at their carrying amount when the restrictions came into force, and no further accruals are to be made for profits or losses of those subsidiary undertakings, unless the parent undertaking still exercises significant influence. In the latter case they are to be treated as associated undertakings.

2.7 The following information should be **disclosed** in the group accounts.

(a) Its **net assets**

(b) Its **profit or loss** for the period

(c) Any amounts included in the **consolidated profit and loss account** in respect of:
 (i) **Dividends received** by the holding company from the subsidiary
 (ii) **Writing down the value of the investment**

Part E: Financial statements

2.8 If **control is temporary** (the investment is held purely for resale), the temporary investment should be included under **current assets** in the consolidated balance sheet at the lower of cost and net realisable value.

2.9 In all cases given above, FRS 2 states that the consolidated accounts should show:

(a) The **reasons** for exclusion
(b) The **names** of subsidiaries excluded
(c) The **premium or discount on acquisition** not written off
(d) **Anything else required** by the Companies Acts

2.10 The CA 1985 requires that when consolidated group accounts are not prepared, or if any subsidiaries are excluded from the group accounts (for any of the reasons given above), a note to the accounts should be given:

(a) To explain the reasons why the subsidiaries are not dealt with in group accounts
(b) To disclose any auditors' qualifications in the accounts of the excluded subsidiaries

A note to the (holding) company's accounts (or the consolidated accounts, if any) should also state, for subsidiaries which are not consolidated in group accounts, the aggregate value of the total investment of the holding company in the subsidiaries, by way of the 'equity method' of valuation.

> **Exam focus point**
> You need to know the criteria for defining a subsidiary and the circumstances under which consolidation is (or is not) required. Do not worry about the alternative accounting treatments applicable when a company's results are not consolidated. They are included here as background.

2.11 **Section summary**

The following table summaries the rules relating to exclusion of a subsidiary.

Reason	Accounting treatment
• Severe long-term restrictions hindering exercise of parent's rights	B/S: equity method up to date of severe restrictions less amounts written off if permanent fall in value
	P&L a/c: dividends received only
• Held exclusively for subsequent resale; has never been consolidated	Current asset at the lower of cost and net realisable value
• Dissimilar activities	Equity method

3 EXEMPTION FROM THE REQUIREMENT TO PREPARE GROUP ACCOUNTS

3.1 The CA 1989 introduced a completely new provision **exempting some groups** from preparing consolidated accounts. There are two grounds.

(a) **Smaller groups** can claim exemptions on grounds of size (see below).

(b) **Parent companies** (*except* for listed companies) **whose immediate parent is established in an EU member country** need not prepare consolidated accounts. The accounts must give the name and country of incorporation of the parent and state the fact of the exemption. In addition, a copy of the audited consolidated accounts of the parent must be filed with the UK company's accounts. Minority shareholders can, however, require that consolidated accounts are prepared.

FRS 2 adds that exemption may be gained if all of the parent's subsidiary undertakings gain exemption under s 229 CA 1985 (see Paragraph 2.1).

3.2 The **exemption** from preparing consolidated accounts is **not available** to:

(a) Public companies

(b) Banking and insurance companies

(c) Authorised persons under the Financial Services Act 1986

(d) Companies belonging to a group containing a member of the above classes of undertaking

3.3 Any two of the following **size criteria** for small and medium-sized groups must be met.

	Small	**Medium-sized**
Aggregate turnover	≤ £2.8 million net/ £3.36 million gross	≤ £11.2 million net/ £13.44 million gross
Aggregate gross assets	≤ £1.4 million net/ £1.68 million gross	≤ £5.6 million net/ £6.72 million gross
Aggregate number of employees (average monthly)	≤ 50	≤ 250

3.4 The aggregates can be calculated either before (gross) or after (net) consolidation adjustments for intra-group sales, unrealised profit on stock and so on. The qualifying conditions must be met:

(a) In the case of the parent's first financial year, in that year
(b) In the case of any subsequent financial year, in that year and the preceding year

If the qualifying conditions were met in the preceding year but not in the current year, the exemption can be claimed. If, in the subsequent year, the conditions are met again, the exemption can still be claimed, but if they are not met, then the exemption is lost until the conditions are again met for the second of two successive years.

3.5 When the exemption is claimed, but the auditors believe that the company is not entitled to it, then they must state in their report that the company is in their opinion not entitled to the exemption and this report must be attached to the individual accounts of the company (ie no report is required when the company *is* entitled to the exemption).

4 CONTENT OF GROUP ACCOUNTS

4.1 The information contained in the individual accounts of a holding company and each of its subsidiaries does not give a picture of the group's activities as those of a single entity. To do this, a separate set of accounts can be prepared from the individual accounts. Remember that a group has no separate (legal) existence, except for accounting purposes.

4.2 There is more than one way of amalgamating the information in the individual accounts into a set of group accounts, but the most common way (and now the legally required way) is to prepare **consolidated accounts**. Consolidated accounts are one form of group accounts which combines the information contained in the separate accounts of a holding company

Part E: Financial statements

and its subsidiaries as if they were the accounts of a single entity. 'Group accounts' and 'consolidated accounts' are often used synonymously, and now that UK law **requires** group accounts to be consolidated accounts, this tendency will no doubt increase.

4.3 In simple terms a set of consolidated accounts is prepared by **adding together** the assets and liabilities of the holding company and each subsidiary. The **whole** of the assets and liabilities of each company are included, even though some subsidiaries may be only partly owned. The 'capital and reserves' side of the balance sheet will indicate how much of the net assets are attributable to the group and how much to outside investors in partly owned subsidiaries. These **outside investors** are known as **minority interests**.

4.4 The CA 1985 requires that group accounts should be prepared whenever a company:

(a) Is a parent company at the end of its financial year

(b) And is not itself a wholly owned subsidiary of a company incorporated in Great Britain.

4.5 Most parent companies present their own individual accounts and their group accounts in a single **package**. The package typically comprises:

(a) A **parent company balance sheet**, which will include 'investments in subsidiary undertakings' as an asset

(b) A **consolidated balance sheet**

(c) A **consolidated profit and loss** account

(d) A **consolidated cash flow statement**

It is not necessary to publish a parent company profit and loss account (s 230 CA 1985), provided the consolidated profit and loss account contains a note stating the profit or loss for the financial year dealt with in the accounts of the parent company and the fact that the statutory exemption is being relied on.

> **Exam focus point**
>
> You only need to be able to produce a simple consolidated balance sheet.

> **Question 1**
>
> During the time until your examination you should obtain as many sets of the published accounts of top quoted companies as possible. Examine the accounting policies in relation to subsidiary companies and consider how these policies are shown in the accounting and consolidation treatment.
>
> Alternatively (or additionally) you should attempt to obtain such information from the financial press, or from the websites of top companies.

5 CANCELLATION AND PART CANCELLATION

5.1 The preparation of a consolidated balance sheet, in a very simple form, consists of two procedures.

(a) Take the individual accounts of the holding company and each subsidiary and **cancel out items** which appear as an asset in one company and a liability in another.

(b) **Add together all the uncancelled assets** and liabilities throughout the group.

21: Group accounts

5.2 **Items requiring cancellation** may include the asset **'shares in subsidiary companies'** which appears in the parent company's accounts will be matched with the liability 'share capital' in the subsidiaries' accounts.

5.3 EXAMPLE: CANCELLATION

H Ltd has one subsidiary company, S Ltd. The balance sheets of the two companies on 31 December 20X6 are given below.

H LIMITED
BALANCE SHEET AS AT 31 DECEMBER 20X6

	£	£	£
Fixed assets			
Tangible assets			35,000
40,000 £1 shares in S Ltd at cost			40,000
			75,000
Current assets			
Stocks		16,000	
Debtors		8,000	
Cash at bank		1,000	
		25,000	
Current liabilities			
Creditors		14,000	
			11,000
			86,000
Capital and reserves			
70,000 £1 ordinary shares			70,000
Reserves			16,000
			86,000

S LIMITED
BALANCE SHEET AS AT 31 DECEMBER 20X6

	£	£	£
Fixed assets			
Tangible assets			45,000
Current assets			
Stocks		12,000	
Debtors		9,000	
		21,000	
Current liabilities			
Bank overdraft		3,000	
Creditors:		4,000	
		7,000	
			14,000
			59,000
Capital and reserves			
40,000 £1 ordinary shares			40,000
Reserves			19,000
			59,000

Prepare the consolidated balance sheet of H Ltd.

5.4 SOLUTION

The cancelling item is H Ltd's asset 'investment in shares of S Ltd' (£40,000) cancels with S Ltd's liability 'share capital' (£40,000).

Part E: Financial statements

The remaining assets and liabilities are added together to produce the following consolidated balance sheet.

H LIMITED
CONSOLIDATED BALANCE SHEET AS AT 31 DECEMBER 20X6

	£	£
Fixed assets		
Tangible assets		80,000
Current assets		
Stocks	28,000	
Debtors	17,000	
Cash at bank	1,000	
	46,000	
Current liabilities		
Bank overdraft	3,000	
Creditors	18,000	
	21,000	
		25,000
		105,000
Capital and reserves		
70,000 £1 ordinary shares		70,000
Reserves		35,000
		105,000

Notes on the example

5.5 (a) H Ltd's bank balance is not netted off with S Ltd's bank overdraft. To offset one against the other would be less informative and would conflict with the statutory principle that assets and liabilities should not be netted off.

(b) The share capital in the consolidated balance sheet is the share capital of the parent company alone. This must **always** be the case, no matter how complex the consolidation, because the share capital of subsidiary companies must **always** be a wholly cancelling item.

Part cancellation

5.6 An item may appear in the balance sheets of a parent company and its subsidiary, but not at the same amounts.

(a) The parent company may have acquired **shares in the subsidiary** at a price **greater or less than their nominal value**. The asset will appear in the parent company's accounts at cost, while the liability will appear in the subsidiary's accounts at nominal value. This raises the issue of **goodwill**, which is dealt with later in this chapter.

(b) Even if the parent company acquired shares at nominal value, it **may not** have **acquired all the shares of the subsidiary** (so the subsidiary may be only partly owned). This raises the issue of **minority interests**, which are also dealt with later in this chapter.

(c) One company may have **issued loan stock** of which a **proportion only** is taken up by the other company.

5.7 The following question illustrates the techniques needed to deal with the third item. The procedure is to cancel as far as possible. The remaining uncancelled amounts will appear in the consolidated balance sheet.

- **Uncancelled loan stock** will appear as a **liability of the group**.

Question 2

The balance sheets of H Ltd and of its subsidiary S Ltd have been made up to 30 June. H Ltd has owned all the ordinary shares and 40% of the loan stock of S Ltd since its incorporation.

H LIMITED
BALANCE SHEET AS AT 30 JUNE

	£	£
Fixed assets		
Tangible assets		120,000
Investment in S Ltd, at cost		
80,000 ordinary shares of £1 each		80,000
£20,000 of 12% loan stock in S Ltd		20,000
		220,000
Current assets		
Stocks	50,000	
Debtors	58,000	
Cash	4,000	
	112,000	
Creditors: amounts falling due within one year		
Creditors	47,000	
Taxation	15,000	
	62,000	
Net current assets		50,000
		270,000
Creditors: amounts falling due after more than one year		
10% loan stock		75,000
		195,000
Capital and reserves		
Ordinary shares of £1 each, fully paid		100,000
Reserves		95,000
		195,000

S LIMITED
BALANCE SHEET AS AT 30 JUNE

	£	£
Tangible fixed assets		100,000
Current assets		
Stocks	60,000	
Debtors	30,000	
Cash	6,000	
	96,000	
Creditors: amounts falling due within one year		
Creditors	28,000	
Taxation	12,000	
	38,000	
		58,000
		158,000
Creditors: amounts falling due after more than one year		
12% Loan stock		50,000
		108,000

Part E: Financial statements

Capital and reserves
80,000 ordinary shares of £1 each, fully paid — 80,000
Reserves — 28,000
108,000

Prepare the consolidated balance sheet of H Ltd.

Answer

H LIMITED
CONSOLIDATED BALANCE SHEET AS AT 30 JUNE

	£	£
Tangible fixed assets		220,000
Current assets		
Stocks	110,000	
Debtors	88,000	
Cash	10,000	
	208,000	
Creditors: amounts falling due within one year		
Creditors	75,000	
Taxation	25,000	
	100,000	
		108,000
		328,000
Creditors: amounts falling due after more than one year		
10% loan stock	75,000	
12% loan stock	30,000	
		105,000
		223,000
Capital and reserves		
Ordinary shares of £1 each, fully paid		100,000
Reserves		123,000
		223,000

Note especially how the uncancelled loan stock in S Ltd becomes a liability of the group.

6 MINORITY INTERESTS

6.1 It was mentioned earlier that the total assets and liabilities of subsidiary companies are included in the consolidated balance sheet, even in the case of subsidiaries which are only partly owned. A proportion of the net assets of such subsidiaries in fact belongs to investors from outside the group (minority interests).

> **KEY TERM**
>
> FRS 2 defines **minority interest** in a subsidiary undertaking as the 'interest in a subsidiary undertaking included in the consolidation that is attributable to the shares held by or on behalf of persons other than the parent undertaking and its subsidiary undertakings'.

In the consolidated balance sheet it is necessary to distinguish this proportion from those assets attributable to the group and financed by shareholders' funds.

6.2 The net assets of a company are financed by share capital and reserves. The consolidation procedure for dealing with partly owned subsidiaries is to **calculate the proportion of ordinary shares, preference shares and reserves attributable to minority interests.**

6.3 EXAMPLE: MINORITY INTERESTS

H Ltd has owned 75% of the share capital of S Ltd since the date of S Ltd's incorporation. Their latest balance sheets are given below.

H LIMITED
BALANCE SHEET

	£
Fixed assets	
Tangible assets	50,000
30,000 £1 ordinary shares in S Ltd at cost	30,000
	80,000
Net current assets	25,000
	105,000
Capital and reserves	
80,000 £1 ordinary shares	80,000
Reserves	25,000
	105,000

S LIMITED
BALANCE SHEET

	£
Tangible fixed assets	35,000
Net current assets	15,000
	50,000
Capital and reserves	
40,000 £1 ordinary shares	40,000
Reserves	10,000
	50,000

Prepare the consolidated balance sheet.

6.4 SOLUTION

All of S Ltd's net assets are consolidated despite the fact that the company is only 75% owned. The amount of net assets attributable to minority interests is calculated as follows.

	£
Minority share of share capital (25% × £40,000)	10,000
Minority share of reserves (25% × £10,000)	2,500
	12,500

Of S Ltd's share capital of £40,000, £10,000 is included in the figure for minority interest, while £30,000 is cancelled with H Ltd's asset 'investment in S Limited'.

The consolidated balance sheet can now be prepared.

H GROUP
CONSOLIDATED BALANCE SHEET

	£
Tangible fixed assets	85,000
Net current assets	40,000
	125,000
Share capital	80,000
Reserves £(25,000 + (75% × 10,000))	32,500
Shareholders' funds	112,500
Minority interest	12,500
	125,000

6.5 In this example we have shown minority interest on the 'capital and reserves' side of the balance sheet to illustrate how some of S Ltd's net assets are financed by shareholders'

Part E: Financial statements

funds, while some are financed by outside investors. You may see minority interest as a deduction from the other side of the balance sheet. The second half of the balance sheet will then consist entirely of shareholders' funds.

6.6 In more complicated examples the following technique is recommended for dealing with minority interests.

Step 1. Cancel common items in the draft balance sheets. If there is a minority interest, the subsidiary company's share capital will be a partly cancelled item. Ascertain the proportion of ordinary shares and the proportion (possibly different) of preference shares held by the minority.

Step 2. Produce a working for the minority interest. Add in the amounts of preference and ordinary share capital calculated in step 1: this completes the cancellation of the subsidiary's share capital.

Add also the minority's share of each reserve in the subsidiary company. Reserves belong to equity shareholders; the proportion attributable to minority interests therefore depends on their percentage holding of *ordinary* shares.

Step 3. Produce a separate working for each reserve (capital, revenue etc) found in the subsidiary company's balance sheet. The initial balances on these accounts will be taken straight from the draft balance sheets of the parent and subsidiary company.

Step 4. The closing balances in these workings can be entered directly onto the consolidated balance sheet.

Question 3

Set out below are the draft balance sheets of H Ltd and its subsidiary S Ltd. You are required to prepare the consolidated balance sheet.

H LIMITED

	£	£
Fixed assets		
Tangible assets		31,000
Investment in S Ltd		
12,000 £1 ordinary shares at cost	12,000	
4,000 £1 preference shares at cost	4,000	
£4,000 10% debentures at cost	4,000	
		20,000
		51,000
Net current assets		11,000
		62,000
Capital and reserves		
Ordinary shares of £1 each		40,000
Revenue reserve		22,000
		62,000

S LIMITED

	£
Tangible fixed assets	34,000
Net current assets	22,000
	56,000
Long-term liability	
10% debentures	10,000
	46,000

21: Group accounts

Capital and reserves	
Ordinary shares of £1 each	20,000
Preference shares of £1 each	16,000
Capital reserve	6,000
Revenue reserve	4,000
	46,000

Answer

Partly cancelling items are the components of H Ltd's investment in S Ltd, ie ordinary shares, preference shares and loan stock. Minorities have an interest in 75% (12,000/16,000) of S Ltd's preference shares and 40% (8,000/20,000) of S Ltd's equity, including reserves.

You should now produce workings for minority interests, capital reserve and revenue reserve as follows.

Workings

1 Minority interests

	£
Ordinary share capital (40% of 20,000)	8,000
Reserves: capital (40% × 6,000)	2,400
revenue (40% × 4,000)	1,600
	12,000
Preference share capital (75% × 16,000)	12,000
	24,000

2 Capital reserve

	£
H Ltd	-
Share of S Ltd's capital reserve (60% × 6,000)	3,600
	3,600

3 Revenue reserve

	£
H Ltd	22,000
Share of S Ltd's revenue reserves (60% × 4,000)	2,400
	24,400

The results of the workings are now used to construct the consolidated balance sheet (CBS).

H GROUP
CONSOLIDATED BALANCE SHEET

	£
Tangible fixed assets	65,000
Net current assets	33,000
	98,000
Long-term liability	
10% debentures	6,000
	92,000
Capital and reserves	
Ordinary shares of £1 each	40,000
Capital reserve	3,600
Revenue reserve	24,400
Shareholders' funds	68,000
Minority interests	24,000
	92,000

Notes

(a) S Ltd is a subsidiary of H Ltd because H Ltd owns 60% of its equity capital. It is unimportant how little of the preference share capital is owned by H Ltd.

(b) As always, the share capital in the consolidated balance sheet is that of the parent company alone. The share capital in S Ltd's balance sheet was partly cancelled against the investment shown in H Ltd's balance sheet, while the uncancelled portion was credited to minority interest.

Part E: Financial statements

(c) The figure for minority interest comprises the interest of outside investors in the share capital and reserves of the subsidiary. The uncancelled portion of S Ltd's loan stock is not shown as part of minority interest but is disclosed separately as a liability of the group.

7 GOODWILL ARISING ON CONSOLIDATION

7.1 In the examples we have looked at so far the cost of shares acquired by the parent company has always been equal to the nominal value of those shares. This is seldom the case in practice and we must now consider some more complicated examples. To begin with, **we will examine the entries made by the parent company in its own balance sheet when it acquires shares.**

7.2 When a company H Ltd wishes to **purchase shares** in a company S Ltd it must pay the previous owners of those shares. The most obvious form of payment would be in **cash**. Suppose H Ltd purchases all 40,000 £1 shares in S Ltd and pays £60,000 cash to the previous shareholders in consideration. The entries in H Ltd's books would be:

DEBIT	Investment in S Ltd at cost	£60,000	
CREDIT	Bank		£60,000

7.3 However, the previous shareholders might be prepared to accept some other form of consideration. For example, they might accept an agreed number of **shares** in H Ltd. H Ltd would then issue new shares in the agreed number and allot them to the former shareholders of S Ltd. This kind of deal might be attractive to H Ltd since it avoids the need for a heavy cash outlay. The former shareholders of S Ltd would retain an indirect interest in that company's profitability via their new holding in its parent company.

7.4 Continuing the example, suppose the shareholders of S Ltd agreed to accept one £1 ordinary share in H Ltd for every two £1 ordinary shares in S Ltd. H Ltd would then need to issue and allot 20,000 new £1 shares. How would this transaction be recorded in the books of H Ltd?

7.5 The simplest method would be as follows.

DEBIT	Investment in S Ltd	£20,000	
CREDIT	Share capital		£20,000

However, if the 40,000 £1 shares acquired in S Ltd are thought to have a value of £60,000 this would be misleading. The former shareholders of S Ltd have presumably agreed to accept 20,000 shares in H Ltd because they consider each of those shares to have a value of £3. This view of the matter suggests the following method of recording the transaction in H Ltd's books.

DEBIT	Investment in S Ltd	£60,000	
CREDIT	Share capital		£20,000
	Share premium account		£40,000

The second method is the one which the Companies Act 1985 requires should normally be used in preparing consolidated accounts.

7.6 The amount which H Ltd records in its books as the cost of its investment in S Ltd may be more or less than the book value of the assets it acquires. Suppose that S Ltd in the previous example has nil reserves, so that its share capital of £40,000 is balanced by net assets with a book value of £40,000. For simplicity, assume that the book value of S Ltd's assets is the same as their market or fair value.

7.7 Now when the directors of H Ltd agree to pay £60,000 for a 100% investment in S Ltd they must believe that, in addition to its tangible assets of £40,000, S Ltd must also have intangible assets worth £20,000. This amount of £20,000 paid over and above the value of the tangible assets acquired is called **goodwill arising on consolidation** (sometimes **premium on acquisition**).

7.8 Following the normal cancellation procedure the £40,000 share capital in S Ltd's balance sheet could be cancelled against £40,000 of the 'investment in S Limited' in the balance sheet of H Ltd. This would leave a £20,000 debit uncancelled in the parent company's accounts and this £20,000 would appear in the consolidated balance sheet under the caption 'Intangible fixed assets. Goodwill arising on consolidation' (although see below for FRS 10's requirements on this type of goodwill).

Goodwill and pre-acquisition profits

7.9 Up to now we have assumed that S Ltd had nil reserves when its shares were purchased by H Ltd. Assuming instead that S Ltd had earned profits of £8,000 in the period before acquisition, its balance sheet just before the purchase would look as follows.

	£
Net tangible assets	48,000
Share capital	40,000
Reserves	8,000
	48,000

7.10 If H Ltd now purchases all the shares in S Ltd it will acquire net tangible assets worth £48,000 at a cost of £60,000. Clearly in this case S Ltd's intangible assets (goodwill) are being valued at £12,000. It should be apparent that any **reserves** earned by the subsidiary **prior to its acquisition** by the parent company must be **incorporated in the cancellation** process so as to arrive at a figure for goodwill arising on consolidation. In other words, not only S Ltd's share capital, but also its pre-acquisition reserves, must be cancelled against the asset 'investment in S Ltd' in the accounts of the parent company. The uncancelled balance of £12,000 appears in the consolidated balance sheet.

7.11 The consequence of this is that **any pre-acquisition reserves of a subsidiary company are not aggregated with the parent company's reserves** in the consolidated balance sheet. The figure of consolidated reserves comprises the reserves of the parent company plus the post-acquisition reserves only of subsidiary companies. The post-acquisition reserves are simply reserves now less reserves at acquisition.

7.12 EXAMPLE: GOODWILL AND PRE-ACQUISITION PROFITS

Sing Ltd acquired the ordinary shares of Wing Ltd on 31 March when the draft balance sheets of each company were as follows.

Part E: Financial statements

SING LIMITED
BALANCE SHEET AS AT 31 MARCH

	£
Fixed assets	
Investment in 50,000 shares of Wing Ltd at cost	80,000
Net current assets	40,000
	120,000
Capital and reserves	
Ordinary shares	75,000
Revenue reserves	45,000
	120,000

WING LIMITED
BALANCE SHEET AS AT 31 MARCH

	£
Net current assets	60,000
Share capital and reserves	
50,000 ordinary shares of £1 each	50,000
Revenue reserves	10,000
	60,000

Prepare the consolidated balance sheet as at 31 March.

7.13 SOLUTION

The technique to adopt here is to produce a new working: 'Goodwill'. A proforma working is set out below.

Goodwill

	£	£
Cost of investment		X
Share of net assets acquired as represented by:		
Ordinary share capital	X	
Share premium	X	
Reserves on acquisition	X	
Group share	a%	(X)
		X
b% preference shares		(X)
Goodwill		X

7.14 Applying this to our example the working will look like this.

	£	£
Cost of investment		80,000
Share of net assets acquired as represented by:		
Ordinary share capital	50,000	
Revenue reserves on acquisition	10,000	
	60,000	
Group share 100%		60,000
Goodwill		20,000

SING LIMITED
CONSOLIDATED BALANCE SHEET AS AT 31 MARCH

	£
Fixed assets	
Goodwill arising on consolidation	20,000
Net current assets	100,000
	120,000
Capital and reserves	
Ordinary shares	75,000
Revenue reserves	45,000
	120,000

FRS 10 *Goodwill and intangible assets*

7.15 FRS 10 *Goodwill and intangible assets* was published in December 1997.

7.16 You should look back to Chapter 16 for a detailed discussion of goodwill. For present purposes, however, you need to know the following.

(a) Goodwill must be amortised if it is expected to last less than 20 years.

(b) Otherwise, goodwill is to remain in the balance sheet (subject to an impairment review).

(c) Negative goodwill is shown as a credit in the balance sheet just below positive goodwill.

7.17 If goodwill is amortised the consolidation adjustment required each year is as follows.

DEBIT   Consolidated profit and loss account
CREDIT   Provision for amortisation of goodwill

The unamortised portion will be included in the consolidated balance sheet under fixed assets.

7.18 FRS 10 contains a presumption that the useful life of the goodwill is less than 20 years. The presumption may be rebutted. If it is greater than 20 years, it must still be amortised. If it is indefinite, it should not be amortised, but a full impairment review should be performed each year. An impairment review should, in any case, be performed at the end of the first full year after acquisition.

> **Exam focus point**
>
> Do not worry too much about this. The examiner will tell you what to do with the goodwill. If it is simply to remain in the balance sheet you need only calculate it as above and show it as an intangible asset in the consolidated balance sheet. If it is to be amortised the treatment will be as in Paragraph 7.17 above. FRS 10 is not examinable, whereas goodwill is.

8 A TECHNIQUE OF CONSOLIDATION   December 2001, December 2002

8.1 We have now looked at the topics of cancellation, minority interests and goodwill arising on consolidation. It is time to set out an approach to be used in tackling consolidated balance sheets. The approach we recommend consists of three steps.

Step 1. Cancel items common to both balance sheets.

Part E: Financial statements

Step 2. Produce working for minority interests as shown in Paragraph 6.6.

Step 3. Produce a goodwill working as shown in Paragraph 7.13 above. Then produce a working for capital and revenue reserves.

8.2 You should now attempt to apply this technique to the following question.

Question 4

The draft balance sheets of Ping Ltd and Pong Ltd on 30 June 20X4 were as follows.

PING LIMITED
BALANCE SHEET AS AT 30 JUNE 20X4

	£	£
Fixed assets		
Tangible assets	50,000	
20,000 ordinary shares in Pong Ltd at cost	30,000	
		80,000
Current assets		
Stock	3,000	
Debtors	20,000	
Cash	2,000	
	25,000	
Creditors: amounts falling due within one year		
Trade creditors	18,000	
	18,000	
Net current assets		7,000
		87,000
Capital and reserves		
Ordinary shares of £1 each		45,000
Capital reserves		12,000
Revenue reserves		30,000
		87,000

PONG LIMITED
BALANCE SHEET AS AT 30 JUNE 20X4

	£	£
Tangible fixed assets		40,000
Current assets		
Stock	8,000	
Debtors	17,000	
	25,000	
Creditors: amounts falling due within one year		
Trade creditors	12,000	
	12,000	
Net current assets		13,000
		53,000
Capital and reserves		£
Ordinary shares of £1 each		25,000
Capital reserves		5,000
Revenue reserves		23,000
		53,000

Ping Ltd acquired its investment in Pong Ltd on 1 July 20X1 when the revenue reserves of Pong Ltd stood at £6,000. There have been no changes in the share capital or capital reserves of Pong Ltd since that date.

Goodwill arising on consolidation is deemed to have an indefinite useful economic life and is to remain in the balance sheet.

Prepare the consolidated balance sheet of Ping Ltd as at 30 June 20X4.

Answer

Stage 1. Cancel common items.

Stage 2. Calculate the minority interest.

21: Group accounts

Minority interest

	£
Ordinary share capital (20% × 25,000)	5,000
Capital reserves (20% × 5,000)	1,000
Revenue reserves (20% × 23,000)	4,600
	10,600

Note. In this particular case, where there are no preference shares or adjustments to Pong Ltd's revenue reserves, the minority interest figure may simply be calculated as 20% of Pong Ltd's net assets, ie 20% × £53,000. Because, however, such adjustments and complications often arise, it is a good idea to get into the habit of producing the working as shown.

Stage 3. Calculate goodwill and reserves.

Goodwill

	£	£
Cost of investment		30,000
Share of assets acquired as represented by:		
Ordinary share capital	25,000	
Capital reserves on acquisition	5,000	
Revenue reserves on acquisition	6,000	
	36,000	
Group share 80%		28,800
Goodwill		1,200

Consolidated capital reserves

	£
Ping Ltd	12,000
Share of Pong Ltd's post acquisition capital reserve	-
	12,000

Consolidated revenue reserves

	£
Ping Ltd	30,000
Share of Pong Ltd's post acquisition revenue reserves: 80%(23,000 - 6,000)*	13,600
	43,600

Note. Post acquisition reserves of Pong Ltd are simply reserves now less reserves at acquisition. The consolidated balance sheet may now be written out.

PING LIMITED
CONSOLIDATED BALANCE SHEET AS AT 30 JUNE 20X4

	£	£
Fixed assets		
Intangible asset: goodwill		1,200
Tangible assets (£50,000 + £40,000)		90,000
Current assets		
Stocks (£3,000 + £8,000)	11,000	
Debtors (£20,000 + £17,000)	37,000	
Cash	2,000	
	50,000	
Creditors: amounts falling due within one year		
Trade creditors (£18,000 + £12,000)	30,000	
	30,000	
Net current assets		20,000
		111,200
Capital and reserves		
Ordinary shares of £1 each		45,000
Capital reserves		12,000
Revenue reserves		43,600
Shareholders' funds		100,600
Minority interests		10,600
		111,200

Part E: Financial statements

9 SUMMARY: CONSOLIDATED BALANCE SHEET

Purpose	To show the net assets which H controls and the ownership of those assets.
Net assets	Always 100% H plus 100% S providing H holds a majority of voting rights.
Share capital	H only.
Reason	Simply reporting to the holding company's shareholders in another form.
Reserves	100% H plus group share of post-acquisition retained reserves of S less consolidation adjustments.
Reason	To show the extent to which the group actually owns net assets included in the top half of the balance sheet.
Minority interest	MI share of S's consolidated net assets.
Reason	To show the extent to which other parties own net assets that are under the control of the holding company.

Chapter roundup

- This chapter has explained the concept of a **group** and introduced several important definitions.

- The principal **regulations** governing the preparation of group accounts have been explained. Many of these are hard to understand and you should re-read this chapter after you have completed your study of this section of the text.

- This chapter has covered the mechanics of preparing simple **consolidated balance sheets**. In particular, procedures have been described for dealing with
    - Cancellation
    - Calculation of minority interests
    - Calculation of goodwill arising on consolidation

- A three-stage drill has been described and exemplified in a comprehensive example.

- The stages are as follows.
    - Cancel items common to both balance sheets
    - Minority interests
    - Goodwill

- It is important that you have a clear understanding of the material in this chapter as this is a key area in the syllabus.

Quick quiz

1. What is the basic objective of consolidation procedures?
2. When might part cancellation of items appearing in individual companies' accounts be required?
3. What are the components making up the figure of minority interest in a consolidated balance sheet?
4. What is 'goodwill arising on consolidation'?
5. Company A holds 40% of the shares of Company B. Company B cannot be a subsidiary of Company A. True or False?
6. Company A holds 100% of the shares of Company B, with a view to a resale. The subsidiary has not been consolidated previously. Which of the following statements is true?

    A Consolidation is compulsory
    B Consolidation is optional
    C Consolidation does not apply, as it is an investment
    D The subsidiary is excluded from consolidation

Answers to quick quiz

1. To show financial information about the group as if it was a single entity.
2. See paragraph 5.6.
3. The proportion of ordinary shares, preference shares and reserves attributable to minority interests.
4. The amount paid over and above what the net assets of the subsidiary are worth.
5. False. B may be a subsidiary if A exerts dominant influence.
6. D. Under FRS 2 a subsidiary must be excluded from consolidation if it is held exclusively for resale **and** the subsidiary has not been consolidated previously.

    (Note: C may be true but there are cases when an investment has to be consolidated.)

Now try the question below from the Exam Question Bank

Question to try	Level	Marks	Time
33	Full exam	10	18 mins

Part F
Interpretation of accounts

Chapter 22

RATIO ANALYSIS

Topic list	Syllabus reference
1 The broad categories of ratios	6(a)
2 Profitability and return on capital	6(a)
3 Liquidity, gearing and working capital	6(a)
4 Shareholders' investment ratios	6(a)
5 Presentation of a ratio analysis report	6(a)

Introduction

So far in this Study Text we have looked at how financial statements are prepared and have described their features and contents.

In this chapter we are concerned with **interpretation of accounts by means of ratios**.

Study guide

Sections 25 and 26 - Interpretation of financial statements

- Revise users of financial statements and their information needs.
- Explain the advantages and disadvantages of interpretation based on financial statements.
- Explain the factors forming the environment in which the business operates.
- Explain the uses of ratio analysis.
- Explain the main ratios to be used in interpreting financial statements to appraise:
    - Profitability
    - Liquidity
    - Working capital efficiency
    - Financial risk
    - Performance from an investor's point of view.
- Explain the working capital cycle (or cash operating cycle).
- Explain normal levels of certain ratios.
- Explain how to formulate comments on movements in ratios between one period and another or on differences between ratios for different businesses.
- Explain the factors which may distort ratios, leading to unreliable conclusions.
- Prepare and comment on a comprehensive range of ratios for a business.

Exam guide

Learn the ratios well. You will use them in this and subsequent exams. Remember the ratios are a tool. As an accountant you must explain the information which ratios provide you with.

Part F: Interpretation of accounts

1 THE BROAD CATEGORIES OF RATIOS

1.1 If you were to look at a balance sheet or P & L account, how would you decide whether the company was doing well or badly? Or whether it was financially strong or financially vulnerable? And what would you be looking at in the figures to help you to make your judgement?

1.2 Your syllabus requires you to appraise and communicate the position and prospects of a business based on given and prepared statements and ratios.

1.3 Ratio analysis involves comparing one figure against another to produce a ratio, and assessing whether the ratio indicates a weakness or strength in the company's affairs.

The broad categories of ratios

1.4 Broadly speaking, basic ratios can be grouped into five categories:

   (a) Profitability and return
   (b) Long-term solvency and stability
   (c) Short-term solvency and liquidity
   (d) Efficiency (turnover ratios)
   (e) Shareholders' investment ratios

1.5 Within each heading we will identify a number of standard measures or ratios that are normally calculated and generally accepted as meaningful indicators. Each individual business must be considered separately, and a ratio that is meaningful for a manufacturing company may be completely meaningless for a financial institution. Try not to be too mechanical when working out ratios and constantly think about what you are trying to achieve.

1.6 The key to obtaining meaningful information from ratio analysis is **comparison**. This may involve comparing ratios over time within the same business to establish whether things are improving or declining, and comparing ratios between similar businesses to see whether the company you are analysing is better or worse than average within its specific business sector.

1.7 It must be stressed that ratio analysis on its own is not sufficient for interpreting company accounts, and that there are other items of information which should be looked at, for example:

   (a) Comments in the Chairman's report and directors' report

   (b) The age and nature of the company's assets

   (c) Current and future developments in the company's markets, at home and overseas;

   (d) Any other noticeable features of the report and accounts, such as post balance sheet events, contingent liabilities, a qualified auditors' report, the company's taxation position, and so on

1.8 In every case, consider also who you are advising, a creditor will not be interested in shareholder's investment ratios.

1.9 **SCENARIO: CALCULATING RATIOS**

To illustrate the calculation of ratios, the following balance sheet and P & L account figures will be used, throughout this chapter.

FURLONG PLC PROFIT AND LOSS ACCOUNT
FOR THE YEAR ENDED 31 DECEMBER 20X8

	Notes	20X8 £	20X7 £
Turnover	1	3,095,576	1,909,051
Operating profit	1	359,501	244,229
Interest	2	17,371	19,127
Profit on ordinary activities before taxation		342,130	225,102
Taxation on ordinary activities		74,200	31,272
Profit on ordinary activities after taxation		267,930	193,830
Dividend		41,000	16,800
Retained profit for the year		226,930	177,030
Earnings per share		12.8p	9.3p

FURLONG PLC BALANCE SHEET
AS AT 31 DECEMBER 20X8

	Notes	20X8 £	20X7 £
Fixed assets			
Tangible fixed assets		802,180	656,071
Current assets			
Stocks and work in progress		64,422	86,550
Debtors	3	1,002,701	853,441
Cash at bank and in hand		1,327	68,363
		1,068,450	1,008,354
Creditors: amounts falling due within one year	4	881,731	912,456
Net current assets		186,719	95,898
Total assets less current liabilities		988,899	751,969
Creditors: amounts falling due after more than one year			
10% first mortgage debenture stock 20Y4/20Y9		(100,000)	(100,000)
Provision for liabilities and charges		(20,000)	(10,000)
		868,899	641,969
Capital and reserves			
Called up share capital	5	210,000	210,000
Share premium account		48,178	48,178
Profit and loss account		610,721	383,791
		868,899	641,969

NOTES TO THE ACCOUNTS

			20X8 £	20X7 £
1	*Turnover and profit*			
	(i)	Turnover	3,095,576	1,909,051
		Cost of sales	2,402,609	1,441,950
		Gross profit	692,967	467,101
		Administration expenses	333,466	222,872
		Operating profit	359,501	244,229

Part F: Interpretation of accounts

(ii) Operating profit is stated after charging:

	20X8	20X7
Depreciation	151,107	120,147
Auditors' remuneration	6,500	5,000
Leasing charges	47,636	46,336
Directors' emoluments	94,945	66,675

2 *Interest*

	20X8	20X7
Payable on bank overdrafts and other loans	8,115	11,909
Payable on debenture stock	10,000	10,000
	18,115	21,909
Receivable on short-term deposits	744	2,782
Net payable	17,371	19,127

3 *Debtors*

Amounts falling due within one year

	20X8	20X7
Trade debtors	884,559	760,252
Prepayments and accrued income	89,822	45,729
Advance corporation tax recoverable	7,200	–
	981,581	805,981

Amounts falling due after more than one year

	20X8	20X7
Advance corporation tax recoverable	9,000	7,200
Trade debtors	12,120	40,260
	21,120	47,460
Total debtors	1,002,701	853,441

4 *Creditors: amounts falling due within one year*

	20X8	20X7
Trade creditors	627,018	545,340
Accruals and deferred income	81,279	280,464
Corporation tax	108,000	37,200
Other taxes and social security costs	44,434	32,652
Dividend	21,000	16,800
	881,731	912,456

5 *Called up share capital*

	20X8	20X7
Authorised ordinary shares of 10p each	1,000,000	1,000,000
Issued and fully paid ordinary shares of 10p each	210,000	210,00

2 PROFITABILITY AND RETURN ON CAPITAL

Pilot paper, December 2001, June 2002

2.1 In our example, the company made a profit in both 20X8 and 20X7, and there was an increase in profit on ordinary activities between one year and the next:

(a) Of 52% before taxation
(b) Of 39% after taxation

2.2 Profit on ordinary activities *before* taxation is generally thought to be a better figure to use than profit after taxation, because there might be unusual variations in the tax charge from year to year which would not affect the underlying profitability of the company's operations.

2.3 Another profit figure that should be calculated is PBIT, profit before interest and tax. This is the amount of profit which the company earned before having to pay interest to the providers of loan capital. By providers of loan capital, we usually mean longer-term loan capital, such as debentures and medium-term bank loans, which will be shown in the balance sheet as 'creditors: amounts falling due after more than one year'.

22: Ratio analysis

2.4 Profit before interest and tax is therefore:

(a) The profit on ordinary activities before taxation
(b) Plus interest charges on long-term loan capital

Published accounts do not always give sufficient detail on interest payable to determine how much is interest on long-term finance. We will assume in our example that the whole of the interest payable (£18,115, note 2) relates to long-term finance.

2.5 PBIT in our example is therefore:

	20X8 £	20X7 £
Profit on ordinary activities before tax	342,130	225,102
Interest payable	18,115	21,909
PBIT	360,245	247,011

This shows a 46% growth between 20X7 and 20X8.

Return on capital employed (ROCE)

2.6 It is impossible to assess profits or profit growth properly without relating them to the amount of funds (capital) that were employed in making the profits. The most important profitability ratio is therefore return on capital employed (ROCE), which states the profit as a percentage of the amount of capital employed.

FORMULA TO LEARN

$$ROCE = \frac{\text{Profit on ordinary activities before interest and taxation}}{\text{Capital employed}}$$

2.7 Capital employed = Shareholders' funds plus 'creditors: amounts falling due after more than one year' plus any long-term provision for liabilities and charges (*or* total assets less current liabilities).

The underlying principle is that we must compare like with like, and so if capital means share capital and reserves plus long-term liabilities and debt capital, profit must mean the profit earned by all this capital together. This is PBIT, since interest is the return for loan capital.

2.8 **EXAMPLE: ROCE**

In our example, capital employed = 20X8 868,899 + 100,000 + 20,000 = £988,899
20X7 641,969 + 100,000 + 10,000 = £751,969

These total figures are the total assets less current liabilities figures for 20X8 and 20X7 in the balance sheet.

	20X8	20X7
ROCE =	$\frac{360,245}{988,899}$	$\frac{247,011}{751,969}$
=	36.4%	32.8%

2.9 What does a company's ROCE tell us? What should we be looking for? There are three comparisons that can be made.

(a) The change in ROCE from one year to the next can be examined. In this example, there has been an increase in ROCE by about 10% or 11% from its 20X7 level.

Part F: Interpretation of accounts

(b) The ROCE being earned by other companies, if this information is available, can be compared with the ROCE of this company. Here the information is not available.

(c) A comparison of the ROCE with current market borrowing rates may be made.

(i) What would be the cost of extra borrowing to the company if it needed more loans, and is it earning a ROCE that suggests it could make profits to make such borrowing worthwhile?

(ii) Is the company making a ROCE which suggests that it is getting value for money from its current borrowing?

(iii) Companies are in a risk business and commercial borrowing rates are a good independent yardstick against which company performance can be judged.

2.10 In this example, if we suppose that current market interest rates, say, for medium-term borrowing from banks, is around 10%, then the company's actual ROCE of 36% in 20X8 would not seem low. On the contrary, it might seem high.

2.11 However, it is easier to spot a low ROCE than a high one, because there is always a chance that the company's fixed assets, especially property, are undervalued in its balance sheet, and so the capital employed figure might be unrealistically low. If the company had earned a ROCE, not of 36%, but of, say only 6%, then its return would have been below current borrowing rates and so disappointingly low.

> **Exam focus point**
> There are different ways of calculating ROCE, and the examiner will give you credit for them. If he tells you how to calculate it you should, of course, follow his instructions.

Return on shareholders' capital (ROSC)

2.12 Another measure of profitability and return is the return on shareholders' capital (ROSC):

> **FORMULA TO LEARN**
> $$\text{ROSC} = \frac{\text{Profit on ordinary activities before tax}}{\text{Share capital and reserves}}$$

2.13 It is intended to focus on the return being made by the company for the benefit of its shareholders, and in our example, the figures are:

$$\begin{array}{cc} 20X8 & 20X7 \\ \dfrac{342,130}{868,899} = 39.4\% & \dfrac{225,102}{641,969} = 35.1\% \end{array}$$

These figures show an improvement between 20X7 and 20X8, and a return which is clearly in excess of current borrowing rates.

2.14 ROSC is not a widely-used ratio, however, because there are more useful ratios that give an indication of the return to shareholders, such as earnings per share, dividend per share, dividend yield and earnings yield, which are described later.

22: Ratio analysis

Analysing profitability and return in more detail: the secondary ratios

2.15 We often sub-analyse ROCE, to find out more about why the ROCE is high or low, or better or worse than last year. There are two factors that contribute towards a return on capital employed, both related to sales turnover.

(a) **Profit margin.** A company might make a high or low profit margin on its sales. For example, a company that makes a profit of 25p per £1 of sales is making a bigger return on its turnover than another company making a profit of only 10p per £1 of sales.

(b) **Asset turnover.** Asset turnover is a measure of how well the assets of a business are being used to generate sales. For example, if two companies each have capital employed of £100,000 and Company A makes sales of £400,000 per annum whereas Company B makes sales of only £200,000 per annum, Company A is making a higher turnover from the same amount of assets (twice as much asset turnover as Company B) and this will help A to make a higher return on capital employed than B. Asset turnover is expressed as 'x times' so that assets generate x times their value in annual turnover. Here, Company A's asset turnover is 4 times and B's is 2 times.

2.16 Profit margin and asset turnover together explain the ROCE and if the ROCE is the primary profitability ratio, these other two are the secondary ratios. The relationship between the three ratios can be shown mathematically.

> **FORMULA TO LEARN**
>
> Profit margin × Asset turnover = ROCE
>
> $$\therefore \frac{PBIT}{Sales} \times \frac{Sales}{Capital\ employed} = \frac{PBIT}{Capital\ employed}$$

2.17 In our example:

		Profit margin		Asset turnover		ROCE
(a)	20X8	$\dfrac{360,245}{3,095,576}$	×	$\dfrac{3,095,576}{988,899}$	=	$\dfrac{360,245}{988,899}$
		11.64%	×	3.13 times	=	36.4%
(b)	20X7	$\dfrac{247,011}{1,909,051}$	×	$\dfrac{1,909,051}{751,969}$	=	$\dfrac{247,011}{751,969}$
		12.94%	×	2.54 times	=	32.8%

2.18 In this example, the company's improvement in ROCE between 20X7 and 20X8 is attributable to a higher asset turnover. Indeed the profit margin has fallen a little, but the higher asset turnover has more than compensated for this.

2.19 It is also worth commenting on the change in sales turnover from one year to the next. You may already have noticed that Furlong plc achieved sales growth of over 60% from £1.9 million to £3.1 million between 20X7 and 20X8. This is very strong growth, and this is certainly one of the most significant items in the P & L account and balance sheet.

Part F: Interpretation of accounts

A warning about comments on profit margin and asset turnover

2.20 It might be tempting to think that a high profit margin is good, and a low asset turnover means sluggish trading. In broad terms, this is so. But there is a trade-off between profit margin and asset turnover, and you cannot look at one without allowing for the other.

(a) A high profit margin means a high profit per £1 of sales, but if this also means that sales prices are high, there is a strong possibility that sales turnover will be depressed, and so asset turnover lower.

(b) A high asset turnover means that the company is generating a lot of sales, but to do this it might have to keep its prices down and so accept a low profit margin per £1 of sales.

2.21 Consider the following.

Company A		Company B	
Sales	£1,000,000	Sales	£4,000,000
Capital employed	£1,000,000	Capital employed	£1,000,000
PBIT	£200,000	PBIT	£200,000

These figures would give the following ratios.

ROCE $= \dfrac{200,000}{1,000,000} = 20\%$ ROCE $= \dfrac{200,000}{1,000,000} = 20\%$

Profit margin $= \dfrac{200,000}{1,000,000} = 20\%$ Profit margin $= \dfrac{200,000}{4,000,000} = 5\%$

Asset turnover $= \dfrac{1,000,000}{1,000,000} = 1$ Asset turnover $= \dfrac{4,000,000}{1,000,000} = 4$

2.22 The companies have the same ROCE, but it is arrived at in a very different fashion. Company A operates with a low asset turnover and a comparatively high profit margin whereas company B carries out much more business, but on a lower profit margin. Company A could be operating at the luxury end of the market, whilst company B is operating at the popular end of the market (Fortnum and Masons v Sainsbury's).

Question 1

Which one of the following formulae correctly expresses the relationship between return on capital employed (ROCE), profit margin (PM) and asset turnover (AT)?

A   PM $= \dfrac{AT}{ROCE}$

B   ROCE $= \dfrac{PM}{AT}$

C   AT $=$ PM × ROCE

D   PM $= \dfrac{ROCE}{AT}$

Answer

ROCE $= \dfrac{Profit}{Capital\ employed}$

PM $= \dfrac{Profit}{Sales}$

$$\text{AT} = \frac{\text{Sales}}{\text{Capital employed}}$$

It follows that ROCE = PM × AT, which can be re-arranged to the form given in option D.

Gross profit margin, net profit margin and profit analysis

2.23 Depending on the format of the P & L account, you may be able to calculate the gross profit margin as well as the net profit margin. Looking at the two together can be quite informative.

2.24 For example, suppose that a company has the following summarised profit and loss accounts for two consecutive years.

	Year 1 £	Year 2 £
Turnover	70,000	100,000
Cost of sales	42,000	55,000
Gross profit	28,000	45,000
Expenses	21,000	35,000
Net profit	7,000	10,000

Although the net profit margin is the same for both years at 10%, the gross profit margin is not.

In year 1 it is: $\dfrac{28,000}{70,000} = 40\%$

and in year 2 it is: $\dfrac{45,000}{100,000} = 45\%$

The improved gross profit margin has not led to an improvement in the net profit margin. This is because expenses as a percentage of sales have risen from 30% in year 1 to 35% in year 2.

3 LIQUIDITY, GEARING AND WORKING CAPITAL

Pilot paper, December 2001, June 2002, June 2003

Long-term solvency: debt and gearing ratios

3.1 Debt ratios are concerned with how much the company owes in relation to its size, whether it is getting into heavier debt or improving its situation, and whether its debt burden seems heavy or light.

(a) When a company is heavily in debt banks and other potential lenders may be unwilling to advance further funds.

(b) When a company is earning only a modest profit before interest and tax, and has a heavy debt burden, there will be very little profit left over for shareholders after the interest charges have been paid. And so if interest rates were to go up (on bank overdrafts and so on) or the company were to borrow even more, it might soon be incurring interest charges in excess of PBIT. This might eventually lead to the liquidation of the company.

These are two big reasons why companies should keep their debt burden under control. There are four ratios that are particularly worth looking at, the **debt** ratio, **gearing** ratio, **interest cover** and **cash flow** ratio.

Part F: Interpretation of accounts

Debt ratio

> **KEY TERM**
>
> The **debt ratio** is the ratio of a company's total debts to its total assets.

3.2 (a) Assets consist of fixed assets at their balance sheet value, plus current assets.

(b) Debts consist of all creditors, whether amounts falling due within one year or after more than one year.

You can ignore long-term provisions and liabilities, such as deferred taxation.

3.3 There is no absolute guide to the maximum safe debt ratio, but as a very general guide, you might regard 50% as a safe limit to debt. In practice, many companies operate successfully with a higher debt ratio than this, but 50% is nonetheless a helpful benchmark. In addition, if the debt ratio is over 50% and getting worse, the company's debt position will be worth looking at more carefully.

3.4 In the case of Furlong plc the debt ratio is as follows.

	20X8	20X7
Total debts	(881,731 + 100,000)	(912,456 + 100,000)
Total assets	(802,180 + 1,068,450)	(656,071 + 1,008,354)
	= 52%	= 61%

3.5 In this case, the debt ratio is quite high, mainly because of the large amount of current liabilities. However, the debt ratio has fallen from 61% to 52% between 20X7 and 20X8, and so the company appears to be improving its debt position.

Gearing ratio

3.6 Capital gearing is concerned with a company's **long-term capital structure**. We can think of a company as consisting of fixed assets and net current assets (ie working capital, which is current assets minus current liabilities). These assets must be financed by long-term capital of the company, which is either:

(a) Share capital and reserves (shareholders' funds) which can be divided into:

   (i) Ordinary shares plus reserves
   (ii) And preference shares

(b) Long-term debt capital: 'creditors: amounts falling due after more than one year'

3.7 Preference share capital is not debt. It would certainly not be included as debt in the debt ratio. However, like loan capital, preference share capital has a prior claim over profits before interest and tax, ahead of ordinary shareholders. Preference dividends must be paid out of profits before ordinary shareholders are entitled to an ordinary dividend, and so we refer to preference share capital and loan capital as prior charge capital.

3.8 The **capital gearing ratio** is a measure of the proportion of a company's capital that is prior charge capital. It is measured as follows:

> **FORMULA TO LEARN**
>
> Capital gearing ratio = $\dfrac{\text{prior charge capital}}{\text{total capital}}$

(a) **Prior charge capital** is capital carrying a right to a fixed return. It will include preference shares and debentures.

(b) **Total capital** is ordinary share capital and reserves plus prior charge capital plus any long-term liabilities or provisions. In group accounts we would also include minority interests. It is easier to identify the same figure for total capital as total assets less current liabilities, which you will find given to you in the balance sheet.

3.9 As with the debt ratio, there is no absolute limit to what a gearing ratio ought to be. A company with a gearing ratio of more than 50% is said to be high-geared (whereas low gearing means a gearing ratio of less than 50%). Many companies are high geared, but if a high geared company is becoming increasingly high geared, it is likely to have difficulty in the future when it wants to borrow even more, unless it can also boost its shareholders' capital, either with retained profits or by a new share issue.

3.10 A similar ratio to the gearing ratio is the **debt/equity ratio**, which is calculated as follows.

> **FORMULA TO LEARN**
>
> Debt/equity ratio = $\dfrac{\text{prior charge capital}}{\text{ordinary share capital and reserves}}$

This gives us the same sort of information as the gearing ratio, and a ratio of 100% or more would indicate high gearing.

3.11 In the example of Furlong plc, we find that the company, although having a high debt ratio because of its current liabilities, has a low gearing ratio. It has no preference share capital and its only long-term debt is the 10% debenture stock.

	20X8	20X7
Gearing ratio	$\dfrac{100{,}000}{988{,}899}$	$\dfrac{100{,}000}{751{,}969}$
	= 10%	= 13%
Debt/equity ratio	$\dfrac{100{,}000}{868{,}899}$	$\dfrac{100{,}000}{641{,}969}$
	= 12%	= 16%

The implications of high or low gearing

3.12 We mentioned earlier that gearing is, amongst other things, an attempt to quantify the degree of risk involved in holding equity shares in a company, risk both in terms of the company's ability to remain in business and in terms of expected ordinary dividends from the company. The problem with a high geared company is that by definition there is a lot of debt. Debt generally carries a fixed rate of interest (or fixed rate of dividend if in the form of preference shares), hence there is a given (and large) amount to be paid out from profits to

Part F: Interpretation of accounts

holders of debt before arriving at a residue available for distribution to the holders of equity. The riskiness will perhaps become clearer with the aid of an example.

	Company A £'000	Company B £'000	Company C £'000
Ordinary share capital	600	400	300
Profit and loss account	200	200	200
Revaluation reserve	100	100	100
	900	700	600
6% preference shares	-	-	100
10% loan stock	100	300	300
Capital employed	1,000	1,000	1,000
Gearing ratio	10%	30%	40%

3.13 Now suppose that each company makes a profit before interest and tax of £50,000, and the rate of corporation tax is 30%. Amounts available for distribution to equity shareholders will be as follows:

	Company A £'000	Company B £'000	Company C £'000
Profit before interest and tax	50	50	50
Interest	10	30	30
Profit before tax	40	20	20
Taxation at 30%	12	6	6
Profit after tax	28	14	14
Preference dividend	-	-	6
Available for ordinary shareholders	28	14	8

3.14 If in the subsequent year profit before interest and tax falls to £40,000, the amounts available to ordinary shareholders will become:

	Company A £'000	Company B £'000	Company C £'000
Profit before interest and tax	40	40	40
Interest	10	30	30
Profit before tax	30	10	10
Taxation at 30%	9	3	3
Profit after tax	21	7	7
Preference dividend	-	-	6
Available for ordinary shareholders	21	7	1

Note the following.

Gearing ratio	10%	30%	40%
Change in PBIT	– 20%	– 20%	– 20%
Change in profit available for ordinary shareholders	– 25%	– 50%	– 87.5%

3.15 The more highly geared the company, the greater the risk that little (if anything) will be available to distribute by way of dividend to the ordinary shareholders.

(a) The example clearly displays this fact in so far as the more highly geared the company, the greater the percentage change in profit available for ordinary shareholders for any given percentage change in profit before interest and tax.

(b) The relationship similarly holds when profits increase, and if PBIT had risen by 20% rather than fallen, you would find that once again the largest percentage change in profit available for ordinary shareholders (this means an increase) will be for the highly geared company.

22: Ratio analysis

(c) This means that there will be greater volatility of amounts available for ordinary shareholders, and presumably therefore greater volatility in dividends paid to those shareholders, where a company is highly geared. That is the risk: you may do extremely well or extremely badly without a particularly large movement in the PBIT of the company.

3.16 The risk of a company's ability to remain in business was referred to earlier. Gearing is relevant to this. A high geared company has a large amount of interest to pay annually (assuming that the debt is external borrowing rather than preference shares). If those borrowings are 'secured' in any way (and debentures in particular are secured), then the holders of the debt are perfectly entitled to force the company to realise assets to pay their interest if funds are not available from other sources. Clearly the more highly geared a company the more likely this is to occur when and if profits fall. **Higher gearing may mean higher returns, but also higher risk.**

Interest cover

3.17 The interest cover ratio shows whether a company is earning enough profits before interest and tax to pay its interest costs comfortably, or whether its interest costs are high in relation to the size of its profits, so that a fall in PBIT would then have a significant effect on profits available for ordinary shareholders.

> **FORMULA TO LEARN**
>
> $$\text{Interest cover} = \frac{\text{profit before interest and tax}}{\text{interest charges}}$$

3.18 An interest cover of 2 times or less would be low, and should really exceed 3 times before the company's interest costs are to be considered within acceptable limits.

3.19 Returning first to the example of Companies A, B and C, the interest cover was as follows.

		Company A	Company B	Company C
(a)	When PBIT was £50,000 =	50,000 / 10,000	50,000 / 30,000	50,000 / 30,000
		5 times	1.67 times	1.67 times
(b)	When PBIT was £40,000 =	40,000 / 10,000	40,000 / 30,000	40,000 / 30,000
		4 times	1.33 times	1.33 times

Note. Although preference share capital is included as prior charge capital for the gearing ratio, it is usual to exclude preference dividends from 'interest' charges. We also look at all interest payments, even interest charges on short-term debt, and so interest cover and gearing do not quite look at the same thing.

3.20 Both B and C have a low interest cover, which is a warning to ordinary shareholders that their profits are highly vulnerable, in percentage terms, to even small changes in PBIT.

Question 2
Returning to the example of Furlong plc in Paragraph 1.9, what is the company's interest cover?

Part F: Interpretation of accounts

Answer

Interest payments should be taken gross, from the note to the accounts, and not net of interest receipts as shown in the P & L account.

	20X8	20X7
PBIT	360,245	247,011
Interest payable	18,115	21,909
	= 20 times	= 11 times

Furlong plc has more than sufficient interest cover. In view of the company's low gearing, this is not too surprising and so we finally obtain a picture of Furlong plc as a company that does not seem to have a debt problem, in spite of its high (although declining) debt ratio.

Cash flow ratio

> **KEY TERM**
>
> The **cash flow ratio** is the ratio of a company's net cash inflow to its total debts.

3.21 (a) Net cash inflow is the amount of cash which the company has coming into the business from its operations. A suitable figure for net cash inflow can be obtained from the cash flow statement.

(b) Total debts are short-term and long-term creditors, together with provisions for liabilities and charges. A distinction can be made between debts payable within one year and other debts and provisions.

3.22 Obviously, a company needs to be earning enough cash from operations to be able to meet its foreseeable debts and future commitments, and the cash flow ratio, and changes in the cash flow ratio from one year to the next, provide a useful indicator of a company's cash position.

Short-term solvency and liquidity

3.23 **Profitability** is of course an important aspect of a company's performance and debt or gearing is another. Neither, however, addresses directly the key issue of **liquidity**.

> **KEY TERM**
>
> **Liquidity** is the amount of cash a company can put its hands on quickly to settle its debts (and possibly to meet other unforeseen demands for cash payments too).

3.24 Liquid funds consist of:

(a) Cash

(b) Short-term investments for which there is a ready market

(c) Fixed-term deposits with a bank or building society, for example, a six month high-interest deposit with a bank

(d) Trade debtors (because they will pay what they owe within a reasonably short period of time)

(e) Bills of exchange receivable (because like ordinary trade debtors, these represent amounts of cash due to be received within a relatively short period of time)

3.25 In summary, **liquid assets** are current asset items that will or could soon be **converted into cash, and cash itself**. Two common definitions of liquid assets are:

(a) All current assets without exception
(b) All current assets with the exception of stocks

3.26 A company can obtain liquid assets from sources other than sales, such as the issue of shares for cash, a new loan or the sale of fixed assets. But a company cannot rely on these at all times, and in general, obtaining liquid funds depends on making sales and profits. Even so, profits do not always lead to increases in liquidity. This is mainly because funds generated from trading may be immediately invested in fixed assets or paid out as dividends. You should refer back to the chapter on cash flow statements to examine this issue.

3.27 The reason why a company needs liquid assets is so that it can meet its debts when they fall due. Payments are continually made for operating expenses and other costs, and so there is a cash cycle from trading activities of cash coming in from sales and cash going out for expenses. This is illustrated by the diagram overleaf.

The cash cycle

3.28 To help you to understand liquidity ratios, it is useful to begin with a brief explanation of the cash cycle. The cash cycle describes the flow of cash out of a business and back into it again as a result of normal trading operations.

3.29 Cash goes out to pay for supplies, wages and salaries and other expenses, although payments can be delayed by taking some credit. A business might hold stock for a while and then sell it. Cash will come back into the business from the sales, although customers might delay payment by themselves taking some credit.

Part F: Interpretation of accounts

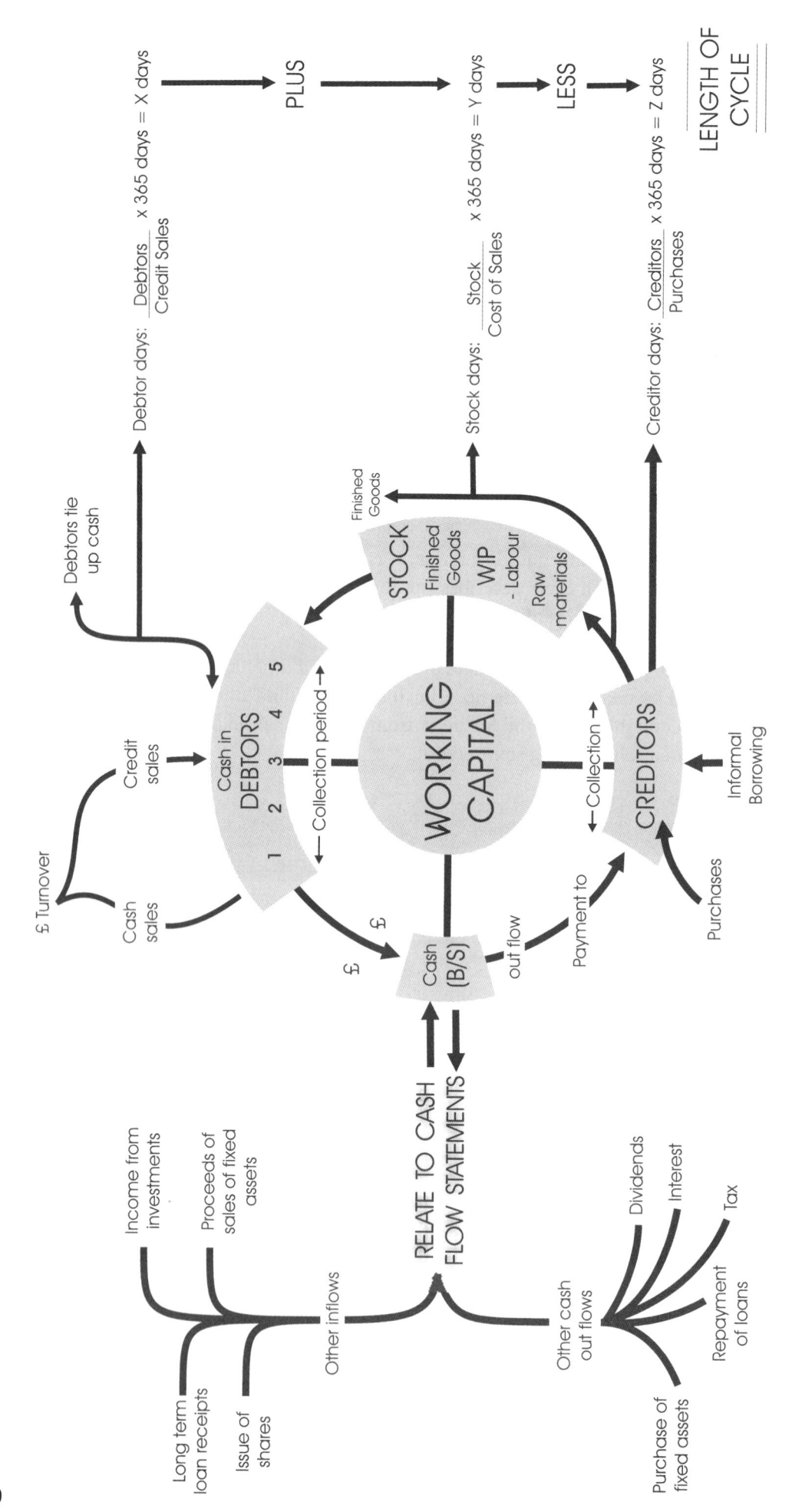

Debtor days: $\frac{\text{Debtors}}{\text{Credit Sales}} \times 365 \text{ days} = X \text{ days}$ → PLUS →

Stock days: $\frac{\text{Stock}}{\text{Cost of Sales}} \times 365 \text{ days} = Y \text{ days}$ → LESS →

Creditor days: $\frac{\text{Creditors}}{\text{Purchases}} \times 365 \text{ days} = Z \text{ days}$

LENGTH OF CYCLE

WORKING CAPITAL

- Debtors tie up cash
- DEBTORS — Cash in — Collection period — 1 2 3 4 5
- £ Turnover: Credit sales, Cash sales
- STOCK: Finished Goods, WIP – Labour, Raw materials
- Finished Goods
- CREDITORS — Collection
- Informal Borrowing
- Purchases
- Payment to
- Cash (B/S) — out flow

RELATE TO CASH FLOW STATEMENTS

Other inflows:
- Income from investments
- Proceeds of sales of fixed assets
- Long term loan receipts
- Issue of shares

Other cash out flows:
- Dividends
- Interest
- Tax
- Repayment of loans
- Purchase of fixed assets

3.30 The main points about the cash cycle are as follows.

(a) The timing of cash flows in and out of a business does not coincide with the time when sales and costs of sales occur. Cash flows out can be postponed by taking credit. Cash flows in can be delayed by having debtors.

(b) The time between making a purchase and making a sale also affects cash flows. If stocks are held for a long time, the delay between the cash payment for stocks and cash receipts from selling them will also be a long one.

(c) Holding stocks and having debtors can therefore be seen as two reasons why cash receipts are delayed. Another way of saying this is that if a company invests in working capital, its cash position will show a corresponding decrease.

(d) Similarly, taking credit from creditors can be seen as a reason why cash payments are delayed. The company's liquidity position will worsen when it has to pay the creditors, unless it can get more cash in from sales and debtors in the meantime.

3.31 The liquidity ratios and working capital turnover ratios are used to test a company's liquidity, length of cash cycle, and investment in working capital.

Liquidity ratios: current ratio and quick ratio June 2003

3.32 The 'standard' test of liquidity is the **current ratio**. It can be obtained from the balance sheet, and is calculated as follows.

> **FORMULA TO LEARN**
>
> $$\text{Current ratio} = \frac{\text{current assets}}{\text{current liabilities}}$$

The idea behind this is that a company should have enough current assets that give a promise of 'cash to come' to meet its future commitments to pay off its current liabilities. Obviously, a **ratio in excess of 1** should be expected. Otherwise, there would be the prospect that the company might be unable to pay its debts on time. In practice, a ratio comfortably in excess of 1 should be expected, but what is 'comfortable' varies between different types of businesses.

3.33 Companies are not able to convert all their current assets into cash very quickly. In particular, some manufacturing companies might hold large quantities of raw material stocks, which must be used in production to create finished goods stocks. Finished goods stocks might be warehoused for a long time, or sold on lengthy credit. In such businesses, where stock turnover is slow, most stocks are not very 'liquid' assets, because the cash cycle is so long. For these reasons, we calculate an additional liquidity ratio, known as the **quick ratio** or **acid test** ratio.

> **FORMULA TO LEARN**
>
> $$\text{The quick ratio, or acid test ratio is:} \quad \frac{\text{current assets less stocks}}{\text{current liabilities}}$$

Part F: Interpretation of accounts

3.34 This ratio should ideally be at least 1 for companies with a slow stock turnover. For companies with a fast stock turnover, a quick ratio can be comfortably less than 1 without suggesting that the company should be in cash flow trouble.

3.35 Both the current ratio and the quick ratio offer an indication of the company's liquidity position, but the absolute figures should not be interpreted too literally. It is often theorised that an acceptable current ratio is 1.5 and an acceptable quick ratio is 0.8, but these should only be used as a guide.

Case example

Different businesses operate in very different ways. Budgens (the supermarket group) for example had (as at 30 April 1993) a current ratio of 0.52 and a quick ratio of 0.17. Budgens has low debtors (people do not buy groceries on credit), low cash (good cash management), medium stocks (high stocks but quick turnover, particularly in view of perishability) and very high creditors (Budgens buys its supplies of groceries on credit).

Compare the Budgens ratios with the Tomkins group which had a current ratio of 1.44 and a quick ratio of 1.03 (as at 1 May 1993). Tomkins is a manufacturing and retail organisation and operates with liquidity ratios closer to the standard. At 25 September 1993, Tate & Lyle's figures gave a current ratio of 1.18 and a quick ratio of 0.80.

3.36 What is important is the **trend** of these ratios. From this, one can easily ascertain whether liquidity is improving or deteriorating. If Budgens has traded for the last 10 years (very successfully) with current ratios of 0.52 and quick ratios of 0.17 then it should be supposed that the company can continue in business with those levels of liquidity. If in the following year the current ratio were to fall to 0.38 and the quick ratio to 0.09, then further investigation into the liquidity situation would be appropriate. It is the relative position that is far more important than the absolute figures.

3.37 Don't forget the other side of the coin either. A current ratio and a quick ratio can get bigger than they need to be. A company that has large volumes of stocks and debtors might be over-investing in working capital, and so tying up more funds in the business than it needs to. This would suggest poor management of debtors (credit) or stocks by the company.

Efficiency ratios: control of debtors   June 2003

3.38 A rough measure of the average length of time it takes for a company's debtors to pay what they owe is the 'debtor days' ratio, or **average debtors' payment period**.

FORMULA TO LEARN

$$\text{Debtors payment period} = \frac{\text{trade debtors}}{\text{sales}} \times 365 \text{ days}$$

3.39 The estimated average **debtors' payment period** is calculated as follows.

3.40 The figure for sales should be taken as the turnover figure in the P & L account. The trade debtors are not the total figure for debtors in the balance sheet, which includes prepayments and non-trade debtors. The trade debtors figure will be itemised in an analysis of the debtors total, in a note to the accounts.

22: Ratio analysis

3.41 The estimate of debtor days is only approximate.

(a) The balance sheet value of debtors might be abnormally high or low compared with the 'normal' level the company usually has.

(b) Turnover in the P & L account is exclusive of VAT, but debtors in the balance sheet are inclusive of VAT. We are not strictly comparing like with like. (Some companies show turnover inclusive of VAT as well as turnover exclusive of VAT, and the 'inclusive' figure should be used in these cases.)

3.42 Sales are usually made on 'normal credit terms' of payment within 30 days. Debtor days significantly in excess of this might be representative of poor management of funds of a business. However, some companies must allow generous credit terms to win customers. Exporting companies in particular may have to carry large amounts of debtors, and so their average collection period might be well in excess of 30 days.

3.43 The trend of the collection period (debtor days) over time is probably the best guide. If debtor days are increasing year on year, this is indicative of a poorly managed credit control function (and potentially therefore a poorly managed company).

3.44 EXAMPLES: DEBTOR DAYS

Using the same examples as before, the debtor days of those companies were as follows.

Company	Date	Trade debtors / turnover	Debtor days (×365)	Previous year	Debtor days (×365)
Budgens	30.4.93	£5,016K / £284,986K =	6.4 days	£3,977K / £290,668K =	5.0 days
Tomkins	1.5.93	£458.3m / £2,059.5m =	81.2 days	£272.4m / £1,274.2m =	78.0 days
Tate & Lyle	25.9.93	£304.4m / £3,817.3m =	29.3 days	£287.0m / £3,366.3m =	31.1 days

3.45 The differences in debtor days reflect the differences between the types of business. Budgen's has hardly any trade debtors at all, whereas the manufacturing companies have far more. The debtor days are fairly constant from the previous year for all three companies.

Stock turnover period   June 2003

3.46 Another ratio worth calculating is the **stock turnover period**, or **stock days**. This is another estimated figure, obtainable from published accounts, which indicates the average number of days that items of stock are held for. As with the average debt collection period, however, it is only an approximate estimated figure, but one which should be reliable enough for comparing changes year on year.

> **FORMULA TO LEARN**
>
> The number of **stock days** is calculated as:
>
> $$\frac{\text{Stock}}{\text{Cost of sales}} \times 365$$

3.47 The reciprocal of the fraction:

Part F: Interpretation of accounts

$$\frac{\text{cost of sales}}{\text{stock}}$$

is termed the stock turnover, and is another measure of how vigorously a business is trading. A lengthening stock turnover period from one year to the next indicates:

(a) A slowdown in trading

(b) A build-up in stock levels, perhaps suggesting that the investment in stocks is becoming excessive

3.48 Presumably if we add together the stock days and the debtor days, this should give us an indication of how soon stock is convertible into cash. Both debtor days and stock days therefore give us a further indication of the company's liquidity.

3.49 EXAMPLES: STOCK TURNOVER

Returning once more to our first example, the estimated stock turnover periods for Budgens were as follows.

Company	Date	$\frac{\text{Stock}}{\text{Cost of sales}}$	Stock turnover period (days × 365)		Previous year	
Budgens	30.4.92	$\frac{£15,554K}{£254,571K}$	22.3 days	$\frac{£14,094K}{£261,368K}$	× 365 =	19.7 days

3.50 The figures for cost of sales were not shown in the accounts of either Tate & Lyle or Tomkins

Question 3

Bingo Ltd buys raw materials on six weeks credit, holds them in store for three weeks and then issues them to the production department. The production process takes two weeks on average, and finished goods are held in store for an average of four weeks before being sold. Debtors take five weeks credit on average.

Calculate the length of the cash cycle.

Answer

The cash cycle is the length of time between paying for raw materials and receiving cash from the sale of finished goods. In this case Bingo Ltd stores raw materials for three weeks, spends two weeks producing finished goods, four weeks storing the goods before sale and five weeks collecting the money from debtors: a total of 14 weeks. However, six weeks of this period is effectively financed by the company's creditors so that the length of the cash cycle is eight weeks.

Question 4

During a year a business sold stock which had cost £60,000. The stock held at the beginning of the year was £6,000 and at the end of the year £10,000.

What was the annual rate of stock turnover?

Answer

$$\text{Stock turnover} = \frac{\text{Cost of goods sold}}{\text{Average stock}} = \frac{£60,000}{£8,000}$$

$$= 7.5 \text{ times}$$

Creditor ratios

June 2003

3.51 Creditors' turnover is ideally calculated by the formula:

$$\frac{\text{Trade creditors}}{\text{Purchases}} \times 365$$

However, it is rare to find purchases disclosed in published accounts and so cost of sales serves as an approximation. The creditors' turnover ratio often helps to assess a company's liquidity; an increase in creditor days is often a sign of lack of long-term finance or poor management of current assets, resulting in the use of extended credit from suppliers, increased bank overdraft and so on.

Question 5

Calculate liquidity and working capital ratios from the accounts of the BET Group, a business which provides service support (cleaning etc) to customers worldwide.

	1997	1996
Turnover	2,176.2	2,344.8
Cost of sales	1,659.0	1,731.5
Gross profit	517.2	613.3
Current assets		
Stocks	42.7	78.0
Debtors (note 1)	378.9	431.4
Short-term deposits and cash	205.2	145.0
	626.8	654.4
Creditors: amounts falling due within one year		
Loans and overdrafts	32.4	81.1
Corporation taxes	67.8	76.7
Dividend	11.7	17.2
Creditors (note 2)	487.2	467.2
	599.1	642.2
Net current assets	27.7	12.2
Notes		
1 Trade debtors	295.2	335.5
2 Trade creditors	190.8	188.1

Answer

	1997		1996	
Current ratio	$\frac{626.8}{599.1}$ = 1.05	$\frac{654.4}{642.2}$ = 1.02
Quick ratio	$\frac{584.1}{599.1}$ = 0.97	$\frac{576.4}{642.2}$ = 0.90
Debtors' payment period	$\frac{295.2}{2,176.2} \times 365$ = 49.5 days	$\frac{335.5}{2,344.8} \times 365$ = 52.2 days
Stock turnover period	$\frac{42.7}{1,659.0} \times 365$ = 9.4 days	$\frac{78.0}{1,731.5} \times 365$ = 16.4 days
Creditors' turnover period	$\frac{190.8}{1,659.0} \times 365$ = 42.0 days	$\frac{188.1}{1,731.5} \times 365$ = 40.0 days

3.52 BET Group is a service company and hence it would be expected to have very low stock and a very short stock turnover period. The similarity of debtors' and creditors' turnover periods means that the group is passing on most of the delay in receiving payment to its suppliers.

Part F: Interpretation of accounts

3.53 BET's current ratio is a little lower than average but its quick ratio is better than average and very little less than the current ratio. This suggests that stock levels are strictly controlled, which is reinforced by the low stock turnover period. It would seem that working capital is tightly managed, to avoid the poor liquidity which could be caused by a high debtors' turnover period and comparatively high creditors.

4 SHAREHOLDERS' INVESTMENT RATIOS

4.1 These are the ratios which help equity shareholders and other investors to assess the value and quality of an investment in the ordinary shares of a company. They are:

(a) Earnings per share
(b) Dividend per share
(c) Dividend cover
(d) P/E ratio
(e) Dividend yield
(f) Earnings yield

4.2 The value of an investment in ordinary shares in a listed company is its market value, and so investment ratios must have regard not only to information in the company's published accounts, but also to the current price, and the fourth, fifth and sixth ratios all involve using the share price.

Earnings per share

4.3 It is possible to calculate the return on each ordinary share in the year. This is the earnings per share (EPS). Earnings are profits after tax, preference dividends and 'extraordinary items' (separately disclosed, large and very unusual items), which can either be paid out as a dividend to ordinary shareholders or retained in the business. You should note that earnings per share will be revisited in Chapter 24 in connection with FRS 3 *Reporting financial performance*.

4.4 EXAMPLE: EARNINGS PER SHARE

Suppose that Draught Ltd reports the following figures:

PROFIT AND LOSS ACCOUNT FOR 20X4 (EXTRACT)

	£
Profit before interest and tax	120,000
Interest	(20,000)
Profit before tax	100,000
Taxation	(40,000)
Profit after tax	60,000
Preference dividend	(1,000)
Profit available for ordinary shareholders (= earnings)	59,000
Ordinary dividend	(49,000)
Retained profits	10,000

The company has 80,000 ordinary shares and 20,000 preference shares.

Calculate earnings per share for Draught Ltd in 20X4.

4.5 SOLUTION

EPS is $\dfrac{£59,000}{80,000}$ = 73.75 pence

Dividend per share and dividend cover

4.7 The **dividend per share** in pence is self-explanatory, and clearly an item of some interest to shareholders.

4.8 **Dividend cover** is calculated as follows.

> **FORMULA TO LEARN**
>
> $$\text{Dividend cover} = \frac{\text{Earnings per share}}{\text{Dividend per (ordinary) share}}$$

4.9 It shows the proportion of profit on ordinary activities for the year that is available for distribution to shareholders has been paid (or proposed) and what proportion will be retained in the business to finance future growth. A dividend cover of 2 times would indicate that the company had paid 50% of its distributable profits as dividends, and retained 50% in the business to help to finance future operations. Retained profits are an important source of funds for most companies, and so the dividend cover can in some cases be quite high.

4.10 A significant change in the dividend cover from one year to the next would be worth looking at closely. For example, if a company's dividend cover were to fall sharply between one year and the next, it could be that its profits had fallen, but the directors wished to pay at least the same amount of dividends as in the previous year, so as to keep shareholder expectations satisfied.

P/E ratio

> **KEY TERM**
>
> The **P/E ratio** is the ratio of a company's current share price to the earnings per share.

4.11 A high **P/E ratio** indicates strong shareholder confidence in the company and its future, eg in profit growth, and a lower P/E ratio indicates lower confidence.

4.12 The P/E ratio of one company can be compared with the P/E ratios of:

   (a) Other companies in the same business sector
   (b) Other companies generally

Dividend yield

4.13 **Dividend yield** is the return a shareholder is currently expecting on the shares of a company. It is calculated as follows.

Part F: Interpretation of accounts

> **FORMULA TO LEARN**
>
> $$\text{Dividend yield} = \frac{\text{Dividend on the share for the year}}{\text{Current market value of the share (ex div)}} \times 100\%$$

4.14 Shareholders look for both dividend yield and capital growth. Obviously, dividend yield is therefore an important aspect of a share's performance.

Question 6

In the year to 31 December 1998, BPP Holdings plc declared an interim ordinary dividend of 5p per share and a final ordinary dividend of 11p per share. Assuming an ex div share price of 432 pence, what is the dividend yield?

Answer

The net dividend per share is (5 + 11) = 16 pence

$$\frac{16}{432} \times 100 = 3.70\%$$

Earnings yield

4.15 Earnings yield is a performance indicator that is not given the same publicity as EPS, P/E ratio, dividend cover and dividend yield.

> **KEY TERM**
>
> **Earnings yield** is measured as the earnings per share, grossed up, as a percentage of the current share price. It therefore, indicates what the dividend yield could be if the company paid out all its profits as dividend and retained nothing in the business.

4.16 It attempts to improve the comparison between investments in different companies by overcoming the problem that companies have differing dividend covers. Some companies retain a bigger proportion of their profits than others, and so the dividend yield between companies can vary for this reason. Earnings yield overcomes the problem of comparison by assuming that all earnings are paid out as dividends.

> **FORMULA TO LEARN**
>
> Earnings yield = dividend yield × dividend cover.

Question 7

	Company P		Company Q	
	£m	£m	£m	£m
Profit on ordinary activities after tax		41.1		5.6
Dividends				
Preference	0.5		-	
Ordinary	20.6		5.4	
		21.1		5.4
Retained profits		20.0		0.2

	Company P	Company Q
Number of ordinary shares	200m	50m
Market price per share	285p	154p

Compare the dividend yield, dividend cover and earnings yield of the two companies.

Answer

	Company P	Company Q
	£m	£m
Profit on ordinary activities after tax	41.1	5.6
Preference dividend	0.5	0
Earnings	40.6	5.6
Number of shares	200m	50m
EPS	20.3p	11.2p
Ordinary dividend per share	10.3p	10.8p
Dividend cover	20.3 / 10.3	11.2 / 10.8
	= 1.97 times	= 1.04 times

	Company P	Company Q
Dividend yield	$\frac{10.3}{285} \times 100\%$	$\frac{10.8}{154} \times 100\%$
	= 3.6%	= 7.0%
Earnings yield	$\frac{20.3}{285} \times 100\%$	$\frac{11.2}{154} \times 100\%$
	= 7.1%	= 7.3%

The dividend yield of Company Q is much higher, but the dividend cover of Company P is greater. (The dividend cover of Q is only just greater than 1. Company Q has just about managed to pay its dividend out of profits made in the year.)

5 PRESENTATION OF A RATIO ANALYSIS REPORT
December 2001, June 2002

5.1 Examination questions on ratio analysis may try to simulate a real life situation. A set of accounts could be presented and you may be asked to prepare a report on them, addressed to a specific interested party, such as a bank. You should begin your report with a heading showing who it is from, the name of the addressee, the subject of the report and a suitable date.

5.2 A good approach is often to head up a 'schedule of ratios and statistics' which will form an appendix to the main report. Calculate the ratios in a logical sequence, dealing in turn with

Part F: Interpretation of accounts

operating and profitability ratios, use of assets (eg turnover periods for stocks and debtors), liquidity and gearing.

5.3 As you calculate the ratios you are likely to be struck by significant fluctuations and trends. These will form the basis of your comments in the body of the report. The report should begin with some introductory comments, setting out the scope of your analysis and mentioning that detailed figures have been included in an appendix. You should then go on to present your analysis under any categories called for by the question (eg separate sections for management, shareholders and creditors, or separate sections for profitability and liquidity).

5.4 Finally, look out for opportunities to suggest remedial action where trends appear to be unfavourable. Questions sometimes require you specifically to set out your advice and recommendations.

Exam focus point
You may be asked to prepare a report on ratios which have already been calculated. Alternatively you may be given a full set of accounts and asked to calculate, evaluate and comment on the ratios.

Planning your answers

5.5 This is as good a place as any to stress the importance of planning your answers. This is particularly important for 'wordy' questions. While you may feel like breathing a sigh of relief after all that number crunching, you should not be tempted to 'waffle'. The best way to avoid going off the point is to prepare an answer plan. This has the advantage of making you think before you write and structure your answer logically.

5.6 The following approach may be adopted when preparing an answer plan.

(a) Read the question requirements.

(b) Skim through the question to see roughly what it is about.

(c) Read through the question carefully, underlining any key words.

(d) Set out the headings for the main parts of your answer. Leave space to insert points within the headings.

(e) Jot down points to make within the main sections, underlining points on which you wish to expand.

(f) Write your full answer, including all numerical calculations in an Appendix.

Exam focus point
You should allow yourself the full time allocation for written answers, that is 1.8 minutes per mark. If, however, you run out of time, a clear answer plan with points in note form will earn you more marks than an introductory paragraph written out in full.

Chapter roundup

- This lengthy chapter has gone into quite a lot of detail about basic **ratio analysis**. The ratios you should be able to calculate and/or comment on are as follows.

    - **Profitability ratios**
        - return on capital employed
        - net profit as a percentage of sales
        - asset turnover ratio
        - gross profit as a percentage of sales

    - **Debt and gearing ratios**
        - debt ratio
        - gearing ratio
        - interest cover
        - cash flow ratio

    - **Liquidity and working capital ratios**
        - current ratio
        - quick ratio (acid test ratio)
        - debtor days (average debt collection period)
        - average stock turnover period

    - **Ordinary shareholders' investment ratios**
        - earnings per share
        - dividend cover
        - P/E ratio
        - dividend yield
        - earnings yield

- With the exception of the last three ratios, where the share's market price is required, all of these ratios can be calculated from information in a company's **published accounts**.

- Ratios provide information through comparison:
    - **Trends** in a company's ratios from one year to the next, indicating an improving or worsening position
    - In some cases, against a **'norm'** or 'standard'
    - In some cases, against the **ratios of other companies**, although differences between one company and another should often be expected

- You may realise that, however many ratios you can find to calculate, **numbers alone will not answer a question**. You **must interpret** all the information available to you and support your interpretation with ratio calculations.

Part F: Interpretation of accounts

Quick quiz

1. Apart from ratio analysis, what other information might be helpful in interpreting a company's accounts?
2. What is the usual formula for ROCE?
3. ROCE can be calculated as the product of two other ratios. What are they?
4. Define the 'debt ratio'.
5. In a period when profits are fluctuating, what effect does a company's level of gearing have on the profits available for ordinary shareholders?
6. What is a company's cash flow ratio?
7. What is earnings per share?
8. What is the P/E ratio?
9. Write down the best approach to answering an interpretation question.

Answers to quick quiz

1. Various other items and notes in the publicised accounts (see paragraph 1.7).

2. $\dfrac{\text{PBIT}}{\text{Capital employed}}$

3. Profit margin × asset turnover = ROCE

4. $\dfrac{\text{The total of a company's debts}}{\text{Total assets}}$

5. See paragraph 3.15.

6. $\dfrac{\text{Net cash inflow}}{\text{Total debts}}$

7. The amount of net profit that is attributable to each ordinary share.

8. $\dfrac{\text{Current share price}}{\text{EPS}}$

9. See paragraph 5.6.

Now try the questions below from the Exam Question Bank

Question to try	Level	Marks	Time
34	Introductory	n/a	36 mins
35	Introductory	n/a	36 mins
36	Full exam	10	18 mins

Other topics

Part G
Miscellaneous topics

Chapter 23

COMPUTER APPLICATIONS IN ACCOUNTING

Topic list	Syllabus reference
1 Accounting packages	3(d)
2 Accounting modules	3(d)
3 Databases	3(d)
4 Spreadsheets	3(d)
5 Practical experience	3(d)

Introduction

We referred briefly to computerised accounting systems in Chapter 12 on control accounts. These days, most accounting systems are computerised and anyone training to be an accountant should be able to work with them.

The most important point to remember is that the **principles of computerised accounting are the same as those of manual accounting**. You should by now have a good grasp of these principles.

The first section of this chapter talks about accounting **packages**. This is a rather general term, but most of us can probably name the accounting package that we use at work.

An accounting package consists of several accounting **modules**, eg sales ledger, cash book. An exam question may take one of these modules and ask you to describe inputs, processing and outputs. Alternatively, you may be asked to outline the advantages of computer processing over manual processing, for example, for debtors or payroll.

Questions may ask you to discuss the advantages and disadvantages of **databases** and **spreadsheets**. These are discussed in Sections 3 and 4. It is likely that you will have used a spreadsheet in your workplace.

Study guide

Section 6 - Computerised accounting systems

- Compare manual and computerised accounting systems.
- Identify the advantages and disadvantages of computerised systems.
- Describe the main elements of a computerised accounting system.
- Describe typical data processing work.
- Explain the use of integrated accounting packages.
- Explain the nature and use of micro-computers.
- Explain other business uses of computers.
- Explain the nature and purpose of spreadsheets.
- Explain the nature and purpose of database systems.

427

Part G: Miscellaneous topics

> **Exam guide**
> If a question on computing comes up, you are likely to get a discursive question on the advantages or disadvantages of a computer system.

1 ACCOUNTING PACKAGES

1.1 The syllabus for this paper requires you to know about the use of computers in financial accounting practice.

> **Exam focus point**
> Questions will *not* be set on the technical aspects of how computers work.

1.2 We shall assume, therefore, that you know that a modern computer generally consists of a keyboard, a television-like screen, a box-like disk drive which contains all the necessary electronic components for data processing, and a printer. This is the computer hardware.

1.3 The computer hardware described above is also known as a personal computer (PC), but the technical name is a **micro-computer**.

> **KEY TERM**
> **Computer programs** are the instructions that tell the electronics how to process data. The general term used for these is **software**.

1.4 Software is what we are concerned with in this text, and in particular 'applications software', that is packages of computer programs that carry out specific tasks.

   (a) Some applications are devoted specifically to an accounting task, for example a payroll package, a fixed asset register or a stock control package.

   (b) Other applications have many uses in business, including their use for accounting purposes. Packages of this sort that we shall describe are databases and spreadsheets.

Accounting packages

> **IMPORTANT!**
> One of the most important facts to remember about computerised accounting is that **in principle, it is exactly the same as manual accounting.**

1.5 Accounting functions retain the same names in computerised systems as in more traditional written records. Computerised accounting still uses the familiar ideas of day books, ledger accounts, double entry, trial balance and financial statements. The principles of working with computerised sales, purchase and nominal ledgers are exactly what would be expected in the manual methods they replace.

1.6 The only difference is that these various books of account have become invisible. Ledgers are now computer files which are held in a computer-sensible form, ready to be called upon.

Advantages

1.7 However, the advantages of accounting packages compared with a manual system are as follows.

(a) The packages can be used by **non-specialists**.

(b) A large amount of **data can be processed very quickly**.

(c) Computerised systems are **more accurate** than manual systems.

(d) A computer is capable of handling and processing **large volumes** of data.

(e) Once the data has been input, computerised systems can **analyse data** rapidly to present useful control information for managers such as a trial balance or a debtors schedule.

Disadvantages

1.8 The advantages of computerised accounting system far outweigh the disadvantages, particularly for large businesses. However, the following may be identified as possible disadvantages.

(a) The initial **time and costs** involved in installing the system, training personnel and so on.

(b) The need for **security checks** to make sure that unauthorised personnel do not gain access to data files.

(c) The necessity to develop a **system of coding** (see below) and checking.

(d) **Lack of 'audit trail'**. It is not always easy to see where a mistake has been made.

(e) Possible **resistance** on the part of staff to the introduction of the system.

Coding

1.9 Computers are used more efficiently if vital information is expressed in the form of codes. For example, nominal ledger accounts will be coded individually, perhaps by means of a two-digit code: eg

00 Ordinary share capital
01 Share premium
05 Profit and loss account
15 Purchases
22 Debtors ledger control account
41 Creditors ledger control account
42 Interest
43 Dividends etc

In the same way, individual accounts must be given a unique code number in the sales ledger and purchase ledger.

Part G: Miscellaneous topics

1.10 EXAMPLE: CODING

When an invoice is received from a supplier (code 1234) for £3,000 for the purchase of raw materials, the transaction might be coded for input to the computer as:

	Nominal ledger			Stock	
Supplier Code	Debit	Credit	Value	Code	Quantity
1234	15	41	£3,000	56742	150

Code 15 might represent purchases and code 41 the creditors control account. This single input could be used to update the purchase ledger, the nominal ledger, and the stock ledger. The stock code may enable further analysis to be carried out, perhaps allocating the cost to a particular department or product. Thus the needs of both financial accounting and cost accounting can be fulfilled at once.

Using an accounting package

1.11 When a user begins to work with an accounting package he will usually be asked to key in a **password**. Separate passwords can be used for different parts of the system, for example for different ledgers if required. The user will then be presented with a 'menu' of options such as 'enter new data' or 'print report' or a Windows-type screen with buttons and icons. By selecting the appropriate option the user will then be guided through the actions needed to enter the data or generate the report.

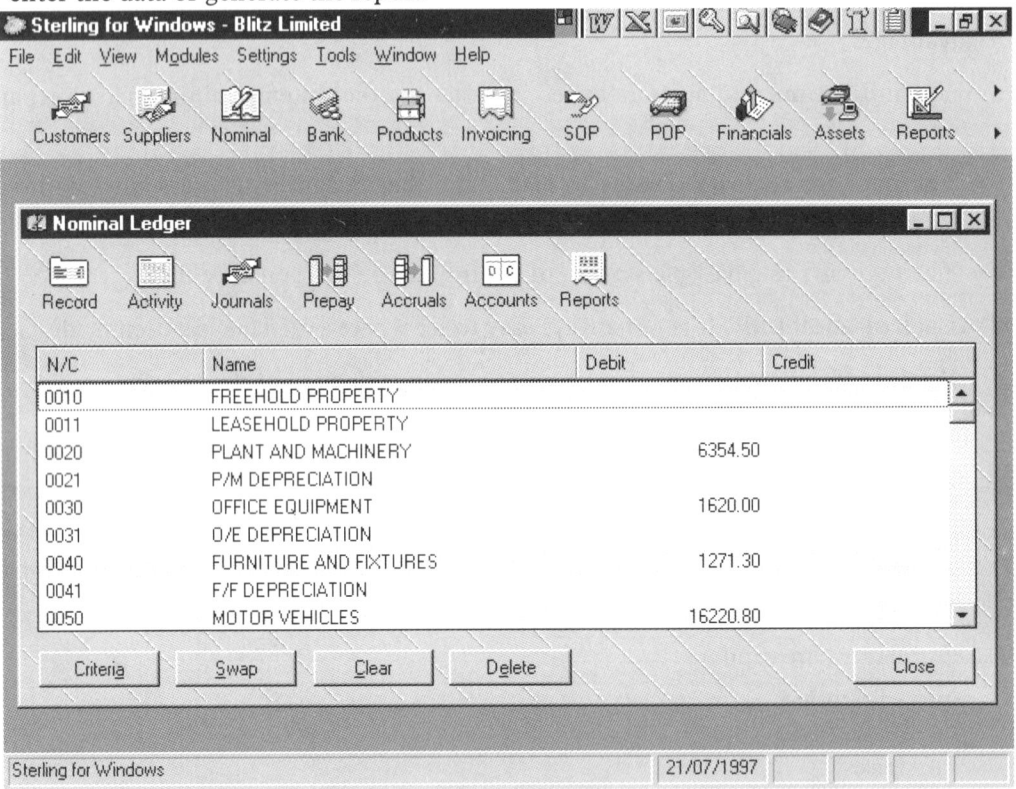

> **IMPORTANT!**
>
> If you are not already using one, get some experience between now and the exam, of using an accounting package.

Modules

> **KEY TERM**
>
> A **module** is a program which deals with one particular part of a business accounting system.

1.12 An accounting package will consist of several modules. A simple accounting package might consist of only one module (in which case it is called a stand-alone module), but more often it will consist of several modules. The name given to a set of several modules is a **suite**. An accounting package, therefore, might have separate modules for:

(a) Invoicing
(b) Stock
(c) Sales ledger
(d) Purchase ledger
(e) Nominal ledger
(f) Payroll
(g) Cash book
(h) Job costing
(i) Fixed asset register
(j) Report generator

Integrated software

1.13 Each module may be integrated with the others, so that data entered in one module will be passed automatically or by simple operator request through into any other module where the data is of some relevance. For example, if there is an input into the invoicing module authorising the despatch of an invoice to a customer, there might be **automatic links**:

(a) To the sales ledger, to update the file by posting the invoice to the customer's account.

(b) To the stock module, to update the stock file by:

   (i) Reducing the quantity and value of stock in hand
   (ii) Recording the stock movement

(c) To the nominal ledger, to update the file by posting the sale to the sales account.

(d) To the job costing module, to record the sales value of the job on the job cost file.

(e) To the report generator, to update the sales analysis and sales totals which are on file and awaiting inclusion in management reports.

Part G: Miscellaneous topics

1.14 A diagram of an **integrated accounting system** is given below.

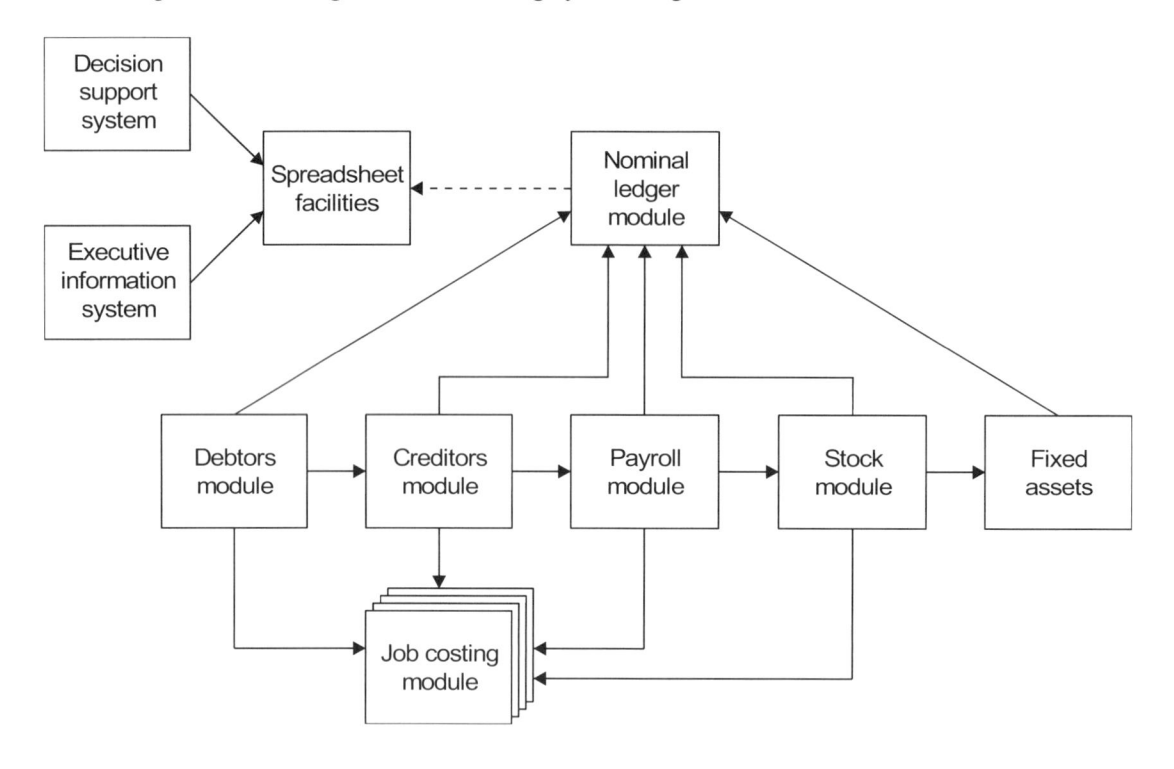

Advantages

1.15 (a) It becomes possible to make just one entry in one of the ledgers which automatically updates the others.

(b) Users can specify reports, and the software will automatically extract the required data from *all* the relevant files.

(c) Both of the above simplify the workload of the user, and the irritating need to constantly load and unload disks is eliminated.

Disadvantages

1.16 (a) Usually, it requires more computer memory than separate (stand-alone) systems - which means there is less space in which to store actual data.

(b) Because one program is expected to do everything, the user may find that an integrated package has fewer facilities than a set of specialised modules. In effect, an integrated package could be 'Jack of all trades but master of none'.

2 ACCOUNTING MODULES

2.1 In this section we shall look at some of the accounting modules in more detail, starting with the sales ledger.

Accounting for debtors

2.2 A computerised sales ledger will be expected to keep the sales ledger up-to-date, and also it should be able to produce certain output (eg statements, sales analysis reports, responses to file interrogations etc). The output might be produced daily (eg day book listings), monthly (eg statements), quarterly (eg sales analysis reports) or periodically (eg responses to file

23: Computer applications in accounting

interrogations, or customer name and address lists printed on adhesive labels for despatching circulars or price lists).

2.3 What we need to do is to have a closer look at the forms that input, output and processing take within a sales ledger. We will begin by thinking about what data we would expect to see in a sales ledger.

Data held on a sales ledger file

2.4 The sales ledger **file** will consist of individual **records** for each customer account. Some of the data held on the record will be **standing data** (ie it will change infrequently). Typical items of standing data are:

(a) Customer account number

(b) Customer name

(c) Address

(d) Credit limit

(e) Account sales analysis code

(f) Account type (there are two different types of account - open item or balance forward - which we will look at shortly)

Each of these items is referred to as a **field** of information.

2.5 Other data held on a customer record will change as the sales ledger is updated. Such data is called **variable data**, and will include:

(a) Transaction data
(b) Transaction description (eg sale, credit note etc)
(c) Transaction code (eg to identify payment period allowed)
(d) Debits
(e) Credits
(f) Balance

2.6 The file which contains these customer records - the sales ledger - is sometimes called a **master file**. If it is updated from another file containing various transactions, then that file is called a **transactions file**. Developments in the way computers store information mean that you are not likely to see these terms much any more - people more often talk about 'databases' of information.

Question 1

What is the relationship between a file, a field and a record?

Answer

A file is made up of records which are made up of fields. Make sure you learn any new terminology like this, because it will make your answers to examination questions far more convincing.

Input to a sales ledger system

2.7 Bearing in mind what we expect to find in a sales ledger, we can say that typical data input into sales ledger system is as follows.

Part G: Miscellaneous topics

(a) **Amendments**

    (i) Amendments to customer details, eg change of address, change of credit limit, etc

    (ii) Insertion of new customers

    (iii) Deletion of old 'non-active' customers

(b) **Transaction data relating to:**

    (i) Sales transactions, for invoicing

    (ii) Customer payments

    (iii) Credit notes

    (iv) Adjustments (debit or credit items)

2.8 Some computerised sales ledgers produce invoices, so that basic sales data is input into the system. But other businesses might have a specialised invoicing module, so that the sales ledger package is not expected to produce invoices. The invoice details are already available (as output from the specialised module) and are input into the sales ledger system rather than basic sales data. So item (b)(i) of the list of typical data should read as follows.

'(b) (i) Sales transactions, for invoicing (if the sales ledger is expected to produce invoices) or invoice details (if already available from a specialised invoicing module).'

Processing in a sales ledger system

2.9 The primary action involved in updating the sales ledger is modifying the amount outstanding on the customer's account. How the amount is modified depends on what data is being input (ie whether it is an invoice, credit note, remittance etc).

2.10 When processing starts, the balance on an account is called the *brought-forward* balance. When processing has finished, the balance on the account is called the *carried-forward* balance. These terms are often abbreviated to b/f and c/f.

2.11 What a computer does is to add or subtract whatever you tell it to from the b/f balance, and end up with a c/f balance.

	£	£
Brought forward account balance		X
Add:		
Invoice value	X	
Adjustments (+)	X	
		X
		X
Deduct:		
Credit note value	X	
Adjustments (-)	X	
Remittances	X	
		X
Carried forward account balance		X

This method of updating customer accounts is called the balance forward method.

2.12 Most systems also offer users the **open item** method of processing the data, which is much neater. Under this method, the user identifies specific invoices, and credits individual payments against specific invoices. Late payments of individual invoices can be identified and chased up. The customer's outstanding balance is the sum of the unpaid open items.

23: Computer applications in accounting

The open item method follows best accounting practice, but it is more time consuming than the balance forward method.

Outputs from a sales ledger system

2.13 Typical outputs in a computerised sales ledger are as follows.

(a) **Day book listing**. A list of all transactions posted each day. This provides an audit trail - ie it is information which the auditors of the business can use when carrying out their work. Batch and control totals will be included in the listing.

(b) **Invoices** (if the package is one which is expected to produce invoices.)

(c) **Statements**. End of month statements for customers.

(d) **Aged debtors list**. Probably produced monthly.

(e) **Sales analysis reports**. These will analyse sales according to the sales analysis codes on the sales ledger file.

(f) **Debtors reminder letters**. Letters can be produced automatically to chase late payers when the due date for payment goes by without payment having been received.

(g) **Customer lists** (or perhaps a selective list). The list might be printed on to adhesive labels, for sending out customer letters or marketing material.

(h) **Responses to enquiries**, perhaps output on to a VDU screen rather than as printed copy, for fast response to customer enquiries.

(i) **Output onto disk file for other modules** - eg to the stock control module and the nominal ledger module, if these are also used by the organisation, and the package is not an integrated one.

The advantages of a computerised debtor system

2.14 The advantage of such a system, in addition to the advantages of computerised accounting generally, is its ability to assist in sales administration and marketing by means of outputs such as those listed above.

Purchase ledger

2.15 A computerised purchase ledger will certainly be expected to keep the purchase ledger up-to-date, and also it should be able to output various reports requested by the user. In fact, a computerised purchase ledger is much the same as a computerised sales ledger, except that it is a sort of mirror image as it deals with purchases rather than sales.

Question 2

What sort of data would you expect to be held on a purchase ledger file?

Answer

The purchase ledger will consist of individual records for each supplier account. Just as for customer accounts, some of the data held on record will be *standing* data, and some will be *variable* data. Standing data will include:

(a) Account number
(b) Name
(c) Address
(d) Credit details

Part G: Miscellaneous topics

   (e) Bank details (eg method of payment)
   (f) Cash discount details, if appropriate

Variable data will include:

   (a) Transaction date
   (b) Transaction description
   (c) Transaction code
   (d) Debits
   (e) Credits
   (f) Balance

Inputs to a purchase ledger system

2.16 Bearing in mind what we expect to see held on a purchase ledger, typical data input into a purchase ledger system is:

   (a) Details of purchases recorded on invoices
   (b) Details of returns to suppliers for which credit notes are received
   (c) Details of payments to suppliers
   (d) Adjustments

Processing in a purchase ledger system

2.17 The primary action involved in updating the purchase ledger is adjusting the amounts outstanding on the supplier accounts. These amounts will represent money owed to the suppliers. This processing is identical to updating the accounts in the sales ledger, except that the sales ledger balances are debits (debtors) and the purchase ledger balances are credits (creditors). Again, the open item approach is the best.

Outputs from a purchase ledger system

2.18 Typical outputs in a computerised purchase ledger are as follows.

   (a) Lists of transactions posted - produced every time the system is run.

   (b) An analysis of expenditure for nominal ledger purposes. This may be produced every time the system is run or at the end of each month.

   (c) List of creditors balances together with a reconciliation between the total balance brought forward, the transactions for the month and the total balance carried forward.

   (d) Copies of creditors' accounts. This may show merely the balance b/f, current transactions and the balance c/f. If complete details of all unsettled items are given, the ledger is known as an **open-ended ledger**. (This is similar to the open item or balance forward methods with a sales ledger system.)

   (e) Any purchase ledger system can be used to produce details of payments to be made. For example:

      (i) Remittance advices (usually a copy of the ledger account)
      (ii) Cheques
      (iii) Credit transfer listings

   (f) Other special reports may be produced for:

      (i) Costing purposes
      (ii) Updating records about fixed assets
      (iii) Comparisons with budget
      (iv) Aged creditors list

Nominal ledger

2.19 The nominal ledger (or general ledger) is an accounting record which summarises the financial affairs of a business. It is the nucleus of an accounting system. It contains details of assets, liabilities and capital, income and expenditure and so profit or loss. It consists of a large number of different accounts, each account having its own purpose or 'name' and an identity or code.

2.20 A nominal ledger will consist of a large number of coded accounts. For example, part of a nominal ledger might be as follows.

Account code	*Account name*
100200	Plant and machinery (cost)
100300	Motor vehicles (cost)
100201	Plant and machinery depreciation
100301	Vehicles depreciation
300000	Total debtors
400000	Total creditors
500130	Wages and salaries
500140	Rent and rates
500150	Advertising expenses
500160	Bank charges
500170	Motor expenses
500180	Telephone expenses
600000	Sales
700000	Cash

2.21 A business will, of course, choose its own codes for its nominal ledger accounts. The codes given in this table are just for illustration.

2.22 It is important to remember that a computerised nominal ledger works in exactly the same way as a manual nominal ledger, although there are some differences in terminology. For instance, in a manual system, the sales and debtors accounts were posted from the sales day book (not the sales ledger). But in a computerised system, the sales day book is automatically produced as part of the 'sales ledger module'. So it may *sound* as if you are posting directly from the sales ledger, but in fact the day book is part of a computerised sales ledger.

Inputs to the nominal ledger

2.23 Inputs depend on whether the accounting system is integrated or not.

(a) If the system is integrated, then as soon as data is put into the sales ledger module (or anywhere else for that matter), the relevant nominal ledger accounts are updated. There is nothing more for the system user to do.

(b) If the system is not integrated then the output from the sales ledger module (and anywhere else) has to be input into the nominal ledger. This is done by using journal entries. For instance.

DEBIT	A/c 300000	£3,000	
CREDIT	A/c 600000		£3,000

Where 600000 is the nominal ledger code for sales, and 300000 is the code for debtors.

Part G: Miscellaneous topics

2.24 Regardless of whether the system is integrated or not, the actual data needed by the nominal ledger package to be able to update the ledger accounts includes:

(a) Date
(b) Description
(c) Amount
(d) Account codes (sometimes called distinction codes)

Outputs from the nominal ledger

2.25 The main outputs apart from listings of individual nominal ledger accounts are:

(a) The trial balance
(b) Financial statements

3 DATABASES

3.1 A database may be described as a 'pool' of data, which can be used by any number of applications. Its use is not restricted to the accounts department. A stricter definition is provided in the *Computing Terminology* of the Chartered Institute of Management Accountants (CIMA).

> **KEY TERM**
>
> 'Frequently a much abused term, in its strict sense a **database** is a file of data structured in such a way that it may serve a number of applications without its structure being dictated by any one of those applications. The idea is that programs are written around the database rather than files being structured to meet the needs of specific programs. The term is also rather loosely applied to simple file management software.'

3.2 The software that runs the database is called the database management system (DBMS). The CIMA's definition is as follows.

> **KEY TERM**
>
> 'Technically, a **database management system** is a system which uses a database philosophy for the storage of information. In practice this term is often used to describe any system which enables the definition, storage and retrieval of information from discrete files within a system. Thus many simple file-handling systems are frequently referred to as "database systems".'

23: Computer applications in accounting

3.3 The database approach can also be summarised diagrammatically.

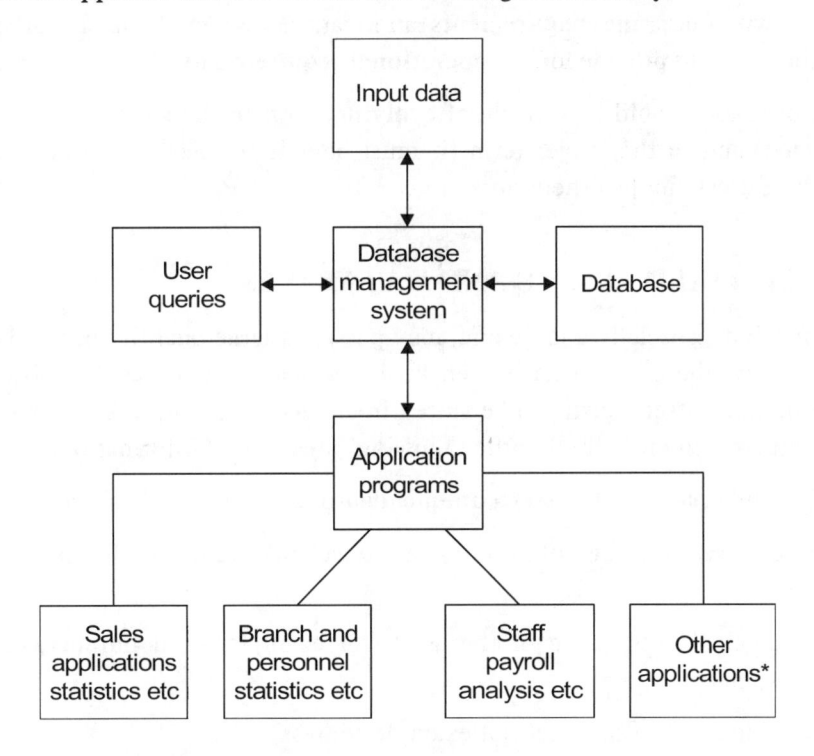

```
                    ┌──────────┐
                    │Input data│
                    └────┬─────┘
                         ↕
    ┌────────┐    ┌────────────┐    ┌──────────┐
    │  User  │◄──►│  Database  │◄──►│ Database │
    │queries │    │ management │    │          │
    │        │    │   system   │    │          │
    └────────┘    └─────┬──────┘    └──────────┘
                        ↕
                 ┌─────────────┐
                 │ Application │
                 │  programs   │
                 └──────┬──────┘
        ┌───────────┬───┴───┬──────────────┐
    ┌───────┐  ┌─────────┐ ┌────────┐  ┌────────┐
    │ Sales │  │Branch & │ │ Staff  │  │ Other  │
    │applic.│  │personnel│ │payroll │  │applic.*│
    │stats  │  │stats etc│ │analysis│  │        │
    │etc    │  │         │ │etc     │  │        │
    └───────┘  └─────────┘ └────────┘  └────────┘
```

* The range of applications which make use of a database will vary widely, depending on what data is held in the database files.

3.4 Note the following from the diagram.

(a) Data is input, and the DBMS software organises it into the database. If you like, you can think of the database as a vast library of fields and records, waiting to be used.

(b) Various application programs (sales, payroll etc) are 'plugged into' the DBMS software so that they can use the database, or the same application used by different departments can all use the database.

(c) As there is only one pool of data, there is no need for different departments to keep many different files with duplicated information.

Objectives of a database

3.5 The main virtues of a database are as follow.

(a) There is **common data** for all users to share.
(b) The extra effort of keeping **duplicate files** in different departments is avoided.
(c) Conflicts between departments who use **inconsistent data are avoided**.

3.6 A database should have four major objectives.

(a) It should be **shared**. Different users should be able to access the *same data* in the database for their own processing applications (and at the *same time* in some systems) thus removing the need for duplicating data on different files.

(b) The **integrity** of the database must be preserved. This means that one user should not be allowed to alter the data on file so as to spoil the database records for other users. However, users must be able to update the data on file, and so make valid alterations to the data.

Part G: Miscellaneous topics

(c) The database system should provide for the needs of different users, who each have their own processing requirements and data access methods. In other words, the database should provide for the **operational requirements of all its users**.

(d) The database should be capable of **evolving**, both in the short term (it must be kept updated) and in the longer term (it must be able to meet the future data processing needs of users, not just their current needs).

3.7 EXAMPLE: FIXED ASSETS AND DATABASES

An organisation, especially a large one, may possess a large quantity of fixed assets. Before computerisation these would have been kept in a manual fixed asset register. A database enables this fixed asset register to be stored in an electronic form. A database file for fixed assets might contain most or all of the following categories of information.

(a) Code number to give the asset a unique identification in the database

(b) Type of asset (for example motor car, leasehold premises), for published accounts purposes

(c) More detailed description of the asset (for example serial number, car registration number, make)

(d) Physical location of the asset (for example address)

(e) Organisational location of the asset (for example accounts department)

(f) Person responsible for the asset (for example in the case of a company-owned car, the person who uses it)

(g) Original cost of the asset

(h) Date of purchase

(i) Depreciation rate and method applied to the asset

(j) Accumulated depreciation to date

(k) Net book value of the asset

(l) Estimated residual value

(m) Date when the physical existence of the asset was last verified

(n) Supplier

Obviously, the details kept about the asset would depend on the type of asset it is.

3.8 Any kind of computerised fixed asset record will improve efficiency in accounting for fixed assets because of the ease and speed with which any necessary calculations can be made. Most obvious is the calculation of the depreciation provision which can be an extremely onerous task if it is done monthly and there are frequent acquisitions and disposals and many different depreciation rates in use.

3.9 The particular advantage of using a database for the fixed asset function is its flexibility in generating reports for different purposes. Aside from basic cost and net book value information a database with fields such as those listed above in the record of each asset could compile reports analysing assets according to location say, or by manufacturer. This information could be used to help compare the performance of different divisions, perhaps, or to assess the useful life of assets supplied by different manufacturers. There may be as many more possibilities as there are permutations of the individual pieces of data.

4 SPREADSHEETS

> **KEY TERM**
>
> A **spreadsheet** is essentially an electronic piece of paper divided into rows and columns with a built in pencil, eraser and calculator. It provides an easy way of performing numerical calculations.

4.1 The intersection of each column and row of a spreadsheet is referred to as a cell. A cell can contain text, numbers or formulae. Use of a formula means that the cell which contains the formula will display the results of a calculation based on data in other cells. If the numbers in those other cells change, the result displayed in the formula cell will also change accordingly. With this facility, a spreadsheet is used to create financial models.

4.2 Below is a spreadsheet processing budgeted sales figures for three geographical areas for the first quarter of the year.

	A	B	C	D	E
1	BUDGETED SALES FIGURES				
2		Jan	Feb	Mar	Total
3		£'000	£'000	£'000	£'000
4	North	2,431	3,001	2,189	7,621
5	South	6,532	5,826	6,124	18,482
6	West	895	432	596	1,923
7	Total	9,858	9,259	8,909	28,026

The use of spreadsheets

4.3 Spreadsheets have many uses, both for accounting and for other purposes. It is perfectly possible, for example, to create proforma balance sheets and P&L accounts on a spreadsheet, or set up the notes for financial accounts, like the fixed assets note.

5 PRACTICAL EXPERIENCE

5.1 Reading about computer systems and packages is no substitute for using them, and you should make every effort to gain experience in using an accounting package.

> **Chapter roundup**
>
> - Computer **software** used in accounting may be divided into two types.
>   - Dedicated accounting packages
>   - General software, the uses of which include accounting amongst many others
> - In principle computerised accounting is the same as manual accounting, but a computerised approach has certain advantages which you should learn thoroughly.
> - An accounting package consists of a number of **'modules'** which perform all the tasks needed to maintain a normal accounting function like purchase ledger or payroll. In modern systems the modules are usually integrated with each other.
> - A **database** is a file of data structured in such a way that it can serve a number of applications without its structure being dictated by any particular function.
> - **Spreadsheets**, too, are often useful both in financial accounting and cost accounting.
> - **Reading about accounting packages is no substitute for using one.**

Part G: Miscellaneous topics

Quick quiz

1. What are the advantages of computerised accounting?
2. What are the disadvantages?
3. What is an accounting suite?
4. What sort of data is input into a sales ledger system?
5. What is the open item method of processing?
6. What should be the four major objectives of a database?
7. What are the advantages of using a database to maintain non-current asset records?
8. What is a spreadsheet?

Answers to Quick Quiz

1. See paragraph 1.7.
2. See paragraph 1.8.
3. A set of several different modules.
4. See paragraph 2.7.
5. Payments are credited to specific invoices, so that late payment of invoices can be identified.
6. See paragraph 3.6.
7. The amount of detail that can be kept about each individual asset and the ease in analysing this information into different reports and calculations (eg depreciation, profit on sale).
8. See paragraph 4.1.

Now try the question below from the Exam Question Bank

Question to try	Level	Marks	Time
37	Introductory	n/a	36 mins

Chapter 24

THE REGULATORY FRAMEWORK

Topic list	Syllabus reference
1 The standard setting process	1(c)
2 Published accounts	5(c)
3 The role of the Stock Exchange	1(c)
4 Generally accepted accounting practice (GAAP)	1(c)
5 Accounting standards and choice	1(d)
6 The need for FRS 3	5(d)
7 Exceptional and extraordinary items	5(d)
8 Structure of the profit and loss account	5(d)
9 FRS 3 statements and notes	5(d)

Introduction

If you recall, at the beginning of your studies (Chapter 1 of this Study Text) we considered some of the influences which have shaped financial accounting. The principal areas identified were company law, accounting standards and GAAP. In this chapter these areas will be considered in more detail. They should make more sense to you now that you know how to prepare financial accounts.

In Chapter 19 you learned how to prepare the accounts of limited companies for internal purposes. In this chapter you learn how to prepare 'published' company accounts for external purposes. In this chapter, you will meet the last standard needed at this stage of your studies: FR3 *Reporting financial performance*.

Study guide

Sections 19, 20 and 21 - Accounting for limited companies 2 - advanced

- Explain the need for regulation of companies in legislation and accounting standards.

- Explain the provisions of legislation and accounting standards governing financial statements (excluding group aspects).

    - Companies Act 1985 including the standard formats for company financial statements.

    - FRS 3 Reporting Financial Performance, including provisions relating to the profit and loss account, the statement of recognised gains and losses and the note of historical cost profits and losses

- Explain the notes to financial statements required for the syllabus.

    - Statement of movements in reserves.
    - Details of fixed assets.
    - Details of post balance sheet events.
    - Details of contingent liabilities and contingent assets (see Section 18).
    - Details of research and development expenditure.

- Prepare financial statements for publication complying with relevant accounting standards and legislation as detailed above.

Part G: Miscellaneous topics

> ## Exam guide
> Learn the published accounts and notes. You need to be able to reproduce them in the exam rapidly so that you can then focus on filling in the figures. Also learn the proforma layout for FRS 3. Try to understand the principles behind this standard, so that you can discuss them.

1 THE STANDARD SETTING PROCESS

1.1 **Limited companies** are required by law (the Companies Act 1985 or CA 1985) to **prepare and publish accounts annually**. The form and content of the accounts are regulated primarily by CA 1985, but must also comply with accounting standards.

1.2 Financial statements are prepared on the basis of a number of fundamental accounting concepts (or accounting principles as they are called in the Companies Act 1985). Many figures in financial statements are derived from the application of judgement in putting those concepts into practice.

1.3 It is clear that different people exercising their judgement on the same facts can arrive at very different conclusions. For example, suppose that a business owns a freehold property which it purchased for £100,000.

   (a) Some people might argue that no depreciation should be charged on the building because property prices are always rising. The building would appear in the accounts permanently at £100,000.

   (b) Others would say that this does not go far enough. If property prices are rising, not only should no depreciation be charged, but the book value of the building should be increased each year by revaluation.

   (c) Still others might say that the £100,000 is expenditure incurred by the business and that all expenditure should at some time be charged to the profit and loss account, perhaps by equal annual depreciation charges over the building's useful life.

1.4 Working from the same data, these different groups of people would produce very different financial statements. If the exercise of judgement is completely unfettered any comparability between the accounts of different organisations will disappear. This will be all the more significant in cases where deliberate manipulation occurs in order to present accounts in the most favourable light.

Old regime: SSAPs

1.5 From 1970 to 1990, the **Accounting Standards Committee** (ASC) developed accounting standards with the aim of narrowing the areas of difference and variety in accounting practice. The ASC published 25 **statements of standard accounting practice** (SSAPs). It came under the control of the Consultative Committee of Accountancy Bodies (CCAB) at an early stage.

1.6 The CCAB's member bodies instructed their members to conform with SSAPs in preparing any accounts which seek to give a true and fair view of an enterprise's results and financial position. This applied in particular to the accounts of limited companies, which are required by law to give a true and fair view; however, SSAPs were intended as authoritative documents whose recommendations might be adopted voluntarily even in the accounts of unincorporated organisations.

24: The regulatory framework

New regime: FRSs

1.7 In 1990, however, a new system came into being for producing standards, following the recommendations of the Dearing Report, produced for the CCAB in 1988. This proposed that a two tier system should be established. The **Financial Reporting Council**, independent of the profession, now guides the standard setting process. The **Accounting Standards Board** (ASB) issues accounting standards, without the previous requirement to obtain agreement from all CCAB members first.

1.8 The ASB is much better staffed and financed than the ASC. The source of this increased finance has been the Stock Exchange, the accountancy bodies and industry.

1.9 The ASB has stated its intention to have a small number of standards 'concerned with principles rather than fine details'. This is a change of direction as the ASC's standards were considered unduly prescriptive in the past. If standards lay down detailed rules then it is often possible, by sticking to the letter rather than the spirit of the rules, to get round them.

1.10 Although there are considerable difficulties in laying down universally agreed principles, the ASB's approach is to emphasise 'substance over form' - the accountant's traditional approach. New standards issued are no longer called SSAPs but financial reporting standards (FRSs). In time all standards will be replaced by or converted to FRSs.

Urgent issues task force

1.11 An important offshoot of the ASB is an **Urgent Issues Task Force**, whose function is 'to tackle urgent matters not covered by existing standards, and for which, given the urgency, the normal standard-setting process would not be practicable' (Sir Ron Dearing, Chairman of the FRC). This was established in March 1991.

Review panel

1.12 The **Review Panel**, chaired by a barrister, is concerned with the examination and questioning of departures from accounting standards by large companies. The Review Panel will be alerted to most cases for investigation by the results of the new CA 1985 requirement that companies must include in the notes to the accounts a statement that they have been prepared in accordance with applicable accounting standards or, alternatively, giving details of material departures from those standards, with reasons.

1.13 Although it is expected that most such referrals will be resolved by discussion, the Panel (and the Secretary of State for Trade and Industry) have the power to apply to the court for revision of the accounts, with all costs potentially payable (if the court action is successful) by the company's directors. The auditors may also be disciplined if the audit report on the defective accounts was not qualified with respect to the departure from standards. Revised accounts, whether prepared voluntarily or under duress, will have to be circulated to all persons likely to rely on the previous accounts. The Review Panel was set up in early 1991.

Current accounting standards

1.14 The following standards are extant at the date of writing (June 2003). The SSAPs which were in force at the date the ASB was formed have been adopted by the Board. They are gradually being superseded by the new Financial Reporting Standards.

Part G: Miscellaneous topics

UK accounting standards

Title			Issue date
		Foreword to accounting standards	Jun 93
FRS 1	#	Cash flow statements (revised Oct 96)	Sep 91
FRS 2		Accounting for subsidiary undertakings	Jul 92
FRS 3	#	Reporting financial performance	Oct 92
FRS 4		Capital instruments	Dec 93
FRS 5		Reporting the substance of transactions	Apr 94
FRS 6		Acquisitions and mergers	Sep 94
FRS 7		Fair values in acquisition accounting	Sep 94
FRS 8		Related party disclosures	Oct 95
FRS 9		Associates and joint ventures	Nov 97
FRS 10		Goodwill and intangible assets	Dec 97
FRS 11		Impairment of fixed assets and goodwill	Jul 98
FRS 12	#	Provisions, contingent liabilities and contingent assets	Sep 98
FRS 13		Derivatives and other financial instruments: disclosures	Sep 98
FRS 14		Earnings per share	Sep 98
FRS 15	#	Tangible fixed assets	Feb 99
FRS 16		Current tax	Dec 99
FRS 17		Retirement benefits	Nov 00
FRS 18	#	Accounting policies	Dec 00
FRS 19		Deferred tax	Dec 00
FRSSE		Financial reporting standard for smaller entities	Nov 97
SSAP 4		Accounting for government grants	Jul 90
SSAP 5		Accounting for value added tax	Apr 74
SSAP 9	#	Stocks and long-term contracts	Sep 88
SSAP 13	#	Accounting for research and development	Jan 89
SSAP 17	#	Accounting for post balance sheet events	Aug 80
SSAP 19		Accounting for investment properties	Nov 81
SSAP 20		Foreign currency translation	Apr 83
SSAP 21		Accounting for leases and hire purchase contracts	Aug 84
SSAP 25		Segmental reporting	Jun 90

Notes

On the Paper 1.1 syllabus (ie the rest are *not* on the syllabus). The group aspects of FRS 1 and FRS 3 are excluded.

The *Statement of Principles for Financial Reporting* (issued December 1999) is also on your syllabus. It was covered in Chapter 14.

Accounting standards and the law

1.15 In June 1993, the ASB published its *Foreword to Accounting Standards* in final form. The Foreword contains a legal opinion from Mary Arden QC on the relationship between accounting standards and the Companies Act requirement to show a true and fair view.

1.16 Miss Arden considered the changes in the Companies Act which, in her view, strengthen the status of accounting standards. These are the granting of statutory recognition to the existence of standards and the introduction of a procedure whereby the Financial Reporting Review Panel can ask the court to determine whether accounts comply with the true and fair requirement.

> 'These factors increase the likelihood that the courts will hold that in general compliance with accounting standards is necessary to meet the true and fair requirement.'

1.17 Miss Arden added that the improved standard setting process also enhances the status of standards since the standard setting body no longer represents the views of the profession alone. The ASB's rigorous practice of discussion, consultation and investigation in producing its standards is another influencing factor.

2 PUBLISHED ACCOUNTS   Pilot paper, December 2001, June 2002, December 2002

2.1 **Statutory accounts** are part of the price to be paid for the benefits of limited liability. Limited companies must produce such accounts annually and they must appoint an independent person to audit and report on them. Once prepared, a copy of the accounts must be sent to the Registrar of Companies, who maintains a separate file for every company. The Registrar's files may be inspected for a nominal fee, by any member of the public. This is why the statutory accounts are often referred to as published accounts.

> **KEY TERM**
>
> **Statutory accounts** are accounts which limited companies are obliged by law to publish in a particular form.

2.2 It is the responsibility of the company's directors to produce accounts which show a **true and fair view** of the company's results for the period and its financial position at the end of the period. The board evidence their approval of the accounts by the signature of one director on the balance sheet (formerly two signatures were required). Once this has been done, and the auditors have completed their report, the accounts are laid before the members of the company in general meeting. When the members have adopted the accounts they are sent to the Registrar for filing.

2.3 The requirement that the accounts show a true and fair view is paramount.

> **IMPORTANT!**
>
> Although statute lays down numerous rules on the information to be included in the published accounts and the format of its presentation, any such rule may be **overridden** if compliance with it would prevent the accounts from showing a **true and fair view**.

2.4 The documents which must be included by law in the accounts laid before a general meeting of the members are:

(a) A profit and loss account (or an income and expenditure account in the case of a non-trading company)

(b) A balance sheet as at the date to which the profit and loss account is made up

(c) A directors' report

(d) An auditors' report addressed to the members (not to the directors) of the company

(e) The group accounts in the case of a company which has subsidiaries at the year end date.

2.5 FRS 1 requires the inclusion of a cash flow statement. This statement was discussed in Chapter 20. Here we will look at the legally required accounting statements, the profit and loss account and balance sheet.

Part G: Miscellaneous topics

2.6 The following example shows a *pro forma* profit and loss account and balance sheet with the notes specified in the Paper 1.1 Study Guide.

STANDARD PLC
PROFIT AND LOSS ACCOUNT FOR THE YEAR ENDED
31 DECEMBER 20X5

	Notes	£'000	£'000
Turnover			X
Cost of sales			X
Gross profit			X
Distribution costs			X
Administrative expenses			X
Operating profit	1		X
Income from fixed asset investments			X
			X
Interest payable and similar charges			X
Profit on ordinary activities before taxation			X
Tax on profit on ordinary activities			X
Profit on ordinary activities after taxation			X
Dividend paid and proposed		X	
Transfer to general reserve		X	
			X
Retained profit for the financial year			X

STANDARD PLC
BALANCE SHEET AS AT 31 DECEMBER 20X5

	Notes	£'000	£'000
Fixed assets			
Intangible assets	2		X
Tangible assets	3		X
Fixed asset investments			X
			X
Current assets			
Stocks		X	
Debtors		X	
Cash at bank and in hand		X	
		X	
Creditors: amounts falling due within one year		X	
Net current assets			X
Total assets less current liabilities			X
Creditors: amounts falling due after more than one year			X
			X
Capital and reserves			
Called up share capital			X
Share premium account	4		X
Revaluation reserve	4		X
General reserve	4		X
Profit and loss account	4		X
			X

Approved by the board on ....

.... Director

The notes on pages XX to XX form part of these accounts.

NOTES TO THE ACCOUNTS

1 *Operating profit*

   Operating profit is stated after charging:

	£'000
Depreciation (see Chapter 10)	X
Amortisation	X
Auditors' remuneration	X
Exceptional items (see Section 7)	X
Directors' emoluments	X
Staff costs	X
Research and development (see Chapter 15)	X

   Notes

   Separate totals are required to be disclosed for:

   (a) Audit fees and expenses
   (b) Fees paid to auditors for non-audit work

   This disclosure is not required for small or medium-sized companies.

Question 1

Arco Ltd receives an invoice in respect of the current year from its auditors made up as follows.

	£
Audit of accounts	10,000
Taxation computation and advice	1,500
Travelling expenses: audit	1,100
Consultancy fees charged by another firm of accountants	1,600
	14,200

What figure should be disclosed as auditors' remuneration in the notes to the profit and loss account?

Answer

	£
Audit of accounts	10,000
Expenses	1,100
Taxation computation and advice	1,500
	12,600

The consultancy fees are not received by the auditors.

2 *Intangible fixed assets*

	Development expenditure £'000
Cost	
At 1 January 20X5	X
Expenditure	X
At 31 December 20X5	X
Amortisation	
At 1 January 20X5	X
Charge for year	X
At 31 December 20X5	X
Net book value at 31 December 20X5	X
Net book value 31 December 20X4	X

   Note

   The above disclosure should be given for each intangible asset.

Part G: Miscellaneous topics

3 Tangible fixed assets

	Freehold land and buildings £'000	Leasehold land and buildings Long leases £'000	Leasehold land and buildings Short leases £'000	Plant and machinery £'000	Fixtures and fittings £'000	Total £'000
Cost (or valuation)						
At 1 Jan 20X5	X	X	X	X	X	X
Additions	X	-	X	-	X	X
Revaluation	X	-	-	-	-	X
Disposals	(X)	-	-	(X)	(X)	(X)
At 31 Dec 20X5	X	X	X	X	X	X
Depreciation						
At 1 Jan 20X5	X	X	X	X	X	X
Charge for year	X	X	X	X	X	X
Revaluation	(X)	-	-	-	-	(X)
Disposals	(X)	-	-	(X)	(X)	(X)
At 31 Dec 20X5	X	X	X	X	X	X
Net book value						
At 31 Dec 20X5	X	X	X	X	X	X
At 31 Dec 20X4	X	X	X	X	X	X

Notes

(a) Long leases are ≥ 50 years unexpired at balance sheet date.

(b) Classification by asset type represents arabic numbers from the standard formats.

(c) Motor vehicles (unless material) are usually included within plant and machinery.

(d) Revaluations in the year: state for each asset revalued:

   (i) Method of valuation

   (ii) Date of valuation

   (iii) The historical cost equivalent of the above information as if the asset had not been revalued.

4 Reserves

	Share premium £'000	Revaluation £'000	General £'000	Profit and loss £'000
At 1 January 20X5	X	X	X	X
Retained profit for the year	-	-	-	X
Revaluation	-	X	-	-
Transfers	-	-	X	X
At 31 December 1995	X	X	X	X

> **Exam focus point**
> The Study Guide requires candidates to prepare balance sheet notes detailing movements on reserves, movements on fixed assets, details of exceptional and extraordinary items, post balance sheet events, contingent liabilities, contingent assets and research and development expenditure. The disclosure notes required for FRS 3, SSAP 13, SSAP 17 and FRS 12 are given in the relevant chapters of this Text.

Question 2

The best way to learn the format and content of published accounts and notes is to practise questions. However, you must start somewhere, so try to learn the above formats, then close this text and write out on a piece of paper:

(a) A standard layout for a balance sheet and profit and loss account.
(b) A standard layout for the notes to these accounts specified by your Study Guide.

3 THE ROLE OF THE STOCK EXCHANGE

3.1 The Stock Exchange is a market for stocks and shares, and a company whose securities are traded on the main market is known as being 'quoted' as a 'listed' company.

3.2 When a share is granted a quotation on The Stock Exchange, it appears on the *Official List* which is published in London for each business day. The Official List shows the 'official quotation' or price for the share for that particular day; it is drawn up by the Quotations Department of The Stock Exchange, which derives its prices from those actually ruling in this market. In practice, the buying and selling prices used by member firms will be within the prices quoted on the Official List.

3.3 In order to receive a listing for its securities, a company must conform with Stock Exchange regulations contained in the **Listing Rules** issued by the Council of The Stock Exchange. The company commits itself to certain procedures and standards, including matters concerning the disclosure of accounting information, which are more extensive than the disclosure requirements of the Companies Acts.

Question 3

To ensure you understand which regulations apply to which type of business, fill in the table below with a 'yes' where compliance is required and 'no' where it is not.

Type of Business	Companies Act	FRSs/ SSAPs	IASs	Stock Exchange Listing Rules
Public Listed Company				
Private Limited Company				
Sole Tradership				

Answer

Your table should look like this.

Type of Business	Companies Act	FRSs/ SSAPs	IASs	Stock Exchange Listing Rules
Public Listed Company	YES	YES	NO	YES
Private Limited Company	YES	YES	NO	NO
Sole Tradership	NO	NO	NO	NO

4 GENERALLY ACCEPTED ACCOUNTING PRACTICE (GAAP)

4.1 This term has sprung up in recent years and it signifies all the rules, from whatever source, which govern accounting. In the UK this is seen primarily as a combination of:

(a) **Company law** (mainly CA 1985)
(b) **Accounting standards**
(c) **Stock Exchange requirements**

4.2 Although those sources are the basis for **UK GAAP**, the concept also includes the effects of non-mandatory sources such as:

Part G: Miscellaneous topics

(a) **International accounting standards**
(b) **Statutory requirements in other countries**, particularly the US

4.3 In the UK, GAAP does not have any statutory or regulatory authority or definition (unlike other countries, such as the US). The term is mentioned rarely in legislation, and only then in fairly limited terms.

4.4 GAAP is in fact a dynamic concept: it changes constantly as circumstances alter through new legislation, standards and practice. this idea that GAAP is constantly changing is recognised by the ASB in its *Statement of aims* where it states that it expects to issue new standards and amend old ones in response to 'evolving business practices, new economic developments and deficiencies identified in current practice.' The emphasis has shifted from 'principles' to 'practice' in UK GAAP.

4.5 The problem of what is 'generally accepted' is not easy to settle, because new practices will obviously not be generally adopted yet. The criteria for a practice being 'generally accepted' will depend on factors such as whether the practice is addressed by UK accounting standards or legislation, or their international equivalents, and whether other companies have adopted the practice. Most importantly perhaps, the question should be whether the practice is consistent with the needs of users and the objectives of financial reporting and whether it is consistent with the 'true and fair' concept.

5 ACCOUNTING STANDARDS AND CHOICE

5.1 It is sometimes argued that companies should be given a **choice** in matters of financial reporting on the grounds that accounting standards are detrimental to the quality of such reporting. There are arguments on both sides.

5.2 **In favour** of accounting standards, the following points can be made.

(a) They reduce or eliminate confusing variations in the methods used to prepare accounts.

(b) They provide a focal point for debate and discussions about accounting practice.

(c) They oblige companies to disclose the accounting policies used in the preparation of accounts.

(d) They are a less rigid alternative to enforcing conformity by means of legislation.

(e) They have obliged companies to disclose more accounting information than they would otherwise have done if accounting standards did not exist. FRS 3 *Reporting financial performance* and FRS 12 *Provisions, contingent liabilities and contingent assets* are examples. The reluctance of companies to disclose information is perhaps evident in the fact that very few companies chose to report the cost of sales in their accounts until legislation enforced the disclosure.

5.3 However, the following arguments may be put forward **against** standardisation and in favour of choice.

(a) A set of rules which give backing to one method of preparing accounts might be inappropriate in some circumstances. For example, SSAP 12 on depreciation was inappropriate for investment properties (in this case, pressure from the property industry secured an exemption from SSAP 12, and SSAP 19 was later issued to deal with this specific case).

(b) Standards may be subject to lobbying or government pressure. For example, an early draft on accounting for research and development (ED 14) was revised (ED 17, subsequently SSAP 13) as a result of pressure from the aerospace and electronics industries. SSAP 16 emerged partly as a result of government pressure. In the USA, the accounting standard FAS 19 on the accounts of oil and gas companies led to a powerful lobby of oil companies, which persuaded the SEC (Securities and Exchange Commission) to step in. FAS 19 was then suspended.

(c) They are not currently based on a conceptual framework of accounting.

(d) There may a trend towards rigidity, and away from flexibility in applying the rules. Michael Alexander, Director of Research and Technical Activities at the FASB in the USA, was quoted as saying (in Accountancy, May 1981) 'The demand for rule-making...comes largely from an insatiable appetite for rules...I am very concerned about this. The reliance on judgement in technical accounting matters seems to have gone.'

6 THE NEED FOR FRS 3

6.1 The introduction of FRS 3 *Reporting financial performance* has meant significant changes to company published accounts. All the changes were intended to improve the quality of information provided to shareholders.

6.2 Before we launch into the details of FRS 3, it is worth considering briefly why the changes were necessary. So what was wrong with the profit and loss account before FRS 3?

Comparisons

6.3 Before FRS 3, it was difficult to make comparisons between one year and another because there was no information about the turnover and profit drawn from activities that ceased during the year (and so will not continue next year) and new activities that did not exist last year.

6.4 To try to deal with this problem, FRS 3 requires an analysis of the profit and loss account as far as the figure of profit on ordinary activities before interest into three elements.

(a) **Continuing operations**
(b) **New acquisitions**
(c) **Discontinued operations**

This is discussed in more detail in Section 8 below.

6.5 Someone needing to make comparisons between this year's and last year's turnover and profit, will thus be **comparing like with like**. Similarly, someone needing to forecast next year's turnover and profit can now see how much of this year's operations will continue into the future.

6.6 To facilitate the comparison with previous years, FRS 3 requires the comparative figures for the previous year (which have to be disclosed alongside those for the current year in published accounts) to be **restated** so as to show as continuing activities only those which are still continuing in the current year.

Part G: Miscellaneous topics

Manipulation

6.7 Another reason for introducing FRS 3 was to put an end to the **manipulation** of the profit and loss account by means of **exceptional and extraordinary items**. These, and the changes introduced in FRS 3 are discussed in more detail in Section 7 of this chapter, but here we just look briefly at the problem which FRS 3 needed to remedy.

Effect on profit after tax

6.8 The forerunner to FRS 3, SSAP 6 *Extraordinary items and prior year adjustments* recognised that large and unusual 'one-off' items in a profit and loss account could distort results and make year-on-year comparisons difficult. It identified two such items, defined informally here, and prescribed two kinds of accounting treatment for the items in question.

   (a) **Exceptional items**. These are part of the normal course of a company's business, but hardly ever happen. They were to be disclosed separately but *included* in the calculation of profit on *ordinary* activities before tax.

   (b) **Extraordinary items**. These hardly ever happen and are *not* part of a company's ordinary activities. They are to be disclosed separately and *excluded* from the calculation of profit on ordinary activities before, and hence after, tax.

Effect on earnings per share

6.9 As you will know from Chapter 22, earnings per share is a way of calculating the return on each ordinary share in the year. It is basically earnings (profit after tax and preference dividends) divided by number of shares. Users of accounts place a great deal of faith in this figure. There is an incentive to make it appear as high as possible.

6.10 Because in pre-FRS 3 times 'earnings' excluded extraordinary items but included exceptional items, there was again an incentive to make 'bad news' extraordinary and 'good news' exceptional, so the earnings per share figure was as high as possible.

6.11 By defining exceptional items very precisely and all **but outlawing extraordinary items** (see Section 7), it was hoped to deal with the above abuse, both as regards the profit and loss account, and as regards earnings per share. It was hoped, furthermore, that earnings per share would decline in importance as an indicator of financial performance.

Main elements of FRS 3

6.12 The main elements of FRS 3 are as follows.

   (a) New structure of the profit and loss account
   (b) Extraordinary items
   (c) Statement of total recognised gains and losses
   (d) Other new disclosures
   (e) Earnings per share

You only need to know about (a) to (d) for your syllabus.

7 EXCEPTIONAL AND EXTRAORDINARY ITEMS

7.1 FRS 3 lays down the rules for dealing with 'out of the ordinary' items and how they are shown in the P & L account. FRS 3 restricts the way companies could manipulate the figures.

Exceptional items

> **KEY TERM**
>
> FRS 3 defines **exceptional items** as:
>
> 'Material items which derive from events or transactions that fall within the ordinary activities of the reporting entity and which individually or, if of a similar type, in aggregate, need to be disclosed by virtue of their *size or incidence* if the financial statements are to give a true and fair view.'

7.2 The definition of ordinary activities is important.

> 'Any activities which are undertaken by a reporting entity as part of its business and such related activities in which the reporting entity engages in furtherance of, incidental to, or arising from these activities. Ordinary activities include the effects on the reporting entity of any event in the various environments in which it operates including the political, regulatory, economic and geographical environments irrespective of the frequency or unusual nature of the event.'

7.3 There are two types of exceptional item and their accounting treatment is as follows.

(a) Firstly, there are **three categories** of exceptional items which must be **shown separately** on the face of the profit and loss account after operating profit and before interest and allocated appropriately to discontinued and continued activities.

   (i) Profit or loss on the sale or termination of an operation.

   (ii) Costs of a fundamental reorganisation or restructuring that has a material effect on the nature and focus of the reporting entity's operations.

   (iii) Profit or loss on disposal of fixed assets.

   For both items (i) and (iii) profit and losses may not be offset within categories.

(b) **Other items** should be allocated to the **appropriate statutory format heading** and attributed to continuing or discontinued operations as appropriate. If the item is sufficiently material that it is needed to show a true and fair view it must be disclosed on the face of the profit and loss account.

7.4 In both (a) and (b) an adequate description must be given in the notes to the accounts.

7.5 FRS 3 does not give examples of the type of transaction which is likely to be treated as exceptional. However, its predecessor on the subject, SSAP 6, gave a useful list of examples of items which if of a sufficient size might normally be treated as exceptional.

(a) Abnormal charges for bad debts and write-offs of stock and work in progress.
(b) Abnormal provisions for losses on long-term contracts.
(c) Settlement of insurance claims.

Extraordinary items

7.6 Under SSAP 6 and SSAP 3 (the replaced standard on earnings per share) the term extraordinary item was one of great significance. However, the ASB publicly stated that it does not envisage such items to appear on a company's profit and loss account and did not provide any examples of things that would be classified as 'extraordinary' rather than 'exceptional'. Its decline in importance has been achieved by tightening of the definition of an extraordinary item.

Part G: Miscellaneous topics

> **KEY TERM**
>
> **Extraordinary items** are defined as material items possessing a high degree of abnormality which arise from events or transactions that fall outside the ordinary activities of the reporting entity and which are not expected to recur.

7.7 Extraordinary items should be shown on the face of profit and loss account before dividends. Tax on the extraordinary item should be shown separately. A description of the extraordinary items should be given in the notes to the accounts.

8 STRUCTURE OF THE PROFIT AND LOSS ACCOUNT

8.1 All statutory headings from turnover to operating profit must be subdivided between that arising from continuing operations and that arising from discontinued operations. In addition, turnover and operating profit must be further analysed between that from existing and that from newly acquired operations. Only figures for turnover and operating profit need be shown on the face of the P & L account; all additional information regarding costs may be relegated to a note. The example below is a simplified version of the example in FRS 3.

PROFIT AND LOSS EXAMPLE 1	1993 £m	1993 £m	1992 as restated £m
Turnover			
Continuing operations	550		500
Acquisitions	50		
	600		
Discontinued operations	175		190
		775	690
Cost of sales		(620)	(555)
Gross profit		155	135
Net operating expenses		(104)	(83)
Operating profit			
Continuing operations	50		40
Acquisitions	6		
	56		
Discontinued operations	(15)		12
Less 1992 provision	10		
		51	52
Profit on sale of properties in continuing operations		9	6
Provision for loss on operations to be discontinued			(30)
Loss on disposal of discontinued operations	(17)		
Less 1992 provision	20		
		3	
Profit on ordinary activities before interest		63	28
Interest payable		(18)	(15)
Profit on ordinary activities before taxation		45	13
Tax on profit on ordinary activities		(16)	(6)
Profit on ordinary activities after taxation		29	7
Extraordinary items - included only to show positioning		-	-
Profit for the financial year		29	7
Dividends		(8)	(1)
Retained profit for the financial year		21	6
Earnings per share		39p	10p

24: The regulatory framework

PROFIT AND LOSS ACCOUNT EXAMPLE 2 (to operating profit line)

	Continuing operations 1993 £m	Acquisitions 1993 £m	Discontinued operations 1993 £m	Total 1993 £m	Total 1992 as restated £m
Turnover	550	50	175	775	690
Cost of sales	(415)	(40)	(165)	(620)	(555)
Gross profit	135	10	10	155	135
Net operating expenses	(85)	(4)	(25)	(114)	(83)
Less 1992 provision	—	—	10	10	—
Operating profit	50	6	(5)	51	52
Profit on sale of properties	9			9	6
Provision for loss on operations to be discontinued					(30)
Loss on disposal of the discontinued operations			(17)	(17)	
Less 1992 provision			20	20	
Profit on ordinary activities before interest	59	6	(2)	63	28

Thereafter example 2 is the same as example 1.

8.2 A note to the profit and loss account will give the analysis of distribution and administrative expenses between continuing and discontinued operations.

8.3 Examples 1 and 2 give slightly different information. It would be difficult to combine the two without producing a profit and loss account so complicated that nobody would understand it.

> **Exam focus point**
>
> For examination purposes, certainly at Paper 1.1, the examiner is likely to settle for Example 1 *or* Example 2, not an attempt to combine the two. FRS 3 itself presents two examples on which the ones given here are based, but does not attempt to combine them. Example 2 emphasises the forward forecasting, and Example 1 emphasises the backward comparison.

Discontinued operations

8.4 A discontinued operation is one which meets all of the following conditions.

(a) The sale or termination must have been completed before the earlier of 3 months after the year end or the date the financial statements are approved. (Terminations not completed by this date may be disclosed in the notes.)

(b) Former activity must have ceased permanently.

(c) The sale or termination has a material effect on the nature and focus of the entity's operations and represents a material reduction in its operating facilities resulting either from:

   (i) Its withdrawal from a particular market (class of business or geographical)
   (ii) Or from a material reduction in turnover in its continuing markets

(d) The assets, liabilities, results of operations and activities are clearly distinguishable, physically, operationally and for financial reporting purposes.

Part G: Miscellaneous topics

Accounting for the discontinuation

8.5 (a) **Results.** The results of the discontinued operation up to the date of sale or termination or the balance sheet date should be shown under each of the relevant profit and loss account headings.

(b) **Profit/loss on discontinuation.** The profit or loss on discontinuation or costs of discontinuation should be disclosed separately as an exceptional item after operating profit and before interest.

(c) **Comparative figures.** Figures for the previous year must be adjusted for any activities which have become discontinued in the current year.

Question 4

B&C plc's profit and loss account for the year ended 31 December 20X2, with comparatives, is as follows.

	20X2 £'000	20X1 £'000
Turnover	200,000	180,000
Cost of sales	(60,000)	(80,000)
Gross profit	140,000	100,000
Distribution costs	(25,000)	(20,000)
Administration expenses	(50,000)	(45,000)
Operating profit	65,000	35,000

During the year the company sold a material business operation with all activities ceasing on 14 February 20X3. The loss on the sale of the operation amounted to £2.2m, which is included in administration expenses in the extract above. The results of the operation for 20X1 and 20X2 were as follows.

	20X2 £'000	20X1 £'000
Turnover	22,000	26,000
Profit/(loss)	(7,000)	(6,000)

In addition, the company acquired a business which contributed £7m to turnover and an operating profit of £1.5m.

Required

Prepare the profit and loss account for the year ended 31 December 20X2 complying with the requirements of FRS 3 as far as possible.

Answer

	20X2 £m	20X2 £m	20X1 £m	20X1 £m
Turnover				
Continuing operations				
(200 - 22 - 7)/(180 - 26)		171.0		154
Acquisitions		7.0		-
		178.0		154
Discontinued		22.0		26
		200.0		180
Cost of sales		(60.0)		(80)
Gross profit		140.0		100
Distribution costs		(25.0)		(20)
Administration expenses (50 - 2.2)		(47.8)		(45)
Operating profit				
Continuing operations* (bal)	72.7		41	
Acquisitions	1.5		-	
	74.2		41	
Discontinued	(7.0)		(6)	
		67.2		35
Exceptional item		(2.2)		-
		65.0		35

* ie 65.0 + 2.2 + 7.0 = 72.7, 35 + 6 = 41

9 FRS 3 STATEMENTS AND NOTES

9.1 FRS 3 introduced a new statement and a variety of new notes to expand the information required in published accounts which we saw in Section 2.

Statement of total recognised gains and losses

> **KEY TERM**
>
> The **statement of total recognised gains and losses** brings together the profit as shown in the profit and loss account and other gains or losses.

9.2 It is important to understand that the profit and loss account can only deal with *realised* profits. An example of realised profits might be profits resulting from the sale proceeds already received or about to be received.

9.3 A company can also make substantial **unrealised profits** and losses, for example through changes in the *value* of its fixed assets. These are **recognised**, in the case of asset revaluation, by increasing the value of the assets in the balance sheet, the double entry being to a revaluation reserve included in shareholders' funds.

Question 5

Can you think of two other types of gains and losses which might be recognised during a period but which are not realised and do not pass through the profit and loss account?

Answer

(a) Gains or losses arising on the translation of foreign currency, for example with overseas investments
(b) Gains or losses on long-term trade investments

> **IMPORTANT!**
>
> Generally speaking, realised profits and losses have been recognised in the profit and loss account; unrealised profits and loses may be recognised in the balance sheet. FRS 3 argues that users of accounts need to know about the unrealised movements. The statement brings all the information together.

9.4 The ASB regards the statement of total recognised gains and losses as very important, and accords it the status of a **primary statement**. This means that it must be presented with the same prominence as the balance sheet, the profit and loss account and the cash flow statement. Below is a specimen statement.

Part G: Miscellaneous topics

STATEMENT OF TOTAL RECOGNISED GAINS AND LOSSES

	£m
Profit for the financial year (ie profit after tax and extraordinary items if any)	29
Unrealised surplus on revaluation of properties	4
Unrealised loss on trade investment	(3)
	30
Foreign currency translation differences	(2)
Total gains and losses recognised since last annual report	28

9.5 The statement is, as you can see, fairly brief, but it is useful in that it brings together information from different sources: the profit and loss account, the balance sheet and the supporting notes for the asset revaluations. The ASB's *Statement of Principles* envisages an even more significant role for the statement of total recognised gains and losses.

Note of historical cost profits and losses

9.6 If a company has adopted any of the alternative accounting rules as regards revaluation of assets then the reported profit figure per the profit and loss account may deviate from the historical cost profit figure. If this deviation is material then the financial statements must include a reconciliation statement after the statement of recognised gains and losses or the profit and loss account.

9.7 The profit figure to be reconciled is profit before tax; however, the retained profit for the year must also be restated.

IMPORTANT!

Note that FRS 3 *requires* the profit or loss on the disposal of a revalued asset to be calculated by reference to the difference between proceeds and the net carrying amount (revalued figure less depreciation on revalued figure).

9.8 The profit or loss based on historical cost will appear in the note of historical cost profits. This is the profit or loss calculated as if the revaluation had not taken place, and will be higher, because the carrying value to be compared with the sale proceeds is lower. Below is an example of a note of historical cost profits and losses.

NOTE OF HISTORICAL COST PROFITS AND LOSSES

	£m
Reported profit on ordinary activities before taxation	45
Realisation of property revaluation gains of previous years	9
Difference between historical cost depreciation charge and the actual depreciation charge of the period calculated on revalued amounts	5
Historical cost profit on ordinary activities before taxation	59

Question 6

A Ltd reported a profit before tax of £162,000 for the year ended 31 December 20X1. During the year the following transactions in fixed assets took place.

(a) An asset with a book value of £40,000 was revalued to £75,000. The remaining useful life is estimated to be five years.

(b) An asset (with a five year useful life at the date of revaluation) was revalued by £20,000 (book value £30,000) was sold one year after revaluation for £48,000.

Show the reconciliation or profit to historical cost profit for the year ended 31 December 20X1.

Answer

RECONCILIATION OF PROFIT TO HISTORICAL COST PROFIT
FOR THE YEAR ENDED 31 DECEMBER 20X1

	£'000
Reported profit on ordinary activities before taxation	162
Realisation of property revaluation gains (see note)	16
Difference between historical cost depreciation charge and the Actual depreciation charge of the year calculated on the revalued Amount (75,000 - 40,000)/5	7
	185

Note: For the revaluation in part (b), original depreciation is $\frac{£30,000}{5}$ = £6,000.

Revalued depreciation is $\frac{£50,000}{5}$ = £10,000.

Revalued NBV is £40,000, giving a profit on sale of £8,000 (£48,000 - 40,000). However, based on original cost, NBV would be £24,000, giving a profit of £24,000 (£48,000 - £24,000). Therefore the difference has to go to the reconciliation ie £16,000 (£24,000 - £8,000).

Chapter roundup

- In this chapter we have looked at the **legal and professional** framework governing the preparation of limited companies' **published accounts**. We also considered the role of the **Stock Exchange**, **GAAP** and the **conceptual framework** of accounting.

- Accounting standards were formerly published by the **Accounting Standards Committee** and called **SSAPs** (statements of standard accounting practice). In future, they will be published by the **Accounting Standards Board** and called **FRSs** (financial reporting standards). Make sure you know the differences between the old system and the new.

- You should also be able to discuss the role of the **Urgent Issues Task Force** and the **Review Panel**.

- All companies must prepare full **statutory accounts** for approval by their shareholders. For large companies, a copy of these accounts must also be made available to the public by filing with the registrar of companies.

- Make sure you know the various **notes to the accounts** from this and previous chapters.

- Listed companies must comply with **Stock Exchange regulations** contained in the *Listing Rules*. The requirements are more stringent than for non-listed companies.

- You should ensure that you understand what is meant by **GAAP**.

- Arguments may be put forward in favour of **choice** in financial reporting as against accounting standards.

- FRS 3 *Reporting financial performance* has introduced radical changes to the profit and loss account of large and medium sized companies.

- You should be aware of the **FRS 3 definitions** of:
  - Extraordinary items
  - Exceptional items
  - Discontinued operations
  - Total recognised gains and losses

- You should be aware of the format of the **statement of total recognised gains and losses**, and the **note on historical cost profits and losses**, and understand their contents. It is not yet clear what type of question will be set concerning these statements.

Part G: Miscellaneous topics

Quick quiz

1. What body currently produces accounting standards?
2. What is the relationship between accounting standards and the Companies Act requirement to show a true and fair view?
3. What do you understand by GAAP?
4. State the arguments in favour of (a) accounting standards; (b) accounting choice.
5. How does FRS 3 define 'ordinary activities'?
6. Which exceptional items must be shown on the face of the P & L account?
7. Define extraordinary items.
8. What components of financial performance should be shown in the profit and loss account according to FRS 3?
9. What conditions must be satisfied for a sold or terminated operation to be classified as discontinued?
10. How should discontinued activities be accounted for?
11. What is shown in the statement of total recognised gains and losses?
12. Which of the following occurrences would be treated as extraordinary under FR3?

    A   Restructuring
    B   Natural disasters
    C   Revaluation
    D   Discontinuing operations

Answers to quick quiz

1. ASB.
2. Council considers that the Companies Act strengthens the status of accounting standards.
3. Generally accepted accounting practice is a combination of company law, accounting standards and stock exchange requirements. It is also influenced by IASs and US requirements.
4. See paragraphs 5.2 and 5.3.
5. See paragraphs 7.2.
6. See paragraphs 7.3.
7. Material items possessing a high degree of abnormality that arise from events outside the ordinary activities and are not expected to recur.
8. A split between continuing activities, acquisitions and discontinued operations.
9. See paragraph 8.4.
10. The results should be separately disclosed, the profit or loss on discontinuance is treated as an exceptional item and prior years figures must be adjusted.
11. See paragraph 9.4.
12. B. The others are normal trading activities.

Now try the questions below from the Exam Question Bank

Question to try	Level	Marks	Time
38	Full exam	10	18 mins
39	Introductory	n/a	39 mins

Chapter 25

USEFULNESS OF FINANCIAL ACCOUNTING

Topic list	Syllabus reference
1 Criticisms of historical cost accounting	2(b)
2 Reasons for continued use of historical cost accounting	2(b)
3 Current purchasing power and current cost accounting	2(b)
4 The nature, purpose and limitations of financial accounting	2(a)
5 Criticisms of accounting conventions	2(a)

Introduction

Occasionally in your Paper 1.1 studies you will have come across criticisms of the conventional financial statements, by which we generally mean the profit and loss account and balance sheet.

You will be introduced to the idea of accounting for changes in price levels, although detailed knowledge of how to do the calculations is not required at this stage.

Study guide

Section 27 - The theoretical and operational adequacy of financial reporting

- Revise the qualitative characteristics of financial information from Sections 1 and 14.

- Explain the advantages and disadvantages of historical cost accounting (HCA) in times of changing prices.

- Explain in principle the main alternatives to HCA:
    - Current purchasing power accounting (CPP)
    - Current cost accounting (CCA)

    Note: computational questions on CPP and CCA will not be set.

- Revise the roles of the ASB in raising standards of financial reporting by setting accounting standards.

Exam guide

In this chapter we also consider the usefulness of financial accounting; you may be required to formulate your own ideas on this (Section 4). You should be able to criticise conventional accounting, giving reasons for your assertions (Section 5).

Part G: Miscellaneous topics

1 CRITICISMS OF HISTORICAL COST ACCOUNTING

1.1 Traditionally, there have been two main reasons for the preparation of accounts:

(a) To fulfil the needs of the owners of a business.

(b) To assist the managers of a business in controlling that business and in making decisions about its future.

1.2 Although the information needs of internal and external users differ considerably, it has become increasingly clear that accounts prepared on a traditional historical cost basis can present financial information in a misleading manner. The greatest criticisms of traditional accounting concepts have stemmed from their inability to reflect the effects of changing price levels.

1.3 Before mentioning the various alternatives, we should first consider the criticisms of historical cost accounting in more detail.

Fixed asset values are unrealistic

1.4 The most striking example is **property**. Although it is a statutory requirement that the market value of an interest in land should be disclosed in the directors' report if it is significantly different from the balance sheet figure, and although some companies have periodically updated the balance sheet values, revaluation's have not been reported consistently.

1.5 If fixed assets are retained in the books at their historical cost, **unrealised holding gains are not recognised**. This means that the total holding gain, if any, will be brought into account during the year in which the asset is realised, rather than spread over the period during which it was owned.

1.6 There are, in essence, two points to be considered.

(a) Although it has long been accepted that a balance sheet prepared under the historical cost concept is an historical record and not a statement of current worth, many people now argue that the balance sheet should at least give an indication of the current value of the company's tangible net assets.

(b) The prudence concept requires that profits should only be recognised when realised in the form either of cash or of other assets the ultimate cash realisation of which can be assessed with reasonable certainty. It may be argued that recognising unrealised holding gains on fixed assets is contrary to this concept.

1.7 On balance, the weight of opinion is now in favour of restating asset values. It is felt that the criticism based on prudence can be met by ensuring that valuations are made as objectively as possible (eg in the case of property, by having independent expert valuations) and by not taking unrealised gains through the profit and loss account.

Depreciation is inadequate to finance the replacement of fixed assets

1.8 Depreciation is not provided for, so there is no retention of profits and so no reserves are available for asset replacement. It is intended as a measure of the contribution of fixed assets to the company's activities in the period. However, an incidental effect of providing for depreciation is that not all liquid funds can be paid out to investors and so funds for asset replacement are on hand. What is important is not the replacement of one asset by an identical new one (something that rarely happens) but the replacement of the operating capability represented by the old asset.

1.9 Another criticism of historical cost depreciation is that it does not fully reflect the value of the asset consumed during the accounting year. Whilst this point is obviously closely related to the first, it can be overcome whilst still retaining insufficient profits to finance replacement.

Holding gains on stocks are included in profit

1.10 During a period of high inflation the monetary value of stocks held may increase significantly while they are being processed. The conventions of historical cost accounting lead to the unrealised part of this holding gain (known as stock appreciation) being included in profit for the year. It is estimated that in the late 1970s nearly half the declared profits of companies were due to stock appreciation.

1.11 EXAMPLE: HOLDING GAINS

This problem can be illustrated using a simple example. At the beginning of the year a company has 100 units of stock and no other assets. Its trading account for the year is shown below:

TRADING ACCOUNT

	Units	£		Units	£
Opening stock	100	200	Sales (made 31 December)	100	500
Purchases (made 31 December)	100	400			
	200	600			
Closing stock (FIFO basis)	100	400			
	100	200			
Gross profit	-	300			
	100	500		100	500

Apparently the company has made a gross profit of £300. But, at the beginning of the year the company owned 100 units of stock and at the end of the year it owned 100 units of stock and £100 (sales £500 - purchases £400). From this it would seem that a profit of £100 is more reasonable. The remaining £200 is stock appreciation arising as the purchase price increased from £2 to £4.

1.12 The criticism can be overcome by using a **capital maintenance concept** based on physical units rather than money values.

Profits (or losses) on holdings of net monetary items are not shown

1.13 In periods of inflation the purchasing power, and thus the value, of money falls. It follows that an investment in money will have a lower real value at the end of a period of time than it did at the beginning. A loss has been incurred. Similarly, the real value of a monetary liability will reduce over a period of time and a gain will be made.

The true effect of inflation on capital maintenance is not shown

1.14 To a large extent this follows from the points already mentioned. It is a widely held principle that distributable profits should only be recognised after full allowance has been made for any erosion in the capital value of a business. In historical cost accounts, although capital is maintained in nominal money terms, it may not be in real terms. In other words, profits may be distributed to the detriment of the long-term viability of the business. This criticism may be made by those who advocate capital maintenance in physical terms and those who prefer money capital maintenance as measured by pounds of current purchasing power (see below).

Part G: Miscellaneous topics

Comparisons over time are unrealistic

1.15 This will tend to an exaggeration of growth. For example, if a company's profit in 1966 was £100,000 and in 1999 £500,000, a shareholder's initial reaction might be that the company had done rather well. If, however, it was then revealed that with £100,000 in 1966 he could buy exactly the same goods as with £500,000 in 1999, the apparent growth would seem less impressive.

1.16 The points mentioned in the last paragraph have demonstrated some of the accounting problems which arise in times of severe and prolonged inflation. Of the various possible systems of accounting for price changes most can be divided into two categories:

(a) General price change bases and in particular current purchasing power (CPP);

(b) Current value bases: the basic principles of all these are:

    (i) To show balance sheet items at some form of current value rather than historical cost

    (ii) To compute profits by matching the current value of costs at the date of consumption against revenue.

The current value of an item will normally be based on replacement cost, net realisable value or economic value.

2 REASONS FOR CONTINUED USE OF HISTORICAL COST ACCOUNTING

2.1 Despite the limitations of historical cost accounting, it is still the accepted basis for the preparation of financial statements. There are a number of reasons why this is so.

(a) It is easy and cheap. Other methods tend to be far more complicated and onerous to use, particularly for small businesses. Also, there is no agreement on an alternative.

(b) The fact that fixed asset revaluation is permitted or encouraged means that there is less likelihood that a serious understatement of actual value will distort the balance sheet valuation of the business.

(c) It is easy to understand and users are aware of its limitations, so make appropriate allowances. Alternative methods generally involve much more complex concepts.

(d) The figures are easy to obtain and are objective and readily verifiable, being tied to actual transactions. Other methods depend more on valuations and are therefore prone to subjectivity.

Question 1

What is meant by the statement that, under historical cost accounting, holding gains are included in stock valuations?

Answer

Look back to paragraph 1.11.

25: Usefulness of financial accounting

3 CURRENT PURCHASING POWER AND CURRENT COST ACCOUNTING

3.1 In the UK an attempt was made to implement a system of **current purchasing power** accounting with the publication in 1974 of provisional statement of standard accounting practice 7 (PSSAP 7). The principal feature of the system was that profit for the year was calculated after an **adjustment** designed to reflect the effect of **general price inflation** on the purchasing power of equity shareholders' funds.

3.2 CPP accounting did not catch on and in 1980 a decisive step was taken in the direction of a current value basis of accounting. SSAP 16 *Current cost accounting* was published for a trial period of three years beginning in March 1980. The system of **current cost accounting** (CCA) advocated by SSAP 16 did not attempt to cater for general price inflation; instead, profit for the year was to be calculated after allowing for the effects of price increases specifically on the operating capability of the particular business.

3.3 The principal features of CCA are as follows.

(a) In the balance sheet, **assets** are stated at their '**value to the business**'. This may be a replacement cost, net realisable value or economic value depending on the circumstances.

(b) In the profit and loss account **holding gains** are **excluded from profit**. A holding gain is the difference between value to the business of an asset and its original cost. If X buys an item for £100 and sells it for £150 there will be an HC profit of £150 - £100 = £50. If the replacement cost of the item at the date of sale is £130, in CC terms there will be an operating gain of £150 - £130 = £20 and a holding gain of £130 - £100 = £30. Current cost accounting recognises operating gains only as profit; historical cost accounting does not differentiate between holding and operating gains, and recognises both as profit.

3.4 SSAP 16 encountered a good deal of criticism on both practical and theoretical grounds. In 1985 the mandatory status of the standard was withdrawn; compliance with its provisions then became only voluntary. The standard itself was finally withdrawn in April 1988.

> **Exam focus point**
> An examination question on CPP or CCA will **not** be computational.

4 THE NATURE, PURPOSE AND LIMITATIONS OF FINANCIAL ACCOUNTING

4.1 You should be able to express your own reasoned opinions on the usefulness of financial accounting.

Question 2

Now that you have nearly reached the end of your Paper 1.1 studies, you should be able to think of a few ideas on this subject. Jot them down on a piece of paper. Now read on.

4.2 Frequently during the course of your studies you will have come across **criticisms** of conventional financial accounting. The following list is not exhaustive; it serves to draw together points which have arisen at various stages in this Study Text.

Part G: Miscellaneous topics

(a) Financial accounts are becoming **increasingly complex**. More and more disclosure is required, much of which is not applicable to small companies.

(b) Increasing complexity means that accounts are **not readily comprehensible** to the layman.

(c) Information which is prepared for external reporting purposes is not generally useful for internal decision making purposes; financial accounts are **backward looking**, while managers must be forward looking.

(d) Financial accounts do not necessarily give a good indication of the suitability of the company for investment and the likelihood of its future success.

(e) The conventional financial statements do not always provide users with the kind of information they want. Employees of a company, for example, will find little of relevance to them.

(f) Financial accounts are prepared under the **historical cost** convention. This information can be misleading especially in times of rapidly rising prices.

4.3 It is important to put these criticisms in perspective by considering alternative views and constructive suggestions which have been made. It is possible to find an answer (of sorts) to each of the points raised in Paragraph 4.2.

Question 3

Your friend Karen Taddup has recently given up her Paper 1.1 studies on the grounds that financial accounting is 'not only difficult but totally useless'. Try to convince her otherwise by answering the criticisms (a) to (f) above.

Answer

(a) This is undeniably true. However, it is desirable that the accounts should provide sufficient detail to give a picture of the company's position. Omissions and oversimplification can lead to distortion.

(b) Some attempts are being made to bridge the gap between layman and expert. The recent ASB Statement on the inclusion of an Operating and Financial Review should go some way towards making accounts more comprehensible.

(c) Financial accounts are not much use for decision making purposes. However, they were not developed for that purpose. The answer lies in timely and relevant *management accounts*.

(d) This criticism is not easy to answer. It is not possible to tell by looking at a set of financial accounts that a company is a 'good bet' for investment. By using ratios such as earnings per share or price to earnings some conclusions can be drawn about a company's performance, but only by comparison with other companies in the same sector and with previous years. Such ratios are not foolproof.

(e) An answer to this criticism lies in the provision of supplementary statements such as value added statements and employee reports. So far, however, these suggestions have not been extensively taken up.

(f) This is a fair criticism. Alternatives to historical costing have not met with any success. FRS 3 *Reporting financial performance* requires a 'statement of total recognised gains and losses' and a 'note of historical cost profits and losses'. This deals with the problem of revaluations that have been undertaken at different times and on different scales. It does not, however, go to the root of the problem of financial reporting in times of rising prices.

4.4 It is hoped that the above exercise will have set you thinking about these issues which are certain to recur in your later studies for Paper 2.5 and Paper 3.6. In the final section of this chapter we consider some criticisms which have been made of accounting conventions.

5 CRITICISMS OF ACCOUNTING CONVENTIONS

5.1 It is easy to assume that the accounting conventions with which we are familiar, and which we have been using in this Study Text, are the best ones we could use. However, this is not necessarily the case. This is potentially a vast topic, so we will confine ourselves to two or three examples.

Criticisms of the prudence convention

5.2 'Prudence' and 'accountant' would appear to go together. Surely this accounting concept is unassailable?

Question 4

Before we go any further, can you remember exactly what prudence is?

Answer

Prudence is, according to FRS 18 *Accounting policies,* a desirable element in financial statements.

The prudence concept lays down that revenue and profits are not anticipated but should only be recorded when earning is reasonably certain. Expenses and liabilities should, however, be recorded when anticipated, as best estimates if no actual figures are available.

Loss in value of assets, whether realised or not, should be recorded when it arises, but a gain in value of an asset should not be recorded except via an unrealised reserve and only then if properly warranted.

An example of the application of the prudence concept is the requirement to value stock at the lower of cost and net realisable value.

5.3 This is all very well, but it can lead to problems, of which the following can be identified as the most significant.

(a) **Prudence** most obviously conflicts with the **matching (or accruals)** concept because it requires that the matching of costs and revenues should not take place if there is any doubt about the future recoverability of deferred costs. This conflict has been summarised as 'should we report the worst possible situation (prudence) or the most likely position (matching)?'

(b) **Prudence** also conflicts with the **going concern** concept because it may not be prudent to assume that a business is a going concern (although it is realistic).

(c) **Prudence** makes it difficult to **treat items consistently** because circumstances in one period may require a different treatment from previous periods in order to be prudent.

(d) **Prudence** also undermines several other conventions not recognised as fundamental accounting concepts. For instance, **objectivity** is regarded as important by most users of accounts but prudence (or conservatism as it is sometimes called) implies a subjectivity in coming to accounting judgements. It is also difficult to reconcile prudence with the use of anything other than the **historical cost convention** for valuing assets.

5.4 The ASB's *Statement of Principles* places little emphasis on prudence - some critics have said too little - and embraces a system of current value accounting. FRS 18 *Accounting policies* relegates prudence to a **desirable quality** of financial statements. Prudence can result in the smoothing of profits and the deliberate understatement of assets or overstatement of liabilities. Prudence is just one element of reliability.

Part G: Miscellaneous topics

Criticisms of the matching concept

5.5 Try this question before you go any further.

Question 5

Can you remember what the matching concept is? A clue: it's the same as the accruals concept.

Answer

Revenue and expenditure are matched under this concept and recorded in the accounts when earned or incurred, rather than on the associated cash movement, provided that it is prudent so to treat them.

This allows most obviously for credit sales, but also results in the identification of stock at the end of each accounting period rather than writing all purchases off to the trading account. Only purchases which result in a sale recorded in the period or are used for promotional or similar purposes should be matched with sales for the period. Therefore, if purchased goods still on hand at the period end are of saleable quality and the company will still be trading in the next period (ie the prudence and going concern concepts are satisfied) then any unsold goods can be treated as current assets and their value can be deducted from purchases and opening stock.

5.6 What could possibly be wrong with that? The main criticism relates to the conflict with historical cost accounting.

5.7 It can be argued that the matching concept is not applied in historical cost accounting. The matching concept states that revenue earned must be matched against expenditure incurred on earning it. The cost of goods sold in the profit and loss account is normally computed on the basis of their historical cost. However, a continuing business will want to replace stocks sold and will have to do so at ever higher prices. This means that some of the 'profit' shown by the accounts is not profit at all, but must be spent in restoring the assets of the business to their previous level.

5.8 It may be argued that the matching concept could be better applied under a system of current cost accounting. This, broadly speaking, values assets at replacement cost. Thus the historical cost profit would be adjusted by the 'cost of sales adjustment' which aims to charge the profit and loss account with the current cost of each item of stock sold at the date of sale.

5.9 Other criticisms of the matching concept include the following.

(a) The nature of the matching process is often **arbitrary**, for example in selecting a depreciation method.

(b) The matching concept **conflicts with the prudence concept** as indicated in Paragraph 5.3 above.

(c) The matching concept is about getting the profit and loss account figure right. This is an admirable aim in itself, but it may mean that the **balance sheet contains** rather **arbitrary figures**. For example, when an asset is depreciated, the balance sheet figure is simply the unexpired cost to be allocated to future accounting periods. In other words, it is what is left over after matching has taken place, not in itself a meaningful figure.

IMPORTANT!

The *Statement of Principles* places less emphasis on matching than has been the convention, partly because it is **more orientated towards the balance sheet** than the profit and loss account.

Depreciation of freehold buildings

5.10 We will now consider a controversial issue: whether depreciation should be provided on freehold buildings.

5.11 It has become common in recent years, particularly in the UK, for companies not to provide any depreciation on freehold buildings. The following points may be made in favour of *not* providing depreciation on freehold buildings.

(a) The value of the asset is the same or greater at the end of the accounting period than at the beginning. To provide depreciation would therefore be unnecessary, if not misleading.

(b) The building is well maintained. The cost of this maintenance has already been charged to the profit and loss account. To charge it again would be 'double counting'.

(c) The value of the building exceeds its cost and if the building were sold the proceeds would be greater than original cost. In other words the net cost of the building, to be allocated over its economic life, is zero.

5.12 However, the following points carry greater weight.

(a) It is irrelevant that the value of the building has not fallen or has risen. The depreciation charge is a means of matching the cost of an asset with the revenue earned over its useful economic life. In charging depreciation no attempt is being made to estimate the current value of an asset.

(b) Depreciation is charged on other fixed assets used in a business, with the exception of freehold land. SSAP 2 demands **consistent** treatment of items.

(c) Like other assets, freehold buildings do not last for ever. The accounting treatment should reflect this.

The case for conventional accounting

5.13 In view of all the criticisms that have been made of accounting conventions, should we go 'back to the drawing board'? It could be argued that the ASB have tried to do this with their *Statement of Principles*. However, there is much to be said for the conventional approach.

(a) **Objectivity**. There is less scope for manipulation of the figures.

(b) **Uniformity**. There is less scope for disagreement than with other, more radical approaches.

(c) **Familiarity**. The importance of familiarity should not be underestimated. Preparers of accounts are more likely to get them right if they are used to them, and the accounts will mean more to users.

The emphasis of Paper 1.1

You may have found some of the foregoing discussions interesting. Perhaps they make all that number crunching worthwhile? Whether or not this is the case, the fact is that Paper 1.1 requires you to think about the issues and concepts underlying accounting. Questions will often require you to 'think' and to express your own views, supported, of course, by reasoned argument. It is a good idea to get into this questioning habit now, as it will become increasingly important in your later studies.

Part G: Miscellaneous topics

Chapter roundup

- **Historical cost accounts** have a number of **deficiencies** in times of rising prices.
- In the UK attempts to deal with the problem have centred mainly on a system of **current cost accounting** introduced by SSAP 16 in 1980. Compliance with SSAP 16 was never widespread even amongst the companies (mainly public companies) within its scope.
- Key elements in the *Statement* are as follows.
  o Financial statements should give financial information useful for assessing stewardship of management and for making economic decisions.
  o Financial information should be relevant, reliable, comparable and understandable.
  o Assets and liabilities have conceptual priority over the profit and loss account.
  o Accounts should move towards current cost valuations.
  o Statement of total recognised gains and losses is for assets held for the business to continue trading.
- You need to be able to express your own ideas on the **usefulness of financial accounting** and to support these ideas with reasoned arguments.
- **Accounting conventions** are not 'set in stone', they can be, and have been, criticised.

Quick quiz

1. Which of the following arguments is not in favour of accounting standards, but is in favour of accounting choice?

   A They reduce variations in methods used to produce accounts
   B They oblige companies to disclose their accounting policies
   C They are a less rigid alternative to legislation
   D They may tend towards rigidity in applying the rules

2. What are the criticisms of the prudence concept?

3. What criticisms can be made of traditional historical cost accounting?

4. Why is a conceptual framework necessary?

Answers to quick quiz

1. D The other arguments are all in favour of accounting standards.

2. - Conflicts with the accrual assumption
   - Conflicts with going concern assumption
   - Difficulty in applying consistency
   - Undermines other assumptions eg objectivity

3. - Non-current asset values are unrealistic
   - Depreciation is inadequate to finance the replacement of non-current assets
   - Holding gains on inventories are included in profit
   - Profits (or losses) on holdings of net monetary items are not shown
   - Time effect of inflation on capital maintenance is not shown
   - Comparisons over time are unrealistic

4. It forms the theoretical basis for determining what is included in accounts, how they are measured and how they are communicated.

Now try the question below from the Exam Question Bank

Question to try	Level	Marks	Time
40	Introductory	n/a	47 mins

Exam question bank

Exam question bank

(Examination standard questions are those accompanied by mark allocations.)

> **Exam focus point**
> The introductory questions are generally **longer** than the approximately 10 mark questions you will meet in the exam. However these questions are intended to **thoroughly practice** the techniques learnt in each lesson. Therefore these questions are well worth doing, and will help to ensure that you can tackle any exam question.

1   USERS OF ACCOUNTING INFORMATION   *18 mins*

The Corporate Report identified many different user groups of accounting information. Identify those who might be interested in financial information about a large public company and describe their information needs.   **10 marks**

2   THE ACCOUNTING EQUATION   *18 mins*

Peter Reid decides he is going to open a bookshop called Easyread, which he does by investing £5,000 on 1 January 20X7. During the first month of Easyread's existence, the following transactions occur.

(a) Bookshelves are purchased for £1,800.
(b) Books are purchased for £2,000.
(c) Half of the books are sold for £1,500 cash.
(d) Peter draws £200 out of the business for himself.
(e) Peter's brother John loans £500 to the business.
(f) Carpets are purchased for £1,000 on credit (to be paid in two months time).
(g) A bulk order of books worth £400 is sold on credit (to be paid in one month's time) for £600.

Required

Write down the accounting equation after each transaction has occurred.   **10 marks**

3   FINANCIAL STATEMENTS   *18 mins*

What is the difference between the balance sheet and the trading, profit and loss account? What is the difference between capital and revenue expenditure? Which of the following transaction is capital expenditure and which revenue expenditure?

(a) A bookseller buys a car for its director for £9,000.
(b) In the first year, the car is depreciated by £900.
(c) The business buys books for £1,500.
(d) The business builds an extension for £7,600.
(e) The original building is repainted, a job costing £1,200.
(f) A new sales assistant is taken on and his salary in the first year is £10,000.   **10 marks**

4   BUSINESS TRANSACTIONS   *18 mins*

The following is a list of typical business transactions.

(a) The purchase of goods on credit.
(b) Allowance to credit customers upon the return of faulty goods.
(c) Refund from petty cash to an employee of an amount spend on entertaining a client.
(d) Credit card sales.

Required

For each transaction identify clearly

(i)   The original document(s) for the data.
(ii) The book of original entry for the transaction.   **10 marks**

Exam question bank

5 BEECHFIELD
18 mins

Beechfield Ltd make use of a petty cash book as part of their book-keeping system. The following is a summary of the petty cash transactions for the month of November 20X9.

			£
November	1	Opening petty cash book float received from cashier	350
	2	Cleaning materials	5
	3	Postage stamps	10
	6	Envelopes	12
	8	Taxi fare	32
	10	Petrol for company car	17
	14	Typing paper	25
	15	Cleaning materials	4
	16	Bus fare	2
	20	Visitors' lunches	56
	21	Mops and brushes for cleaning	41
	23	Postage stamps	35
	27	Envelopes	12
	29	Visitors' lunches	30
	30	Photocopying paper	40

Required

Draw up the petty cash book for the month using analysis columns for stationery, cleaning, entertainment, travelling and postages. Show clearly the receipt of the amount necessary to restore the float and the balance brought forward for the start of the following month. Folio numbers are not required. **10 marks**

6 HYPER
18 mins

The following extracts are taken from Hyper Ltd's accounts for the quarter ended 30 June 20X1.

	£
Debtors balance, 1 April 20X1	40,000
Creditors balance, 1 April 20X1	22,000
VAT creditor, 1 April 20X1	4,100

Transactions during the quarter were as follows.

	£
Invoiced sales, including VAT	141,000
Purchases on credit, including VAT	84,600
Payments made for credit purchases	92,700
Receipts from debtors	128,300
Payment to VAT creditor	4,100

The rate of VAT during the quarter was 17.5% and this rate applied to all purchases and sales.

Required

Prepare the ledger account entries necessary to give effect to these transactions. **10 marks**

7 J OCKEY
27 mins

Mr J Ockey commenced trading as a wholesale stationer on 1 May 20X4 with a capital of £5,000 with which he opened a bank account for his business.

During May the following transactions took place.

May	1	Bought shop fittings and fixtures for cash from Store Fitments Ltd for £2,000
	2	Purchased goods on credit from Abel £650
	4	Sold goods on credit to Bruce £700
	9	Purchased goods on credit from Green £300
	11	Sold goods on credit to Hill £580
	13	Cash sales paid intact into bank £200
	16	Received cheque from Bruce in settlement of his account
	17	Purchased goods on credit from Kaye £800
	18	Sold goods on credit to Nailor £360
	19	Sent cheque to Abel in settlement of his account
	20	Paid rent by cheque £200
	21	Paid delivery expenses by cheque £50
	24	Received from Hill £200 on account
	30	Drew cheques for personal expenses £200 and assistant's wages £320
	31	Settled the account of Green.

Required

(a) Record the foregoing in appropriate books of original entry.
(b) Post the entries to the ledger accounts.
(c) Balance the ledger accounts where necessary.
(d) Extract a trial balance at 31 May 20X4.

Note. You are not required to complete any entries in personal accounts, nor are folio references required.

8 **OMEGA** *27 mins*

At 1 May 20X3 amounts owing to Omega by his customers in respect of their April purchases were:

	£
Alpha	210
Beta	1,040
Gamma	1,286
Delta	279
Epsilon	823

The amounts owing by Omega to his suppliers at 1 May were:

	£
Zeta	2,173
Eta	187
Theta	318

Sales made by Omega during May were as follows:

	£
Gamma	432
Epsilon	129
Beta	314
Epsilon	269
Alpha	88
Delta	417
Epsilon	228

Purchases during May:

	£
Eta	423
Zeta	268
Eta	741

Returns inwards: (ie sales returns)

	£
Epsilon	88

Exam question bank

Cash payments:

	£
Eta	187
Theta	318
Zeta	1,000

Cash receipts:

	£
Beta	1,040
Delta	279
Gamma	826
Epsilon	823

Required

(a) Open accounts for Omega's customers and suppliers and record therein the 1 May balances.

(b) Record the transactions in the appropriate personal and impersonal accounts.

(c) Balance the personal accounts where necessary.

(d) Extract a list of debtors at 31 May showing in separate columns:

    (i) The total amounts owing.
    (ii) Amounts owing in respect of May.
    (iii) Amounts owing in respect of April.

Note. You need not enter dates or narrative in the accounts.

9 HUBBLE *36 mins*

On 28.2.20X8, which is one month before the end of his financial year, the ledger accounts of A Hubble were as follows.

CASH

	£		£
Capital	9,500	Rent	2,750
Bank loan	3,000	Creditors	700
Sales	11,200	Interest	350
Debtors	400	Electricity	400
		Telephone	180
		Drawings	1,300

CAPITAL

	£		£
		Cash	9,500

BANK LOAN

	£		£
		Cash	3,000

SALES

	£		£
		Cash	11,200
		Debtors	4,600

DEBTORS

	£		£
Sales	4,600	Cash	400

RENT

	£		£
Cash	2,750		

PURCHASES

	£		£
Creditors	2,100		

CREDITORS

	£		£
Cash	700	Purchases	2,100

INTEREST

	£		£
Cash	350		

ELECTRICITY

	£		£
Cash	400		

TELEPHONE

	£		£
Cash	180		

DRAWINGS

	£		£
Cash	1,300		

During the last month of his financial year, A Hubble recorded the following transactions.

(a) He bought goods for £2,000, half for credit and half for cash.

(b) He paid the following:
- Interest £20
- Electricity £25
- Telephone £12

(c) He made sales of £3,500 of which £500 were for cash.

(d) He received £220 from debtors.

Required

(a) Post the transactions for March 20X8 into the ledger accounts.

(b) Balance off the ledger accounts and draw up a trial balance.

(c) Prepare a balance sheet as at 31.3.20X8 and a trading, profit and loss account for the year ended 31.3.20X8.

10 RENT, RATES AND INSURANCE   *36 mins*

From the information given below you are required:

(a) To calculate the charge to the profit and loss account for the year ended 30 June 20X6 in respect of rent, rates and insurance.

(b) To state the amount of accrual or prepayment for rent, rates and insurance as at 30 June 20X6.

The accruals and prepayments as at 30 June 20X5 were as follows.

	£
Rent accrued	2,000
Rates prepaid	1,500
Insurance prepaid	1,800

Payments made during the year ended 30 June 20X6 were as follows.

Exam question bank

20X5		£
10 August	Rent, three months to 31 July 20X5	3,000
26 October	Insurance, one year to 31 October 20X6	6,000
2 November	Rates, six months to 31 March 20X6	3,500
12 December	Rent, four months to 30 November 20X5	4,000
20X6		
17 April	Rent, four months to 31 March 20X6	4,000
9 May	Rates, six months to 30 September 20X6	3,500

11 HACKER *45 mins*

Hacker commenced business as a retail butcher on 1 January 20X0. The following is a summary of the transactions which took place during the first three months of trading.

(a) Cash sales amounted to £3,000, including £500 of sales on credit cards.

(b) Credit sales totalled £1,600 and of this £300 was outstanding at the end of the period.

(c) On the commencement of business Hacker had paid £4,000 into the business, and a full year's rent of £600 had been paid immediately.

(d) A delivery van was purchased on 1 January at a cost of £900. It was agreed that this should be depreciated at the rate of 20% per annum.

(e) During the period suppliers had been paid £1,600 for meat and invoices totalling £400 remained unpaid at 31 March.

(f) The stock of meat at the close of business on 31 March was valued at cost at £360.

(g) Sundry expenses (all paid during the period and relating to it) amounted to £400, and during March Hacker drew £200 from the business.

Required

(a) Write up the ledger accounts and cash book of Hacker.

(b) Extract a trial balance.

(c) Prepare a trading and profit and loss account for the three months ending 31 March 20X0, and balance sheet at that date.

Tutorial note. Keep firmly in your mind the fact that you are preparing quarterly accounts, whereas some expenses are given as an annual amount.

You might also be interest in the new idea given in (a), that sales on credit cards can be treated in the same way as sales paid by cheque - ie as cash sales.

12 JAMES *27 mins*

James opened a shop on 1 July 20X2 and during his first month in business, the following transactions occurred.

20X2

1 July   James contributes £20,000 in cash to the business out of his private bank account.
2 July   He opens a business bank account by transferring £18,000 of his cash in hand.
5 July   Some premises are rented, the rent being £500 per quarter payable in advance in cash.
6 July   James buys some second-hand shop equipment for £300 paying by cheque.
9 July   He purchases some goods for resale for £1,000 paying for them in cash.
10 July   Seddon supplies him with £2,000 of goods on credit.
20 July   James returns £200 of the goods to Seddon.
23 July   Cash sales for the week amount to £1,500.
26 July   James sells goods on credit for £1,000 to Frodsham.
28 July   Frodsham returns £500 of the goods to James.
31 July   James settles his account with Seddon by cheque, and is able to claim a cash discount of 10%.
31 July   Frodsham sends James a cheque for £450 in settlement of his account, any balance remaining on his account being treated as a cash discount.

31 July   During his initial trading, James has discovered that some of his shop equipment is not suitable, but he is fortunate in being able to dispose of it for £50 in cash. There was no profit or loss on disposal.

31 July   He withdraws £150 in cash as part payment towards a holiday for his wife.

Required

(a) Enter the above transactions in James' ledger accounts, balance off the accounts and bring down the balances as at 1 August 20X2.

(b) Extract a trial balance as at 31 July 20X2.

13 GEORGE   27 mins

George is a wholesaler and the following information relates to his accounting year ending 30 September 20X2.

(a) Goods are sold on credit terms, but some cash sales are also transacted.

(b) At 1 October 20X1 George's trade debtors amounted to £30,000 against which he had set aside a provision for doubtful debts of 5%.

(c) On 15 January 20X2 George was informed the Fall Ltd had gone into liquidation, owing him £2,000. This debt was outstanding from the previous year.

(d) Cash sales during the year totalled £46,800, whilst credit sales amounted to £187,800.

(e) £182,500 was received from trade debtors.

(f) Settlement discounts allowed to credit customers were £5,300.

(g) Apart from Fall Ltd's bad debt, other certain bad debts amounted to £3,500.

(h) George intends to retain the provision for doubtful debts account at 5% of outstanding trade debtors as at the end of the year, and the necessary entry is to be made.

You are required to enter the above transactions in George's ledger accounts and (apart from the cash and bank and profit and loss accounts) balance off the accounts and bring down the balances as at 1 October 20X2.

14 SAIGON   36 mins

(a) Minh Ltd makes and sells two products, the Ho and the Chi. The following data relates to the company's year end stock of finished goods.

	Direct materials and labour £	Production overheads £	Transport to customers £	Sales value £
Ho	1,235	1,050	240	2,300
Chi	4,680	1,365	75	6,220
	5,915	2,415	315	8,520

Calculate the total figure for stock at the year end.

(b) Saigon, a trader dealing in one product only, has the following transactions over a six month period.

	Date	Quantity Units	Unit cost £
Purchases	1 June 20X2	1,500	90
	1 August 20X2	2,000	92
	1 October 20X2	3,000	93
Sales	June 20X2	340	140
	July 20X2	700	140
	August 20X2	800	144
	September 20X2	450	144
	October 20X2	900	144
	November 20X2	630	145

The trader held no stock at 31 May 20X2.

Exam question bank

Applying the following principles of stock valuation, calculate Saigon's gross profit or loss for the six months ended 30 November 20X2.

(i) First in, first out
(ii) Last in, first out

(Ignore other expenses which may have been incurred for the period.)

(c) Reproduced below is Paragraph 39 of SSAP 9 *Stocks and long-term contracts*.

'In particular, the use of the LIFO method can result in the reporting of current assets at amounts that bear little relationship to recent costs. This may result in not only a significant misstatement of balance sheet amounts but also a potential distortion of current and future results. This places a special responsibility on the directors to be assured that the circumstances of the company require the adoption of such a valuation method in order for the accounts to give a true and fair view.'

Applying this comment to your calculations in part (b) of this question, discuss the extent to which you agree with it.

15 A COMPANY'S PLANT AND MACHINERY   45 mins

A company's plant and machinery account at 31 December 20X8 and the corresponding depreciation provision account broken down into years of purchase, are as follows.

Year of purchase	Plant and machinery at cost £	Depreciation provision £
20X0	20,000	20,000
20X2	30,000	30,000
20X4	100,000	90,000
20X6	70,000	35,000
20X7	50,000	15,000
20X8	30,000	3,000
	300,000	193,000

Depreciation is at the rate of 20% per annum on cost. It is the company's policy to assume that all purchases, sales or disposals of plant occurred on 30 June in the relevant year for the purposes of calculating depreciation, irrespective of the precise date on which these events occurred.

During 20X9 the following transactions took place.

(a) Purchase of plant and machinery amounted to £150,000.
(b) Plant that had been bought in 20X2 for £17,000 was scrapped.
(c) Plant that had been bought in 20X4 for £9,000 was sold for £500.
(d) Plant that had been bought in 20X6 for £24,000 was sold for £8,500.

Required

(a) Calculate the provision for depreciation of plant and machinery for the year ended 31 December 20X9. In calculating this provision you should bear in mind that it is the company's policy to show any profit or loss on the sale or disposal of plant as a completely separate item in the profit and loss account.

(b) Show the following as at 31 December 20X8 and 31 December 20X9:

(i) Plant and machinery, at cost
(ii) Depreciation provision (ie accumulated deprecation)
(iii) The net book value of plant and machinery
(iv) The profit or loss on sales or disposals of plant and machinery

Tutorial note. It would help you to reconcile the figures as at 31 December 20X8 with the figures as at 31 December 20X9 for items (i) and (ii) by calculating the 1 January figures, and then making adjustments for disposals and additional purchases during 20X9 in order to arrive at the figures for 31 December 20X9.

Exam question bank

16 SPARK   *54 mins*

Spark has been trading for a number of years as an electrical appliance retailer and repairer in premises which he rents at an annual rate of £1,500 payable in arrears. Balances appearing in his books at 1 January 20X1 were as follows.

	£	£
Capital account		1,808
Motor van		1,200
Fixtures and fittings		806
Provision for depreciation on motor van		720
Provisions for depreciation on fixtures and fittings		250
Stock at cost		366
Debtors for credit sales		
Brown	160	
Blue	40	
Stripe	20	
		220
Cash at bank		672
Cash in hand		5
Loan from Flex		250
Creditors for supplies		
Live	143	
Negative	80	
Earth	73	
		296
Amount owing for electricity		45
Rates paid in advance		100

Although Sparks has three credit customers the majority of his sales and services are for cash, out of which he pays various expenses before banking the balance.

The following transactions took place during the first four months of 20X1.

	January £	February £	March £	April £
Suppliers' invoices				
Live	468	570	390	602
Negative	-	87	103	64
Earth	692	-	187	-
Capital introduced		500		
Bankings of cash (from cash sales)	908	940	766	1,031
Expenditure out of cash sales before banking				
Drawings	130	120	160	150
Stationery	12	14	26	21
Travelling	6	10	11	13
Petrol and van repairs	19	22	37	26
Sundry expenses	5	4	7	3
Postage	12	10	15	19
Cleaner's wages	60	60	65	75
Goods invoiced to credit customers				
Brown	66	22	10	12
Blue	120	140	130	180
Stripe	44	38	20	48
Cheque payments (other than those to suppliers)				
Telephone	40	49	59	66
Electricity	62	47	20	106
Rates	-	-	220	-
Motor van (1 February 20X1)	-	800	-	-
Unbanked at the end of April	-	-	-	12

Spark pays for goods by cheque one month after receipt of invoice, and receives a settlement discount of 15% from each supplier.

Credit customers also pay by cheque one month after receipt of invoice, and are given a settlement discount of 10% of the invoice price.

Exam question bank

Required

(a) Write up the ledger accounts of Spark for the four months to 30 April 20X1, and extract a trial balance after balancing off the accounts.

(b) Prepare:

(i) A trading and profit and loss account for the four months
(ii) A balance sheet on 30 April 20X1

after dealing with the following matters.

(i) The payment of £800 for a new motor van represents the balance paid to the garage after being granted a part-exchange value of £500 on the old van.

(ii) Depreciation is provided at the rate of 20% per annum on the cost of motor vans and at the rate of 10% on the cost of fixtures and fittings. No depreciation is to be provided in the period of disposal.

(iii) Interest on the loan from Flex is to be accrued at 10% per annum and credited to his account.

(iv) Amounts owing at 30 April 20X1 were electricity £22, and telephone £15. The payment for rates was for six months in advance from 1 March.

(v) Included in the payments for telephone was one of Spark's private bills of £37 which is to be charged to him.

(iv) Stock at cost on 30 April 20X1 amounted to £390.

17 FRANK MERCER I
18 mins

On 10 January 20X9, Frank Mercer received his monthly bank statement for December 20X8. The statement showed the following:

MIDWEST BANK PLC
F Mercer: Statement of Account

Date 20X8	Particulars	Debits £	Credits £	Balance £
Dec 1	Balance			1,862
Dec 5	417864	243		1,619
Dec 5	Dividend		26	1,645
Dec 5	Bank Giro Credit		212	1,857
Dec 8	417866	174		1,683
Dec 10	417867	17		1,666
Dec 11	Sundry Credit		185	1,851
Dec 14	Standing Order	32		1,819
Dec 20	417865	307		1,512
Dec 20	Bank Giro Credit		118	1,630
Dec 21	417868	95		1,535
Dec 21	416870	161		1,374
Dec 24	Bank charges	18		1,356
Dec 27	Bank Giro Credit		47	1,403
Dec 28	Direct Debit	88		1,315
Dec 29	417873	12		1,303
Dec 29	Bank Giro Credit		279	1,582
Dec 31	417871	25		1,557

His cash book for the corresponding period showed:

Exam question bank

CASH BOOK

20X8		£	20X8		Cheque no	£
Dec 1	Balance b/d	1,862	Dec 1	Electricity	864	243
Dec 4	J Shannon	212	Dec 2	P Simpson	865	307
Dec 9	M Lipton	185	Dec 5	D Underhill	866	174
Dec 19	G Hurst	118	Dec 6	A Young	867	17
Dec 26	M Evans	47	Dec 10	T Unwin	868	95
Dec 27	J Smith	279	Dec 14	B Oliver	869	71
Dec 29	V Owen	98	Dec 16	Rent	870	161
Dec 30	K Walters	134	Dec 20	M Peters	871	25
			Dec 21	L Philips	872	37
			Dec 22	W Hamilton	873	12
			Dec 31	Balance c/d		1,793
		2,935				2,935

Required

Bring the cash book balance of £1,793 up to date as at 31 December 20X8. **10 marks**

18 FRANK MERCER II *18 mins*

Using the information in question 17 above, draw up a bank reconciliation statement as at 31 December 20X8. **10 marks**

19 APRIL SHOWERS *18 mins*

April Showers sells goods on credit to most of its customers. In order to control its debtor collection system, the company maintains a sales ledger control account. In preparing the accounts for the year to 31 October 20X3 the accountant discovers that the total of all the personal accounts in the sales ledger amounts to £12,802, whereas the balance on the sales ledger control account is £12,550.

Upon investigating the matter, the following errors were discovered.

(a) Sales for the week ending 27 march 20X3 amounting to £850 had been omitted from the control account.

(b) A debtor's account balance of £300 had not been included in the list of balances.

(c) Cash received of £750 had been entered in a personal account as £570.

(d) Discounts allowed totalling £100 had not been entered in the control account.

(e) A personal account balance had been undercast by £200.

(f) A contra item of £400 with the purchase ledger had not been entered in the control account.

(g) A bad debt of £500 had not been entered in the control account.

(h) Cash received of £250 had been debited to a personal account.

(i) Discounts received of £50 had been debited to Bell's sales ledger account.

(j) Returns inwards valued at £200 had not been included in the control account.

(k) Cash received of £80 had been credited to a personal account as £8.

(l) A cheque for £300 received from a customer had been dishonoured by the bank, but no adjustment had been made in the control account.

Required

Prepare a corrected sales ledger control account, bringing down the amended balance as at 1 November 20X3. **10 marks**

20 CHI KNITWEAR *36 mins*

Chi Knitwear Ltd is an old fashioned firm with a hand-written set of books. A trial balance is extracted at the end of each month, and a profit and loss account and balance sheet are computed. This month however the trial balance will not balance, the credits exceeding debits by £1,536.

485

Exam question bank

You are asked to help and after inspection of the ledgers discover the following errors.

(a) A balance of £87 on a debtors account has been omitted from the schedule of debtors, the total of which was entered as debtors in the trial balance.

(b) A small piece of machinery purchased for £1,200 had been written off to repairs.

(c) The receipts side of the cash book had been undercast by £720.

(d) The total of one page of the sales day book had been carried forward as £8,154, whereas the correct amount was £8,514.

(e) A credit note for £179 received from a supplier had been posted to the wrong side of his account.

(f) An electricity bill in the sum of £152, not yet accrued for, is discovered in a filing tray.

(g) Mr Smith whose past debts to the company had been the subject of a provision, at last paid £731 to clear his account. His personal account has been credited but the cheques has not yet been entered in the cash book.

Required

(a) Write up the suspense account to clear the trial balance difference.
(b) State the effect on the accounts of correcting each error.

21 ACCOUNTING CONCEPTS (PILOT PAPER) *18 mins*

If the information in financial statements is to be useful, regard must be had to the following accounting concepts.

(a) Materiality (4 marks)
(b) Substance over form (3 marks)
(d) Money measurement (3 marks)

Required

Explain the meaning of each of these concepts, including in your explanation one example for the application of each of them. **10 marks**

22 INTANGIBLE *18 mins*

The accounts of Intangible Ltd at 1 January 20X6 include deferred development costs of £26,500. During the year ended 31 December 20X6 Intangible Ltd purchased a new business. The consideration paid to the proprietor included £4,800 in respect of goodwill. The company also spent £7,900 in research and £3,500 on development activities.

The directors of Intangible Ltd intend to write off goodwill evenly over its estimated economic life of four years. They believe that £22,600 of development costs should be carried forward at 31 December 20X6.

Show the ledger accounts for goodwill and research and development in the books of Intangible Ltd.
10 marks

23 FABRICATORS *36 mins*

Fabricators Ltd, an engineering company, makes up its financial statements to 31 March in each year. The financial statements for the year ended 31 March 20X1 showed a turnover of £3m and trading profit of £400,000.

Before approval of the financial statements by the board of directors on 30 June 20X1 the following events took place.

(a) The financial statements of Patchup Ltd for the year ended 28 February 20X1 were received which indicated a permanent decline in that company's financial position. Fabricators Ltd had bought shares in Patchup Ltd some years ago and this purchase was included in unquoted investments at its cost of £100,000. The financial statements received indicated that this investment was now worth only £50,000.

(b) There was a fire at the company's warehouse on 30 April 20X1 when stock to the value of £500,000 was destroyed. It transpired that the stock in the warehouse was under-insured by some 50%.

(c) It was announced on 1 June 20X1 that the company's design for tank cleaning equipment had been approved by the major oil companies and this could result in an increase in the annual turnover of some £1m with a relative effect on profits.

The following points have also to be taken into consideration.

(d) Bills receivable of £150,000 were discounted on 15 March 20X1 and are due for maturity on 15 September 20X1.

(e) The company is expecting to receive orders worth up to £2 million for a new item of equipment which is at present on field trials. The equipment is being imported by the company at selling price less a trade discount of 25%. A quantity of this new equipment was held in stock on 31 March 20X1.

You are required to explain how, if at all, items (a) to (e) above should be reflected in the accounts of Fabricators Ltd for the year ended 31 March 20X1.

24 MISS TEEK
36 mins

Miss Anne Teek runs a market stall selling old pictures, china, copper goods and curios of all descriptions. Most of her sales are for cash, although regular customers are allowed credit. No double entry accounting records have been kept, but the following information is available.

SUMMARY OF NET ASSETS AT 31 MARCH 20X8

	£	£
Motor van		
Cost		3,000
Depreciation		2,500
Net book value		500
Current assets		
Stock	500	
Debtors	170	
Cash at bank	2,800	
Cash in hand	55	
	3,525	
Current liabilities		
Creditors	230	
Net current assets		3,295
Net assets		3,795

Additional information

(a) Anne bought a new motor van in January 20X9 receiving a part-exchange allowance of £1,800 for her old van. A full year's depreciation is to be provided on the new van, calculated at 20% on cost.

(b) Anne has taken £50 cash per week for her personal use. She also estimates that petrol for the van, paid in cash, averages £10 per week.

(c) Other items paid in cash were:

Sundry expenses	£24
Repairs to stall canopy	£201

(d) Anne makes a gross profit of 40% on selling prices. She is certain that no goods have been stolen but remembers that she appropriated a set of glasses and some china for her own use. These items had a total selling price of £300.

(e) Trade debtors and creditors at 31.3.X9 are £320 and £233 respectively, and cash in hand amounts to £39. No stock count has been made and there are no accrued or prepaid expenses.

A summary of bank statements for the twelve months in question shows:

Exam question bank

	£
Credits	
Cash banked (all cash sales)	7,521
Cheques banked (all credit sales)	1,500
Dividend income	210
	9,231

	£
Debits	
Purchase of motor van	3,200
Road fund licence	80
Insurance on van	323
Creditors for purchases	7,777
Rent	970
Sundry	31
Accountancy fees (re current work)	75
Bank overdraft interest (6 months to 1.10.X8)	20
Returned cheque (bad debt)	29
	12,505

The bank statement for 1 April 20X9 shows an interest charge of £27.

Required

Prepare Anne's trading and profit and loss account for the year to 31 March 20X9 and a balance sheet as at that date.

(Assume a 52 week year)

25 HIGHTON
45 mins

A Highton is in business as a general retailer. He does not keep a full set of accounting records; however it has been possible to extract the following details from the few records that are available.

	1 April 20X1 £	31 March 20X2 £
Freehold land and buildings at cost	10,000	10,000
Motor vehicle (cost £3,000)	2,250	
Stock, at cost	3,500	4,000
Trade debtors	500	1,000
Prepayments: motor vehicle expenses	200	300
property insurance	50	100
Cash at bank	550	950
Cash in hand	100	450
Loan from Highton's father	10,000	
Trade creditors: accruals	1,500	1,800
electricity	200	400
motor vehicle expenses	200	100

Extract from a rough cash book for the year to 31 March 20X2

	£
Receipts	
Cash sales	80,400

	£
Payments	
Cash purchases	17,000
Drawings	7,000
General shop expenses	100
Telephone	100
Wages	3,000

Extract from the bank pass sheets for the year to 31 March 20X2

	£
Receipts	
Cash banked	52,850
Cheques from trade debtors	8,750

	£
Payments	
Cheques to suppliers	47,200
Loan repayment (including interest)	10,100
Electricity	400
Motor vehicle expenses	1,000
Property insurance	150
Rates	300
Telephone	300
Drawings	1,750

Note. Depreciation is to be provided on the motor vehicle at a rate of 25% per annum on cost.

You are required to prepare a trading and profit and loss account for the year to 31 March 20X2, and a balance sheet as at that date.

26 CHURCH   45 mins

The summarised balance sheet of Richard Church, photographic retailer, as at 31 March 20X2, is as follows.

	Cost £	Dep'n £	NBV £
Fixed assets			
Shop equipment and fittings	15,000	3,000	12,000
Motor vehicles	6,000	1,500	4,500
	21,000	4,500	16,500
Current assets			
Stock		10,420	
Debtors		6,260	
Rent prepaid		650	
Bank		6,690	
		24,020	
Current liabilities			
Trade creditors		4,740	
Accrued expenses: heating and lighting		380	
		5,120	
Net current assets			18,900
			35,400
Long term liabilities			
Loan from S Chappell			3,000
			32,400
Capital			32,400

Despite professional advice, Richard Church has not maintained an accounting system, but produces the following information regarding the financial year ended 31 March 20X3.

(a) Total sales and sales returns were £152,600 and £3,500 respectively. An average gross profit to sales ratio of 30 per cent is maintained during the year.

(b) The trade debtors figure at 31 March 20X3 was £5,620, on which figure it has been decided to make a provision for doubtful debts of 5 per cent at the year end. During the course of the year trade debts amounting to £470 had been written off.

(c) The trade creditors figure at 31 March 20X3 was £6,390. Discounts received from suppliers amounted to £760.

(d) Stock at 31 March 20X3 indicates an increased investment of £4,000 in stock over that one year earlier. Drawings from stock by Richard Church during the year amounted to £600 and were included in payments made to suppliers; otherwise no records of these drawings were made.

Exam question bank

(e) Payments for shop salaries for the year were £15,840, and for heating, lighting, rent and rates and other administration expenses amounted to £3,460. At 31 March 20X3 rent paid in advance amounted to £480, and heating bills outstanding were £310.

(f) Shop fittings acquired during the year, and paid for, amounted to £2,000. Depreciation on shop equipment and fittings is provided annually at the rate of 10 per cent on the original cost of assets held at the year end. Similarly, depreciation on the motor vehicle is to be provided at the rate of 25% on original cost.

(g) On 31 March 20X3 the loan from S Chappell was repaid.

(h) Cash drawings by Richard Church amounted to £9,000.

Required

(a) Prepare a trading, profit and loss account for the year ended 31 March 20X3. (15 marks)

(b) Prepare a balance sheet as at 31 March 20X3. (10 marks)

27 SNAKES AND LADDERS I   *18 mins*

E Snakes and R Ladders have been trading in partnership as furniture dealers for several years sharing profits and losses in the proportion three-fifths to Snakes and two-fifths to Ladders.

The partnership's draft balance sheet as at 30 April 20X1 was as follows.

	£	£		£	£
Capital accounts			Fixtures & fittings		
Snakes	23,000		at cost	32,000	
Ladders	10,000		Provision for		
		33,000	depreciation		
			at 30 April 20X0	12,800	
Current accounts					19,200
Snakes	2,300		Motor vehicles at cost	8,800	
Ladders	1,600		Provision for		
		3,900	depreciation		
Bank overdraft		5,450	at 30 April 20X1	2,200	
Trade creditors		4,610			6,600
			Stock in trade at cost		14,830
			Trade debtors, less		
			provision for		
			doubtful debts		6,330
		46,960			46,960

After the preparation of the above balance sheet, the following discoveries were made.

(a) A loan to the partnership of £6,000 from Snakes at 5% pa on 1 May 20X0 has been credited inadvertently to Snakes' capital account.

(b) Depreciation for the year ended 30 April 20X1 has not been provided on the fixtures and fittings.

Note. The partnership's policy is to provide depreciation on fixed assets at the following annual rates on the cost of assets held at the end of each financial year.

| Fixtures and fittings | 10% |
| Motor vehicles | 25% |

(c) The provision for doubtful debts at 30 April 20X1 is £470, despite the fact that it has been decided that this provision should be at the rate of 5% of trade debtors at the end of each financial year.

(d) The bank overdraft figure of £5,450 is before allowance has been made for bank charges of £60 debited in the partnership's bank account on 27 April 20X1.

(e) Partners' drawings for the year ended 30 April 20X1 were as follows.

			£
(i)	Cash:	Snakes	4,300
		Ladders	3,900

(ii) Goods withdrawn from own use, at cost price:
Snakes 500
Ladders 600

It has now been established that cash drawings for the year under review had been posted from the cash book to the debit of the cost of goods sold whilst no entry has been made in the accounting records for goods withdrawn for partners' own use.

(f) Provision has not been made in the draft accounts for the following outstanding items at 30 April 20X1:

	£
Electricity charges accrued due	280
Insurance premiums prepaid	460

(g) Motor vehicle expenses of £400 incurred in August 20X0 have been debited inadvertently to motor vehicles at cost.

(h) The stock in trade valuation at 30 April 20X1 included a book case at cost £500 which had been acquired in January 20X1 for the partnership's offices.

Note. The purchase of the bookcase in January 20X1 was recorded correctly in the partnership's books of account.

Required

The journal entries correcting for items (c) and (e) above. Journal narratives are required. **10 marks**

28 SNAKES AND LADDERS II *18 mins*

Using the information in question 27 above, prepare the corrected partnership balance sheet as at 30 April 20X1. **10 marks**

29 HANOI *32 mins*

You are the assistant to the financial controller of Hanoi Ltd, a manufacturing company. The company's year end is 31 March 20X4. The following balances have been extracted as at that date.

	£'000
Freehold land	200
Leasehold premises: cost	150
accumulated amortisation	6
Plant and equipment: cost	120
accumulated depreciation	48
Trade debtors	100
Provision for doubtful debts	2
Trade creditors	76
Operating expenses accrual	10
Stocks	62
Bank balance (positive)	20
10% debentures	110
8% preference shares	100
Share capital (ordinary £1 shares)	200
Profit and loss account	100

The following information is also available.

(a) During the year, a boring machine was found to be past its best. It was decided to write down the machine from its net book value of £20,000 to its scrap value of £5,000. The original cost of the machine was £40,000.

(b) On 31 March 20X4 the preference dividend for the year was paid. Debenture interest was also all paid on 31 March 20X4.

(c) On 1 April 20X3 50,000 £1 ordinary shares were issued at a premium of 50p per share.

(d) An ordinary dividend of 10p per share was paid on 31 March 20X4.

(e) In the year ended 31 March 20X4, the following transactions took place.

Exam question bank

	£
Sales	305,000
Purchases	108,000
Contras between debtors and creditors accounts	25,000
Operating expenses paid	58,000
Bad debts written off	12,000

(f) The lease on the premises, when originally taken out, was for fifty years. The premises are to be amortised over the period of the lease. Plant and equipment is depreciated at 20% pa on the straight line basis.

(g) Stock at 31 March 20X4 amounted to £45,000.

(h) The following balances were available as at 31 March 20X4.

	£
Accrued operating expenses	15,000
Trade creditors	58,000
Trade debtors	96,000

Required

Prepare the profit and loss account of Hanoi Ltd for the year ended 31 March 20X4 and a balance sheet at that date.

Note. While you are not required to comply with all statutory disclosure requirements, your financial statements should be clearly and informatively presented and be in accordance with generally accepted principles.

---

30 PRIDE (PILOT PAPER)   *18 mins*

The following extracts have been taken from the trial balance of Pride Limited at 31 March 20X1:

	£'000	£'000
Issued share capital		
500,000 ordinary shares of 50p each		250
Share premium account 1 April 20X0		180
Profit and loss account 31 March 20X1		34
Land at cost	210	
Buildings - cost 1 April 20X0	200	
- accumulated depreciation at 1 April 20X0		120
Plant and equipment - cost	318	
- accumulated depreciation at 1 April 20X0		88
Debtors	146	
Cash at bank	50	
Creditors		94
10% debentures issued 20W5		100
Allowance for doubtful debts		10
Suspense account		166

Notes:

1. The profit and loss account balance of £34,000 shown above is the final balance of retained profit for the year and may be incorporated into your answer as such.

2. The balance on the suspense account is made up as follows:

	£'000
Receipt of cash on 8 January 20X1 on the issue of 200,000 ordinary shares of 50p each at a premium of 30p per share	160
Proceeds of sale of plant*	6
	166

* This plant had originally cost £18,000 and had been written down to £6,000 at 31 March 20X0. The company's policy is to provide depreciation for a full year in the year of acquisition of assets and none in the year of sale.

3. Depreciation is to be provided for on the straight line basis at the following annual rates:

Land	Nil
Buildings	2 per cent
Plant and equipment	20 per cent

4. the provision for doubtful debts is to be increased to £12,000.

5. Prepayments and accruals at 31 March 20X1 were:

	£000
Prepayments	8,000
Accruals	4,000

6. The closing stock was £180,000.

Required

Prepare the balance sheet of Pride Limited as at 31 March 20X1 for publication complying as far as possible with the provisions of the Companies Acts. **10 marks**

31 BUTTHEAD *45 mins*

Butthead Ltd is a small trading company. From the information below, you are required to prepare a trading, profit and loss account and a balance sheet in a form suitable for presentation to the directors. You should show all your workings and your financial statements should provide as much information as is helpful. Taxation is to be ignored.

(a) BUTTHEAD LIMITED
TRIAL BALANCE AS AT 31 DECEMBER 20X7

	£	£
Sales		160,800
Purchases	82,400	
Stock at 1 January 20X7	10,800	
Suspense account	2,800	
Freehold building	56,000	
Fixtures and fittings: cost	52,000	
depreciation 31.12.X7		18,800
Ordinary shares of 25p each		20,000
10% debentures		16,000
5% preference shares of 25p each		8,000
Profit and loss reserve at 1.1.X7		15,200
Cash at bank	1,200	
Cash in hand	1,200	
Sundry expenses*	37,600	
New issue account		12,000
Debtors control account	21,200	
Creditors control account		14,400
	265,200	265,200

*Note. This figure includes depreciation for the year.

(b) The following details relate to the company's bank reconciliation.

(i) The balance per the bank statement was £1,200 overdrawn.

(ii) A cheque for £2,000 had been accepted by the bank as being for £2,000, but had been entered in the cash book as £1,600.

(iii) Bank charges appear on the bank statement, but are not shown in the cash book.

(iv) On 31 December 20X7 there were unpresented cheques totalling £800, all of which cleared in the first week of the next accounting period.

(c) Stock at 31 December 20X7 was £13,600.

(d) In January 20X7 12,000 25p shares were issued at £1 each. The cash received was treated correctly, but the corresponding credit was made to a 'share issue account', as the bookkeeper was unsure of the correct treatment.

Exam question bank

(e) As at 31 December 20X7, the building is to be revalued to £60,000.

(f) The directors propose a dividend on the ordinary share capital as at 31 December 20X7 of 20p per share. No dividends were paid during the year.

(g) Debenture interest for the six months to 30 June 20X7 has been paid and is included in the figure for sundry expenses.

(h) The debtors and creditors ledgers do not reconcile with the debtors and creditors control accounts. Balance totals are as follows.

Debtors ledger
Debit balances £20,000
Credit balances £1,200

Creditors ledger
Credit balances £16,000
Debit balances £800

In reconciling the accounts you discover the following errors.

(i) The total on the debtors control account should be £22,400, not £21,200.

(ii) Contras of £1,600 have been correctly entered in the individual ledger accounts but not in the control accounts.

(iii) The list of debit balances on the sales ledger has been understated by £400.

(iv) The balance owed to Beavis plc of £800 has not been included in the list of ledger balances.

(v) During the year, a credit note was issued for £800. This has been treated like an invoice in both the individual ledger account and the control account.

After adjusting for the above errors, any remaining differences should be dealt with by transferring from the control accounts to the suspense account. If there is still a balance on the suspense account, this must be transferred to sundry expenses.

32 CRASH (PILOT PAPER) *18 mins*

The balance sheets of Crash Limited at 31 March 20X0 and 31 March 20X1 were as follows:

	Reference to notes	31 March 20X0 £'000	20X0 £'000	31 March 20X1 £'000	20X1 £'000
Fixed assets	1				
Cost or valuation		9,000		10,950	
Accumulated depreciation		(3,300)	5,700	(3,600)	7,350
Current assets					
Stock		1,215		1,350	
Debtors		1,350		1,290	
Cash		60		105	
Total assets		2,625		2,745	
Less: Current liabilities					
Trade creditors		(990)		(1,080)	
Bank overdraft		(195)		(270)	
		(1,185)		(1,350)	
			1,440		1,395
Net current assets			7,140		8,745
Less: 10% debentures			(1,500)		(750)
			5,640		7,995
Called up share capital			2,250		3,000
Share premium account			750		1,200
Revaluation reserve			-		750
Profit and loss account			2,640		3,045
			5,640		7,995

Notes:

1. Fixed assets

    (a) During the year fixed assets, which had cost £1,500,000 and which had a book value of £300,000 at 31 March 20X0, were sold for £375,000.

    (b) Land acquired in 20W7 was revalued upwards by £750,000 in preparing the balance sheet at 31 March 20X1.

2. Debentures

    Interest is due half-yearly on 30 September and 31 March and was paid on the due dates. The company repaid £750,000 debentures on 31 March 20X1.

3. Profit before interest for the year ended 31 March 20X1 was £555,000. No dividends were paid during the year.

4. Ignore taxation.

Required

Prepare a cash flow statement for Crash for the year ended 31 March 20X1 using the indirect method, complying as far as possible with the requirements of FRS 1 *Cash Flow Statements*.

The note reconciling net cash with movement is net debt is NOT required. **10 marks**

33 PORT *18 mins*

You have been told that your employer Port plc acquired 45,000 ordinary shares of Starboard Ltd on the 31 December 20X5 when the balance on Starboard's profit and loss account was £250,000. In addition Port plc is able to appoint four of the five directors of Starboard Ltd thus exercising control over their activities.

The balance sheets of Port plc and Starboard Ltd for the year ended 31 December 20X6 are shown below.

	Port plc £'000	Port plc £'000	Starboard Ltd £'000	Starboard Ltd £'000
Fixed assets				
Freehold properties		400		300
Plant and machinery		200		150
Investments: Starboard Ltd		450		
		1,050		450
Current assets				
Stock	150		100	
Debtors	170		80	
Bank	40		20	
	360		200	
Less current liabilities				
Creditors	170		120	
	170		120	
Working capital		190		80
		1,240		530
Share capital		500		100
Profit and loss account		740		430
		1,240		530

You are given the following additional information.

(a) Share capital of Port plc is 500,000 shares of £1 each and the share capital of Starboard is 100,000 ordinary shares of £1 each.

(b) The goodwill on acquisition is to be capitalised and not amortised.

Required

Prepare the draft consolidated balance sheet of Port plc as at 31 December 20X6. **10 marks**

Exam question bank

34 WAXEN WAYNE
36 mins

Waxen Wayne plc is a well-established company. Its board of directors is committed to a programme of expansion, commencing in 20X1. Unfortunately, there are unlikely to be enough retained profits to finance the expansion, and so it will be necessary to raise new capital from outside sources. The amount of finance which the board of directors wishes to raise is £2,000,000. There are three possible courses for raising the money, and each is thought to be practicable.

(a) *Scheme 1:* to issue £2,000,000 10% debenture stock 20X7 - 20X9 redeemable at par;

(b) *Scheme 2:* to issue 2,000,000 14% redeemable preference shares of £1 each, redeemable at par;

(c) *Scheme 3:* to issue 800,000 ordinary shares of £1 each at a premium of £1.50 per share. It would be hoped to pay an annual dividend of 12% of the nominal share value, which is the rate currently paid to existing ordinary shareholders.

Extracts from the current balance sheet of Waxen Wayne plc are as follows.

	£
Ordinary share capital (£1 shares fully paid)	10,000,000
General reserve	4,000,000
Profit and loss account	2,000,000
8% debentures	12,000,000

It is estimated that without the proposed expansion, the company's profit before interest and tax would remain static at about £3,710,000 for at least five more years.

The proposed expansion would be expected to earn an additional annual profit before interest and tax of £400,000 and would increase the total sales turnover of the company to £80 million per annum.

Corporation tax is payable at the rate of 40% on profits after interest and before tax.

'Earnings per share' is defined as the profits after tax and preference dividend, and extraordinary items, divided by the number of ordinary shares issued and ranking for dividend. The EPS for the current year is 16.5 pence, calculated as follows:

	£
Profit before interest and tax	3,710,000
Interest (8% of £12,000,000)	960,000
Profit before tax	2,750,000
Corporation tax (40%)	1,100,000
Profit after tax	1,650,000
Preference dividend	0
Earnings for ordinary shareholders	1,650,000
Number of ordinary shares	10,000,000
Earnings per share (EPS)	16.5p

Required

(a) Why might a company wish to issue redeemable debentures or preference shares?

(b) When would the debenture stock in scheme 1 be redeemed?

(c) The intention is to pay dividends of 12% on nominal value to ordinary shareholders. What would this imply for the new shareholders subscribing for the 800,000 new shares?

(d) What would be the earnings per share:

    (i) If scheme 1 were adopted?
    (ii) If scheme 2 were adopted?
    (iii) If scheme 3 were adopted?

(e) What would be the gearing ratio of the company after one full year:

    (i) If scheme 1 were adopted?
    (ii) If scheme 2 were adopted?
    (iii) If scheme 3 were adopted?

(f) Calculate the ROCE for each scheme, in two different ways, taking capital employed at the end of one full year of operations as your measure of capital employed.

(g) Analyse one of your ROCE calculations between profitability and asset turnover.

35 EFFICIENT *36 mins*

The financial statements of Efficient Ltd for the year 20X3 contain the following information:

On 31 December 20X3

Ratio of current assets to current liabilities	1.75 to 1
Liquidity ratio - total of debtors and bank balances to current liabilities	1.25 to 1
Net current assets	£37,500
Issued capital in ordinary shares	£50,000
Fixed assets - percentage of shareholders' equity and reserves	60%
Average age of outstanding debts (based on a year of 52 weeks)	7 weeks

For the year 20X3

Net profit - percentage of issued share capital	15%
Annual rate of turnover of stock (based on cost on 31 December 20X3)	4.16 times
Gross profit - percentage of turnover	20%

On 31 December 20X3, there were:

(a) No current assets other than stock, debtors and bank balances
(b) No liabilities other than shareholders' funds and current liabilities
(c) No assets or debit balances other than fixed and current assets

You are required to reconstruct in as much detail as possible:

(a) The balance sheet as on 31 December 20X3.
(b) The trading and profit and loss accounts for the year 20X3.

Ignore taxation.

Exam question bank

36 BROOD (PILOT PAPER) *18 mins*

The balance sheets of Brood Limited, at 30 April 20X0 and 30 April 20X1 are given below:

	30 April 20X0 £000	£000	30 April 20X1 £000	£000
Assets				
Tangible fixed assets				
Cost of valuation	51,000		63,000	
Accumulated depreciation	(12,500)	38,500	(16,300)	46,700
Current assets				
Stocks	16,400		18,400	
Trade debtors	19,100		20,600	
Sundry debtors and prepayments	3,100		4,000	
Total Assets	38,600		43,000	
Less: current liabilities				
Trade creditors	(11,400)		(8,400)	
Accruals	(3,400)		(4,200)	
Overdraft at bank	(13,700)		(4,800)	
	28,500		17,400	
Net current assets		10,100		25,600
		48,600		72,300
Less: 7% Debentures (£20m issued 1 May 20X0)		(20,000)		(40,000)
		28,600		32,300
Called up share capital		10,000		10,000
Share premium account		5,000		5,000
Revaluation reserve		5,000		5,000
Profit and loss account		8,600		12,300
		28,600		32,300

The summarised profit and loss accounts of Broad for the years ended 30 April 20X0 and 20X1, ignoring tax, are:

	Year ended 30 April	
	20X0 £000	20X1 £000
Sales	58,000	66,000
Cost of sales	(43,000)	(49,000)
Gross profit	15,000	17,000
Operating expenses	(10,000)	(10,500)
Profit from operations	5,000	6,500
Interest payable	(1,400)	(2,800)
Net profit for the period	3,600	3,700

Required

(a) Calculate the following ratios for each of the two years:

   (i)   Return on total capital employed
   (ii) Return on owners' equity
   (iii) Current ratio
   (iv) Quick ratio (acid test)
   (v)   Gearing (leverage)
   Use year-end figures for all ratios. (5 marks)

(b) Comment briefly on the movements in these ratios between the two years. (5 marks)

10 marks

Exam question bank

37 HELPFUL COMPUTERS
36 mins

Computers are increasingly being used for accounts work in all types of business.

(a) What makes accounting systems relatively easy to computerise?
(b) Why are computers so helpful in processing accounting data?

38 SSAP 2
18 mins

(a) 'The drawbacks of SSAP 2 have led to calls for a conceptual framework of accounting.'

Discuss this statement in light of the introduction of FRS 18. **(5 marks)**

(b) 'The going concern concept is fundamental to the preparation of financial statements. If a company cannot be assumed to be a going concern, the effect on those statements is dramatic.'

Discuss and illustrate your arguments with an example. **(5 marks)**

10 marks

39 STUD-U-LIKE
39 mins

Stud-U-Like Ltd is a publisher of Study Packs for various accountancy bodies. The packs are printed in-house and contained in ring binders which are made to a distinctive design in a small factory at the company's main site near Wormwood Scrubs, London. During the year ended 30 June 20X7, it was found necessary to shut down this factory and the workers were made redundant. The binders were to be bought in from an external supplier.

The following trial balance is available as at 30 June 20X7.

	£'000	£'000
Share capital - £1 ordinary shares		20
10% preference shares, 25p nominal value		20
Profit and loss account		38
Sales and purchases	85	300
Sales/purchase returns	4	8
Land and buildings (cost)	80	
Plant: cost/depn to 1 July 20X6	100	20
10% debentures		60
Opening stock	30	
Operating expenses	18	
Cost of factory closure (including redundancy)	75	
Sales/purchase ledger control	40	18
Provision for doubtful debts		2
Bank	54	
	486	486

In preparing the financial statements, the following information needs to be taken into account.

(a) No debenture interest has been accrued for.
(b) The provision for doubtful debts is to be 2½% of debtors.
(c) Depreciation at 10% on cost should be provided on plant.
(d) Sales returns of £2,000 were entered in the sales day book as if they were sales.
(e) Closing stock was valued at £35,000.
(f) The corporation tax charge for the year is £30,000.

Required

(a) Prepare a profit and loss account for the year ended 30 June 20X7. Your profit and loss account should be in good form, although it need not conform to the exact requirements of the Companies Act 1985. It must show clearly the items: gross profit, net operating profit, net profit before tax and profit for the year available to ordinary shareholders. Your workings should be set out clearly.

(b) 'FRS 3 *Reporting financial performance* aimed to improve the quality of financial information provided to shareholders.'

  (i) How might FRS 3 be applied to the profit and loss account you prepared in part (a)?

  (ii) What further information would you need in order to prepare the profit and loss account in accordance with FRS 3?

40 MEETING NEEDS 47 mins

(a) Explain the meaning of value added and its uses.

(b) Discuss the extent to which published financial statements meet the needs of shareholders and employees.

(c) Discuss any other statements which you feel might better fulfil employees' requirements.

(d) What is the purpose of the ASB's *Statement of Principles*?

Multiple choice questions

1   MCQS (PILOT PAPER)   *90 mins*

(i)   In a sales ledger control account, which of the following lists is composed only of items which would appear on the credit side of the account?

   A   Cash received from customers, sales returns, bad debts written off, contras against amounts due to suppliers in the purchase ledger

   B   Sales, cash refunds to customers, bad debts written off, discounts allowed

   C   Cash received from customers, discounts allowed, interest charged on overdue accounts, bad debts written off

   D   Sales, cash refunds to customers, interest charged on overdue accounts, contras against amounts due to suppliers in the purchases ledger.

(ii) Y purchased some plant on 1 January 2000 for £38,000. The payment for the plant was correctly entered in the cash book but was entered on the debit side of plant repairs account.

   Y charges depreciation on the straight line basis at 20% per year, with a proportionate charge in the year of acquisition and assuming no scrap value at the end of the life of the asset.

   How will Y's profit for the year ended 31 March 2000 be affected by the error?

   A   Understated by £30,400
   B   Understated by £36,100
   C   Understated by £38,000
   D   Overstated by £1,900

(iii) The trial balance of Z failed to agree, the total being: debit   £836,200
                                                                   credit £819,700

   A suspense account was opened for the amount of the difference and the following errors were found and corrected:

   1   The totals of the cash discount columns in the cash book had not been posted to the discount accounts. The figures were Discount Allowed £3,900 and Discount Received £5,100.

   2   A cheque for £19,000 received from a customer was correctly entered in the cash book but was posted to the customer's account as £9,100.

   What will be the remaining balance on the suspense be *after* the correction of these errors?

   A   £25,300 credit
   B   £7,700 credit
   C   £27,700 debit
   D   £5,400 credit

(iv) The trial balance of C Limited did not agree, and a suspense account was opened for the difference. Checking in the bookkeeping system revealed a number of errors.

   1   £4,600 paid for motor van repairs was correctly treated in the cash book but was credited to motor vehicles asset account

   2   £360 received from B, a customer, was credited in error to the account of BB

   3   £9,500 paid for rent was debited to the rent account as £5,900

   4   The total of the discount allowed column in the cash book had been debited in error to the discounts received account

   5   No entries has been made to record a cash sale of £100.

   Which of the errors above would require an entry to the suspense account as part of the process of correcting them?

   A   3 and 4
   B   1 and 3
   C   2 and 5
   D   2 and 3

Multiple choice questions

(v) B acquired a lorry on 1 May 2000 at a cost of £30,000. The lorry has an estimated useful life of four years, and an estimated resale value at the end of that time of £6,000. B charges depreciation on the straight line basis, with a proportionate charge in the period of acquisition.

What will the depreciation charge for the lorry by in B's accounting period to 30 September 2000?

- A £3,000
- B £2,500
- C £2,000
- D £5,000

(vi) SSAP 9 'Stocks and Long Term Contracts' defines the items that may be included in computing the value of a stock of finished goods manufactured by a business.

Which one of the following lists consists only of items which may be included in the balance sheet value of such stock, according to SSAP 9?

- A Foreman's wages, carriage inwards, carriage outwards, raw materials
- B Raw materials, carriage inwards, costs of storage of finished goods, plant depreciation
- C Plant depreciation, carriage inwards, raw materials, foreman's wages
- D Carriage outwards, raw materials, foreman's wages, plant depreciation

(vii) The closing stock of X Limited amounted to £116,400 *excluding* the following two stock lines:

1 400 items which had cost £4 each. All were sold after the balance sheet date for £3 each, with selling expenses of £200 for the batch.

2 200 different items which had cost £30 each. These items were found to be defective at the balance sheet date. Rectification work after the balance sheet amounted to £1,200, after which they were sold for £35 each, with selling expenses totalling £300.

Which of the following total figures should appear in the balance sheet of X for stock?

- A £122,300
- B £121,900
- C £122,900
- D £123,300

(viii) The Accounting Standards Board's 'statement of Principles for Financial Reporting' gives five qualitative characteristics which make financial information reliable.

These five characteristics are:

- A Prudence, consistency, understandability, faithful representation, substance over form
- B Accruals basis, going concern concept, consistency, prudence, true and fair view
- C Faithful representation, neutrality, substance over form, completeness, consistency
- D Freedom from material error, prudence, faithful representation, neutrality, completeness

(ix) The following attempt at a bank reconciliation statement has been prepared by Q Limited:

	£
Overdraft per bank statement	38,600
Add: deposits not credited	41,200
	79,800
Less: outstanding cheques	3,300
Overdraft per cash book	76,500

Assuming the bank statement balance of £38,600 to he correct, what *should* the cash book balance be?

- A £76,500 overdrawn, as stated
- B £5,900 overdrawn
- C £700 overdrawn
- D £5,900 cash at bank

(x) After checking a business cash book against the bank statement, which of the following items could require an entry in the cash book?

1 Bank charges
2 A cheque from a customer which was dishonoured
3 Cheque not presented
4 Deposits not credited
5 Credit transfer entered in bank statement

6 Standing order entered in bank statement.

- A 1, 2, 5 and 6
- B 3 and 4
- C 1, 3, 4 and 6
- D 3, 4, 5 and 6

(xi) The following information is relevant to the calculation of the sales figure for Alpha, a sole trader who doers not keep proper accounting records:

	£
Opening debtors	29,100
Cash received from credit customers and paid into the bank	381,600
Expenses paid out of cash received from credit customers before banking	6,800
Bad debts written off	7,200
Refunds to credit customers	2,100
Discounts allowed to credit customers	9,400
Cash sales	112,900
Closing debtors	38,600

The figure which should appear in Alpha's trading account for sales is:

- A £525,300
- B £511,700
- C £529,500
- D £510,900

(xii) A sole trader who does not keep full accounting records wishes to calculate her sales revenue for the year.

The information available is:

		£
1	Opening stock	£17,000
2	Closing stock	£24,000
3	Purchases	£91,000
4	Standard gross profit percentage on sales revenue	40%

Which of the following is the sales figure for the year calculated from these figures?

- A £117,600
- B £108,000
- C £210,000
- D £140,000

(xiii) A business compiling its accounts for the year to 31 January each year pays rent quarterly in advance on 1 January, 1 April, 1 July and 1 October each year. After remaining unchanged for some years, the rent was increased from £24,000 per year to £30,000 per year as from 1 July 2000.

Which of the following figures is the rent expense which should appear in the profit and loss account for year ended 31 January 2001?

- A £27,500
- B £29,500
- C £28,000
- D £29,000

(xiv) On 31 December 2000 the stock of V Limited was completely destroyed by fire. The following information is available:

1. Stock at 1 December 2000 at cost £28,400
2. Purchases for December 2000 £49,600
3. Sales for December 2000 £64,800
4. Standard gross profit percentage on sales revenue 30%

Based on this information, which of the following is the amount of stock destroyed?

- A £45,360
- B £32,640
- C £40,971
- D £19,440

Multiple choice questions

(xv) Which of the following statements concerning the accounting treatment of research and development expenditure are true, according to SSAP 13 'Accounting for Research and Development'?

1. If certain criteria are met, research expenditure may be recognised as an asset.
2. Research expenditure, other than capital expenditure on research facilities, should be recognised as an expense as incurred.
3. In deciding whether development expenditure qualifies to be recognised as an asset, it is necessary to consider whether there will be adequate finance available to complete the project.
4. Development expenditure recognised as an asset must be amortised over a period not exceeding five years.
5. The financial statements should disclose the total amount of research and development expenditure recognised as an expense during the period.

A   1, 4 and 5
B   2, 4 and 5
C   2, 3 and 4
D   2, 3 and 5

(xvi) D, E and F are in partnership, sharing profits in the ratio 5:3:2 respectively, after charging salaries for E and F of £24,000 each per year.

On 1 July 2000 they agreed to change the profit-sharing ratio 3:1:1 and to increase E's salary to £36,000 per year, F's salary continuing unchanged.

For the year ended 31 December 2000 the partnership profit amounted to £480,000.

Which of the following correctly states the partners' total profit shares for the year?

	D	E	F
A	£234,000	£135,800	£109,200
B	£213,000	£157,800	£109,200
C	£186,000	£171,600	£122,400
D	£237,600	£132,000	£110,400

(xvii) At 1 January 2000 the capital structure of Q Limited was as follows:

	£
Issued share capital 1,000,000 ordinary shares of 50p each	500,000
Share premium account	300,000

On 1 April 2000 the company made an issue of 200,000 50p shares at £1.390 each, and on 1 July the company made a bonus (capitalisation) issue of one share for every four in issue at the time, using the shares premium account for the purpose.

Which of the following correctly states the company's share capital and share premium account at 31 December 2000?

	Share capital	Share premium account
A	£750,000	£230,000
B	£875,000	£285,000
C	£750,000	£310,000
D	£750,000	£610,000

(xviii) A company compiles its accounts for the year to 31 March. In May 2000 the company sold its northern division, making a profit of £4m. The company's trading profit for the year to 31 March 2000 was £11m, to which the northern division has contributed £3m.

Which of the following treatments of the profit on the sale of the northern division and of its trading results is correct according to FRS 3 'Reporting Financial Performance'?

Multiple choice questions

	Trading results of northern division in profit and loss account for year ended 31 March 2000 as:	Profit on sale of northern division in profit and loss account as an exceptional item separately disclosed for year ended:
A	Discontinuing activity	31 March 2000
B	Discontinuing activity	31 March 2001
C	Art of continuing activities	31 March 2000
D	Part of continuing activities	31 March 2001

(xix) FRS 1 'Cash Flow Statements' requires the cash flow statement to be accompanies by a note reconciling operating profit to net operating cash flow.

Which of the following lists consists only of items which could appear in such a reconciliation?

- A   Depreciation, increase in debtors, decrease in creditors, interest paid, increase in stocks
- B   Increase in creditors, decrease in stocks, profit on sale of plant, depreciation, decrease in debtors
- C   Increase in creditors, equity dividends paid, depreciation, decrease in debtors, increase in stock
- D   Depreciation, interest paid, equity dividends paid, decrease in stocks.

(xx) SSAP 17 'Accounting for Post Balance Sheet Events' regulates the extent to which events after the balance sheet date should be reflected in financials statements.

Which of the following lists of such events consists only of items that, according to SSAP 17, should normally be classified as non-adjusting?

- A   Insolvency of a debtor whose balance was outstanding at the balance sheet date, issue of shares or debentures, a major merger with another company
- B   Issue of shares or debentures, changes in foreign exchange rates, major purchases of fixed assets
- C   A major merger with another company, destruction of a major fixed asset by fire, discovery of fraud or error which shows that the financial statements were incorrect
- D   Sale of stock, giving evidence about its value at the balance sheet date, issue of shares or debentures, destruction of a major fixed asset by fire

(xxi) An analysis of its financial statements revealed that the debtor collection period of R Limited was 100 days, when 60 days is a reasonable figure.

Which one of the following could NOT account for the high level of 100 days?

- A   Poor performance in R's credit control department
- B   A large credit sale made just before the balance sheet date
- C   R's trade is seasonal
- D   A downturn in R's trade in the last quarter of the year

(xxii) Which of the following correctly defines working capital?

- A   Fixed assets plus current assets minus current liabilities
- B   Current assets minus current liabilities
- C   Fixed asserts plus current assets
- D   Share capital plus reserves

(xxiii) At 1 January 1998 Limited acquired 80% of the share capital of s for £160,000. At that date the share capital of S consisted of 100,000 ordinary shares of £1 each and its reserves totalled £40,000. Goodwill on acquisition of subsidiaries is amortised on the straight line basis over five years.

in the consolidated balance sheet of H and its subsidiary S at 31 December 2000 the amount appearing for goodwill should be:

- A   £16,000
- B   £19,200
- C   £28,800
- D   £4,000

Multiple choice questions

(xxiv) At 1 January 1998 H Limited acquired 60% of the share capital of S for £180,000. At that date the share capital of S consisted of 200,000 shares of 50p each. The reserves of and S are stated below:

	At 1 January 1998 £	At 31 December 2000 £
H	280,000	240,000
S	50,000	180,000

In the consolidated balance sheet of H and its subsidiary S, what amount should appear for the minority interest in S?

- A £92,000
- B £280,000
- C £152,000
- D £112,000

(xxv) H Ltd acquired 75% of the share capital of S for £280,000 on 1 January 1994. Goodwill arising on consolidation has been fully amortised.

Details of the share capital and reserves of S are as follows:

	At 1 January 1994 £	At 31 December 2000 £
Share capital	200,000	200,000
Profit and loss account reserve	120,000	180,000

At 31 December 2000 the profit and loss account reserve of H amounted to £480,000.

What figure should appear in the consolidated balance sheet of H and S for the profit and loss account reserve at 31 December 2000?

- A £530,000
- B £525,000
- C £485,000
- D £575,000

2 MCQs

(i) Who issues Financial Reporting Standards?

- A The auditing practices board
- B The stock exchange
- C The accounting standards board
- D The government

(ii) Which of the following *not* an accounting concept?

- A Prudence
- B Consistency
- C Depreciation
- D Accruals

(iii) When preparing financial statements in periods of inflation, directors

- A Must reduce asset values
- B Must increase asset values
- C Must reduce dividends
- D Need make no adjustments

(iv) The following information relates to a bank reconciliation.

(i) The bank balance in the cashbook before taking the items below into account was £8,970 overdrawn.

(ii) Bank charges of £550 on the bank statement have not been entered in the cashbook.

(iii) The bank has credited the account in error with £425 which belongs to another customer.

(iv) Cheque payments totalling £3,275 have been entered in the cashbook but have not been presented for payment.

Multiple choice questions

(v) Cheques totalling £5,380 have been correctly entered on the debit side of the cashbook but have not been paid in at the bank.

What was the balance as shown by the bank statement *before* taking the items above the account?

- A   £8,970 overdrawn
- B   £11,200 overdrawn
- C   £12,050 overdrawn
- D   £17,750 overdrawn

(v) W Ltd bought a new printing machine from abroad. The cost of the machine was £80,000. The installation costs were £5,000 and the employees received specific training on how to use this particular machine, at a cost of £2,000. Before using the machine to print customers' orders, a test was undertaken and the paper and ink cost £1,000.

What should be the cost of the machine in the company's balance sheet?

- A   £80,000
- B   £85,000
- C   £87,000
- D   £88,000

(vi) The electricity account for the year ended 30 June 20X1 was as follows.

	£
Opening balance for electricity accrued at 1 July 20X0	300
Payments made during the year	
1 August 1999 for three months to 31 July 20X0	600
1 November 1999 for three months to 31 October 20X0	720
1 February 2000 for three months to 31 January 20X1	900
30 June 2000 for three months to 30 April 20X1	840

Which of the following is the appropriate entry for electricity?

	Accrued At 30 June 20X1	Change to profit and loss account year ended 30 June 20X1
A	£Nil	£3,060
B	£460	£3,320
C	£560	£3,320
D	£560	£3,420

(vii) The year end of M plc is 30 November 20X0. The company pays for its gas by a standing order of £600 per month. On 1 December 20W9, the statement from the gas supplier showed that M plc had overpaid by £200. M plc received gas bills for the four quarters commencing on 1 December 20W9 and ending on 30 November 20X0 for £1,300, £1,400, £2,100 and £2,000 respectively.

Which of the following is the correct charge for gas in M plc's profit and loss account for the year ended 30 November 20X0.

- A   £6,800
- B   £7,000
- C   £7,200
- D   £7,400

(viii) S & Co. sell three products - Basic, Super and Luxury. The following information was available at the year end.

	Basic £ per unit	Super £ per unit	Luxury £ per unit
Original cost	6	9	18
Estimated selling price	9	12	15
Selling and distribution costs	1	4	5
	units	units	units
Units of stock	200	250	150

The value of stock at the year end should be

- A   £4,200
- B   £4,700
- C   £5,700
- D   £6,150

507

Multiple choice questions

(ix) A car was purchased by a newsagent business in May 20W7 for:

	£
Cost	10,000
Road tax	150
Total	10,150

The business adopts a date of 31 December as its year end.

The car was traded in for a replacement vehicle in August 20X0 at an agreed value of £5,000.

It has been depreciated at 25% per annum on the reducing-balance method, charging a full year's depreciation in the year of purchase and none in the year of sale.

What was the profit or loss on disposal of the vehicle during the year ended December 20X0?

- A Profit: £718
- B Profit: £781
- C Profit: £1,788
- D Profit: £1,836

(x) A summary of the balance sheet of M Ltd at 31 March 20X0 was as follows

	£000
Total assets less current liabilities	120
Ordinary share capital	40
Share premium account	10
Profit and loss account	10
5% debentures 20Y0	60
	120

If the operating profit for the year ended 31 March 20X0 was £15,000, what is the return capital employed?

- A 12.5%
- B 25%
- C 30%
- D 37.5%

(xi) The annual sales of a company are £235,000 including VAT at 17.5%. Half of the sales are on credit terms; half are cash sales. The debtors in the balance sheet are £23,500.

What are the debtor days (to the nearest day)?

- A 37 days
- B 43 days
- C 73 days
- D 86 days

(xii) The concept of capital maintenance is important for

- A The sources of finance
- B The measurement of profit
- C The relationship of debt to equity
- D The purchase of fixed assets

(xiii) A stock record card shows the following details.

February	1	50 units in stock at a cost of £40 per unit
	7	100 units purchased at a cost of £45 per unit
	14	80 units sold
	21	50 units purchased at a cost of £50 per unit
	28	60 units sold

What is the value of stock at 28 February using the FIFO method?

- A £2,450
- B £2,700
- C £2,950
- D £3,000

(xiv) A particular source of finance has the following characteristics: a fixed return, a fixed repayment date, it is secured and the return is classified as an expense.

Is the source of finance

A	Ordinary share	
B	Hire purchase	
C	Debenture	
D	Preference share	

(xv) Which of the following statements gives the best definition of the objective of accounting?

- A To provide useful information to users
- B To record, categorise and summarise financial transactions
- C To calculate the taxation due to the government
- D To calculate the amount of dividend to pay to shareholders

(xvi) A company has been notified that a debtor has been declared bankrupt. The company had previously provided for this doubtful debt. Which of the following is the correct double entry?

	DR	CR
A	Bad and doubtful debts account	The debtor
B	The debtor	Bad and doubtful account
C	Provision for doubtful debts	The debtor
D	The debtor	Provision for doubtful debts

(xvii) W Ltd is registered for value added tax. The managing director has asked four staff in the accounts department why the output tax for the last quarter does equal 17.5% of sales (17.5% is the rate of vat). Which one of the following four replies she received was *not* correct?

- A The company had some exports that were not liable to VAT
- B The company made some sales of zero-rated products
- C The company made some sales of exempt products
- D The company sold some products to businesses not registered for VAT

(xviii) Which of the following is *not* the purpose of a sales ledger control account?

- A A sales ledger control account provides a check on the arithmetic accuracy of the personal ledger
- B A sales ledger control account helps to locate errors in the trial balance
- C A sales ledger control account ensures that there are no errors in the personal ledger
- D Control accounts deter fraud

(xix) The net book value of a company's fixed assets was £200,000 at 1 August 20X0. During the year ended 31 July 20X1, the company sold fixed assets for £25,000 on which it made a loss of £5,000. The depreciation charge of the year was £20,000. What was the net book value of fixed assets at 31 July 20X1?

- A £150,000
- B £155,000
- C £160,000
- D £180,000

Multiple choice questions

(xx) The draft balance sheet of B Ltd at 31 March 20X0 is set out below.

	£	£
Fixed assets		450
Current assets		
Stock	65	
Debtors	110	
Prepayments	30	
	205	
Current liabilities		
Creditors	30	
Bank overdraft (Note 1)	50	
	80	
		125
		575
Long-term liability		
Loan		(75)
		500
Ordinary share capital		400
Profit and loss account		100
		500

Note 1: The bank overdraft first occurred on 30 September 20W9.

What is the gearing of the company?

A   13%
B   16%
C   20%
D   24%

(xxi) According to the ASB 'statement of principles' which of the following is not an objective of financial statements?

A   Providing information regarding the financial position of a business
B   Providing information regarding the performance of a business
C   Enabling users to assess the performance of management to aid decision making
D   Helping to assess the going concern status of a business

(xxii) The ASB statement of principles identified user groups. Which of the following is not an information need for the 'Investor' group?

A   Assessment of repayment ability of an entity
B   Measuring performance, risk and return
C   Taking decisions regarding holding investments
D   Taking buy/sell decisions

(xxiii) The role of the Financial Reporting Council is to

A   Oversee the standard setting and regulatory process
B   Formulate accounting standards
C   Review defective accounts
D   Control the accountancy profession

(xiv) Which of the following items does not appear under the heading 'reserves' on a company balance sheet?

A   Share premium account
B   Retained profits
C   Revaluation surpluses
D   Proposed dividends

(xxv) Which of the following statements regarding a company profit and loss account is correct?

A   The Companies Act 1985 defines the expenses which are reported under 'cost of sales'
B   'Depreciation' appears as a separate heading
C   Interest payable is deducted from profit after taxation
D   Bad debts will be included under one of the statutory expense headings (usually administrative expenses)

Exam answer bank

Exam answer bank

1 USERS OF ACCOUNTING INFORMATION

The people who might be interested in financial information about a large public company may be classified as follows.

(a) *Managers of the company*. These are people appointed by the company's owners to supervise the day-to-day activities of the company. They need information about the company's financial situation as it is currently and as it is expected to be in the future. This is to enable them to manage the business efficiently and to take effective control and planning decisions.

(b) *Shareholders of the company*, ie the company's owners. These will want to assess how effectively management is performing its stewardship function. They will want to know how profitably management is running the company's operations and how much profit they can afford to withdraw from the business for their own use.

(c) *Trade contacts*, including suppliers who provide goods to the company on credit and customers who purchase the goods or services provided by the company. *Suppliers* will want to know about the company's ability to pay its debts; *customers* need to know that the company is a secure source of supply and is in no danger of having to close down.

(d) *Providers of finance to the company*. These might include a bank which permits the company to operate an overdraft, or provides longer-term finance by granting a loan. The bank will want to ensure that the company is able to keep up with interest payments, and eventually to repay the amounts advanced.

(e) *The Inland Revenue*, who will want to know about business profits in order to assess the tax payable by the company, and also the *Customs and Excise*.

2 THE ACCOUNTING EQUATION

Transaction	Assets		=	Capital		+	Liabilities	
		£			£			£
Start of business	Cash	5,000	=		5,000	+		0
(a)	Cash	3,200	=		5,000	+		0
	Shelves	1,800						
		5,000						
(b)	Cash	1,200	=		5,000	+		0
	Shelves	1,800						
	Books	2,000						
		5,000						
(c)	Cash	2,700	=		5,000	+		0
	Shelves	1,800		Profit	500			
	Books	1,000						
		5,500			5,500			
(d)	Cash	2,500	=		5,000	+		0
	Shelves	1,800		Profit	500			
	Books	1,000		Drawings	(200)			
		5,300			5,300			
(e)	Cash	3,000	=		5,000	+ Loan	500
	Shelves	1,800		Profit	500			
	Books	1,000		Drawings	(200)			
		5,800			5,300			500
(f)	Cash	3,000	=		5,000	+ Loan	500
	Shelves	1,800		Profit	500	Creditor	1,000
	Books	1,000		Drawings	(200)			
	Carpets	1,000			5,300			1,500
		6,800						

513

Exam answer bank

Transaction	Assets		=	Capital		+	Liabilities	
		£			£			£
(g)	Cash	3,000	=		5,000	+	Loan	500
	Shelves	1,800		Profit	700		Creditor	1,000
	Books	600		Drawings	(200)			
	Carpets	1,000			5,500			1,500
	Debtor	600						
		7,000						

3 FINANCIAL STATEMENTS

A balance sheet is a 'snapshot' of the financial position of a business. It is a statement of the liabilities, assets and capital of the business at a given moment in time. It is basically the same as the accounting equation, but written out in more detail.

The trading profit and loss account is not a static picture like the balance sheet, but is a record of income generated and expenditure incurred over the relevant accounting period.

Capital expenditure is expenditure which results in the acquisition of fixed assets (or an improvement in their earning capacity). It is not charged as an expense in the trading, profit and loss account.

Revenue expenditure is any other expenditure such as purchase of goods and expenses incurred to keep the business running (for example repairs, wages, electricity and so on). It is accounted for in the trading, profit and loss account.

Capital expenditure: (a), (d)
Revenue expenditure: (b), (c), (e), (f)

(Note that the value of the transactions is irrelevant.)

4 BUSINESS TRANSACTIONS

(a) *Purchase of goods on credit*

    (i) The supplier's invoice would be the original document.
    (ii) The original entry would be made in the purchase day book.

(b) *Allowances to credit customers on the return of faulty goods*

    (i) The usual documentation is a credit note. Occasionally, however, a customer may himself issue a debit note.
    (ii) The book of original entry would be the sales returns day book.

(c) *Petty cash reimbursement*

    (i) The original documents for the data would be receipts and a petty cash voucher.
    (ii) The transaction would be entered in the petty cash book.

(d) *Credit card sale*

    (i) The original document would be the credit card sales voucher or, strictly speaking, a copy of it.
    (ii) The original entry would be made in the cash book. This is because a credit card sale is like a cash sale as far as the retailer is concerned. The credit card company pays immediately, or very soon after the transaction has taken place. There is no need to set up a debtor.

Exam answer bank

5 BEECHFIELD

PETTY CASH BOOK

Receipts £	Date 20X9 Nov	Narrative	Total £	Stationery £	Cleaning £	Enter-tainment £	Travel £	Postages £
350	1	Cash						
	2	Materials	5		5			
	3	Stamps	10					10
	6	Envelopes	12	12				
	8	Taxi fare	32				32	
	10	Petrol	17				17	
	14	Typing paper	25	25				
	15	Materials	4		4			
	16	Bus fare	2				2	
	20	Visitors' lunch	56			56		
	21	Mops and brushes	41		41			
	23	Stamps	35					35
	27	Envelopes	12	12				
	29	Visitors' lunches	30			30		
	30	Photocopying paper	40	40				
			321	89	50	86	51	45
321	30	Cash						
	30	Balance c/d	350					
671			671					
	Dec							
350	1	Balance b/d						

6 HYPER

Initial workings

1 Invoiced sales excluding VAT = $\dfrac{£141{,}000}{117.5} \times 100 = £120{,}000 \therefore \text{VAT} = £21{,}000$

2 Purchases excluding VAT = $\dfrac{£84{,}600}{117.5} \times 100 = £72{,}000 \therefore \text{VAT} = £12{,}600$

DEBTORS

	£		£
Balance b/f	40,000	Bank	128,300
Sales and VAT creditor	141,000	Balance c/f	52,700
	181,000		181,000

CREDITORS

	£		£
Bank	92,700	Balance b/f	22,000
Balance c/f	13,900	Purchases and VAT creditor	84,600
	106,600		106,600

VAT CREDITOR

	£		£
Creditors (W2)	12,600	Balance b/f	4,100
Bank	4,100	Debtors (W1)	21,000
Balance c/f	8,400		
	25,100		25,100

SALES

	£		£
		Debtors (W1)	120,000

Exam answer bank

PURCHASES

	£		£
Creditors (W2)	72,000		

BANK ACCOUNT (EXTRACT)

	£		£
Debtors	128,300	Creditors	92,700
		VAT creditor	4,100

7 J OCKEY

(a) The relevant books of prime entry are the cash book, the sales day book, the purchase day book.

CASH BOOK (RECEIPTS)

Date	Narrative	Total £	Capital £	Sales £	Debtors £
May 1	Capital	5,000	5,000		
May 13	Sales	200		200	
May 16	Bruce	700			700
May 24	Hill	200			200
		6,100	5,000	200	900

CASH BOOK (PAYMENTS)

Date	Narrative	Total £	Fixtures and fittings £	Creditors £	Rent £	Delivery expenses £	Drawings £	Wages £
May 1	Store Fitments Ltd	2,000	2,000					
19	Abel	650		650				
20	Rent	200			200			
21	Delivery expenses	50				50		
30	Drawings	200					200	
30	Wages	320						320
31	Green	300		300				
		3,720	2,000	950	200	50	200	320

SALES DAY BOOK

Date	Customer	Amount £
May 4	Bruce	700
May 11	Hill	580
Mat 18	Nailor	360
		1,640

PURCHASE DAY BOOK

Date	Supplier	Amount £
May 2	Abel	650
May 9	Green	300
May 17	Kaye	800
		1,750

(b) and (c)

The relevant ledger accounts are for cash, sales, purchases, creditors, debtors, capital, fixtures and fittings, rent, delivery expenses, drawings and wages. Because this is not the end of the accounting period, balances on sales and expense accounts are not transferred to P & L but are simply carried down to be continued in the next month.

CASH ACCOUNT

	£		£
May receipts	6,100	May payments	3,720
		Balance c/d	2,380
	6,100		6,100

SALES ACCOUNT

	£		£
Balance c/d	1,840	Cash	200
		Debtors	1,640
	1,840		1,840

PURCHASES ACCOUNT

	£		£
Creditors	1,750	Balance c/d	1,750

DEBTORS ACCOUNT

	£		£
Sales	1,640	Cash	900
		Balance c/d	740
	1,640		1,640

CREDITORS ACCOUNT

	£		£
Cash	950	Purchases	1,750
Balance c/d	800		
	1,750		1,750

CAPITAL ACCOUNT

	£		£
Balance c/d	5,000	Cash	5,000

FIXTURES AND FITTINGS ACCOUNT

	£		£
Cash	2,000	Balance c/d	2,000

RENT ACCOUNT

	£		£
Cash	200	Balance c/d	200

DELIVERY EXPENSES ACCOUNT

	£		£
Cash	50	Balance c/d	50

DRAWINGS ACCOUNT

	£		£
Cash	200	Balance c/d	200

WAGES ACCOUNT

	£		£
Cash	320	Balance c/d	320

Exam answer bank

(d) Trial balance as at 31 May 20X4:

Account	Dr £	Cr £
Cash	2,380	
Sales		1,840
Purchases	1,750	
Debtors	740	
Creditors		800
Capital		5,000
Fixtures and fittings	2,000	
Rent	200	
Delivery expenses	50	
Drawings	200	
Wages	320	
	7,640	7,640

8 OMEGA

(a),(b),(c)

ALPHA

	£		£
Opening balance	210		
May sales	88	Balance c/d	298
	298		298

BETA

	£		£
Opening balance	1,040	Cash	1,040
May sales	314	Balance c/d	314
	1,354		1,354

GAMMA

	£		£
Opening balance	1,286	Cash	826
May sales	432	Balance c/d	892
	1,718		1,718

DELTA

	£		£
Opening balance	279	Cash	279
May sales	417	Balance c/d	417
	696		696

EPSILON

	£		£
Opening balance	823	Cash	823
May sales	129	Returns	88
May sales	269	Balance c/d	538
May sales	228		
	1,449		1,449

ZETA

	£		£
Cash	1,000	Opening balance	2,173
Balance c/d	1,441	May purchases	268
	2,441		2,441

Exam answer bank

ETA

	£		£
Cash	187	Opening balance	187
Balance c/d	1,164	May purchases	423
		May purchases	741
	1,351		1,351

THETA

	£		£
Cash	318	Opening balance	318

SALES ACCOUNT

	£		£
		May sales	1,877

PURCHASES ACCOUNT

	£		£
May purchases	1,432		

RETURNS ACCOUNT

	£		£
May returns	88		

CASH ACCOUNT

	£		£
May receipts	2,968	May payments	1,505

(d) DEBTORS AS AT 31 MAY

	April £	May £	Total £
Alpha	210	88	298
Beta	-	314	314
Gamma	460	432	892
Delta	-	417	417
Epsilon	-	538	538
	670	1,789	2,459

9 HUBBLE

Rather than write out the ledger accounts all over again, the question may be answered as follows.

(a) The postings necessary for each transaction are:

		£	£
DEBIT	Purchases	2,000	
CREDIT	Cash		1,000
CREDIT	Creditors		1,000
DEBIT	Interest	20	
CREDIT	Cash		20
DEBIT	Electricity	25	
CREDIT	Cash		25
DEBIT	Telephone	12	
CREDIT	Cash		12
DEBIT	Cash	500	
DEBIT	Debtors	3,000	
CREDIT	Sales		3,500
DEBIT	Cash	220	
CREDIT	Debtors		220

Exam answer bank

(b) Once these have been posted and the accounts balanced off, the trial balance is:

Account	Dr £	Cr £
Cash	18,083	
Capital		9,500
Bank loan		3,000
Sales		19,300
Debtors	6,980	
Rent	2,750	
Purchases	4,100	
Creditors		2,400
Interest	370	
Electricity	425	
Telephone	192	
Drawings	1,300	
	34,200	34,200

(*Note.* If you are not confident of your arithmetic, you may find it safer to write out and balance off all the ledger accounts individually.)

PROFIT AND LOSS (LEDGER) ACCOUNT

	£		£
Rent	2,750	Sales	19,300
Purchases	4,100		
Interest	370		
Electricity	425		
Telephone	192		
Balance (net profit taken to balance sheet)	11,463		
	19,300		19,300

(c) A HUBBLE BALANCE SHEET AS AT 31 MARCH 20X8

	£	£
Assets		
Cash	18,083	
Debtors	6,980	
	25,063	
Current liabilities		
Creditors	(2,400)	
		22,663
Long-term liabilities		
Loan		(3,000)
		19,663
Capital		
Capital as at 1.4.20X7		9,500
Add profit for year		11,463
Less drawings		(1,300)
Capital as at 31.3.20X8		19,663

Exam answer bank

A HUBBLE
TRADING, PROFIT AND LOSS ACCOUNT
FOR THE YEAR ENDED 31 MARCH 20X8

	£	£
Sales		19,300
Less cost of sales		4,100
Gross profit		15,200
Less other expenses		
Rent	2,750	
Interest	370	
Electricity	425	
Telephone	192	
		3,737
Net profit		11,463

10 RENT, RATES AND INSURANCE

(a) *Rent for the year ending 30 June 20X6*

	£
1 July 20X5 to 31 July 20X5 = £3,000/3	1,000
1 August 20X5 to 30 November 20X5	4,000
1 December 20X5 to 31 March 20X6	4,000
Accrued, 1 April 20X6 to 30 June 20X6 = 3/4 × £4,000	3,000
Charge to profit and loss for year ending 30 June 20X6	12,000

Rates for the year ending 30 June 20X6

	£	£
Rates prepaid last year, relating to this year		1,500
1 October 20X5 to 31 March 20X6		3,500
1 April 20X6 to 30 September 20X6	3,500	
Less prepaid July to September (3/6)	1,750	
April to June 20X6		1,750
Charge to profit and loss for year ending 30 June 20X6		6,750

Insurance for the year ending 30 June 20X6

	£	£
Insurance prepaid last year, relating to this year		1,800
1 November 20X5 to 31 October 20X6	6,000	
Less prepaid July to October (4/12)	2,000	
		4,000
Charge to profit and loss for year ending 30 June 20X6		5,800

(b) The accrual or prepayment for each expense can be summarised from the workings in part (a).

	£
As at 30 June 20X6	
Rent accrued	3,000
Rates prepaid	1,750
Insurance prepaid	2,000

Exam answer bank

11 HACKER

(a)

CASH BOOK

	£		£
Capital	4,000	Rent	600
Debtors - cash received	1,300	Delivery van	900
Cash sales	3,000	Creditors	1,600
		Sundry expenses	400
		Drawings	200
		Balance c/d	4,600
	8,300		8,300
Balance b/d	4,600		

SALES

	£		£
Trading a/c *	4,600	Cash book	3,000
		Debtors - credit sales	1,600
	4,600		4,600

DEBTORS

	£		£
Sales - on credit	1,600	Cash book	1,300
		Balance c/d	300
	1,600		1,600
Balance b/d	300		

CAPITAL

	£		£
Drawings *	200	Cash book	4,000
Balance c/d *	6,165	Profit and loss a/c *	2,365
	6,365		6,365
		Balance b/d	6,165

RENT

	£		£
Cash book	600	Profit and loss a/c *	150
		Prepayment c/d *	450
	600		600
Balance b/d	450		

DELIVERY VAN

	£		£
Cash book	900		

CREDITORS

	£		£
Cash book	1,600	∴ Purchases *	2,000
Balance c/d	400		
	2,000		2,000
		Balance b/d	400

PURCHASES

	£		£
Creditors	2,000	Trading a/c*	2,000

SUNDRY EXPENSES

	£		£
Cash book	400	Profit and loss a/c *	400

DRAWINGS

	£		£
Cash book	200	Capital a/c*	200

(b)
TRIAL BALANCE

	Dr £	Cr £
Cash book	4,600	
Sales		4,600
Debtors	300	
Capital		4,000
Rent	600	
Delivery van	900	
Creditors		400
Purchases	2,000	
Sundry expenses	400	
Drawings	200	
	9,000	9,000

Note. The asterisked entries will be made after the trial balance has been extracted.

(c) TRADING AND PROFIT AND LOSS ACCOUNT
FOR THE THREE MONTHS ENDING 31 MARCH

	£	£
Sales		4,600
Purchases	2,000	
Less closing stock	360	
Cost of sales		1,640
Gross profit		2,960
Rent	150	
Sundry expenses	400	
Depreciation on van ($3/12 \times 20\% \times £900$)	45	
		595
Net profit (to capital account)		2,365

STOCK ON HAND AT END OF THREE MONTHS

	£		£
Trading a/c	360		

PROVISION FOR DEPRECIATION

	£		£
		Profit and loss a/c	45

Exam answer bank

BALANCE SHEET AT 31 MARCH

	£	£
Fixed assets		
Van: cost	900	
less depreciation	45	
		855
Current assets		
Stock at cost	360	
Debtors	300	
Prepayments	450	
Cash	4,600	
	5,710	
Creditors	400	
		5,310
		6,165
Hacker's capital		
Original capital		4,000
Profit	2,365	
Less drawings	200	
Retained profit		2,165
		6,165

12 JAMES

Tutorial note. This question introduces a distinction between the cash account (representing cash in hand) and the bank account (representing cash at bank). When cash in hand is paid into the bank the transaction is accounted for as a payment from the cash account and a receipt of cash by the bank account.

(a)

CASH ACCOUNT

			£			£
1.7.X2	Capital		20,000	2.7.X2	Bank	18,000
23.7.X2	Sales		1,500	5.7.X2	Rent	500
31.7.X2	Equipment		50	9.7.X2	Purchases	1,000
				31.7.X2	Drawings	150
					Balance c/d	1,900
			21,550			21,550
1.8.X2	Balance b/d		1,900			

CAPITAL ACCOUNT

		£			£
31.7.X2	Balance c/d	20,000	1.7.X2	Cash	20,000
			1.8.X2	Balance b/d	20,000

BANK ACCOUNT

		£			£
2.7.X2	Cash	18,000	6.7.X2	Equipment	300
31.7.X2	Debtors	450	31.7.X2	Creditors	1,620
				Balance c/d	16,530
		18,450			18,450
1.8.X2	Balance b/d	16,530			

RENT ACCOUNT

		£			£
5.7.X2	Cash	500	31.7.X2	Balance c/d	500
31.7.X2	Balance b/d	500			

EQUIPMENT ACCOUNT

			£				£
6.7.X2	Bank		300	31.7.X2	Cash		50
					Balance c/d		250
			300				300
1.8.X2	Balance b/d		250				

PURCHASES ACCOUNT

			£				£
9.7.X2	Cash		1,000	31.7.X2	Balance c/d		3,000
10.7.X2	Creditors (Seddon)		2,000				
			3,000				3,000
1.8.X2	Balance b/d		3,000				

CREDITORS ACCOUNT

			£				£
20.7.X2	Purchase returns		200	10.7.X2	Purchases		2,000
31.7.X2	Bank		1,620				
	Discounts received		180				
			2,000				2,000

PURCHASES RETURNS ACCOUNT

			£				£
31.7.X2	Balance c/d		200	20.7.X2	Creditors		200
				1.8.X2	Balance b/d		200

SALES ACCOUNT

			£				£
31.7.X2	Balance c/d		2,500	23.7.X2	Cash		1,500
				26.7.X2	Debtors (Frodsham)		1,000
			2,500				2,500
				1.8.X2	Balance b/d		2,500

DEBTORS ACCOUNT

			£				£
26.7.X2	Sales		1,000	28.7.X2	Sales returns		500
				31.7.X2	Bank		450
					Discounts allowed		50
			1,000				1,000

SALES RETURNS ACCOUNT

			£				£
28.7.X2	Debtors		500	31.7.X2	Balance c/d		500
1.8.X2	Balance b/d		500				

DISCOUNTS RECEIVED ACCOUNT

			£				£
31.7.X2	Balance c/d		180	31.7.X2	Creditors		180
				1.8.X2	Balance b/d		180

DISCOUNTS ALLOWED ACCOUNT

			£				£
31.7.X2	Debtors		50	31.7.X2	Balance c/d		50
1.8.X2	Balance b/d		50				

Exam answer bank

DRAWINGS ACCOUNT

			£				£
31.7.X2	Cash		150	31.7.X2	Balance c/d		150
1.8.X2	Balance b/d		150				

(b) TRIAL BALANCE AS AT 31 JULY 20X2

	Debit £	Credit £
Cash	1,900	
Capital		20,000
Bank	16,530	
Rent	500	
Equipment	250	
Purchases	3,000	
Purchase returns		200
Sales		2,500
Sales returns	500	
Discounts received		180
Discounts allowed	50	
Drawings	150	
	22,880	22,880

13 GEORGE

DEBTORS ACCOUNT

		£			£
1.10.X1	Balance b/f (b)	30,000	15.1.X2	Bad debts-Fall Ltd (c)	2,000
30.9.X2	Sales (d)	187,800	30.9.X2	Cash (e)	182,500
				Discounts allowed (f)	5,300
				Bad debts (g)	3,500
				Balance c/d	24,500
		217,800			217,800
1.10.X2	Balance b/d	24,500			

SALES ACCOUNT

		£			£
30.9.X2	Trading P & L a/c	234,600	30.9.X2	Cash (d)	46,800
				Debtors (d)	187,800
		234,600			234,600

BAD DEBTS ACCOUNT

		£			£
15.1.X2	Debtors-Fall Ltd (c)	2,000	30.9.X2	Trading P & L a/c	5,500
30.9.X2	Debtors (g)	3,500			
		5,500			5,500

PROVISION FOR DOUBTFUL DEBTS ACCOUNT

		£			£
30.9.X2	Balance c/d (h) 5% × £24,500	1,225	1.10.X1	Balance b/f (b) 5% × £30,000	1,500
	Trading P & L a/c - reduction in provision	275			
		1,500			1,500
			1.10.X2	Balance b/d	1,225

Exam answer bank

DISCOUNTS ALLOWED ACCOUNT

			£				£
30.9.X2	Debtors		5,300	30.9.X2	Trading P & L a/c		5,300

CASH ACCOUNT (EXTRACT)

			£
30.9.X2	Debtors		182,500
	Sales		46,800

TRADING PROFIT AND LOSS ACCOUNT (EXTRACT)

		£			£
30.9.X2	Bad debts	5,500	30.9.X2	Sales	234,600
	Discounts allowed	5,300		Provision for doubtful debts	275

14 SAIGON

(a) *Ho*

	£
Cost: materials and labour	1,235
production overhead	1,050
	2,285
NRV: sales value	2,300
less transport	240
	2,060

∴ Value of this item is £2,060.

Chi

	£
Cost: materials and labour	4,680
production overhead	1,365
	6,045
NRV: sales value	6,220
less transport	75
	6,145

∴ Value of this item is £6,045.

∴ Total value of year end stock is £2,060 + £6,045 = £8,105.

(b) Total purchases are as follows.

		£
1 June	1500 × £90	135,000
1 August	2,000 × £92	184,000
1 October	3,000 × £93	279,000
		598,000

Total sales are as follows.

		£
June and July	(340 + 700) × £140	145,600
August to October	(800 + 450 + 900) × £144	309,600
November	630 × £145	91,350
		546,550

Total purchases are 6,500 units and total sales are 3,820 units. Closing stock is therefore 0 (opening stock) + 6,500 − 3,820 = 2,680 units.

(i) *First in, first out (FIFO)*

Using FIFO, the 2680 units in closing stock will all be deemed to come from the October purchase of 3000 units at £93 a unit.

Exam answer bank

	£	£
Sales		546,550
Opening stock	0	
Purchases	598,000	
	598,000	
Less closing stock 2,680 × £93	249,240	
Cost of goods sold		348,760
Gross profit		197,790

(ii) *Last in, first out (LIFO)*

	Purchases (units)		
	1 June	1 August	1 October
	1,500	2,000	3,000
Sales (units)			
June	(340)		
July	(700)		
August		(800)	
September		(450)	
October			(900)
November			(630)
	460	750	1,470

Value of closing stock

	£
460 × £90	41,400
750 × £92	69,000
1,470 × £93	136,710
	247,110

	£	£
Sales		546,550
Opening stock	0	
Purchases	598,000	
	598,000	
Less closing stock	247,110	
Cost of goods sold		350,890
Gross profit		195,660

(c) It will be observed from part (b) that, under LIFO, closing stock and profit are lower than under FIFO. This is because LIFO assumes that the oldest (and therefore usually, but not always) the cheapest stock is 'left behind'. (Note that we are concerned with valuation, not physical movement of stock.)

It could be argued that LIFO follows the matching concept more closely than FIFO. By calculating cost of sales on the basis of the more recent purchase price, FIFO matches costs and revenues more closely. By giving a more conservative profit figure in this case, although not, of course, if prices are falling, it could also be argued that LIFO is more prudent than FIFO.

However, it should be observed that, because one period's closing stock is the next period's opening stock, any effect on profit will be reversed in the following accounting period. In the long term, therefore, from the point of view of the profit and loss account it makes no difference whether FIFO or LIFO is used.

When it comes to the balance sheet, however, LIFO has serious drawbacks. The period end balance of stock represents the earliest purchases of the item which means that the figure for stocks in the balance sheet bears little relationship to recent cost levels. For this reason SSAP 9 outlaws LIFO, although it is permitted under companies legislation.

15 A COMPANY'S PLANT AND MACHINERY

(a) (i) Fixed assets purchased in 20X0 and 20X2 cannot be depreciated further, because they are already fully depreciated.

Exam answer bank

(ii) Fixed assets purchased in mid-20X4 had been depreciated by 90% (4½ years) by 31 December 20X8. All these assets will be fully depreciated by mid-20X9, when some of them are sold for £500.

(iii) Fixed assets purchased in 20X6 and sold in 20X9 would be 60% depreciated at the time of sale. Fixed assets purchased in 20X6 and not sold would be 70% depreciated by the end of the year.

Year of purchase		Plant and machinery at cost £	Depreciation charge as a % of cost		Depreciation charge P & L account £
20X0		20,000	(fully depreciated)	0%	0
20X2		30,000	(fully depreciated)	0%	0
20X4		100,000	(note (ii) above)	10%	10,000
20X6	Assets sold in 20X9	24,000	(sold in mid-year)	10%	2,400
	Assets not sold in 20X9	46,000		20%	9,200
20X7		50,000		20%	10,000
20X8		30,000		20%	6,000
20X9		150,000	(bought in mid-year)	10%	15,000
Total provision for depreciation for the year					52,600

(b) (i) Plant and machinery

Year of purchase	At cost, as at 31 Dec 20X8 £	Disposals during 20X9 £	Additions during 20X9 £	At cost, as at 31 Dec 20X9 £
20X0	20,000			20,000
20X2	30,000	(17,000)		13,000
20X4	100,000	(9,000)		91,000
20X6	70,000	(24,000)		46,000
20X7	50,000			50,000
20X8	30,000			30,000
20X9	-		150,000	150,000
Total	300,000	(50,000)	150,000	400,000

(ii) Provision for depreciation

Year of purchase	Accumulated depreciation as at 31 Dec 20X8 £	Accumulated depreciation on items disposed of in 20X9 £	Provision for depreciation £	Accumulated depreciation as at 31 Dec 20X9 £
20X0	20,000	-	-	20,000
20X2	30,000	(17,000)	-	13,000
20X4	90,000	(9,000)	10,000	91,000
20X6	35,000	(14,400) *	11,600	32,200 **
20X7	15,000	-	10,000	25,000
20X8	3,000	-	6,000	9,000
20X9	-	-	15,000	15,000
Total	193,000	(40,400)	52,600	205,200

* 60% depreciated at time of sale, 60% × £24,000 = £14,400.
** 70% depreciated 70% × £46,000 = £32,200.

(iii)
	31 Dec 20X8 £	31 Dec 20X9 £
Fixed assets		
Plant and machinery at cost	300,000	400,000
Provision for depreciation	193,000	205,200
Net book value	107,000	194,800

Exam answer bank

(iv)

	Disposal of item of plant purchased in		
	20X2 £	20X4 £	20X6 £
Cost of plant disposed of	17,000	9,000	24,000
Accumulated depreciation on plant disposed of (see (ii))	17,000	9,000	14,400
Net book value of plant at date of disposal	0	0	9,600
Net sale price	0	500	8,500
Profit/(loss) on disposal	0	500	(1,100)

There is a total loss of £600 on sale/disposal of the three items.

16 SPARK

(a) Check the balances on your ledger accounts with the trial balance shown below.

	Debit £	Credit £
Cash book		
Bank (note below) (W1)	1,703	
Cash (unbanked at end of period) (W2)	12	
Nominal ledger		
Drawings	560	
Postage and stationery	129	
Travelling expenses	40	
Motor expenses	104	
Cleaning expenses	260	
Sundry expenses	19	
Telephone	214	
Electricity	190	
Motor vans	2,000	
Rates	320	
Fixtures and fittings	806	
Capital		2,308
Purchases	3,163	
Discounts received		419
Credit sales		830
Cash sales		4,764
Discount allowed	81	
Provision for depreciation:		
motor van		720
fixtures and fittings		250
Stock at 1 January 20X1	366	
Loan - Flex		250
Sales ledger		
Brown	12	
Blue	180	
Stripe	48	
Purchase ledger		
Live		602
Negative		64
Earth		
	10,207	10,207

Workings

1 **Cash at bank**

	£
Opening balance	672
Bankings of cash (908+940+766+1,031)	3,645
Capital introduced	500
Received from customers	
90% × (160+66+22+10+40+120+140+130+20+44+38+20) = 90% of 810	729
	5,546
Less cheque payments (telephone, electricity, rates, van)	(1,469)
Payments to suppliers	
85% × (143+468+570+390+80+87+103+73+692+187) = 85% × 2,793	(2,374)
Closing balance	1,703

2 **Cash in hand**

	£		£
Balance b/d	5	Bank	3,645
∴ Sales	4,764	Drawings	560
		Stationery	73
		Travel	40
		Petrol and van	104
		Sundry	19
		Postage	56
		Cleaner	260
		Balance c/d	12
	4,769		4,769

(b) (i) **SPARK - TRADING AND PROFIT AND LOSS ACCOUNT FOR THE FOUR MONTHS ENDED 30 APRIL 20X1**

	£	£	£
Sales			5,594
Opening stock		366	
Purchases		3,163	
		3,529	
Closing stock		390	
			3,139
Gross profit			2,455
Discount received			419
Profit on sale of motor van			20
			2,894
Rent (W1)		500	
Rates (W2)		174	
Electricity		212	
Telephone (W3)		192	
Motor expenses		104	
Travelling		40	
Postage and stationery		129	
Cleaning		260	
Sundry expenses		19	
Depreciation (W4)			
Motor van	65		
Fixtures and fittings	27		
		92	
Discount allowed		81	
Loan interest (W5)		8	
			1,811
Net profit			1,083

Workings

1 Rent: 4/12 × £1,500 = £500; Accrual of £500 at 30 April
2 Rates: £100 + 2/6 × £220 = £174; Prepayment of £146 at 30 April
3 Telephone: £214 + £15 − £37 = £192

Exam answer bank

    4   Depreciation: Motor van: 20% × £1,300 × 3/12 = £65
          Fixtures: 10% × £806 × 4/12 = £27

    5   Loan interest: 10% × £250 × 4/12 = £8

(ii) SPARK - BALANCE SHEET AS AT 30 APRIL 20X1

	Cost £	Dep'n £	£
Fixed assets			
Motor van	1,300	65	1,235
Fixtures and fittings	806	277	529
	2,106	342	1,764
Current assets			
Stock at cost		390	
Debtors		240	
Payments in advance		146	
Cash at bank		1,703	
Cash in hand		12	
		2,491	
Current liabilities			
Trade creditors	666		
Accrued expenses	537		
		1,203	
			1,288
			3,052
Loan account: Flex			258
			2,794
Capital account			£
Balance at 1 January			1,808
Capital introduced			500
Profit for the four months			1,083
			3,391
Less drawings			597
			2,794

17 FRANK MERCER I

CASH BOOK

20X8		£	20X8		£
Dec 31	Balance b/f	1,793	Dec 31	Bank charges	18
Dec 31	Dividend	26	Dec 31	Standing order	32
			Dec 31	Direct debit	88
				Balance c/d	1,681
		1,819			1,819

18 FRANK MERCER II

BANK RECONCILIATION AS AT 31 DECEMBER 20X8

	£	£
Balance per bank statement		1,557
Add unrecorded lodgements:		
V Owen	98	
K Walters	134	
		232
Less unpresented cheques:		
B Oliver (869)	71	
L Philips (872)	37	
		(108)
Balance per cash book (corrected)		1,681

Exam answer bank

19 APRIL SHOWERS

> *Tutorial note.* The question specifically requires the correction of the control account before the correction of the list of balances. You should of course follow the examiner's requirements, even though the opposite order was recommended in the text.

SALES LEDGER CONTROL ACCOUNT

	£		£
Uncorrected balance b/f	12,550	Discounts omitted (d)	100
Sales omitted (a)	850	Contra entry omitted (f)	400
Bank - cheque dishonoured (l)	300	Bad debt omitted (g)	500
		Returns inwards omitted (j)	200
		Amended balance c/d	12,500
	13,700		13,700
Balance b/d	12,500		

Note. Items (b), (c), (e), (h), (i) and (k) are matters affecting the personal accounts of customers. They have no effect on the control account.

20 CHI KNITWEAR

(a)

SUSPENSE ACCOUNT

	£		£
Opening balance	1,536	Debtors - balance omitted	87
Sales - under-recorded	360	Cash book - receipts undercast	720
		Creditors: credit note posted to wrong side	358
		Cash book: Mr Smith's debt paid but cash receipt not recorded	731
	1,896		1,896

Notes

(i) Error (b) is an error of principle, whereby a fixed asset item (capital expenditure) has been accounted for as revenue expenditure. The correction will be logged in the journal, but since the error did not result in an inequality between debits and credits, the suspense account would not have been used.

(ii) The electricity bill has been omitted from the accounts entirely. The error of omission means that both debits and credits will be logged in the journal, but the suspense account will not be involved, since there is equality between debits and credits in the error.

(b) (i) The error means that debtors are understated. The correction of the error will increase the total amount for debtors to be shown in the balance sheet.

(ii) The correction of this error will add £1,200 to fixed assets at cost (balance sheet item) and reduce repair costs by £1,200. The P & L account will therefore show an increased profit of £1,200, less any depreciation now charged on the fixed asset.

(iii) The undercasting (ie under-adding) of £720 on the receipts side of the cash book means that debits of cash will be £720 less than they should have been. The correction of the error will add £720 to the cash balance in the balance sheet.

(iv) This transposition error means that total sales would be under-recorded by £8,514 - £8,154 = £360 in the sales account. The correction of the error will add £360 to total sales, and thus add £360 to the profits in the P & L account.

(v) The credit note must have been issued for a purchase return to the supplier by the business. It should have been debited to the creditor's account, but instead has been credited. Assuming that the purchase returns account was credited correctly, the effect of the error has been to overstate total creditors by 2 × £179 = £358, and this amount should be credited from the suspense account and debited to the creditors account. The effect will be to reduce the total for creditors in the balance sheet by £358.

(vi) The electricity bill, when entered in the accounts, will increase creditors by £152, and reduce profits (by adding to electricity expenses) by £152, assuming that none of this cost is a prepayment of electricity charges.

(vii) Since the cheque has not yet been recorded in the cash book, the correction of the error will add £731 to the cash balance in the balance sheet. At the same time, the provision for doubtful debts can be reduced, which will increase the net amount for debtors in the balance sheet by £731 (ie debtors less provision for doubtful debts, although the reduction in gross debtors by £731 has already been accounted for, due to the cash received) and increase profits by £731.

21 ACCOUNTING CONCEPTS

Tutorial note. Be prepared for written questions. Many students practise the numbers in questions but they skimp on the written questions. This is a mistake as there is a significant written element in each exam.

(a) **Materiality**. This concept involves assessing amounts to ensure that importance is not attached to figures which are not large enough to have an **effect** on the financial statements or on the user's **understanding** of them.

An example is that **only material** discontinued business segments are disclosed separately **under FRS 3**.

(b) **Substance over form**. This concept highlights the importance of the **underlying transactions** which make up the financial statements. The **legal form** of the transaction is not as important as the **commercial reality**: its substance.

An example of this is where a lease is identified as an operating lease. The commercial reality is that the lessee takes the risks and gains the rewards of ownership and so the lease should be treated as a finance lease.

(c) **Money measurement**. This concept states that only items which can be valued in monetary terms should be included in the financial statements.

An example of this is internally generated goodwill. The business may have generated goodwill over many years but there is no way to accurately place a value on it.

22 INTANGIBLE

Tutorial note. The important point is to distinguish between the amounts actually spent during the year and the amounts charged to profit and loss account.

PURCHASED GOODWILL

	£		£
Cash	4,800	P & L a/c - amortisation	1,200
		Balance c/d	3,600
	4,800		4,800
Balance b/d	3,600		

RESEARCH AND DEVELOPMENT EXPENDITURE

	£		£
Balance b/f	26,500	∴ P & L a/c *	15,300
Cash: research	7,900	Development expenditure c/d	22,600
development	3,500		
	37,900		37,900
Balance b/d	22,600		

* The P & L charge includes the £7,900 spent on research. The balance (£15,300 - £7,900) = £7,400 consists of amortisation of development expenditure.

23 FABRICATORS

The treatment of the events arising in the case of Fabricators Ltd would be as follows.

(a) The fall in value of the investment in Patchup Ltd has arisen over the previous year and that company's financial accounts for the year to 28 February 20X1 provide additional evidence of conditions that existed at the balance sheet date. The loss of £50,000 is material in terms of the trading profit figure and, as an adjusting event, should be reflected in the financial statements of Fabricators Ltd as an exceptional item in accordance with FRS 3.

(b) The destruction of stock by fire on 30 April (one month after the balance sheet date) must be considered to be a non-adjusting event (ie this is 'a new condition which did not exist at the balance sheet date'). Since the loss is material, being £250,000, it should be disclosed by way of a note to the accounts. The note should describe the nature of the event and an estimate of its financial effect. Non-reporting of this event would prevent users of the financial statements from reaching a proper understanding of the financial position.

(c) The approval on 1 June of the company's design for tank cleaning equipment creates a new condition which did not exist at the balance sheet date. This is, therefore, a non-adjusting event and if it is of such material significance that non-reporting would prevent a proper understanding of the financial position it should be disclosed by way of note. In this instance non-disclosure should not prevent a proper understanding of the financial position and disclosure by note may be unnecessary.

(d) The bills would have been discounted with recourse and hence there is a possibility of a liability arising if the bills are not honoured. Under FRS 12, the contingent liability of £150,000 in respect of bills discounted should be disclosed by way of a note in the financial statements.

(e) In these circumstances, if the field trials are not successful, then there is a possibility that it will be difficult to sell the equipment. Therefore, consideration should be given as to whether the equipment should be written down in the accounts to net realisable value. If the loss is not probable, a provision would not be required but consideration should be given as to whether the contingent liability should be disclosed by way of note. In the circumstances given, it would appear that the possibility of loss is remote and therefore, under FRS 12, no disclosure would be required. The expected future sales which might arise should not be included in the financial statements.

24 MISS TEEK

> *Tutorial note.* The opening balance sheet is given and so need not be reconstructed: Miss Teek's capital at 31 March 20X8 is £3,795. Accounts should be opened for the trading account, debtors, creditors and cash. Since some payments are in cash from cash takings, a two column cash book should distinguish between cash transactions and bank transactions.

Exam answer bank

MISS TEEK
TRADING AND PROFIT AND LOSS ACCOUNT
FOR THE YEAR ENDED 31 MARCH 20X9

	£	£
Sales: cash (W1)		10,850
credit (W2)		1,650
		12,500
Opening stock	500	
Purchases (W3)	7,600	
	8,100	
Closing stock (W4)	(600)	
Cost of sales		7,500
Gross profit		5,000
Expenses		
Rent	970	
Repairs to canopy	201	
Van running expenses (520 + 80 + 323)	923	
Depreciation	1,000	
Sundry expenses (24 + 31)	55	
Bank interest	47	
Accounting fees	75	
Bad debts	29	
		3,300
		1,700
Profit on disposal of van		1,300
		3,000

MISS TEEK
BALANCE SHEET AS AT 31 MARCH 20X9

	£	£	£
Fixed assets			
Motor van: cost (W5)			5,000
depreciation (W5)			1,000
net book value			4,000
Current assets			
Stock (W4)		600	
Debtors (W2)		320	
Cash in hand (W1)		39	
		959	
Current liabilities			
Bank overdraft (W1)	474		
Bank interest (presumably not paid until 1 April)	27		
Creditors (W3)	233		
		734	
Net current assets			225
			4,225
Proprietor's capital			
Balance at 31 March 20X8			3,795
Profit for the year		3,000	
Less drawings		2,570	
Retained profit for the year			430
Balance at 31 March 20X9			4,225

Exam answer bank

Workings

1 CASH BOOK

	Cash £	Bank £		Cash £	Bank £
Balance b/d	55	2,800	Drawings (52 × £50)	2,600	
Cash takings banked			Petrol (52 × £10)	520	
(contra entry)		7,521			
Cheques banked		1,500	Sundry expenses	24	
Dividend income -			Repairs to canopy	201	
drawings a/c		210	Taking banked (contra		
Cash takings (balancing			entry)	7,521	
figures)	10,850		Purchase of van		3,200
			Road fund licence		80
			Insurance on van		323
			Creditors		7,777
			Rent		970
			Sundry		31
			Accounting work		75
			Bank interest		20
			Returned cheque - bad debt		29
Balance c/d (overdraft)		474	Balance c/d	39	
	10,905	12,505		10,905	12,505
Balance b/d	39		Balance b/d		474

2 DEBTORS

	£		£
Balance b/d	170	Cash	1,500
Credit sales - balancing figure	1,650	Balance c/d	320
	1,820		1,820

3 CREDITORS

	£		£
Bank	7,777	Balance b/d	230
Balance c/d	233	Purchases (balancing figure)	7,780
	8,010		8,010

Goods taken as drawings:

		£
Selling price	(100%)	300
Gross profit	(40%)	120
Cost	(60%)	180

Therefore, purchases taken to the trading account = £7,780 - £180 = £7,600.

4 Closing stock

			£
Sales (10,850 + 1,650)	(100%)		12,500
Gross profit	(40%)		5,000
Cost of goods sold	(60%)		7,500
Opening stock			500
Purchases (W3)			7,600
			8,100
Cost of goods sold			7,500
Closing stock (balancing figure)			600

5 New van

The bank statement shows that the cash paid for the new van was £3,200. Since there was a part exchange of £1,800 on the old van, the cost of the new van must be £5,000 with first year depreciation (20%) £1,000.

Exam answer bank

6 Disposal of van

	£		£
Van at cost	3,000	Provision for depreciation at date of sale	2,500
Profit on disposal	1,300	Asset account (trade in value for new van)	1,800
	4,300		4,300

7 Drawings

	£		£
Cash	2,600	Dividend income	210
Stock	180	Capital account (balance)	2,570
	2,780		2,780

Since there are no investments in the business balance sheet, the dividend income must be separate from the business. However, since it is paid into the business bank account, it should be accounted for, in effect, as a reduction in drawings.

25 HIGHTON

TRADING PROFIT AND LOSS ACCOUNT
FOR THE YEAR ENDED 31 MARCH 20X2

	£	£
Sales: cash	80,400	
credit (W1)	9,250	
		89,650
Cost of sales		
Opening stock	3,500	
Purchases: cash	17,000	
credit (W2)	47,500	
	68,000	
Less closing stock	4,000	
		64,000
Gross profit		25,650
Expenses		
Depreciation of motor vehicle (25% × £3,000)	750	
Motor vehicle expenses (W3)	800	
Property insurance £(50 + 150 - 100)	100	
Loan interest	100	
Electricity £(400 + 400 - 200)	600	
General shop expenses	100	
Telephone £(100 + 300)	400	
Wages	3,000	
Rates	300	
		6,150
Net profit		19,500

Exam answer bank

BALANCE SHEET AS AT 31 MARCH 20X2

	£	£
Fixed assets		
Freehold land and buildings at cost		10,000
Motor vehicle: cost	3,000	
accumulated depreciation	1,500	
		1,500
		11,500
Current assets		
Stock	4,000	
Trade debtors	1,000	
Prepayments	400	
Cash at bank	950	
Cash in hand	450	
	6,800	
Current liabilities		
Trade creditors	1,800	
Accruals	500	
	2,300	
Net current assets		4,500
		16,000
Proprietor's capital		
At 1 April 20X4 (W4)*		5,250
Net profit for the year	19,500	
Less drawings £(7,000 + 1,750)	8,750	
Profit retained in business		10,750
		16,000

*The opening capital could be inserted as a balancing figure; W4 is included merely to prove the figure.

Workings

1   DEBTORS CONTROL ACCOUNT

	£		£
Opening balance	500	Bank	8,750
∴ Credit sales	9,250	Closing balance	1,000
	9,750		9,750

2   CREDITORS CONTROL ACCOUNT

	£		£
Bank	47,200	Opening balance	1,500
Closing balance	1,800	∴ Credit purchases	47,500
	49,000		49,000

3   MOTOR VEHICLE EXPENSES

	£		£
Prepayment b/f	200	Accrual b/f	200
Bank	1,000	∴ P & L account	800
Accrual b/f	100	Prepayment c/f	300
	1,300		1,300

Exam answer bank

4 PROPRIETOR'S CAPITAL AT 1 APRIL 20X1

	£	£
Assets		
Freehold land and buildings	10,000	
Motor vehicle	2,250	
Stock	3,500	
Debtors and prepayments	750	
Cash at bank and in hand	650	
		17,150
Liabilities		
Loan	10,000	
Creditors and accruals	1,900	
		11,900
		5,250

26 CHURCH

(a) TRADING PROFIT AND LOSS ACCOUNT
FOR THE YEAR ENDED 31 MARCH 20X3

	£	£
Sales (less returns)		149,100
Opening stock	10,420	
Purchases (balancing figure)	108,370	
	118,790	
Closing stock £(10,420 + 4,000)	14,420	
Cost of goods sold		104,370
Gross profit (30% × £149,100)		44,730
Add discounts received		760
		45,490
Expenses		
Bad debts	470	
Provision for doubtful debts (5% × £5,620)	281	
Salaries	15,840	
Heat, light etc (W5)	3,560	
Depreciation:		
shop fittings 10% × £(15,000 + 2,000)	1,700	
motor vehicle 25% × £6,000	1,500	
		23,351
Net profit		22,139

Exam answer bank

(b) BALANCE SHEET AS AT 31 MARCH 20X3

	Cost £	Depreciation £	Net £
Fixed assets			
Shop equipment and fittings	17,000	4,700	12,300
Motor vehicle	6,000	3,000	3,000
	23,000	7,700	15,300
Current assets			
Stock		14,420	
Trade debtors less provision		5,339	
Rent paid in advance		480	
Bank		16,100	
		36,339	
Current liabilities			
Trade creditors		6,390	
Accrued expenses		310	
		6,700	
Net current assets			29,639
			44,939
Proprietor's capital			
Balance at 31 March 20X2			32,400
Profit for year		22,139	
Less drawings £(9,000 + 600)		9,600	
			12,539
			44,939

Workings

Note. No distinction is made in the question between cash transactions and bank transactions. A 'total cash account' must therefore be constructed instead of the more usual columnar bank and cash account.

1 TOTAL CASH ACCOUNT

	£		£
Balance b/f	6,690	Creditors (Working 3)	106,560
Debtors (W2)	149,270	Salaries	15,840
		Heat, light etc	3,460
		Shop fittings	2,000
		Loan - repayment	3,000
		Drawings	9,000
		Balance c/d	16,100
	155,960		155,960
Balance b/d	16,100		

2 TOTAL DEBTORS ACCOUNT

	£		£
Balance b/f	6,260	Bad debts	470
Sales	152,600	Returns inwards	3,500
		Cash (balancing figure)	149,270
		Balance c/d	5,620
	158,860		158,860
Balance b/d	5,620		

Exam answer bank

3

TOTAL CREDITORS ACCOUNT

	£		£
Discounts received	760	Balance b/f	4,740
Cash (balancing figure)	106,560	Purchases (W4)	108,970
Balance c/d	6,390		
	113,710		113,710
		Balance b/d	6,390

4

PURCHASES ACCOUNT

	£		£
Creditors	108,970	Trading account	108,370
		Drawings	600
	108,970		108,970

5 *Heat, light etc*

	£	£
Amounts paid in year		3,460
Add: rent prepayment at 31 March 20X2	650	
heating accrual at 31 March 20X3	310	
		960
		4,420
Less: rent prepayment at 31 March 20X3	480	
heating accrual at 31 March 20X2	380	
		860
P & L charge for year		3,560

27 SNAKES AND LADDERS I

		Debit £	Credit £
(i)	Provision for doubtful debts	130	
	Profit and loss account		130

Being: the correction of a provision for doubtful debts, which is to be reduced from £470 to £340.

(ii)	Drawings account: Snakes	4,300	
	Drawings account: Ladders	3,900	
	Trading account		8,200

Being: the correction of an error whereby cash drawings of £8,200 were treated as a cost of sales.

(iii)	Drawings account: Snakes	500	
	Drawings account: Ladders	600	
	Trading account		1,100

Being: the correction of an error whereby stocks taken for personal use were not accounted for.

Notes

1 The current value of debtors is:

	£
Debtors less provision for doubtful debts	6,330
Provision for doubtful debts (current)	470
Debtors	6,800
Provision should be (5% of £6,800)	£340
Decrease in provision needed (£470 - £340)	£130

2   The posting from the cash book for cash drawings should have been to the debit of the drawings account, not the cost of goods sold account. The correction can be made by a transfer between the drawings account and the trading account.

3   The goods taken by the partners for their own use should have been debited to the drawings account and credited to the purchases account. The correction can be made by crediting the trading account.

28 SNAKES AND LADDERS II

Notes

(i) Fixtures and fittings

	£
At cost, in draft balance sheet	32,000
Depreciation for year (10%)	£3,200

The bookcase is presumed to be a fixture and fitting.

(ii) Motor vehicles

	£
At cost, in draft balance sheet	8,800
Less motor vehicle expenses	400
Corrected balance	8,400

Reduction in depreciation for the year (25% of £400) = £100.

(iii) Alterations to net profit

	Increase £	Decrease £
Depreciation: fixtures and fittings		3,200
Depreciation: motor vehicles	100	
Motor vehicle expenses		400
Reduction in provision for doubtful debts	130	
Bank charges		60
Drawings treated as cost of sales (4,300 + 3,900 + 500 + 600)	9,300	
Accruals - electricity		280
Prepayment - insurance	460	
Loan interest - Snakes 5% × £6,000		300
Overstatement of closing stock		500
	9,990	4,740
Increase in net profit		£5,250

(iv) Appropriation of increase in net profit

	£
Snakes (60%)	3,150
Ladders (40%)	2,100
	5,250

(v) Adjustments to current accounts

	Snakes £	Ladders £
Loan interest	300	
Share of extra net profit	3,150	2,100
Less drawings not yet accounted for	(4,800)	(4,500)
Reduction in current accounts	(1,350)	(2,400)
Current account as per draft balance sheet	2,300	1,600
Amended current account balance	950	(800)

Exam answer bank

The corrected partnership balance sheet is shown below.

SNAKES AND LADDERS
BALANCE SHEET AS AT 30 APRIL 20X1

	Cost £	Dep'n £	Net £
Fixed assets			
Fixtures and fittings	32,000	16,000	16,000
Motor vehicles	8,400	2,100	6,300
	40,400	18,100	22,300
Current assets			
Stock £(14,830 - 500)		14,330	
Trade debtors (£6,800 - £340 provision)		6,460	
Prepayment		460	
		21,250	
Current liabilities			
Bank overdraft £(5,450 + 60)		5,510	
Trade creditors		4,610	
Accrual		280	
		10,400	
Net current assets			10,850
			33,150
Loan			(6,000)
			27,150

Partners' accounts

	Capital £	Current £	Total £
Snakes	17,000	950	17,950
Ladders	10,000	(800)	9,200
	27,000	150	27,150

Tutorial note. This question is quite tricky. Although some of the adjustments might seem fairly obvious, there are quite a number of items which are easily overlooked.

(a) Charging motor vehicles expenses against net profit, as well as reducing the fixed asset value and depreciation charge.

(b) Remembering to adjust the overdraft (bank charge) stock (bookcase) and trade debtors, as well as including the accrual and prepayment.

(c) Calculating all the adjustments to net profit.

(d) Appropriating the change in net profit.

(e) Remembering to charge drawings against the partners' current accounts

If you solved this problem correctly, you are to be congratulated.

29 HANOI

> *Tutorial note.* In a manufacturing company you would expect to see work in progress as well as stocks, but this is ignored here as the purpose of this question is to test incomplete records techniques and presentation aspects.

Exam answer bank

HANOI LIMITED
TRADING, PROFIT AND LOSS ACCOUNT
FOR THE YEAR ENDED 31 MARCH 20X4

	£'000	£'000
Sales		305
Cost of sales		
Opening stock	62	
Purchases	108	
	170	
Closing stock	45	
		125
Gross profit		180
Operating expenses (W4)	63	
Plant depreciation (W5)	31	
Lease amortisation	3	
Bad debt expense	12	
		109
Operating profit		71
Debenture interest		11
		60
Dividends: ordinary		25
preference		8
Retained profit for the year		27

HANOI LIMITED
BALANCE SHEET AS AT 31 MARCH 20X4

	Cost £'000	Depn £'000	NBV £'000
Fixed assets			
Freehold land	200	–	200
Leasehold premises	150	9	141
Plant and equipment	85	44	41
		(W6)	
	435	53	382
Current assets			
Stocks		45	
Debtors (96 – 2)		94	
Bank (W1)		164	
		303	
Current liabilities			
Trade creditors		58	
Accrual		15	
		73	
Net current assets			230
			612
10% debentures			110
			502
Capital and reserves			
Ordinary £1 shares			250
Share premium			25
8% preference shares			100
Profit and loss a/c (100 + 27)			127
			502

545

Exam answer bank

Workings

1. **Bank balance**

   BANK A/C

	£'000		£'000
Balance b/d	20	Creditors (W3)	101
Debtors (W2)	272	Dividends: ordinary	25
Share capital	50	preference	8
Share premium	25	Debenture interest	11
		Operating expenses	58
		Balance c/d	164
	367		367

2. **Receipts from debtors**

   DEBTORS CONTROL A/C

	£'000		£'000
Balance b/d	100	Contra with CCA	25
Sales	305	Bad debts written off	12
		Bank (bal fig)	272
		Balance c/d	96
	405		405

3. **Payments to creditors**

   CREDITORS CONTROL A/C

	£'000		£'000
Contras with DCA	25	Balance b/d	76
Bank (bal fig)	101	Purchases	108
Balance c/d	58		
	184		184

4. **Operating expenses**

	£'000
Owed 1.4.X3	10
Paid during year	58
Owed 31.3.X4	15
P & L charge	63

5. **Plant cost and depreciation**

	£'000
Plant at cost b/d	120
Less fully depreciated item	40
Depreciable amount	80

   Depreciation charge £80,000 × 20% = £16,000

   (*Note*. Plant at cost for balance sheet includes fully depreciated item £(80 + 5) = £85,000.)

   Write down on machine (20 – 5) = £15,000.
   ∴ Total depreciation charge on plant (16 + 15) = £31,000.

6. **Plant: accumulated depreciation**

	£'000
B/d	48
Less fully depreciated item	20
	28
Add charge for year	16
	44

30 PRIDE

> *Tutorial note.* This is a straightforward question. Make sure you know the proforma balance sheet well enough to throw it down as you start the question. The allowance for doubtful debts increases to £12,000 so you can ignore the original £10,000.

Exam answer bank

PRIDE LIMITED
BALANCE SHEET AS AT 31 MARCH 20X1

	Cost £'000	Accumulated depreciation £'000	Net book value £'000
Fixed assets			
Land	210	-	210
Buildings	200	(124)	76
Plant and equipment	300	(136)	164
			450

Current assets
Stock		180	
Debtors (146 – 12)		134	
Prepayments		8	
Cash		50	
		372	

Liabilities: amounts falling due in one year
Creditors		94	
Accruals		4	
		98	

Net current assets			274
Less 10% debenture			(100)
			624

Capital and reserves
Issued share capital (250 + 100)		350
Share premium account (180 + 60)		240
Profit and loss account		34
		624

Workings

1 Plant and equipment

	£'000
Original cost	318
Disposal	(18)
Cost at year end	300
Depreciation @ 20%	60
Accumulated depreciation	88
Disposal (18 – 6)	(12)
	136

31 **BUTTHEAD**

> *Tutorial note.* The best approach to this question is to set out proformas for your workings leaving plenty of space. You will find yourself slotting figures into several different workings before any of them are complete.

547

Exam answer bank

BUTTHEAD LIMITED
TRADING, PROFIT AND LOSS ACCOUNT
FOR THE YEAR ENDED 31 DECEMBER 20X7

	£	£
Sales (160,800 – 1,600)		159,200
Cost of goods sold		
Opening stock	10,800	
Purchases	82,400	
	93,200	
Closing stock	(13,600)	
		(79,600)
Gross profit		79,600
Sundry expenses (W1)		(46,400)
Operating profit		33,200
Debenture interest		(1,600)
Net profit		31,600
Dividends: preference	400	
ordinary (92,000 × 0.20)	18,400	
		(18,800)
Retained profit for the year		12,800
Retained profit brought forward		15,200
Retained profit carried forward		28,000

BUTTHEAD LIMITED
BALANCE SHEET AS AT 31 DECEMBER 20X7

	£	£
Fixed assets		
Freehold building		60,000
Fixtures and fittings: cost	52,000	
depreciation	18,800	
		33,200
		93,200
Current assets		
Stock	13,600	
Debtors	17,600	
Cash in hand	1,200	
	32,400	
Current liabilities		
Creditors	16,000	
Debenture interest ($^6/_{12} \times 1,600$)	800	
Dividends	18,800	
Bank overdraft	2,000	
	37,600	
Net current liabilities		(5,200)
Total assets less current liabilities		88,000
10% debentures		(16,000)
		72,000
Share capital and reserves		
Ordinary shares of 25p		23,000
5% preference shares of 25p		8,000
Share premium		9,000
Revaluation reserve		4,000
Profit and loss reserve		28,000
		72,000

Exam answer bank

Workings

1   *Sundry expenses*

		£
Per trial balance		37,600
Less debenture interest (16,000 × 10% × $^6/_{12}$)		(800)
Suspense account (W4)		6,400
Bank (2,800 + 400)		3,200
		46,400

2   *Debtors control account and debtors ledger*

DEBTORS CONTROL ACCOUNT

	£		£
Balance b/d	21,200	Sales	1,600
Suspense	1,200	Contra	1,600
		Suspense	1,600
		Balance c/d	17,600
	22,400		22,400

Debtors ledger

	Dr	Cr
	£	£
Balances b/d	20,000	1,200
Understatement	400	
Sales		1,600
	20,400	2,800

Net corrected balance: £17,600

3   *Creditors control account and creditors ledger*

CREDITORS CONTROL ACCOUNT

	£		£
Contra	1,600	Balance b/d	14,400
Balance c/d	16,000	Suspense a/c	3,200
	17,600		17,600

Creditors ledger

	Dr	Cr
	£	£
	800	16,000
Beavis plc		800
	800	16,800

Net credit balances: £16,000

4   *Suspense account*

SUSPENSE ACCOUNT

	£		£
Balance b/d	2,800	Debtors control	1,200
Creditors control	3,200	Sundry expenses (bal fig)	6,400
Debtors control	1,600		
	7,600		7,600

Exam answer bank

5 Bank

	£	
Balance per bank statement	(1,200)	o/d
Unpresented cheques	(800)	
	(2,000)	o/d
Cash book balance per t/b	1,200	
Cheque difference (to sundry expenses)	(400)	
Bank charges (bal fig)	(2,800)	
	(2,000)	

32 CRASH

> *Tutorial note.* Always get your proforma cash flow down on paper first. This helps you to focus on the job in hand. Remember to look at both share capital and share premium for the proceeds of any share issue.

CRASH LIMITED
CASHFLOW STATEMENT FOR THE YEAR ENDED 31 MARCH 20X1

Note. Reconciliation of operating profit to net cash inflow from operating activities

	£'000
Operating profit	555
Depreciation (1.5m – 0.3m + 3.6m – 3.3m)	1,500
Profit on sale of fixed assets (375 – 300)	(75)
Increase in stocks	(135)
Decrease in debtors	60
Increase in creditors	90
Net cash inflow from operating activities	1,995

CASH FLOW

		£'000
Net cash inflow from operating activities		1,995
Returns on investments and servicing of finance		
Interest paid		(150)
Capital expenditure		
Purchase of fixed assets (W1)	(2,700)	
Proceeds from sale of fixed assets	375	
		(2,325)
Financing		
Repayment of debentures	(750)	
Proceeds from issue of shares	1,200	
		450
Outflow of cash		(30)

Workings

1 Fixed assets

	£'000
Opening cost	9,000
Disposal: cost	(1,500)
Closing balance	(10,950)
Movement before revaluation	3,450
Revaluation	(750)
Movement in the year	2,700

Exam answer bank

33 PORT

> *Tutorial note.* This question is straightforward, but you should remember to approach the question methodically so that you don't make any silly mistakes.

PORT PLC
CONSOLIDATED BALANCE SHEET AS AT 31 DECEMBER 20X6

	£'000	£'000
Fixed assets		
Goodwill		293
Freehold properties (400 + 300)		700
Plant and machinery (200 + 150)		350
		1,343
Current assets		
Stock (150 + 100)	250	
Debtors (170 + 80)	250	
Bank (40 + 20)	60	
	560	
Current liabilities		
Creditors (170 + 120)	290	
	290	
Net current assets		270
		1,613
Capital and reserves		
Share capital		500
Profit and loss account (W3)		821
		1,321
Minority interests (W2)		292
		1,613

Workings

1 Goodwill

	£'000
Cost of investment	450
Net assets acquired: 45% × (100 + 250)	(157)
	293

2 Minority interests

	£'000
55% × 530	292

3 Profit and loss account

	£'000
Port plc	740
Starboard plc 180 (W4) × 45%	81
	821

4 Post acquisition reserves of Starboard plc

	£'000
Profit and loss reserve at 31.12.20X6	430
Less profit and loss reserve on acquisition	(250)
	180

34 WAXEN WAYNE

(a) A company might wish to issue redeemable debentures and preference shares:

    (i)   In order to ensure that the higher gearing will not be for the long term.

Exam answer bank

(ii) In the hope that interest rates will come down in the future, so that when the debentures or preference shares are redeemed, new debentures or shares can be issued to replace them, but at a lower interest rate/dividend yield.

(iii) Redeemable items give greater flexibility for choosing a suitable capital structure.

(b) The debentures would become redeemable from 20X7, at the option of the company, but by 20X9 at the very latest. The company could redeem the debentures piecemeal from 20X7, all at once from 20X7 or not until all at once in 20X9.

(c) If shareholders receive a dividend at the 'coupon rate' of 12% or 12 pence per £1 share, then new shareholders who have paid a premium of £1.50 to buy each share would have an annual dividend on their investment of:

$$\frac{12p}{£1 + £1.50} \times 100\% = 4.8\%$$

(d)

	Scheme 1 £	Scheme 2 £	Scheme 3 £
Profit before interest and tax:			
Current operations	3,710,000	3,710,000	3,710,000
New scheme	400,000	400,000	400,000
	4,110,000	4,110,000	4,110,000
Interest			
8% debentures	(960,000)	(960,000)	(960,000)
10% debentures (10% × £2m)	(200,000)	-	-
Profit before tax	2,950,000	3,150,000	3,150,000
Corporation tax (40%)	(1,180,000)	(1,260,000)	(1,260,000)
Profit after tax	1,770,000	1,890,000	1,890,000
Preference dividend (14% of £2m)	-	(280,000)	-
Earnings for ordinary shareholders	1,770,000	1,610,000	1,890,000
Ordinary dividend (12p per share):			
10,000,000 shares	(1,200,000)	(1,200,000)	-
10,800,000 shares	-	-	(1,296,000)
Retained profits	570,000	410,000	594,000
Earnings per share	£1,770,000	£1,610,000	£1,890,000
	10,000,000	10,000,000	10,800,000
	17.7p	16.1p	17.5p

(*Note 1*. Scheme 1 provides a higher earnings per share because profits are boosted by the fact that corporation tax is charged on profits after interest. In other words interest is an 'allowable' expense for company tax purposes.)

(e)

	Scheme 1 £	Scheme 2 £	Scheme 3 £
8% debentures	12,000,000	12,000,000	12,000,000
10% debentures	2,000,000	-	-
Preference shares	-	2,000,000	-
Prior charge capital	14,000,000	14,000,000	12,000,000
Ordinary share capital	10,000,000	10,000,000	10,800,000
Share premium (800,000 × £1.5)			1,200,000
General reserve	4,000,000	4,000,000	4,000,000
P & L account b/f	2,000,000	2,000,000	2,000,000
Extra retained profit after one year	570,000	410,000	594,000
Total capital after one year	30,570,000	30,410,000	30,594,000
Gearing	14,000,000	14,000,000	12,000,000
	30,570,000	30,410,000	30,594,000
	45.8%	46.0%	39.2%

Exam answer bank

(f) ROCE

(i) as $\dfrac{\text{PBIT}}{\text{Total long - term capital}}$ $\dfrac{4{,}110{,}000}{30{,}570{,}000}$ $\dfrac{4{,}110{,}000}{30{,}410{,}000}$ $\dfrac{4{,}110{,}000}{30.594{,}000}$

         13.4%   13.5%   13.4%

(ii) as $\dfrac{\text{Earnings}}{\text{Equity capital and reserves}}$ $\dfrac{1{,}770{,}000}{15{,}670{,}000}$ $\dfrac{1{,}610{,}000}{16{,}410{,}000}$ $\dfrac{1{,}890{,}000}{18{,}594{,}000}$

         10.7%   9.8%   10.2%

(g) Taking the ROCE in (f) (i)

(i) PBIT/sales $\dfrac{4{,}110{,}000}{80{,}000{,}000}$ same   same

         5.1%   5.1%   5.1%

(ii) Sales/capital employed $\dfrac{80{,}000{,}000}{30{,}570{,}000}$ $\dfrac{80{,}000{,}000}{30{,}410{,}000}$ $\dfrac{80{,}000{,}000}{30{,}594{,}000}$

         2.62 times   2.63 times   2.61 times

35 EFFICIENT

(a) BALANCE SHEET AS AT 31 DECEMBER 20X3

	£	£
Fixed assets		56,250
Current assets		
Stock	25,000	
Debtors	17,500	
Bank balances	45,000	
	87,500	
Less current liabilities	50,000	
Net current assets		37,500
		93,750
Capital and reserves		
Issued share capital		50,000
Unappropriated profits:		
Balance at 1 January 20X3	36,250	
Net profit for year	7,500	
		43,750
		93,750

(b) TRADING AND PROFIT AND LOSS ACCOUNT FOR THE YEAR ENDED 31 DECEMBER 20X3:

	£
Sales	130,000
Cost of sales	104,000
Gross profit	26,000
Overheads	18,500
Net profit	7,500

Exam answer bank

Workings

1. $\dfrac{\text{Current assets}}{\text{Current liabilities}} = \dfrac{1.75}{1}$

   $\therefore \dfrac{\text{Current assets - current liabilities (ie net current assets)}}{\text{Current liabilities}}$

   $= \dfrac{1.75 - 1}{1}$

   $= \dfrac{0.75}{1}$

   $\therefore$ Current liabilities $= \dfrac{1}{0.75} \times$ net current assets

   $= \dfrac{1}{0.75} \times £37,500$

   $= £50,000$

   $\therefore$ Current assets $= 1.75 \times £50,000 = £87,500$

		£
2	Debtors and bank balances are 125% of current liabilities = 125% of £50,000	62,500
3	Stock is therefore £87,500 - £62,500	25,000
4	If stock is £25,000, then turnover at cost is 4.16 × £25,000	104,000
	Gross profit = 25% on cost (= 20% on turnover)	26,000
	Sales	130,000
5	Net profit is 15% of share capital	7,500
	∴ Overheads are £26,000 - £7,500	18,500
6	Debtors are 7/52 × turnover = 7/52 × £130,000	17,500
7	Bank balances constitute balance of current assets	
	ie £87,500 - (£25,000 + £17,500)	45,000
8	Fixed assets are 60% of shareholders' equity	
	Shareholders' equity = total net assets	
	Net current assets = £37,500 and must be 40% of total net assets	
	∴ Fixed assets = 60/40 × £37,500	56,250

36 BROOD

> *Tutorial note.* You should be able to calculate the ratios. If not, then make sure you learn them well. Calculating the ratios is only ever half the battle (if that). You must use the ratios to make relevant and useful comments about Brood's results.

(a)
			20X0	20X1
(i)	Return on capital employed		10.3%	9.0%
	$\dfrac{5,000}{28,600 + 20,000}$	$\dfrac{6,500}{32,300 + 40,000}$		
(ii)	Return on owners' equity		12.6%	11.5%
	$\dfrac{3,600}{28,600}$	$\dfrac{3,700}{32,300}$		

Exam answer bank

				20X0	20X1
(iii)	Current ratio			1.35:1	2.47:1
	$\dfrac{38{,}600}{28{,}500}$	$\dfrac{43{,}000}{17{,}400}$			
(iv)	Quick ratio			0.78:1	1.41:1
	$\dfrac{38{,}600 - 16{,}400}{28{,}500}$	$\dfrac{43{,}000 - 18{,}400}{17{,}400}$			
(v)	Gearing			41.1%	55.3%
	$\dfrac{20{,}000}{28{,}600 + 20{,}000}$	$\dfrac{40{,}000}{32{,}300 + 40{,}000}$			

(b) The first two ratios show that the **returns** from both capital and equity have **fallen** slightly. It may be that the **additional debenture loan** has been used to expand the business but the **rewards of the additional investment** have yet to be seen.

The current and quick ratios have **improved significantly**, moving from slightly low to slightly too high. Two major changes within working capital are the **overdraft** (reduced by the debenture loan) and **trade creditors** (which have also bucked the trend and gave down instead of up).

The gearing ratio has **increased** due to the additional debenture loan. Brood is probably as highly geared as it can safely be with **43% of its profit** going to pay **interest** in 2001.

37 HELPFUL COMPUTERS

(a) A computer always has to be told what to do. It will not think for itself. The instructions which tell it what to do (and when to do it) are given in programs - or in a collection of programs (depending on the complexity of the application being used on the computer). The easiest way to think of a program is that it is made up of a set of rules. So a computer operates within a framework of rules which tell it exactly what to do.

Accounting systems also exist within a framework of clearly defined, standard rules. The rules govern the regular, routine movement of transaction data through the accounting system. Although the actual accounting system might differ from business to business, the rules on which they are based do not. If a credit sale is made, for instance, then the relevant entries are made in the sales ledger and the debtors ledger. All businesses would make the same entries, although how they go about doing so might differ.

It is because both computer and accounting systems are based on clearly defined rules that accounting systems are relatively easy to computerise. The logical steps already existing within the accounting system can be transcribed into logical steps within the computer system. It would be much harder to computerise a system which was not based on standard rules, because first such rules would have to be created (in order to be able to set the program rules for the computer).

(b) Computers are widely used today because of their ability to process large volumes of data quickly, accurately and economically. Faced with an enormous load of paperwork, a company no longer has to employ an equally enormous army of clerks. It buys a computer instead.

Unlike clerks, computers never suffer from fatigue, or boredom, or even hangovers. They are capable of processing large volumes of data accurately for long periods of time without ill-effects - apart from the occasional failure of an electronic component, or hiccup in the software.

So computers are particularly good at repetitive, time-consuming tasks on large amounts of data. Accounting data tends to occur in such a way that large volumes of data require similar processing (eg invoice details, or payroll details). Standard programs can be developed fairly easily to deal with these volumes of data (eg invoice application, payroll package). In other words, accounting data happens to be the sort of data for which a standard computer program can be produced fairly easily.

Computers are also able to store and summarise large quantities of data. Once the accounting data has been captured (ie put into a form suitable for the computer) it can be stored on (for example) disk or tape, from which:

(i) It can be quickly retrieved for amendment for inspection
(ii) Records can be summarised and printed on request

Exam answer bank

(iii) Exceptions can be reported whenever they occur

All of the above would be repetitive and time-consuming in a manual accounting system, but are the very activities at which a computer excels.

38 SSAP 2

> *Tutorial note.* The introduction of FRS 18 has helped to address the shortcomings of SSAP 2. FRS 18 isn't a huge departure from SSAP 2 but you should highlight the way it has brought accounting policies in line with the *Statement of Principles*. Remember FRS 18 comes into force for accounting periods **beginning** on or after 24 December 2001 and so SSAP 2 still applies for years up to and including 23 December 2002.

(a) SSAP 2 *Disclosure of accounting policies*, was probably the most fundamental accounting standard. Its overall objectives were to further the user's understanding of financial statements by promoting an improvement in the quality of information disclosed. To achieve this it established as generally accepted accounting practice the disclosure in financial statements of clear explanations of the accounting policies followed.

However, it was never the intention behind SSAP 2 to develop a coherent conceptual framework. The need for such a framework has been recognised for some time. In the United States, the Financial Accounting Standards Board (FASB) has defined a framework as:

> 'a constitution, a coherent system of interrelated objectives and fundamentals that can lead to consistent standards and that prescribe the nature, function and limits of financial accounting and financial statements'.

The *Statement of Principles* has been introduced to provide a conceptual framework for accounting. This has helped put a stop to the firefighting approach which was typical of early accounting standards. The *Statement of Principles* is an underlying basis for consistent accounting principles which allows new standards to fit within a framework. FRS 18 *Accounting policies* has been introduced to replace SSAP 2 and bring accounting policies in line with the requirements of the framework provided by the *Statement of Principles.*

(b) The going concern concept is that an enterprise will continue in operational existence for the forseeable future. This means that the financial statements of an enterprise are prepared on the assumption that the enterprise will continue trading. If this were not the case, various adjustments would have to be made to the accounts: provisions for losses; revaluation of assets to their possible market value and so forth.

Unless it can be assumed that the business is a going concern, the other three fundamental accounting concepts cannot apply. This can be seen by considering each concept in turn as follows.

Consistency

It is meaningless to speak of consistency from one accounting period to the next when this is the final accounting period.

Accruals

The accruals or matching concept states that revenue and expenses which are related to each other are matched, so as to be dealt with in the same accounting period, without regard to when the cash is actually paid or received. This is particularly relevant to the purchase of fixed assets. The cost of a fixed asset is spread over the accounting periods expected to benefit from it, thus matching costs and revenues. In the absence of the going concern convention, this cannot happen, as an example will illustrate.

Suppose a company has a machine which cost £10,000 two years ago and now has a net book value of £6,000. The machine can be used for another three years, but as it is obsolete, there is no possibility of selling it, and so it has no market value.

If the going concern concept applies, the machine will be shown at cost less depreciation in the accounts, as it still has a part to play in the continued life of the enterprise. However, if the assumption cannot be applied the machine will be given a nil value and other assets and liabilities will be revalued on the basis of winding down the company's operations.

Prudence

The prudence concept as we normally understand it cannot apply if the business is no longer a going concern. A more drastic approach than mere caution is required when it is known that the business must cease trading.

39 STUD-U-LIKE

> *Tutorial note.* This is the kind of question you can reasonably expect to be asked on FRS 3 for Paper 1.1. Note that the emphasis is on understanding and explaining. The accounts preparation part of this question does not require a great deal of 'number crunching'.

(a) STUD-U-LIKE LIMITED
PROFIT AND LOSS ACCOUNT FOR THE YEAR ENDED 30 JUNE 20X7

	£'000	£'000
Turnover (W1)		292
Cost of sales (W2)		72
Gross profit		220
Operating expenses	18	
Decrease in doubtful debt provision (W3)	(1)	
Depreciation (10% × 100)	10	
		27
Net operating profit		193
Closure and redundancy costs	75	
Debenture interest (10% × 60)	6	
		81
Net profit before tax		112
Tax		30
Net profit after tax		82
Preference dividend (10% × 20,000)		2
Profit for the year available to ordinary shareholders		80

Workings

1 Turnover

	£'000
Sales per trial balance	300
Less returns incorrectly included	2
	298

	£'000
Sales returns per trial balance	4
Add returns incorrectly excluded	2
	6

Turnover = sales less returns = 298 − 6 = 292

2 Cost of sales

	£'000
Opening stock	30
Purchases less returns (85 − 8)	77
	107
Closing stock	35
	72

3 Decrease in doubtful debt provision

	£'000
Provision as at 1 July 20X6	2.0
Provision required: 2½% × (40 − 4)	0.9
∴ Decrease needed	1.1

For purposes of accounts say £1,000

Exam answer bank

(b) (i) The major change to the profit and loss account brought in by FRS 3 *Reporting financial performance* was to highlight certain key aspects of financial performance. It does this by requiring the following.

(1) All statutory headings from turnover to operating profit must be subdivided between that arising from continuing operations and that arising from discontinued operations.

(2) The following categories of exceptional items must be shown separately on the face of the profit and loss account after operating profit and before interest and allocated appropriately to discontinued and continued activities.

- Profit or loss on the sale or termination of an operation.

- Costs of a fundamental re-organisation or restructuring that has a material effect on the nature and focus of the reporting entity's operations.

- Profit or loss on disposal of a fixed asset.

The item to which FRS 3 could apply in the profit and loss account of Stud-U-Like is the closure/redundancy costs. The figure of £75,000 is material in the context of the accounts. If the factory making the ring binders is to be regarded as a discontinued operation, it will be necessary to separate out revenues and expenses associated with it from other revenues and expenses and show them separately as required by FRS 3. It will, in any case, be necessary to separate the profit or loss on the sale of fixed assets from the other costs as, if material, this is required to be shown separately as an exceptional item.

(ii) It is not clear, however, whether the manufacture of the special ring binders can be regarded as a separate operation which has now been discontinued. It appears that the ring binders were not sold separately, giving rise to separate revenues and costs, but were part of the cost of the Study Pack products. Further information on this point would be needed to determine exactly how FRS 3 should be applied.

40 MEETING NEEDS

(a) Value added is the difference between sales revenue in a period and the cost of bought-in materials and services. It is a performance measure of the wealth created by the company and emphasises the return made to those creating the wealth, namely employees, shareholders, lenders and the government. It differs from profit in that personnel costs, interest and depreciation are deducted from sales revenue. In other words value added is generally equal to pre-tax profit plus personnel costs, interest and depreciation. Value added has a number of uses, including:

(i) Forming the basis of the company's financial objective besides profit, and measuring the company's performance.

(ii) Communicating the company's financial results to employees and shareholders by means of a value added statement.

(iii) Forming the basis of an employee productivity scheme.

(b) The main concern of shareholders is generally the security of their investment. Institutional shareholders invariably have access to investment analysts, whose skill and understanding of accounts is such that any information provided by company reports can be readily assimilated and interpreted. The concern of investment analysts, in their capacity as agents for existing and potential institutional shareholders, is usually to obtain more information, in particular about matters such as future plans and prospects, cash flow and the relative profitability of different segments of a company or group. Many large companies do now provide some information of this type.

Private shareholders have the same interest in security. An academic study (Lee and Tweedie: *The Private Shareholder and the Corporate Report*) found that their main needs were:

(i) Income information (eg current profit and trend of profits).
(ii) Information on the future prospects of the company.
(iii) Dividend information (eg cover, amount and trend).

The study also revealed widespread lack of knowledge among private shareholders, many of whom clearly did not read annual reports because they were unable to understand them. Annual reports do contain considerable information relating to the requirements listed above, but they also contain much other information that often obscures the points of interest to the private shareholder. It is also significant that annual reports are inevitably based on past results, which are often of interest only in so far as they indicate possible future trends. In the past, the chairman's report has tended to be the most popular part of the report as it is generally understandable and contains future predictions. The Companies Act 1985 requires the directors' report to include details of important events since the balance sheet date, an indication of likely future developments in the business of the group, and an indication of any activities in research and development. This might help to add to the shareholders' understanding.

The same lack of knowledge is true to a great extent of employees, whose understanding of the full annual report is generally minimal. Conventional company accounts are prepared for the benefit of shareholders and do not meet the needs of employees. These needs could be summarised as:

(i) Information on managerial performance, efficiency and objectives, including employment plans.

(ii) Information on the company's future prospects, including its capacity to pay remuneration, meet pension obligations and maintain or increase employment.

(iii) Information on pay, conditions and terms of employment of various groups of employees.

Many large companies now produce employee reports designed to provide information of this type. In almost all cases, however, the provision of meaningful and detailed information about future prospects (both for shareholders and employees) is hindered by management's fear of revealing too much to competitors.

(c) *The Corporate Report* (1975 ASC discussion paper) suggested that companies should produce, among other things, value added statements, and employment reports. Employment reports would contain the following information:

(i) Numbers employed, average for the financial year and actual on the first and last day.

(ii) Broad reasons for changes in the numbers employed.

(iii) The age distribution and sex of employees.

(iv) The functions of employees.

(v) The geographical location of major employment centres.

(vi) Major plant and site closures, disposals and acquisitions during the past year.

(vii) The hours scheduled and worked by employees giving as much detail as possible concerning differences between groups of employees.

(viii) Employment costs including fringe benefits.

(ix) The costs and benefits associated with pension schemes and the ability of such schemes to meet future commitments.

(x) The cost and time spent on training.

(xi) The names of unions recognised by the entity for the purpose of collective bargaining and membership figures where available or the fact that this information has not been made available by the unions concerned.

(xii) Information concerning safety and health including the frequency and severity of accidents and occupational diseases.

(xiii) Selected ratios relating to employment.

Many companies do produce reports containing some of this information; however, reports about employment are not necessarily adequate for the information of employees. Value added statements are often given prominence, as these emphasise the importance of employees rather than shareholders and can be presented diagrammatically and colourfully (pie-charts, bar-charts etc). However, an ASC study (A E Hamill: *Simplified Financial Statements*) concluded that:

'Those employee reports that are currently issued are largely irrelevant to employee needs. Reports to employees might more usefully consist of basic simplified financial statements, supplemented by special reports that contain information that is of particular interest to employees at unit or site level.'

(d) The following are the main reasons why the ASB developed the *Statement of Principles*.

(i) To assist the ASB by providing a basis for reducing the number of alternative accounting treatments permitted by accounting standards and company law

Exam answer bank

(ii) To provide a framework for the future development of accounting standards

(iii) To assist auditors in forming an opinion as to whether financial statements conform with accounting standards

(iv) To assist users of accounts in interpreting the information contained in them

(v) To provide guidance in applying accounting standards

(vi) To give guidance on areas which are not yet covered by accounting standards

(vii) To inform interested parties of the approach taken by the ASB in formulating accounting standards

The role of the *Statement* can thus be summed up as being to provide consistency, clarity and information.

Multiple choice answers

1 MCQ 1

(i) **A**

(ii) **B**

			£	£
DEBIT	Fixed assets		38,000	
CREDIT	Plant and repairs			38,000
DEBIT	Dep'n expense		1,900	
CREDIT	Accumulated dep'n			1,900

Profit is understated by £38,000 – £1,900 = £36,100

(iii) **D**

	£
Suspense account	(16,500)
Discount allowed	(3,900)
Discount received	5,100
Transposition of cash received	9,900
	(5,400)

(iv) **B** Only errors 1 and 3 involve a single entry to correct them.

(v) **B** $\dfrac{£30,000 - £6,000}{4 \text{ years}} \times \dfrac{5 \text{ months}}{12 \text{ months}} = £2,500$

(vi) **C**

(vii) **C**

	£
	116,400
Line 1: (400 × £3) – £200	1,000
Line 2: (200 × £35) – £300 – £1,200	5,500
	122,900

(viii) **D**

(ix) **C** The bank is overdrawn.

	£
Overdraft	(38,600)
Deposits	41,200
	2,600
Unpresented cheques	(3,300)
Overdraft	(700)

(x) **A**

(xi) **A**

	£
Opening debtors	(29,100)
Cash from credit customers	381,600
Cash sales	112,900
Closing debtors	38,600
Expenses paid out of cash	6,800
Bad debts written off	7,200
Discounts allowed	9,400
Refunds	(2,100)
	525,300

(xii) **D** Cost of sales: £17,000 + £91,000 – £24,000 = £84,000

Sales	100%
Cost of sales	60%
Gross profit	40%

Sales: $\dfrac{£84,000}{60\%} = £140,000$

Multiple choice answers

(xiii) A $\dfrac{5 \text{ months}}{12 \text{ months}} \times £24{,}000 = £10{,}000$

$\dfrac{7 \text{ months}}{12 \text{ months}} \times £30{,}000 = £17{,}500$

Total rent: £10,000 + £17,500 = £27,500

(xiv) B

	£
Stock out: 64,800 × 70%	(45,360)
Stock in: purchases	49,600
Stock at 1 December	28,400
Stock @ 31 December	32,640

(xv) D

(xvi) A

	D £	E £	F £
Salaries	-	30,000	24,000
PSR to 1.7.20X0 (240,000 – 24,000) 5:3:2	108,000	64,800	43,200
PSR to 31.12.20X0 (240,000 – 30,000) 3:1:1	126,000	42,000	42,000
	234,000	136,800	109,200

(xvii) C

	£
Share capital @ 1.1.20X0	500,000
Issue on 1.4.20X0 (200,000 @ 50p)	100,000
Bonus issue (1.2m ÷ 4) @ 50p	150,000
Share capital as at 31.12.20X0	750,000

	£
Share premium @ 1.1.20X0	300,000
1.4.20X0 200,000 shares @ (130p – 50p)	160,000
Bonus issue (as above)	(150,000)
	310,000

(xviii) B

(xix) B

(xx) B

(xxi) D

(xxii) B

(xxiii) B

	£
Consideration	160,000
Shares and reserves acquired (100,000 + 40,000) @ 80%	(112,000)
Goodwill	48,000

Goodwill remaining: $\dfrac{2 \text{ years}}{5 \text{ years}} \times £48{,}000 = £19{,}200$

(xxiv) D

MI	£
Shares	100,000
Reserves	180,000
	280,000
MI @ 40%	112,000

Multiple choice answers

(xxv) C

	£
Consideration	280,000
Acquired 320,000 @ 75%	240,000
Goodwill	40,000

Profit and loss account

	£
H Ltd	480,000
S Ltd's post acq reserves (180,000 – 120,000) @ 75%	45,000
Fully amortised goodwill	(40,000)
	485,000

2 MCQ 2

(i) C

(ii) C

(iii) D

(iv) B

Cash book	£	Bank statement	£
Balance	(8970)	Balance	(11,200)
Bank charges	(550)	Credit in error	(425)
		Unpresented cheques	(3,275)
		Outstanding deposits	5,380
	(9,250)		(9,250)

(v) D

	£
Cost of machine	80,000
Installation	5,000
Training	2,000
Testing	1,000
	88,000

(vi) C

Electricity Account

		£		£
			Balance b/fwd	300
20X0:				
1 August	Paid bank	600		
1 November	Paid bank	720		
20X1:				
1 February	Paid bank	900		
30 June	Paid bank	840		
30 June	Accrual c/d £840 × ²/₃	560	Profit and loss account	3,320
		3,620		3,620

(vii) A

Gas supplier account

	£		£
Balance b/fwd	200	28 February invoice	1,300
Bank £600 × 12	7,200	31 May invoice	1,400
		31 August invoice	2,100
		30 November invoice	2,000
		30 November bal. c/d	600
	7,400		7,400

Multiple choice answers

Gas account

		£			£
28 February	invoice	1,300			
31 May	invoice	1,4004			
31 August	invoice	2,100			
30 November	invoice	2,000	30 November Profit and loss account		6,800
		6,800			6,800

(viii) B

	Cost	Net realisable value	Lower of cost & NRV	Units	Value
	£	£	£		£
Basic	6	8	6	200	1,200
Super	9	8	8	250	2,000
Luxury	18	10	10	150	1,500
					4,700

(ix) B

	£
Cost	10,000
20W7 Depreciation	2,500
	7,500
20W8 Depreciation	1,875
	5,625
20W9 Depreciation	1,406
	4,219
20X0 Part exchange	5,000
Profit	781

(x) A

$$\frac{\text{Operating profit}}{\text{Capital employed}} = \frac{£15,000}{£120,000} \times 100 = 12.5\%$$

(xi) C

$$\frac{\text{Debtors including VAT}}{\text{Credit sales including VAT}} = \frac{£23,500}{£117,500} \times 365 \text{ days} = 73 \text{ days}$$

(xii) B

(xiii) C

(xiv) C

(xv) A

(xvi) C

(xvii) D

(xviii) C

(xix) A

	£	£
Net book value at 1st August 20X0		200,000
Less depreciation		(20,000)
Proceeds	25,000	
Loss	5,000	
Therefore net book value		(30,000)
		150,000

(xx) A Gearing =

$$\frac{\text{debt}}{\text{debt} + \text{equity}} = \frac{75}{75+500} = 13\%$$

(xxi) D Correct. This is not an objective from the statement of principles. Additional data is required to assess this.

Multiple choice answers

	A	This is a primary objective.
	B	Again, a major objective.
	C	All Classes of users require information for decision making.
(xxii)	A	Correct. This information is a need for the 'lender' group.
	B	This is an important need, particularly relative to other investment opportunities.
	C	A primary need.
	D	A major need for existing (and prospective) investors.
(xxiii)	A	This is correct, the FRC also raises funds and controls the strategic direction of its subsidiary bodies such as the Accounting Standards Board.
	B	This is the role of the Accounting Standards Board.
	C	This is the role of the Financial Reporting Review Panel.
	D	Each professional body is essentially self regulatory. The only avenue for consultation is via the Consultative Committee of Accountancy Bodies.
(xiv)	D	This is correct because proposed dividends are current liabilities.
	A	This is statutory reserve.
	B	Otherwise known as the profit and loss reserve.
	C	This is an unrealised reserve.
(xxv)	D	Correct, company will usually include this under distribution costs or administrative expenses.
	A	Incorrect, the contents of cost of sales are not defined by statute.
	B	Depreciation will be included under the relevant statutory expense heading. (eg office equipment depreciation will go into administrative expenses).
	C	Incorrect, net profit is calculated after interest.

Index

Index

Note: **Key Terms** and their references are given in **bold**

Accounting concepts, 12
Accounting estimates, 248
Accounting equation, 25, 26, 68
Accounting for VAT, 87
Accounting information, 4
Accounting policy, 248
Accounting standards and choice, 452
Accounting Standards and the law, 14, 446
Accounting Standards Board (ASB), 13, 445
Accounting Standards Committee, 13, 444
Accounting standards, 12, 445
Accruals and prepayments, 288, 299
Accruals concept, 238
Accruals, 111, 115, 194
Accruals, 112
Acid test ratio, 411
Adjusting events, 272
Administration expenses, 48
Alternative accounting, 178
Alternative accounting rules, 178
Alternative accounting valuation, 180
Appropriation of net profits, 320
ASB, 459
Asset turnover, 401
Asset, 23
Assets, 8, 28, 39, 254
Audit trail, 429
Auditing, 10
Auditors' report, 9
Authorised (or nominal) capital, 329
Average cost, 147
Average cost, 155

Bad and doubtful debts, 194
Bad debt, 126
Bad debts, 48, 122, 127, 134, 290
Balance sheet, 38, 46, 99, 100, 129, 218, 256, 448
Balance sheet, 8, 38
Balancing ledger accounts, 94
Bank charges, 201
Bank interest, 201
Bank overdraft, 40
Bank reconciliation, 201
Bank reconciliation, 202, 205
Bank statements, 63
Bills of exchange, 40
Bonus issues, 343
Books of prime entry, 58
Books of prime entry, 79

Brought forward, 39
Business equation, 28, 68

Calculating ratios, 396
Called-up capital, 330
Capital, 26
Capital, 39
Capital account, 319
Capital expenditure, 16
Capital gearing ratio, 404, 405
Capital income, 17
Capital transactions, 17
Capitalisation of finance costs, 181
Carriage costs, 107
Carriage inwards, 109
Carriage outwards, 109
Carried forward, 39
Cash, 43
Cash book, 58, 61, 83, 288, 296
Cash book, 61
Cash cycle, 409
Cash discount, 123
Cash discounts, 124, 125
Cash flow ratio, 408
Cash flow statement, 256
Chairman's report, 9, 396
Class of fixed assets, 189
Coding, 429
Companies Act 1985, 154, 178, 334
Compensating errors, 225
Compensating errors, 95, 222, 225
Computer programs, 428
Conceptual framework, 249
Conceptual framework, 249, 250
Consistency concept, 242
Consolidation, 372
Constructive obligation, 278
Consultative Committee of Accountancy Bodies (CCAB), 444
Contingent assets, 281
Contingent liabilities, 281
Continuing operating, 453
Contributions from owners, 254
Control account, 210
Control accounts, 210, 218
Control, 371
Correction of errors, 80, 225
Cost, 181
Cost of goods sold, 108
Costing module, 431
Credit note, 57
Credit sales and debtors, 288

569

Index

Credit, 70
Creditor, 30
Creditors control account, 211
Creditors' turnover, 415
Creditors, 74, 214
Credits, 94
Cumulative weighted average costing, 151
Current account, 319
Current assets, 40, 42, 43, 46
Current assets, 42
Current cost accounting (CCA), 467
Current liabilities, 39
Current purchasing power (CPP);, 466
Current ratio, 411
Current replacement cost, 144
Customs and Excise, 85

Database management system, 438
Database, 438
Day book analysis, 80
Dearing Report, 445
Debenture loans, 337
Debentures, 40
Debit note, 57
Debit notes, 57
Debit, 70
Debits, 94
Debt ratio, 404
Debt/equity ratio, 405
Debtor days ratio, 412
Debtor days, 413
Debtor, 31
Debtors control account, 211
Debtors control account, 214
Debtors ledger, 217
Debtors payment period, 412
Debtors, 30, 43, 74, 211, 432
Deferred development costs, 263
Depreciation of freehold buildings, 471
Depreciation, 182
Depreciation, 182, 194
Derecognition, 255
Directly attributable finance costs, 181
Directors' report, 8, 396
Disclosure requirements of FRS 15, 185
Discontinued operations, 453, 457
Discount, 123
Disposal of a fixed asset, 173
Disposal of fixed assets, 172, 174
Distributions to owners, 254
Dividend cover, 417
Dividend per share and dividend cover, 417
Dividend yield, 417, 418

Dividends, 331
Dividends, 48
Dominant influence, 371
Double entry bookkeeping, 70
Double entry bookkeeping, 72
Double entry, 94
Drawings account, 319
Drawings, 27
Drawings, 27, 28, 288, 300, 316
Duality, 247

Earnings per share, 416, 454
Earnings yield, 418
Efficiency ratios, 412
Elements of financial statements, 251, 254
Entity concept, 25
Error of commission, 228
Error of omission, 228
Error of principle, 224
Error of transposition, 223
Errors of commission, 222, 224
Errors of commission, 224
Errors of omission, 222, 223
Errors of principle, 95, 222, 224
Errors of transposition, 222, 223
Errors, 80
Error of omission, 223
Exceptional items, 454, 455
Exceptional items, 455
Exempt activities, 87
Exemption of subsidiary undertakings from preparing group account, 374
Extraordinary items, 454, 455
Extraordinary items, 456

Factors affecting depreciation, 183
FIFO (first in, first out), 147
FIFO (first in, first out), 148, 156
Final accounts questions, 197
Finance expenses, 48
Financial Accounting Standards Board (FASB), 250
Financial accounts, 9
Financial adaptability, 252
Financial management, 10
Financial Reporting Review Panel, 446
Financial reporting standards, 445
Financial statements, 8
Fixed assets and databases, 440
Fixed assets valuation: alternative accounting rules, 178
Fixed assets, 40, 41, 177

Fixed assets: disclosure, 179
Foreword to Accounting Standards, 446
Format of a ledger account, 69
Framework on the preparation and presentation of financial stat, 250
FRED 12, 387
FRS 1 Cash flow statements, 354
FRS 11 Impairment of fixed assets and goodwill, 185
FRS 12 Provisions, contingent liabilities and contingent assets, 181, 277
FRS 15 Tangible fixed assets, 178, 180, 182
FRS 2 Accounting for subsidiary undertakings, 369, 373
FRS 3 Reporting financial performance, 184, 453, 454

GAAP, 15

Gains, 254
Gearing ratio, 404
General ledger, 68
Generally Accepted Accounting Practice (GAAP), 15, 451
Going concern concept, 237
Goods destroyed, 293
Goods received notes, 57
Goods sold, 47
Goods stolen, 294
Goods written off, 110
Goodwill and pre-acquisition profits, 385
Goodwill arising on consolidation, 384
Goodwill, 260
Goodwill, 263
Gross profit margin, 403
Gross profit, 46, 47
Gross profit, 47

Historical cost accounting, 464

Historical cost, 144
Historical cost, 244
Holding company, 369

Impersonal accounts, 82

Implications of high or low gearing, 405
Imprest system, 64
Incomplete records, 288, 301
Indirect costs, 46
Indirect method, 353
Initial recognition, 255
Inland Revenue, 85
Input and output VAT, 86

Input VAT, 86
Intangible assets, 177
Intangible fixed asset, 261
Intangible fixed asset, 41
Intangible fixed assets, 336, 449
Integrated accounting, 432
Integrated software, 431
Interest cover, 407
Interest held on a long-term basis, 371
Internal audit, 11
Internal check, 218
International Accounting Standards Committee (IASC)., 14
Inventory, 194
Investments, 41, 177, 337
Invoice, 56
Invoices and credit notes, 56
Irrecoverable VAT, 86
Issued capital, 330

Journal entries, 79, 225

Journal, 58, 79
Journal, 79

Layout of fixed assets register, 192

Ledger accounting for stocks, 141
Ledger accounts, 70
Ledger file, 433
Liabilities, 39, 254
Liability, 24
Liability, 31, 277
LIFO (last in, first out), 147
LIFO (last in, first out), 149
Limitations of financial accounting, 467
Limited companies, 24, 318, 326, 447
Limited company accounts, 334
Limited liability, 327
Liquidity, 403, 408, 411
Liquidity, 408
Loans by partners, 320
Long-term liabilities, 40
Long-term liability, 40
Long-term solvency, 403
Losses, 254

Machine hour method, 184

Management (or cost) accounting, 10
Management accounting, 9
Management reports, 431
Market value of shares, 334
Materiality concept, 243

Index

Measurement in financial statements, 251, 255
Methods of calculating, 184
Methods of depreciation, 184
Minority interest, 380
Minority interests, 380
Module, 431
Money measurement concept, 242

Need for accounts, 5
Net assets, 38
Net book value (NBV), 183
Net current assets, 46
Net profit margin, 403
Net profit, 46, 47
Net profit, 47
Net realisable value, 110, 144
New acquisitions, 453
Nominal ledger, 68
Nominal ledger, 68, 437
Nominal value, 339
Non-adjusting events, 273
Non-deductible inputs, 87
Non-financial statements, 8
Non-registered persons, 86
Notes to the accounts, 449

Objective of financial statements, 251
Objectivity, 245
Omission of a transaction, 95
Opening and closing stocks, 141
Opening balance sheet, 288
Operating profit, 449
Ordinary activities, 455
Ordinary shares, 333
Other new disclosures, 454
Output VAT, 86
Ownership interest, 254

P/E ratio, 417
Paid-up capital, 330
Parent undertaking, 369
Participating interest, 370
Partnership accounts, 314
Partnership Act 1890, 315
Partnership agreement, 315
Partnership, 315
PBIT, profit before interest and tax, 398
Personal accounts, 82
Petty cash book, 63
Petty cash book, 64
Post balance sheet events, 272

Preference shares, 332
Prepayments, 112
Prepayments, 44, 111, 113, 116, 194
Presentation of financial information, 251, 256
Primary profitability ratio, 401
Primary statement, 459
Private companies, 328
Profit analysis, 403
Profit and loss account, 46, 47, 87, 129, 256, 448
Profit and loss account, 8
Profit and loss reserve, 340
Profit before interest and tax, 399
Profit margin, 401
Profit smoothing, 277
Profit, 28
Profit, 5
Profitability, 398
Profit-sharing ratio, 315
Provision for depreciation, 169
Provision for doubtful debts, 128
Provision for doubtful debts, 135
Provision, 129, 277
Provisions, 122, 277
Provisions, 277, 343
Prudence concept, 129
Prudence concept, 239
Prudence, 469
Public companies, 328
Published accounts, 447
Purchase day book, 58, 59
Purchase day book, 59
Purchase ledger, 84
Purchase ledger, 84, 219, 435
Purchase order, 56
Purchase returns day book, 60
Purchase returns day book, 61
Purchased goodwill, 260, 262
Purchased goodwill, 261
Purchases and trade creditors, 288
Purchases returns day book, 58
Purchases, stocks and the cost of sales, 288
Purpose of control accounts, 218

Qualitative characteristics of financial information, 251, 253
Quick ratio, 411

Ratio analysis, 396
Real accounts, 192
Realisation concept, 245
Realised profits, 459

Recognition in financial statements, 251, 255
Reducing balance method, 163, 165, 184
Reporting entity, 251
Research and development, 263
Reserve, 343
Reserves, 339, 450
Restructuring, 279
Return on capital employed (ROCE), 399
Return on shareholders' capital (ROSC), 400
Revaluation reserve, 179, 189
Revaluations, 188
Revenue expenditure, 16
Revenue income, 17
Rights issues, 344
ROCE, 399, 401
Role of the accountant in society, 9
ROSC, 400

Sales and purchase ledgers, 82
Sales day book, 58
Sales day book, 58, 83
Sales ledger, 83
Sales ledger, 83
Sales order, 56
Sales returns day book, 58, 60
Sales returns day book, 60
Secondary ratios, 401
Selling and distribution expenses, 48
Separate valuation principle, 243
Settlement discount, 123
Settlement discounts, 124, 125
Share capital, 339
Share premium account, 341
Share premium account, 342
Short-term investments, 44
Short-term solvency, 408
Small and medium-sized groups, 375
Solomons report, 250
Source documents, 56
Spreadsheet, 441
SSAP 12, 183, 188
SSAP 13 Accounting for research and development, 263
SSAP 17 Accounting for post balance sheet events, 272, 275
SSAP 2 Disclosure of accounting policies, 236
SSAP 3, 455
SSAP 6 Extraordinary items and prior year adjustment, 454, 455
SSAP 9, 154, 155
Standard setting process, 443

Standard setting, 14
Statement of Principles for Financial Reporting, 251
Statement of Principles, 250, 251, 469
Statement of recognised gains and losses, 459
Statement of total recognised gains and losses, 256, 454
Statement of total recognised gains and losses, 459
Statements of standard accounting practice, 444
Statements, 435
Statutory accounts, 447
Statutory books, 329
Statutory provisions relating to all fixed assets, 177
Stock days, 413
Stock destroyed, 295
Stock Exchange, 451
Stock module, 431
Stock turnover period, 413
Stocks, 43, 144
Stocktaking, 143
Stolen goods or goods destroyed, 288
Stolen goods, 293
Straight line method, 163, 164, 184
Subsequent expenditure, 181
Subsequent remeasurement, 255
Subsidiary undertaking, 369
Subsidiary, 369
Substance over form, 247
Substance over form, 247, 445
Sum of digits method, 163, 184
Suspense account, 227
Suspense account, 227, 229

'T' accounts, 69
Tangible assets, 177
Tangible fixed asset, 41
Tangible fixed assets, 336
Taxation, 338
Time differences, 201
Time interval, 247
Trade debtors, 44
Trade discount, 123
Trading account, 46, 47
Trading and profit and loss account, 46, 49, 97
Transposition error, 219, 228
Trial balance, 92, 218
Trial balance, 93
True and fair view, 15

Index

True and fair view, 16
Two column cash book, 296
Types of error, 222

Unlimited liability, 327
Unpresented cheques, 204
Unrealised profits, 459
Urgent Issues Task Force and the Review Panel, 13
Urgent Issues Task Force, 445
Usefulness of financial accounting, 463
Users of accounting information, 5
Users of financial statements, 252

Valuation of fixed assets, 178
Value added tax, 85
Valuing stocks, 144
Variable data, 433
VAT on motor cars, 87
VAT, 87, 89
Wages and salaries, 211

Working capital, 46
Wrong account, 95

See overleaf for information on other
BPP products and how to order

ACCA Order

To BPP Professional Education, Aldine Place, London W12 8AW
Tel: 020 8740 2211   Fax: 020 8740 1184
email: publishing@bpp.com   online: www.bpp.com

Mr/Mrs/Ms (Full name) _____
Daytime delivery address _____
Postcode _____
Daytime Tel _____   Date of exam (month/year) _____   Scots law variant Y / N

	6/03 Texts	1/03 Kits	1/03 Passcards	MCQ Cards	Tapes	8/03 i-Learn	8/03 i-Pass	Virtual Campus
PART 1								
1.1 Preparing Financial Statements	£20.95	£10.95	£6.95	£5.95	£12.95	£34.95	£24.95	£90.00
1.2 Financial Information for Management †	£20.95	£10.95	£6.95	£5.95		£34.95	£24.95	£90.00
1.3 Managing People	£20.95	£10.95	£6.95		£12.95	£34.95	£24.95	£90.00
PART 2								
2.1 Information Systems	£20.95	£10.95	£6.95		£12.95	£34.95	£24.95	£90.00
2.2 Corporate and Business Law **	£20.95	£10.95	£6.95		£12.95	£34.95	£24.95	£90.00
2.3 Business Taxation FA 2002 (for 12/03 exams)	£20.95	£10.95	£6.95		£12.95	£34.95	£24.95	£90.00
2.4 Financial Management and Control †	£20.95	£10.95	£6.95		£12.95	£34.95	£24.95	£90.00
2.5 Financial Reporting	£20.95	£10.95	£6.95		£12.95	£34.95	£24.95	£90.00
2.6 Audit and Internal Review	£20.95	£10.95	£6.95		£12.95	£34.95	£24.95	£90.00
PART 3								
3.1 Audit and Assurance Services	£20.95	£10.95	£6.95		£12.95	£34.95	£24.95	
3.2 Advanced Taxation FA 2002 (for 12/03 exams)	£20.95	£10.95	£6.95		£12.95		£24.95	
3.3 Performance Management †	£20.95	£10.95	£6.95		£12.95		£24.95	
3.4 Business Information Management	£20.95	£10.95	£6.95		£12.95		£24.95	
3.5 Strategic Business Planning and Development	£20.95	£10.95	£6.95		£12.95		£24.95	
3.6 Advanced Corporate Reporting	£20.95	£10.95	£6.95		£12.95		£24.95	
3.7 Strategic Financial Management	£20.95	£10.95	£6.95		£12.95		£24.95	
INTERNATIONAL STREAM								
1.1 Preparing Financial Statements	£20.95	£10.95	£6.95	£5.95				
2.2 Corporate and Business Law (International Variant-9/03)	£20.95							
2.5 Financial Reporting	£20.95	£10.95	£6.95					
2.6 Audit and Internal Review	£20.95	£10.95	£6.95					
3.1 Audit and Assurance Services	£20.95	£10.95	£6.95					
3.6 Advanced Corporate Reporting	£20.95	£10.95	£6.95					
Success in your Research and Analysis Project – Tutorial Text (8/03)	£19.95							
Learning to Learn (7/02)	£9.95							

Subtotal £ _____

POSTAGE & PACKING

Study Texts
	First	Each extra	Online
UK	£5.00	£2.00	£2.00
Europe*	£6.00	£4.00	£4.00
Rest of world	£20.00	£10.00	£10.00

£ ___
£ ___
£ ___

Kits
	First	Each extra	Online
UK	£5.00	£2.00	£2.00
Europe*	£6.00	£4.00	£4.00
Rest of world	£20.00	£10.00	£10.00

£ ___
£ ___
£ ___

Passcards/Success Tapes/MCQ Cards/CDs
	First	Each extra	Online
UK	£2.00	£1.00	£1.00
Europe*	£3.00	£2.00	£2.00
Rest of world	£8.00	£8.00	£8.00

£ ___
£ ___
£ ___

Grand Total (incl. Postage)   **£** _____

I enclose a cheque for
(Cheques to BPP Professional Education)

Or charge to Visa/Mastercard/Switch

Card Number _____

Expiry date _____   Start Date _____

Issue Number (Switch Only) _____

Signature _____

We aim to deliver to all UK addresses inside 5 working days; a signature will be required. Orders to all EU addresses should be delivered within 6 working days. All other orders to overseas addresses should be delivered within 8 working days.
* Europe includes the Republic of Ireland and the Channel Islands. † 6/02 for 12/03 exam. The new edition published in 8/03 is for the 6/04 exam only. ** For Scots law variant students, a free Scots Law Supplement is available with the 8.8 Text

ACCA – Paper 1.1 Preparing Financial Statements (6/03)

REVIEW FORM & FREE PRIZE DRAW

All original review forms from the entire BPP range, completed with genuine comments, will be entered into a draw on 31 January 2004 and 31 July 2004. The names on the first four forms picked out will be sent a cheque for £50.

Name: _____ **Address:** _____

How have you used this Text?
(Tick one box only)
- ☐ Home study (book only)
- ☐ On a course: college _____
- ☐ With 'correspondence' package
- ☐ Other _____

Why did you decide to purchase this Text?
(Tick one box only)
- ☐ Have used complementary Kit
- ☐ Have used BPP Texts in the past
- ☐ Recommendation by friend/colleague
- ☐ Recommendation by a lecturer at college
- ☐ Saw advertising
- ☐ Other _____

During the past six months do you recall seeing/receiving any of the following?
(Tick as many boxes as are relevant)
- ☐ Our advertisement in *ACCA Student Accountant*
- ☐ Our advertisement in *Pass*
- ☐ Our advertisement in *PQ*
- ☐ Our brochure with a letter through the post

Which (if any) aspects of our advertising do you find useful?
(Tick as many boxes as are relevant)
- ☐ Prices and publication dates of new editions
- ☐ Information on Text content
- ☐ Facility to order books off-the-page
- ☐ None of the above

Which BPP products have you used?

Text	☑	MCQ cards	☐	i-Learn	☐
Kit	☐	Tape	☐	i-Pass	☐
Passcard	☐	Video	☐	Virtual Campus	☐

Your ratings, comments and suggestions would be appreciated on the following areas.

	Very useful	Useful	Not useful
Introductory section (Key study steps, personal study)	☐	☐	☐
Chapter introductions	☐	☐	☐
Key terms	☐	☐	☐
Quality of explanations	☐	☐	☐
Case examples and other examples	☐	☐	☐
Questions and answers in each chapter	☐	☐	☐
Chapter roundups	☐	☐	☐
Quick quizzes	☐	☐	☐
Exam focus points	☐	☐	☐
Question bank	☐	☐	☐
Answer bank	☐	☐	☐
List of key terms and index	☐	☐	☐
Icons	☐	☐	☐

	Excellent	Good	Adequate	Poor
Overall opinion of this Text	☐	☐	☐	☐

Do you intend to continue using BPP Products? ☐ Yes ☐ No

Please note any further comments and suggestions/errors on the reverse of this page. The BPP author of this edition can be e-mailed at: janiceross@bpp.com

Please return to: Katy Hibbert, ACCA Range Manager, BPP Professional Education, FREEPOST, London, W12 8BR

REVIEW FORM & FREE PRIZE DRAW (continued)

Please note any further comments and suggestions/errors below.

FREE PRIZE DRAW RULES

1. Closing date for 31 January 2004 draw is 31 December 2003. Closing date for 31 July 2004 draw is 30 June 2004.

2. No purchase necessary. Entry forms are available upon request from BPP Professional Education. No more than one entry per title, per person. Draw restricted to persons aged 16 and over.

3. Winners will be notified by post and receive their cheques not later than 6 weeks after the draw date.

4. The decision of the promoter in all matters is final and binding. No correspondence will be entered into.